THE BOOK OF
AMERICAN CLOCKS

THE BOOK OF AMERICAN CLOCKS

BY

BROOKS PALMER

WITH 312 ILLUSTRATIONS

MACMILLAN PUBLISHING CO., INC.

NEW YORK

Fourteenth Printing 1979

Macmillan Publishing Co., Inc.
866 Third Avenue, New York, N.Y. 10022

For permission to quote short extracts from Penrose Hoopes' " Connecticut Clockmakers of the Eighteenth Century" (copyright, 1930, by Edwin
Valentine Mitchell, Inc.) thanks are due to both author and publisher.

TO

JULIE

ACKNOWLEDGMENTS

The author wishes to express his gratitude to the many friends who by their knowledge and advice have helped him in the preparation of this book, and in particular to those listed below. Special thanks are due to the National Association of Watch and Clock Collectors, whose encouragement and cooperation have been invaluable.

Vincent D. Andrus
Mr. and Mrs. Amos G. Avery
Dr. H. Sheridan Baketel
Barny
Lockwood Barr
Samuel H. Barrington
E. A. Battison
Mr. and Mrs. Frank Beaven
Dr. Anthony Benis
Harry Birnbaum
Dr. M. A. Bissell
Albert H. Bosshart, Jr.
John J. Bowman
Mr. and Mrs. Bernard W. Brandt
Francis D. Brinton
Mrs. Yves Henry Buhler
E. E. Burt
Ernest Carsner
Mrs. Joseph Carson
Edward E. Chandlee
Ben Cohen
J. E. Coleman
Clarence D. Collins
John T. Collins
James G. Conlon
Dr. Alfred Cossidente
Ernest A. Cramer
George B. Cutten
Paul N. Dann
Paul G. Darrot
George B. Davis
Mr. and Mrs. Raymond B. Davison
Robert Dickey
Albert O. Dodge
L. R. Douglas

Lewis A. Dyer
George H. Eckhardt
Laurits Eichner
Charles D. Fenstermacher
Omar D. Fisher
H. K. Fleisher
Robert Franks
Henry B. Fried
Jack Fuchs
H. H. Funk
James W. Gibbs
Harrold E. Gillingham
Ralph E. Gould
Phillipse Greene
C. Wesley Hallett
Stuart W. Havens
Frederick B. Hicks
David C. Hill
Robert H. Hill
Edwin J. Hipkiss
Rev. Paul Hollingshead
Penrose Hoopes
George Hull
George L. Hunt
Dudley Ingraham
Edward Ingraham
Jerome Paul Jackson
Russell Leigh Jackson
Dr. Arthur E. James
Samuel W. Jennings
James A. Jensen
Mr. and Mrs. Walter Keller
Dr. Charles Kennedy
Rhea Mansfield Knittle
John K. Lamond
Mrs. Bella C. Landauer
C. E. Landis

Oscar T. Lang
Ira W. Leonard
Dr. Lev
Anne Lockett
Mrs. John B. Mason
Mark F. Massey
Douglas K. Merrill
Mr. and Mrs. Willis Michael
Mr. and Mrs. Willis I. Milham
Edward Mitchell
Peter Mitchell
Carl Mitman
C. Fred Muth
Richard Newcomb
James J. Niehaus
Olin S. Nye
Donald K. Packard
Albert L. Partridge
Jesse Perlman
Mrs. A. E. Prime
J. Russell Putnam
Dr. Arthur Rawlings
Mrs. Oscar Ritter
Walter Roberts
S. C. Robinson
Jean Louis Roehrich
Oscar Roesen
Eugene Rossi
John Lowry Ruth
Rev. Roland Sawyer
A. C. Scott
John Schenk
Frederick Mudge Selchow
Andrew Shiland
L. S. Spangler

L. D. Stallcup
Dr. W. Barclay Stephens
Mr. and Mrs. Charles Messer
   Stow
Earl T. Strickler
Fred C. Sweinhart
Frank A. Taylor

John H. Thompson
Floyd L. Thoms
Charles Terry Treadway
Dr. Carl Vogel
Ray Walker
Norman E. Webster
J. Cheny Wells

George C. White
Daniel E. Whitford
Jack Willey
Alice Winchester
H. LeBarre Williams, Jr.
H. Ogden Wintermute
Harry W. Yaseen

For permission to reproduce Ill. Nos. 5, 6, 7, 53, and 54 thanks are due to Edward E. Chandlee, author of "Six Quaker Clockmakers."

Edward Ingraham was most helpful in providing a number of key photographs, as were Messrs. F. M. Selchow, B. W. Brandt, Frank Beaven, Robert Franks, Raymond B. Davison, J. E. Coleman, Richard Newcomb, Lockwood Barr, and Ray Walker.

THE BOOK OF
AMERICAN CLOCKS

INTRODUCTION

THE following pages are not intended in any way to be a formal history of American clockmaking. A great deal more research than has yet been attempted remains to be done before such a book can be written. Yet today there is more interest than ever before in American clocks and timepieces. The Kitchen Clock of 1850 is now reverently set on the mantel of the living room after passing years in the attic or barn. With its reestablishment in an honored place in the family circle, there is a natural desire to find out all that can be known about its date, its maker, and its value. And the same is true of great-grandfather's watch, which has turned up in some safety deposit box.

What has been attempted in this book is to establish the known background of clock and watch making in America; to show, by means of the illustrations, the development of the more important types of clocks and watches; and to provide a list of makers with as much information about them as is currently obtainable. Particular attention has been paid in the illustrations to clock movements, because what is inside the clock case is at least as important in dating a clock as the case itself. It is hoped that by a careful examination of the list and the illustrations, any American clock or watch can be identified as to its date and its maker.

To those of us today in search of an interest to take our minds away from the confused present and teach us something of our country's past, there is no pastime which offers such opportunities as the collecting of clocks. Once embarked on it, any number of fascinating questions will arise. For instance, who were the men who printed the old clock labels, and what adhesive did they use to make them stick so well these many years? If the collector is interested in larger questions, did the manufacture of clocks help the brass industry, or was it the other way around?

If this book answers some of the questions which the beginning collector will ask, if it enrolls into the growing list some new collectors, and if in addition it gives to its readers something of the beauty and romance attached to the clocks themselves, the author will feel that he has done his part.

HISTORY

The story of American Timekeeping begins shortly after the separate colonies were settled. Public, or Tower, clocks are mentioned in town records as early as 1650;

but we know little or nothing about them, or who made them, installed them, and kept them running. A clock marked a definite advance for a town formerly dependent for the marking of noon on the sound of a bell or a cannon. In the seventeenth century, the golden age of clockmaking in England, pendulums with anchor or deadbeat escapements replaced the less accurate foliot balance, giving accuracy never before dreamed of in any time machine made by man. By 1690 the Tall Clock, much as we now know it, was an accomplished success, so well made and so efficient a timekeeper that there has been little change in its movements to the present day.

In America the eighteenth century was marked by the appearance of clocks in homes as symbols of prosperity. Clockmaking was still a craft operation; all the work was done by the clockmaker. Metals were scarce and hard to procure, and so was glass. Therefore many early advertisements called for old metal, to be used in making new clock movements.

The Early Clockmaker

Let us pause for a moment and consider just what had to be done to make a clock.

The craftsman working alone, or aided by an apprentice or two, used only the simplest of hand tools—hammer, drill, and file—with sand for casting. It was tedious, painstaking, wearing labor. Brass plates and blanks for the wheels were cast, using molds of sand. The brass was an alloy of copper and zinc and, on occasion, tin, for which each craftsman had his own formula. After the casting had cooled, it was still too soft and had to be beaten for a long period with light blows of the hammer until hard. This "planishing" could go on for days. Early manuals gave exact instructions, and one of them advised that, if a crack developed in the plate, the brass should be put under water and the planishing continued. This must have furnished a fine shower bath on a cold winter's day at a time long before central heating.

After the brass was of suitable hardness, it was filed smooth and polished to the necessary thickness. A later process for casting brass between two polished marble slabs gave it a more uniform thickness and reduced the amount of tedious filing. Later still the clockmaker was able to buy brass castings and blanks ready for filing, cutting, and finishing; some of them came from Europe, some were made here.

Gears had to be cast in blank, cut, and filed; some of the old clocks still bear the marks of the lines used for cutting the teeth; all this was hand work. Despite the scarcity of metals and the amount of time involved, some few clocks were made in this country in the eighteenth century; but they were made only at the order of a purchaser. In those days there were no trains to catch and split second accuracy was not necessary.

Since it took months to make a clock, and there were not too many people who could and would buy one, most clockmakers engaged also in other occupations. Everything needed in the national economy had to be made by hand; there was no going to a store and buying parts or articles ready-made. The gunsmith and the blacksmith frequently tried their hands at clockmaking in colonial days, and their names are found on some of the oldest clocks. It should be noted that these crafts. men were necessary and important citizens.

A piece of machinery devised by Elisha Purington, who was making clocks in Kensington, New Hampshire, in the second quarter of the eighteenth century, enabled him to cut the teeth on the gears of his clocks. After casting the brass in blank, he put the blanks on this lathelike device and turned them by a foot treadle, connected by a linen cord which ran over a spiked pulley to prevent slipping.

Through the eighteenth century Tall Clocks were made in small but increasing numbers, particularly in Philadelphia and the surrounding area. The brass movements were housed in splendid examples of the cabinet and case maker's art. They were treasured then as they are today.

Then came the War of the Revolution, and clockmakers turned to making guns, bullets, and war material. Many a lead clock weight was converted into bullets. The part of the clockmaker, blacksmith, and gunsmith in this successful campaign has never been fully told or appreciated.

Clockmaking After the Revolution

At the end of the war, clockmaking was resumed. Tall Clocks in the price levels of the day were expensive. There was a need for a less costly, smaller clock, and a number of makers, independently and in several places occupied themselves with the problem. Up to now, American clockmaking had closely followed the English pattern. Now New England ingenuity developed native American types and styles.

The Willards in Grafton, Massachusetts, developed various new types of clocks, culminating in the final perfection of the Banjo Clock, which sold for about thirty-five dollars. Although the use of metal movements still made production slow, Simon Willard made about four thousand clocks from 1802 until 1840.

The same thought of a moderate-priced, small clock engaged the minds of a number of ingenious Connecticut Yankees, but their idea was of a clock mass produced by machines that would enable every home owner to afford it.

Wood was plentiful and metal scarce. A wood-movement clock could be built to sell in quantity for less than one of metal. Dial, hands, weights, and a wood movement were the essentials in producing the Wag-on-Wall Clock. This at first sold for about twenty dollars; the tall case cost another twenty dollars. After 1790 Gideon Roberts began to make this kind of clock in quantity. He had lived in the Wyoming Valley of Pennsylvania, and perhaps learned from German and Dutch settlers how to build clocks with wooden movements. He was the first Bristol, Connecticut, clockmaker. He may have used mass production principles in making more than one part of a clock at the same time. His clock No. 511 is shown in illustration No. 63 and its movement in No. 65. Roberts's place in American clock history is yet to be determined. He owned an assembly plant in Richmond, Virginia, after 1800, operated by one of his sons.

(3)

John Rich of Bristol made the same kind of clock at the same time and a little later, and is recorded as having made more than 100 clocks. So did some of the Merrimans and the Ives, and certainly Levi Lewis. But the man who has received the credit for the first mass-produced, low-priced clock is Eli Terry. Data on his life and clockmaking can be found in the List of Makers. He had the enterprise to accept and fill an order for four thousand clocks in 1806 and to devise a sales technique that would ensure their distribution—the first recorded instance of the use of mass production for peacetime products. (Eli Whitney's firearm contract with the United States government in 1798 was the first mass production contract for war material.)

This was the beginning of factory production. Machines making identical parts could produce a hundred clocks in the time that the hand craftsman could make a single part, and brought clocks within the purchasing power of the people. The second problem, how to sell them, also was solved by Eli Terry, who deserves much of the credit for a faster growing America. Up to this time, if a purchaser needed an article, it was ordered or "bespoke," and then made by hand. Connecticut clockmakers, with considerable assistance from the fabled Yankee Peddler, changed all this. From now on clocks were first made and then sold. On the 1806 order for four thousand clocks, finished clocks were coming off the "assembly line" at the rate of about sixty a day. They were all sold, and more were made and sold.

A new era had begun, and the era of the craftsman ended. Water power was harnessed to drive machines, replacing muscle and toil. Penrose Hoopes calls Eli Terry "the last of the Craftsmen and the first of the Industrialists."

Terry had other ideas. By diligent hard work his Shelf Clock, about twenty inches high, was in being by 1814 and was patented in 1816. This became the beautiful Pillar and Scroll Clock, which sold for about fifteen dollars and ran thirty hours on a winding. It and the Shelf Clocks which followed were promoted by aggressive selling methods, and eventually captured the market. The Pillar and Scroll Clock inspired many good imitations by inventors who went on to design and produce Shelf Clocks of their own pattern. Seth Thomas purchased the right to make Terry Shelf Clocks. Merriman, Birge & Company, of which Joseph Ives was a member, made large numbers of Wall Mirror Clocks from 1819 to 1822. In 1824 Chauncey Jerome made a taller but plainer Shelf Clock with a longer pendulum which he called the Bronze Looking Glass Clock. In Connecticut by the 1820's there was a real boom in clockmaking, and the clocks were sent all over the country. The eight-day wooden movement Shelf Clock followed. Cast-brass eight-day Shelf Clocks were made. Clocks were used for barter in place of money. Houses were bought and sold for so many clock movements. But the inevitable aftermath occurred, and the depression of 1837 brought clockmaking to a complete standstill. With it came the end of the wooden clock movement.

Noble Jerome, brother of Chauncey, used rolled-brass strips or stampings to produce a thirty-hour, weight-driven movement in an OG case, shown in No. 250, that sold at a new low price and started the clock business booming again in 1838.

Connecticut clocks captured the market, and by 1845 clocks were made in Connecticut at the rate of nearly a million a year. Many of these are still in use.

Although the Willards and Howard of Boston fought successfully to maintain their markets, the Connecticut Shelf Clocks brought an end to the making of Tall Clocks in Pennsylvania about 1840 or 1860. The low prices and the fact that they were good clocks caused them to be sold all over the globe.

As an example of foreign merchandising, the story of the exploit of Chauncey Jerome deserves more than this brief mention. With his factories producing tremendous numbers of the brass-movement, weight-driven OG's, he cast an eye on sales possibilities in England. He dispatched an agent, Epaphroditus Peck, with a shipload of clocks, which was promptly seized and purchased at his price by the British custom officials as representing unfair competition. As soon as Jerome heard of this very profitable business with the British government, over went another load of OG's, which was equally promptly seized. The third shipload convinced the customs, and Jerome sold these without help.

The period 1838 to 1857 was prosperous for Connecticut clockmakers. Factories and mass production had taken over. The financial panic of 1857 put an end to clockmaking for a time and started the trend toward consolidation of clockmaking within a few large companies. This trend has continued to the present day. In this, clockmaking has followed the usual pattern of American industry.

In 1845 coiled springs for motive power began to be used by the Connecticut clockmakers. This allowed the case maker, hitherto restrained by the sober lines of the weight-driven movement, to indulge his fancy in any shape. Around 1850, clocks controlled by a balance wheel, called "Marine Movement" in Connecticut, began to appear on the market. This oscillating balance wheel was of the general type used to regulate watches. The principle was developed independently by Charles Kirke, Silas Burnham Terry, Bainbridge Barnes, and others. One advantage of Marine Movement clocks over pendulum-controlled clocks was that they would continue to run while being moved from place to place. From them the round, metal-cased, lever escape alarm clock, first produced in 1875, was developed, the ancestor of the modern, functionally designed alarm. In 1914 Henry Warren of Ashland, Massachusetts, perfected a clock powered by electric alternating current with synchronous motor.

The last two types provide the bulk of modern American clock production.

TYPES OF CLOCKS

There are four major types of clock—Tower, Tall, Wall, and Shelf.

Tower or Turret Clock is the name given to the large type set in steeples, towers and public buildings for all to see. The earliest European Tower Clocks had neither hands nor face, but merely caused a bell to sound at stated regular intervals. The dial and the hands were added later. After 1658 the pendulum and improved escapements increased their accuracy.

Aside from a very few foreign-made house clocks imported into the colonies, the first American clocks were Tower Clocks. This is as yet a comparatively unexplored chapter in our history. In Massachusetts, town records speak of them in vague terms, for example:

The 9th mo., 1650.
At a Generall towne meting upon warning, it was agreed that the Bells Capt. Crumwell gave the Towne should be by the Selectmen disposed of to the Best Advantage, and the produce Laid out for one Bell for a Clocke.

25:11:1657.
. . . Richard Taylor is allowed thirty shillings for repairing the clock for his direction to ring by, and is to have five pounds per annum for the future, provided hee bee att charges to keepe a clock and to repayre itt.

July 28th [1684].
Agreed with Wm Sumner blacksmith to pay him 4^lds in mony to keepe the clocke at ye North end of the Towne for one yeare to begin the 1st of Augt next & to pay him for worke done about s^d clocke the yeare past, 14^s. mony.*

According to *The Old Clock Book*, by Mrs. N. Hudson Moore, a Tower Clock was set up in the steeple of the New Meeting House in Ipswich in 1704. Diligent research has failed to uncover any other data about this clock. Newburyport had Tower Clocks as early as 1734. One, damaged by lightning in 1754, was examined by Benjamin Franklin. Ebenezer Parmalee made a wooden-movement Tower Clock in Guilford, Connecticut, in 1726, since replaced; the old movement is still preserved in the Guilford Historical Society. In later records mention is made of other Connecticut Tower Clocks.

There must have been earlier Tower Clocks in New York before the one built for the Old Dutch Church at the corner of Liberty and Nassau streets by Benjamin Hanks of Litchfield, Connecticut. Hanks, an ingenious inventor, is worthy of further study.

Philadelphia, Baltimore, and Charleston all possessed early Tower Clocks, exact information about which is hard to locate.

William Bentley of Salem, Massachusetts, in his Diary published by the Essex Institute tells us: "1792—June 25 . . . By Caesar I learn that the Bell in the East Meeting House was put up in October 1772. & the clock on the 22nd May 1773 made by a Mr. Liscombe belonging to the Town . . ."

Many famous clockmakers made Tower Clocks, and the long and honorable register of names would include Simon Willard, Eli and Samuel Terry, and Seth Thomas. In 1842 Edward Howard founded a business which even today mainly concerns itself with making and maintaining them.

Two movements of Tower Clocks are shown in Nos. 71, 72.

* Quotations from the *Report* and the *Second Report of the Record Commissioners of the City of Boston*.

Tall Clocks are the second major type. The English prefer the name Long Case. Floor and Hall are two other names. The most popular nickname is "grandfather" clock. In this book we will refer to them as Tall Clocks. Tall Clocks, as opposed to Shelf or Wall Clocks, stand unsupported on the floor. The case for the movement hides the pendulum and weights, and keeps out the dust. They range from five to as much as nine feet in height; the cases are of various woods, in designs which vary according to the taste of the cabinetmaker.

In 1660, forty years after the Pilgrims landed, English and Dutch makers completed a Tall Clock mechanism with pendulum and anchor escapement that kept very accurate time. At first the dial had only an hour hand, with the dial ring divided into forty-eight segments for the quarter-hours. Some of these one-handed clocks were made in America; a few have survived. In Europe the minute hand was added around 1680, and the second hand around 1690 to complete the dial with which we are familiar today.

In early America, Tall Clocks were made wherever clockmakers flourished, but especially in Pennsylvania. Of the fifty-five Tall Clocks illustrated in three standard books on American clocks—Moore (1911), Milham (1923), and Nutting (1924)—the makers are distributed by states as follows: Pennsylvania, 14; Massachusetts, 14; Connecticut, 11; Rhode Island, 6; New Hampshire, 3; New York, 1; unknown, 6. While this shows that Tall Clocks were made all over the eastern seaboard, it does not point out the predominance of Pennsylvania. In fact, Tall Clocks continued be made in that state up to the middle of the nineteenth century.

In the earliest Tall Clocks the dials were of metal, about 10½ inches square, with no arch, the cases frequently without ornamentation, probably because of Quaker influence. Frequently attachments such as the calendar, the phases of the moon, the rocking ship at the end of the pendulum, and even musical devices were added. In later times the dials were made larger.

Four different types of movement were used: the thirty-hour brass movement with endless chain or rope, the eight-day brass movement with two weights, the thirty-hour Connecticut wood movement, and the scarce eight-day wood movement.

Dwarf Tall Clocks

A later derivation of the Tall Clock is the Dwarf, Miniature, or Small Tall Clock, nicknamed "grandmother." Of the few that were made, most were in the early nineteenth century. Preserving the exact proportions of the corresponding Tall Clocks, they attained a height of four feet or less. Correctly, the name is never applied to a Shelf Clock. Pictures of some of them by the Baileys, the Wilders, Benjamin Morrill, and other fine makers are shown in Nos. 90–105.

Clocks that hang on the wall are called Wall Clocks. They are of many shapes and styles, the earliest of which is the Wag-on-Wall, shown in No. 2. American Wag-on-Wall Clocks as can be seen from the illustration are in effect Tall Clock movements without the protecting case.

Around 1783 Simon Willard made a few of the delightful thirty-hour brass-movement Wall Clocks shown in No. 108. The evolution of this clock is an interesting piece of American history. In the second stage of their development they were cased in Massachusetts Shelf or Half Clock cases. Then the "Coffin" Clock was developed, and finally the Banjo, the unique clock shape and movement which Willard patented in 1802. Banjo Clocks are still made because of their pleasant appearance and accurate timekeeping, although some of them have lost the fine case proportions of the originals. Most Banjo Clocks were "timepieces," recording time only, whereas a true "clock" strikes the hours in addition. Some contained an alarm mechanism. Some were arranged to strike one hammer blow on the side of the case every hour; this required only a single weight. Later some striking Banjo Clocks were made with a wider throat to accommodate the necessary two weights. Some were housed in ornate gilded cases with brackets; these were called Presentation Banjos. Most of the Willard Banjos were made with a throat tablet. In later models mahogany panels were used, because these hand-painted tablets were difficult to produce. Bezels were of brass, later of wood. Willard Banjo Clocks are shown in Nos. 149–153.

After 1842 a late type of Banjo with a plain wood case, wood bezels, no side arms, and a curved side box was made by Edward Howard of Boston and others. This was made in at least five sizes, and tradition has it that the largest were used as timepieces in the stations of the Pennsylvania and Reading railroads. The simple eight-day brass movements of the Banjo Clocks kept splendid time.

Certain Boston clockmakers developed two "cousins" of the Banjo. The first, the Lyre, contained a Banjo-type eight-day brass movement; these were either clocks or timepieces, with or without tablets. The maker originally responsible for the design is not known; they were made by Aaron Willard, Jr., John Sawin, Sawin & Dyer, Lemuel Curtis, and others. Examples of the Lyre Clock are shown in Nos. 159–168.

The second "cousin" is the Girandole, rightly called America's most beautiful clock. It was designed by and bears the name of Lemuel Curtis. Perhaps twenty-five in all were made by him.

Connecticut makers made five styles of Wall Clocks deserving of mention—the early "Wag-on-Wall," the "Lyre" Wall Clock, the "Wall Wagon Spring," the "Wall Regulator," which ticked away in so many schoolrooms and offices, and certain splendid weight-driven regulators, some with maintaining power, of which a few are still in existence.

New Hampshire produced its own unusual type of Wall Clock. Its movement was of brass, eight-day, and it was usually a timepiece. The door, which ran the full length of the clock, was divided to display the dial at the top and a mirror below. The design may have resulted from the stiff business competition of the period; a good timepiece and an attractive mirror must have been a salable package. Benjamin Morrill, Joseph Chadwick, James Collins, and others made examples. In 1822 Joseph Ives of Connecticut received a patent on a similar though much taller style of clock. These New Hampshire clocks are illustrated in Nos. 211–214.

A number of the Wall Clocks known in England as Act of Parliament Clocks were made in America, but few have survived.

An example of the Columbus Clock properly labeled as to its 1892 origin is shown in No. 281.

Shelf Clocks

The Shelf Clock is the fourth important type. Shelf clocks are made to stand on shelves, mantels, tables, but not on the floor. As a type, they represent an extraordinary variety of styles, from the bracket clock of the 1600's to the round tin alarm clock of the 1900's. Their popularity and variety arose from the desire of the clock-makers to produce a timepiece that would be smaller and less expensive than the Tall Clock. The English type of early bracket clock was not made in any considerable numbers in this country. The earliest American Shelf Clock was the type known as the Massachusetts Shelf or Half Clock, made by the Willards and others after the Revolutionary War. The movements are brass, both thirty-hour and eight-day, timepiece and clock, alarm and strike. Many have "kidney" dials, some have "dish" dials where the metal dial is convex. They were good timekeepers, usually powered by a movement like the simple efficient Banjo movement. Simon Willard is believed to have given up their manufacture after the perfection and popularity of the Banjo. His brother Aaron and others continued making them into the first quarter of the nineteenth century. A good assortment of styles of Massachusetts Shelf Clocks is shown in Nos. 109–133.

Simon Willard's "Lighthouse" Clock (Nos. 150, 151), which he patented and made in 1822, is perhaps best called a Shelf Clock. It never became popular, and he abandoned the idea after making a few.

A rare type of Shelf Clock made in Massachusetts, the Shelf Lyre, is shown in Nos. 157, 158.

The largest number and variety of Shelf Clocks were produced by Connecticut makers. By 1808 Eli Terry had made his first thirty-hour wood Shelf Clock and was working hard on the idea of producing wood-movement clocks in quantity. Some examples of his early experiments are in the collection of Charles Terry Treadway of Bristol. The Box Case Clock, shown in No. 179, is the one on which he received a patent in 1816. Through evolution of case design this became the Pillar and Scroll Clock, finally reaching the standard model about 1818–1819.

Stages in the evolution of this clock are, in order, the Outside Escapement, the Off-Center Pendulum, and the Inside Outside, all shown in Nos. 179–188. They sold for $15, important money in those days after the War of 1812, when business was depressed. Later two-third-sized miniatures by such makers as Mark Leavenworth were made. The Pillar and Scroll Clock remained the most popular Shelf Clock until about 1825 and survived well into the 1830's. It was widely pirated and copied, especially in Plymouth and Bristol, Connecticut.

Inventive clockmakers like Silas Hoadley produced different designs to avoid infringing on Eli Terry's patents. In Torrington a group of clockmakers developed the Torrington type movement, running horizontally the complete width of the case and housed in a Pillar and Scroll case, shown in No. 192. Massachusetts had its own variety of Pillar and Scroll, made by William Sherwin and others, shown in No. 204. All these clocks were fitted with thirty-hour, wood movements.

With the immense popularity of the Pillar and Scroll Clocks some makers turned to a cast brass eight-day movement, which the owner had to wind only once a week, instead of every day. These were made from about 1820 into the 1830's. There were at least three distinct styles; the first is shown in No. 195; the second, a giant size, is not illustrated; the third, the Pennsylvania style, is shown in No. 205, made by J. D. Custer and other Pennsylvania clockmakers, evidently in an attempt to compete with the aggressively sold, mass-produced Connecticut Shelf Clocks.

It is a sad commentary on the transience of public taste that the beautiful Pillar and Scroll Clock was eventually replaced by the Bronze Looking Glass Clock "invented" by Chauncey Jerome. He says in his autobiography: "In 1825, I invented the Bronze Looking Glass Clock which soon revolutionized the whole business. It could be made for one dollar less, and sold for two dollars more than the Patent Case [Pillar and Scroll]." A clock, similar in design, is shown in No. 207. It has a thirty-hour, wood movement with a taller case to fit the longer pendulum. Despite its inferior design, it quickly became popular; thousands were made and sold.

At about this time, the OG clock appeared, the largest-selling Connecticut Shelf Clock, which continued to be made until 1914. It was made in six or more sizes, at first with wood movements, after 1837 with brass, both thirty-hour and eight-day, weight- and spring-driven. Its title is derived from the wavelike molding of its plain, rectangular case. Examples are shown in Nos. 250, 251. Up to 1845 the case maker had to design a clock case that would accommodate the vertical fall of the weights. Inexpensive springs for motive power then became available, and henceforth the design was restricted only by the whim of the maker. Probably the first and most popular style was the Steeple Clock designed by Elias Ingraham, and shown in Nos. 252, 253. Later came the standard production models, illustrated in No. 255. The Bee Hive was another popular style, as was the small eight-day clock shown in No. 258. After this the styles of Connecticut shelf clocks are too numerous to list. Many are shown in the later illustrations, along with the iron-cased clocks, imitations of French Shelf Clocks, and the once popular Calendar Clocks.

In No. 276 is shown an early tin, lever-escape alarm clock, the ancestor of the modern, functionally designed plastic-cased Shelf Clock.

Despite the verdict of Wallace Nutting in *The Clock Book* that this country has contributed nothing to the art of case design with the solitary exception of the Girandole, the author asserts that these later clocks not only are worthy of being illustrated, but represent a notable example of American ingenuity and inventiveness. How the passage of time can alter an aesthetic judgment is a larger question than can be discussed in this book.

AMERICAN WATCHES

Because watches fascinate a large group of people who frequently take no interest in clocks these notes, and Nos. 289–312, are included.

Portable timekeepers came into being in Europe with the invention of a coiled spring after 1500. Improved control devices and, around 1700, jeweled movements made them more accurate and reduced their size, until man had a timekeeper he could comfortably carry.

"Watchmakers" came early to the colonies, from England, Scotland, Ireland, Holland, France, Germany, and Switzerland, and set themselves up in business even though the number of clocks and watches owned in America could not have been large.

Few watches appear to have been made in this country before 1850, but there is little exact information on the subject. Before 1850 the majority of watches were imported from Europe. In some instances parts may have been brought in and assembled here, for American names appear on both dial and movement. We can only guess how much the owners of these names had to do with the making of the watch. The materials and metals used were such as the craftsman could make or procure, and each watch was patiently finished by hand work. Illustration No. 291 shows a watch of the late eighteenth century marked both on the dial and on the movement "Ephraim Clark" (of Philadelphia).

Nathaniel Hurd's will mentions "my watch—Brown, Boston, on the face of it," probably referring to Gawen Brown. The History of Norwich, Connecticut, mentions that "Thomas Harland's factory produced 200 watches and 40 clocks a year" around 1800. None of these watches is now known. The entire subject of early American watchmaking offers a splendid field for future research.

Perhaps the first attempt to produce watches in volume in America was undertaken by Luther Goddard (1762–1842) at Shrewsbury, Massachusetts. Goddard began the manufacture of watches in 1809, when imports had been blocked off by tariff restrictions. He employed other watchmakers and made watches up to 1817. When the "Jefferson Embargo" was lifted in 1815 foreign watches again deluged the American market at prices lower than he was able to meet, and he returned to preaching the gospel. It has never been accurately ascertained whether these were imported in finished condition or were assembled in Shrewsbury from foreign-made parts, or were actually made in Shrewsbury. A Goddard watch No. 155, owned by Frank Bogenrief, Hinton, Iowa, is shown in Nos. 289, 290.

In 1837 the second American attempt to make watches in volume was started in East Hartford by the brothers Henry and J. F. Pitkin. They used machinery which they had invented and constructed to produce between 800 and 1,000 watches, and were helped by N. P. Stratton. Abbott described the watches as of "three quarter plate, slow train, about size 16, known as the Pitkin Watch." Again, competition by foreign-made watches proved too stiff. In 1841, after moving the plant to New York City, the Pitkins abandoned watchmaking.

According to S. H. Barrington, Jacob Custer (1805–1872), the ingenious clock-maker of Norristown, Pennsylvania, made at least twelve watches in or about the year 1843. The Custer Watch, shown in Nos. 292, 293, is owned by Mr. Barrington, who states that Custer himself made all the parts except the hairspring and the fusee chain. Jewels were used in the pallets only. Custer eventually received a patent.

What eventually became the Waltham Watch Company received its start in 1850. Edward Howard (1813–1904) and Aaron L. Dennison (1812–1895) successfully combined to make a watch, using specially designed machinery for production in volume, forty years after Terry's success with clockmaking. Documentation of the tremendous difficulties they overcame is given by Charles W. Moore in *Timing a Century: History of the Waltham Watch Company*. This company, having successfully met foreign competition from time to time, discontinued business in 1950, after a life of one hundred years. George V. White of Wollaston, Massachusetts, has an excellent collection of watches of Waltham make. His research provided the early numbering for identification given in the List of Makers.

The Elgin National Watch Company of Elgin, Illinois, has been making jeweled movement watches since it was first organized in 1864 as "The National Watch Company." Its first watches, produced in 1867 and described as "an 18 size, full plate, quick train, and straight line escapement," are shown in Nos. 297, 298. The public insisted on having the name Elgin on the watch, and the present name was adopted in 1874, one year after the company produced its first stem wind watch. Formerly watches were wound by separate keys, which are today collector's items. The Elgin Company continues to make fine jeweled watches today.

In the 1870's fine American-made watches were successful but not inexpensive. The minds of some inventors now turned to the problem of producing a low-priced but accurate watch, just as the Connecticut clockmakers had produced their low-priced clocks.

The first attempt in 1875 by Jason R. Hopkins of Washington, D.C., W. B. Fowle, and the Auburndale (Massachusetts) Watch Co. to produce a watch to sell for about fifty cents ended in failure.

On May 21, 1878, D. A. Buck received a patent on a watch. Overcoming terrific obstacles, he finally succeeded in making what became at its first production in 1880 the Waterbury Watch, illustrated in No. 306. It was first made by Benedict and Burnham, and a subsidiary company, the Waterbury Watch Company, incorporated in 1880. There were only fifty-eight parts. A seven- to nine-foot spring was coiled about the movement with the watch case serving as the barrel, as shown in No. 307. A simplified duplex escapement and modified tourbillon movement was used. The dial, printed on celluloid-covered paper was fastened to the plate. The movement carried the minute hand and made one revolution per hour. Waterbury watches were originally sold for $3.50 to $4.00, and by 1888 almost half a million watches a year were turned out. Total production before discontinuance in 1891 was well over a million.

Many stories are told about the Waterbury watch, for 140 half-turns of the stem were needed to wind fully. One of the best known is: "Here, wind my Waterbury for a while. When you are tired, I'll finish winding." The deathblow to the Waterbury was its use as a premium to sell men's suits: a watch was given away free with a suit of clothes. This was fatal to its prestige.

The next chapter in the history of the inexpensive watch is provided by "R. H. Ingersoll & Bro." who in 1892 began to sell "the watch that made the dollar famous." See Nos. 308, 310. The story of the Ingersoll watch is fully documented in H. G. Brearley's *Time Telling Through the Ages*, to which the reader is referred.

The complete story of watchmaking in America cannot be told within the confines of this Introduction. Organizing watch companies was a popular form of American business venture from the 1860's through the 1890's. All these companies and their organizers are to be found in the List of Makers. Some few met with success, many more with immediate failure. No history of American watchmaking would be complete without the story of the Hamilton Watch Company, organized in 1892, and today one of the greatest manufacturers of jeweled watches in America.

For the story of the manufacture of modern non-jeweled watches, the reader is particularly referred to the List of Makers, under Ingraham Company, Western Clock Manufacturing Company, United States Time Corporation of Waterbury, Connecticut, and New Haven Clock Company of New Haven.

The Mechanics of a Watch

A Watch is a portable time-telling machine composed of four basic divisions that act together to release the source of power in such a way that the passage of time may be scaled and read. These divisions are: power—mainspring; train—gears; escapement—so called because it allows a tooth to escape from a pallet at regular intervals; and indication—dial and hands.

Coiled springs of tempered steel up to two feet in length produce the power. The spring is usually contained in a round housing called a barrel, with teeth on the rim. This is the first or great wheel. As the spring uncoils, the barrel revolves, turning the assemblage of wheels and pinions known as the train. The train is usually composed of the center, second, third, fourth, and escape wheels. The power is released to the escape (balance) wheel or regulator under control of the escapement. The most widely used types of escapement are detached lever, cylinder, duplex, and chronometer.

Correctly proportioned gears under the dial turn the hour and minute hands at a 1 to 12 ratio.

Dials are made of enamel, metal, or printed paper. The cases that house the movements are made of various metals, ranging from tin to gold.

The Measurement of Watch Movements

There are two systems of measurement of watch movements—the American, and the French or Swiss.

Watches made in America are measured by a system devised by Aaron L. Dennison. Zero (0) is the base size and equals 35/30 of an American inch. Movements larger than 0 are numbered 1, 2, 3, etc. Movements smaller than 0, 2/0, 3/0, 4/0, etc. 6/0 size is exactly an inch.

The ligne is the unit of measurement of the size of a foreign watch. It is one-twelfth of an inch, and there are 12 inches in a Paris foot. It equals 2.26 millimeters or .0888 inch (American).

LIST OF MAKERS

About six thousand names which have appeared on clocks or watches made in America are listed in this book.

The list is not and probably never can be made complete. Much unrecorded time has passed since early days, and as a result, much history has been lost. Much more needs to be explored about all the men mentioned here, but this is the most thorough and detailed list of American clock and watch makers now in print.

It originally came into being because of ignorance, distress, and then stubbornness. The first two clocks in the author's collection bore on their labels the name "Wm. L. Gilbert, Winchester, Conn." A check of published sources (and there are a great many in the New York Public Library) revealed little. But with the cooperation of the Gilbert Company and with persistent inquiry of other authorities, exact names and dates were established, so that the name "Wm. L. Gilbert" became not just a name on an old Connecticut clock, but a recovered and rewarding piece of history.

Gradually, the author added to his collection of clocks. The additions bore new names. In time he tracked their makers down. They in turn pointed to other names. Thus from the collecting of old clocks developed a second and equally fascinating hobby, the discovery of the work and lives of the men who made them. Eventually the thought came to him that he might embody the information he was collecting into a list which would include all hitherto published names.

Some of the men listed may not have been in the strict sense clockmakers. But just what is a "clockmaker"? Before the advent of the factory, the following craftsmen were necessary in the making of a clock: the brass founder; the steel forger; the maker of springs; the caster of weights; the gear cutter; the movement maker who, if he himself did not cut the gears, had to mount them on proper axles and assemble the mechanism between the plates; the bell caster; the dial maker; (if jewels were used for pivots) the jeweler; the case maker; the glazier for the glass parts of the case; the maker of chain, cat, gut, or cord; the gilder or painter of tablets and dials; and lastly the man who sold the complete clock. Some few men may have performed all these functions, but in most cases there was a man for each function. So we encounter difficulty in an exact definition of "clockmaker."

Further confusion came from the old descriptive term "watchmaker," which seems to have been the title preferred by certain clockmakers. Benjamin Bagnall, probably Boston's first authenticated clockmaker, called himself "watchmaker," though there seems to be no record that he ever made what we know as a watch. At least none bearing his name is known.

Some of the names in the list were found in early advertisements by men calling themselves clockmakers or watchmakers, though their work may have been confined to repair.

Later, when clocks and watches were made in factories and the craftsman gave way to the machine, the development of selling technique produced men who were simply dealers, though the clocks and watches they sold are marked with their names.

The list began with names of clocks which were not to be found in Wallace Nutting's *The Clock Book*. Later the expanded list of about seventeen hundred in the third volume of *Furniture Treasury* was consulted. Both of Nutting's lists were inadequate to answer the persistent questions of this particular collector. Other lists, other books were explored; authorities who themselves had never written were probed for their often priceless knowledge. The author's list began to take shape.

The earliest list of American makers, containing several hundred names, was compiled by Charles T. Crossman and ran serially in the *Jewelers' Circular* from 1889 to 1891.

Mrs. N. Hudson Moore's *The Old Clock Book*, published in 1911, contains the first workable list of American clockmakers. This splendid pioneering work is still generally accurate, although much additional information has been uncovered since. On many disputed points, it is stimulating to refer back to what Mrs. Moore has to say.

Mention has already been made of the two Wallace Nutting lists.

American Clocks and Clockmakers, by Carl W. Drepperd, published in 1947, contains a list of about three thousand names. Other names appeared in the magazine *Timepieces*. The material contained in the thirty numbers of the *Bulletin* of the National Association of Watch and Clock Collectors has been helpful. Also consulted were directories of cities and towns, special monographs by various historical societies, and such other sources as *Arts and Crafts in Philadelphia, Maryland, and South Carolina*, by Prime; *Arts and Crafts in New England*, by Dow; *Arts and Crafts in New York*, by Gottesman; *Maryland Silversmiths*, by Pleasants and Sill; George Cutten's books on silversmiths in New York, Massachusetts, and North Carolina; *Six Quaker Clockmakers*, by Chandlee; *Chester County Clocks and Their Makers*, by

James; *Connecticut Clockmakers of the Eighteenth Century* and "Early Clockmaking in Connecticut," by Hoopes; the Minutes of the Boston Clock Club as told by Albert L. Partridge; *Antique Watches, and How to Establish Their Age,* by Abbott; *A History of Simon Willard, Inventor and Clockmaker,* by Willard; the Ingraham, Buell, Barr study of Bristol Makers; and *Time and Timekeepers,* by Milham. A list of sources will be found in the Bibliography.

Names of some American makers were found in two English lists, *Old Clocks and Watches and Their Makers,* by Britten, and *Watchmakers and Clockmakers of the World,* by Baillie.

After ten years of active research, six thousand names have been compiled. Particular attention has been paid to the detailed history and changes in ownership of the larger clock companies, so that the dates of their clocks can be more accurately identified.

GLOSSARY OF CLOCK TERMS

Acorn Clock: So called because of its shape.

alarm: An attachment to a clock or watch that marks a predetermined time. Found on some early Tall Clocks, as well as Shelf Clocks, even with wood movements. The Connecticut pendulum Shelf alarm clocks have the brass ring with numbers at the center post of the dial.

arbor: Axle on which gears and pinions are mounted.

balance: The oscillating wheel with the hairspring that regulates the escape of power.

balance cock: The support for the top of the balance staff of a watch.

Banjo: Nickname given to Willard's Improved Timepiece.

barrel: The round container of the mainspring.

beat: The ticking sound of the teeth of the escape wheel on the pallets. A clock or watch is "out of beat" when the intervals of the tick are uneven.

bezel: The part that holds the glass over the dial of a clock or watch.

bob: A complete pendulum has three parts: the pendulum rod, the pendulum ball, often wrongly called "bob," and the bob, which is the wire loop, threaded for the regulating nut.

bushing: The point where the arbor, or axle pivot, extends through the clock plate for its "bearing" is called a "bushing" when additional metal is added to make the bearing surface longer than the mere thickness of the plate. The removal and replacement of worn bushings with new metal, or cutting them larger and replacing them with heavier metal, is called "rebushing."

calendar: An attachment on Tall Clocks to tell the day of the month. A type of Wall or Shelf Clock made in large numbers after 1860.

cannon tubes: An inaccurate designation of the hour pipe (carrying the hour hand) and the minute post, or "center post" (carrying the minute hand). The seconds post carries the second hand whether it is center seconds or otherwise.

case: That which contains the clock or watch.

center seconds hand, or *sweep second hand:* This type of hand is mounted at the center of the dial. Used on eighteenth century Tall Clocks as well as on some modern watches.

chronometer: A very accurate timekeeper; as, the marine chronometer.

clepsammia: "Sand thief," an hour glass.

clepsydra: "Water thief," early form of timekeeper.

clock: A machine that records the passing of time and also strikes at least the hours — differing from a "timepiece," which keeps time only.

count wheel: Locking plate which controls the number of blows struck on the bell or gong. Does not allow for repeat striking.

dial: The face of a clock or watch.

drum: The round barrel on which the weight cord is wound.

escape: The method of regulating the release of power.

escape wheel: Regulator of the running of the clock.

fly: The fan on the strike train which slows the rate of striking.

full plate: Top plate of a watch in full round diameter. Clocks are also referred to as "full plate" when the plates are not pierced or otherwise cut out.

gadget clock: A timekeeper with extra accessories.

gimbal: Any support used to keep a timekeeper level, like the universal joints on a marine chronometer.

Girandole: Beautiful American Wall Clock designed by Lemuel Curtis.

hairspring: The balance spring of a watch or clock.

hands: Used on dials to mark hours, minutes or seconds.

Hollow Column Clock: A Shelf Clock so named because the weights of the pendulum movement rise and fall through hollowed columns. Believed to have been first made by the Bartholomews in Bristol, Conn., about 1828, using a smaller than standard wooden thirty-hour movement. See No. 215. Had the advantage in shipping to the buyer that the weights could be wedged into the columns rather than left loose or shipped separately. Many case designs extant. Another type, made by George Marsh & Co., is shown in No. 216. This style has an eight-day brass movement. The third design, made by the Mungers in Auburn, N.Y., is shown in No. 221. The hollow columns are made of sheet iron.

horologiographer: "Describer of timepieces."

hourglass: A device for measuring time, constructed of two cone-shaped or similar glass globes connected at their apexes by a small opening, containing just the right quantity of sand to flow in a certain time interval from the upper to the lower globe.

interchangeable parts: Parts which will fit equally well in any two machines of the same model.

Iron-Front Clock: Connecticut Shelf Clock with cast-iron front. See Nos. 273–275.

jack: A spit or moving figure turned by a clock mechanism. See No. 113.

jewel: Usually a semiprecious or synthetic stone used for bearings. Precious stones are now encountered only as end stones of good chronometers, for which diamonds are used.

kidney dial: Opening in front of dial in Massachusetts Shelf Clocks named possibly because of its shape.

labels: Labels used in Connecticut Shelf Clocks originally were of plain paper and used as dust blocks. Later they were engraved, lithographed or printed with the maker's name and served as an advertisement.

leaves: The teeth of the pinion gears.

Lighthouse Clock: Made by Simon Willard in 1822. See Nos. 150, 151.

Lyre: Form of Wall Clock.

mainspring: A long ribbon of coiled steel, providing power for clocks and watches. Not generally used on American clocks until the middle 1840's.

maintaining power: A booster power to keep the clock running while being wound.

Mantel Clock: Name later used for Shelf Clock.

Massachusetts Shelf Clock: Style of clock sometimes called Half Clock, or Box on Box Clock.

movement: The mechanism of the clock or watch.

OG, or *ogee* (used in architecture and furniture as well as clocks): A wavelike molding one side convex, the other concave, shaped like the letter S. The OG clock case is a plain rectangle. Mahogany or other wood veneer was used over the pine case. The result was simple, dignified, and pleasing, particularly when the graining was good. Made from about 1825 to about 1914 in six or more sizes, with wood and brass movements, both thirty-hour and eight-day, weight- and spring-driven. This is the clock case that housed the thirty-hour brass movement that Jerome used to revive the clock industry after the 1837 depression. "OG" or "ogee" is also applied to clock dials like those on the brass movement Shelf Clocks made by Seth Thomas, with a raised curve under the hour numerals, to distinguish them from "flat dials."

orrery: Machine showing the relative positions of the planets—a planetarium.

pallet: The part through which the escape wheel gives the impulse to the pendulum or balance wheel.

Pillar and Scroll: Shelf Clock design attributed to Eli Terry.

pinion: A small toothed wheel usually driven by a gear. The lantern pinion was made of two collars or plates joined by short steel wires called staves.

plates: The front and back of the movement.

Position Clock: A Regulator.

quick train: A watch movement beating five times per second, or 18,000 per hour.

"rack and snail": A striking mechanism which allows the strike to be repeated. The rack is a bar with teeth on one edge. The snail is a snail-shaped cam.

Regulator: Originally used to designate an accurate wall clock. Later applied to many Connecticut Wall Clocks.

Roman strike: Instead of one bell, two bells of different tone were used for striking the hours, a "one" bell and a "five" bell. Hours one, two, and three were struck on the "one" bell. Six was struck by one strike on the "five" bell, and one on the "one," thus following the Roman numerals which appear on the clock dial as VI. Four was struck by one strike on the "one" bell and one on the "five" bell, since "four" appears on these dials as IV, instead of the usual IIII.

Shelf Clock: One that stands on a shelf. In colonial days there were shelves in the kitchen, but no mantel over the fireplace in the living room. These came later, as did the term Mantel Clock.

slow train: A watch movement beating four times a second, or 14,400 an hour.

spring clocks: In such clocks springs, rather than weights, are the motive power.

stem wind: Up to about the 1870's watches were wound with separate keys.

sweep second hand: See center seconds hand.

Tall Clock: Hall, floor, or long-case clock, nicknamed "grandfather."

timepiece: A time-telling machine which does not strike.

Tower, or *Turret, Clock:* A public clock, as in steeples or buildings.

train: The series of gears and pinions that carry the power to the escapement.

verge: The pallet axis of the clock.

wagon spring: Flat-leaved springs used to power a clock movement, invented by Joseph Ives.

watch paper: The round paper which fitted into the watch case. Watchmakers and repairers used them for advertising.

weights: The fall of weights was used to power early clock movements.

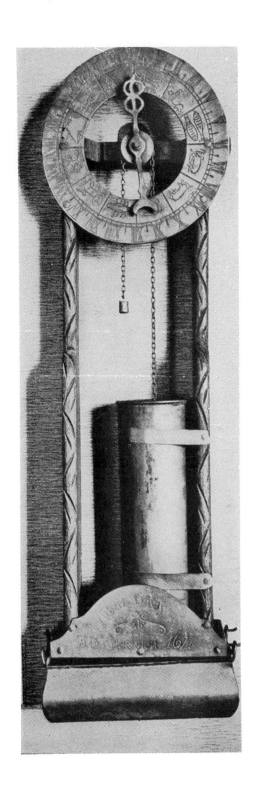

1. Water clock, or clepsydra, an early form of timekeeper.

2. By R. T. Manning, Ipswich, Mass., 1767. Wag-on-Wall clock. Essex Institute, Salem, Mass.

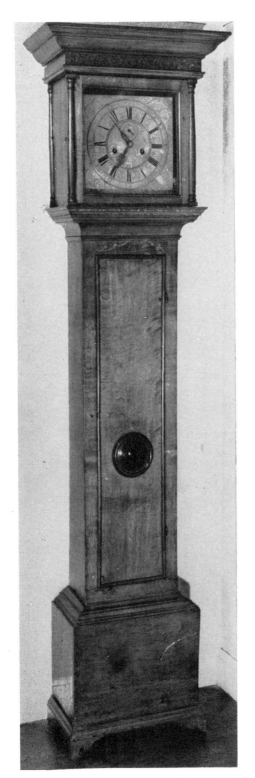 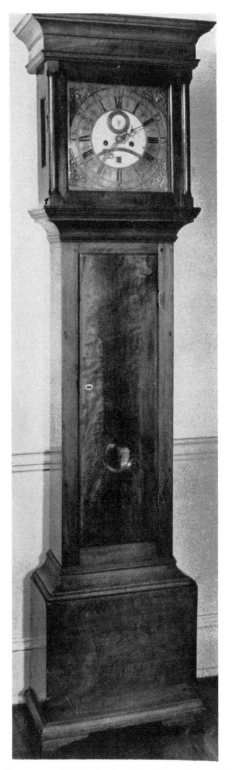

3. By Abel Cottey, who worked in Philadelphia, 1682–1711. Tall clock. Possibly the earliest extant American-made clock. Collection of Mrs. Joseph Carson, Bryn Mawr, Pa.

4. By Benjamin Chandlee, Nottingham, Md., *ca.* 1714. Square dial, walnut case, 81½ inches tall.

(5)

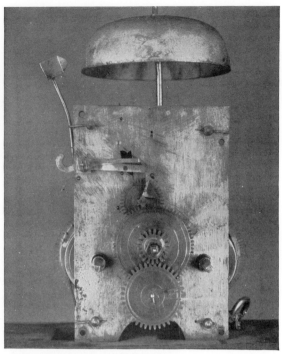

(6)]

(7)

5. Brass eight-day movement of clock shown in No. 3.
6. Movement of clock shown in No. 4.
7. Dial of clock shown in No. 4.

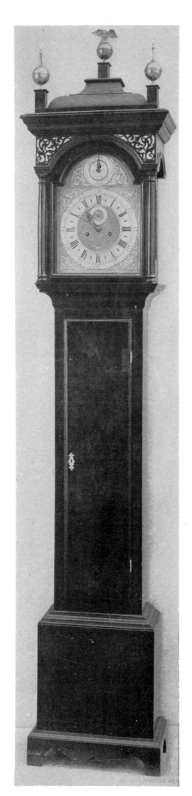

8. By Benjamin Bagnall, possibly Boston's first authenticated clockmaker,
ca. 1712–1740. Metropolitan Museum.

9. By Benjamin Bagnall.

10. Side view of No. 9.

11. By Samuel Bagnall, Boston, *ca.* 1740. Domed cherry case, 12-inch brass dial.

12. William Claggett dial. Newport, R.I., *ca.* 1730–1749.

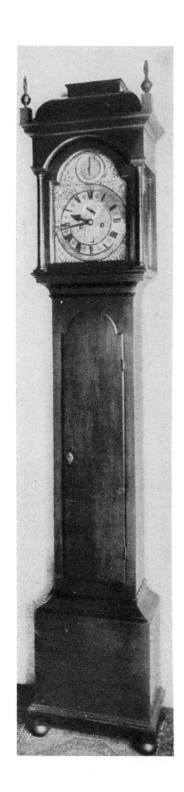

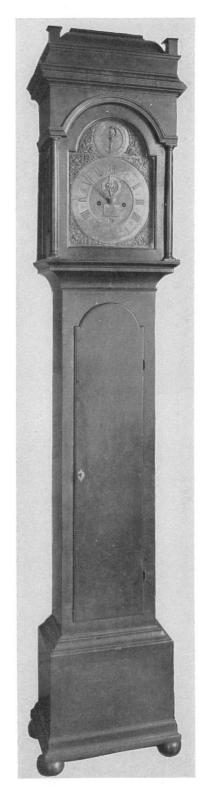

13. By William Claggett. Sarcophagus hood mahogany case. R.I. Historical Society.

14. By William Claggett.

15. Claggett dial. Moon phase in arch. Small corner dials: upper left, probably for time of tunes; lower left, calendar for days; upper right, "Britons Strike Home" and "Happy Swain," two musical tunes played by the clock; lower right, months. Inner circle shows the number of days in the month.

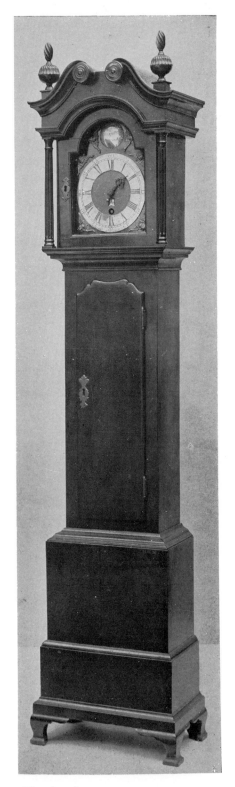

16. By William Claggett. Flat hood.

17. By Thomas Claggett, Newport, R.I., *ca.* 1730–1749. Metropolitan Museum.

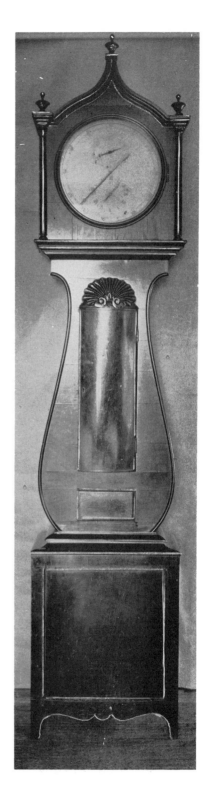

18. By John Townsend, Newport, R.I. Case *ca.* 1760–1770. Movement by William Tomlinson, England, *ca.* 1700–1741. Metropolitan Museum.

19. Maker unknown. Block Front with Shell.

 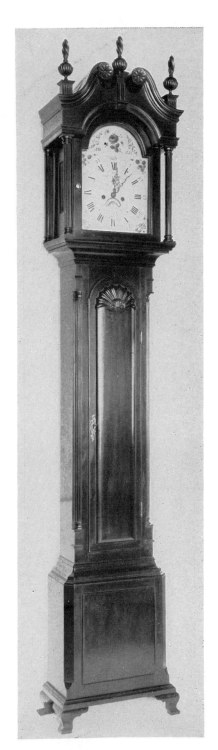

20. Boxed top. Case by John Goddard. Garvan Collection.

21. Case by John Goddard, *ca.* 1760–1775.

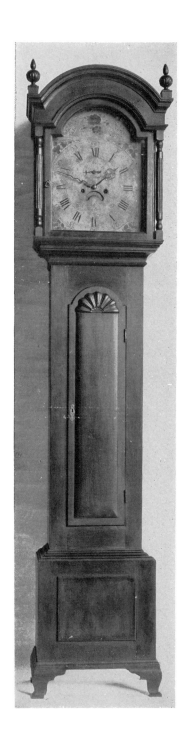

22. Case by John Goddard.

23. By David Williams, Newport, R.I., *ca.* 1800–1825. Seven feet tall, no side columns.

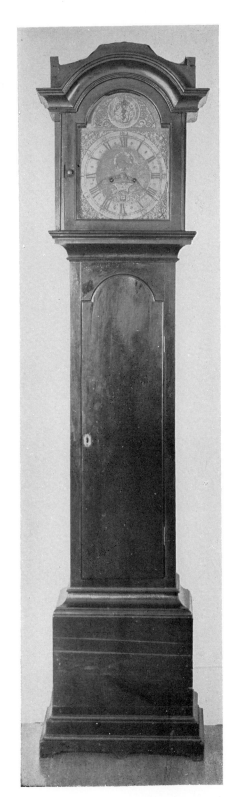

24. By Gawen Brown, Boston, *ca.* 1749–1773.

25. Maker unknown.

26. By Thomas Johnson, copper-plate dial. (1708–1767.) On the back are engraved four pages of music. Essex Institute, Salem, Mass. Preserved Clapp was a clockmaker of Amherst, Mass.

27. By David Blasdel (Blaisdell), Almsbury (Amesbury), Mass. Dial of metal movement hang-up clock, 1747. Haverhill Historical Society.

28. Dial of David Rittenhouse clock. "General Wayne" engraved in the arch, above which is the figure of Wayne in the circle.

29. By David Rittenhouse. A masterpiece, nine feet tall.
Owned by Drexel Institute and in Pennsylvania Museum.

30-31-32. Three David Rittenhouse clocks. The cases present a contrast in cabinet making.

33. By David Rittenhouse.

34. By Benjamin Rittenhouse, brother of David, who was reported to have made clocks *ca.* 1765. Dial is marked "Worcester."

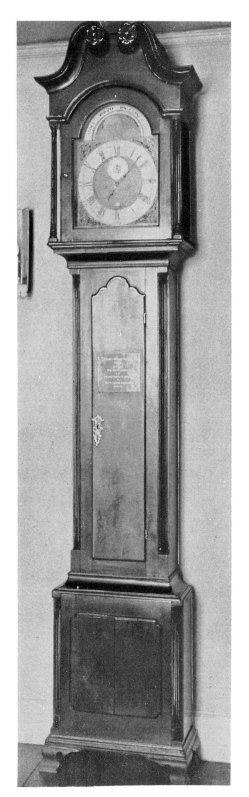

35-36. Two clocks by John Wood, Philadelphia, 1760-1793.
Old Garrison House, Trenton, N.J.; Metropolitan Museum.

 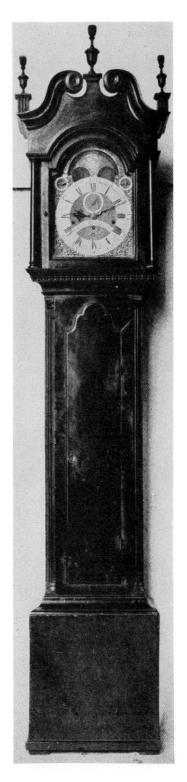

37. Maker unknown. Pennsylvania Museum.

38. By Henry Flower, Philadelphia, *ca.* 1753–1775.

39. By Daniel Rose, Reading, Pa., *ca.* 1779–1820.

40. By D. H. Solliday, Sumneytown, Pa., *ca.* 1800.
It is unusual to find glass of this type in the case door.

42. Dial of No. 41. Pewter. One hand. Inscription reads "HARK; WHAT'S THE CRY: PREPARE, TO MEET THY GOD TODAY."

41. By Nathaniel Dominy, East Hampton, Long Island. Dated "1789." Made for Capt. David Fithian, July 1, 1789. Eight-day brass movement.
Collection of Frederick Mudge Selchow.

43. By Timothy Chandler, Concord, N.H., *ca.* 1800.

44. Maker unknown, made for Capt. Thomas Marshall. Case of cherry and pine with satinwood inlay.

45. By Caleb Wheaton, Providence, R.I., *ca.* 1800.

46. By E. Storrs, Utica, N.Y. Early nineteenth century. Metropolitan Museum.

47. By Isaac Brokaw, Bridgeton, N.J. Garvan Collection, Yale University.

48. Maker unknown. Mahogany case, 8 feet tall. Garvan Collection.

49. By Eli Porter, Williamstown, Mass., *ca.* 1790–1800.

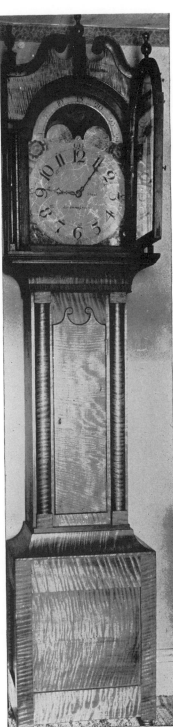

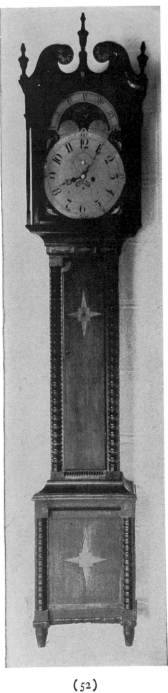

(51)

(52)

51. Daniel Scheid, Sumneytown, Pa.

52. By Jacob Cope, Watsontown, Pa. Three clocks with broken arch hoods and dials with arabic numerals and moon phase in the arch, *ca.* 1800.

50. Maker unknown.

53. By Isaac Chandlee. Brass eight-day movement. *ca.* 1807.

54. By Goldsmith Chandlee. Eight-day brass movement. Made at Stevensburg and Winchester, Va. Showing all the separate parts that make up a movement of this type. 1803.

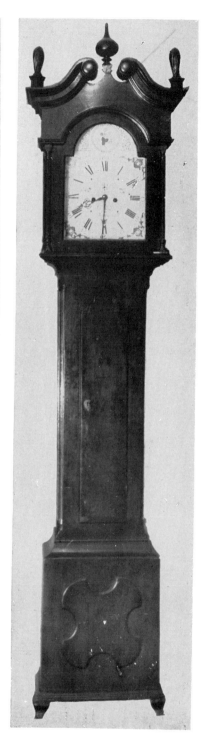

55. By Enos Doolittle, Hartford, Conn., *ca.* 1790.

56. By Ashel Cheney.

57. Maker unknown.

58. By Peregrine White, Woodstock, Conn. Dial and weights of musical tall clock.

59. By Thomas Harland, Norwich, Conn. Metropolitan Museum.
60. By Thomas Harland. Collection of William H. Putnam.

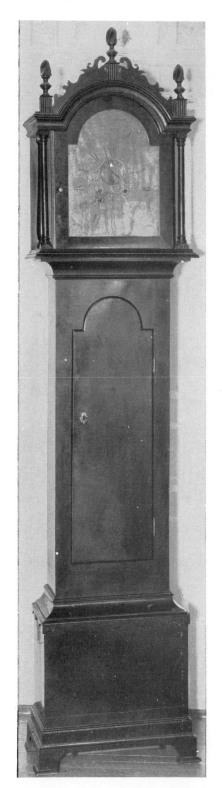

61. By Thomas Harland. 7 feet 3 inches tall.

62. By Thomas Harland. The "whales' tails" motive on the hood is used on these four Harland clocks.

63. By Silas Hoadley, Plymouth, Conn. Good example of this type of clock with wooden movement. Essex Institute, Salem, Mass.

64–65. Side and back view of the wooden movement in No. 66.

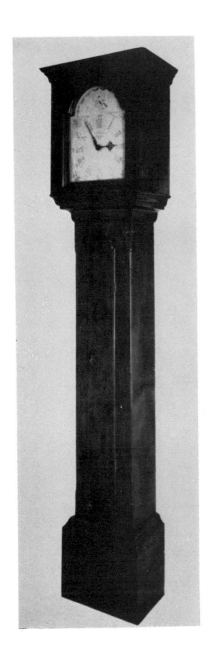

66. By Gideon Roberts, Bristol, Conn. Bristol's earliest clockmaker, *ca.* 1790 to his death in 1813. Clock numbered 511.

67. Dial, paper on wood, of No. 63.

68. Wooden movement of No. 63.

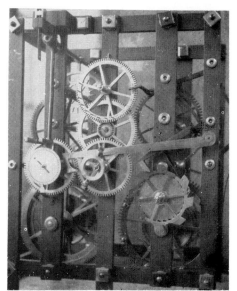

69. By Joseph Ives, wood movement for tall clock, *ca.* 1810. Collection of Edward Ingraham.

70. Details of the roller pinions used by Joseph Ives to reduce friction in movements similar to No. 69.

71. By Isaiah Lukens, Philadelphia, *ca.* 1820. Tower-clock movement for Second Bank of the United States, later the Customhouse. Reconditioned 1949 by Robert Franks and Philadelphia chapter of National Association of Watch and Clock Collectors.

72. Movement for tower clock originally in the First Presbyterian Church, Morristown, N.J., erected in 1738. Maker unknown. Movement now at Morristown National Historical Park, N.J.

73. By J. D. Custer, Pa. Movement of Pillar & Scroll Clock shown in No. 205. S. H. Barrington Collection.

74. Brass dial marked "E. Willard" with iron painted top. The slot in the iron above figure "XII" may have been for a rocking ship.

75. By Ephraim Willard, *ca.* 1777–1805.

76. By Benjamin Willard, Grafton, *ca.* 1790.

 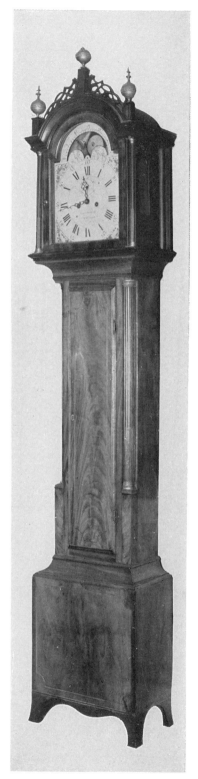

77. By Simon Willard, enameled iron dial. Tall clocks were the earliest clocks made by him.

78. By Simon Willard, dial with moon phase. Mahogany case 7 feet 10½ inches tall. The fret on the hood is similar to that on No. 77.

79. By Aaron Willard. Case 6 feet 4 inches tall, mahogany, with inlay in base.
80. By Aaron Willard, "Watchman's Clock." Essex Institute.

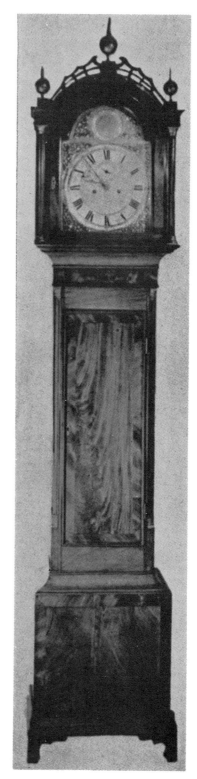

81. Maker unknown. Case attributed to Duncan Phyfe.

82. Maker unknown.

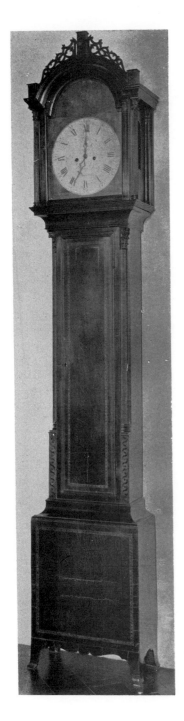
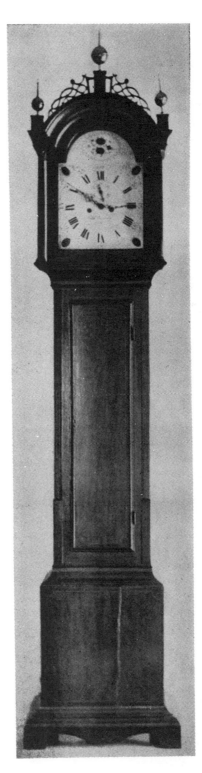

83. By James Doull, Charlestown, Mass., later in Philadelphia, *ca.* 1790–1820.
84. By Nathan Edwards, Acton, Mass., early nineteenth century.
85. By "S. M. Taber." Stephen M. Taber (1777–1862) worked at New Bedford, Mass., and Providence, R.I.

86. By David Williams, Newport and Providence, R.I., first quarter nineteenth century.

87. By William Cummens (1768–1834), Roxbury, Mass., *ca.* 1789–1834. Similar to tall clock in Edwin Hale Abbot Collection.

88. Friesland clock, not American. Essex Institute. See "Dutch Clocks" in list.

89. Dutch hood clock, not American. See "Dutch Clocks" in list.

90. Dwarf tall timepiece attributed to Benjamin Willard.

91. By Joshua Wilder. Dwarf tall clock.

92. No. 91 with rear door open to show mechanism of pendulum behind the back plate.

93. Attributed to Samuel Mulliken. Less than two feet tall. Kidney dial, Pallet arbor with no suspension spring, similar to small early Simon Willard clocks.

94. By Joshua Wilder. Dwarf tall timepiece.
95. By Joshua Wilder. Dwarf tall clock.

96. By John Bailey, Jr., Hanover, Mass. Dwarf tall clock.
97. By Reuben Tower, Hanover and Plymouth, Mass., *ca.* 1810–1830.

Four beautiful examples of dwarf tall clocks.

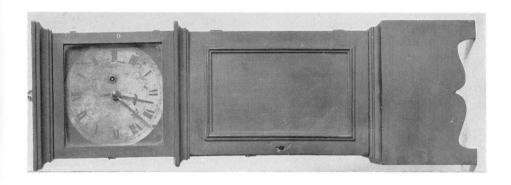

98-99-100-101. By unknown makers. Four different types of dwarf tall clocks.

102. By H. Bower, Philadelphia, *ca.* 1800 or later.
103. Maker unknown. Similar to No. 102.

104. Maker unknown.   Similar to one made by Benjamin Morrill
of Boscawen, N.H. Essex Institute.

105. By Joshua Wilder.

106. By Simon Willard. Shelf clock 18 inches high, with "Willard" on name plate. Pendulum attached directly to the anchor. Thirty-hour, weight-driven. Collection of Mr. Barny.

107. All the parts that make up the Simon Willard movement in No. 106.

108. By Simon Willard, *ca.* 1783. Thirty-hour wall clock. Fifteen are known.

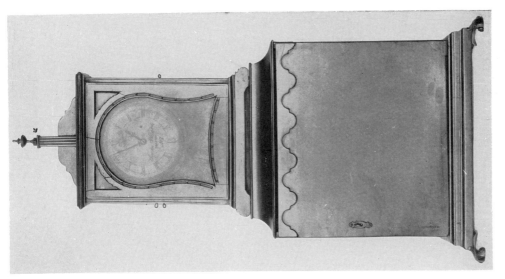

109. By Simon Willard. Brass dial.
110. By Simon Willard. "Made and Warranted for Dr. Dix; Simon Willard, fecit." Pennsylvania Museum.
111. "Willard, Grafton." Whereabouts of this clock now unknown. These three clocks are the beginning of the type called Massachusetts shelf or half clock.

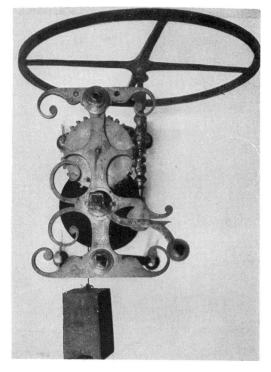

113. Clockwork roasting jack of type made
and advertised by Simon Willard, sold
by Paul Revere and others.

112. Banjo-type movement enclosed in coffin case. Dial and hands similar to No. 109, except for Arabic numerals. Winds at II.

116. Maker unknown. Massachusetts shelf clock. Dial shows through round opening in painted tablet.

114. Maker unknown. Kidney dial.
115. Label of Simon Willard, Roxbury, Mass.

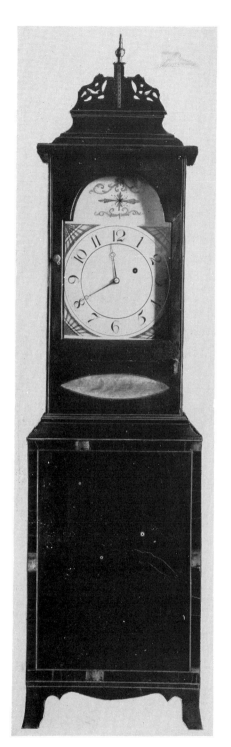

117. A Willard Massachusetts shelf clock.

118. By Simon Willard. Massachusetts shelf clock, kidney dial. Bottom panel a tablet.

Four different types of the Massachusetts shelf case design.

119. By Aaron Willard.
120. By Aaron Willard. Pennsylvania Museum.
Maker unknown.

121. By Aaron Willard.
122. By Aaron Willard, Jr.

123. By Aaron Willard, Boston. Timepiece, kidney dial.

124. By David Williams, Newport, R.I. Kidney dial. Timepiece *ca.* 1800.

125. By Elnathan Taber (1768–1854), *ca.* 1790. Timepiece.

126. By John Sawin, clock with dished (convex) dial, *ca.* 1825. Upper and lower tablets.

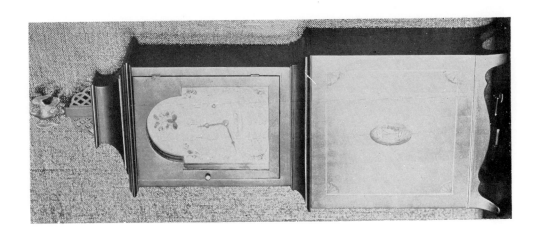

127–128–129. Three Massachusetts shelf clocks by David Wood, Newburyport, Mass., *ca.* 1790–1830.

130. Attributed to Elnathan Taber. Thirty inches high, kidney dial timepiece.

131. By Ebenezer Belnap, Boston, *ca.* 1810–1830. Timepiece.

132. By David Studley, Hanover, Mass. Clock *ca.* 1815.

133. By Ezekiel Jones, Boston. Timepiece *ca.* 1810.

134. Label used by Aaron Willard, Boston.   135. By Aaron Willard. Wall timepiece.   136. By Aaron Willard. Wall regulator timepiece.

137. By Simon Willard, movement of "Improved Timepiece." Patented by him in 1802, now commonly called "banjo."

138. Timepiece movement of No. 137, with front plate removed.

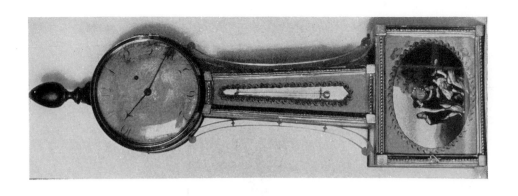

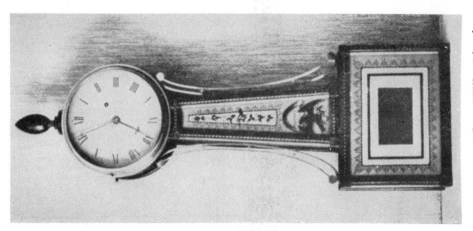

139–140–141. Three Willard banjos.

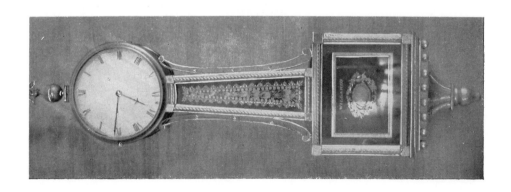

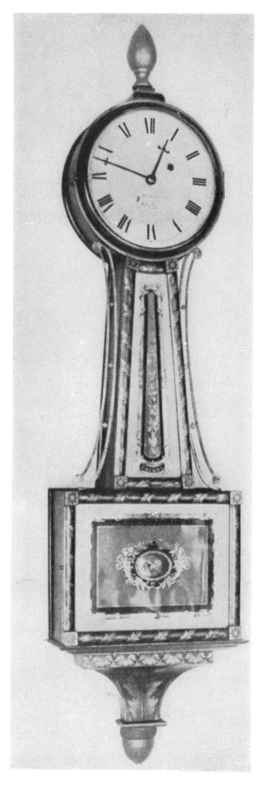

142. Willard banjo with bracket (the part under the box).

143. S. Willard & Sons, Boston, *ca.* 1824–1832. Banjo with bracket.

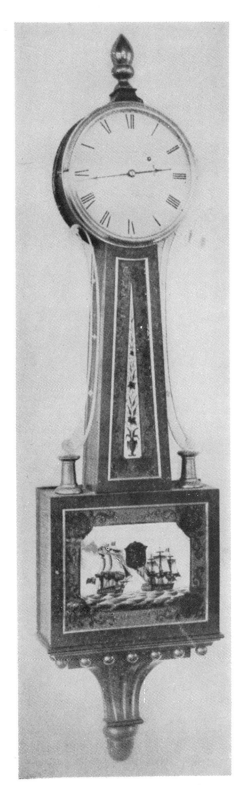

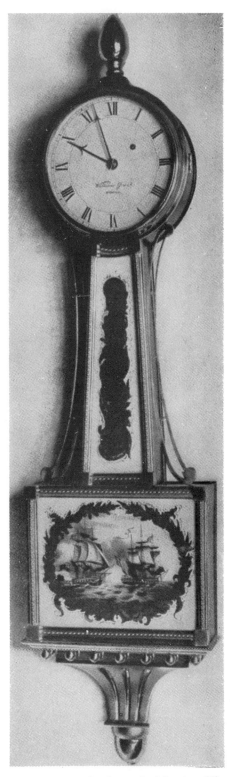

144. By William Cummens, Roxbury, Mass. One of his tall clocks is shown in No. 87. The spools beneath the side arms are unique.

145. By William Grant, Boston, *ca.* 1815.

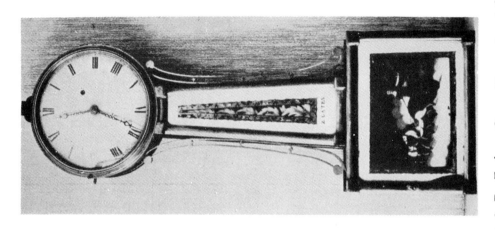

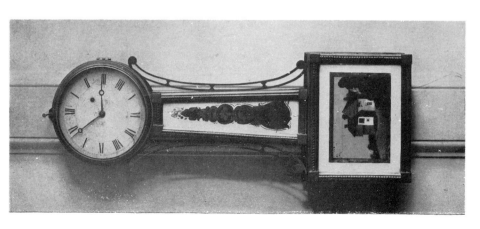

148. By Zacheus Gates, Harvard and Charlestown, Mass., *ca.* 1815.
149. By "Aaron Willard, Boston." Striking banjo. Collection of Frank Beaven.

146. By David Wood, Newburyport, Mass.
147. By John Sawin, Boston. Alarm timepiece.

150. By Simon Willard. "Lighthouse Clock," patented and advertised from Roxbury, Aug. 10, 1822. An eight-day alarm timepiece, 16 inches tall.

151. Lighthouse alarm timepiece with cast brass weight. Collection of Ginsberg & Levy.

DIRECTIONS FOR PUTTING UP THE TIMEPIECE.

Drive a hook in the wall where it is to be placed and suspend the Time
piece upon it. Open the lower door which is unfastened by turning the
button a little forward with the key. Screen the pendulum by which the
Timepiece may be plumbed, observing that it hangs free of the case and
in line with the point where it was confined, then screw it to the wall at those
screws thro' the back. Put the pendulum in motion. The weight is already
wound up. Set it with the minute hand which may be moved
backwards or forwards. To make the Timepiece go faster raise
the pendulum ball by the screw at the bottom, to make it go slower
lower the ball with the same screw.

These Timepieces are an improvement upon all others,
as they go by a Weight instead of a Spring, and the pendulum being
of a longer calculation than in any other small Pieces, renders it more
accurate and has proved is keep better time. The President of the United States
having granted a Patent for them, they are made by access from the
Patentee by Aaron Willard Jun. Washington St. Boston.
near Roxbury.
MASSACHUSETTS.

152. Label of Aaron Willard, Jr., Boston.   153. By Aaron Willard, Jr. Large flying eagle finial.

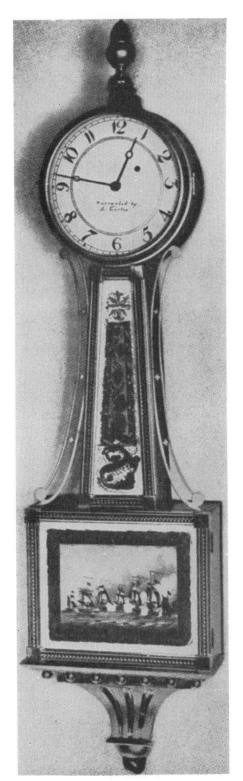

154. By Lemuel Curtis, Concord, Mass., *ca.* 1811–1818.

155. By Lemuel Curtis. Lyre clock. Strikes on two wires which run diagonally under "XI" to lower right side of the case. Pendulum about 3 inches shorter than usual. Spiraled hands are typical of Curtis. Collection of Donald K. Packard.

157. By Lemuel Curtis. Shelf lyre time-piece. Collection of F. M. Selchow.

156. By Lemuel Curtis. Girandole. One of America's most beautiful clocks

158. Shelf lyre clock, similar to No. 157, with doors open and center panel removed to show mechanism. Waist of the clock is shown on the left.

159. By Sawin and Dyer, Boston. Lyre timepiece. Metropolitan Museum.

160. By Sawin & Dyer, Boston. Lyre clock.
161. By John Sawin. Timepiece.

162. Maker unknown.

163. By Abiel Chandler, Concord, N.H., *ca.* 1829–1844. Striking lyre.

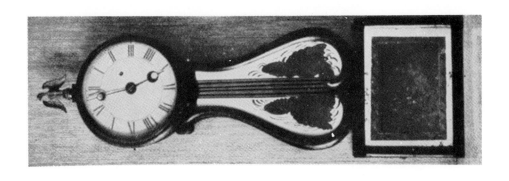

164–165–166–167. Makers unknown. Four lyres of different design.

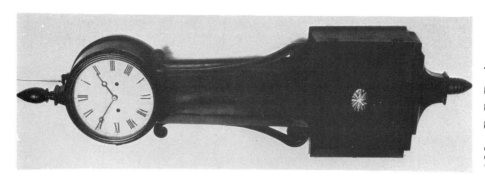

168. Lyre wall regulator. Collection of Peter Mitchell.
169. By "Forestville Mfg. Co.," *ca.* 1850. Connecticut lyre (wall acorn). Eight-day brass movement timepiece. Collection of L. S. Spangler.
170. Howard banjo. Collection of Mr. and Mrs. R. B. Davison.
171. Howard square box striking banjo with bracket and wood side arms. Collection of J. C. Harvey.

172. Howard gallery timepiece. Ray Walker Collection.
173. Movement of Howard gallery timepiece, No. 172.
174. By "E. Howard & Co., Boston." Lyre timepiece. Collection of F. M. Selchow.
175. Howard-type banjo with bracket.
176. By George D. Hatch, North Attleboro, Mass., 1850's. Wall regulator with striking banjo movement.

177. Three sizes of Howard banjos. Ray Walker Collection.

178. Maker unknown.

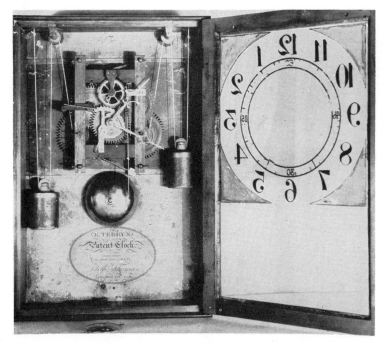

179. Eli Terry. Wood movement rack and snail strike shelf clock, patented in 1816.

180. Second type of strap wood movement used by Eli Terry, *ca.* 1816–1817. The count wheel in the center has replaced the rack and snail strike.

181. Box clock with door open showing the first type of movement used by Eli Terry. Forerunner of the pillar and scroll clock. Seth Thomas label.

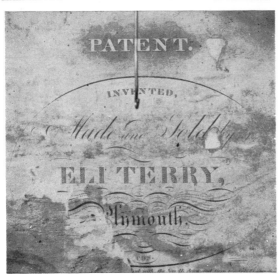

182. *Top left.* Eli Terry. Outside escapement pillar and scroll, *ca.* 1817–1818.
183. *Lower left.* Label of outside escapement pillar and scroll. Mitchell Collection.
184. *Top right.* Seth Thomas inside outside escapement. Terry's date, *ca.* 1818–1819.
Collection of R. B. Davison.
185. *Lower right.* Off-center pendulum pillar and scroll. Mitchell Collection.

186. Eli Terry. Standard pillar and scroll, *ca.* 1818–1819 and later.

187. Eli Terry. Standard pillar and scroll with door open and dial removed, showing the standard thirty-hour wood movement and the label. Peter Mitchell Collection.

188. Seth Thomas. Pillar and scroll, *ca.* 1820–1830.

189. Group of Connecticut shelf clocks. Mitchell Collection.

190. E. Terry & Sons, 1818–1824. Box case, alarm wood movement. Mitchell Collection.

191. Miniature and standard pillar and scroll clocks. Walter Keller Collection.

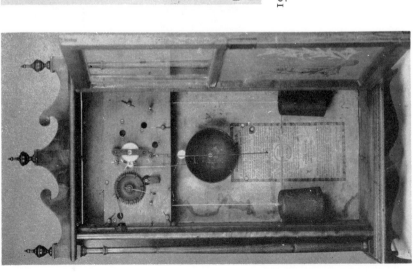

193. By Ethel North (left) and Norris North (right), *ca.* 1820. Pillar and scroll clocks with "Torrington Type" thirty-hour wood movement. Mitchell Collection.

194. By Rodney Brace, North Bridgewater, Mass., *ca.* 1825. Trained in Torrington, he continued to use that type of wood movement. Brandt Collection.

192. By Ethel North. Pillar and scroll, door open. Collection of L. S. Spangler.

195. H. Clark, Plymouth, Conn., *ca.* 1820 or later. Pillar and scroll with eight-day brass
movement. Collection of Frank Beaven.
196. Door open showing movement and label of No. 195.
197. Bishop & Bradley, Watertown, Conn., *ca.* 1823 to 1830. Pillar and scroll. Collection of
Richard Newcomb.
198. L. B. Bradley, Watertown, Conn., *ca.* 1823. Pillar and scroll. Newcomb Collection.
199. L. B. Bradley. Column shelf eight-day brass timepiece. Label dated "1823." Collection
of J. K. Lamond.

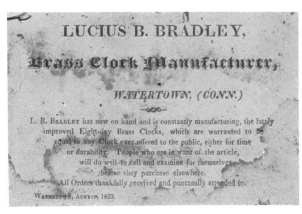

200. L. B. Bradley, *ca.* 1823. Column clock eight-day brass movement.

201. Label of No. 199. Dated "August, 1823."

202. Door open showing movement of No. 200.

203. Movement of No. 199. Heavy weight with compound pulley. Off-center pendulum.

204. By William Sherwin, Buckland, Mass., *ca.* 1830. Massachusetts type pillar and scroll with thirty-hour wood movement. Selchow Collection.

205. By Jacob D. Custer, Norristown, Pa. Pennsylvania type pillar and scroll. About thirty of these were made. Moon phase in round opening under center post. Eight-day brass movement. See No. 73.

206. Atkins & Downs, Bristol, Conn., 1831–1832. Transition type thirty-hour wood movement with carved columns and top.

(207) (208) (209)

(210)

207. Pratt & Frost, Reading, Mass., 1832–1835. Mirror or looking-glass shelf clock. Thirty-hour movement with 18-inch pendulum. Hour and minute wheels in front of front plate. Collection of Ernest Carsner.

208. Silas Hoadley, Bristol, Conn. Franklin alarm clock. George B. Davis Collection.

209. E. Terry & Sons. Eight-day wood movement. Mitchell Collection.

210. Label of No. 209.

211–212–214. Makers unknown. Three examples of New Hampshire mirror clocks, all with eight-day brass movements, *ca.* 1830. Strikers.

213. By Benjamin Morrill, Boscawen, N.H., *ca.* 1825. Eight-day timepiece brass movement. Ray Walker Collection.

215. E. & G. Bartholomew, Bristol, Conn., 1828–1832. Hollow column clock with thirty-hour wood movement. Collection of Frank Beaven.

216. George Marsh & Co. No place name—Conn. Hollow column, with eight-day brass movement. Frank Beaven Collection.

217. "Probably by E. Terry & Son or Eli Terry, Jr." "Connecticut Banjo," standard type thirty-hour wood movement. Frank Beaven Collection. A similar clock is in the Collection of F. M. Selchow.

218. C. & L. C. Ives, Bristol, Conn., 1830–1838. Three-decker eight-day strap brass movement with rolling pinions. Small mirror opening above center post. B. W. Brandt Collection.

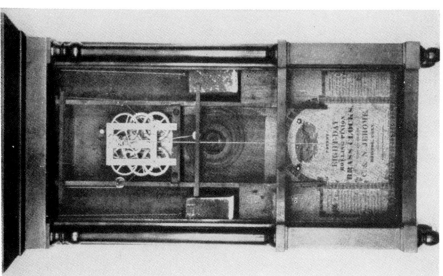

219. C. & N. Jerome, Bristol, Conn., 1830–1839. Black and gold
painted wood dial. Empire case.

220. No. 219 with door removed to show eight-day movement and label.

221. Asa Munger, Auburn, N.Y. Hollow column clock with sheet-
iron columns. Beaven Collection.

222. Maker unknown. Double-decker, *ca.* 1830. Movement similar to No. 220.

223. A. (Asa) Munger, Auburn, N.Y., *ca.* 1833. New York State design of Empire shelf clocks. Eight-day brass movement.

224. No. 223 with the door open, showing label. Similar clocks have Munger & Benedict labels. Eagle pendulum frequently used by Munger.

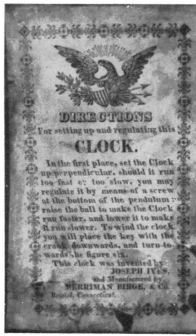

225. Merriman, Birge & Co., Bristol, Conn. Long wall mirror clock, *ca.* 1818–1819. First of
a series of clocks designed by Joseph Ives.

226. Iron plate movement of No. 225.

227. Merriman, Birge & Co., *ca.* 1822. Mirror wall clock. Collection of Frank Beaven.

228. Label of No. 227.   229. No. 227 with door open.

230. Joseph Ives, 1825–1830. Four wagon spring clocks. Case design shows possible Duncan Phyfe influence. Collection of F. M. Selchow.

231. Joseph Ives. Experimental wagon spring in pillar and scroll case. Showing mechanism. Three now known. Collection of Dr. M. A. Bissell. Others owned by Richard Newcomb, Jerome Jackson.

232. Wagon spring movement in No. 230. Movement is brass eight-day with rolling pinions.

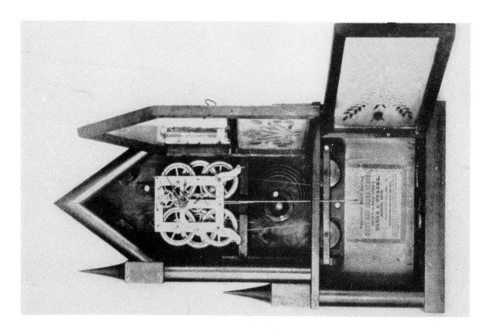

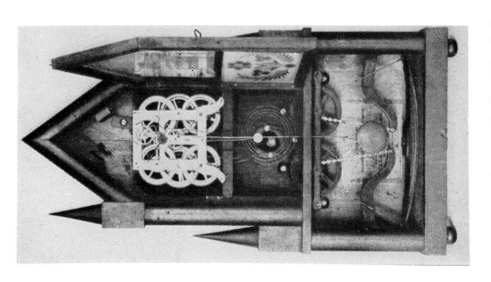

233–234–235. Birge and Fuller, Bristol, Conn., 1844–1848. Steeple on steeple clocks. No. 233 shows eight-day wagon spring power;

No. 234, case; No. 235, eight-day fusee. Both types of power are found in these clocks.

236. Birge & Fuller. Steeple on steeple clock with thirty-hour wagon spring power. Beaven Collection.

237. Birge & Fuller. Thirty-hour wagon spring movement. Beaven Collection.

238. Birge & Fuller. Three wagon spring clocks. Left and right, eight-day movement; center, thirty-hour with overpasted label of Daniel Pratt, Jr. Selchow Collection.

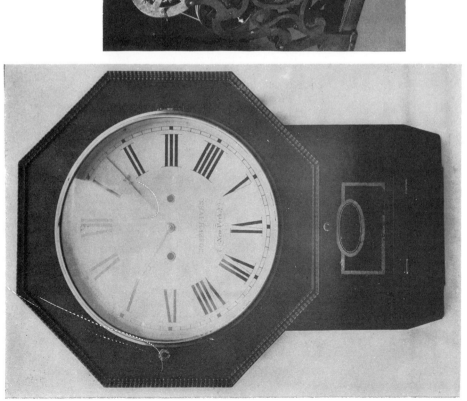

239. Atkins, Whiting & Co., Bristol, Conn., 1850–1855. Wall cased thirty-day wagon spring clock, invention of Joseph Ives.

240. Joseph Ives. Thirty-day wagon spring movement. Found in clock case No. 239 or No. 241.

241. Atkins Clock Mfg. Co., Bristol, Conn., 1855–1858. Shelf clock with thirty-day wagon spring movement.

(242)

(243)

(244)

(245)

(246)

(247)

242. Atkins Clock Mfg. Co., Bristol, Conn., 1856–1858. Wall clock. When Joseph Ives refused further use of his wagon spring, this thirty-day fusee was used.   Selchow Collection.

243. Joseph Ives. Selchow Collection.

244. The unusual eight-day brass movement of No. 243.

245. Joseph Ives, *ca.* 1853. Hourglass clock, thirty-hour. L. S. Spangler Collection.

246. N. L. Brewster & Co., Bristol, Conn., *ca.* 1861. Shelf clock with Ives tin-plate movement. Wire gong instead of bell.   Selchow Collection.

247. A Joseph Ives tin-plate movement, patented in 1859.

248. Silas Burnham Terry, Plymouth, Conn., *ca.* 1848. Balance-wheel escapement clock. This clock had an overpasted label of J. J. & W. Beals, Boston. Essex Institute.

249. *Top Right.* Balance escapement movement as in No. 248. Mitchell Collection.

250. *Lower left.* Thirty-hour rolled-brass movement, 1838, used by Chauncey Jerome to revivify clock business after the 1837 depression. Edward Ingraham Collection.

251. The OG which cased the movement in No. 250.

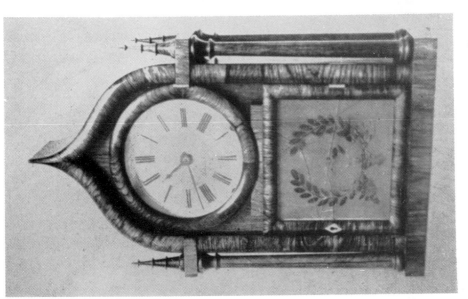

252–253. Brewster & Ingrahams, Bristol, Conn., 1844–1852. Round and sharp gothic twin-steeple shelf clocks. Elias Ingraham designed the cases, which became extremely popular and have remained so to the present time.

254. J. C. Brown, Bristol, Conn., 1842–1849. Rippled steeple clock. On the etched tablet there is a ballon ascension. Author's Collection.

255. Three steeple clocks. Sperry & Bryant, Williamsburg, L. I., C. Boardman, and New Haven Clock Co. The end clocks are 15 inches high; the center, 19 inches. Selchow Collection.
256. By Chauncey Jerome. Two rounded-top shelf clocks. Brandt Collection.
257. Smith & Goodrich, Bristol, Conn., 1847–1852. Eight-day clock. Brandt Collection.
258. Three beehive clocks. Brewster & Ingrahams, J. C. Brown, E. N. Welch & Co.
259. Group of Small Connecticut shelf clocks. George B. Davis Collection.

260. Forestville Mfg. Co., Bristol, *ca.* 1845. Acorn clock.
261. Mechanism of acorn clock, No. 260, showing fusees near bottom of case.
262. Crane year clock. Essex Institute.
263. Movement of Crane year clock. Wound once a year. Selchow Collection.

264. Seth Thomas, after 1860. Calendar clock. Eight-day.
265. By Southern Clock Co., St. Louis, Mo., 1875. "Fashion" calendar clock.
J. E. Coleman Collection.
266. Ithaca Calendar Clock Co., 1865–1914. Box skeleton calendar clock. Many have
movements by E. N. Welch, Bristol. Brandt Collection.
267. Gale patent wall calendar clock. Edward Ingraham Collection.
268. Seth Thomas. Wall calendar clock. Brandt Collection.

269. T. R. Timby, Saratoga Springs and Baldwinsville, N.Y. Solar timepiece, patented 1863.

270. Connecticut wall regulator. Thousands of these were made. Mitchell Collection.

271. Juvet time globe. Patented by Louis P. Juvet, 1867. Made also *ca.* 1879–1886 at Canojaharie, N.Y. Brandt Collection.

272. Seth Thomas Co., Thomaston, Conn., *ca.* 1890. Violin clock. Selchow Collection.

273. Metal-cased Connecticut clock with mother-of-pearl inlay, *ca.* 1860 and later.
274. American Clock Co., 1859. Iron-front thirty-hour time strike and alarm. Collection of
Miss Edythe Clark.
275. Metal-cased clock referred to as "Iron Front." Conn., *ca.* 1860 and later.
276. Seth Thomas, 1879. Drum alarm brass case. Paul Darrot Collection.
277. E. Ingraham and Co., *ca.* 1880. One of the first "Marblized" clocks.
Edward Ingraham Collection.
278. Briggs Conical clocks, patented 1856. Made in Bristol, *ca.* 1875.
George B. Davis Collection.

279. H. J. Davis, New York, N.Y., *ca.* 1880. Illuminating Alarm Clock.
Mitchell Collection.
280. American Screw clock, "made for J. C. Kennedy." Wesley Hallet Collection.
281. Columbus Clock, 1892. Brandt Collection.
282. "Continental" blinking-eye clock.
283. Blinking-eye clocks made in Connecticut, *ca.* 1875. "Topsey & Sambo."
Peter Mitchell Collection.
284. "Ignatz," in New Haven Clock Co. Catalogue, 1885. A one-day timepiece, whose ball on
the end of a string escapement winds and unwinds on each of two poles like a tether ball.
Probably for the store window. Patented 1883 by A. C. Clausen. Selchow Collection.

285. Part of the Mitchell Collection, Middletown, N.Y.

286. Collection of Willis Michael, Red Lion, Pa.

287. Part of the Mitchell Collection, Middletown, N.Y.

288. Small section of the Collins Clock Museum, Georges Mills, N.H.

289–290. *Top left and lower left.* Watch by Luther Goddard (1762–1842), Shrewsbury, Mass., *ca.* 1809–1817, of which about five hundred were made. The hour hand is like those used on Connecticut shelf clocks of the period. Watch No. 155. In the Collection of Frank Bogenrief, Hinton, Iowa.

291. *Top right.* Watch marked "Ephraim Clark," Philadelphia, *ca.* 1780–1800. Dr. Anthony Benis Collection.

292–293. *Middle and lower right.* Watch by Jacob D. Custer, Norristown, Pa. He received a U.S. patent, 1843, and may have made a dozen or more. Collection of S. H. Barrington.

(294)

(295)

(297)

(296)

(298)

(299)

(300)

(301)

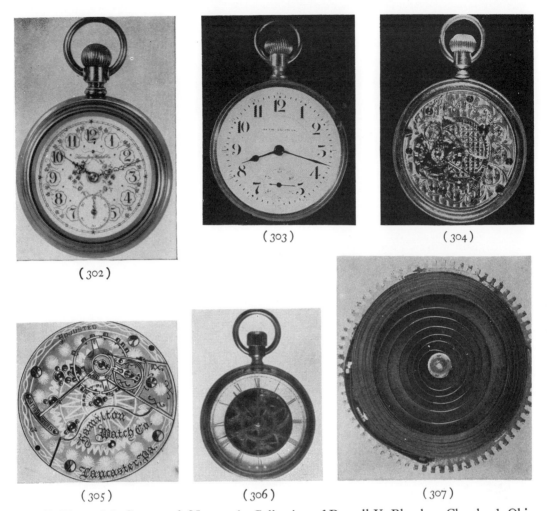

(302)　(303)　(304)

(305)　(306)　(307)

294. E. Howard & Co., watch No. 4446. Collection of Russell V. Bleecker, Cleveland, Ohio.

295. Watch movement of E. Howard & Co., Boston, No. 20,685. (J. E. Coleman)

296. Elgin lady's watch. This type popular from 1904 till *ca.* 1920, when wrist watches came into vogue.

297. "LADY ELGIN." The first lady's watch made in Elgin factory, 1867.

298. "B. W. RAYMOND," No. 714. Watch made by Elgin in 1867, named after a founder of the company. (Courtesy of Elgin National Watch Co.)

299. Ezra Bowman watch movement. Lancaster, Pa. Bowman Technical School Collection. (J. E. Coleman)

300. J. P. Stevens & Co., Atlanta, Ga. (J. E. Coleman)

301. The fifteenth watch made by Elgin, 1867.

302. The first Hamilton watch, 1892. Hamilton Watch Co., Lancaster, Pa.

303. Seth Thomas "Maiden Lane" watch, 25 jewels, size 18. They made watches 1884–1914. Collection of Paul Darrot.

304. Movement of No. 303.

305. Movement of the first Hamilton watch. Size 18, about 1¾ inches diameter. (Courtesy of Hamilton Watch Co.)

306. Waterbury Watch Co., *ca.* 1880. Simplified duplex escapement and modified Tourbillon movement. 1⅞ inches diameter, ⅝ inches thick, 58 parts, spring 7 to 9 feet long, taking 140 half-turns to wind. Willis Milham Collection.

307. Mainspring of Waterbury watch, 7–9 feet long.

(308)   (309)

(310)   (311)

308. "R. INGERSOLL & BRO. New York" 1893 watch No. 309,499.
309. "Pocket Clock" made by the Waterbury Clock Co. in 1895, No. 177,738.
310. Movement of Ingersoll No. 309,499.
311. Movement of No. 177,738.
312. Patent Office model of a Waterbury watch, 1885.
(Illustrations on this page courtesy of Smithsonian Institution.)

LIST OF CLOCKMAKERS

ABBREVIATIONS

Sources of information or references where additional material can be found are listed in parentheses at the end of each entry.

AAJ: *American Antiques Journal*
Abb.: Henry G. Abbott, *Antique Watches*, list of makers, 1897
adv.: advertised
AJ: *Antiques Journal*
ALP: Albert L. Partridge, Boston
Ant.: *The Magazine Antiques*
apt.: apprentice
astro.: astronomical
Avery: Dr. and Mrs. Amos G. Avery, Amherst, Mass.
aw.: at work
b.: born
Baillie: G. H. Baillie
BCC: Boston Clock Club, 1934–1940
BCL: Mrs. Bella C. Landauer Collection of Watch Papers
Bir.: Harry Birnbaum Collection of Watch Papers
Bowman: John J. Bowman, Lancaster, Pa.
Brandt: Mr. and Mrs. Bernard W. Brandt, Montrose, N.Y.
bro.: brother
Buhler: Mrs. Yves Henry Buhler, Museum of Fine Arts, Boston
Bul.: *Bulletin* of the National Association of Watch and Clock Collectors
Burt: Edwin B. Burt, Auburndale, Mass.
C.: clock or clockmaker
ca.: circa or about
cal.: calendar
C. D. Collins: Clarence Dexter Collins, Curator, Collins Clock Museum, Georges Mills, N.H.
Chandlee: Edward E. Chandlee, Philadelphia
Childs: Andrew L. Childs, New York City
chron.: chronometer
Col.: collection
Coleman: J. E. Coleman, Nashville, Tenn.
Conrad: Henry C. Conrad
Cramer: Ernest A. Cramer, Philadelphia. Collection of Watches, Watch Papers
Crossman: Charles T. Crossman
Cutten: George B. Cutten

D.: dealer
d.: died
DCH: David C. Hill
dir.: directory
DKP: Donald K. Packard
Dre.: Carl W. Drepperd
EI: Edward Ingraham, Bristol, Conn.
engr.: engraved
Evans: Charles T. Evans, Secretary, American National Retail Jewelers Association
Ex.: example
f.: failed
FMS: Frederick Mudge Selchow, Jericho, N.Y.
Franks: Robert Franks, Bryn Mawr, Pa.
FT: *Furniture Treasury*, Wallace Nutting
G.: goldsmith
g.: gold
Gen. Time Col.: Collection of General Time Corporation, New York City
Gil.: Harrold E. Gillingham, Philadelphia
Hist.: town history
Hob.: *Hobbies*, a magazine
Hoopes: Penrose R. Hoopes, Philadelphia
Hull: George W. Hull, historian of Bristol, Conn.
IBB.: Ingraham, Buell, Barr study of Bristol Makers, 1936
ill.: illustration
Imp.: importer
Ingraham: Edward Ingraham, Bristol, Conn.
insts.: instruments
J.: jeweler
James: Dr. Arthur E. James, West Chester, Pa.
JWW: John Ware Willard
Keller: Walter F. Keller, Scarsdale, N.Y.
Knittle: Rhea Mansfield Knittle, Ohio historian
Lan. Co.: Papers of Lancaster County History
LB: Lockwood Barr

Lockett: Miss Anne Lockett
LSS: L. S. Spangler, Hagerstown, Md.
marr.: married
MFM: Mark F. Massey, Washington, D.C.
mfr.: manufacturer
Milham: Willis I. Milham, Williamstown, Mass.
min.: minute
MMA: Metropolitan Museum of Art, New York City
Moore: Mrs. N. Hudson Moore, *The Old Clock Book*, 1911
movt.: movement
mus.: musical
NAWCC: National Association of Watch and Clock Collectors
n/d: no date
n/p: no place
PG: Phillipse Greene
pos.: possibly
Prime: Alfred Coxe Prime
prob.: probably
pub.: published
R.: repairer
rep.: repeating
S.: silversmith
sd.: signed
sig.: signature
6QC: *Six Quaker Clockmakers*, Edward E. Chandlee
Smiths. Inst.: Smithsonian Institution
Stout: Arthur Stout, Stanfordville, N.Y.
Stow: Mr. and Mrs. Charles Messer Stow, New York City
str.: striking
Stretch: Miss Carolyn Stretch, Philadelphia
tall: tall clock or floor, hall or long case clock
Timepieces: magazine of that name
Twp.: township
(tx): tax records shown in Ingraham, Buell, Barr study of Bristol Makers, 1936
W.: watch or watchmaker
Williams: Carl M. Williams
WRM: Willis R. Michael

LIST OF MAKERS

ABBETS, JAMES: Albany, N.Y. Adv. 1760, "Shortly to remove."

ABBEY, DAVID: Pittsburgh, Pa. *Ca.*1830.

ABBOTT & BRO., H. C.: Birmingham, Ala. *Ca.*1901.

—, GEORGE: Phila. Dir. 1822.

—, HENRY: N.Y.C., 18 Maiden Lane, Pat. Jan. 1, 1881, No. 236748 stem-winding device. Adv. 1892, "Patent Self Winding Device on market 11 years, about 50,000 in use; price reduced 50%."

—, MOSES: Sutton, N.H. *Ca.*1820. Tall maple-cased clock known. Moved to Pomfret, Vt.

—, SAMUEL: Boston, Pitt St. *Ca.*1810–1832. Prolific maker of Shelf, Banjo, Tall (few) and N.H. Mirror clocks. Also other place names on dials. Wide-waisted Lyre, 1810 on dial, "Montpelier, Vt.," in Gen. Time Col. N.H. Mir. LSS Col.

ABEL, ROBERT K.: Phila. Dir. 1840–1841.

ACKER, JOSEPH D.: West Chester, Pa. Dir. *ca.*1850.

ACORN CLOCK: See ill. Nos. 260, 261.

ADAMS (Wm.) & EATON (Samuel A.): Boston. Dir. 1816–1821.

— (Wm.) & HARLAND (Henry): Boston. Dir. 1813.

— & PERRY WATCH MFG. CO.: Lancaster, Pa. Org. 1874–1876. f. None made. Reorganized as Lancaster Penna. Watch Co. Later reorganized with same name and "Ltd." Control passed to Abram Bitzner and Oppenheimer Bros. & Veith, N.Y.C., selling agents; f. 1890. Sold to Hamilton Watch Co. 1892.

"— STREET," used by Waltham Watch Co. after 1878.

— (Wm.) & TROTT (Andrew C.): Boston. Dir. 1810.

—, CHARLES: Erie, Pa. *Ca.*1860. Marketed Calendar clock marked "Liberty."

—, E. W.: Seneca Falls, N.Y. *Ca.*1830–1850. Of MARSHALL AND ADAMS. Mfrs. of Tower, Shelf, and Regulator clocks. Brass movt., 8-day Shelf of type like Conn.

—, H. B.: Elmira, N.Y. Adv. 1842.

—, JOHN C.: Early promotor of watch factories in Chicago in 1870's. Six locations. "The Great American Starter."

—, "J.C.," used by Cornell Watch Co. 1871–1874.

—, JOHN P.: 1812–. Newburyport, Mass. 1858–1860.

—, JONAS: Rochester, N.Y. 1834.

—, NATHAN: 1755– b. Newbury, Mass. As "joiner" to Danvers, 1783, and Andover, 1784. Back to Danvers 1786 as C. Probably apprenticed to Ezra Batchelder. Probably to Wiscasset, Me., 1792; activity there unknown. Abbott, Baillie, and others date Boston 1796–1825.

—, SAMUEL: Boston. Dir. 1825.

—, THOMAS F.: Boston. Dir. 1810.

—, THOMAS F.: Baltimore, Market St. Petersburg, Va., 1804. Adv. 1807. Then Edenton, N.C. Adv. 1809–1810.

—, WALTER: 1810–1880. Bristol. Spent greater part of life here. Identified with clock business except for Civil War service. Worked for C. Boardman many years, then Atkins Clock Co. Probably no clocks with his name. (Hist.)

—, WILLIAM: Boston. Dir. 1809–1825. Of the firm of ADAMS & EATON. (Baillie)

ADOLPH, DUFF: Phila. Dir. 1837.

AGAR, EDWARD: N.Y.C. Dir. 1761.

AHERNS, ADOLPH: Phila. Dir. 1837.

AIRD, DAVID: Middletown, Conn. 1785. Not a maker; name possibly changed from "Charles Brewster." Adv. as W. 1785. Careless acquisition of other people's property reported.

AITKEN, JOHN: Phila. Adv. 1785; Dir. 1813. Clocks and musical inst.

AITKINSON: See Atkinson.

AKERS, EDWARD: Baltimore. 1843–1882.

ALBEE, WILLARD W.: Newburyport, Mass. Dir. 1860.

ALBERT, JOHN: Huntington, Pa. *Ca.*1816. Three Tall clocks WRM Col.

ALBRIGHT, R. E.: Flushing, N.Y. *Ca.*1860.

—, THOMAS F.: Phila. Dir. 1837–1845.

ALDEN & ELDRIDGE: Bristol. *Ca.*1820.

ALDER, W. D.: N.Y.C. "With De Mory GRAY, successor to Geo. C. A. BAKER." Chron. dated "1868" in BCL Col.

"ALEXANDER," used by U.S. Watch Co. *ca.*1869–1870.

—, SAMUEL: Phila., 213 N. 2 St. 1787–1808.

ALLEBACH, HENRY: Reading, Pa. Adv. 1829.

—, JACOB: Phila. 1825–1840. Tall clocks.

—, M. B.: Phila. *Ca.*1800.

ALLEN, ALEXANDER: Rochester, N.Y., 1 Buffalo St. Dir. 1860. "Mfger. & R small mchy. & C."

—, JAMES: –1684. Boston.

—, JARED T.: Batavia, N.Y. Adv. 1832–1836.

—, J. T.: Rochester, N.Y. Dir. 1844–1846. S.

—, JOHN: N.Y.C. 1798.

—, WILLIAM: Adv. 1772. "From Birmingham and has joined Jacob & Claude." Drepperd adds, at Port Tobacco, Md., 1773 to 1780's.

ALLENTOWN: Pa. William Allen (b. Phila. 1704–), owner of 3370 acres in Northampton Co., Pa. Laid out town of Northampton, 1762. Name was used till 1800. From 1800–1811 name used was Allentown. Then incorporated as Borough of Northampton till 1838, when the present name Allentown was adopted. (Funk)

ALLISON, GILBERT: Pa. Tall clocks. n/p. n/d.

ALLOWAY, WILLIAM: Ithaca, N.Y. Adv. 1823.

ALLYN, JOHN: Hartford, Conn. "1657." Name may have been Van Allen, Dutch trader. Probably not C.

—, NATHAN: Hartford, Conn. "The Hartford W." Doolittle's business turned over to him. Seems to have sold it 1808 to Heydorn & Imlay. Disappears 1811. (Hoopes)

ALMY, JAMES: New Bedford, Mass. 1836.

ALRICHS, JACOB: 1775–1857. Wilmington, Del. Apprenticed to uncle Jonas 1793–1797. Started alone 1797 and adv. for apprentice. C. and W. many years, but not full time after 1810. Elijah Hollingworth an apprentice. To 311 Mkt. St. bet. 3rd and 4th Sts. City Council 1823, Del. Senate 1830. Son Henry. (Conrad)

— (Jacob) & McCLARY (Samuel): Wilmington, Del. 1793–1797. First Wilmington mchy. shop. (Baillie)

—, JONAS & JACOB: Wilmington, Del. 1793–1797. Dissolved 1797. Uncle and nephew. Tall clocks. (Conrad) (Baillie)

—, HENRY S.: Wilmington, Del. Son of Jacob. After 1857 continued his father's W. and C. business. (Conrad)

—, JONAS: 1759–1802. Wilmington, Del. First C. of this name. 1772–1802. Possibly apt. of Thomas Crow and succeeded him in old 2nd St. store. Uncle of Jacob; together 1793–1797. Tall clocks. (Conrad)

—, WESSELL: *Ca.*1670–1734. New Castle, Del., before 1697, then Salem, N.J. Doubt about him as C., S. and G. *Ca.* 1719. (Williams)

ALSOP, THOMAS: Phila. Dir. 1842, 1849–1850.

ALTMORE, MARSHALL: Phila. 1819–1832.

ALVORD, PHILO: 1812–1878. Utica, N.Y. Dir. 1834.

AMANA: Buffalo, N.Y., 1843–1855, then Iowa Co., Iowa. n/d. Hooded Wall clock ill. in Drepperd.

AMANT, PETER (or Fester): Phila. Dir. 1794. (Moore)

AMBERMAN, JOHN S.: Bklyn., N.Y.C., 135 Nassau St. Dir. 1856–1857.

AMERICAN CLOCK CO.: N.Y.C., 3 Cortlandt St. Org. 1849 to succeed Conn. Protective Clock Co. 1850 credit report, "A Clock Co. consisting of John Birge, Brewster & Ingrahams, J. C. Brown, E. Manross, Smith & Goodrich, Terry & Andrews, and Chauncey Jerome and William L. Gilbert of Winchester. Large dealers in clocks; have opened a large depository in N.Y.C. for the sale of clocks, and I understand that it is there called The American Clock Co. They have a factory in Bristol, where they make 30,000 clocks annually. They must be and are good and safe to trust." Took over N.Y.C. sales for Bristol

Brass & Clock Co. 1857. Adv. 1859 N. Haven and Forestville, Conn. "Composed of New Haven Clock Co., formerly Jerome Mfg. Co., and E. N. Welch, Forestville." 1870 catalogue says Seth Thomas Co. & W. L. Gilbert added. Chicago office 1868, 115 Lake St.; 1877, 172 State St. Added offices *ca.*1880 at Phila., 625 Chestnut St., and San Francisco, 7 Montgomery St. Many extant clocks. (EI) (Hull)

—, Cuckoo Clock Co.: Phila. n/d. Ex. Essex Inst.

— Horologe Co., The: Boston (Roxbury). 1850. Warren Mfg. Co. 1850; then Boston Watch Co. 1853. Early start Waltham Watch Co.

— National Watch Co., The: South Bend, Ind. 1902 only. W. Name changed 1902 to South Bend W. Co. "Never used except on paper." (Evans) (MFM)

— Mfg. & Supply Co., Ltd.: N.Y.C., 10 Dey St. Electric battery self-winders under Pond patents. Shelf, Tall, Regulator, Gallery clocks.

— Repeating Watch Factory: Elizabeth, N.J. 1885–1892. 5-minute repeater attachment for watches under patent Jan. 27, 1885. Three similar names 1892–1905. (MFM)

— Watch Co.: Waltham, Mass. Feb. 4, 1859–1885. Absorbed Nashua Watch Co., Apr. 1862. Entire factory rebuilt and enlarged 1878–1883. Became 1885, American Waltham Watch Co.; 1906 became Waltham Watch Co. (1906–1950). (Crossman) (Evans)

AMES, Horace: N.Y.C. *Ca.*1860.

AMIDON, L.: Bellows Falls, Vt. *Ca.*1860.

ANDERSON, David D.: Marietta, O. 1821–1824. C. (Abbott)

—, David M.: *Ca.*1795–1862. Waynesburg, Pa. Later Honey Brook. Aw. *ca.*1820. Marked Tall clocks "David M." or "D.M." Apprenticed to local maker. Had as apprentices J. Clemens McConnell and Isaac Landis of Coatsville, Pa. Made first town clock at Waynesburg. Continued making Tall clocks despite competition of Conn. Shelf clocks. (James)

—, Jesse: Pennsville, ? n/d.

—, John: "Md." Adv. 1746. Clock cases. (MFM)

ANDREW, John: 1747–1791. Salem, Mass. "At the sign of Gold Cup on Long Wharf." G. J. W. 1769.

ANDREWS, L. (Lucius) M. & F. (Franklin) C.: Bristol. (tx) 1837–1843. In 1837 leased Treat's mechanic shop south side Pequabuck River west of Main St. with right to use casting room as needed for their work. Shelf clocks with this label extant. (Hist.)

—, N. & T.: Meriden, Conn. 1832.

—, D. B.: Cincinnati, O. n/d.

—, Franklin C.: N.Y.C., 46 Maiden Lane and 3 Cortlandt St. Also listed Bristol, Conn., in L. M. & F. C. Andrews. Dir. 1848. Brass movt. Shelf clock owned by Mrs. J. E. Hamilton, Edgewood, Md.

—, Hu: Washington, Pa. n/d. Tall clock Lewis Dyer Col.

—, James: N.Y.C. *Ca.*1815.

ANDRUS & BEACH: Watertown, Conn. n/d. Wood movt. Shelf clock in Fred E. Quick Col., Watertown, Conn. Label printed by "Joseph Hurlbut, Hartford, Conn."

ANGELL, Otis N.: Johnston, R.I. Patented "alarm bell self-acting clock," June 20, 1834.

ANGELUS Clock Co.: Phila. Inc. 1874. Made 8-day str. clock which sounded angelus at 6, noon, and 6; cases like cathedral door and 4″ spire finial.

ANNIN, M.: N.Y.C. "1786." (MFM) (Baillie)

ANNISTON, Isaac: Phila. Dir. 1785. (Prime)

ANSONIA Brass & Battery Co.: Ansonia Conn. Reported made clocks *ca.*1870.

ANSONIA Brass & Clock Co.: Ansonia, Conn. 1851–1878. Other name for —

ANSONIA Clock Co.: Ansonia, Conn., 1851–1878. N.Y.C. 1879–*ca.*1930. Both names used in Conn. Started by Anson G. Phelps (Ansonia named for him) 1851 as subsidiary of Ansonia Brass Co. to increase use of brass. Boston office (Dir. 1854), 43 Hanover St. Successful; became separate company *ca.*1859. Inc. 1873. Usual styles of Conn. clock, Wall and Shelf, some wgt, mostly spring driven; with or without alarms; some marine lever escapements. Clocks marked "Ansonia, Conn." Brooklyn, N.Y., factory acquired 1878 and all operations moved there. Clocks marked "New York." Fire 1879 destroyed plant; going again 1880. Good

ANSONIA CLOCK CO. (cont'd)
clocks, Gallery, Shelf, Mantel; wood and china cases. Some unusual clocks: "Bobbing Doll," pat. 1886, "Swinging Doll," pat. 1889. Some similar to French imports. Identifying trade mark "A" inside circle. Making new clocks ceased ca.1930. Machinery sold to Russia. Many collectibles still available. Can usually be repaired. (AJ May 1950)

ANSP[T]ETH, J. ROLLIN: Buffalo, N.Y. Ca.1880. Alarm dials.

ANTAME, JOSEPH AMEEL: Phila. Ca.1784. Lived in two-story brick house east side Germantown Rd. above 4th St. in Penn. Twp. Aw. shop near home Benj. Franklin; tradition repaired clocks and watches for him. (Hob. Dec. 1946)

ANTHONY, ISAAC: Newport, R.I. Ca.1750.

—, JACOB, SR.: Phila., 227 No. 2nd St. Dir. 1802.

—, JACOB, JR.: Phila., 35 Brewers Alley. 1802.

—, L. D.: Providence, R.I. Dir. 1848.

ANTRIM, CHARLES: Phila. Dir. 1837–1839, 1844–1847.

—, CHARLES W.: Dir. 1840.

APP, SAMUEL: Phila. Dir. 1835, ca.1850.

APPEL, JOHN ELLIS: Dover, Pa. Aw. 1778–1780.

APPLETON, TRACY & CO.: Waltham Watch Co. 1858–1859.

—, W., & CO.: Boston. Movt. No. 2398, "Swiss appearance" in Ira Leonard Col.

—, GEORGE B.: Salem, Mass., 179 Essex St. 1859–1864.

—, JAMES: Marblehead, Mass. Adv. 1823.

APPLEWHITE, WILLIAM: Columbia and Camden, S.C. 1830's.

ARBUCKLE, JOSEPH: Phila. Dir. 1847–1848.

"ARCHAUMBAULT, F. A.," on dial Fredonia Watch Co., antimagnetic spring. Cramer Col.

ARCHER, WILLIAM: N.Y.C. Ca.1830.

—, WILLIAM, JR.: Salem, Mass., 222 Essex St. in 1846; 188 in 1850.

ARKELL, JAMES: Canajoharie, N.Y. Partner Louis Juvet (Time Globe Clock), 1880–1886.

ARMSTRONG, THOMAS: N.Y.C., Bklyn. Ca. 1830.

ARNOLD, JACOB: Phila. Dir. 1848. C.

—, JARED: Amber, N.Y. Ca.1830.

ARNOLD, JARED, JR.: Amber, N.Y. Ray Walker Col.

ARRISON, JOHN: Phila. Dir. 1837.

ARTHUR, H. G.: Boston. Dir. 1830.

—, JAMES: 1842–1930. N.Y.C. Several clocks (see Herring, Lure of the Clock). Gave clock collection (created James Arthur Foundation), to New York University, New York City.

ARWIN, WILLIAM: Albany, N.Y. Dir. 1837–1838.

ASH, LAWRENCE: Phila. Adv. 1762–1763, "Late from Mr. Edward Duffield's, 2 Front St., 6 doors above High (Market) St." Baltimore 1773; possibly Boston later. C. W.

ASHBY, JAMES: Boston, King St. From Cumberland, Eng. Adv. 1769, 1771, 1772, 1773. W. and finisher. Imported clocks and watches. Left during Rev. War. Adv. Moore. (Ant. Jan. 1929)

ASHCRAFT, O.: N.Y.C., 53 Nassau St. Dir. 1840.

ASHTON, W. & C.: Phila. "Front St., 6 doors above Market St. C & W makers."

—, ARTHUR S.: Lynn, Mass. n/d. Watch paper BCL Col.

—, C.: Phila. Dir. 1762–1797. (MFM)

—, ISAAC: Phila. Census 1790.

—, SAMUEL: Phila. 1790's.

—, W.: Phila. 1762–1797. Clocks and watches. (MFM)

ASHWIN & CO.: Pa. n/d.

ASKEW, JAMES: Charleston, S.C. 1770–1790.

ASPENWALL, SAMUEL: Pittstown, Pa. n/d. (Burt)

ASPINWALL, ZALMON: Boston. Dir. 1809–1813.

ASTON, THOMAS: Newburyport, Mass. J. D. 1860.

"ATHERTON, FREDERICK," used by U.S. Watch Co. 1867.

—, MATTHEW: Phila. Dir. 1837–1840.

—, NATHAN, JR.: Phila. Dir. 1825.

—, OTIS: N.Y.C. 1798.

ATHLETIC WATCH CO.: Chicago. "Made by Swiss." n/d. (MFM)

ATKINS & ALLEN: f. 1846, succeeded by Smith & Goodrich. (Abbott)

— CLOCK CO.: 1859–1879. Org. to carry on business of Atkins Clock Mfg. Co. Made Calendar clocks inv. by William Terry,

Marine and 30-hr. Shelf clocks. Rough going 1873 but survived. Priest Atkins went totally blind by 1879; did not fail, all claims paid in full; carried on as Barnes Brothers Clock Co. till 1884. Ex. Essex Inst. (IBB) (LB) (Ant. March 1949) (Hoopes) (Hull)

— Clock Mfg Co.: 1855–1858. Joint stock company to succeed Atkins, Whiting & Co. June 23, 1856. Ives declared contracts forfeited over royalty dispute. f. 1858; became Atkins Clock Co.

— (Alden A.) & Co.: 1837–1846. As Atkins & Allen. f. 1846; succeeded by Smith & Goodrich. (Abbott)

— & Downs (Anson): 1831–1832. Empire Shelf clock. One paper reads, "for George Mitchell."

—, I. (Irenus) & Co.: 1847–1857. Clocks, cotton gins, and other mchy. Joseph Ives 1850 assigned to them and Adna Whiting of Farmington exclusive right to use his "reciprocal escapement" and "improvements in the dial works of clocks." Made 8-day and 30-hr. clocks under style of Atkins, Whiting & Co.

—, Merritt W. & Co.: 1846–1856. Included Merritt W. Atkins, Henry H. Porter, and Irenus and Thomas Atkins. f. Made 8-day and 30-hr. spring clock and 30-hr. wgt. clock. Label read, "M. W. Atkins & Co."

— & Norton: Bristol. n/d.

— & Porter: Bristol. 1840–1846. Merritt W. Atkins and Henry H. Porter made clocks in shop east side Stafford Ave. Shelf clock labels printed by "Wells & Willard, 184½ Main St., Hartford." Reorganized 1846 as Atkins, Merritt W. & Co.

—, R. (Rollin) & I.: Brothers. 1833–1837. Till 1847 in company making saws.

— & Son: Bristol. Ca.1870.

— & Welton: Bristol. 1835–1836. Making clocks in saw mill on North Branch Creek. Norman Allen became partner. He and Alden Atkins made clocks and spool stands as Atkins & Allen.

—, Whiting & Co.: 1850–1854. Joseph Ives made assignments 1850–1853 which included right to use Ives roller pinions and wagon spring clocks. 30-day wagon spring in both Wall (see ill. No. 239) and Shelf (see ill. No. 241). Some bear labels of Atkins Clock Mfg. Co.

—, Alden A.: Bristol. 1835–1846. Mfgr. began 1835 with Eldridge G. Atkins and Noah E. Welton as Atkins & Welton.

—, Alvin: Rochester, N.Y. Dir. 1849–1850.

—, Eldridge G.: Bristol. 1835–1842. After Atkins & Welton continued making clocks under own name.

—, George: Bristol. n/d. (Hoopes)

—, Irenus: 1792–1882. Bristol. Aw. 1830–1879. Ordained Baptist minister. Combined preaching with long career as C. in various firms in "Atkins shop." Started 1830 as Mitchell (Geo.) & Atkins; put out of business 1837 by panic. At same time was partner in Atkins & Downs.

—, Jearum: Joliet, Ill. Inv. "perpetual" clock 1848 powered by expanding and contracting metal rods geared to endless chain. (Scien. Am. Oct. 21, 1848)

—, Joel: Middletown, Conn. Adv. 1777. Tall clock 7′7″, mahogany case, bronze dial with Roman hours and Arabic minutes. Engraved "Joel Adkins, Middletown." Moon and Calendar clocks reported. (Hoopes)

—, John H.: Chicago. n/d. J. C. Adams and apprentice. (MFM)

—, Rollin: 1790–1844. Bristol. Brother of Irenus. Son, Elias, founded Atkins Saw Co. of Indianapolis, Ind.

Atkinson, M. & A.: Baltimore. "1804." (Baillie)

—, Matthew & William: Baltimore. Possibly brothers; William, father of Leroy. Adv. 1787, moved from Gay St. to corner Market and Holliday Sts.

—, Anna Maria Leroy: –1823. Baltimore, 33 Market Space. Wife of Wilmer, mother of William. Either from father or husband learned how to make clocks, first in 1750. Widowed, she continued till ca.1819. Possibly first of her sex to make American clocks. Tall clock owned by Dr. George Rohrer. Described as "fine finish, brass dial, with the date on moon dial." (Baillie)

—, James: –1756. Boston. Town Records Jan. 2, 1744, "James Atkinson, Watchmaker from London, Appeared & desired to be Admitted an Inhabitant & to open a Shop in this Town, which is here by granted, he having brought with him upwards of Five Hundred Pounds Sterling & being a Gentleman of Good Character." Adv. Jan. 8, 1745, "Watchmaker from London. Made in a compleat manner of his own name warranted." Adv. Aug. 6, 1745, "Moved to King St. from Cornhill." Adv. 1748, "All sorts of repeating and plain clocks with or without cases at reasonable rates." Notice, Nov. 15, 1756, "Deceased late of Halifax; estate administered by Philip Freeman of Boston." None known extant.

—, LEROY: Baltimore. 1824–1830. Probably grandson of Wilmer (or Matthew). Son of William. Brought up as C. and W. Silver plate assayer.

—, PEABODY: Concord, N.H. 1790. Apprentice of Levi Hutchins. (Baillie)

—, W.: N.Y.C. 1865–1875. Made clock transfer tablets.

—, WILMER: Lancaster, Pa. Ca.1748. b. Baltimore, 1748 marr. Anna Maria Leroy, dau. Abraham Leroy, C. Began life as cutler. At least one Tall clock extant. Wife learned C., later went to Baltimore.

ATLAS WATCH Co.: Chicago. n/d. W., possibly Swiss parts. (MFM)

ATMAR, RALPH: Charleston, S.C. Ca.1800.

ATTMORE, MARSHALL: Phila. Dir. 1821–1837. C. and W. (Baillie)

ATWOOD & BRACKETT: Littleton, N.H. Ca.1850.

—, ANSON L.: 1816–1907. Bristol. Came to Bristol 1838 with Birge & Mallory; period of contracts or jobs. Contracted to make parts for such firms as Brewster, Manross and Ingraham. Brewster & Ingrahams contracted with him 1848 to make in one year 12,000 spring clock movts. after pattern of those made by Pomeroy & Robbins. Also enjoyed farming. Clocks doubtful. (Hist.)

—, B.W.: Plymouth, Mass. Ca.1860.

AUBURNDALE WATCH Co.: Auburndale, Mass. Org. 1879. Bought mchy. of U.S. Watch Co. of Marion, N.J. Voluntary assignment 1883. Used names "Auburndale Rotary," "Auburndale Timer," "Bentley," "Lincoln." (Evans)

AURORA WATCH Co, THE: Aurora, Ill. Inc. 1883. Began operations 1885. f. 1886.

Mchy. sold to Hamilton Watch Co. 1892. First watch No. 1 but possibly several No. 1's; true No. under balance bridge. (MFM) (Evans) ("Timing a Century")

AUSTIN, BENJAMIN: Kalamazoo, Mich. Ca.1850.

—, ISAAC: Upper Delaware Ward, Pa. "1783."

—, ISAAC: Phila., 7 Arch St., north side, 1785–1799, then 176 Oxford St. to 1801. May be same as above. d. 1801. Adv. 1781. Dir. 1785–1801. (Baillie) (Prime)

—, JOHN: Phila. ca.1830–1840. (MFM)

—, JOSIAH: 1828–. Salem, Mass., 147 Essex St., 1853–1855; 243, 1857. J. D. W. Adv. 1857 as W.; later to Boston.

—, ORKIN: Waterbury, Conn. Ca.1820. Movts. or parts of clocks at plant on Beaver Pond Brook.

—, SEYMOUR: Hartford, Conn. Ca.1800. Later at Western Reserve.

AVERY, JOHN: Boston. Moore says "1726." Made clock inside North Church of Paul Revere fame. Ill. Moore No. 88. "Shaped like Act of Parliament clock put in gallery 1726. Cost 22 pounds. Still good timekeeper. Dial refinished. Long body case needed for seconds pend." (Origin of "John" unknown.)

—, JOHN, JR.: 1732–1794. Preston, Conn. Son of John and Ann. Inventive; self-taught C and S. d. 1794, leaving tools listed pg. 49 (Hoopes). Tall clocks, one owned by Mrs. J. A. Migel, Pelham, N.Y.

AVISE, M.: Reading, Pa. Adv. 1827.

AVISSE, CHARLES: Baltimore. 1812. J. W.

AYRES (E.) & BEARD (Evans C.): Louisville, Ky. Adv. Dir. 1816–1831; Beard then continues alone through Dir. 1875.

—, ALEXANDER: –1824. Lexington, Ky. Before 1776 Essex Co., Va.; Lex., 1790–1823, Danville, Ky., 1823–1824. Aw. 1770–1824.

—, E.: Louisville, Ky. Ca.1816–1831.

—, HAMILTON: New Holland, Pa. Ca.1820. "Made Tall clock owned by Theodore Glass." "Little known." (Lan. Co.)

—, SAMUEL: Lexington, Ky., then Danville, Ky. 1776–1824. Adv. 1790 to 1824. C. W. S. J. (MFM) (LB)

BABBITT, H. W.: Providence, R.I. Dir. 1849.

BABCOCK & Co.: Phila., 71 Richmond St., 44 Richmond St., 111 Broad St. Dir. 1831–1833. C., W., pos. D.

BABCOCK, ALVIN: Boston. Dir. 1810–1813.

BACHELDER: See Batchelder.

BACHELOR, N.: July 10, 1846, patent assignee of H. Biggins on "design for clock frame."

BACHMAN, JACOB: Lampeter, Pa. Father of John, who later worked with him. Tall clocks extant with name on dial. Believed to have been Cabinetmakers after 1766.

—, JOHN: 1798–. Bachmanville (near Soudersburg), Pa. Marr. 1822. Cases for Bowman & Baldwin. Sold some with his name on dial, but "made no pretence to making or assembling movts." Made two cases, exchanged for one movt., cased the movt. and sold with his name. Aw. ca.1820. (Baillie) (Lan. Co.)

—, JOSEPH: N.Y.C. Dir. 1855.

BACKES, J. P.: Charleston, S.C. Ca.1850.

BACON, JOHN: Bristol. (tx) 1833–1845. Bought out E. M. Barnes and Orrin Hart. With Chauncey Boardman eight years. Built shop. As Barnes & Bacon 1833–1840, then under own name to 1845. (Hist.)

—, SAMUEL: Annapolis, Md. Adv. 1752, "From London."

BADDER, ISAAC: Dayton, O. Ca.1830.

BADELY, THOMAS: (Not Bradley) –1720. Adv. 1712, "with J. Essex in Boston," then "late of Boston." W. Insolvent estate 1720. (Baillie)

BADGER, JAMES: Bklyn, N.Y. Ca.1840.

BADLAM, STEPHEN: 1751–1815. Boston, Lower Mills, and Dorchester, Mass. Cabinetmaker for clocks of Wm. Cummens and others. (JWW)

BADMAN, JOSEPH: Colebrookdale, Pa. Fourth group. Ca.1800. Tall clocks. (Steinmetz)

BADOLLET, PAUL: N.Y.C. "1798."

BAERR, WILLIAM: Weaverdale, Cai. Ca.1860.

BAGNALL, BENJAMIN: 1689–1773. Probably Boston's first authenticated C. b. England. Formerly believed to have learned C. there and to Boston ca.1710; now thought to have come to Phila. first, there learned C. from Peter Stretch or others, then to Boston. Marr. Elizabeth Shove, 1712; seven children; two sons, Benj. Jr.

and Samuel. Tall clocks in Metropolitan Museum of Art. and in Brandt Col. Casemaker unknown, Quaker, important in Boston affairs, later as merchant and in real estate, probably gave up C. ca.1730. Lived in Boston rest of life. Not to be confused with Benj. Jr. (See ill. Nos. 8, 10)

—, BENJAMIN, JR.: 1715–. Apprentice to father. Had hard life. Probably Tall clocks at Boston, later Phila., Providence, and Newport, R.I. Tall clock at Metropolitan Museum of Art. Marr. (1) Anne Hawden, 1737, (2) Anne Peaslee of Haverhill, Mass., 1742. (Baillie)

—, SAMUEL: Ca.1740–1760. Brother Benj. Jr. Apt. to father. Tall clock at Metropolitan Museum of Art. Abbott lists 100 years too early.

—, WILLIAM: C. Stretch said he was C. at Boston early 18th century. Not known.

BAILEY, BANKS, & BIDDLE: Phila. Started as Bailey & Kitchen, 1832–1846; then Bailey & Co., 1846–1878; then Bailey, Banks, & Biddle. All records burned 1893.

—, BANKS, & BIDDLE CO.: 1894 to present. Some clocks made, others imported and purchased. Tall, Shelf, Banjo, European, etc. Tall clock owned by Mrs. F. W. Floyd, Gloucester City, N.J., with their plate on dial moon (rosewood inlaid case, brass dial). Banjo in mahogany case and brass side arms owned by Mrs. Wm. F. Waugh, Chicago. This data to help date extant clocks. (Gillingham)

— & BROTHERS: Utica, N.Y. Adv. 1846–1852, "at the sign of the big watch."

— (also Bayley) FAMILY: Hanover, Mass.

—, G. S., & CO.: Danbury, Conn. Ca.1860.

— & OWEN: Abbeville, S.C. Adv. 1848 as W. and J.

—, CALVIN: 1761–1835. Son of John I. Hanover, Mass., to Bath, Me., Nov. 4, 1828. Doubtful if C. there.

—, GAMALIEL: Mt. Holly, N.J. W. Main St. 1807. At Phila. till 1833, then possibly in Ohio. W. and S. succeeded 1821 by Peter Hill, Negro C. (Williams)

—, I. G.: Conn. or N.H. R. Ca.1848.

—, J. T.: Phila. Dir. 1828–1833.

—, JOHN I: Father of three clockmakers; John II, Calvin, Lebbeus.

—, JOHN II: 1751–1823. Hanover and Lynn, Mass. Aw. Ca.1770. Tall, Dwarf Tall,

BAILEY, JOHN II (cont'd)
and Mass. Shelf. Several examples, D. K. Packard Col. N.Y. Hist. Soc. has a surveyor's compass by him. Marr. 1780 Mary Hall of Berwick, Me. Clock at Hingham inscribed in back of case, "Made in 1801, running parts made in F. Burr's store by John Bayley. A case made by Theodore Cushing 1808." David Studley, an apprentice, and sons, John III and Joseph. John Bailey or Bayley listed Boston Dir. 1803–1816.

—, JOHN III: 1787–1883. Hingham, Mass. 1815–1820. (Abbott)

—, CAPT. JOHN S.: Pa. Ca.1855–1890. Sun dials; dealer in Tall clocks. Wrote "Early Clockmakers," 1885. (Bucks Co. Hist. Soc.)

—, JOSEPH: Hingham, New Bedford, and Lynn, Mass. Ca.1800–1840.

—, LEBBEUS: 1763–1827. Hanover. Son of John I. At early date to No. Yarmouth, Me., where prior to 1824 made Tall clocks. Tall clock owned by Dr. A. R. Mitchell, Yarmouth, at Gore Mansion, Waltham. Short pendulum clock movt., kidney dial, fine hands. Dial minute markings in faint red and 5-minute triangle marks. On bottom dial gilt work in black, "L. Bailey–N. Yarmouth." Housed in top of desk. Lead weight with 2½' fall for week's run.

—, PARKER: Rutland, Vt. Ca.1860.

—, PUTNAM: No. Goshen, Conn. Ca.1830. Square case, side rounded column, broken arch top, in Flint Sale 1926. Crowing rooster clock in EI Col.

BAILY & WARD: N.Y.C. "1832."

—, EMMOR: London Grove, Pa. Son of Joel. Apprentice to Phila. W. d. Ohio. (James)

—, JOEL: 1732–1797. W. Bradford, Pa. Yeoman, Gunsmith, Surveyor, Astronomer, and Mathematician. Marr. 1759. Quaker. One Tall clock known. (James)

—, WILLIAM: Phila. Dir. 1816–1822. (Baillie)

—, WILLIAM: Phila. Dir. 1820.

BAIRD CLOCK CO.: Plattsburg, N.Y. Ca.1892–1893. Used Seth Thomas movts. Shelf clock in G. B. Davis Col.

—, EDWARD P.: Plattsburg, N.Y. In above company.

BAKER, ALEXANDER: N.Y.C., 370 2nd Ave. Dir. 1854.

BAKER, BENJAMIN F. (or H.): Phila. 1825. (Baillie)

—, BENJAMIN H.: Dir. 1823–1825.

—, ELEAZAR: 1764–1849. Ashford, Conn. Marr. 1787. Adv. 1793, C. W. G., and for apprentice 15 or 16 yrs. old; apprentice Edmund Hughes had "run away." Hughes later S. and C. in Hampton and Middletown, Conn. (Hoopes)

—, ELIAS: New Brunswick, N.J. Ca.1840. W. D. S. (Williams)

—, GEORGE: 1790–. b. Ipswich, Mass. W. J. Salem, Mass. Later he (or one of same name) in Providence, R.I., ca.1825. (Baillie)

—, GEO. C. A.: N.Y.C. 1868. Chron. Succeeded by DeMory Gray and W. A. Alder.

—, JAMES M.: Phila. Dir. 1842.

—, JOSEPH: Phila. Provincial Tax List 1772.

—, SAMUEL: 1787–1858. New Brunswick, N.J. C. W. J. S. Watch paper mentioned; sold variety of articles. Active 1855 as J., 17 Peace St. (Williams)

—, STEPHEN: Salem, Mass. 1791–. b. Beverly, Mass. Marr. 1827. J., W., Justice of the Peace, Postmaster in Salem, Mass. Wilmington, N.C., where adv. 1817, "watches for sale"; also Sheffield, Ill.

—, THOMAS, JR.: 1793–1820. Haverhill, Mass. Salem, Essex St., 1815, G. S. Partner Jabez Baldwin, 1817. Probate records, "of Concord, N.H."

—, WILLIAM: Boston. Dir. 1820.

BALCH, B., & SON: Salem, also Boston, Mass. 1832–1842.

— (Daniel) & CHOATE (John): Boston. Dir. 1816.

— (James) & LAMSON (Charles): Salem, Mass., 1842–1864.

— (Benjamin) & SMITH (Jesse, Jr.): Salem, Mass. Org. 1818.

—, BENJAMIN: 1774–. Salem, Mass. b. Bradford, Mass.; learned Clockmaking from cousin Daniel Balch; to Salem 1796. Listed 1807 as W.; 1818 partner with Jesse Smith, Jr., as Balch & Smith.

—, CHARLES HODGE: 1787–. Newburyport, Mass., shop on Merrimack St. 1808. Superintendent town clocks 1817.

—, DANIEL: 1734–1790. Newburyport, Mass. b. Bradford, Mass., son of Rev.

(142)

William Balch. Probably apprentice to Samuel Mulliken. Made Tall clocks in Bradford. To Newburyport 1756; kept town clock 1781–1783. Tall clocks, some musical. Two sons, apprentices, Daniel and T. H. (Moore) (AJ Feb. 1950)

—, DANIEL: 1761–1835. Newburyport, Mass. Tall and Mass. Shelf clocks. Continued father's business after 1790. Ex. J. C. Wells Col.

—, EBENEZER: 1723–1808. Apprenticed Boston; 1744, to Hartford, Conn. Wethersfield, Conn., 1756. Nine children. (Hoopes)

—, JAMES: 1806–. Salem, Mass. With Charles Lamson org. 1842, Balch & Lamson.

—, JOSEPH: 1760–1855. Son and apprentice to Ebenezer. Drummer boy in Rev. War; later C. and S. in Wethersfield, Conn.; 1794 to Williamstown, Mass.; 1810 to Johnstown, N.Y.

—, MOSES PHIPPEN: 1810–. Lowell, Mass., Dir. 1832; Lynn, Mass., 1844.

—, THOMAS HUTCHINSON: 1771–1817. Newburyport, Mass. Contemporary with brother Daniel. Tall clocks. Ex. in Dalton House, Newburyport, Mass., ill. Moore.

BALDWIN, S. S., & SON: N.Y.C. Ca.1830. "D. in C. W. S. J., etc." (FT)

— (Jedidiah) & STORRS (Nathan): Northampton, Mass. 1792–1794.

—, ANTHONY: 1783–1867. Lampeter Sq., Pa. b. Strasburg, Pa., apprentice of Joseph Bowman. Aw. Lampeter Sq. from 1810. "Big frame, fifteen children. Made number of clocks . . . of good handiwork. Just when he ceased is hard to determine." (Lan. Co.)

—, EBENEZER: Nashua, N.H. Ca.1810–1830.

—, EDGAR: Troy, N.Y. Dir. 1848–1850.

—, GEORGE W.: Sadsburyville, Pa. 1777–1844. Possibly brother of Anthony. Seven tall clocks known. Probably did not make cases (see Thomas Ogden); cherry and mahogany, "New Holland" for Australia on dial on hemisphere. Two sons, Oliver P. and Robert. (James) (Baillie) (Abbott)

—, HARLAND: Sadsburyville, Pa. Brother of Geo. W. Classed as C. 1809, but possibly cases only. (James)

BALDWIN, JABEZ: Ca.1777–1829. Apprentice of Thomas Harland. C. W. S. Succeeded W. Cleaveland, Salem, Mass. Boston, 1815 with John Jones as partner in Baldwin & Jones.

—, JEDIDIAH: Brother of Jabez. Apprenticed to Thomas Harland. To Northampton, Mass., 1791 as member of Stiles & Baldwin, 1791, and Stiles & Storrs, 1792. To Hanover, N.H., postmaster, where Dartmouth College records his death; but to Morrisville, N.Y., 1818–1820; Fairfield, N.Y., and Rochester, N.Y. (Dir. 1834–1844).

—, MATTHAIS: W. before 1830, when he turned to building steam locomotives and formed Baldwin Locomotive Co., Phila. (Mittman, HIA Journal Jan. 1948)

—, OLIVER P.: Coatesville, Pa. Ca.1860–1890. Son of Geo. W., brother of Robert. W. and J. (James)

—, ROBERT: Coatesville, Pa. Ca.1860. W. and J. (James)

—, THOMAS F. H.: 1807–. Downington and Coatesville, Pa. Adv. 1829–1858. Henry B. Freeman was apprentice. (James)

BALER, JOHN: Northampton, Pa. n/d.

BALL, WEBB C. Co., THE: Cleveland, Ohio. W. Co. Founded 1879. Inc. mfg. after 1894. (Evans) ("Timing a Century")

—, ALBERT: Poughkeepsie, N.Y. Adv. 1832–1835.

—, CHARLES: Poughkeepsie, N.Y. Adv. 1840–1842.

—, S.: Black Rock, N.Y. Adv. 1826.

—, WILLIAM: 1729–1810. Phila., High St. Adv. 1752–1810.

BANCROFT, G. P.: Granville, O. Clock cases and furniture. Adv. 1831. (Knittle)

BANDELL, I., & Co.: also Bandell & Co. n/d. Name on Banjo clocks. W. Keller Col.

BANKS, EDWARD P.: Portland, Me. Dir. 1834.

—, JOSEPH: Phila., Pa. Grassell's Alley. Dir. 1819.

BANNATYNE WATCH Co.: Waterbury, Conn. Inc. 1905. Inexpensive watches, as low as $1.50. Out of business 1911, purchased 1912 by The Ingraham Co. of Bristol.

BANNEKER, BENJAMIN: Baltimore, Md. Ca. 1754. Negro. Fine Clockmaking; no apprenticeship or previous experience. Later became distinguished Mathematician in field of Astronomy. (Franks)

BANSTEIN, JOHN: Phila. Dir. 1791.

BANTEL, PHILIP: N.Y.C. Patent July 21, 1858. 100-day Tall clock, James Arthur Col. (See ill. 28 and p. 44, *Lure of the Clock*)

BARBECK, C. G.: Phila. Dir. 1835.

BARBER, EPHRAIM: Marlborough, Mass. n/d. (BCC)

—, JAMES: Phila. Dir. 1842.

—, WILLIAM: Phila. *Ca.*1846.

BARGER, GEORGE: Phila. Dir. 1844.

BARKER & MUMFORD: Newport, R.I. n/d. "A" shaped Banjo with David Williams movt.

— (Jonathan) & TAYLOR (Samuel): Worcester, Mass. Until 1807.

—, B. B.: N.Y.C. 1786–1790. (Baillie)

—, JAMES F.: Palmyra, N.Y. Adv. 1826–1827.

—, JONATHAN: d. 1807. Worcester, Mass. Senior partner Barker & Taylor.

—, WILLIAM: Boston. Dir. 1800, 1825. Two of same name 1807–1809.

BARKLAY, J. & S.: Baltimore, 44 (or 46) Baltimore St. 1812–1816.

—, J.: Baltimore, 46 Baltimore St. 1817–1824. In firm of J. &. S. Barklay, 1812–1816.

BARNARD, SAMUEL: Utica, N.Y. Dir. 1844–1845.

BARNES (Wallace, Carlyle F., Harry) BROTHERS CLOCK CO., THE: Bristol. 1880–1884. Wallace Barnes and two sons. Liquidated as "too much new capital needed for new mchy." (Hull)

— (Thomas, Jr., Alphonso), DARROW (Elijah) & Co.: David and Edwin Matthews were the other members of firm.

— (Alphonso) & JEROME (Andrew J.): 1833–1837. f.

— (Thomas, Jr.) & JOHNSON (William): Bristol. 1819–1823.

—, THOMAS, JR., & Co.: Bristol. 1819–1823. Also known as Barnes & Johnson. With Wyllis Roberts, son of Gideon, and William Johnson. "Took over privilege of the water works." Tall clocks, brass movt. After 1823 Barnes may have continued for himself at same site; no proof.

— (Thomas, Jr.) & WATERMAN (Samuel): 1811–1812.

—, ALPHONSO: Bristol. 1804–1877. Father of Wallace. In Barnes and Jerome.

BARNES, CARLYLE F.: Bristol. 1880–1884. Son of Wallace. In The Barnes Brothers Clock Co.

—, HARRY: Bristol. 1880–1884. Son of Wallace. In The Barnes Brothers Clock Co.

—, JOHN: Phila. *C.*1759.

—, STEPHEN: 1771–1810. Bristol. Recorded as trader. Taxed 1804 as tinner. "When he died the estate had 576 wood wheeled clocks." Possibly product of Gideon Roberts or his son Elias. (Hull)

—, THOMAS, JR.: 1773–1855. Bristol. "Local merchant, Yankee trader, mfgr., private banker, real estate operator, transportation leader, shrewd investor, Clockmaker with George Mitchell, most successful." Solvent through 1837 depression. In Barnes & Johnson, Thomas Barnes, Jr., & Co., Barnes & Waterman, Joseph Ives & Co. Partner 1838–1850, Barnes, Darrow & Co. (Hull)

—, WALLACE: 1827–1893. Bristol. Son of Alphonso. "Druggist, farmer, trader, real estate operator, inventor, developed springs; at least three patents." Trustee Dec. 25, 1879, in liquidation of Atkins Clock Co.

—, WILLIAM H: New Haven, Conn. 1840–1850.

BARNHART, SIMON: Kingston, O. *Ca.*1850.

BARNHILL, ROBERT: Phila. W. Adv. 1776–1778, for stolen watch 1777.

BARNITZ, A. E.: York, Pa. *Ca.*1850.

BARNS, JOHN: West River, Md. Adv. 1756, "Clockmaker by trade." (Md. Gazette, Sept. 30, 1756)

BARNY: N.Y.C. 20th century.

BARR MFG. CO.: Weedsport, N.Y. Battery-operated Shelf clock under dome, "Barr" on dial, owned by Roy John Hayward, N.Y.C.

—, JOHN: Port Glasgow, N.Y. *Ca.*1840.

BARRAGANT, PETER: Phila. *Ca.*1820.

BARRELL, COLBORN: Boston, Mass. "Store on the Dock." Adv. 1772, "A fine 8-day spring clock with alarm, good silver watches with chains, seals. A fine watch for a Physician, with second hand." (FT)

BARRETT & SHERWOOD: San Francisco, Cal. *Ca.*1850–1888. Clocks, Chron.

—, J. A.: n/p. Clock Patent No. 235655, Dec. 21, 1880, model Smiths. Inst.

BARRINGTON, JOSEPH: Salisbury, N.C. Adv. 1792, Dumfries, Va. Began business Dumfries July 12, 1792. Adv., "Makes clocks of various descriptions such as wind themselves up without manual assistance, regulate themselves according to inclemency of the weather, and show the day on all parts of the globe at one time; watches such as wind up by being carried on a fob, also the key to effect the same being turned either way." Adv. 1826 Salisbury, N.C.; 1832, 1839, Tarboro, N.C.

BARROW, SAMUEL: Phila., Chestnut St. bet. 2nd and Front; Adv. 1771, Pa. *Chronicle*, Oct. 7, 1771, "to make all kinds of watches and clocks including stop watches." Came over in *Betsey* from Liverpool, Eng. Set up complete shop. Apprenticed to famous John Harrison, Eng. (Prime)

BARROWS, JAMES M.: Tolland, Conn. 1832. "Mfr. of silver spoons and dealer in watches and jewelry." (FT)

BARRY, STANDISH: 1763–1844. Baltimore, Market and Gay Sts. Adv. 1784. Apprentice of David Evans. Adv., "W and Clockmakers and engravers." 1810.

BARTBERGER, BEN: Pittsburgh, Pa. n/d. Name on Watch Paper BCL Col.

BARTELS, FRANZ: Jersey City, N.J. After Civil War.

BARTENS & RICE: N.Y.C. 1878.

BARTHOLOMEW: Famous name in Bristol clock history.

— & BARNES: Bristol. (See Barnes, Bartholomew & Co.)

— (William G.), BROWN (Jonathan C.) & Co.: Bristol. (tx) 1833–1834. Sometimes referred to as Bartholomew, Hills & Brown. Brown and William Hills bought land, water rights; built dam and factory in "wilderness" of Forestville near site of present Sessions Clock Co., successor company. Later Forestville Mfg. Co.

—, ELI, & Co.: Bristol. No tax record; believed to be before 1828. Looking-glass Shelf clock extant.

—, E. (Eli) & G. (George): Bristol. (tx) 1828–1832. Made 30-hr. wood movt., hollow column clock. Plant in Edgewood section. Here Barnes, Bartholomew & Co. made clocks till 1836, when George sold out and name was changed to Upson, Merriman & Co.

BARTHOLOMEW, GEORGE W.: 1805–1897. Bristol. Peddler at 18 of Bristol clocks and other products on Eastern Seaboard as far south as Ala. and Miss. In E. & G. Bartholomew, 1828–1832; Barnes, Bartholomew & Co., 1832–1836; 1836–1845, making clocks, painted wood dials, and clock tablets. Joined Gold Rush to Cal. 1849. Back to Bristol, 1853, with son in hardware business until 1884, when plant burned. Other interests included successful operation of Bristol Copper Mine. (AJ June 1948, May 1949) (Am. Col. Sept. 1948)

—, HARRY SHELTON: 1832–1902. Bristol. Son of George W.; with him as G. W. & H. S. Bartholomew, hardware and possibly some clocks. After fire business transferred to "old clock factories."

—, WILLIAM G.: Bristol. One of organizers of Forestville Mfg. Co. Little data available.

BARTLETT, ISRAEL: Haverhill, Mass. n/d. "—, P. S.," used by predecessor companies of Waltham Watch Co. 1854–1878.

BARTON BROTHERS & Co.: New Haven, Conn. Steeple on Steeple clocks with C. Boardman movt. in F. D. Cooley Col., Windsor, Vt.

—, BENJAMIN: Alexandria, Va. *Ca.*1830.

— (should be Bartow), JOHN: Haverhill, Mass.

—, JOHN: 1808–. Salem, Mass., 1846–1848; Newburyport, State St., 1849–1850.

—, JOS.: Stockbridge, Mass., 1764–1804. Then Utica, 1804–1832. (Packard)

—, O. G.: Fort Edward, N.Y. *Ca.*1830. Watch Paper BCL Col.

—, WILLIAM CLEVELAND: 1813–. Salem, Mass., 142 Essex St. By 1846 in grocery business.

BARTOW, JOHN: Haverhill, Mass. Dir. 1853.

BARWELL, BARTHOLOMEW: N.Y.C. Adv. 1749–1760. From Bath, Eng. Tall clock in Museum of City of N.Y.; in I. Sack Col.

BASCOM (Asa) & NORTH (Noah): Torrington, Conn. Sued Sept. 1813, on claimed default of note of $300 by H. Clark and Calvin Butler, both of Plymouth. (Avery)

BASIL: Baltimore to Albany, N.Y. *Ca.*1773.

BASSETT, J., & W. H.: Cortland, N.Y. *Ca.* 1815. Albany, 1820.

—, CHARLES: n/d. Bennington or Burlington, Vt., or Binghamton, N.Y. Tall clocks; one known.

BASSETT, GEORGE FRANCIS: 131 So. Front St., Phila. Dir. 1791–1798. (Prime)

—, NEHEMIAH: Albany, N.Y. Adv. 1795–1800. Dir. 1813–1819.

BATCHELDER, E. & A.: Danvers, Mass. Name on Tall clock 8-day brass movt. owned by Fred Landry, Plaistow, N.H.

—: Family of Danvers, Mass., Clockmakers.

—, ANDREW: 1772–1845. Danvers, Mass. Marr. 1802. Combined Clockmaking with blacksmithing ca.1795.

—, EZRA: Father of Ezra and Andrew. Blacksmith, farmer; operated first express service to Boston.

—, EZRA, JR.: 1789–1840. Blacksmith, C. Account book 1803–1830 in existence; in 27 years sold 36 Tall clocks, $35 to $65; names of original purchasers given. Possibly imported movts. "Having developed into fine cabinetmakers, the Batchelders made their cases themselves." Nathan Adams, son-in-law, apprentice. (Frank Damon) (BCC)

BATCHELOR & BENSEL: N.Y.C., 101 Reade St. Dir. 1848; Bensel in Dir. 1854. Mfr. "metallic" clocks.

—, CHARLES: N.Y.C., 233 Broadway. Dir. 1854.

—, N.: N.Y.C. Patent 1846.

BATEMAN, JOSEPH: Morristown, Pa. n/d. Tall clocks. (Orr)

—, VALENTINE: Reading, Pa. n/d. Tall clocks. (Orr)

BATES, JAMES C.: Haverhill, Mass., 79 Merrimack St. Dir. 1879–1889. Aw. 1865 for Kimball & Gould; 1879 own business.

BATESON, JOHN: –1727. Boston. "After his death there was left in his shop an 8-day clock movt. and a silver repeating watch." (Moore)

BATH, BARTEN: N.Y.C. Dir. 1850.

BATTELL, GEORGE E.: Newburyport, Mass. Dir. 1860.

BATTERSON, JAMES: –1727. Philadelphia, Boston, N.Y.C., Charleston, S.C. Moore: "Another early clockmaker." Boston Town Records, Sept. 29, 1707: "James Batterson, Clockmaker being present Says he came from Pensilvania into theis Town abt a month Since & desires to dwell here. the Select men do now warn him to depart out of Town to finde Suretyes to Save the Town from Charge." Must have found

them, for twice adv. from Boston as "lately from London," and "for new clocks or old ones turned into pendulums."

—, JOHN: Annapolis, Md. Purchased real estate 1723; described as "watchmaker."

BATTING, JOSEPH: Phila. Dir. 1850.

BATTLES, A. T.: 1795–. Utica, N.Y. Adv. 1846.

BAUER, JOHN R. (or N.): N.Y.C. 1832.

BAUGH, VALENTINE: Abington, Va. 1820–1830. (Abbott)

BAUMAN, GEORGE: Sugar Creek, O. 1815. (Knittle)

BAUR, JOHN: Northampton, Pa. n/d. Tall clocks. (Funk)

BAWD & DOTTER: N.Y.C., Barclay St. After 1800. "Elliott movts. in American Tall cases."

BAYLEY: See Bailey.

—, SIMEON C.: Phila., 2nd and Chestnut Sts. Dir. 1794.

BAYNES, B. B.: Lowell, Mass., 44 Merrimack St. Dir. 1835.

BEACH & BYINGTON: Plymouth, Conn. Ca. 1840.

— & HUBBELL (or HUBBELL & BEACH): Bristol. (tx) 1859–1863. Brass movts. with balance wheel and marine clocks.

—, HUBBELL & HENDRICK: Bristol. 1853–1854. See Hubbell.

— (Miles) & SANFORD (Isaac): Litchfield, Conn. 1785. Brass movts. Sanford engraver. To Hartford, 1785; dissolved June, 1788. Beach Sr., C. Apprentice James Ward as partner 1790–1797; other activities. Alone 1797–1813. Son John partner in Beach & Son 1813–1828.

— (Miles) & SON (John): 1813–1828.

— (Miles) & WARD (James): Hartford. 1790–1797.

—, CHARLES: 1816–1894. Bristol. "Many years loyal, efficient assistant in several clock factories." (Hist.)

—, EDMUND: Brooklyn, N.Y., Remsen St. n/d.

—, JOHN: 1813–1828. Son of Miles; in Beach & Son.

—, MILES: 1743–1828. First cousin Macock Ward, probably his apprentice. Major in Rev. War. Selectman Litchfield, Conn., 1777. In Beach & Sanford 1785–1788, Beach & Ward 1790–1797, Beach & Son 1813–1828. Father of John. Partners probably not Clockmakers, though Sanford and Ward versatile mechanics. (Hoopes)

—, NATHAN: 1806–. Painted clock dials "for 17 years" for Terry, Hoadley, and others.

—, WILLIAM: Adv. 1834. "M'F'G'R clocks for sale by the box, Peddlars and others are requested to give him a call." Mahogany Shelf clock, two-panel door, carved eagle top, half side columns, standard 30-hr. wood movt., and label printed by P. Canfield, Hartford, printer, owned by Guy Christian, Georgetown, Mass.

BEALS, J. J., CLOCK ESTABLISHMENT: Boston. Adv. Dir. 1847. Store in "Circular Building at the junction of Blackstone and Union Sts." Lists 22 types of clocks, mostly Conn. type, but including "Willard Timepieces."

—, J. J., & Co.: Boston. Dir. 1848, 1850–1853; 1849–1850 without "& Co."

—, J. J., & SON: Boston. Dir. 1854. Badly proportioned Steeple clock with this overpasted label, owned by Herbert Marble, Orleans, Mass.

—, J. J. & W.: Boston, Haymarket Sq. Dir. 1848. Sold Silas B. Terry marine movt. clocks, overpasted label. Ex. Essex Inst.; also Flint Sale.

—, WILLIAM & J. J.: Boston, 1846. Overpasted label on Birge & Fuller 8-day wagon spring, Steeple on Steeple clock in Ray Walker Col.

—, J. J.: Boston, 16 Hanover St. Dir. 1874.

—, WILLIAM: Boston. Dir. 1838, "clockmaker," 21 Merrimac St.; 1843, 4th St.; 1845, 81 Hanover St.; 1854, no address.

BEARD, DUNCAN, & C. WEAVER: Appoquinimink, Del. Tall clock reported with name on dial.

—, DUNCAN: –1797. Made clocks possibly as early as 1755 at Appoquinimink (near Cantwell's Bridge), now Odessa, Del. During Rev. War may have made gun locks. Conrad listed in 1897, 15 known Tall clocks; one at National Bank of Smyrna, Del.

—, EVAN C.: Ca.1816–1875. Louisville, Ky. With E. Ayer & Co., 1816–1831, then alone. (LB)

—, ROBERT: Md. 1774.

"—, S. M.," used by U.S. Watch Co. 1869–1870.

BEARDSLEY, H. P.: Curonna, Mich. Ca. 1870.

BEASLEY, JOHN M.: 1815–1889. Baptist Minister. Adv. 1838 as W., R. and J. Retired 1886.

BEATH & ELLERY: Boston. Ca.1810. (Burt)

—, JOHN: Boston. Dir. 1805.

BEATTIE, GEORGE: Columbus, O. Ca.1850. "From Baltimore." (Knittle)

BEATTY, ALBERT L.: Phila. Dir. 1833.

—, CHARLES A.: "Georgetown, 1812" on Tall clock dial. (Burt)

—, GEORGE: 1808–1850. Harrisburg, Pa. Tall clocks.

BECHEL, CHARLES: Bethlehem, Pa. Ca.1850. Tower clocks. (Funk)

BECHTEL, HENRY: Phila. Dir. 1817.

BECHTLER, C., & SON: Spartanburg, S.C. Ca.1857.

—, CHRISTOPHER, SR.: Phila. 1830–1831. N.Y.C. 1829. To Rutherford, N.C., 1831. Adv., "Long experience in mending J. and repairing clocks and watches." d. 1842.

—, CHRISTOPHER, JR.: N.Y.C. 1829, from Europe. Rutherford, N.C., 1831. Associated with father until 1842; later at Spartanburg, S.C., to ca.1857, as C. Bechtler & Son.

BECK, HENRY: Phila. Dir. 1837–1839.

—, JACOB: Hanover, Pa. Ca.1820. Tall clocks.

—, THOMAS: Phila.; to Trenton, N.J., ca.1784. Adv. "watch cases repaired."

BECKER, CHARLES: Cleveland, O. Ca.1830. Poss. mfr.

BECKWITH, DANA: Bristol, North Main St. Assessed as C., 1818–1823. "Skilled mechanic" 1824–1837.

BECTEL, NAZARETH: Bethlehem, Pa. n/d. (Funk)

BEDFORD, E.: Batavia, N.Y. Adv. 1816.

BEEBE, WILLIAM: N.Y.C. Patent with Samuel Blydenburg April 26, 1833. "Clocks."

BEECHER, WM.: Southbridge, Mass. Violet Watch Paper Bir. Col.

BEER, ALFRED: Versailles, Ind. Ca.1870.

—, ROBERT: Olean, Versailles, Ind. 1825.

BEHN, M. H.: N.Y.C. Ca.1860. Invented Alarm clock combined with lamp which lit up when alarm went off. (See ill. No. 279.)

BEIDT, JULIUS: Phila. Dir. 1848.

BEIGEL, HENRY: Phila. Dir. 1816–1817.

BEITEL, JOSIAH O.: Nazareth, Pa. n/d.

BELK, WILLIAM: Phila., 76 Front St. Dir. 1797–1800.

BELKNAP, EBENEZER: Boston. Dir. 1809–1830. Mass. Shelf clocks. (See ill. No. 131.)

—, WILLIAM: Boston. *Ca.*1820.

BELL, JAMES: N.Y.C. "1804."

—, JOHN: N.Y.C. Adv. 1734, "8-day Tall clocks with japanned cases."

—, M.: Mateo, N.C. *Ca.*1880.

—, SAMUEL: Boston. Dir. 1813.

—, S. W.: Phila. Dir. 1837.

—, THOMAS W.: Phila. Dir. 1837.

—, WILLIAM: Phila. Dir. 1805.

—, WM. W.: Mrs. R. R. Henning owns Tall clock, mahogany case, moon, date, and center seconds hand, "Looks like work of Wilmington, Del., cabinetmaker." Some sources say D.

BELLEROSE, G. I. H.: Three Rivers, Quebec. *Ca.*1790–1807. Tall clock LSS Col.

BEMIS, AUGUSTUS: Paris, Me. *Ca.*1810.

—, JONATHAN: Paris Hill, Me. Apprentice of Enoch Burnham. Beautiful Tall clocks with rocking ship; one in Hamlin Memorial Library. (Ruth S. Brooks)

—, MERRICK: n/d. Patent No. 26,008, Nov. 8, 1859, model Smiths. Inst.

—, SAMUEL: 1789–1881. Boston. "Made Clocks and watches." Dentist 1822–1861. At 72 proprietor Hart's Location, N.H. Had fine collection Watch Papers.

BENEDICT BROTHERS: N.Y.C. 1836. (BCL)

— (Deacon Aaron) & BURNHAM: Waterbury, Conn. Org. 1850. Bone and ivory buttons. Mr. Burnham of N.Y.C., Noble Jerome, making movts., Edward Church making cases. Arad W. Welton partner 1855, in the firm. Starting point of several interesting American developments. Waterbury Clock Co. established 1857 as division or separate company; now United States Time Corp. These firms have made millions of clocks. Parent company later became Benedict & Burnham Co., and Benedict & Burnham Mfg. Co., name used 1870's. *Illustrated Phila.* 1889, says, "started in 1812 and made since a variety of products of brass and copper"; became American Brass Co. This company provided funds and set up in 1880 The Waterbury Watch Co., which produced famous Waterbury watch. (See ill. No. 306.)

— & BURNHAM Co.: Formerly Benedict & Burnham.

— & BURNHAM MFG. Co.: *Ca.*1870. Illustrated Phila. 1889.

— & SCUDDER: N.Y.C. *Ca.*1830.

—, A.: Syracuse, N.Y. Adv. 1835.

—, ANDREW: N.Y.C., 23 Bowery. *Ca.*1810–1830.

—, MARTIN: N.Y.C. *Ca.*1830.

—, SAMUEL: N.Y.C., 5 Wall St. Aw. 1845.

—, S. W.: N.Y.C., 30 Wall St. Probably Samuel. His adv. 1845, 5 Wall St. at Museum of City of N.Y. Another source, "a shop where he sold clocks made in Conn. on which he put his name."

BENHAM, AUGUSTUS: New Haven, Conn. *Ca.*1840.

—, JOHN H.: New Haven, Conn. Printed clock labels. Dir. 1840, home 36 Grand Ave. Dir. 1846, business 55 Orange St., 1856 to Glebe Bldg., cor. Church and Chapel Sts.; took over from J. Madison Patton publishing of city directory, thereafter Benham's New Haven Directory.

BENJAMIN, E. (Everard), & Co.: New Haven, Conn. 1846–1847.

— (Everard) & FORD (George H.): New Haven, Conn. 1848.

—, BARZILLAIC: New Haven, Conn. Adv. 1823. Possibly Tower clocks.

—, EVERARD: New Haven, Conn. 1846–1847 in E. Benjamin & Co.; 1848 in Benjamin & Ford.

—, JOHN: 1730–1796. Stratford, Conn. Marr. 1753. Active in Christ Episcopal Church, organist 1758–1773. Rev. War; wounded Battle of Ridgefield. Town treasurer 1777. Later owned and operated ropewalk. (Hoopes)

BENNETT & CALDWELL: Phila. Dir. 1843–1848.

— & THOMAS: Petersburg, Va. *Ca.*1820.

—, ALFRED: Phila. Dir. 1837–1847.

—, JAMES: N.Y.C. Adv. 1768–1773.

—, T. N.: Canandaigua, N.Y. *Ca.*1860.

BENNY, JONATHAN: Easton, Md. 1798.

BENRUS MFG. Co.: Waterbury, Conn. 1936. (L B)

—, PETER C.: N.Y.C., 1 Cortlandt St. Dir. 1874.

BENSEL, LEONARD: N.Y.C. 1880's. Illuminated clocks.

"BENTLEY," used by Auburndale Watch Co. 1879.

—, CALEB: York, Pa., Leesburg, Va. n/d. Brother of Eli. (James)

—, ELI: 1752–. West Whiteland, Pa. Marr. 1772. First cousin Thomas Shields, Phila. Eight Tall clocks known, one 30-hr., seven 8-day, all brass movts. To Taneytown, Md. after 1778. (James)

—, THOMAS: Gloucester and Boston, Mass. 1764–1804. "Brother of the celebrated Rev. William Bentley. He was later employed by Emery of Boston."

BERHULT, JOHN: N.Y.C. Ca.1860.

BERKLY, J.: Lewisburg, Pa. Ca.1800–1820. Name appears on Tall clock dials. May have made Wag-on-Wall movts. cased by him and others.

BERRGANT, PETER: Phila. Dir. 1829–1833.

BERRINGER, A. J.: Albany, N.Y. Dir. 1834–1835.

—, JACOB: Albany, N.Y. Dir. 1835–1843.

BERRY, JAMES: N.Y.C. "Making Tall clocks with Osborne dials in the 1790's." (Stow)

BERWICK, ABNER: 1820. Probably Abner Rogers. (Abbott)

BESSONET, JOHN P.: N.Y.C. "1793."

BEST, THOMAS: Lebanon, O. Adv. 1808 "made Clocks and watches, and sharpened swords and dirks." Adv. 1822, "Clock and Watchmaker and silversmith 1 door So. of Wm. Lowry's store on Broadway, and returns his sincere thanks to the public for that liberal support which he has received for upwards of 14 years." Adv. 1826, "moved across the street." (Phillips)

BEVENS, WILLIAM: Phila. Dir. 1810–1813. Norristown till 1816.

"BEVIN, EDWARD," used by Newark Watch Co., 1867–1869.

BICHAULT, JAMES: Boston. Adv. 1729, "Lately arrived from London, makes and mends . . ."

BICKFORD, D.: n/p. Patent No. 19479, March 2, 1858, model Smiths. Inst.

BIDDLE, OWEN: 1737–1799. North Ward, Phila. Sold watch and clock parts and tools. Adv. 1764–1770, "Clockmaker and scientist, statesman and patriot." Associated with David Rittenhouse in his ob-

servations of the transit of Venus. Dr. Babb paid him high tribute. Shop next to Roberts' warehouse. (Stretch)

BIEGEL, HENRY W.: Phila. 191 N. 3rd St. Dir. 1810–1813.

BIERSHING, HENRY: Hagerstown, Md. 1815–1843. (LSS)

BIGELOW & BROS.: Boston. Dir. 1842.

— & KENNARD: Boston. Tall 8-day brass clock, brass dial, mahogany case, James Conlon Col.

—, JOHN B.: Boston. Ca.1840.

BIGGER (Gilbert) & CLARKE: Baltimore, Market St. Adv. 1783–1784, "Watch & Clock makers from Dublin." Adv. 1784, dissolved.

—, GILBERT: Baltimore. Continued alone. 115 Baltimore St. 1784–1816.

—, WILLIAM: Baltimore. 1802.

BIGGINS, H.: Assigned to N. Bachelor, patent for "design for clock frame" July 10, 1846.

BIGGS, THOMAS: Phila. Early 19th century. C. and Math. insts.

BILL, JOSEPH R.: Middletown, Conn. "1841."

BILLINGS, ANDREW: Poughkeepsie, N.Y. Ca.1810.

"—, FREDERICK," used by New York Watch Co. 1871–1875.

—, I.: Acton, Mass. Apprenticed to Aaron Willard. Made and sold a few clocks, putting his name on movt.; Lyre clock known. (H. M. Baker)

—, JONATHAN: Reading, Pa. Ca.1730.

—, JOSEPH: Reading, Pa. Adv. 1770.

—, L.: Northampton, Mass. Opened shop "Bloody Brook" 1837. (Cutten)

BILLON, CHARLES, & Co.: Phila., 20 S. 3rd St. Dir. 1795–1797. Also spelled Billow. Moore listed this firm in Boston.

BILLON (Billow), CHARLES: Phila. Dir. 1798–1819. d. St. Louis 1822.

BILLS, ELIJAH: Plymouth and Colebrook, Conn. Label of Shelf clock owned by Elizabeth Gaylord, Torrington, Conn., "Improved clocks mfg. by" Edward Terry, Printer. Mahogany Shelf clock in Flint Sale 1926, 31½ × 16¼. Another in Woodstock, Vt., wooden movt.

—, RODGER: Colebrook River, Conn. Flint Sale 1926, "Square case, carved columns and top."

BILLY BROS.: St. Lucas, Iowa. n/d. Iron-cased clocks.

BINGHAM & BRICERLY: Phila. 1778–1799.

—, B. D.: Nashua, N.H. 1830–1840. Tall and Banjo clocks. Many sold as "Warranted by L. W. Noyes."

BINNEY, HORACE: Phila. 1780–1875. C. Ca.1800–1840.

BIRDSLEY, E. C., & Co.: Meriden, Conn. Adv. 1831, "Clock and wood comb makers, Manufacturers of improved clocks." (Moore)

BIRGE (John), CASE (Hervey, Erastus) & Co.: Bristol. (tx) 1833–1834. With Joseph Ives. Brass 8-day weight-driven clocks, Empire, two- and three-decker cases. Dissolved 1834; Birge formed 1834 Birge, Gilbert & Co.

BIRGE (John) & FULLER (Thomas): 1844–(Feb.) 1848. Successful partnership; terminated with death of Fuller. Steeple on Steeple cases, fuzee and 1- and 8-day wagon-spring power plants. (See ill. Nos. 233–238.) "Puffin' Betsy," nickname given quaint old steam locomotive, used on some labels.

— (John) & GILBERT (Wm. C.): Bristol. 1837.

— (John), GILBERT (Wm. C.) & Co.: Bristol. 1834–1837. Gilbert later one of the more successful men in the business. Company still in existence in Winsted. By the tax records this became 1837 Birge & Gilbert; 1838 Birge, Mallory & Co.

— (John) & HALE: Bristol. 1823.

— -HAYDEN Co.: St. Louis, Mo. Ca.1850.

— (John) & IVES: Ca.1832–1833. Used Ives patents on brass movts.

—, JOHN, & Co.: (tx) 1848.

—, MALLORY (Ransom), & Co.: 1838–1843, with Sheldon Lewis and Thomas F. Fuller.

— (John), PECK (Ambrose) & Co.: 1849–1859. Prospered, made large number of clocks. Samuel Taylor (not the one in Worcester, Mass.) and William R. Richards partners. Credit report 1850, "... good no doubt, though Mr. Birge is involved in an unpleasant law suit with Mr. Joseph Ives ... a good man if the lawyers would let him alone ... the real and personal property must be worth say $25,000 at least. You can safely trust them all you wish." Birge retired from firm 1855

to continue farming, in which he had all his life been interested. This company was later merged with J. C. Brown enterprises and after several successor firms is now Sessions Clock Co. Many Birge clocks are extant, all of them varying types of Conn. Shelf clocks. (AAJ June, July 1949)

— & TUTLE: (tx) 1823.

—, JOHN: 1785–1862. Bristol. Important and successful. b. Torringford. Cabinet-maker. Fought in War of 1812. Successful wagon builder, listed 1820–1821. Possibly took clock selling trips. Probably making clocks 1820–1821. In Henderson & Birge 1822. Merriman (Titus) and Birge may have been producing as early as 1819 to 1823. (See ill. No. 225 for mirror clock and label.) Various enterprises, 1825–1830, including wagon building. To N.Y.C. 1830, according to tradition, to rescue Joseph Ives from debtor's prison and bring him back to Bristol. Reported to have purchased for $10,000 rights to certain Ives patents used in his clocks. Clocks possibly under own name 1830–1831. Alone 1848. John Birge died at Bristol June 6, 1862, aged 77, 49 days after death of former associate and partner, Joseph Ives. One of organizers of The Conn. Protective Clock Co. 1849.

—, J.: Brattleboro, Vt. "Early 19th century." Probably one of John Birge's clocks found there.

—, JOHN, JR.: 1815–1818.

BIRNIE, LAURENCE: Philadelphia, Pa. Adv. October 24, 1774, "Watchmaker from Dublin, Ireland, at Arch Street near Second." Adv. June 21, 1775, for Journeyman Watchmakers. Adv. Nov. 25, 1777.

BISBEE, J.: Brunswick, Me. 1798–1825. C. (Abbott)

BISHOP (James) & BRADLEY (Lucius B.): Watertown and Plymouth, Conn. Ca. 1823–1830. (See ill. No. 197.) Clock factory, large production. Label, "Patent clocks invented by Eli Terry made and sold by," Wood movts., most with 8-day brass wind; pillar and scroll and columned cases. Plant burned ca.1830, fire "consumed a large quantity of clocks awaiting shipment."

BISHOP (Daniel E., Dan F.) & NORTON (Charles): Bristol. (tx) 1853–1855. Assessed as having 50 clocks; no assessment of "investments in mfg."

—, DANIEL E.: Bristol. 1853–1855. In Bishop & Norton.

—, DAN F.: Bristol. 1853–1855. In Bishop & Norton.

—, HOMER: Bristol. After 1837.

—, J.: Allentown, Pa. *Ca.*1810. Tall clocks.

—, JAMES: Watertown, Conn. *Ca.*1825–1830. Flint Sale 1926 mahogany Shelf clock 32½ × 16¾.

—, JOSEPH: Wilmington, N.C. Adv. 1817–1822.

—, JOSEPH: Phila. Dir. 1829–1833.

—, MORITZ: Easton, Pa. 1786–1788. (Roberts)

—, RUFUS: Mt. Joy, Pa. *Ca.*1850.

BISPHAM, SAMUEL: Phila. and So. N.J. Tall 8-day brass clocks. Purchased building land Phila. 1696.

BISSELL, DAVID E.: Windsor, Conn. C., W., and dentist. *Ca.*1830.

BIXLER, CHRISTIAN I: 1710–1762. Lancaster Co., Pa. Son of Johann Jacob Bixler, Swiss, who came to America *ca.*1702. No record of Clockmaking.

—, CHRISTIAN II: 1737–1811. Reading, Pa. Natural aptitude for clocks. Varied activities; "clock store" 1760–1800. No record of Clockmaking, but in the business.

—, CHRISTIAN III: 1763–1840. Reading and Easton, Pa. C. Learned either at father's store or from John Keim of Reading. Account book states he made 50 Tall clocks for John Keim in Reading. Shop in Easton 1785. Records making 465 clocks by 1812. Active in civic affairs; one of those responsible for growth of Easton. Ledger contains plans for clock movts., drawings for hands, personal notes on trade. "He made many Tall clocks from 1783 to 1830 or possibly a bit later, which were then in great demand, till the Conn. clock became a stiff competitor. He was most particular and critical as to the materials used and sought the best methods of building the movts. so as to avoid irregular timekeeping, which was a common fault of some of the clocks of that period. Due to skillful drilling and polishing and filing of the tiny holes with delicate drills of his own make, his process worked quite as successfully as though jewels had been used." Beginning of Bixler firm now in Easton, Pa. (Norman E. Webster) (Kenneth H. Mittman)

—, DANIEL: Pa. Member Bixler family. Only data, "Entered his father's business *ca.*1810."

BLACK, JOHN: Phila. Dir. 1839–1850 and later. "Watchmaker."

BLACKFORD, EDWARD: N.Y.C. *Ca.*1830.

BLACKNER, JOHN L.: Cleveland, O. Adv. 1837, "Movt. for clocks and watches."

BLACKSLEY, RICHARD: Dayton, O. Adv. 1829, "Shelf and Mantel clocks."

BLAIR, ELISHA: Brooklyn, N.Y. *Ca.*1840.

BLAISDELL (Earlier spelled BLASDEL): Family of twelve clockmakers.

—, ABNER: Chester, N.H. 1771–1812. Possibly cases only. Son of Isaac.

—, CHARLES C.: 1838–1924. Ossipee, N.H. Later generation. Made in one year fine timekeeper, cherry case, "richly colored with rusty nails in vinegar," artistic pendulum, brass scroll work, owned by George Moody, Rumford, Me. (Blaisdell Papers)

—, DAVID: 1712–1756. Amesbury, Mass. Son of Jonathan. Famous for ingenuity and mechanical skill. House and shop adjoining property of Josiah Bartlett, signer of Declaration of Independence. Possibly 50 clocks. (See ill. No. 27.) Of his five children, David II, Nicholas, and Isaac were clockmakers. He served in French and Indian Wars.

—, DAVID II: 1736–1794. Amesbury, Mass. Son of David. C., blacksmith. Made all metal work for *Alliance* and other boats built at Amesbury for American Navy. May have made metal movt. Wag-on-Wall clock at Haverhill Hist. Soc. (See ill. No. 27.)

—, DAVID III: 1767–1807. Chester, N.H. and Peacham, N.H. Son of Isaac. One source, "evidently expert C."; another, "doubtful if made any clocks."

—, EBENEZER: 1778–1813. Chester, N.H. Son of Isaac; father d. when Ebenezer 13. Apprentice of Timothy Chandler, Concord, N.H. d. at Ackworth, N.Y. "on his way to the front to join the Army at Canadian frontier."

BLAISDELL, ISAAC: 1738–1791. Chester, N.H. Son of David. Aw. 1762. C. S. Tall clocks extant with endless rope drive, single weight, system he may have used in most of his Tall clocks. Prolific mfr. Some clocks sold without cases "for people who could not afford the extra expense for the case." Two Tall clocks in Derry, N.H., and two in Brookline, Mass. Transmitted skill to five sons—Abner, David III, Ebenezer, Isaac II, Richard.

—, ISAAC II: 1760–1797. Chester, N.H. Son of Isaac. Salisbury, Mass. Worker in metals; may have made clocks; some marked "Isaac" may be his.

—, JONATHAN: 1678–1748. Amesbury, Mass. Father of David. Clock in Hopkington, N.H., possibly by him, "brought to that town by a Daniel Kimball ... the first complete clock there"; possibly made by a later Jonathan.

—, NICHOLAS: Amesbury, Mass., Portland, Me. 1743–1800. Son of David. C. S. Tall clock owned by Paul C. Loring, Yarmouth, Me., endless rope drive, two hands, no seconds hand, brass wheels, n/d., maker's name on plate on dial.

—, RICHARD: 1762–1790. Chester, N.H. Son of Isaac. Some Tall clocks, and even at his premature death had established for himself an honored place in the community. (Blaisdell Papers)

BLAKE, E.G.: Farmington, Me. *Ca.*1850.

BLAKESLEE, M., & Co.: n/d. Terryville, Conn. 30-hr. brass Shelf clock.

—, M. & E.: Heathenville, Conn. Stencil case, 30-hr. wood movt. in C. D. Collins Col.

—, MARVIN & EDWARD: Plymouth, Conn. 1832. Flint Sale 1926, No. 46 square case, pt. columns and top, claw feet.

—, EDWARD K.: Cincinnati, O. *Ca.*1840–*ca.*1850. Patented marine timepiece "on lever clock for steamboats, canal packets, and railroad cars, for use like a watch in any position, serving as *admiral* chronometer." Later representative of Seth Thomas. Sold clock parts. Assembled and sold complete clocks.

—, JEREMIAH: Plymouth, Conn. 1841–1849. With Myles Morse.

—, MILO: Plymouth, Conn. *Ca.*1824. Employed by Eli Terry, Jr.; later partner till death of Terry 1841, then back to farming.

—, R., JR.: N.Y.C., 54 John Street. Dir. 1848. Clocks.

—, WILLIAM: Newtown, Conn. 1820–. Apprenticed to father, Ziba; partner after 1820. Successful J.

—, ZIBA: 1763–1834. Newtown, Conn. b. Plymouth, Conn., July 9, 1768; d. Newtown, Conn., Nov. 9, 1834. Son of Abner and Thankfull (Peeter) Blakeslee; father of William. Freeman's oath 1791. Marr. Mehitable Botsford of Newtown May 3, 1792. C., J., Bell founder, and joiner. Church clocks, Tall and Turret clocks, clocks and watches of all kinds. Adv. Farmers Journal, Newtown. Shortly after 1820 took son William into partnership.

BLAKESLY, HARPER: Cincinnati, O. *Ca.*1830.

BLAKEWELL, JOHN P.: Pittsburgh, Pa. Glass mfr. Patent 1830 "glass wheels for clocks."

BLANC, LEWIS: Phila., 172 North 2nd St. *Ca.*1810.

BLANCHARD, ASA: 1808–1838. Lexington, Ky. One of best known Kentucky Silversmiths. Movts. for Tall clocks, mahogany inlay case made possibly by Egerton of N.J., now in Metropolitan Museum of Art. Will mentions two apprentices, George Early and Eli C. Garnor, to whom left tools and shop.

BLAND, SAMUEL: Phila. Dir. 1837, 1845–1850. W.

BLANKFORD, WILLIAM: 1838–1920. Chicago. b. London, to U.S. 1879.

BLATT, JOHN: Phila. *Ca.*1841. Clock dealer.

BLAUS, SAMUEL: n/p. n/d. Clock owned by Mrs. Robert J. Thomas, Williamsport, Pa.

"BLINKING EYE CLOCKS": Sold 1875 for $5.75. (See ill. Nos. 282, 283.) (Hobb. June 1946)

BLISS & Co., JOHN: N.Y.C., 128 Front St. *Ca.*1891 to Dec. 1898. Adv. as chron. maker.

— & CREIGHTON: Brooklyn, N.Y. n/d.

—, H. A.: Bennington, Vt.

—, JOHN: Zanesville, O. Adv. 1815 as C.

—, WILLIAM: Cleveland, O. *Ca.*1810.

BLOMESBURG, PETER: Trenton, N.J. Watch movt. No. 5833, Cramer Col.

BLOOMER & SPERRY: N.Y.C. *Ca.*1840.
—, GEORGE: Northampton, Pa.
BLOWE, GEORGE: Phila. Dir. 1837, 1846–1850, and later.
BLUMER, JACOB, & JOSEPH GRAFF: Allentown, Pa. 1799. Tall clock, "1799" engraved on dial.
—, JACOB: Allentown, Pa. 1798–1820. "Worked all week and finished completely 30-hour clock which was $16 clear to me" (from one of his letters). In 1814 assessed $25 on occupation. Joseph Graff partner few years. One Tall clock, "Jacob Blumer and Joseph Graff," 1799.
—, JOSEPH: Allentown, Pa. 1798–*ca.*1820.
BLUNDY, CHARLES: Charleston, S.C., Church St. Adv. 1750, "Makes and mends all kinds of watches and thermometers." Away from Charleston 1753–1760. Adv. 1760 had returned to Clockmaking.
BLUNT & Co.: N.Y.C. Adv. 1869, Mfrs. marine Chron.
—, E. & G. W.: N.Y.C. *Ca.*1850.
BLYDENBURG, SAMUEL: N.Y.C. Patent with William Beebe "clocks" April 26, 1833.
BOARDMAN (Chauncey) & DUNBAR (Butler): Bristol. (tx) 1811.
— (Chauncey) & SMITH (Samuel B.): Bristol. 1832.
— (Chauncey) & WELLS (Col. Joseph A.): Bristol. 1832–1843. Clocks with 30-hour and 8-day wood movts.; brass movts. after 1837. Name on Conn. map 1837. Some labels printed by "C. E. Moss, Litchfield." Prosperous. Large numbers of clocks extant. Many types of Conn. Shelf clocks, including OG's and Steeple-on-Steeple Gothics. "One of the most important firms of that time." Received patent No. 4914, Jan. 7, 1847, model at Smiths. Inst. for "reversed fuzee" mechanism, "by placing the driving spring and fuzee on the same shaft, connecting same to the movement frame of the clock." Used in Acorn clocks. Wells must have left the firm, for by 1850 a credit report said, "Makes 30,000 clocks annually, pays his bank notes well, others not so well. has mortgages . . . owes considerable but is supposed to be worth a fair country property. A good man and very industrious. His son-in-law Dr. Charles F. Foote, I am told, is about to meet with him in the

clock business. This will be of help." f. 1850; Charles F. Foote purchased assets. Fuzee Shelf clock, "Patent Equalizing and Retaining Power Spring Brass clocks, warranted good if well used, made and sold by Chauncey Boardman, Bristol, Conn., U.S.," in G. B. Davis Col. Movt. has wood cones fronted by brass disk about size of half dollar; cord attached at point of largest diameter. (Ant. March 1949) (EI) (Hull)
—, CHAUNCEY: 1789–1857. For forty years prominent Bristol Clockmaker *ca.*1810–1850. Began making wood hang up movements with Butler Dunbar. Bristol History refers to them as "primitive wall pattern." Small shop near site of Humason Mfg. Co. Boardman bought out Dunbar 1812 and continued alone. Made movements for others including Chauncey Jerome. 1832 of Boardman, Smith & Co. with Samuel B. Smith. 1832–1843 in Boardman and Wells, with Joseph A. Wells one of largest mfr. of period operating as many as four factories at one time. Wood movements till 1837, then of rolled brass. Early makers of spring-driven clocks, of which they were proud. In 1844 firm split and each continued at clockmaking under his own name. Jointly received patent on a fuzee Jan. 8, 1847. Patent model in Smiths. Inst. Charles Foote, Boardman's son-in-law, acquired assets 1850.
—, CHESTER: Plymouth, Conn. 1842–1845. Label in standard Steeple clock with brass springs, "movt. by E. C. Brewster, Bristol," Col. of Mr. and Mrs. E. D. Cooley, Windsor, Vt.
—, GEORGE: Bristol. No dates no tx data. Flint Sale 1926, "mahogany Shelf clock 25½ × 15½, plain case OG."
BOCHEMSDE, FREDERICK: Boston. Dir. 1809–1821.
BODE, WILLIAM: Phila., 10th and Market, and High and Market Sts. 1796–1806.
BODELEY, THOMAS: Boston. *Ca.*1720.
BOEHME, CHARLES: 1774–1868. Baltimore. 1799–1812. W. C. R.
BOFENSCHEN, CHARLES: Camden, S.C. Adv. 1854–1857. C. W.
BOGARDUS, EVERARDUS: N.Y.C. 1675. Grandson of Dominie Everardus Bogardus

BOGARDUS, EVERARDUS (*cont'd*)
and Anneke Jans. Freeman 1698. Marr. Anna Dally 1704. C. S.

—, JAMES: 1800–1874. N.Y.C. and Henrietta, N.Y. b. Catskill, N.Y., Mar. 14, 1800. Apprenticed to W. 1814; expert Die maker and Engraver. Constant 8-day 3-wheeled chron. clock 1820; 8-day clocks without dials. Patent, Henrietta, N.Y., March 2, 1830, "Clocks"; N.Y.C. May 18, 1832, "Striking part of Clock"; 1833, for first dry gas meter; for machine for making postage stamps. Constructed N.Y.C. 1847 cast iron five-story factory building. d. N.Y.C.

BOGER (John R.) & WILSON (Wm. R.): Salisbury, N.C. Adv. 1846–1853, Watch repairers.

—, JOHN E.: Salisbury, N.C. Adv. 1845–1853, dealer in and repairer of watches. In Boger & Wilson 1846; sold out 1853.

BOIS-DE-CHESNE, JOHN FRANCIS: Charleston, S.C. Adv. Oct. 1, 1750, "Clock and Watchmaker from London. Had shop in Tradd Street."

BOLKMAN, EBENEZER: Attleboro, Mass. Tall clock owned by George F. Fiske, "in family since 1750." (Dr. S. Baketel)

BOLLMAN, WILLIAM: Atlanta, Ga. *Ca.*1870.

BOLOQUET, MARCEL: New Bern, N.C. *Ca.* 1760. "A Swiss clockmaker."

BOLTE, H. N.: Atlantic City, N.J. "Estb. 1864." (BCL Col.)

BON FANTI, JOSEPH: N.Y.C., 305 Broadway. *Ca.*1823. Probably importer French and German clocks.

BOND & SON: Boston, "Exchange Coffee House, Congress St." Brown Watch Paper, Bir. Col.

—, WILLIAM, & SON: Boston. Dir. 1813–1842 and later.

—, CHARLES: Boston. Dir. 1830–1842.

"— ST.," used by American Watch Co. from 1886.

—, WILLIAM: Boston. Dir. 1800–1810 and later. Reported 1812 to have made first Am. weight-driven Chronometer; "no springs could be imported during the War." Also Wall clocks.

—, WILLIAM: Portland, Me. *Ca.*1785. May be same man; later to Boston.

BONNARD (Bounard), M.: Phila., 62 Race St. Dir. 1799.

BOOTH, HIRAM N.: N.Y.C. Dir. 1849.

"BORDEN, GAIL," used by National Watch Co., Chicago 1871–1875.

BORHEK, EDWARD: Phila. Dir. 1829–1840.

BOSS & PETERMAN: Rochester, N.Y. Adv. Dir. 1841. D.

—, JAMES: Phila. Dir. 1846–1847. Invented, patented, gold-filled watch case 1859.

BOSTON CLOCK CO.: Chelsea, Mass. 1888–1897. Was Eastman Clock Co.; became Chelsea Clock Co. Overpasted label on clock with Crane 12-month movt. in Selchow Col. Also Ex. Essex Inst.

BOSTON WATCH CO.: Boston and Waltham. 1850. Beginning of Waltham Watch Co. *ca.* same time as Dennison, Howard, & Davis. To Waltham 1853; 1857 became Waltham Improvement Co. Howard back into business for himself at Roxbury in old plant. Became 1858 Baker Tracy and Co. for a few months, then Appleton, Tracy, & Co., then American Watch Co. (Crossman) (Evans) ("Timing a Century")

BOSTWICK & BURGESS MFG. CO.: Norwalk, O. 1892–1893. Makers of some 20,000 famous wood movt. Columbus Clocks. (See ill. No. 281.) Head of Columbus on wood dial and date "1492"; frequently mistaken for date of clock. (See pamphlet by Willis I. Milham for full story.) Souvenirs at Chicago World Fair 1893 at $5; later reportedly sold for $1. Face 13" tall, 5½" dial diameter, one hand, Arabic numbers, folio balance, weight driven. Waitley of Worthington, O., believed to have purchased business 1894.

BOTSFORD, J. S.: Troy, N.Y. *Ca.*1840.

—, L. F.: Albany, N.Y. Dir. 1830–1831.

—, PATRICK: New Haven, Conn. *Ca.*1840.

—, S. N.: Hampden, Whitneyville, Conn. *Ca.*1850.

BOTTOMLEY, T.: Boston. 1784. (Baillie)

BOUDINOT, ELIAS: 1706–1770. S., probably no clocks. (Williams)

BOUGHELL, JOSEPH: N.Y.C. 1786–1797. (Moore)

BOULT (Thomas A.) & JOHNSON (Arthur J.): Hagerstown, Md. (LSS)

BOUSTON, JOHN: Phila. "1790."

BOUTE, LEWIS CHARLES: Phila. Dir. 1839.

BOUVRIER, DANIEL: Zanesville, O. Adv. 1816, "From France." C. W. (Knittle)

BOUVRIER, M.: Pittsburgh, Pa. Also Baltimore and Zanesville, O.

"BOWEN, C. T.," used by Cornell Watch Co. 1871–1874.

—, GEORGE A.: Boston. Dir. 1842.

BOWER, HENRY, (HY), (BAUER, HIRAM or HENRY): Phila. Early 19th Century. Dwarf Tall clock. (See ill. No. 102.)

—, MICHAEL: Phila., 72 N. 2nd St. Dir. 1799.

—, WILLIAM: Charleston, S.C., 28 Broad St. Adv. 1772–1783.

BOWERS, GEORGE: Phila. Dir. 1850.

BOWMAN: Famous name in Pa. Horological history.

— (Joseph) & BALDWIN (Anthony): Lampeter, Pa. Tall clocks.

—, EZRA F.: Lancaster, Pa. 1847–1901. Apprenticed to Swiss watchmaker 1867–1870. Invented and introduced watchmaking tools and technical processes. Designed 1874 model for watch of Adams & Perry Mfg. Co. Began 1879 making fine watches. (See ill. No. 299.) Watches good but business unprofitable; sold out to J. P. Stevens, Atlanta, Ga.; developed retail and wholesale watch business and invented and mfd. tools; several patents. Founded 1887 Bowman Technical School; carried on by son John J. Many distinguished graduates. Dr. Daniel Herring, "This pioneer has done his work . . . well."

—, GEORGE: Columbus, O. Adv. 1840's, "Clockmaker." (Knittle)

—, JOSEPH: New Holland and Elliott's Corner, Pa. Ca.1800. Father of Joseph. (Baillie)

—, JOSEPH: 1799–1892. Strasburg, Pa. Aw. 1821–1844. Marr. 1820. Apprenticed to Anthony Wayne Baldwin. Tall clocks.

BOWNE (Browne), SAMUEL: –1819. N.Y.C., 81 John St. Aw. 1799. S. Sold japanned and walnut cased clocks. Marr. Mary Steeker 1778.

BOYCE, BENJAMIN M.: Boston, 49 Cornhill, later 119 Hanover St. till Aug. 25, 1895. Aw. 1880–1895. Marr. Delia Pratt, daughter of Daniel Pratt, Jr., of Reading and Boston. Later Daniel Pratt & Son, 339 Washington St. and 53 Franklin St. 1895–1916. Old tag inside Tall clock, "W. B. King" on dial.

BOYD & RICHARDS: Phila., 315 North Front St. Dir. 1808.

—, H.: Blairsville, Pa. Ca.1830. C. W. S. Made 8-day Tall clocks.

—, JOHN: Lowell, Mass. Dir. 1861.

—, JOHN: 1805–. Sadsburyville, Pa. Ca. 1830–1860. Listed tax rolls 1830 as "Watchmaker." Last of the makers with Anderson. Four Tall clocks known. (James)

—, THOMAS: Phila., 41 Cannonhill St. Dir. 1807–1809.

BOYER, JACOB: 1754–1790. Boyertown, Pa. "Father of the founders." In Rev. War. Tall clock owned by George W. Collins, Du Pont, Wash., walnut case, "Jacob Boyer" on dial, moon, day of month, sweep seconds hand, 8-day brass movt.

BOYNTON, CALVIN: Buffalo, N.Y. Dir. 1859.

—, JOHN E.: Manchester, Iowa. Ca.1870.

BOYTER, DANIEL: Boston Dir. 1800, and Poughkeepsie, N.Y. Adv. 1803.

BRABNER, WILLIAM A.: Boston. Dir. 1825.

BRACE (Rodney) & PACKARD (Isaac): Brockton, Mass. Ca.1825.

—, JARED: Newtown, Conn. "Not much known." (Hoopes)

—, RODNEY: Torrington, Conn., No. Brockton, Mass. Ca.1825. (See ill. No. 194.) Evidently trained in Torrington; clocks used horizontal "Torrington" type wood movt. Ca.1825 to Brockton (North Bridgewater); with Isaac Packard making Shelf Empire cased clocks, wood movts. "They sent them to all parts of the country in wagons." Ex. Essex Inst. of Shelf clock, carved case, 3-panel door, Torrington type wood 30-hr. movt., claw feet.

—, WILLIAM H.: St. Albans and Greenville O. 1826–1827. "At Knowles Linnell's Clock factory." Possibly from Conn. 1827–1828. (Knittle) (Lockett)

BRACKETT, J. R.: Boston. Dir. 1842.

—, O.: "Vassalboro, Me." Small Shelf clock owned by Teina Baumstone, N.Y.C., 29″ tall, 8″ wide.

—, R.: Vassalboro, Me. "Shelf clock made in form of Dwarf Tall, 29″ tall, original red paint, dial painted and lettered as above. Runs well"; Mrs. B. K. Little Col. Tall rocking ship clock owned by P. E. Bearse, Bklyn.

BRADBURY, JACOB: N.Y.C. Dir. 1847.

BRADFORD, O. C.: Binghamton, N.Y. Adv. 1841.

BRADIER, JOHN: Phila. Dir. 1802–1804.

BRADLEY, B., & Co.: Boston, 147 Hanover St. "Successors to Jerome Mfg. Co., Wholesale Dealers in clocks of every style and variety." Receipted bill 1862 in Mitchell Col. shows prices then charged for various clocks.

— & BARNES: Boston. Dir. 1856.

— & HUBBARD: Meriden, Conn. Blinking Eye Clocks patented 1856. (See ill. Nos. 282, 283.) Fancy clock cases before 1854. Name in small box clock in Ray Walker Col., 30-hr. brass spring movt.

— & HUBBARD MFG. Co.: Meriden, Conn. After 1854, to ca.1915. Fancy cast iron clock cases, movts. from Ansonia and New Haven Clock Cos. (Charles Parker)

—, Z., & SON: New Haven, Conn. 1840.

—, COL. ANER: Watertown, Conn. Shop at Hamilton Ave. and Woodbury Rd. Originally from New Haven. Father of Lucius B. S., spoons, gold beads, gold rings, gold and silver shoe and knee buckles; mended clocks and watches. Fought with distinction Rev. War.

—, D. W.: N.Y.C. Ca.1850.

—, DIMON: Patent with Joel Curtis from Cairo, N.Y., Aug. 22, 1814, for "wheels, teeth, and pinions."

—, FREDERICK: N.Y.C. n/d. Possibly Casemaker only.

—, G. C.: Binghamton, N.Y. Adv. 1841.

—, H.: Marietta, O. Late 1810's.

—, HORACE P.: Rochester, N.Y. Dir. 1832–1840.

—, LUCIUS B.: 1800–1870. Watertown, Conn. Son of Col. Aner Bradley. Clock factory "near Barlow's Pond," extensive operations. Also with James Bishop. Ca.1830 plant burned; many clocks lost; discontinued. Pillar and Scroll and Pillar clocks, 8-day brass movts., weight driven; dividers inside case, channel weights. One label, "Lucius B. Bradley, Brass Clock Manufacturer, Watertown, Conn. L. B. Bradley has now on hand and is constantly manufacturing, the lately improved Eight-day Brass Clocks, which are warranted to be equal to any Clock ever offered to the public, either for the time

or durability. People who are in want of the article, will do well to call and examine for themselves before they purchase elsewhere. All Orders thankfully received and punctually attended to. Watertown, August, 1823." (See ill. Nos. 198–203.)

—, NELSON: Plymouth, Conn. 1840.

—, RICHARD: Hartford, Conn. 1825–1839.

BRADY, JOHN: Phila. Dir. 1835.

BRADYCAMP, LEWIS: Lancaster, Pa. Aw. 1836–1860. Apprentice of Martin Shreiner. Tall clocks.

BRAKE, FREDERICK: Albany, N.Y. Dir. 1840–1844.

BRAMBLE, G. A.: n/p. Ca.1858. Repaired J. Masters Tall clock. (Mrs. B. K. Little)

BRAND, JAMES: Boston. Adv. 1711, "From London."

—, JOHN: Boston, Anne St. Adv. 1711–1712, "Watchmaker from London who maketh and mendeth all sorts of clocks and watches." Adv. 1713 servant had run away. Adv. 1714, "several compleat new pocket watches, London made." Adv. 1714, "designs for a time to go to England."

BRANDEGEE, ELISHANA: Berlin, Conn. Ca.1830. "Mfr. of cotton thread, clocks of all descriptions, and dealer in American goods."

BRANDT, A., & Co.: Phila., 129 N. 2nd St. Ca.1803–1804.

—, AIME & CHARLES: Phila. Dir. 1800–1814. Watch ca.1809 Ira Leonard Col. has center seconds hands, Calendar circle, good painted enamel dial.

—, BROWN & LEWIS: Phila., 158 N. 2nd St. Dir. 1795–1796.

— & MATHEY: Phila., 138 New St. at cor. N. 2nd, 158 S. 2nd St. Adv. 1795–1799.

— (Brant, Brent), ADAM: New Hanover, Pa. Ca.1750. "One of the early makers." A. Sanford Craven, Mrs. Elva Hanley own Tall clocks by him.

—, AIME: Phila. Dir. 1816–1831. Watches with center seconds hands.

—, JACOB: New Hanover, Pa. Early 19th century.

BRASHER, ABRAHAM: N.Y.C., Wall St. 1786–1805.

BRASTOW, A., & Co.: Lowell, Mass., "on Central St." Yellow Watch Paper Bir. Col.

BRASTOW, ADISON & CO.: Lowell, Mass. 1832–1837.

BRAZIER, AMABLE: Phila., 7 and 23 N. 3rd St. Dir. 1794–1828. "A French Watchmaker."

BREADY, C. L.: Phila. Dir. 1808.

BREARLEY, JAMES: Phila., 79 N. 2nd St.; 67 Mulberry; 67 Arch St.; 78 N. 3rd St. Dir. 1795–1822.

BRECKEL, RICHARD: N.Y.C. Adv. 1755, "Mechanical puppet show . . . makes and cleans all sorts of clocks reasonably."

BRECKENRIDGE, J. M.: 1809–1896. New Haven and Meriden, Conn. "Clockmaking all his life. His death removed the last one of the original Conn. Makers [sic]. He learned the trade at age 19 and lived through the wonderful growth of the Clockmaking business, saw wood works crowd out cast brass, and sheet brass take the place of wood. Although a maker for many years he never gained a fortune as many of his contemporaries did, and was at his bench at New Haven Clock Co. till within a few months of his death. His last work was making dies for clock hands, which requires special skill. During his long career he made many improvements in Clockmaking tools. Invented wire gong." (Moore)

BRECKWELL, JOHN: Pikeland Twp., Pa. Chester Springs 1831–1835. Doubtful he made clocks in Chester Co. (James)

BREESE, LYMAN: Wellsburg, Va. Ca.1830.

BREIDENBACH, L.: Phila. Dir. 1807.

BREITINGER & KUNZ: Phila., 37 N. 9th St. Name on dial Wall clock in Geiger Col.

BRENEISER, SAMUEL: Adamstown and Reamstown, near Reading, Pa. Adv. 1799. Many Tall clocks. Brother William, Womelsdorf, Pa. Mrs. Benjamin Harrigan, Phila., owns Tall clock in case, excellent inlay, moon, no place name on dial.

—, SAMUEL II: Reamstown and Reading, Pa. Ca.1830–1860. "Fourth Group. One of the last makers." Possibly son of Samuel. Dr. D. G. Robinson, Forty Fort, Pa., owns Tall clock, 8′ walnut case 21″ wide, 8-day brass movt., moon-days, hour strike. (Steinmetz)

—, WILLIAM: Womelsdorf, Pa. Ca.1800. Brother of Samuel. Tall clocks.

BRENER, WILLIAM: Yeadon, Pa. n/d. Tall clocks.

BRENFTER, WALTER: Canterbury, Conn. Ca.1800. Brass movt. Tall clocks.

BRENKELEAR, JAN: N.Y.C. Reports and traditions date ca.1660 to 1750's. None now known.

BRENNAN, BARNABAS: Phila. Dir. 1843.

BREWER, —: Middletown, Conn. 1800–1803. (Hoopes)

—, ISAAC: Phila. 1813.

—, THOMAS A.: Phila. Dir. 1830 to ca.1850.

—, WILLIAM: Phila., Chestnut St. between Front and 2nd. Adv. 1774 opened shop.

BREWSTER & BROWN: Bristol. (tx) 1839–1840.

— & CO., ELISHA C.: Bristol, Race St. (tx) 1840–1843. Among first users of coiled springs. Shaylor Ives, partner. Firm sometimes known as Brewster & Ives, became 1844 Brewster & Ingrahams.

— & CO., N. L.: Bristol. Org. 1861 to make Joseph Ives patent round tin movt. Shelf clock. Ex. in Selchow Col., round top rosewood Shelf clock, two circles on one-piece door, 8-day coiled spring, not wagon spring. (See ill. No. 246.)

—, E. C., & SON: Bristol. (tx) 1855. With son Noah L. After this Elisha retired. Ex. in Museum of City of N.Y.

— (Elisha) & IVES: Bristol. Became 1844 Brewster & Ingrahams.

— (Elisha) & INGRAHAMS (Elias and Andrew): Bristol. 1844–1852. N.Y.C. office, 46 Cortlandt St. Dir. 1848. One of most prolific producers of clocks of the period. Several Bristol plants. Elias Ingraham's design of Sharp Gothic (now called Steeple) widely copied. (See ill. Nos. 252, 253.) Large export business to England. Report 1850, "Good, no doubt. Make 20 to 30,000 clocks annually and pay very well. Have real estate and buildings belonging to the Company, all clear . . . I fully believe they are to be trusted." Twin Steeple, overpasted label, "Pond & Barnes, 71 Hanover St., Boston," Ray Walker Col. Label in another in Geo. B. Davis Col., "Patent Spring eight day Repeating Brass Clocks mfged by"; brass coiled springs. (EI)

— MFG. CO.: Bristol. (tx) 1852–1854. Partners, Elisha Brewster, Wm. Day,

BREWSTER MFG. CO. (cont'd)
Augustus Norton, Noble Jerome. Succeeded Brewster & Ingrahams. Good foreign trade. Ex. Essex Inst.

— & WILLARD: Portsmouth, N.H. 1830's. Possibly to sell Willard clocks.

—, ABEL: 1775–1807. Canterbury, Conn., few rods So. First Soc. Meeting House. Aw. 1796. S. Adv. 1796, various types of clocks and timepieces. By 1797 began to feel effect of long term credits then customarily extended, "those who trust long cannot sell inexpensively long"; and asked for immediate settlement of all accounts more than 3 months out. Took apprentice 1799 and announced different types of 8-day repeating clocks. "Glad to exchange merchandise for a saddle horse." To Norwich Landing 1800. Adv. 1805 for successor; sold out to Judah Hart and Alvin Wilcox. (Hoopes)

—, CHARLES E.: Portsmouth, N.H. Ca.1840.

—, ELISHA C.: 1791–1880. Pos. first Conn. Clockmaker to mass produce clocks with American-made springs, though Charles Kirke may have preceded him. Clothmaker by trade; learned clock business by traveling through South as "Yankee clock pedlar" for Thomas Barnes Jr. & Co. Purchased 1833 Charles Kirke's clock manufactory; made clocks till ca.1855, first hiring Kirke to run it for him. Connected with Brewster & Brown, Elisha C. Brewster & Co., Brewster & Ives, Brewster & Ingrahams, E. C. Brewster & Son.

—, GEORGE G.: Portsmouth, N.H. Ca.1850.

—, W.: Middlebury, Vt. n/d. Watch Paper BCL Col.

BRIGDON, GEORGE S.: Norwich, Conn. Ca.1810–1830.

"BRIGGS, J. A.," used by N.Y. Watch Co. 1870.

—, JOHN C.: No Concord records. Patents 1855 and 1856 from Concord, N.H., on "Briggs Rotary." (See ill. No. 278.) Patents 13451 Aug. 21, 1855, 15456 July 15, 1856. Many by E. N. Welch Mfg. Co. 1870's; "made a specialty of rotary clocks, and it is claimed that they are the only American makers of reliable clocks having this escapement." S. B. Terry did not make them. Movts. 30-hr.; one 8-day known. Keep "pretty good time" despite

51 mm. pendulum. Ex. in Edward Ingraham, S. R. Rector, Rev. Charles Brewer, Selchow, and G. B. Davis Cols. See *Am. Horologist and Jeweler*, Aug. 1946, for article by J. E. Coleman.

—, NATH'L: Boston. Dir. 1820.

BRINCKERHOFF, C.: N.Y.C. Bell founders; bells and brass blanks for clocks. Succeeded after 1800 by Sayre & Force.

—, DIRK: N.Y.C. "1756." "Sign of Golden Clock."

BRINDLE, G. B.: Norwich, Conn. n/d. Watch Paper BCL Col.

BRINGHURST, JOSEPH: Phila. Dir. 1813.

BRINTZINGHOFFER, F.: Phila. Dir. 1804.

BRISTOL BRASS CLOCK MANUFACTORY, THE: Bristol. 1818–1819. Elias and Curtis Roberts and Joseph Ives. Brass movt. Mirror clocks. Extant is a contract to buy 60. Examples, 9″ pendulums, Edward Ingraham and A. L. Partridge Cols.

— BRASS & CLOCK CO., THE: Bristol, on site of old Atkins & Welton toy shop. 1850–1903. Store N.Y.C. Joint stock company; Bristol and Waterbury makers who joined to make clocks and brass for clock industry. Headed by Israel Holmes; E. N. Welch first president. Name changed 1903 to Bristol Brass Co., later Bristol Brass Corp.; long since given up Clockmaking. Early 1853 trade agreement, "every brass mill in Naugatuck Valley signed a price agreement to bring their business out of the 1857 depression."

— CLOCK CO., THE: Bristol. N.Y.C., 48 Dey St. Dir. 1854. Org. 1843 "with small capital" by Chauncey Jerome, Elisha Hotchkiss, Edward Fields, Elisha Manross, E. C. Brewster, Joseph A. Wells, and Augustus Jerome to do foreign business, particularly China.

— CLOCK CASE CO.: Bristol. (tx) 1854–1857. Joint stock company org. March 1854, $20,000 capital by 35 prominent men, J. C. Brown, president. "A large shop was built on No. side of Doolittle's cor. near RR on land now owned by Sessions Foundry. Soon abandoned, and shop stood idle a number of years." (LB)

— MFG. CO.: Bristol. Org. Sept. 4, 1837. Pos. first Bristol Corporation to make satinetts, etc. March 2, 1842, rechartered to make satinetts, clocks, etc.; Chauncey

Ives, pres. Leased for short time part of "Eureka Shop" from Brewster & Ingrahams. Dissolved, n/d.

BRITTAIN, JOSEPH: Bakerstown, Pa. *Ca.*1830.

BROADBRIDGE, JAMES: Newburgh, N.Y. Adv. 1806–1832.

"BROADWAY," used by American Watch Co. 1872.

BRODERSEN, CHRISTIAN: 1834–1887. Russellville, Ky. Bro. of Emil. (LB)

—, EMIL: Cincinnati, O. b. Denmark, one of four brothers to this country before 1860. Aw. for Duhme & Co. (LB)

BROGAN, JOHN: N.Y.C. *Ca.*1810.

BROKAW, AARON: 1768–185–. Elizabethtown, N.J. Son of Isaac. Continued father's business. Tall clocks, brass 8-day movts., some with cases by John Scudder.

—, ISAAC: 1746–1826. Hillsborough Twp., Bridgetown (Rahway), N.J. Late 18th century. Prominent N.J. Tall C. Making clocks by 1776, when according to minutes of Provincial Congress and Com. of Safety July 26, 1776, given "30 lbs. of lead as he could not carry on his trade of Clockmaking without that quantity." Continued to ca.1810. *Ca.*125 Tall clocks, 8-day brass movts., cases by various casemakers, Rosett & Mulford and John Scudder; 30 known; some dials marked "Elizabethtown." (See ill. No. 47.) Marr. Betsy Miller, dau. of Aaron Miller, C., from whom he learned trade. Two sons, Aaron and John. Mrs. J. S. Frelinghuysen, Far Hills, N.J., owns two; 7 ft. Tall, 3 brass ball finials, fine mahogany case, plain fluted columns; one darker mahogany inlay in door 8½' tall, broken arch top, brass dial. (Ant. July 1943) (M.H. Greene)

—, JOHN: (pos.) Woodbridge, N.J. Bro. of Aaron, son of Isaac. "Known that he made one or two Tall clocks but more than that are not known." (PG)

BROKESMIELD, JOSEPH: Cincinnati, O. *Ca.* 1830.

BRONSON, BENNET: Waterbury, Conn. *Ca.* 1800. "Clockmaker." (Anderson)

—, I. W.: Buffalo, N.Y. 1825–1830.

—, PHARRIS: Waterbury, Conn., Cairo, N.Y. Patent with Joel Curtis 1814 on "pinions."

BROOK, JOHN: N.Y.C. *Ca.*1830.

BROOKER, JOHN: Germantown, Pa. n/d. (Fred Muth)

BROOKS, B. F., & Co.: Utica, N.Y. Adv. 1831.

— & GRISWOLD: Utica, N.Y. Adv. 1832.

—, B. F.: Utica, N.Y. Dir. 1828–1837.

—, BERNARD: Salem Crossroads, Pa. *Ca.* 1830. Tall clocks, none extant.

—, CHARLES V.: Utica, N.Y. Dir. 1834–1840.

—, F. O.: Madison, Ind. *Ca.*1860.

—, HERVEY: Goshen, Conn. Father of Watts. Pottery business. Adv. "exchange for clocks." Prob. made none. Tall clock, "BROOKS" on dial, also painting of original buildings at Yale, John H. Thompson Col. Clock Label reads "Sold by H. Brooks." Other example in Whitney Brooks Col., Torrington, Conn.

—, JOHN: Germantown, Pa. n/d.

—, L. S.: Mass. or N.H., n/p. b. Temple, N.H. W. and J. before 1848.

—, WATTS: Son of Hervey. Mentioned 1830's leaving for South or West with shipments of clocks to be sold.

—, WILLIAM PENN BEAL: Boston, 118 Blackstone St. Dir. 1856, "Watchmaker." This was author's grandfather; successful furniture business; certainly never made clock or watch; had them for sale.

BROOMALL, LEWIS R.: Phila. Dir. 1846–1850.

BROUGHHAM, GEORGE: Baltimore. Adv. by David Evans, Baltimore C. and W., "If he, native of London, by profession a Watchmaker who arrived Baltimore 1774, and who lived with me 4 years, will apply to me either personally or by letter, will learn something greatly to his advantage."

BROWER, S. DOUGLAS: Troy, N.Y. Dir. 1841–1842.

BROWN (Thomas W.) & ANDERSON: Wilmington, N.C. 1850–1871.

—, BACON & Co.: Bristol. Pos. C. n/d.

— & BUCK: Columbus, O. Adv. 1850.

— & BUTLER: Bristol. (tx) 1853. Pos. C.

— & GOODRICH: Bristol. No exact data.

— & KIRBY: New Haven, Conn. 1840. (Moore)

— & LEWIS: Bristol. (tx) 1839. Pos. C.

— & MARSTERS: N.Y.C., 112 Chatham St. Watch Paper Cramer Col.

BROWN, ROBERT, & SON: Adv. 1833 and later.

—, (J.R.) & SHARPE: Providence, R.I., 115 S. Main St. Adv. 1856, "Clock and Watch makers and mfgers. of small machinery."

—, ALBERT: Columbia, Pa. Ca.1850.

—, DAVID: Providence, R.I. 1834–1850. (Abbott)

—, EDWARD L.: Newburyport, Mass. Dir. 1860.

—, GAWEN: 1719–1801. Boston. Adv. 1762–1773 King St. b. England. At Boston by 1749. Tall and Tower clocks. In Rev. War. Reported made and installed Tower clock Old South Church ca.1770. At least 15 advs.; 1768 "Exhibit at Town Meeting, frames and principal movts. of superb and stately Town Clock, 8-day, maintaining power, dead beat, steel pinions, teeth polished abating friction, the math. pendulum may be altered 3,500th part of an inch while going. Masterpiece of the Kind, and an Honor to America." Metropolitan Museum of Art. Ill. No. 24. (BCC) Boston Records: "May 3d 1758 . . . Gawen Brown Informs the Selectmen that he has taken into his service John Cross Smith, a young man a watchmaker who came as a passenger with Capt. Partridge from London." Oct. 5, 1767 . . . "Mr. Gowen Brown appeared, and agreed with the Selectmen to rectify the Hand of the Dyal of the Clock at the Brick Church, and to clean said Clock, for Forty Shillings lawful money." Nathaniel Hurd's will 1778, ". . . my watch, Brown, Boston on the face of it."

—, GEORGE: Bristol. (no tx) Standard OG in Geiger Col. 30-hr. brass weight-driven mahogany OG in Selchow Col.

—, J. H.: Des Moines, Ia. Ca.1850.

—, JOHN: Lancaster, Pa. Late 18th century. "Early maker, not many Tall clocks." (Lan. Co.)

—, JOHN: Phila., 359 N. 2nd St. Dir. 1819–1822.

—, JOHN JAMES: Andover, Mass. Ca.1840.

—, JONATHAN CLARK: 1807–1872. Bristol. 1831–1855. Sept. 1832 purchased interests of Elias Ingraham and William G. Bartholomew, clock cases; firm became Bartholomew, Brown & Co. Complete clocks, their label. Also 1835–1839 in "Forestville Mfg. Co." with Bartholomew, Wm. Hills, Chauncey Pomeroy, Jared Goodrich, Lora Waters. First clocks 8-day strap movt., weight-driven, veneered mahogany Empire cases; escape wheel solid brass, good timekeepers. One in author's collection; label, "Improved Eight Day Brass Clocks made and sold by the Forestville Manufacturing Co., Bristol, Conn., warranted if well used — etc. Wm. Hills, J. C. Brown, C. Pomeroy, O. J. Goodrich." Hills, Brown & Co. firm name 1840–1842. Brown bought out Hills, became J. C. Brown & Co., 1842–1849; used *both* own name and "Forestville Mfg. Co."; label, "Eight Day Brass Clocks, springs with equalizing power warranted not to fail, mfg. & sold by The Forestville Mfg. Co., J. C. Brown, Bristol, Conn."; printed by J. G. Wells, 26 State St., Hartford. Used "Forestville Clock Manufactory, J. C. Brown, Proprietor," 1850–1855. Adv. 1851, Conn. Business Dir.; inc. 1852. Started hardware business 1853, Forestville Hardware & Clock Co., possibly separate firm, some clocks. Bad fire and approaching depression of 1857, all Brown's enterprises failed 1855, purchased by E. N. Welch, who combined them with various Birge and Manross firms; since 1903 Sessions Clock Co. Brown to other industries; not again in clock business. d. 1872, Nyack, N.Y.

Difficult to date clocks with any of these names. Some mix-up on dates of Conn. Shelf clocks marked "Forestville Mfg. Co." Rolled brass one-day weight-driven movt. ca.1838, mostly later. Etched glass tablets after 1840. Coiled springs, first brass, later steel, in fuzee wood cones, later metal, ca.1842 and later. OG 30-hour brass movt. ca.1838 and after. Sharp and round Gothic steeples late 1840's. Acorn clocks ca.1847–1850. Wall Conn. Lyre clocks ca.1850. House, Maple St., Bristol, purchased from L. C. Ives 1847 (still standing), frequently pictured on his clock tablets. Some clock tablets have his portrait. (See ill. No. 254.) (Am. Col. Sept. 1947) (EI) (LB)

—, JOSEPH R.: Providence, R.I. Ca.1850.

—, LAMONT (or Laurent): Utica, N.Y. 1838–1841. Rochester, N.Y. 1841.

BROWN, ROBERT: Baltimore, 21 No. Gay St. Adv. 1829–1831; 1833 and after as Robert Brown & Son.

—, S.: Norristown, Pa. *Ca.*1850.

—, SAMUEL: N.Y.C. *Ca.*1820.

—, SAMUEL A.: Lowell, Mass., Exchange Bldg., Central St., Dir. 1835; 40 Merrimack St., Dir. 1837.

—, THOMAS: Zanesville, O. Adv. 1813, "Clock cases." (Knittle)

—, THOMAS WILLIAM: 1803–1872. Marr. 1822. Learned trade N.Y.C., opened shop 1830, "where he lived for the rest of his life." In Brown & Anderson.

—, WILLIAM: Phila. Dir. 1823, 1824, 1837.

—, WILLIAM: York, Pa. *Ca.*1840.

BROWNE, LIBERTY: Phila. n/d.

BROWNING, SAMUEL: Boston, 77 Broad St. Adv. 1815. Math. instrs.

BRUFF, CHARLES OLIVER: N.Y.C. Adv. 1769, "At the Sign of the Teapot . . . cleans watches and puts in glass for one shilling." Son of James. (MFM)

—, JAMES: –1780. Elizabeth, N.J.; first S., did private coining. b. Talbot Co., Md. *Ca.*1748 to N.Y.C., adv. 1766, "at the Sign of the Clock and Two Watches opp. to Mr. Roorback at the Fly Market." To Md. before 1776, d. there 1780. (Williams)

BRUGHNER, JACOB: Brooklyn, N.Y. *Ca.* 1840–1850.

BRYANT, E. D.: N.Y.C. Dir. 1850.

—, THOMAS: Rochester, N.Y. *Ca.*1800.

BUARD, CHARLES W.: Phila. Dir. 1849.

BUCHER, JESSE: Dayton, O. *Ca.*1830.

BUCK, D. A. A.: Basic patent May 21, 1878; devised what became long-winding, inexpensive Waterbury watch, after months of patient effort; patent model at Smith. Inst. (See ill. Nos. 306, 309, 311, 312.) Only 58 parts, coiled spring about 9' long, about movt. inside case, which served as barrel; old duplex escapement improved so that all parts could be stamped out easily. Whole movt. carrying minute hand made one revolution an hour. Dial printed on paper. Sold initially at $4. (See Waterbury)

—, SOLOMON: Glens Falls, N.Y. Adv. 1827–1828.

BUCKLE, JACOB: Pittsburgh, Pa. *Ca.*1830.

BUCKLEY, SAMUEL: Phila. Dir. 1811.

BUCKMAN, GEORGE W.: Baltimore, 30 Gould St. "1802."

BUDD, JOSEPH: New Mills (now Pemberton), N.J. *Ca.*1806–1820. Tall clocks, broken arch hood, mahogany cases, owned by D. K. Bennett, Collingswood, N.J. ("Osborne" dial); R. P. von de Selde, Wilton, Conn.; Mrs. Herbert E. Harper, Merchantville, N.J.

BUELL, ORLANDO: New Preston, Conn., and Staten Island, N.Y. n/d. Tall clocks.

BUERK, J. E.: Boston. Patented time clock Jan. 1, 1861, like Imhauser clock 3½″ diameter, 1½″ thick; punctured paper charts with keys.

BUFFET, GEORGE FRANCIS: Phila., 131 Front St. *Ca.*1796.

BULKLEY, JOSEPH: 1755–1815. Fairfield, Conn. Pos. apt. of John Whitear, Jr. After Whitear's death became leading C. Marr. 1778. In Rev. War. Some clocks still extant in vicinity. (Hoopes)

BULL, JAMES P.: Newark, N.J. 1850–1857. (PG)

—, JOHN: York, Pa. Early 19th century.

BULLARD, CHARLES: 1794–1871. Boston Neck, at or near 843 Washington St. 1816–1844. Painted dials and tablets for Simon Willard and others. Marr. 1822. Apt. and successor of English artist who did tablets and dials for Willard and surrounding Cs. Adv., "ornamental painter." *Ca.*1844 to Dedham, Chestnut Hill St. Exquisite work, especially dials. Last work for Simon Willard, Jr., on their books Oct. 16, 1865, "for clock dials." Probably had apts; no successor. (JWW)

BULOVA WATCH CO.: 1875–. N.Y.C. Since *ca.*1946 American watches N.Y.C., stamped "Made in U.S.A." Also plant in Switzerland.

BUMMEL & SCOVILLE: Owego, N.Y. Arthur H. Torrence, Indiana, Pa., owns wood movt. Shelf clock marked "Made & Sold wholesale & retail by . . ."; label printed by "Gazette Office, Owego, N.Y."

BUNDY (W. L.) TIME RECORDING CO.: Binghamton, N.Y. Adv. 1893. Time recorders, Seth Thomas movts.

BUNKER, BENJAMIN: Nantucket, Mass. Early 19th century.

"BUNN," used by Illinois Springfield Watch Co. 1870–1872.

BUNNELL, EDWIN: Bristol. Sold land 1850 to Smith & Goodrich. Assessed 1851 for "47 clocks"; clocks extant with his label.

BUNTING, DANIEL: Phila. Dir. 1844.

BURDICK, M. H.: Bristol. *Ca.*1849. Son H. M. moved to Cleveland, O., wholesale distributor of clocks and watches.

BURDICT, S. P.: n/p. *Ca.*1880. Inventor patent lever 8-day Cathedral gong musical clock.

BURG, JACOB: Lancaster Co., Pa. n/d. "Noted maker Tall clocks." (Lan. Co.)

BURGER, JOSEPH: N.Y.C. n/d. Pos. dial maker.

BURGI, FREDERICK: Trenton. 1774–July 2, 1775. Journeyman with John Fitch. In Hurtin & Burgi.

—, JACOB: Lancaster, Pa. *Ca.*1750. Tall clocks.

BURITT, P.: Ithaca, N.Y. Patent with P. Burdick Oct. 25, 1821 on "clocks."

BURK, CHARLES: Phila. Dir. 1848.

BURKELOW, SAMUEL: Phila., Shippen St. Census 1790. Dir. 1791–1793, 1796–1813.

BURKMAR, THOMAS: Prob. Boston. 1776.

BURLINGTON, VT.: "Seems to have been Clockmaking center after War of 1812. Little data; worthy of further research."

BURNAP (Ela) & JAMES (Joshua): Boston. Dir. 1809–1810.

—, DANIEL: 1759–1838. East Windsor, Conn. *Ca.*1780. Apt. of Thomas Harland. Tall clocks, pos. mass production. Eli Terry apt. "Unusually fine workmanship; skilful engraver, dials splendid." Pos. wood movt. Cheney type Tall clocks. Brass movts. 8-day specialty. Adv. 1791 for two apts. Account book in existence. Tall clocks considered among most interesting and valuable of late 18th century. Made 8-day musical Tall clock in own home. To Coventry (now Andover), Conn. after 1800; built house 1805 where he lived rest of his life. Justice of Peace many years; court in own house. Continued to make clocks, silver spoons, etc. Later gave shop to apprentice, fitted up attic for occasional work on clocks and watches; few clocks after 1815. Broke hip 1825. Kindly but taciturn. Fed wild animals and protected them; "even the quail would congregate in his farmyard for the grain he scattered for them." d. 1838, prosperous and respected. (Hoopes)

—, ELA: Boston. Dir. 1810.

BURNES CLOCK CO.: Conn., n/d. In G. B. Davis Co. Label, "Improved 8-day Calendar Clocks, guaranteed Springs and Bushed Movements sold by the Burnes Clock Co." Simple Calendar clock, good movt., by Gilbert Clock Co., Winsted, Conn., prob. assembled.

BURNET, SMITH: 1770–1830. Newark, N.J. Adv. 1793, Broad St., N.W. cor. Market St., "Watch Store." Practical C. (Williams)

BURNHAM, —: Danvers, Mass. 1831. With Robinson, Burnham & Co., watch and math. inst. makers.

—, E. B.: Salisbury, N.C. Adv. 1821, "Elliott & Burnham." Prob. not N.Y.C. 1814–1821, though one listed by same name.

—, ENOCH: Paris Hill and Rumford, Me. Portland 1806–1835. Tall clocks with rocking ship. Jonathan Bemis an apt. (Ruth S. Brooks)

—, J. W.: Salisbury, Conn. *Ca.*1825–1835. Shelf clocks, 8-day brass movt. (LB)

—, P. B.: Greenville, S.C. Adv. 1856.

BURNS, HUGH: Phila., 94 Chestnut St., 1812. Dir. 1809–1811.

BURR & CHITTENDEN: Lexington, Mass. 1831–1837. Many clocks with these labels. Assemblers; or may have made some. Also overpasted labels on Conn. clocks. Burr to Chicago, business ceased 1837. (AAJ May 1949)

—, EZEKIEL & WILLIAM: Providence, R.I. 1792. (MFM)

—, C. A.: Rochester, N.Y. 1841. Pos. D.

—, JONATHAN: Lexington, Mass. Of Burr and Chittenden 1831–1837.

BURRAGE, JOHN: Baltimore. Adv. 1769, C. and had left Francis Knapp.

BURRITT, JOSEPH: 1795–1889. Ithaca, N.Y. Adv. 1819–1838, S. Patent from Ithaca with T. Burritt Oct. 21, 1821 "clocks." Adv. 1819–1835.

BURROUGHS, THOMAS: Lowell, Mass., 44 Merrimack St. Dir. 1834. With Wm. Moulton and James Carr.

BURROWES, JOHN: Strasbourg, Pa. *Ca.*1808. Tall clock owned by James J. Jackson, Woodbury, N.J., walnut case, calendar, moon.

BURROWES, THOMAS: –1839. Strasbourg, Pa. "Made some clocks" 1787–1810. b. County Cavan, Ire., to Del. 1784, Lancaster Co. 1787. Father of Thomas H. Burrowes, founder public school system in Pa. "Did not make many Tall clocks." To Ireland 1810 for inheritance; returned U.S.A. 1822.

BURT & CADY: Kansas City, Mo. *Ca.*1870.

BURTON, WOLSEY: Phila., also pos. Dover, Del. Early 18th century. Quaker. Pos. C.

BURTT, THOMAS F.: Stoneham, Mass., 1855. Danvers, Portsmouth 1872; Stoneham till 1890. With Waltham Watch Co. 1879. Tall, Banjo, Wall regulator, and others.

BURUT, ANDREW: Baltimore, 97 Broad St. 1819–1837.

BURWELL (Elias) & CARTER (W. W., L. E.): Bristol, Race St. (tx) 1859–1861. Calendar clocks.

—, ELIAS: Bristol, Race St. (tx) 1851–1867. With Terry, Downs & Burwell 1851–1852; Burwell & Carter 1859–1861; alone to 1867. Made Lewis patent Calendar clocks. Purchased patent. Calendar clock owned by Dr. Howard B. Seyfert, Media, Pa.

BUSH, GEORGE: Easton, Pa. 1812–1837. C. Great-grandfather of William A. Bush, East Orange, N.J., who has Tall clock No. 213, moon and calendars. (Abbott)

—, HENRY: Cincinnati, O. Dir. 1841.

—, MICHAEL: Easton, Pa. Tall clocks. n/d.

BUTLER (Henry W.) & BARTLETT (Edward M.): West Chester, Pa. Adv. 1834. S. J. W. "Clocks and watches repaired." Dissolved Sept. 9, 1834. Bartlett continued till 1840 as Silversmith. "Bought case from Ogden June 17, 1835, and assembled at least one clock." (James)

—, HENDERSON & Co.: Clement, Nova Scotia. n/d. Pillar and Scroll clock owned by James R. Joy, 29 Perry St., N.Y.C. Label, "Patent Clock / invented by / Eli Terry / made and sold at / Clement, Nova Scotia by / Butler, Henderson & Company / etc. Printed by Stubs & Son, Printers, Saint Andrews."

—, ROMAN M., & Co.: Annapolis, Nova Scotia. Typical Mirror clock, wood movt. 34½ × 16½ × 5½, tablet, not mirror, in door, owned by Mrs. A. L. Stiegelmen, Bera, O.

—, FRANKLIN: Phila. *Ca.*1850. Dir. 1846.

BUTLER, JAMES: 1713–1776. Boston. G. S. Marr. Elizabeth Davie before 1739.

—, NATHANIEL: 1760–1829. Utica, N.Y. Aw. 1799–1815. S. W.

BYAM, C. C.: Amesbury, Mass. *Ca.*1850. W. D.

BYINGTON (Loring) & Co.: Bristol. (tx) 1843–1849.

— (Loring) & GRAHAM: Bristol. 1852–1853. Shop at "Edgewood." Made cases.

—, LORING (Lawler): 1797–1889. Bristol, and Newark, N.Y. Sold for E & G. Bartholomew 1828–1832. Hollow column sample clock he carried owned by Mrs. Frank B. Colvin, Bristol, Conn. In Byington & Co. 1843–1849; Byington & Graham 1852–1853. Shop Newark, N.Y., *ca.*1830 selling clocks by C. Boardman, though his name on paper and dial.

BYRAM, EPHRAIM: Sag Harbor, N.Y. Aw. *ca.*1840–1860. b. to family of Clockmakers, excelled in art. N.Y.C. City Hall clock, West Point Chapel clock, numerous Tower clocks on Long Island.

BYRNE, JAMES: Phila., N.Y.C., Elizabeth, N.J. Adv. Phila. 1784, N.Y.C. 1789–1797, Elizabeth, N.J., 1799, "Watches and Clocks for sale." S. (Williams)

CABLE, STEPHEN: N.Y.C., 25 Albany St., Dir. 1848; 424 Grand St., Dir. 1854.

CACHOT, FELIX: –1839. Bardstown, Ky. S. W. C. Formerly Trappist monk.

CADWELL, EDWIN: N.Y.C. Aw. 1840.

"C. M. CADY," used by Cornell Watch Co. 1871–1874.

CAIN, C. W.: N.Y.C., 157 William St.

—, MICHAEL: Albany, N.Y. Dir. 1831–1832.

CAIRNS, JOHN: Providence, R.I. 1784. Shop near St. John's Church, next door Saunders Pitman. Adv., "watches of any fashion required for $25. warranted for two years without expense except in case of accident." Some running 1911. Accidentally drowned in Moshasseck River. (Moore)

—, JOHN, II: 1800–. Providence, R.I. Aw. 1840–1853.

CALAME, OLIVIER: Frederick, Md. Aw. 1819.

CALDERWOOD, ANDREW: Phila., 22 Steuben St. Dir. 1800–1822.

CALDWELL (James E.) & Co.: Phila. Dir. 1850. "Often imported French and German clocks."

—, JAMES E.: Phila. Dir. 1840–1850.

CALENDAR & AUGER: Meriden, Conn. *Ca.* 1860.

— CLOCK CO., THE: Glastonbury, Conn. Aw. 1856.

CALHOUN, W. H.: Nashville, Tenn. n/d. "Has window in Balance Cock." Watch in Ira W. Leonard Col.

"CALIFORNIA," used by Otay Watch Co. 1889.

— WATCH CO.: Berkeley, Calif. Succeeded Cornell Watch Co. San Francisco 1876 but closed same year. Tradition some movts. stamped "Berkeley," Mark Massey has seen those stamped "California Watch Co." Sold out 1877 to Independent Watch Co., Fredonia, N.Y. (Evans) ("Timing a Century") (MFM)

CALOR, C. H.: Plainville, N.J. 1888–1889. Clock-case maker. (MFM)

CALVERT (T. G.) & BURNETT (B. L.): Lexington, Ky. Adv. 1855 on Main St. as "Practical Watch Makers, French Clocks cleaned and adjusted." (LB)

CAMBRIDGE WATCH CO.: N.Y.C., 37 Maiden Lane. Adv. 1900, "American movts." (MFM)

CAMERDEN & FORSTER: N.Y.C. Late 1800's. French clocks, this name on dial; one in author's col.

CAMP, EPHRAIM: Salem Bridge, Conn. *Ca.* 1830. Brass movt. 8-day Shelf clock in Newcomb Col.

—, HIRAM: 1811–1893. Son Samuel and Jeannette Jerome. b. Plymouth, Conn., April 9, 1811. Aw. 1829–1844 for uncle, Chauncey Jerome, Plymouth and Bristol. Hist. Plymouth says last of C. to leave Plymouth. To New Haven 1844. Built shop 1851 to make movts., sold to Jerome Mfg. Co., origin of New Haven Clock Co., still in business. Camp first president; retired 1892, d. 1893. Wrote March, 1893, "Sketch of the Clock Making Business, 1792–1892," reprinted NAWCC Bul.

CAMPBELL, ALEXANDER: Phila. Dir. 1798–1799.

—, ALEXANDER: Brooklyn, N.Y. *Ca.* 1840–1850.

CAMPBELL, BENJAMIN: 1749–. Hagerstown, Md., 1775–1792; Uniontown, Pa., 1792–1830. (LSS)

—, CHARLES: Phila., 3 So. 3rd St. Dir. 1794–1803. Later 55 So. Front St.; 1799 to Germantown, opp. King of Prussia Inn, Germantown Rd. Astro. & Musical clocks reported. (Gillingham)

—, CHARLES: N.Y.C. Imported 1798 four boxes clocks, watches, watch glasses.

—, ISAAC: Phila. "Watchmaker." Dir. 1813, watch-case maker; Dir. 1818–1822, W.; Dir. 1821–1824.

—, JOHN: Hagerstown, Md. *Ca.*1773. Few Tall clocks. (LSS)

—, JOHN: Campbell's Town, Md. Adv. 1773. No. 12 watch known.

—, JOHN: N.Y.C. and Brooklyn. *Ca.*1840.

—, ROBERT: Baltimore, 1799–1872. 1819–1838.

—, ROBERT G.: Ravenna, O. Adv. 1829. (Knittle)

—, THOMAS: N.Y.C. *Ca.*1810.

—, WILLIAM: Carlisle, Pa. Adv. 1763. Abbott placed one same name Phila. 1799. No other data.

CANBY & NIELSON (Alex): West Chester, Pa. Adv. 1819. (James)

—, CHARLES: 1792–1883. Wilmington, Del., 311 Market St. C. Crippled for life, possibly polio; walked with two canes. Fond of swimming. Apprentice 1808 of Ziba Ferris; Tall clocks by 1813. Sold business *ca.*1853 to apprentice George Elliott. Apprentices: Elliott, P. Sheward Johnson, Jacob F. Johnson, 3rd and Market Sts., Thomas Conlyn, later Carlisle, Pa., John A. Rankin (d. Elkton 1896), Thomas S. Dawson. (Conrad)

CANDEE & McEWAN: Edgefield, S.C. Adv. 1858.

CANFIELD (Samuel) & FOOTE (Wm.): Middletown, Conn. 1795–1796.

—, SAMUEL: Middletown, Conn., Lansingburg, N.Y. 1780 S. Partner Wm. Foote 1795 to *ca.*1800. One Tall clock extant, running. (Hoopes)

CANNON, WILLIAM: Phila. Pos. C. 1738.

CAPPER, MICHAEL: Phila., 99–119 Race St. Dir. 1798–1800.

CAPRON, J. B.: New Milford, Conn. Watch Paper BCL Col.

CARLETON: Bradford, Mass. After Mulliken and Balch, third family Clockmakers. Farm on Merrimack R. included author's birthplace. "Squire" Dudley Carleton, 1721–1807, had two clockmaking sons, Dudley and Michael.

—, DUDLEY: 1748–. Bradford, Newbury, Vt. (1776). Pos. apprentice to Mulliken family. Tall clocks. Skilled cabinetmaker. Son Dudley.

—, JAMES H.: Haverhill, Mass. Dir. 1853.

—, JOHN C.: Bradford, Vt. Ca.1800. C.

—, MICHAEL: 1757–1836. Bradford, Mass. Haverhill, Mass., Water St. Son of first Dudley. C. Also tinsmith. Marr. 1795. Mrs. F. B. Pierce, Haverhill, owns Tall clock, maple case, Osborne dial, no moon, 8-day brass movt., brass pendulum rod. (Mrs. J. B. Mason)

CARMAN, SAMUEL: Brooklyn, N.Y. Ca.1850.

CARNEY (Kearney), HUGH: Wolcottville, Ind. Pillar and Scroll clocks known, one in Richard Newcomb Col.

CARPENTER, ANTHONY: 1790–1868. New Holland, Pa. German parentage. C. Aw. 1820. "Business continued by his son, A. W." (Lan. Co.)

—, A. W.: 1814–1869. New Holland, Pa. Son of Anthony. C. till 1860. Not many clocks. (Lan. Co.)

—, C. H.: Middleboro, Mass. Ca.1870. Watch Paper Bir. Col.

—, JOSEPH: 1747–1804. Norwich, Conn. Pos. apt. Mass. Ca.1769 to Norwich, Conn., C. and S.; rented shop from stepfather, Joseph Peck, £1 10s. yearly. Leased land 1773 from pastor of church, built shop, still standing 1933. Marr. 1775 to Eunice Fitch. William Cleveland appraised shop contents 1804. (Hoopes)

—, LUMEN: Oswego, N.Y. Adv. 1845–1847.

CARR, FRANK B.: Fall River, Mass. Ca. 1870.

—, J. P.: N.Y.C. Ca.1820.

—, JAMES: Ohio. Ca.1830. Drove through country selling clocks and bee "palaces" (rye straw beehives). (Knittle)

—, JAMES: Lowell, Mass., 44 Merrimack St. Dir. 1834. W. with Wm. Moulton.

—, JAMES: Halifax, Nova Scotia. n/d. "Successor to late Alex Troup, Argyle St." Gray Watch Paper Bir. Col.

—, LYMAN: Manchester, N.H. Dir. 1855.

CARR, NORMAN G.: Concord, N.H. Watch Paper BCL Col.

CARRELL, JOHN & DANIEL: Phila., Market St. Dir. 1785. Adv. 1785, "Clocks and watches made." (Gillingham)

—, DANIEL: Phila. before 1790; Charleston, S.C., to ca.1801; then Phila. Dir. 1806.

—, JOHN: Phila. Census 1790. Dir. 1792–1793. Adv. 1794. Clock movts., watch dials, chains. Some imported 1789–1790. (Gillingham)

CARRINGTON, WILLIAM: Charleston, S.C. Ca.1830. Aw. 1830–. b. Conn., d. N.Y. 1901. Studied Watchmaking under Benedict, N.Y.C. Friend of Tiffanys. Marr. Harriet E. Simonds, Mar. 19, 1845.

CARRYL, PATRICK: N.Y.C. 1758. "Clockmaker."

CARSON, GEORGE: York, Pa. Ca.1819.

—, THOMAS: Albany, N.Y. Ca.1830.

CARTER, W. W., & L. F.: Bristol., No. Main and North Sts. (tx) 1863–1868. Calendar clocks, Lewis and Burwell patents. (EI)

—, JACOB: Concord, N.H. Ca.1840.

—, JACOB: Phila., 21 No. Alley St. Dir. 1806–1808.

—, THOMAS: Phila. Dir. 1823–1824.

—, WILLIAM: –1738. Phila. Ca.1683. (Brix)

CARVALKS, D. N.: Phila. Dir. 1846.

CARVALLO, N.: Charleston, S.C. Ca.1780.

CARWITHIN, WILLIAM: Charleston, S.C. Cabinetmaker ca.1733. Clock cases. (MFM)

CAR(E)Y, JAMES, (Jr.?): Belfast and/or Brunswick, Me. Aw. 1806–1850. Apprentice of Robert Eastman 1805; partner 1806–1809; bought firm 1809; his apprentice Aaron L. Dennison became partner 1830. (Abbott)

CASE (Erastus, Harvey) & BIRGE (John): Bristol. (tx) 1830–1837. See Birge & Case.

—, DYER, WADSWORTH & Co.: Augusta, Ga. Ca.1835. After 1837, Dyer, Wadsworth & Co. Assembled and sold Seth Thomas movts. and cases.

— (Everett G.) & ROBINSON (Abel T.): Bristol. (tx) 1850–1851. Clock cases and toys.

— (Erastus, Harvey), WILLARD (Sylvester) & COX: Bristol. (tx) 1835. Ives roller pinion 8-day brass; separate alarm movt. lower right corner.

CASE, ERASTUS: Bristol. (tx) 1830–1837. Aug. 24, 1834, one of purchasers J. Ives patents. In Birge, Case & Co. 1833–1834, Case, Willard & Co. 1835–. Bro. Harvey Case. (Hist.)

—, HARVEY: Bristol. Aw. 1830–1837. In Birge, Case & Co. 1833–1834; Case, Willard & Co. 1835–. Aug. 28, 1834, one of purchasers J. Ives patents. With bro. Erastus started Bristol Mine Co. 1837 with G. W. Bartholomew; shortly sold property. (tx) (Abbott)

CASSAL, ABRAHAM: Phila. W., Pawnbroker. Dir. 1835. (Brix)

CASTAN, STEPHEN & Co.: Dir. 1819. W. J.

—, STEPHEN: Phila. Dir. 1818. Watchcase maker.

CASTENS, J. M.: Charleston, S.C. Ca. 1770.

CASWELL, A.: N.Y.C. Ca. 1860.

CATE, COL. SIMEON: Sanbornton, N.H. Early 19th century. Bought out T. Gridley.

CATER, STEPHEN: Charleston, S.C., Elliott St. Adv. 1744, 1748, "Clock and Watchmaker, also repairs all sorts of watches and clocks." (Prime)

CATHCART, A. H.: Marshall, Mich. Ca. 1870.

CATHERWOOD, JOHN: Charleston, S.C. Ca. 1760.

CATLIN, JOEL: Augusta, Ga. Ca. 1820.

CAVE, JOSEPH: 1799–1847. West Goshen Twp. 1812, West Chester 1824, Marshallton, Pa. Adv. 1825. West Chester. Adv. 1826–1835; to Phila. Dir. 1837–1847. (James)

CECIL, CHARLES: Phila. "Clocksmith." Dir. 1808–1809.

CELLERS, JOHN: Chillicothe, O. 1814. "Goldsmith, Clock and Watchmaker." (Knittle)

CHADWICK, JOSEPH: Boscawen, N.H. 1787. Pos. apt. of Timothy Chandler. Related by marriage to Benjamin Morrill. Aw. 1810–1831. Original shop one-story building on site now occupied by Post Office; moved across street. With Morrill, may have originated "N.H. Mirror." When machine-made clocks available, retired to Vt. (See ill. Nos. 211–214.) (DKP) (Abbott)

CHAMBERLAIN, BENJAMIN MOSES: Salem, Mass., 300 Essex St. 1842, 291 Essex St. 1846, 201 Essex St. 1850, 207 Essex St.

1861. Junior partner Smith & Chamberlain. J., S. In business till 1870. Marr. Mary Elizabeth Low Oct. 29, 1843.

—, CHARLES: Phila. Dir. 1833–1839.

—, LEWIS: Phila. Dir. 1829–1842.

—, WILLIAM: Towanda, Pa. Ca. 1830–1850.

CHAMBERLIN, CYRUS: New Haven, Conn. Ca. 1850.

—, LEWIS: Elkton, Md. Ca. 1824. Phila. Dir. 1831–1840.

CHAMPLIN, JOHN: New London, Conn. Adv. 1773, "Materials for repairing clocks and watches."

CHAMPNEY & FELTON: Troy, N.Y. Ca. 1860.

—, L. C.: Troy, N.Y. Aw. 1830. Watch Paper BCL Col.

—, LEWIS C.: Phila. Dir. 1845 and later.

CHANDLEE: Clockmaker family Pa. and Md. Carefully documented, splendidly illustrated in *Six Quaker Clockmakers* by Edward E. Chandlee.

—, ELLIS & ISAAC: Tall clocks so marked from 1792–1804. Ellis made movts., Isaac did finishing.

—, ELLIS, & BROTHERS: "Chandlee & Sons" before 1790.

— (Benjamin III) & HOLLOWAY (Robert): Baltimore, 98 High St. 1818–1823.

— & SONS: 1770–1790. Formed by sons of Benjamin, Jr.

—, BENJAMIN, JR.: 1723–1791. Third Quaker C. Fifth child of Benj., Sr. Succeeded father; expert craftsman. More of his clocks have been found than any of the others.

—, BENJAMIN, SR.: 1685–1745. Second Quaker C. 1714–1730. b. Ire., to Phila. 1702, Nottingham, Md. Feb. 1712. Apt. to Abel Cottey seven years. Marr. Sarah Cottey Feb. 28, 1710. 7' walnut cases. Sons helped 1732–1741. First clocks marked "B" or "Benj'n" or "Benjamin Chandlee-Nottingham." To Wilmington, Del. 1741. (See ill. No. 4.)

—, BENJAMIN III: Winchester, Va., and Baltimore. Son of Goldsmith. Continued father's business in Winchester for a time; to Baltimore; joined Holloway in S. shop; repaired clocks and watches with father's tools. Conn. clock competition too much for further production of Tall clocks.

—, ELLIS: 1755–1816. Nottingham, Md. Son of Benjamin, Jr., bro. Goldsmith and

Isaac. Fifth Quaker C. Aw. with father. Few clocks during Rev. War. Under own name before 1791.

—, GOLDSMITH: –1821. Fourth Quaker C. Eldest son of Benj., Jr. Worked for father. To Stephensburg, Va.; later built house in Winchester, Va. Signed dials "G. Chandlee, Winchester or Stephensburg, Va." Tall clocks, brass 8-day movts. rack and snail strike, dials white painted iron. (See ill. No. 54.)

—, ISAAC: 1760–1813. Sixth Quaker C. Tall clocks marked "Isaac Chandlee." Unmarr. (See ill. No. 53.)

—, JOHN: 1757–1813. Nottingham, Md. Not mechanical but artistic. "Left some tools." Conrad said that a John Chandlee watchmaker at Wilmington, Del. "1741 moved to Wilmington and carried on the business of Watchmaker and limner at his new store nearly opposite the Academy." Either in error or two John Chandlees.

—, VEAZEY: 1804–. Brick Meeting House, Md. Son of Ellis. Ca.1846 repaired clocks and watches. No Tall clocks known.

CHANDLER, ABIEL: 1807–1881. Concord, N.H. Son and successor of Timothy. Aw. 1829–1846. N.H. Mirror and striking Banjo clocks in D. K. P. Col. (See ill. No. 163.)

—, JOHN: Suffolk, Md. 1774.

—, PERLEY: Barre, Vt. Ca.1870–1890. W. and J. Three watches in possession of heirs.

—, MAJOR TIMOTHY: 1760–1846. Concord, N.H. Son of Wm. and Annis Chandler. Apprenticed at 8 to Major Jonathan Hale, wool card maker; after father d., mother had to place her son "in trade." Hale to Pomfret, Conn., 1781, taking Timothy with him. Became master at wool card making 1783. Returned to Concord. Learned Clockmaking. Eventually ca.1800 built Concord factory employing Clockmakers and apprentices. Factory burned 1809, loss over $5,000; Concord citizens raised $1,200 to rebuild. Retired 1829; son Abiel continued to 1846. Title "Major" from enlisting Minute Men 1797; commissioned in N.H. Militia 1799. Marked clocks with sharp steel die; sup-

ported movt. by board, semicircular "T. Chandler." Splendid Tall clocks. (See ill. No. 43.) One in LSS Col.; one owned by Edward Mitchell; one by Mrs. Henry Nevins, Pelham, N.Y. (DKP)

"GEORGE CHANNING," used by U.S. Watch Co. 1868.

CHAPIN, AARON & ELLIPHALET: Windsor and Hartford, Conn. 1780–1800. May have made Tall clock cases with whales-tails motive. (LB)

—, AARON, & SON: Hartford, Conn. 1825–1838.

—, S. & A.: Northampton, Mass. Opened shop South Hadley Canal 1834. W. S. J. Continued 1835.

—, EDWIN G.: Buffalo, N.Y. Dir. 1836.

CHAPMAN, C. H.: Easthampton, Mass. Ca.1860.

—, CHARLES: Troy, N.Y. Dir. 1838–1839. W.

CHAPPEL (Samuel) & SARTWELL (James): Jamestown, N.Y. Ca.1840. Wag-on-Wall and Tall clocks.

CHARLES, LEWIS: Phila. Dir. 1837.

CHARTER, —: Pa. 1785. Watchcase maker.

CHASE, GEORGE: N.Y.C., 159 East 21st St. Dir. 1854.

—, JOHN F.: Newark, N.J. Aw. 1851–1854.

—, SAMUEL: 1794–. Newburyport, Mass. Dir. 1851.

—, TIMOTHY: Belfast, Me. 1826–1840.

—, WILLIAM H.: Salem, Mass. Ca.1840.

CHAUDRON & RASCH: Phila. Ca.1830. Clock importers.

—, SIMON, & Co.: Phila. W., J. Dir. 1807–1811.

—, EDWARD: Phila. J., W. Dir. 1816.

—, J.: Phila. Adv. 1798.

—, P.: Phila. Adv. 1797.

—, SIMON: Phila., 12 South 3rd St. W., J. Dir. 1798–1814.

CHEESEMAN, JAMES L.: N.Y.C. Ca.1830.

CHELSEA CLOCK Co.: 1897–. Chelsea, Mass. Patent Nos. 229,646 and 229,647, dated 1904, models Smiths. Inst.

CHENEY, ASHEL: 1759–. E. Hartford, Conn. Eldest son of Benjamin. Followed father's trade of C. Moved Northfield, Mass., 1790, there listed as property owner. Many Tall clocks, wood and brass movts. (See ill. No. 56.) Also Putney, Vt. (Battisen) (Ill. Hoopes)

CHENEY, BENJAMIN: 1725–1815. East Hartford, Conn. Son of Benjamin and Elizabeth Long Cheney. Probably apprentice of Seth Youngs, Hartford, *ca.*1739. Own business *ca.*1745, brass and wood movt. clocks, small brass articles. Apts., bro. Timothy, John Fitch, sons Ashel, Elisha, Martin, Russell. Most famous apprentice Benjamin Willard. John Fitch says, "Pretty good sort of man with many oddities, though deformed by rickets during youth." Nails and tacks 1778 for Rev. War. Later to Berlin, Conn. (Hoopes)

—, BENJAMIN, JR.: East Hartford or Manchester, Conn. Son of Benjamin, Sr. Tall clocks, cherry cases, wood movts.

—, ELISHA: Middletown and Berlin, Conn. Aw. 1793–1833. Son of Benjamin, Sr. First screws for pistol factory of bro.-in-law Simeon North, Worthington Parish. North moved to Middletown, Cheney engaged in clockmaking, first Tall then Shelf. Pos. later at Vandalia, Springfield, Ill. (Hoopes)

—, MARTIN: Windsor, Vt. *Ca.*1790. Son and apt. of Benjamin, Sr.

—, OLCOTT: Middletown and Berlin, Conn. Son of Elisha, grandson of Benjamin, Sr. Aw. with Elisha till 1835, purchased business. Lived in Berlin. Factory over town line, clocks marked "Middletown." (Transition Shelf clock in Moore)

—, RUSSELL: East Hartford, Conn., Putney and Thetford, Vt. Son of Benjamin, Sr. Skilled C. (Hoopes)

—, TIMOTHY: 1731–1795. Bro. Benjamin, Sr. Blacksmith, joiner, C. and S. Wood and brass movts. "There is nothing to indicate these two brothers were together." John Fitch aw. for Benjamin, Sr., later for Timothy. Appointed 1768 Lieut. to train soldiers; led Hartford troops in Rev. War but relieved of duty to make gunpowder. Built grist mill 1790 on stream south of what is now So. Manchester, Conn., and homestead (standing 1933). d. East Hartford; considerable estate. (Hoopes)

CHERRY, JAMES: Phila. Dir. 1849 and later.

CHESHIRE CLOCK Co.: Cheshire, Conn. *Ca.*1880.

— WATCH Co., THE: Cheshire, Conn. 1883–*ca.*1893. (Frustader)

CHESTER, GEORGE: N.Y.C. Adv. 1757, "At the sign of the dial on the New Dock, next door to Mr. Van Dyck, the Hatter."

—, RICHARD: Hanover, Pa. 1795–1816.

CHILD, S. T. & T. T.: Phila., 452 No. 2nd St. Dir. 1848 and later. Watch Paper "So T.," Cramer Col.

—, HENRY T.: Phila. Dir. 1840–1842.

—, JOHN: Phila., "452 N. 2nd St." Dir. 1813–1847. English type Shelf clock. Watch Paper Cramer Col.

—, S. J.: Lyons, N.Y. *Ca.*1830. Watch Paper BCL Col.

—, SAMUEL T.: Phila. Dir. 1843–1848. Watch Paper Cramer Col.

—, THOMAS T.: Phila. Dir. 1845.

—, TRUE W.: Boston. 1823.

CHILDS, EZEKIEL: Phila. Dir. 1830–1835. Built one of five experimental steam locomotives for B. & O. *ca.*1829–1830.

CHIPPERFIELD, N. W., & Co.: N.Y.C., 198 Division St. Dir. 1854.

—, N. W.: N.Y.C. *Ca.*1860.

CHITTENDEN, AUSTIN: Lexington, Mass. 1831–1837. See Burr & Chittenden. Assemblers; pos. made Shelf clocks. Many extant. Shelf clock owned by Louis Reilly, Kingfisher, Okla., label, "Austin Chittenden, Lexington, Mass., warranted if well cared"; also American eagle, 13 stars in background and different 14th star separated. "Still keeping good time, wood works, iron weights." (Complete story AAJ May 1949)

CHOLLOT (Cholliet), JOHN B.: Phila., 148 No. 4th St. Dir. 1816–1819.

CHRIST, DANIEL: Kutztown, Pa. 4th Group. Early 19th century.

CHRYSTLER, WILLIAM: Phila. Dir. 1828–1835.

CHURCH, EDWARD: New Haven, Conn. *Ca.*1850.

—, JOSEPH: Hartford, Conn. 1825–1838.

—, LORENZO: Hartford, Conn. 1846.

—, WILLIAM F.: Skowhegan, Me. "Clocks and watches." *Ca.*1830. Watch Paper BCL Col.

CINCINNATI TIME RECORDER Co.: Cincinnati, O. 1936.

CITO, J. C.: Boston. *Ca.*1820. Lyre clock.

CLACKNER, JOHN: Troy, N.Y. Dir. 1833–1837.

CLAGGETT, H.: Newport, R.I. "Father of Thomas, classed with Benjamin Bagnall. 1726–1740." (FT) "No record of H. Claggett." (BCC)

—, THOMAS: Newport, R.I. Son of William. 1730–1749. (See ill. No. 17.) (BCC)

—, WILLIAM, JR.: 1696–1749. b. Wales. Marr. Boston 1714 Mary Armstrong. Adv. 1715. To Newport 1716. Engraver; paper money for Rhode Island 1738. Dau. Mary marr. Clockmaker James Wady of Newport. Mus. insts.; pos. clock cases. Interested in electricity 1746. Referred to as merchant, C., engraver, author. (See ill. Nos. 12–16.) (BCC)

CLAPP, JOHN: 1764–1840. Roxbury, Mass. b. Rochester, N. Y., d. Roxbury, Mass. Cabinetmaker ca.1800. Apt. was Deacon Nehemiah Munroe.

—, PRESERVED: 1731–. Amherst, Mass. Eldest son Preserved and Sarah West Clapp. Corporal in French-Indian War. "Dr." Ingenious. Invented 1776 gun carriage used in Revolutionary War. Small Wag-on-Wall clock owned by Emerson G. Gaylord, Chicopee, Mass. as in ill. No. 2. Dial plate by Thomas Johnson 1708–1767. Four pages of music engraved on back. At Essex Inst. (See ill. No. 26.)

"CLARK": Woodstock, Vt. Name burned in label on Wag-on-Wall clock. (A. B. Wilder, Jr.)

—, BENJAMIN & ELLIS: Phila., 1 S. Front St. Dir. 1811–1840. Mentioned at Providence, R.I., ca.1820. Tall clock owned by Miss Jane F. Mills, Phila.

— & BROTHERS: Rutland, Vt. Ca.1830. Watch Paper BCL Col.

— & Co.: Augusta, Ga. Ca.1820.

— (Daniel), COOK (Zenas) & Co. Waterbury, Conn. Ca.1815.

— (A. N.) & COWLES: Plainville, Conn. Ca.1870–1889. "Clock hands and other delicate hardware."

— & ENGLE: Hazelton, Pa. n/d. "Wonder clock." (Joel Biestel)

—, EPHRAIM & CHARLES: Phila. Dir. 1806–1811.

—, GILBERT & BROWN: N.Y.C. Ca.1840. Pos. dealers in Conn. clocks.

—, JESSE W., & Co.: Phila., 2nd and Lombard Sts. Dir. 1809–1814.

— & LATHAM: Charleston, S.C. 1780.

CLARK & MORSE: Plymouth, Conn. Ca.1820–1830. E. C. Kimball, Boston, ca.1940, owned 8-day brass movt. Shelf clock, rack strike. (BCC)

—, RUSSELL & RANDALL: Woodstock, Vt., Central St. Dir. 1869, "Next door to Murdock & Mellish." (A. B. Wilder, Jr.)

— & TURNER (Franklin): Fayetteville, and Wadesboro, N.C. Dir. 1820–1823. Turner operated store both places. William Widdifield supt. Fayetteville store, bought out business; adv. 1823. (Cutten)

—, A. J.: Circleville, O. "Clockmaker." (Knittle)

—, A. N.: Plainville, Conn. Ca.1888. "Makes watch makers' goods and watch cases." Watch keys and watchcase springs 1888–1889.

—, Amos: Lewisberry, Pa. Ca.1780–1800.

—, B. H.: Newcomerstown, O. 1846. "Maker of clocks." (Knittle)

—, BENJAMIN: Phila., Front and Market Sts., later 36 Market St. Adv. 1791. Dir. 1793–1848.

—, BENJAMIN S.: Wilmington, Del., 407 Market St. Succeeded George Jones ca.1850. "The stand so long occupied by Jones." (Conrad)

—, BENJAMIN W.: Phila. Dir. 1831.

—, CHARLES: Phila. Dir. 1809–1814.

—, DANIEL: Waterbury, Conn. C. Member Abel Porter & Co. 1808; 1810–1815 with Zenas Cook and William Porter.

—, DAVID: Charleston, S.C. Ca.1770.

—, EDWARD: Phila., So. 5th St. between South and Shippey Sts. W. Dir. 1797.

—, ELIAS: Phila. Dir. 1802.

—, ELLIS: Phila. Dir. 1816–1848.

—, EPHRAIM: –1822. Phila., 2nd St. 1780; Front and Market 1785, 1793. Adv. 1780–1800. Dir. 1785–1811. Succeeded John Wood 1793. Adv. 1800, "Has received clocks via *Kensington*." English type Bracket clock. Watch Dr. Anthony Benis Col. See ill. No. 291. (Gillingham) (LB)

—, GABRIEL: Baltimore, 1831–1839. "Apprentice of Foxcroft."

—, GEORGE D.: –1935. Coosada, Ala. Ca.1878. From Conn. Clock owned near Montgomery, Ala. (Peter A. Brannon)

— (Clarke), GEORGE G.: Providence, R.I., 27 Cheapside. Ca.1824.

CLARK, HEMAN: 1783–1838. Early career not known. Apt. of Eli Terry; according to Henry Terry bought from Eli Terry, in Plymouth, Conn., 1807, 20′ square shop and water-power, as Eli had purchased from Calvin Hoadley larger building at Greystone. Made clocks or wooden hang-up-movts. (See ill. No. 67.) Sold shop to Seth Thomas 1813. Built "two shops" in Plymouth; continued alone or as Clark & Morse (Myles) or Curtis & Clark, to ca.1823 or later. May have left Plymouth about then. Probably not too successful. d. New Haven Jan. 22, 1838. No record of patents.

Pillar and Scroll clock in Mr. and Mrs. Frank Beaven Col. ill. No. 195, 8-day brass movt. ill. No. 196; label, "Patent Improved / Eight day Brass Clocks / made by H. CLARK / Plymouth, Connecticut." Ill. Nos. 195 and 199 Pillar and Scroll clocks, 8-day brass movts. by H. Clark and Lucius Bradley (1800–1870). Date uncertain of manufacture of this type of brass movt. by Clark and others. Eli Terry patent 1816 covered wood and brass movts. Specifications included placing escape wheel and verge on front plate of movt. (see ill. Nos. 196 and 201), also arrangement whereby weights "run the whole length of the case," features which Henry Terry said were new and contributed to "a new *form* of clock." Accordingly there should be no warrant for attributing to any clock construction with those features (e.g., so-called Clark movt.), origin antedating Terry patent and production.

—, HORACE G.: Weston, Vt. *Ca.*1830. Watch Paper BCL Col.

—, JOHN: N.Y.C. 1770–1790. "Maker of Shagreen cases."

—, JOSEPH: *Ca.*1821. N.Y.C. 1768–1777, Danbury, Conn., 1777. C. W. Adv. 1787, 1791. Good 8-day Tall clocks, neat mahogany cases. Bore arms in Danbury raid 1777. Marr. Anna Stedman of Danbury 1787. Later shop near printing office. "Shipping, Houses, Country Produce &c will be received in payment of clocks." Adv. 1795, 8-day clocks with or without cases. To N.Y. State 1811; later to Alabama. (Hoopes)

CLARK, LEVI: Norwalk, Conn. Watch Paper Bir. Col.

—, PHILIP: Albany, N.Y. Dir. 1837–1843.

—, RICHARD: –1772. Charleston, S.C. Adv. 1767 opened shop King St. Richard Yeadon bought stock 1772. (MFM)

—, ROBERT: Charleston, S.C., 5½ Church St., and Tradd and Church Sts. Adv. 1785, "Math., Optical and Philosophical Instruments maker and Clockmaker from London." Aw. for Lang & Wyles.

—, RUSSELL: Woodstock, Vt. Either 1830 or Dir. 1869. Watch Paper, O. Hockenson, N.Y.C.

—, THOMAS: Boston, So. side Court House. Adv. 1764, "Clock and Watchmaker from London. Warrants clocks and watches, as same are of his own make."

—, THOMAS W.: Phila. Dir. 1830–1850.

—, WILLIAM H.: Palmer, Mass. *Ca.*1860.

CLARKE (Lucius), GILBERT (Wm.) & Co.: Winsted, Conn., 1841 and later. Weight-driven one-day brass clocks, OG cases. Revived Riley Whiting business, quiet since he d. 1835; became present William L. Gilbert Clock Corp.

—, GILBERT & Co.: N.Y.C., 46 Cortland St. Dir. 1848. Sales office.

— & HUTCHINSON: Phila. Dir. 1813.

—, AMBROSE: Baltimore. With Bigger & Clarke 1783. Alone 1784. Last adv. as W. 1787.

—, C. W.: "Pa." Tall clock. (Orr)

—, E. M.: Lowell, Mass. Watch Paper BCL Col.

—, GEORGE R.: Utica, N.Y. *Ca.*1820.

—, JOHN: Phila. 1797. "Clark" listed as silverplater. Dir. 1837. Pos. two: 1, 1790–1811; 2, *ca.*1837–1845.

—, LUCIUS: Winsted, Conn. From Bristol. Purchased business 1841 after death of Riley Whitney and associated with William L. Gilbert and Ezra Baldwin. "Baldwin a Clockmaker. Clarke a merchant." (Vail)

—, SYLVESTER: Salem Bridge, Conn. 1830. Brass 8-day clock, carved top, Pillar case, claw feet, label, "S. CLARKE's improved Brass / CLOCKS / warranted / IF well used / Salem-Bridge, / Conn." Metal dial, seconds hand. No. 54 in Flint Sale 1926, square column sides, carved top, claw feet, 8-day brass movt.

CLATON, ELIAS B.: Phila. Dir. 1848 and later.

CLAUDE (Abraham) & FRENCH: Annapolis, Md. Adv. 1773–1775; 1783, "Abraham Claude has formed a partnership for conducting Clock and watch making business with one FRENCH." Pos. James Ormsby French. Baltimore 1771. (Prime)

—, ABRAHAM: Annapolis, Md. Ca.1779. Had apt. Also in Jacob & Claude. Adv. 1773–1775. From London. C. J. Adv. alone 1775.

CLAUDON, JOHN-GEORGE: Charleston, S.C., Church St. Adv. 1743, "Lately come to town a watchmaker from London." (Prime)

CLAUSEN, A. C.: Patent Oct. 9, 1883, for "Ignatz" made by "Jerome & Co." New Haven Clock Co. In Cols. of H. G. Rowell, F. Selchow, F. J. Watters. (See Bul. Vol. III, p. 316) (Am. Col. Aug. 1935). (See ill. No. 284.)

CLAYMORE, ROBERT: Germantown, Pa. 1765–1780. Slave of Dr. Christopher Witt, freed by master's will and received Witt's Clockmaking tools and apt.

CLAYTON, JOHN: Charleston, S.C. Adv. 1743, "Watchmaker from London, who cleans, mends and repairs both clocks and watches either plain or repeating."

—, RICHARD: Cincinnati, O. Young Englishman here 1834. Shop 1834–1856. Ballooning for recreation, great fame by 1839. (Ant. Sept. 1928) (BCC)

—, SAMUEL: Brooklyn, N.Y. Ca.1850.

CLEIN, JOHN: Phila. Dir. 1830–1833.

CLEMENS, MOSES: N.Y.C. 1749. "In the Broadway."

CLERC, HENRY: N.Y.C. Ca.1820.

CLEVELAND, BENJAMIN HORTON: Newark, N.J. 1767–1837. C. Son of Joseph and Mary Horton Cleveland. Marr. Mary Gardner 1789. Shop mentioned 1792 in Wood's Gay, east side Broadway near Market. Dial, "B. CLEVELAND, NEWARK."

—, FRANCIS: Zanesville, O. Adv. 1815, "Clockmaker." (Knittle)

—, WILLIAM: 1770–1837. Norwich, New London, Conn., etc. Son of Aaron and Abiah Hyde Cleveland. Pupil of Thomas Harland. C. 1792–ca.1800. Aug. 1792 New London partnership with John Proc-

tor Trott, Trott & Cleveland; took over vacant shop of Gurdon Tracy; adv. "clocks and watches"; dissolved early 1796; Trott continued at Norwich. Cleveland reported at Salem, Mass., ca.1800 (pos. uncle of same name); probably Salem, O., ca.1808; New York State; Putnam (now part of Zanesville), O.; later to Norwich; dates uncertain. Clockmaking ceased ca. 1800. d. Black Rock, N.Y. Grandfather of Pres. Grover Cleveland. (Hoopes) (Knittle)

—, WILLIAM: Salem, Mass. No definite data; pos. uncle or relative of other Wm. Cleveland.

CLIFFORD, EBENEZER: 1746–. Kensington, Exeter, N.H. b. Kensington, to Exeter 1788. Built first Exeter church and first diving bell. Tall clock cases for Fellows. (Ant. July, 1948)

COAD, REV. FRANK A. M.: Hillsboro, N.H. Ca.1800. Case for miniature Tall clock in S. C. Robinson Col., Stamford, N.Y.

COATES, ISAAC: Phila. Dir. 1835–1839.

—, WILLIAM: Buffalo, N.Y. Dir. 1835–1839.

COBB, Z. B.: Cincinnati, O. Adv. 1850. (Knittle)

COCHRAN, GEORGE: –1807. West Chester, Pa. Taxed as "Watchmaker" 1799. "One of Chester county's first Clockmakers." Little known; nephew, his apt., continued business. (James)

—, L.: Northfield, Vt. n/d. Watch Paper George K. Eckhardt Col.

COCHRANE, A. T.: N.Y.C. n/d. 2″ diameter yellow gold engraved case No. 5421–15519 owned by George A. Firestone, Collingswood, N.J.

—, THOMAS: N.Y.C. Ca.1810.

COCKRELL, JAMES: Phila. Dir. 1843 and later.

COE & Co.: N.Y.C., 52 Dey St. Dir. 1854.

—, RUSSELL: Meriden, Conn. "1856."

COGGESHALL, G.: Bristol. Early 19th century. Tall clocks.

COGSWELL, HENRY: Salem, Mass. Marr. 1847. With father, John C. Store robbed Dec. 30, 1845.

—, JOHN CLEAVELAND: 1793–. Salem, Mass., 179 Essex St. Prob. father of Henry; partnership with him 1849; alone 1853.

COGSWELL, JOSEPH: Norwich, Conn. Late 18th century.

—, ROBERT: 1791–1862. b. Haverhill, Mass., Mar. 12, 1791. Marr. Salem 1815. Pos. dry goods business *ca.*1837. Watch Paper owned by William Cogswell, N.Y.C.

COHEN, THOMAS: Chillicothe, O. "G. and maker of Tall clock movts." Possibly bro. Barrow Cohen, S., N.Y.C. Adv. 1814. St. Louis *ca.*1845. (Knittle)

COLE, DAVID: N.Y.C. *Ca.*1840.

—, JAMES C.: Rochester, N.H. Aw. 1812. Apt. of Edw. Moulton. Watch Paper, "Watch & Clock Maker. Turn regulator with this side to go faster, slow against it." Two in Bir. Col. Son, Shubael.

—, SHUBAEL: Rochester, N.H. *Ca.*1830–1850. Son of James C. Some clock dials have "Great Falls, N.H."

—, R. P.: Ludlow, Vt. *Ca.*1830. Watch Paper BCL Col.

COLEBROOK: Conn. *Ca.*1840. Some Clockmaking; documented details lacking. Pos. cases only. (Henry Hart Vining)

COLEMAN, J. E.: Nashville, Tenn. 20th century C., author, historian. Tremendous collection of pictures and data on American timekeepers.

—, JAMES: Phila. Dir. 1833.

—, JOHN: Phila. Dir. 1848.

—, NATHANIEL: 1765–1842. Burlington, N.J. Aw. 1787–1835. Bro. Samuel. S.; pos. no clocks or watches. (Williams)

—, SAMUEL: 1761–after 1842. Trenton, N.J. Bro. of Nathaniel. Pos. C. (Williams)

COLLETTE, JOSHUA: Lebanon, O. Watch Paper dated Oct. 1825.

COLLINS & CO.: Cranston, R.I. Brass movt. Shelf. Pos. Dealer *ca.*1840.

— METAL WATCH FACTORY: N.Y.C., 335 Broadway. Adv. 1873. "Made imitation gold hunting-case watch of the Collins Gold Metal."

—, ELIJAH: Boston. Listed as W.; adv. 1727, "Pickled Fish in bbls. suitable to send to West Indies."

—, JAMES: 1802–1844. Goffstown, N.H. Aw. 1821, with father. Son of Stephen and Abigail. N.H. Mirror clocks, many with dished dials. Good example in Collins Museum. Shop burned 1847. (C. D. Collins)

COLLINS, STEPHEN: Goffstown, N.H. 1847. With son James.

—, W. A.: Troy, N.Y. Dir. 1840–1841.

—, WILLIAM: N.Y.C., 103 Fulton St. Dir. 1854.

COLLOM, DAVID W.: Phila. Dir. 1846.

COLONIAL CLOCK Co.: N.Y.C., W. 47 St. n/d. (MFM)

— MFG. Co.: Zeeland, Mich. 1929–1942. Tall clocks.

COLUMBUS (COLUMBIA) WATCH Co., THE: Columbus, O. Succeeded Gruen & Savage (org. 1876). Imp. watch movts. 1882. Sold 1902 to South Bend Watch Co.

"— WATCH Co., THE NEW," Pos. used by The Columbus Watch Co. 1902.

COLVIN, WALTER: Trenton, N.J. Adv. 1785, "Opened his shop in Trenton where he carries on the clock and watchmaking business." Adv. 1785–1790.

COMPTON, WILLIAM: Rochester, N.Y. W. Dir. 1844–1846.

CONANT & SPERRY: N.Y.C. *Ca.*1840.

—, ELIAS: Bridgewater, Mass., 1776–1812; Lynn, Mass., 1812–1825. (Abbott)

—, H.: N.Y.C. 1889. Inventor of Isochronal clock mfd. by Tiffany & Co. Five or six extant. (NAWCC. Bul. No. 26)

—, NATHANIEL PEABODY: 1819–. Danvers, Mass. W. *ca.*1850.

—, W. S.: N.Y.C., 177 Pine St. *Ca.*1820.

CONING, RICHARD: Boston. C., founder. Dir. 1796.

CONLYN, THOMAS: Pos. Carlisle, Pa. n/d. Apt. of Charles Canby, Wilmington, Del.

CONN. CLOCK Co.: N.Y.C., 69 Nassau St. after 1850; prob. office. Dir. 1872.

—, PROTECTIVE CLOCK Co.: Bristol (tx) 1849. Combination of eleven principal names of the time; pos. early cartel. Elias and Andrew Ingraham, E. C. Brewster, John Birge, Elisha Manross, J. C. Brown, Theodore Terry, Samuel B. Smith, Chauncey Goodrich, Bristol; Wm. L. Gilbert, Winsted; Chauncey Jerome, New Haven, "Large dealers in clocks; have opened a large depository in N.Y.C. for the sale of clocks . . . called The American Clock Co. . . . factory in Bristol where they make 30,000 clocks annually." Most had own plants; prob. no separate factory. (EI) (Hull)

CONOVER, DAVID F.: Phila. n/d. Chron. maker. (MFM)

CONRAD, OSBORNE & Co.: Phila. *Ca.*1850.

—, OSBORNE: Phila. Dir. 1841 and later. "Clockmaker and J. at 96 N. 2nd St., corner Quarry below Race."

CONSTANT, FRANCIS: Kingston, N.Y. 1860.

CONVERSE & CRANE: Boston. *Ca.*1870.

—, PASCAL: New Haven, Conn. *Ca.*1850.

CONWAY, THOMAS A.: Baltimore, Hawk St. "1819–1824."

COOK & STILLWELL: Rochester, N.Y. *Ca.* 1850.

—, ALEX: "CANNONSBURG, 1841" on dial, Tall clock, mahogany case, steel movt. in Omar Fisher Col., Pittsburgh, Pa.

—, BENJAMIN: Northampton, Mass. *Ca.* 1846.

—, ERASTUS: Rochester, N.Y. Dir. 1815–1845.

—, FREDERICK: Columbia, Pa. 1825–1832; York, Pa. 1832–1842.

—, HARRY: Poughkeepsie, N.Y. Adv. 1815–1817.

—, WILLIAM G.: Baltimore, 3 Baltimore St. "1817–1824."

—, ZENAS: Waterbury, Conn. "Bought part of a clock factory in 1811." With Daniel Clark and William Porter on Great Brook 1814 to *ca.*1820. (Hist.)

COOKE, F. B.: Columbia, Pa. n/d. Pos. "agent." Name in 1-day Shelf clocks, wood and brass movts.

COOKE'S SONS, B. G.: Phila. Dir. 1853. Clock wholesalers.

COOLEY, HENRY P.: Cooperstown and Troy, N.Y. Adv. 1834. Dir. 1842–1843.

COOLIDGE, HENRY J.: New Haven, Conn. Adv. 1787, "opened a shop, 3rd bldg. So. of Church in Church St. where he makes and sells repeating, horizontal, seconds, day of month, and plain watches, Spring, Chime, and Spring Quarter clocks, with moon, age, day of month, and seconds; to stand on desks. Also Common 8-day clocks with weights." (Hoopes)

COOPER, CHARLES: Lebanon, Pa. Early 19th century.

—, JOHN: N.Y.C. Dir. 1846.

—, JOSEPH: Columbia, S.C. 1843–1854; Greenville, S.C. *ca.*1855; Columbia, S.C. Dir. 1860.

—, JOSEPH B.: Phila. Dir. 1842–1846.

COOPER, ROBERT H.: Phila. Dir. 1850 and later.

—, SAMUEL B.: Phila. Dir. 1840.

COPE, JACOB: Watsontown, Pa. *Ca.*1800. Tall clocks, one owned in Quakertown, Pa., another by Henry S. Miller, Jr., name and "No. 223," on pendulum. (See ill. No. 52.)

—, JOHN: Lancaster, Pa. *Ca.*1800.

COPELAND, ROBERT: Baltimore, 9 Thames St., Fells Pt. W. 1796.

COPPERT, T.: Olneyville, R.I. *Ca.*1840. Pos. Cooper.

COPPUCK, G. W.: 1804–1882. Mt. Holly, N.J., Mill St. Son of James and Elizabeth. Adv. 1826. Tall clocks. Dial, "G. W. Coppuck, Mount Holly." "Sheraton or Empire cases — lavish use of mahogany veneer." (Williams)

COREY, P.: Providence, R.I. *Ca.*1850.

CORGEE, ARTHUR: Phila. Dir. 1823–1824.

CORL, ABRAHAM: –1842. East Nantmeal, Pa. Twelve Tall clocks known. One marked "Coventry," where he was after 1829. Cases, 7–8' high, pos. by Elias Hall. Tall clock owned by Richard Berheim, N.Y.C. (James)

CORLISS, JAMES: Weare, N.H. *Ca.*1800. "Learned trade by peeking in Emery's window."

CORNELL WATCH Co.: Chicago. Org. 1870, taking over Newark Watch Co. Sold and to San Francisco 1874; to Berkeley and reorganized as California Watch Co. 1875. Sold 1877 to Independent Watch Co., Fredonia, N.Y. In Chicago used names "Paul Cornell, J. C. Adams, John Evans, E. S. Williams, C. M. Cady, 'Ladies Stem Wind,' Geo. F. Root, H. N. Hibbard, C. T. Bowen, Geo. C. Waite." In Cal. used "C. & L. Kidder."

—, WALTER: Newport, R.I. *Ca.*1800. Tall clock, 8-day brass movt. owned by Mrs. Bradley Randall, Newton, Conn., formerly owned by William Jones, Gov. R.I. in 1812.

CORNWELL, NATHAN: Darien, Ga. *Ca.*1820.

CORONA WATCH Co.: N.Y.C. Adv. Dec. 1900. (MFM)

CORTELYOU, JACQUES: 1781–1822. W. J. S. D. Aw. 1805. (Williams)

"CORTLAND": Cortland, N.Y. Makers not named. Aw. 1840's. Pos. Conn. movts. Sold in surrounding country.

CORVAZIER, EDWARD: Phila. Dir. 1846.

CORWIN, EBEN M.: n/p. Patent No. 185,-106, Dec. 5, 1867, model, Smiths. Inst.

CORY, LEWIS: Rahway, N.J. *Ca.*1830.

COSTELL, STACEY: Phila. W. Built one of five experimental steam locomotives for B. & O. trial 1830. (Mitman) (HIA Jan. 1948)

COTTEY, ABEL: 1655–1711. Phila. Prob. first authenticated C. in America. b. Eng., to Phila. 1682 with William Penn on ship *Welcome*. Listed as C. 1682. Tall clocks, 8-day brass movts. (See ill. No. 3.) Prob. no watches. First of "Six Quaker Clockmakers." James Logan's Journal, "For scouring the clock £0–15–02, 4 mo.–17–1704." William Penn paid him for clock repair 1701. Owned much real estate; prosperous and successful. Sister Sarah marr. Benjamin Chandlee, apt. (Mrs. Joseph Carson) (Chandlee) (Gillingham)

COUPAR, JOHN: Phila. Aw. *ca.*1774. "Sold skeleton watches from London, as did Robert." (Mrs. Joseph Carson)

—, ROBERT: Phila. Adv. 1774.

COVELL, GRAY & Co.: N.Y.C., 554 Broadway. Dir. 1872. Imp. French clocks; one in author's Col.

COWAN, WILLIAM: Richmond, Va. *Ca.*1819.

COWLES, IRVING C.: n/p. Patent No. 184,230, Nov. 14, 1876, model Smiths. Inst.

COWLEY, L. D.: La Grange, Ind. *Ca.*1870.

COX & CLARK: N.Y.C. Dir. 1832.

—, BENJAMIN: Phila., 136 Front St. Dir. 1809–1813.

—, JAMES: N.Y.C. *Ca.*1810.

COZENS, J. B. (or Joseph): Phila. Dir. 1823–1829.

—, JOSIAH: Phila., 73 N. Front St. Dir. 1819–1824.

CRAFT (Kraft), JACOB: Shepperdstown, W. Va. Aw. 1775–1815. Tall clock owned by Robert McCauley, Hagerstown, Md., brass dial, sweep seconds, cherry case well made; one with "New Holland" for Australia on dial owned by Mrs. Horace Sanderson, Pasadena, Calif. (LSS)

CRAIG, JAMES: Williamsburg, Va. *Ca.*1772.

—, JOHN B.: Pittsburgh, Pa. *Ca.*1845.

CRANCH, RICHARD: Salem, Mass. *Ca.*1754–1767. W. from Eng. Adv. Boston, "near Mill Bridge . . . 1775, Watchmakers' tools for sale . . . clocks cleaned and mended by a Clockmaker lately from London at this shop, . . . imported watches for sale." Adv. 1773, "moved to Braintree, Mass., carrying on Watchmaker's business as usual." Adv. 1789. Father Justice Cranch of Washington, bro.-in-law Pres. John Adams.

—, WILLIAM: Boston. n/d. "Astronomer."

CRANE, AARON D.: Caldwell, N.J. Invented Crane's Patent Year Clock. Patents from Caldwell on "Clocks" March 18, 1829, and from Newark, N.J., No. 1973, Feb. 10, 1841. These clocks later made by The Year Clock Co., 35 Cortlandt St., N.Y.C.; J. R. Mills & Co., 109 Fulton St., N.Y.C.; Boston Clock Co. Runs year on one winding. (See ill. Nos. 262, 263.)

—, JOHN E.: Lowell, Mass. *Ca.*1850.

—, JONAS: Newark, N.J. 1850–1855. (PG)

—, SIMEON: Canton, Mass. *Ca.*1810. Mass. Shelf clock ill., Milham No. 274.

—, WILLIAM: Mass., Canton *ca.*1780, Stoughton *ca.*1800. Tall clocks. Watch Paper Charles Thomas, N.Y.C.

CRAVEN, ALFRED: Phila. Dir. 1843.

CRAWFORD, WILLIAM: 1745–. Oakham, Mass. From Rutland, Mass. Excellent Dwarf Tall clocks. House still standing, with "clock room." (Effie Swindell)

CRAWLEY, ABRAHAM: Boston. *Ca.*1815.

—, C.: Phila. Dir. 1829–1833.

CREHORE, CHARLES CRANE: 1793–1879. Milton, Roxbury, Mass. Son of John Sheppard and Hannah Lyon Crehore. Clock casemaker Roxbury *ca.*1815. Cabinetmaker, mus. insts.; prob. no clocks. Cases for S. Willard, Jr., B. F. Willard, Simon Willard, and others. To Boston *ca.*1828, 98 Charles St.; d. Boston; no successor. Fine cases. (JWW) (BCC)

"CRESCENT GARDEN," used by American Watch Co. 1869–1877.

"CRESCENT STREET," used by American Watch Co. 1869–1877.

— WATCH CASE Co., THE: Newark, N.J. 1923. (Evans)

CREUSE, BENJAMIN: Phila. Adv. 1772.

CRISSWELL, ISAAC: Phila. *Ca.*1840.

CRITCHETT, JAMES: Candia, N.H. Early 19th century.

CRITTENDEN, CHARLES: Tallmage, O. *Ca.* 1830. (Knittle)

—, SIMEON: 1796–1867. Guilford, Conn. Mass. type Pillar and Scroll Shelf clocks. One owned by Thomas Fowler, N.Y.C. (See ill. No. 204.) (Ant. Sept. 1944)

CROCKER, J. R.: Valley Falls, R.I. Adv. 1860's, "Clocks for toy banks."

—, ORASMUS: East Meriden (Bangall), Conn. *Ca.*1831–1837. "Built a factory for making clocks." f.

—, WILLIAM: Phila. Dir. 1834; N.Y.C. *Ca.*1840.

CROMWELL, WM.: N.Y.C. 1820.

CROSBY & WASHBURGH: N.Y.C. *Ca.*1860.

—, C. A. W.: Boston. Late 19th century. Name on dial small marble-cased French clock owned by Elisabeth Palmer, Bradford, Mass.

—, CHARLES: Angelica, N.Y. Adv. 1835–1836.

—, D. S.: N.Y.C. *Ca.*1850. Pos. of Crosby & Washburgh.

CROSS, JAMES: Rochester, N.H. n/d. C.

—, THEODORE: Boston. Before 1775. (Ant. Jan. 1929)

CROUCHLEY, THOMAS: N.Y.C. *Ca.*1840.

CROW, GEORGE: –1772. Wilmington, Del. Father of Thomas and George, Jr. Aw. 1754–1772. Marr. 1746. Tall clocks (six known), surveyors' insts. Clock owned by Atty. Gen. P. Warren Green; one by Samuel H. Robinson, calendar slot on dial, at top woman's head with eyes that move as pendulum swings. (Conrad)

—, GEORGE, JR.: –1802. Wilmington, Del.

—, JOHN: Wilmington, Del. Aw. 1770–1798. Adv. 1797, "Clock and Watch maker announces a great variety of jewelled high wheel and plain watches for sale at wholesale and retail at cor. Market and 2nd Sts." Tall clock at Old Town Meeting House, Wilmington. (Conrad)

—, THOMAS: Wilmington, Del., 2d St. 1770–1824. Phila. (*ca.*1797, 1805–1807), West Chester (1808), Pa. Son and apt. of George. "Like his father, in favor with the public. Elected town clerk. From the number of extant Tall clocks he was an industrious maker, a Watchmaker, and a worthy man." Tall clock dials both brass and enameled, including "Osborne."

More than 25 known. Adv. Pa. *Gazette* 1782, "Clock & Watchmaker in Wilmington hath for sale Watch Springs by the dozen. He Puts Springs in Watches at 12 shillings each, warranted for one year. Clockmakers may be supplied with large Springs for Table or Musical Clocks of any size." Tall clock in Old Town Hall, Wilmington; one owned by Mrs. Helen B. Stewart, Wilmington. (Conrad) (James) (Abbott) (Baillie)

CRUM & BARBER: Unionville, Conn. 1830–1840. Wood movt. Shelf clock, nicely carved case in Geo. B. Davis Col.

"CULVER, H. Z.," used by National Watch Co., Chicago, 1867–1875.

CUMMENS, WILLIAM: 1768–1834. Boston (or Roxbury, Mass.), Taber and Winslow Sts. Apt. of Simon Willard. Aw. 1789–1834. Marr. 1793. Tall, Mass. Shelf, Banjo clocks. "Made a very good clock." (J. W. Willard) Tablets prob. by C. Ballard; on dials, "Warranted by W. Cummings, Roxbury." Tall clock in Edwin Hale Abbot, Jr. Col., Ventnor, N.J., painted iron dial, hood with N.E. fret, mahogany inlay. (See ill. No. 87.) (BCC)

—, WILLIAM, JR.: 1793–. Apt. to father; helped him to *ca.*1816. No further record. (BCC)

CUMMING, JOHN: Albany, N.Y. 1774–1779. Pos. to Europe 1780; in wreck. Apt. to bro. Alex Cumming. (Ant. Jan. 1949)

CUMMINGS, S.: Concord, N.H. Late 18th century. Aw. for Timothy Chandler.

CUNNINGHAM, A. J.: Charleston, S.C. "Primarily a Watchmaker." Aw. 1830–1850.

CURE, JULE F.: Phila. Dir. 1839–1840.

—, LOUIS (Lewis): Phila., 154 Race St. Dir. 1811–1819. Brooklyn 1830's.

CURRIER (Edmund) & FOSTER: Salem, Mass., 11 Derby St. 1831–1837. Pine-cased Dwarf Tall clock ill. in L.B. Col.

— & TROTT: Boston. 1833–1839. Aaron Dennison worked for them. (Crossman)

—, E.: Hopkinton, N.H. n/d. (Burt)

—, EDMUND: Salem, Mass., 7 Derby St. 1828. C. S. J. W.; timepieces, Galley clocks, regulators. Head of Currier & Foster, 1831; left firm 1837. Lyre clock ill. Am. Col. Sept. 1939.

—, JOHN: Salem, Mass. Pos. related to Edmund. W. Dir. 1831.

CURRIER, ELIPHALET: 1774–1831. Haverhill, Mass. "Watchmaker."

CURTIS & CLARK: Plymouth, Conn. *Ca.* 1825. Shelf clock label. Pos. 8-day brass shelf clocks. "Best springs are imported from Geneva." Movt. with solid plates, going barrels with springs, rack and snail strike, escape wheel on front plate, shorter pendulum, iron dial, carved column case, carved feet. Label penciled, "bought 1825." Exs. in F.M.S. and Walter Keller Cols.

— (Lemuel) & DUNNING (J. L.): Concord, Mass., *ca.*1813–1818; Burlington, Vt. Some excellent clocks with this name.

—, H., & Co.: Meriden, Conn. *Ca.*1830. Pillar Shelf clocks.

—, J., & Co.: Cairo, N.Y. Tall clock, 1-day wood movt. *ca.*1830 in Walter Keller Col.

— (Lewis) & MARSH (George): Farmington, Conn. "Clock shop" now caddy house on golf links.

"— MFG. Co., SAMUEL," used by forerunner company of Waltham Watch Co. 1853.

—, BENJAMIN B.: Boston (Roxbury), Mass. Son of Samuel, bro. Lemuel and Samuel, Jr. Painted clock tablets; ornamental gilding and painting. (BCC)

—, CHARLES: Roxbury, Mass. Dial maker.

—, JOEL: Three patents: Waterbury, Conn., 1814, "pinions"; with Dimon Bradley, Cairo, N.Y., Aug. 22, 1814, "wheels, teeth, and pinions"; Cairo, N.Y., Aug. 22, 1814, "mode of boring plates."

—, LEMUEL: 1790–1857. Concord, Mass. "One of the best known and finest makers" (H. G. Rowell). Apt. of Willards; Adv. 1811. Four types of Wall clocks: Banjo, Girandole, Lyre, Shelf Lyre. (See ill. Nos. 154–158.)

Originated Girandole (see ill. No. 156), masterpiece of design; "America's most beautiful clock." One known with center seconds hand. Round tablets by Benjamin Curtis and others. "Commerce" most frequent; others "Perry's Victory," "Shipwreck of St. Paul," "Lady of the Lake." Iron dials, slightly convex, "L. Curtis" or "L. Curtis Patent." Generally Roman numerals; some Arabic may be earlier. Wooden balls of two sizes; 26 of larger, 35 to 37 of smaller. Bezel of brass, rarely wood.

Lyre clock (see ill. No. 155) has unusual striking wire, can be tuned, diagonally from under the dial at "9" to lower right corner of case. DKP Col.

Cases more ornate than Willards'. Patent July 12, 1816 on improvement on Willard TP. Some Banjo movts. with rounded top plates, name stamped. Movts. well designed and finished; plates high polish like French movts., cast brass, planished, scraped, filed. Pallets well made.

Son of Samuel and Sarah Partridge Curtis, nephew of Aaron Willard, Abel Hutchins, Elnathan Taber, first cousin of Aaron Willard, Jr., and John Sawin. Bro. Samuel, Jr., dial painter in Roxbury. Apt. J. L. Dunning, partner *ca.*1813; to Burlington, 1818; prob. made clocks. d. Burlington 1857. (Ant. Dec. 1923) (Am. Col. Mar. 1938) (ALP) (DKP)

—, LEWIS: 1774–1845. Farmington, Conn., Main St. Apt. of Daniel Burnap. C. S. Aw. 1795–1820. Father paid carpenter Judah Woodruff 13 shillings to make show window. Adv. 1797, robbed of silver. Adv. 1799, for shop on Main St. "Still continues to carry on Clock making Business such as chime clocks that play a number of different tunes and clocks that exhibit the moon's age and common 8-day clocks and time-pieces of various kinds." 1820 to St. Charles, Mo.; d. Hazel Green, Wis., 1845. (Hoopes) (Hartford Times, July 21, 1928)

—, SAMUEL: 1788–1879. Boston. Bro. Lemuel. Dial mfg. 1807 with Spencer Nolan, son-in-law of Aaron Willard; dials, tablets, mirrors, paintings. Dir. 1820, "Clock dial painter, 73 Market St., house Batterymarch." Pos. ran Lemuel's shop 1818 (after Lemuel went to Vt.) till taken over by Joseph Dyer. Pos. with Lemuel in Vt. (BCC)

—, SOLOMON: Phila. Dir. 1793.

—, W.: Newburyport, Mass. Early 19th century. Little data, Banjo clock with bracket with this maker's name extant. (BCC)

CUSHING, PETER H.: Braintree, Mass. n/d. (Burt)

—, THEODORE: Hingham, Mass. *Ca.*1808. Cases for John Bailey. (DKP)

CUSTER, DANIEL: Reading, Pa. *Ca*.1810–1820.

—, ISAAC: Norristown, Pa. *Ca*.1830–1850. Younger bro. of Jacob; with him in clock shop. Later to St. Louis; S.; prob. sold Jacob's clocks and watches. (S. H. Barrington) (Conrad)

—, JACOB D.: 1805–1872. Jefferson, Norristown, Pa. Son of John and Barbara Ann Detweiler Custer; b. Worcester Twp., Pa. Self-taught. Repaired father's watch, fame spread, 1825 aw. Jefferson, Pa. Marr. 1842 Mary B. Carlisle. Adv. Norristown, 1832, "J. D. Custer has commenced Clock and Watch Repairs one door above Thomas & Hoovens store at Main and Swede Sts." Built factory near Main and Green Sts. Nov. 20, 1830, Patent on "Clocks." Good business man, never made much money, but inventive genius. Made and invented grease cup, revolving lights for Govt.; pos. castings for ironclad *Monitor*. Tall clocks *ca*.1830, Penna. Pillar and Scroll clocks (see ill. Nos. 73, 205). Tower clocks, and about 14 watches (see ill. Nos. 292, 293). Early movts., wood plates, brass wheels. Tower clocks cast iron and steel, later all brass. At least three different striking controls. Patent on watches Feb. 1, 1843; model at Smiths. Inst. Made all parts except hair spring and fuzee chain. d. Norristown. (S. H. Barrington) (Bul.) (Abbott)

CUTLER, JOHN N.: Albany, N.Y. Dir. 1829–1850.

—, JOHN N., JR.: Albany, N.Y. Dir. 1842 and later.

CUTLEY, ABLE: –1710. Phila.

CYCLO CLOCK CO.: N.Y.C. "Sold by sheriff sale, 1892." (MFM)

DADIN, LOUIS: Charleston, S.C. *Ca*.1840.

DAFT, THOMAS: Phila. Adv. 1775, "Late of London." N.Y.C., 1786–1790.

DAGGETT, JAMES: St. Louis, Mo. *Ca*.1820.

—, T.: Providence, R.I. *Ca*.1840.

DAKIN, JAMES: Boston. Dir. 1796. Mass. Shelf ill. in Drepperd. Ex. in J. C. Wells Col.

DALRYMPLE, JAMES: 1765–1839. Salem, Mass., Court St. b. Ireland, marr. 1806. Continued 1795 watch business of Joseph Mulliken. Essex St. near Court 1802–1813, Essex St. till 1836.

DALZIEL, JOHN: N.Y.C. 1798.

DANA (George) & WHITTAKER (Thomas): Providence, R.I. 1805 to *ca*.1825.

—, PAYTON & NATHANIEL: Providence, R.I. *Ca*.1830.

—, DANIEL: Providence, R.I. Early 19th century.

—, GEORGE: Providence, R.I. 1805–*ca*.1825. With Thomas Whittaker bought out N. Dodge.

—, PAYTON: Providence, R.I. Early 19th Century. Tall clocks, pine case, brass dial, TP alarm, I. Sack Col.

DANIEL, G.: Cincinnati, O. Pos. worked for Luman Watson. Wag-on-Wall clock, "As model for L. Watson," usual Conn. type, wood dial, long pendulum. (See ill. No. 68.)

—, G. L.: Rome, N.Y. Adv. 1840–1843.

—, GEORGE C.: Elizabeth City, N.C. Adv. 1829, "Opened shop for watch & clock making." Adv. 1831, "Moved to Halifax and employed a Watchmaker."

—, HENRY H.: White River Village, Vt. Watch Paper E. Wood Gauss, N.Y.C.

DANNER, ALEXANDER: Lancaster, Pa. *Ca*. 1800. "Had a factory." Cases for Shreiners and other Lancaster makers; prob. no complete clocks. (Lan. Co.)

DARLINGTON, BENEDICT: Westtown Twp., Pa. 1810–1812. Wood movt. clocks; other activities. "Three men from Conn.," Jonathan B. Hatch, Russell Vibber, Thomas DeWolf, fitted up wood movts., he cased them. Prob. case maker only. (James)

DARROW & MATTHEWS: Bristol. (tx) 1824–1826. Pos. clockmakers.

—, WILLIAM, & CO.: Bristol. (tx) 1834–1836. Pos. C.

—, ELIJAH: 1800–1857. Bristol. (tx) 1824–1856. Glass tablet and dial painter; clock tablets of "his own invention and design" (decal type?). In Jeromes & Darrow. Later made 30-hr. clocks. (A. J. Sept., 1950)

—, FRANKLIN C.: Bristol. (tx) 1857–1865. Clock tablets. Org. Darrow Mfg. Co., rawhide doll heads.

DART, LEWIS: Jersey City, N.J. *Ca*.1850.

DAVENPORT, JAMES: Salem, Mass. "Watch & Clockmaker on the Paved St. 1784."

DAVENPORT, JOSEPH: 1773–1849. Newton Upper Falls, Mass. "Brass movt. Tall clock in mahogany veneer case. Dial about 12″ square, no lunette, mounted directly on the movt. without the intervening false plate." (E. A. Battison)

—, WILLIAM: Phila. Early 1800's.

DAVIDSON, BARZILLAI: Norwich, Conn. 1775. "Worker in gold and silver and offered for sale handsome assortments of jewelry and fine timekeepers." (Hist.)

—, BARZILLAI: New Haven, Conn. 1825. Prob. son of preceding. Tower clock for New Haven Meeting House for $260.

—, C.: N.Y.C., 42 Fulton St. 1830. Mentioned in adv. of Ives Clocks in Conn. *Courant.*

—, SAMUEL: "Md." 1774.

DAVIES, B. F. & T. M.: Ithaca, N.Y. ca.1870. Very large wall Ithaca Calendar clock from Oneida Co. Court House made under Horton patents.

— & HODGENS: N.Y.C. 1873. Succeeded James Wood & Co.

—, THOMAS: Utica, N.Y. Ca.1820.

—, THOMAS: N.Y.C. Patent Aug. 12, 1846, for lever clock listed as "improvement." OG extant with this patent, label "Terryville." Patent also used by Seth Thomas. Also patent for "improvement in clocks," Jan. 15, 1846. (FMS)

DAVIS & BABBITT: Providence, R.I. *Ca.* 1810.

— & BARBOUR: Bristol. No tx. Elias Ingraham contracted to make cases for them. Shipped South movts. and cases to avoid tax. (Hist.)

— CLOCK CO.: Columbus, Miss., ca.1880.

—, PALMER & CO.: Boston. Dir. 1842.

— POLSEY CO.: Boston. n/d. Square top Dwarf Tall clock, Boxford, Mass.

—, TOKLAS & CO.: San Francisco, Cal. Ca. 1880.

—, ARI: Boston. Ca.1840. Mfr. and R. Chrons., surveyors' insts., etc. Elias Howe was apt. (Mitman) (HIA Jan. 1948)

—, C. P.: Elizabethport, N.J. n/d. Watch Paper Clarence Goss, N.Y.C.

—, CALEB: Woodstock, Va. b. Annapolis. Eldest son John crossed mountains into Harrison Co., W. Va., ca.1816, later brought father and family to Clarksburg.

DAVIS, D. P.: Boston. 1842–1849. In Howard & Davis.

—, GABRIEL: Manheim, Pa. Ca.1780. "Little known." (Lan. Co.)

—, H. J.: N.Y.C., 5 Cortlandt St. Illuminated alarm clock. (See ill. No. 279.) Ex. in Mitchell, G. B. Davis, Ray Walker Cols.

—, JOHN: Pos. 1730–. Fairfield, Conn. Pos. apt. of John Whitear. Church records 1750, "Clockmaker, a stranger and said Davis is to Keep the Church Clock in good repair for 2 years. £5 a year providing it goes well the said time, if not, he is to have nothing for his labor, and the first 5 pounds to be paid at the end of the first year and the other at the 2nd year, and that the Church Wardens are not put to more trouble about paying the money than to pay it either in Stratford or Fairfield and to be paid in old tenor money." (Hoopes)

—, JOHN: New Holland, Churchtown, Pa., Phila. Dir. 1818. Ca.1802–1805. Dials of Tall clocks enameled with floral designs in corners, "J. Davis, New Holland." (Lan. Co.)

—, JOHN WHEELWRIGHT: 1800–. Salem, Mass. Jr. partner Moulton & Davis, 1824.

—, JOSIAH S.: Patent on "Watch Key," Providence, R.I., April 3, 1827.

—, PETER: Jaffrey, N.H. n/d.

—, PHINEAS: York, Pa. Apt. of Jonathan Jessop, who befriended him 1809 when parents d. Aw. on first coal-burning B. & O. locomotive. (Michael)

—, RICHARD: Phila. Dir. 1837.

—, RILEY A.: New Bern, N.C. Adv. 1850.

—, SAMUEL: Boston. Dir. 1830. "Imported watches and clocks."

—, SAMUEL: Pittsburgh, Pa. Dir. 1815–1850. (Gillingham)

—, W. M.: Morrisville, N.Y. Adv. 1825.

—, WILLIAM: "Arrived at Boston 1683— had a large family and small amount of money. One David Edwards became surety that he would not become a charge on the town." (Moore)

DAVISON, C.: N.Y.C., 42 Fulton St. near Pearl. Adv. 1830. Ives patent lever spring clocks.

DAWES, ROBERT: Boston. Dir. 1842.

DAWREY, CHARLES D.: Brooklyn, N.Y. Dir. 1850. Clock and dial painter.

DAWSON, JONAS: Phila., 418 High (now Market) St. Dir. 1813–1824.

—, THOMAS S.: Wilmington, Del. n/d. Apt. of Charles Canby. (Conrad)

DAY, D. N. & R.: Westfield, Mass. *Ca.*1830. Stenciled 30-hr. Shelf clock in Collins Museum.

—, ISRAEL: Baltimore, Anne St., Fells Pt. 1802–1807.

DAYTON WATCH CO.: Dayton, O. n/d. (MFM)

—, JOHN D.: Brooklyn, N.Y. *Ca.*1840–1850.

"DEACON, J. W.," used by U.S. Watch Co. *ca.*1870.

DEAN (Wm.) & Co. (George): Salem, Mass., 307 Essex St. 1800–1837. Dir. 1837, "hardware."

—, GEORGE: *Ca.*1778–1831. Salem, Mass. In Dean & Co.

—, WILLIAM: *Ca.*1775–1846. Salem, Mass. 1797–1800. Then Dean & Co. to 1837.

—, WILLIAM: Pleasant Valley, N.Y. Patent on "clock machinery" Dec. 21, 1821.

DEARDOFF & TURNER: Lebanon, O. n/d. Watch Paper. W. S. J.

DEARDORFF, PETER: Lebanon, O. n/d. Watch Paper.

DEBENNEVILLE, N.: Phila. Dir. 1820–1822.

DEBERARD, —: Utica, N.Y. *Ca.*1820.

DEBRUHL, MICHAEL SAMUEL: Charleston, S.C., 35 Union St. Listed 1806. Aw. 1798–1806. Pos. to Abbeville, S.C. Partnership with Mary Matilda Dunseeth as Dunseeth & Debruhl dis. 1804.

DEEMS, JOHN: Baltimore. Dir. 1842. (MFM)

DEFOREST & Co.: Salem Bridge (Naugatuck), Conn. Adv. 1832, C. W. "and buttons of all kinds." Shelf clocks, 8-day brass movts.

DEGIY, LEWIS: Boston. *Ca.*1800.

DEHUFF, A.: York, Pa. *Ca.*1850.

DEIBERT, S. F.: Catawissa, Pa. n/d. Tall clock Brandt Col.

DELACHAUX, PHILIP H.: Phila. Dir. 1820–1822.

DELAPLAINE, JAMES R.: N.Y.C. 1786–1799.

DE LONG, CHARLES: 1871–. W. Age 15 apt. Glens Falls, N.Y. 1886. With Jones & Bardmore, Troy, N.Y., 1887; M. Eliasoff & Co., Albany, N.Y., 1880–1889; Marsh & Hoffman, Albany, N.Y.; Fred McIntyre Watch Co., Kankakee, Ill. (Chamberlain)

DELONG, PETER ANGLE: 1839–. "Little known." (Chamberlain)

DELONGUEMAIRE, —: Charleston, S.C. *Ca.* 1700.

DELOSTE, FRANCIS: Baltimore. "1817."

DELUXE CLOCK & MFG. CO.: N.Y.C. *Ca.* 1929. Six clocks in Arthur James Col., New York University.

DELVIN, MARK H.: Salem, Mass., 136 Derby St. Dir. 1864. R.

DE MILT, THOMAS & BENJAMIN: N.Y.C. Dir. 1805.

—, BENJAMIN: N.Y.C. 1802–1818.

—, SAMUEL: N.Y.C. Aw. 1820–1840. (H. R. Fairbanks)

—, THOMAS: N.Y.C. 1798–1818. Pos. Phila.

DENHAM, JOHN: Phila. Dir. 1848.

"DENNISON (Aaron L.), HOWARD (Edward) & DAVIS": On first watches produced at Waltham 1854. Forerunner Waltham Watch Co. (G. V. White)

—, AARON L.: 1812–1895. Brunswick, Me., 1830; Boston, 1833; Roxbury, Mass., 1849; Waltham, Mass., 1854; Switzerland 1864; England 1868. "Father of the American watch industry." With Edward Howard, first to use successfully interchangeable parts system and machinery to make watches. b. Freeport, Me., March 6, 1812, son of shoemaker; little schooling, much hard work. Apt. of James Carey, C. and W., Brunswick, Me., 1830–1833. To Boston aw. for Currier & Trott, then Jones, Low, & Ball. Alone Boston 1839, J. and general watch business. Invented "Dennison Standard Gauge" 1840.

Edward Howard (1813–1904) C. as Howard & Davis from 1842. Both had idea of mass-producing watches; partnership 1849. Financed by Samuel Curtis, began to design and make needed machinery. Model watch to run 8 days made 1850, size 18; unsuccessful. Concentrated on one-day watch of English type. Org. "The American Horologe Co." 1850 in concrete factory in Roxbury; before 1853 watches on market. Plant 1854 to Waltham—beginning of Waltham Watch Co. First watches marked "Dennison, Howard,

DENNISON, AARON L. (*cont'd*)
& Davis." Financial trouble 1857; business reorganized; Dennison superintendent till 1862; Howard reestablished watch business at old Roxbury plant.

Dennison org. Tremont Watch Co. 1864. To Zurich, Switz., 1864 to study and get watch parts made; returned 1866. Tremont Watch Co. f. 1868. Dennison to Birmingham, Eng.; d. there January 9, 1895. Made watch cases as "Dennison, Wigley, & Co." ("Timing a Century") (Abbott) (Brearley) (G. V. White)

DERBY, CHARLES: Salem, Mass., 203 and 180 Essex St. 1846–1857.

—, CHARLES, JR.: Salem, Mass. Three in Dir. 1859, one "Watchmaker."

—, JOHN: N.Y.C. 1816.

DE REIEMER & MEAD: Ithaca, N.Y. Adv. 1830–1831.

DERRY MFG. CO.: Derry, N.H. n/d. Banjo clock with this name stamped on movt., nicely decorated throat and door, brass bezel and side arms, in Herbert Marble Col., Orleans, Mass.

DE SAULES & CO.: N.Y.C. Ca.1830. Pos. D.

DESCHAMPS, FRANCIS: Phila. Dir. 1846–1849.

DES COMBES, EDWARD J.: Baltimore. Patent Apr. 30, 1840, on watch escapement.

DE ST. LEGER, —: New Bern, N.C. Adv. 1790, "Continued the watchmaking business in all its branches."

DEUCONNER, G.: Phila. Dir. 1817.

DEVACHT, FRANÇOIS: Gallipolis, O. Missionary John Heckewelder 1792, "The most interesting shops of the workmen were those of the Goldsmiths and Watchmakers. They showed us work on watches, compasses and sun dials finer than I have ever beheld." None survive. (A. Lockett)

—, JOSEPH: Gallipolis, O. With bro. François.

DEVELIN, J. & M.: Phila. Dir. 1848 and later.

DEVERELL, JOHN: Boston. Adv. 1790, "Next door to the Treasury." W. C. "Very neat new silver watches for $16, etc." Adv. Baltimore 1789 display of springs made by him.

DEWEY, I.: Chelsea, Vt. n/d. N.H. Mirror clock, larger and different style, 4' high, scroll top, at Collins Museum. (BCC)

DEWITT, GARETT: Sparta, Ga. Ca.1840.

DE WOLF, THOMAS: Westtown, Pa. 1810–1815. With Jonathan Hatch and Russell Vibber cased fitted wooden movts. by Henry Darlington. (James)

DEXTER, DANA: Boston. Ca.1870.

—, H.: Stockbridge, N.Y. Ca.1840. Pos. with Conn. movts.

—, JOSEPH W.: Providence, R.I. 1824.

—, WILLIAM: Stockbridge, N.Y. Ca.1830 or later.

DE YOUNG, MICHAEL: Baltimore. Ca.1830.

DIALS, IMPORTED: Names found on false plate of Tall clocks believed to be English. Osborne & Wilson, Thomas Osborne, Osborne Mfg. Co., James Wilson, Walker & Hughes, E. Owen, W. L. Price, Wilson & Osborne.

DICKENSON, —: Boston. Early 19th century. Tall clock, 8-day brass movt., enameled dial, oak case, in Albert Col. (Baillie)

—, CHARLES: Zanesville, O. Adv. 1815. (Knittle)

—, JOHN: Phila. Dir. 1822–1825.

—, RICHARD: Mt. Holly, N.J. 1760–1770. Tall clocks. (Stow)

—, WILLIAM: Phila. Dir. 1843–1848.

DICKERSON, JOHN: 1755–1828. Morristown, N.J. and Phila., 411 No. Front St. Dir. 1797. Pos. apt. Cary Dunn. S. Adv. 1778 for apt. and watch repairer. Later in Indiana. (Williams)

DICKSON, WHITE, & CO.: Phila. Dir. 1837.

DIDIER, PIERRE: Gallipolis, Ohio. W. with De Vacht. Later to St. Louis; pos. C. and W. Elected Mo. State Treasurer. (Lockett)

DIEFENBACH, PETER: N.Y.C. n/d. Watch Paper BCL Col.

DIEHL, JACOB: 1776–1858. Reading, Pa. Ca.1800. 4th group. Operated shop of Daniel Rose till 1804 during absence of Rose; then alone. Tall clocks owned by E. T. Hollinger, Hagerstown, Md.; Maurice Walter, N.Y.C., Robert S. Anderson, Washington, D.C.; "Bedford, Pa." on metal dial; frame of movt. marked "William Whittacker, Halifax"; on back of dial and on moon phase "No. 70" painted; broken arch top, cherry case. (Steinmetz)

DIKEMAN, EDWARD B.: Grand Rapids, Mich. Ca.1840–1860.

DILLON & CO. (E. Openshaw), T. E.: N.Y.C. 1869. Succeeded Dillon & Tuttle.

— & TUTTLE: N.Y.C. Mfg. Chrons. till 1869; became T. E. Dillon & Co.

DINSMORE, JAMES: Hopkinton, N.H. n/d. Tall clock, inlaid cherry case, 12" enamel dial, Metropolitan Museum of Art.

DISTURNELL, WILLIAM: New Haven and Middletown, Conn. Adv. 1784, from London, C. and W. opened shop on College St., New Haven. Later to Middletown. Adv., W. and R. Extent of Clockmaking not known. (Hoopes)

DITTMYIR, JOHN: Rochester, N.Y. Patent No. 218,945, Aug. 26, 1879, model Smiths. Inst.

DIX, JOSEPH: Phila., Lombard St. W. Adv. 1769. (Prime)

DIXON, ISAAC: Phila. Dir. 1843 and later.

DOBBELAAR, M. J.: N.Y.C. n/d. Watch Paper BCL Col.

DOBBS, HENRY M.: N.Y.C. 1794–1802. (MFM)

DOBSON, JOHN A.: Baltimore. Ca.1860–1870.

DODD, ABNER: Newark, N.J. 1830–1849. (PG)

DODGE & WHITAKER: Providence, R.I. Ca. 1800. Pos. Nehemiah Dodge and Thomas Whitaker.

— (Nehemiah) & WILLIAMS (Stephen): Providence, R.I. 1799–1800. "Of short duration."

—, EZRA: 1766–1798. New London, Conn., Main St. 1789. Apt. of Thomas Harland. Took apt. to "location occupied by John Champlin, noted G." Built own shop 1790 opp. Winthrop's Wharf. Marr. Elizabeth Hempstead 1790. Adv. 1798, "General assortment of groceries, rum, brandy, molasses, flour, and still carries on Clock and Watchmaking." Penrose Hoopes, "Ingenious mechanic, good man, and valuable citizen." (Am. Col. Sept. 1947) (Hoopes)

—, EZRA: Providence, R.I. Ca.1820.

—, GEORGE, JR.: 1779–. Salem, Mass. Dir. 1837.

—, JOHN: Catskill, N.Y. Adv. 1818–1819.

—, NEHEMIAH: Providence, R.I., North Main St. 1796. Aw. 1796–ca.1820. To Seril Dodge's shop. With Stephen Williams, 1799. Member Mechanic's Assn. 1803. Retired ca.1820; sold out to George Dana and Thomas Whitaker.

DODGE, SERIL: –1802. Providence, R.I., "2 doors North of Baptist Meeting House." Aw. 1788. Apt. Thomas Harland. Clocks, Watches, Silversmith. To Pomfret, Conn., 1796.

DOGGET, JOHN: 1780–. Boston. Cabinet-maker. Roxbury 1812 at Eustis St. opp. burial ground. Clock cases, mirror frames, gold leaf, carving. Not Clockmaker. Later joined by Samuel, younger bro.; both successful. Retired 1850. (BCC)

—, SAMUEL: Roxbury and Boston. Cabinet-maker with bro. John. Larger quarters later on Market St., then Washington St. Added line of imp. rugs. Retired 1854.

DOLE, H. L., & CO.: Haverhill, Mass., 4 Merrimack St. Dir. 1865–1877.

DOLL, JOSEPH: Lancaster, Pa. Ca.1800–1820. Harrisburg later.

DOMINICK, BERNHARDUS: Phila. Adv. 1775.

—, FREDERICK: Phila., 2nd and Vine Sts. Adv. 1768, "from Germany"; adv. to ca. 1777. Miss C. Stretch reported one Tall clock; pos. movt. by Peter Stretch.

DOMINY, CAPT. NATHANIEL: 1732–1812. Sag Harbor and East Hampton, N.Y. Ca.1764–1809. Long Island C.; also whaler. Ledger records 41 clocks; prob. 30 more. First clocks had only one hand; next, with two hands, either timepieces or clocks. Most elaborate and expensive was "telltale, alarm, and repeating clock." Adv. 1804. Several extant; two in E. C. Kerr family, Mrs. John F. Erdmann, N.Y.C. See ill. Nos. 41, 42 for one in Selchow Col. (L. B. Keim) (Mrs. D. P. O'Sullivan) (FMS)

DOMMETT, JOHN: Phila. Wm. Rawle's Book, Pa. Hist. Soc., May 8, 1736, "To cash paid John Dommett for cleaning my clock yesterday £0–3–0." (Gillingham)

DON, ALEXANDER: Albany. Dir. 1815–1817.

DONALDSON, GEORGE E.: Doylestown, Pa. n/d. Watch Paper James Jensen Col.

DOOGAL & RUSSEL: N.Y.C. 1805.

DOOLITTLE, ENOS: 1751–1806. Hartford, Conn. Aw. 1772–ca.1790. Aptd. to bro. Isaac, New Haven; first clock by 1771. Adv. 1772, "All kinds of clocks, Surveyor's Instruments, Marine Compasses, etc." Apr. 1773 had "London trained Journeyman Watchmaker"; soon adv. for another

DOOLITTLE, ENOS (con't)
instead. Fine engraving. Adv. 1785, still repaired watches. Adv. 1786 clock for sale. Interested in brass foundry 1787; 1788 bell casting with Jesse Goodyear of Hampden. Other "branches of his business." After 1791 cast bells under own name; by 1793 making them for stock. Retired 1802; son James continued bell casting. Tall clock ill. No. 55. (Hoopes)

—, ISAAC: 1721–1800. New Haven, Conn., Chapel St. b. Wallingford, Conn.; pos. apt. of Macock Ward. To New Haven ca.1742. Penrose Hoopes, "One of the leading manufacturers and most versatile mechanic of the State." Diversified business life over half century; Clocks, S., chocolate, clock glasses, powder mill, etc. Ca.1785–1788 poor health. Bell casting 1788–1797. Son Isaac, Jr., succeeded him. Tall clocks at Metropolitan Museum of Art; John K. Lamond Col., Havertown, Pa.; Mrs. Perrin C. Galpin, Pelham, N.Y. (Hoopes)

—, ISAAC, JR.: 1759–1821. New Haven, Conn. Ca.1780. Aw. 1780 and later. Son of Isaac. Adv. 1781, "Compasses, Sea and Land Surveyors scales and protractors, gauging rods, walking sticks, Silver and Plated Buttons turned upon a horn, also Clocks and Watches, etc." Not too active maker of clocks. Just before father's death adv. had taken over shop. (Hoopes)

—, JAMES: Hartford, Conn. Son of Enos. Continued bell foundry. Not C. (Hoopes)

—, LUCIUS F.: N.Y.C., 264 Eighth Ave. Dir. 1854.

DORCHESTER CLOCK & BELL FOUNDRY: Dorchester, Mass. Clocks and parts; organs. Ten employes in 1830's.

DOREY, JOSEPH L.: East Caln Twp., Pa. (Taxed) as W. 1824. (James)

DORFLINGER, JOSEPH: Phila. Dir. 1837.

DORON, JNO: Vincentown, N.J. Ca.1849. Watch Paper BCL Col.

DORSEY, PHILIP: Baltimore. Ca.1800.

DOTY, GEORGE: Buffalo, N.Y. Dir. 1835.

—, JOHN F.: Albany, N.Y. Dir. 1813–1823; Rochester, N.Y. Dir. 1844.

DOUGHTY, S. H.: N.Y.C., 28 John St. Dir. 1854.

DOUGLASS, JOHN: New Haven, Conn. 1800–1820. (Baillie)

—, THOMAS: Niles, Mich. Ca.1870.

DOULL, JAMES: Charlestown, Mass. Ca. 1790–1820; Phila. Dir. 1823–1840, 1843–1849. Tall and Mass. Shelf clocks. (See ill. No. 83.)

DOUTY, HENDRICK: Phila. Adv. 1774.

DOVER, THOMAS: Dayton, O. 1830's.

DOWDNEY, BURROWS: Phila., Front St. Adv. 1768–1771.

—, NATHANIEL: Phila. n/d. Tall clock, handwritten label. (Am. Col. Oct. 1939)

DOWIG, GEORGE: Baltimore. Adv. 1784.

DOWLE, ROBERT: N.Y.C. 1793.

DOWLING, G. R. & B., Co.: Newark, N.J. Adv. 1832–1838.

DOWNES, ARTHUR: Charleston, S.C., "On The Bay." 1762–1765 with Joshua Lockwood. Adv. 1765. Adv. 1768 "moved." (Prime)

DOWNING & DYER: St. Johnsbury, Vt. n/d.

— (Geo.) & PHELPS (Silas): Newark, N.J. Ca.1815. To N.Y.C. 1825, J. (Williams)

—, D.: St. Johnsbury, Vt. n/d. George Watts, N.Y.C., owns Watch Paper.

—, GEORGE R.: Richmond, Va. Ca.1819.

DOWNS, ANSON: 1797–1876. Bristol. Pos. apt. of Seth Thomas; pos. with bro. Ephraim 1816–1822 in Cincinnati, O., and with Luman Watson (no dir.). At Plymouth, Conn. 1821. To Bristol 1829. In Atkins & Downs 1831–1832. Later at Waterville making buttons and knives. (LB)

—, EPHRAIM: 1787–1860. Bristol. Aw. 1810–1842. Important C. b. Wilbraham, Mass. Dec. 20, 1787, son of David and Mary Chittenden Downs. Bro. Anson. Carpenter. Clock cases 1810 for Harrisons. Tall clocks, 30-hour wood movts.; Pillar and Scroll cases; successful C. Reported to have made two horseback trips to Cincinnati, O.; 1816–1821 with Luman Watson. Pos. took with him parts and patterns of Conn. clocks, or shipped for assembly. To Hoadleyville or Greystone, Conn., 1822 with Silas Hoadley, pos. Eli Terry and Seth Thomas. Marr. Chloe Painter 1822, becoming bro.-in-law Silas Hoadley and Butler Dunbar. To Bristol in fall of 1825; with George Mitchell. Many wood movt. Shelf clocks. (See ill.

No. 206); his mill ill. in *History of Bristol.*
Mitchell 1825 sold Downs a house, half
sale price to be in wood clock movts. at $3.
Settled suit in 1830 with Eli Terry. Did
not fail in 1837 depression. Retired 1842,
poor health. d. Bristol. Extant clock
labels include "EPHRAIM DOWNS for
George Mitchell," "for Eli Terry &
Sons," "for Mitchell & Atkins," "for
George Mitchell, case by Elias Ingraham." (LB)

DRAWBAUGH, DANIEL: Eberly's Mills, Pa.
Adv. 1874. Invented telephone device
pos. earlier than Bell's. Electric clocks
"like Alexander Bain's."

DREYFOUS, JOSEPH: Phila. Dir. 1825. "Importer of Watches." (Brix)

DRING, THOMAS: West Chester, Pa. Aw.
*ca.*1790. Three tall clocks known. Returned to Eng. before 1800. (Brinton)
(James) (Gillingham)

DROPSIE, M. A.: Phila. Dir. 1842–1849.

DROWN, CHARLES LEONARD: 1824–. Newburyport, Mass. Aw. 1849. With bro.
John 1850–1860.

—, JOHN BOARDMAN: 1826–. Newburyport,
Mass., 36 Merrimack St. With bro.
Charles 1850–1860. Green Watch Paper
Bir. Col.

—, RICHARD: *Ca.*1795–. Newburyport,
Mass., Merrimack St. Came in 1810 at
age 15. Apt. of David Wood. Successful.
Banjo clock known. (BCC) (AJ. July
1950)

DROZ & SONS, CHARLES: Phila., 149 Walnut
St. Dir. 1806–1814.

—, CHARLES A.: Phila. Dir. 1811–1841.

—, FERDINAND HUMBERT: Pittsburgh, Pa.,
*ca.*1840. Cleveland, O., *ca.*1850. Son of
Humbert.

—, HANNAH: Phila. Dir. 1842 and later.
Another woman craftsman.

—, HUMBERT: Phila., 10 Arch St. Dir.
1793–1811. Father of Ferdinand.

—, JOHN: Cincinnati, O. Adv. 1824, "From
Switzerland." (Knittle)

DRUMMOND, LEVIN J.: Baltimore. *Ca.*1875.
C. Goss, N.Y.C., owns Watch Paper.

DRYER, C.: Louisville, Ky. *Ca.*1850. Clocks
and thermometers.

DRYSDALE, WILLIAM: Phila., 144 So. Front
St. Dir. 1816–1851.

—, WILLIAM, JR.: Phila. Dir. 1842–1845.

DU BOIS & FOLMAR: N.Y.C. 1816.

—, B. F.: Pos. Chester Co., **Pa.** n/d.

—, GABRIEL: N.Y.C. *Ca.*1810.

—, P. C.: 1845–1925. Alameda, Cal. Several Tall and Shelf clocks of English style
mostly with chimes or bells. (Dr. W. B.
Stephens)

DUCOMMAN, A. L.: Phila. Dir. 1795–1798.
"Watchcase maker." (Baillie)

DUCOMMUN, HENRY, JR., & Co.: Phila. Dir.
1843–1844.

DUDLEY WATCH Co.: Lancaster, Pa., West
End Ave. 1923–1924. W. W. Dudley
made watch with Masonic symbols; did
not sell well. Succeeded by Fulton Watch
Co. 1924. (Bowman)

DUDLEY, ——: Phila. 1784. Adv.

—, BENJAMIN: 1785–1820. Newport, R.I.
(Abbott)

—, THOMAS: Boston or Roxbury, Mass.,
near Boston line. Cabinetmaker, large
patronage. Adv. 1807, "Wanted immediately 2 or 3 journeymen cabinet makers
to whom constant work and good wages
will be paid." (BCC)

DUEBER-HAMPDEN WATCH Co., THE: Can-
ton, O. 1888–1927. Merger of J. C.
Dueber Watch Case Mfg. Co. and Hamp-
den Watch Co. of Springfield, Mass.
Names used, "Hayward," "Perry," and
"State Street." (Bowman)

—, JOHN C., WATCH Co.: Canton, O. M. F.
Massey says this name used by Dueber.

— WATCH CASE MFG. Co.: Newport, Ky.
*Ca.*1877–1888.

—, JOHN C.: *–ca.*1925. Newport, Ky., Canton, O. Successful watchcase mfr. bought
control 1886 of The Hampden Watch Co.
Merged and moved to Canton, O., 1888
as Dueber-Hampden Watch Co.; grew to
be one of largest in America. Receiver
appointed *ca.*1925; machinery sold *ca.*1925
to Russia. (Bowman)

DUFF, GEORGE: Phila. Dir. 1837.

—, GEORGE C.: New Bern, N.C. Adv. 1846
claiming thorough knowledge of business.

DUFFIELD, EDWARD: West Whiteland Twp.,
Pa. Brinton and James find no trace.

—, EDWARD: 1720–1803 or 1730–1805. Adv.
1756–1775. Succeeded Thomas Stretch
1762 in care of State House clock to 1775.
To Moreland Twp. to devote time to an-
cestral estate. Friend and executor of

DUFFIELD, EDWARD (cont'd)
Benjamin Franklin. Tower clocks; fine Tall clocks in cases by best cabinetmakers. Tall clocks owned by Mrs. James B. White, Newcastle, Del., Hubert Somers, Atlantic City, N.J.; B. Boric, Whitemarsh, Pa. owns two, one 5' high. (Stretch)

DUFFNER, VINCENT: Cincinnati, O. Adv. 1850. (Knittle)

DUHME & Co.: Cincinnati, O. *Ca.*1850.

DULTY, JOHN: Zanesville, O. *Ca.*1810.

DUMESNIL, ANTHONY: Boston. Dir. 1796–1809.

—, ANTHONY: Lexington, Ky. Dir. 1818. W. J. (LB)

DUMOTETTE, J. B.: Phila. Early 19th century.

DUNBAR, JACOBS, & WARNER: Bristol. *Ca.* 1850.

— (Butler) & MERRIMAN (Titus): Bristol. Wood clocks. *Ca.*1810.

— & WARNER: Bristol. 1850–1852. Pos. C.

—, BUTLER: 1791–. Bristol. b. Plymouth, Conn., Feb. 1, 1791; to Bristol *ca.*1810 as partner of Dr. Titus Merriman making clocks. To Springvale, Pa. 1815; back to Bristol. Father of Edward L., bro.-in-law Ephraim Downs and Silas Hoadley.

—, EDWARD BUTLER: 1842–. Bristol. Aw. 1866. Clock spring maker. As Dunbar Brothers 5,000–8,000 per day. *Ca.*1885 clock factories making own springs; turned to other types. (Hull)

—, COL. EDWARD L.: 1815–1872. Bristol. Son of Butler. Marr. 1840 Julia Warner, Bristol. Among first to specialize in making clock springs. Apt. of Silas Hoadley, Greystone, R.I. Credit report *ca.*1850, "Real estate is worth $10,000 and all clear . . . does a great deal of business . . . I should trust him readily. He makes clock trimmings." Purchased 1847 Silas Burnham Terry process, later changed to Pomeroy process. Purchased 1845 Chauncey Jerome residence Main St. (Jerome's business all at New Haven after Bristol fire). (Hull) (Ingraham)

—, JOHN: Baltimore. 1796. W. and math. insts.

DUNCAN, ALEX: Elgin, Ill. n/d. Name on Tall clock owned by M. D. Grant, Pt. Hope, Ont.

DUNGAN & KLUMP: Phila., 1208 Chestnut St. *Ca.*1910. Mouse clock ("Hickory, dickory, dock" in action). Two in Peter Mitchell Col.

DUNHEIM, ANDREW: N.Y.C. 1775.

DUNLAP, ARCHIBALD: N.Y.C. 1802.

DUNN, CARY: N.Y.C. 1776–1782; Morristown, N.J., 1782; Newark, N.J., 1782–1783. S., prob. not C. or W. (Williams)

DUNNE, ROBERT: N.Y.C. *Ca.*1840.

DUNNING (Julius N.) & CRISSEY (Elnathan F.): Rochester, N.Y. Adv. 1847.

— & CURTIS: Concord, Mass. *Ca.*1812–1817. Name on Banjo clocks.

—, J. L.: Concord, Mass. 1811–1817. Apt. of Lemuel Curtis, later partner. Active C. after War of 1812. Good Banjo clocks. Went with or followed Curtis to Burlington, Vt., leaving Concord shop to Joseph Dyer, their apt. High hopes for good clock business Lake Champlain and Eastern N.Y. not fully realized. (BCC)

DUNNINGS: Wolcottville, Conn. n/d.

DUNSEATH, W. G.: Pittsburgh, Pa. n/d.

DUPEE, ODRIAN: Phila., then Boston. Adv. 1735, "Watch finisher." Boston, Selectmen's Records 1739, "Odrain Dupee, Appearing, Informs . . . that he is by Trade a Watch Maker and Works at present with Mr. Bagnall, Sr."; 1740, "Florentia, the wife of Odrian Dupee, . . . lately imported into this Town from New York by Albertus Bosch . . . are admitted Inhabitants; Mr. Benjamin Bagnall having given Bond to the Town Treasurer." (Buhler)

DUPUY, JOHN: –1803. Phila., 2nd St. Adv. 1769–1774. Adv. 1777, Reading, Pa. (Prime)

DURAND, ASHER BROWN: 1796–1886. Boston. "Father was a watchmaker and in his shop the future artist learned to cut cyphers on spoons, whence the transition to engraving was, with his artistic aptitudes, a natural process . . ." (Tuckerman)

DURANT, JOHN H. G.: New Haven, Conn. n/d.

DUREN, H.: N.Y.C. *Ca.*1820–1840.

DURFEE, WALTER H.: Providence, R.I., 283 High St., 270 Washington St. Late 19th century. Good Tall clocks, some inlaid, brass 8-day movts., 102" high, broken arch hood, oak case, owned by John McGinley, 2nd, New Canaan, Conn.; J. P. Campbell, Springfield, O.

DURGIN, F.: Andover, N.H. n/d.

DURYEA, W.: N.Y.C., 48 Dey St. Dir. 1854.

DUSENBERRY, D. C.: Middletown, N.Y. Early 19th century. Clock at Museum of the City of N.Y.

DUTCH CLOCKS: Made in Holland. *Ca.*1650–1800. Many owned in America. Included for identification only. Wall clocks, three general types:

Friesland (ill. No. 88). Named for Dutch province where first made. Ornate cases, deep-carved or molding decoration, sometimes gilded. Ill. Britten, 6th ed., No. 714; Milham, p. 167. Ex. in Mitchell Col.

Dutch Hood (ill. No. 89). Oval brass ornament near bottom of case. Ill. Milham No. 131. Ex. in Mitchell Col.

Zaandam. Named for city where prob. first made. Comparatively few. Unlike Friesland type. Ill. Milham No. 134; Britten No. 715.

Ex. all three types in Oscar Roesen Col., Scarsdale, N.Y.

DUTCH, STEPHEN: Boston. Dir. 1809–1816.

DUTENS, CHARLES: Phila. D. J. Adv. 1757, "From London, removed from Market St. to the Ring and Door of 2nd St. near Arch St."

DUTTON, DAVID, & SONS: Mont Vernon, N.H. *Ca.*1840. Shelf clock, 30-hour wood movt. owned by J. A. Masey, Hellertown, Pa.

—, DAVID: 1792–1882. Mont Vernon, N.H. Aw. 1830's–1840's. Numbers of Mirror Shelf clocks with this name on label; like those of Daniel Pratt, Reading, Mass. Wood movts., usually 30-hour, type varying from Terry patent. Alice Wilson of Nahant, Mass., said he made cases and movts. Some labels dated.

—, REED: Milford, N.H. *Ca.*1840. Shelf clock labels known.

DYAR (DYER), GEORGE WILD: Boston, 33 Market St. In Sawin & Dyer; partnership with John Sawin dissolved 1828. (See ill. Nos. 160, 161.) (BCC)

—, GILES: Boston. Appointed town clock keeper 1673.

—, HARRISON D.: N.Y.C. Patent for "Clocks" Dec. 6, 1827.

—, WARREN: Lowell, Mass. *Ca.*1831. Dir. 1832. Listed as D.; looking glasses and crockery.

DYE, WILLIAM: Fayetteville, N.C. *Ca.*1805. Aptd. to William Hillard.

DYER, WADSWORTH & Co.: Augusta, Ga. *Ca.*1838–1843. Prob. followed Case, Dyer, Wadsworth & Co. Used Birge & Mallory 8-day movts., shutter 3-decker cases. Label like Birge, Mallory & Co. except for American eagle. (S. W. Havens)

—, JOSEPH: Concord, Mass., Middlebury, Vt. Aw. 1816–1820. C. Journeyman or apt. employed by Lemuel Curtis and J. L. Dunning; succeeded them. Followed them to Vermont after 1820. (BCC)

DYFFER, DANIEL: Reading, Pa. *Ca.*1820. Tall clock owned by Charles D. Fenstermacher, Turbotville, Pa.

DYKE, ALBERT: N.Y.C. 1926–. W., Chrons.

DYSART, JAMES P.: Lancaster, Pa. *Ca.*1850.

EARP, ROBERT: Phila. 1811. (Prime)

EASTERLY, JOHN: New Holland, Pa. "1825–1840." (Moore)

EASTMAN (Robert) & CAREY (James): Belfast and Brunswick, Me. 1806–1809.

— CLOCK Co.: Chelsea, Mass. 1886–1888. Became Boston Clock Co., then Chelsea Clock Co. (J. F. McDonald)

—, ABEL B.: Concord, N.H., aptd. *ca.*1800–1806; Belfast, Me., 1806–*ca.*1821. Abbott lists him at "Haverhill, Mass., 1816–1821." Research showed only that some ancestors once lived there; to Concord, N.H.

—, ROBERT: Belfast and Brunswick, Me. 1805–1808. In Eastman & Carey. (Abbott)

EATON, ELON: Grand Rapids, Mich. *Ca.* 1860.

—, JAMES: Boston. Dir. 1807.

—, JOHN H.: Boston. Dir. 1809–1810.

—, SAMUEL A.: Boston. Dir. 1825–1842.

EBERMAN FAMILY: Lancaster, Pa. Many fine Tall clocks. John, Sr., 1749–1835, father of three sons: Jacob 1773–1837; John II 1776–1846; Joseph 1780–1844, who had son Charles and pos. Joseph, Jr. Also "Gottlieb"; relationship not clear. (Lan. Co.)

—, CHARLES: *Ca.*1820–. Lancaster, Pa. Son of Joseph. W. J. "In later years at No. Queens St. store." (Lan. Co.)

—, GOTTLIEB: Lancaster, Pa. 1782. (Brix)

EBERMAN, JACOB: 1773–1837. Lancaster, Pa. Bro. John and Joseph. With father. Aw. 1775–1820. Few Tall clocks known.

—, JOHN, SR.: 1749–1835. Lancaster, Pa. Aw. 1773–1820. Son of John, who came U. S. 1749. Uncertain whether he or son John II made all clocks bearing name "John Eberman." Made town clock 1784 in Lancaster Court House Belfry in Penn Sq., Pa.

—, JOHN II: 1776–1846. Prob. made most of clocks so marked. Aw. 1797–ca.1840. Bro. Joseph and Jacob.

—, JOSEPH: 1780–1844. Son of John. C. Aw. ca.1791–1820 and later.

—, JOSEPH II: Dir. 1857–1860. Pos. son of Joseph.

EBY, CHRISTIAN: Manheim, Pa. Aw. ca. 1799–1837. Many Tall clocks. In Stauffer & Eby ca.1800. Sons Jacob and George. One Tall clock with months and days for full year in circle around face. Tall 30-hour clock owned by Mrs. Robert H. Stickley, Memphis. Tall clock extant, "C. Eby, Manheim 1799." Tall clock business at height before 1830; declined as competition with Conn. Shelf clocks increased. Prob. mostly repairing after 1837, though still made clocks. (Lan. Co.) (Bowman)

—, GEORGE: Manheim, Pa. Aw. 1830–1860. Son of Christian, bro. Jacob. Tall clock owned by Robert H. Snyder, N.Y.C.

—, JACOB: Manheim, Pa. Aw. 1830–1860. Son of Christian, bro. George. Fine Tall clocks graceful hands, especially sweep seconds, inlay case. (Bowman)

ECKEL, ALEXANDER PERRY: 1821–1906. Greensboro, N.C. From Front Royal, Va. Adv. 1845, "House fitted up for carrying on clock and watch and jewelry business, of which he had a thorough knowledge." (Cutten)

ECKSPEWEN, WILLIAM: Pa. n/d. Tall clocks. (Orr)

EDGEMERE WATCH CO.: Chicago. n/d. "Some sold by Sears Roebuck." (MFM)

EDGERLY, SYLVESTER: Roxbury, Mass. Aw. ca.1820–1840. Willard apprentice. All wood Banjo clocks in Lewis Dyer and DKP Cols.; plain wood bezel, no side arms, square box, glass tablets.

EDMANDS & HAMBLETT: Boston. Ca.1865. Electric clocks.

EDMOND, WILLIAM: Phila. Dir. 1848.

EDMUNDS, JAMES: Charleston, S.C., Broad St. Adv. 1745, "From London." (Baillie)

EDMUNDSON, THOMAS: Warrington Twp., Pa. 1794–1800. Tall clocks.

EDSON, JONAH: 1792–1874. Bridgewater, Mass. Aw. 1815–1830. (Abbott)

EDWARDS, A. (Abraham) & C. (Calvin): Ashby, Mass. Aw. 1794–1797. Calvin d. 1797. (L. L. Barber) (JWW)

—, ABRAHAM: 1761–1840. Ashby, Mass. C. G. Aw. 1794–1840. Father of John, bro. Calvin. "When he came to Ashby, he made pewter buttons. Afterwards, after taking an old clock to pieces, he established Clockmaking. On dials of one of his clocks was a picture of his house with a horse chestnut tree on each side. West of the house was a shed, a clock shop, a store, and a barn, all connected. When he first came to Ashby, he boarded with a Lt. Barrett. He abandoned Goldsmithing 1794 and made clocks until his death in 1840." (Barber)

—, CALVIN: –1797. Son of Samuel. G. S. 1789–1797, C. 1792–1797. "He might possibly be related to the celebrated S. John Edwards (ca.1700–1746) of Boston." (JWW)

—, JOHN: 1787–. Son of Abraham. Aw. 1809–1812. Some clocks; none after 1812. (Barber)

—, JOHN: Annapolis, Md. 1735. (Baillie)

—, NATHAN: Acton, Mass. Early 19th Century. "Good Tall clocks." (See ill. No. 84.)

—, SAMUEL, SR.: 1715–1783. b. Wrentham, Mass. Father of Calvin. Pos. C.

—, SAMUEL, JR.: Ashby, Mass., 1804–1808; Gorham, Me., 1808–1830. C. Wood movts.

EELLS, EDWARD, SR.: 1739–. Stonington, Preston, Conn. Aw. 1773. Pos. C. Son Edward, Jr.

—, EDWARD, JR.: 1773–1832. Middlebury, Vt., Medina, N.Y. b. Preston, Conn. Pos. aptd. Conn. Marr. 1802. Tall clocks, one 7½' high, mahogany inlay case, 8-day brass movt.

EFFEY, WILLIAM: Davenport, Ia. Ca.1850.

EGAN, ROBERT: Williamsburg, Va. *Ca.*1772. (MFM)

EGERTON, MATTHEW, SR.: 1739–1802. New Brunswick, N.J. Aw. *ca.*1765–1802. Label, "Cabinetmaker in Burnett St." Clock cases, fine furniture.

—, MATTHEW, JR.: –1837. New Brunswick, N.J., Burnett St. With father, Matthew, Sr. Aw. *ca.*1787–1837. Fine Tall clock cases for many N.J. makers. Label, "Made and sold by —, joiner and cabinetmaker, New Brunswick, N.J."

EGG, EDWARD: Columbia, S.C. Dir. 1860–*ca.*1879. (Cutten)

EGGERT, D.: N.Y.C. 1826–1827. Taught Chron. bus. to Simon Willard, Jr. (BCC)

ELECTIME CORP.: Brooklyn, N.Y. 1949.

ELECTRIC SELF-WINDING CLOCK CO.: Bristol. (tx) 1903. Forestville, Central St.

"ELGIN, LADY," used by National Watch Co. of Elgin 1869 and later.

— NATIONAL WATCH CO.: Elgin, Ill. Aurora, Lincoln, Neb. 1864–. Successors to National Watch Co., org. 1864. First in wooden factory; partly burned 1865; new building 1866. First movt. (see ill. No. 298) April 1, 1867, "B. W. Raymond," 18 size full plate, quick train, straight line, escapement jeweled movt. Also 1867 "J. Ryerson," "H. H. Taylor," "G. M. Wheeler," 1868 "Mat Laflin." Four lower grade movts. 1869–1870 "W. H. Ferry," "M. G. Ogden," "J. V. Farwell," "Charles Fargo." First "Lady Elgin," see ill. No. 297, 1867 by National Watch Co. Became Elgin National Watch Co. 1874. First stem-wind watch 1873. By 1884, 96 distinct grades watches made at Elgin. Wrist watches introduced *ca.*1910. "The quick train balance wheel is 18,000 instead of 14,800 beats an hour, a smaller balance wheel being lighter and a longer main spring." Elgin watch has 150 parts. (Company records)

   Serial Nos. and year of mfr. (This is only approximate—watch of lower no. may be made later than one of higher no., depending on size, style and demand):

Serial No.	Year
101	1867
100,000	1870
200,000	1874
300,000	1874
400,000	1874
500,000	1877
600,000	1879
700,000	1880
800,000	1881
900,000	1881
1,000,000	1882
2,000,000	1886
3,000,000	1888
4,000,000	1890
5,000,000	1893
6,000,000	1895
7,000,000	1897
8,000,000	1899
9,000,000	1900
10,000,000	1903
11,000,000	1904
12,000,000	1905
13,000,000	1907
14,000,000	1909
15,000,000	1910
16,000,000	1911
17,000,000	1912
18,000,000	1914
19,000,000	1916
20,000,000	1917
21,000,000	1918
22,000,000	1919
23,000,000	1920
24,000,000	1921
25,000,000	1922
26,000,000	1923
27,000,000	1924
28,000,000	1925
29,000,000	1926
30,000,000	1927
31,000,000	1927
32,000,000	1928
33,000,000	1929–1930–1931–1932–1933
34,000,000	1933–1934–1935
35,000,000	1934–1935
36,000,000	1936–1937
37,000,000	1937–1938–1939
38,000,000 (X)	1939–1940
39,000,000 (C)	1940–1941
40,000,000 (E)	1941–1942
41,000,000 (Y)	1942–1943
42,000,000 (T)	1943–1944
43,000,000 (L)	1945–1946
44,000,000 (U)	1947
45,000,000 (J)	1948
46,000,000 (V)	1949
47,000,000 (H)	1950

ELIASOFF, M., & Co.: Albany, N.Y. *Ca.* 1888. Charles E. DeLong worked for them. (Chamberlain)

ELIOT, WILLIAM: Baltimore. 1799. (Moore)

ELLERY, E.: Pos. Newburyport, Mass. n/d. Name on Mass. Shelf clock owned by Tiena Baumstone, N.Y.C. "Found in Mass."

"—, WM.," used by American Watch Co. after 1861.

ELLICOTT, ANDREW: 1754–1820. Solebury, Pa. Son of Joseph and Judith Bleaker Ellicott; professor at West Point after 1812. Aw. 1774–1780. Surveying on Mason-Dixon Line. No clocks extant. (Gillingham) (Roberts)

—, ANDREW, SR.: Baltimore. Adv., 1775, 1780. C. and math. insts.

—, ANDREW, JR.: Phila. n/d. Father of Joseph. Pos. C. (Gillingham)

—, JOSEPH: 1732–1780. Buckingham, Pa. Ellicott's Mills, Md. Aw. 1750–1780. Famed C. Tall clocks. Steinmetz said he made No. 60 in 1774, but N. R. Hoover, N.Y.C., owns No. 67 with "1770" engraved on movt. Tall clock 9' high owned by Mrs. Frank M. Acton, Elkins Park, Pa. E. G. Paisly, N.Y.C., owns No. 35 with "Buckingham" on dial.

ELLIOTT (Zebulon) & BURNAM: Salisbury, N.C., Main St. Adv. 1821, "Clock and Watchmakers from N.Y.C." (Cutten)

—, B.: Phila. W., teacher. Dir. 1818–1822.

—, BENJAMIN P.: Phila. Dir. 1843 and later.

—, B. R.: Farmington, Me. *Ca.*1850.

—, G. M.: Patterson, N.J. n/d. Watch Paper BCL Col.

—, GEORGE: Wilmington, Del. Pos. after 1856. Apt. and successor of Charles Canby.

—, HAZEN: Lowell, Mass. Dir. 1832.

—, J.: Plymouth, Pa. *Ca.*1770.

—, JOHN A.: Sharon, Conn. Green Watch Paper Bir. Col.

—, LUTHER: Amherst, N.H. *Ca.*1840.

—, ZEBULON: N.Y.C. Dir. 1814–1921. Salisbury, N.C. Adv. 1821. In Elliott and Burnam. (Cutten)

ELLIS, BENJAMIN: Phila. Dir. 1829–1833.

ELLIS, GEORGE: Phila. Dir. 1850.

ELLSWORTH, DAVID: 1742–1821. Windsor, Conn. Son of David and Jemima Leavitt

Ellsworth. Bro. Oliver was U.S. Chief Justice. Apt. of either Seth or Ben Youngs in Windsor. Aw. *ca.*1763. Made muskets for Rev. Army. Craftsman and mechanic like Lowrey in Wethersfield. (Hoopes)

ELMORE, M. W.: Ottawa, Kan. *Ca.*1860.

ELSON, HERMAN N.: Phila. Dir. 1843–1848.

—, JULIUS: Phila. Dir. 1842–1844.

ELVINS, WILLIAM: Baltimore, Fells Point; 4 Fell St., 10 Bond St., 12 Fell St., 32 Thames St. 1796–1808. (Moore)

ELWYN, GEORGE: Bristol. n/d.

ELY, HUGH: New Hope, Pa., 1799–1803; Trenton, N.J., 1803–1820. (Stow)

—, JOHN: Mifflinburg, Pa. Early 19th century. (Conrad)

EMBREE, EFFINGHAM: N.Y.C. Dir. 1794. Aw. 1785. Tall clock in Museum of City of N.Y. C. P. Wicks, Stamford, Conn. owns Tall clock with "Osborne's Manufactory, Birmingham" on false plate of dial.

EMERSON, DUDLEY: 1765–. Lyme, Conn. Son of Broadstreet and Jemima Emerson. Adv. 1788, "Clock and watchmaking and jewelry carried on in Lyme, East Society, on road to New London, East Haddam, makes chime clocks with hours, minutes and seconds, day, moon's age 8-day repeating ditto, 30-hour ditto, and 8-day tp. Watches, repairing. Served regularly his apprenticeship at the above branches. Flatters himself that he will be able to give satisfaction." Adv. for apt. (Hoopes)

—, GEORGE W.: Newport, Me. n/d. (Burt)

—, WILLIAM G.: Newport, Me. *Ca.*1830. N.H. Mirror clock in James Conlon Col. (BCC)

EMERY, JESSE: Weare, N.H. 1800. See Emory. (Moore)

—, SAMUEL: Salem, Mass., 12 Waters St., 1809, 162 Derby St., 1855–1864. Math. insts. Prob. no clocks.

EMMERY, JOHN: N.Y.C. Late 1800's. A. O. Dodge, Schenectady, N.Y., owns 11-jeweled key wind and set movt. No. 21892, steel balance.

EMMET, EDWARD TILLET: Boston. Adv. 1764, "Opened shop at side town house on King St., C.W.R."

EMMONS, C. G.: Boston. Dir. 1842.
—, ERASTUS: Trenton, N.J. 1800–1820. (PG)
EMORY, JESSE: 1759–1838. Weare, N.H. (not Emery) E. A. Battison examined four wood movt. Tall clocks where name is spelled "Emory." Two dated "1800."
EMPIRE CITY WATCH CO.: N.Y.C. n/d. Watch Paper BCL Col.
— CLOCK CO.: Bristol. Inc. May 13, 1854, Noble Jerome president.
ENGARD, SAMUEL: Phila. Dir. 1837–1842.
ENGLAND, JAMES: Baltimore, Fells Point, 24 Bond St., 1807–1819. G. S. W. J. 22 Broad St. 1818–1829 pos. another man.
ENGLE, STEPHEN D.: n/d. Watchmaker and inventor of Engle clock, exhibited in United States cities by Capt. J. Reid.
ENSIGN, CHARLES: Troy, N.Y. Dir. 1842 and later.
ENT (ENDT), THEOBALD (THEODORE): Phila. Ca.1742. Son John.
—, JOHN: –1794. N.Y.C., Bayard St.; Phila., 2nd St. Adv. 1756, "John Ent, clock and watchmaker, at the sign of the dial, has moved to the house of Mr. John Wright, watchmaker in Bayard St., where he continues to make and repair in the newest manner all sorts of clocks and watches with repeating, horizontal or the plain kind. Gentlemen and ladies that are pleased to honor him with their employ may depend on the greatest care and dispatch imaginable." Phila., ca.1760–1790. Adv. 1763–1794. (Gillingham) (Prime)
—, JONATHAN: Phila. No data.
ENTWISTLE, EDMUND: Boston. Adv. 1742, "Imported to be sold a fine clock, 8–9 days, one winding up, repeats hour it struck last when you pull it. Dial is 13″ square and arched with a semi-circle on the top, around which is plate with this motto, 'Time Shews the Way of Life's Decay.' Well engraved and silvered within motto ring. Shows from behind two semi-spheres, moons increase and decrease by two curious painted faces ornamented with golden stars between on a blue ground, and a white circle on the outside. Divided into days, figures at every third on which Divisions is shewn, the age by a fixed index from the top as they pass the

great circle which is divided into 31 equal parts, figured at every other on which is shewn the day of the month by a hand from the dial plate as the hour hand is; it also shews the seconds as a common and is ornamented with various engravings in the most fashionable manner. Case made of good mahogany with quarter columns in the body, raised panels with quarter rounds. The head is ornamented with gilded Brasses and frieze with new fashioned Balls composed of mahogany with gilt leaves and flames. Also a silvered watch." Prob. not maker.
EOFF & HOWELL: N.Y.C. 1805. (Baillie)
—, GARRETT: 1785–1858. N.Y.C., 23 Elm St. 1814; 3 New St. 1819. Partnership with Howell, Connor, Phyfe, Morris.
ERB, JOHN: 1814–. Conestoga Center, Pa. Aw. 1835–1860. "Made few Tall clocks mainly repairing. Came into Tall clock making when it was pretty well at an end." (Lan. Co.)
ERNST, —: Cooperstown, N.Y. Ca.1810–1840.
ERWIN, HENRY: Phila. S., Dir. 1817–1829. W., Dir. 1837–1842.
ESSEX, JOSEPH: Boston, King St. Adv. 1712, "Lately arrived from Great Britton, performs all sorts of new clocks and watch works, 30 hour clocks, week clocks, month clocks, spring table clocks, chime clocks, quarter clocks, turret clocks and new pocket watches, new repeating watches, guaranteed for 12 months."
ESSLINGER, CHARLES: Buffalo. Dir. 1840–1848.
EST (pos. "ENT"), JOHN: N.Y.C. Ca.1760.
ESTELLE, SAMUEL: Germantown, O. Ca. 1870.
ESTERLIE, JOHN: 1778–. New Holland and Lebanon, Pa. Aw. ca.1812, retired 1830. (Lan. Co.)
EUBANK (Joseph) & JEFFERIES (James): Glasgow, Ky. Adv. 1820–1834. (LB)
—, JAMES: 1805–. Glasgow, Ky. Aw. 1826. In Joseph & William Savage. Alone after 1834. (LB)
—, JOSEPH: Glasgow, Ky. In Eubank & Jefferies, 1820–1834. Joseph & James Eubank, 1834–1841. Alone 1841–1855.
EUREKA MFG. CO.: Boston. Adv. 1860's. Astro., marine, school, hotel, office, cal-

EUREKA MFG. CO. (cont'd)
endar, house clocks, clockwork-driven coffee roasters.
— MFG. CO., THE: Bristol, North St. (tx) 1864–1868. Clocks and coffee roasters in Eureka Shop. F. 1868; Horace Partridge of Boston purchased bus. See also above.
— SHOP, THE: Bristol, North St. before 1837. Later known as "Blue Shop." (IBB)
EVANS, DAVID & ELIJAH: Baltimore. Adv. 1789. (Prime)
—, (S.) & FURNISS (Wm.): Newport, Del. Ca.1746. Tall clock so marked.
—, ALFRED: Kirkwood, N.Y. Ca.1850.
—, DAVID: Phila., 1770–1773. Baltimore, 1773–1784, where he adv. "At the sign of the arch dial and watch, Gay St. late of Phila." Nephew of David Rittenhouse; made Tall clock case for him. (Prime)
—, E.: Cincinnati, O. Adv. 1850. (Knittle)
—, HENRY: Newark, N.J. Ca.1850.
—, JAMES: Chenango Point, N.Y. Adv. 1821. (Cutten)
"—, JOHN": Used by Cornell Watch Co. Ca.1871.
—, JOHN: Charles Co., Md. 1754.
—, S.: Newport, Del. Ca.1746. Pos. belonged to same family as Oliver Evans, famous millwright and inventor. Name on Tall clock dial.
—, SEPTIMUS: Warwick, Pa. Ca.1810.
—, STEPHEN: Warwick, Pa. Ca.1810. (J. S. Bailey)
—, THOMAS: N.Y.C. Ca.1760.
—, WILLIAM M.: Cincinnati, O. Adv. 1850. (Knittle)
—, WILLIAM M.: Phila. Dir. 1813–1848.
EVARD, CHARLES C. (or E.): Phila. Dir. 1837.
EVENS, WM., JR.: Kensington, N.H. Ca. 1770. Blacksmith, also aw. in Purington Shop. (Ant. July 1948)
EVERMAN, JACOB: Lancaster, Pa. 1773 and later. Pos. Eberman.
EVES, WILLIAM: Cincinnati, O. Prob. Evans.
EYRE, JOHANN: Phila. n/d.
—, MATTHAIS: Phila. Adv. 1775. Made watch springs. Mentioned in adv. of John Wood 1775. (Prime)

FABER, GEORGE: Sumneytown and Reading, Pa. Aw. ca.1780. Tall clocks, No. 23 made in 1805 owned by William H.

Bergey, Sumneytown, Pa.; No. 13 owned by Louis A. Holton, Coatesville, Pa. (Abbott)
FABER, S.: New Bedford, Mass. Pos. Taber.
FABIAN, H.: Chester and Lancaster, Pa. S.C. Adv. 1853. Pos. from Charleston. (James)
FADELEY, J. M.: Louisville, Ky. Adv. 1842.
FAFF, AUGUSTUS P.: Phila. Dir. 1835.
FAHRENBACH, PIUS: Boston. Ca.1850.
FAINSTERN, J.: Boston. n/d. Watch Paper BCL Col.
FAIRBANKS, JOSEPH O.: Newburyport, Mass. Dir. 1860.
FAIRHAVEN CLOCK CO.: Fairhaven, Vt. Ca. 1891–1910. "Made lever escapement and also pendulum clocks. At peak, employed 400 workmen." (Burt)
FAIRMAN, GIDEON: 1774–1827. Newburyport, Mass. With William Hooker in Hooker & Fairman before 1810. Math. insts. Phila. 1810 in Draper, Murray, & Fairman, engravers.
FALES, G. S.: New Bedford, Mass. Ca.1820. (Abbott)
—, JAMES: New Bedford, Mass. 1810–1820. (Abbott)
—, JAMES, JR.: New Bedford, Mass. Ca. 1830.
"FARGO, CHAS.," used by Elgin National Watch Co. from 1872.
FARIS, CHARLES: 1764–1800. Adv. 1796, "Clocks and Watches." Aw. 1795–1800. Silver tea or coffee service in Metropolitan Museum of Art.
—, HYRAM: 1769–1800. Son and apt. of William. Tall clocks. Aw. ca.1790–1800. d. of yellow fever.
—, WILLIAM, JR.: 1762– ca.1815. Annapolis, Md. Apt. to father, Wm., Sr. Norfolk, Va., ca.1790; in Havana, Cuba, 1792–1794; Edenton, N.C., 1798. Marr. 1803. (LB)
—, WILLIAM, SR.: Phila. 1749; Annapolis, Md. 1757. Son of famous London C., William Faris, who d. 1728. Mother brought him to Phila. 1729, with several of his father's clocks. Aptd. to Peter Stretch in Phila. Many talents. Trained numerous apts. Skilled at cabinet designing, chair making, tulip growing, tavern keeping, dentistry, portrait painting. Best known as S. and C. Tall clocks have fine 8-day, one-month, and one-year brass

movts. with brass dials, some with musical attachments, beautiful cases. Adv. 1757, "Watchmaker from Phila., had a shop near the church next to Mr. Wallace's in Church St., Annapolis." Adv. 1759, "Procured a clockmaker." Adv. 1764, "Opened a tavern." Adv. 1770, "Clock and watch maker." Adv. 1791, "Death slightly exaggerated, in full health. Watch and Clockmaking." Adv. 1792, "looking glass factory for his son, Jr." Approximately 17 advs. Nine clocks in inventory of estate. Among apts. pos. Henry Flower of Phila., and William McParlin, who succeeded him. (LB)

FARMER, JOHN: Phila. "Watchmaker." Mentioned 1699 in will of Anne Cox. Pos. aw. 1693. (Prime)

—, M. G.: Salem, Mass. *Ca.*1849. Ex. Galvanic clock at Charitable Mechanics' Assn., Salem.

FARNHAM, HENRY & RUFUS: Boston. 1780. Bros. (Moore)

—, HENRY: Boston. *Ca.*1780. Apt. of Thomas Harland.

—, RUFUS: Boston. Aw. 1780. Apt. of Thomas Harland.

—, SAMUEL H.: 1813–. Oxford, N.Y. Adv. 1840–1842.

FARR & OLMSTEAD: Brandon, Vt. n/d. C. (BCL)

—, BELA: Norwich, N.Y. Adv. 1829.

—, JOHN: Utica, N.Y. Dir. 1834.

—, JOHN C.: Phila. Dir. 1824–1840.

FARRAR, C. & D.: Lampeter, Pa. n/d. Tall clock with applied carving under scroll top; case pos. by Jonathan Gostelowe. (FT)

FASBENDER, JOHN H.: Richmond, Va. *Ca.* 1819. Pos. Charleston, S.C., *ca.*1800.

FASIG, CONRAD: Reading, Pa. Late 18th and early 19th century. 4th Group. (Steinmetz)

FASOLDT (E. C.) MFG. CO. (H. J. T. HALSEY): Albany, N.Y. Dir. 1884. "Tower clocks, regulators and microscopes."

—, CHARLES: 1818–1898. N.Y.C., Albany, N.Y. b. Germany; to N.Y.C. 1849. W. Aw. *ca.*1850. To Albany 1861. Employed 50 on watch, clock, and precision work. Inventive; four patents; one on escapement improvement No. 44652 Mar. 7, 1865, others through 1877. Patent No.

6765991, model at Smiths. Inst. Tower clock at Centennial Exposition Phila. 1876. Son Otto. (Chamberlain)

FASOLDT, DUDLEY: Albany, N.Y. n/d. Son of Otto, grandson of Charles.

—, JOHN G.: Albany, N.Y. Dir. 1869.

—, MAX: Albany, N.Y. Dir. 1869.

—, OTTO H.: Albany, N.Y. Son of Charles. Son Dudley.

FATMAN, BROS.: Phila. Dir. 1843.

FATTON & CO.: Phila. Dir. 1840–1841.

—, FREDERICK: Phila. Dir. 1830–1839.

FAULKNER, JAMES: N.Y.C. *Ca.*1840.

FAVER, CHRISTIAN: Lampeter, Pa. n/d. Pos. Forrer.

FAVRE, JOHN JAMES: Phila. Dir. 1797.

FAY, HENRY: Albany, N.Y. *Ca.*1850.

FEDDERSEN, H. F.: Lancaster, Pa. *Ca.*1850.

FEHLINGER, SAMUEL: Gettysburg, Pa. Early 19th century. Tall clocks.

FELIX, J.: Columbia, Pa. *Ca.*1840.

FELLOWS, ABRAHAM: Troy and Waterford, N.Y. Adv. 1810–1850 and later. (BCL)

FELLOWS, I. W. & J. K.: Lowell, Mass. Dir. 1834 and later.

—, REED & OLCOTT: N.Y.C. Adv. 1829, "Fancy hardware, Watches, Jewelry, Watch Materials, Tools, etc." (Moore)

— (Louis) & SCHELL: N.Y.C., Maiden Lane. *Ca.*1856–1857 exclusive agency for sale of watches made in Waltham; lapsed with assignment 1857. Fellows "caught the watch factory fever" and started what became Newark Watch Co., first in N.Y.C., later Newark 1863. (Stephens)

—, STORM & CURGILL: N.Y.C. Adv. 1832. "Watches, Silverware, and fancy goods." (Moore)

—, IGNATIUS W.: Lowell, Mass. Dir. 1834.

—, JAMES: Kensington, N.H. *Ca.*1800. Son and apt. of Jeremiah. A few Tall clocks. (Ant. July 1948)

—, JAMES K.: Lowell, Mass. Dir. 1832–1834.

—, JEREMIAH, JR.: 1749–1837. Kensington, N.H. Purchased 1788 property of Puringtons. Enlarged workshop. Kept tavern, which burned 1876. Made some cases for own Tall clocks, other cases by Ebenezer Clifford, which sold for $25 more than his own. Sons took over blacksmith shop *ca.*1825. Excellent Tall clocks extant. One in Lewis Dyer Col. (Ant. July 1948)

FELTON, A. C.: Boston. *Ca.*1860.

FENLESTER, ALEXANDER: Baltimore, No. Calvert St. 1807.

FENN, WILLIAM B.: 1813–. Plymouth, Conn. Marr. 1864. Extensive maker of clock tablets for Conn. Cs. Employed women.

FENNO, JAMES: Lowell, Mass., "4 Cottage Road and Merrimac St." Dir. 1834–1837. Violet Watch Paper Bir. Col.

FERGUSON, ELIJAH: New Bern, N.C. Marr. 1833. Adv. 1845–1850, "Old North State Jewelry Store."

—, GEORGE: Phila. Dir. 1820–1822.

FERRIS, BENJAMIN C. & W.: Phila., 17–20 No. Second St. Dir. 1808–1811.

— (Benjamin) & McELWEE (J.): Phila. Dir. 1813.

FERRIS, —: Norwalk, Conn. "1889." Watch Paper Bir. Col.

—, BENJAMIN: Waterford, N.Y. Adv. 1811.

—, BENJAMIN C.: Phila., 1802–1811; Wilmington, Del., 1811–1813. Elder bro. of Ziba. Aptd. Phila., No. Second St. Pos. C. (Conrad)

—, EDWARD B.: Phila. Dir. 1846–1848.

—, ZIBA: 1786–1875. Wilmington, Del. Younger bro. and apt. of Benjamin in Phila. Marr. 1816. Aw. *ca.*1810–1850. Apts.: Ziba, Jr., Thomas J. Megear, William F. Rudolph, Charles Canby. Tall, Wall, Shelf clocks.

—, ZIBA, JR.: n/d. Apt. of father. (Conrad)

FERTIG, BENJAMIN: Phila. 1811. (Baillie)

—, JACOB: 1778–1823. Vincent, Pa., 1802–1808; Phila., 18 No. 4th St. Dir. 1810–1811. Patented "bellows mender." To Pikeland, Pa. 1815; also kept tavern there. (James)

FESSLER & SON, JOHN: Frederickton, Md. Early 19th century. Name on Tall clock owned by Mrs. Phillip Tillion, New Milford, Conn.

—, JOHN: –1820. Frederickton, Md. Aw. 1782–1820. "Used lantern pinion of early date." Succeeded by his son in 1820. (Crossman)

—, JOHN, JR.: Frederick, Md. Aw. 1820–1840.

FEST & BRO.: Phila. Dir. 1850 and later.

—, ALFRED: Phila. Dir. 1815 and later.

—, EDWARD: Phila. Dir. 1842 and later.

FETON, J.: Phila. 1828–1840.

FIELD, F., & Co.: Boston. n/d. Mahogany plain cased Banjo clock, original tablets, Flint Sale 1926.

— JOHN: Poughkeepsie, N. Y. Early 19th century. Brass founding; pos. clocks.

—, JOHN H.: Batavia, N.Y. Adv. 1811.

—, PETER: Hudson, N.Y., 1785; N.Y.C. 1802; Newburgh, N.Y. 1807–1810. Adv. 1795–1800.

—, PETER, JR.: 1802–1825.

FIFFE, H.: Pos. Tifft. n/p. *Ca.*1810. Banjo clock owned by E. J. Patterson, Phila.; another "in Mrs. Brownell Col. in 1911." (Moore)

FIFIELD, JOHN: Kingston and Kensington, N.H. 1758–1759. Blacksmith; one of buyers of Purington Shop; pos. C. only. (Ant. July 1948)

FILBER, JOHN: Yorktown and Lancaster, Pa. 1810–1825. Tall clock, enameled dial, mahogany case, owned by Mills-Schuyler family, Pelham, N.Y. (Abbott)

FINLEY, JOHN: Baltimore. C. Adv. 1754. (Prime)

FINNEY, JOHN: Charlestown, Md. Adv. 1754, "Living in Charlestown in Md. Makes and mends all sorts of clocks and watches in the best and cheapest manner and likewise makes and mends all sorts of gold and silverware." (Prime)

FISH, ISAAC: Utica, N.Y. Dir. 1843 and later.

—, ISAAC, JR.: Utica, N.Y. 1850 and later.

FISHER ELECTRIC CLOCK CO.: N.Y.C. Inc. Sept. 1896. (MFM)

—, GEORGE: Frederick, Md. Aw. early 19th century. Adv. 1800 for journeyman helper. Bro.-in-law Arthur Johnston, Hagerstown. (LSS)

—, GEORGE: Troy, N.Y. Dir. 1837–1846.

—, JOHN, SR.: –1808. York, Pa. b. Germany, Johannes Fischer; to Phila. with parents Oct. 4, 1749. Family d. of yellow fever. To York 1759. C., engraver, portrait painter, organ builder. Fine Tall clocks. Astro. Tall clock at Yale U.; another Tall owned by Dr. E. A. Glatfelter, York, Pa. Also pos. at Lampeter Sq., Pa., Tall clock, walnut case. The town's finest clockmaker. (Miss Jane Kell)

—, LOUIS: N.Y.C. *Ca.*1800.

FISK, SAMUEL: 1769–1797. Boston. Bro. William. Marr. 1794. Cabinetmaker. Aw. *ca.*1790–1797. (JWW)

—, WILLIAM: 1770–1844. Boston Neck. Son of Samuel and Abigail White Fisk. Marr. 1794. Pos. Apt. of some cabinetmaker in Roxbury. With bro. Samuel, till 1797. "Made nearly all of Simon Willard clock cases 1800–1834." Cases for Aaron and other Willards. Excellent reputation. Fine work; specialty furniture and clock cases, especially with inlay. After 1792 "next to Aaron Willard's." Bought 1798 "a lot of land with shop 40 × 20 next to Aaron Willard and a lot of land with dwelling house, barn, etc. next to the land of John Davis, Washington St., Boston Neck." Called "surveyor" in will. Large family. (JWW)

FISTER, AMON: Phila. Adv. 1794.

FITCH, EUGENE: N.Y.C. Patents Dec. 16, 1902. Four in all. Inventor of "Plato clock, a modern gadget clock with leaves with numbers on them turning to indicate the passing of time"; later made in Germany. Basic patent No. 733,180. (Coleman)

—, JOHN: 1743–1798. Inventor of the steamboat. b. Windsor, Conn. Apt. to Cheney Bros. *ca.*1763. At 21, brass worker. To Trenton 1769; worked for Matthew C. Lunn and others as S. Joined Continental Army as Lt. 1776. Captured by Indians, British prisoner at Detroit. Freed, to N.Y.C. 1782; Bucks Co., Pa., making buttons, spoons, etc. Experimented on steamboat engines 1783. Also an engraver. To France to sell steamboat idea. S. in Phila.; to Bardstown, Ky., *ca.*1789. S. mark, "J. F." or "I. F." Apparently no clockmaking. No clocks or watches extant. (LB)

—, JONAS: Pepperell, Mass. Late 18th century.

FITCHBURG WATCH CO.: Fitchburg, Mass. *Ca.*1874. "Discontinued after a few years without producing any watches." (Crossman)

FITE, JOHN: 1783–1818. Baltimore, 227 Baltimore St., 1807–1817. Lived 8 German St.

FITTS, GEORGE: Bangor, Me. *Ca.*1830–1860.

FITZ, WILLIAM: Portsmouth, N.H. *Ca.*1780 and later. Mass. Shelf clock, cherry case, described in N.Y. *Telegram* 1939. Mass. Shelf clock in Flint Sale 1926. From style of work pos. followed Simon Willard.

FIX, GEORGE: Reading, Pa. C. 1802 and later. Fourth group. Tall clock owned by S. S. Wisser, Ozone Park, N.Y. (Steinmetz)

—, JOSEPH: Reading, Pa. Early 19th century. (Steinmetz)

FLACH, GEORGE W.: 1818–1877. Charleston, S.C., 115 King St. From Hessen, Germany. Aw. *ca.*1840–1870.

FLAIG, E.: Danville, Ky. Aw. early 1860's. W. With Lapsley & Finck, J., who sold out 1865. Flaig started own business. (LB)

FLETCHER, CHARLES & THOMAS: Phila. Prob. Importers. 1830.

—, J. & S. W.: Phila. n/d.

—, CHARLES: Phila. Dir. 1817–1833. "Imports watches, jewelry, and mantel clocks."

—, THOMAS: Phila. Dir. 1814–1850 and later. Pos. D. and J. "Manufacture of jewelry and silverware and furnishings. Extensive assortment of watches and mantel clocks."

FLING, DANIEL: Phila., 97 No. 2nd St. Dir. 1809–1822. Pos. later at Mt. Holly, N.J.

FLOOD, WILLIAM: Phila. Dir. 1837.

FLOTO, WILLIAM: Phila. Dir. 1849.

FLOURNAY: Late 18th century Va. family of C. (MFM)

FLOWER, HENRY: Phila., 2nd St. near Chestnut. Adv. 1753–1775. "A watchmaker and fine cabinet work." Miss C. Stretch knows of Tall clock. Pos. movts. from Peter Stretch. (See ill. No. 38.)

FLOYD, THOMAS: Charleston, S.C., Church St. Adv. 1767, "Makes and cleans all sorts of clocks, also gunsmith. From London. Late from Mr. Smith's, Clockmaker, in Upper Moorfields, makes and cleans . . . including turret clocks." Adv. 1767–1770's.

FOLE, NATHANIEL: Northampton, Mass. Aw. 1819–1820. (Cutten)

FOLGER, PETER: Nantucket, Mass. 1617–1690. Grandfather of Walter, Jr. From Norwich, Eng., *ca.*1635. Seventh child, Abiah, was mother of Benjamin Franklin.

FOLGER, PETER (cont'd)

"Inventive, mechanical, and scientific, mastered Indian dialect, also surveyor, schoolmaster, and fine blacksmith. Could have repaired or made a better watch." Master of many trades. No timepiece known. (Stevens, *Nantucket*)

—, WALTER, JR.: Nantucket, Mass. 1765 1849. Fourth of 12 children. First cousin of Benjamin Franklin. Little schooling. "At age 22 he devised and built a Tall astronomical clock (most complicated domestic timepiece on record), gold ball for the sun rises and sets exactly at the right time each day, plus the place in the ecliptic and moon phases by a silver ball, and times of full tide for Nantucket. The calendar adjusted for leap year. Dials to record the year. It did everything but predict the weather." Exceptional C. and W. Self-taught. Practiced medicine and surgery, and inoculated for small-pox without charge. Engraved Bank of Nantucket bills. Lawyer; judge. Great scientific interest; invented and experimented. During War of 1812 set up factory at Nantucket for carding and spinning cotton and wool; power-driven looms. At General Court everything he wore came from own factory. Reflecting telescope *ca.*1818, finest in country. Discovered new spots on Venus. Indifferent about making money. Made clock oil. Kind to apts., fed them at home. A remarkable man. Daniel Webster said, "On the island of Nantucket met with a philosopher, mathematician, and astronomer in Walter Folger, worthy to be ranked among the great discoverers in science. He preferred to live quietly in his home town among his old friends." (Stevens, *Nantucket*)

FOLKROD, WILLIAM: Phila. Dir. 1849 and later.

FOLLET, MARVILL M.: Lowell, Mass. Dir. 1835.

FOLLETT, N. M.: Madrid, N.Y. 19th cent.

FOLMAR, ANDREW: N.Y.C. Early 19th century.

"FOOT, HOMER," used by N.Y. Watch Co. *ca.*1870.

FOOTE, CHARLES F.: Bristol. (tx) 1852– 1855. Bought in 1850 assets of Chauncey Boardman, operated his old clock factory few years.

FOOTE, WILLIAM: 1772–*ca.*1836. Middletown and East Haddam, Conn. Son of Charles and Jerusha Foote. With Samuel Canfield 1795 as Canfield & Foote; dissolved 1796. East Haddam "shop near the landing." Later to Mich. (Hoopes)

FORBACH, JOSEPH: N.Y.C. Dir. 1854.

FORBES & TUCKER: Concord, N.H. Hoadley type wood movt. label "1841," printed by "Asa McFarland, opposite State House, Concord, N.H."; case like David Dutton's of Mt. Vernon. N.H. Hist. Soc., "no record." (ALP) (Ant. Aug. 1946)

—, JOHN: Hartford, Conn. "A clock and watchmaker from Phila." Settled Hartford 1770, adv., "Set up a business of clock and watch making at the shop of Steven Taylor and will treat them in the best English manner with a three year guarantee," in reply to Lambier Lescoit, who announced his work guaranteed for three years. (Hoopes)

—, WELLS: Bristol, N.H.; Conn. Pos. in Forbes & Tucker. C. Clock paper *ca.* 1842. Wood movts.; one in J. P. Jackson Col.

FORD, GEORGE: Lancaster, Pa., West King St. Aw. 1811–1840. C.; surveyors' insts., compasses, etc.; R. At least 30 Tall clocks. Of English descent. Concentrated on instrument making. (Magee) (Bowman)

—, GEORGE II: Lancaster, Pa. Aw. 1840. Son and successor of George. Tall clocks. (Bowman) (Franks)

—, GEORGE H.: New Haven, Conn. 1850's. In Benjamin & Ford. Watch Paper BCL Col.

—, HENRY: Detroit, Mich. "Apprentice at watchmaking at age 16 to a Mr. Magill in 1871. Never lost his love of watchmaking. He originally planned about 1880 to produce a watch for 30¢." (Carl Mittman) (HAJ Jan. 1948)

—, HENRY O.: Athol Depot, Mass. n/d. Watch Paper BCL Col.

—, PETER: Lancaster, York, Pa. Aw. 1783– 1820. (Bowman)

—, SOUTHERLAND: Charleston, S.C. Adv. 1741, "From London." Adv. 1742, "Clocks and watches carefully mended and taken care of by the year. Clock-maker."

FORD, WILLIAM: Phila. Dir. 1848.

FORESTVILLE CLOCK CO.: Bristol. 1840's. Label in 30-hour brass movt. OG printed by Calhoun Co., Hartford.

FORESTVILLE CLOCK MANUFACTORY: Bristol. (tx) 1849–1853. One of J. C. Brown's trade names. Adv. 1851, "The Forestville Clock Manufactory, J. C. Brown, Proprietor. 8-day and 30-hour Marine clocks, 8-day OG carved top, round top, carved and plain, silver top carved and plain, 8-day Jenny Linds, Prince Alberts and Victorias, etc."

— HARDWARE CO.: Bristol. (tx) 1852–1853. Joint stock company, another operation of J. C. Brown, pres. Name changed 1853 to Forestville Hardware & Clock Co.

— HARDWARE & CLOCK CO.: Bristol. (tx) 1853–1855. J. C. Brown, pres. "100,000 clocks a year." Absorbed by E. N. Welch.

— MFG. CO.: Bristol. One of long line of continuous companies now Sessions Clock Co. Started with Ingraham (Elias) & Bartholomew (William C.) who made clock cases, 1831. Bartholomew, Brown, & Co., J. C. Brown having bought Ingraham interest, 1832–1834. Factory built in Forestville by J. C. Brown, Jared Goodrich, L. Waters, Chauncey Boardman, and William Hills of Plainville, as The Forestville Manufacturing Company. (tx) 1835–1839. Made brass 8-day movts., solid escape wheels, Empire cases; fine timekeepers. Became 1840 Hills, Brown & Co. Brown bought out Hills; became 1842 J. C. Brown & Co.; used "Forestville Mfg. Co." and "J. C. Brown" as labels, 1842–1849. One label, "Forestville Mfg. Co., J. C. Brown, S. B. Smith and C. Goodrich," on 8-day OG strap brass movt. Steeple Shelf clock, also "patent pending 1848" (Barny Col.). Some labels printed by "Wells Steam Press, 26 State St., Hartford." Other Forestville labels with other men's names. Became 1850 The Forestville Clock Manufactory Co., and 1853 the Company above. Name changed 1853 to Forestville Hardware and Clock Co. after fire. f. 1855. Purchased by E. N. Welch. Later became Sessions Clock Co. (Am. Col. Sept. 1947)

FORRER, CHRISTIAN & DANIEL: Newberry and Lampeter, Pa. Aw. 1754–1774. Tall clock, Backman case. (Lan. Co.)

—, CHRISTIAN: 1737–1738. Lampeter and Newberry, Pa. b. Switzerland. Bro. Daniel. C. Came to U.S., 1754. Aw. 1754–1783. To Pa. 1774. Ran ferry on Susquehanna River; farmer. (Lan. Co.)

— (not Farrar), DANIEL: Lampeter and Newberry, Pa. Ca.1755–1780. b. Switzerland. Bro. Christian. Tall clocks.

FORT DEARBORN WATCH AND CLOCK CO.: Chicago, Ill. 1918. (BCL)

FOSTER, N. & T.: Newburyport, 1820–1886. Bros.

—, GEORGE B.: Boston. Dir. 1842.

—, JOHN C.: Portland, Me. Dir. 1803–1804. (Moore)

—, JOSEPH H.: Bristol, Pa. n/d. Watch Paper Cramer Col.

—, NATHANIEL: Newburyport, Mass. 1797–1893. In charge of town clocks April 1818 to 1828. Bro. Thomas; together 1820–1886; aw. till age 89. (AJ June, July, 1950)

—, THOMAS: Newburyport, Mass. 1799–1887. Bro. Nathaniel; together 1820–1886.

—, THOMAS WELLS: Newburyport, Mass. Dir. 1860. With father in N. & T. Foster. (AJ, June, July, 1950)

FOURNIER, STANISLAUS: New Orleans, La. 1849. Made a public electric clock, operated by electric impulses from a master clock in his shop; powered by galvanic battery, hands moved each half minute.

FOUSTON, JOHN: N.Y.C. 1805. (MFM)

FOWELL, J. & N.: Boston. Dir. 1805–1809.

FOWLE, JOHN: Boston. Dir. 1805–1813.

—, J. H.: Northampton, Mass. Ca.1850.

—, NATHAN: Charleston, S.C. Ca.1840.

— (FOWELL), NATHANIEL: Boston. Dir. 1803.

FOWLER, JOHN C.: Boston. Dir. 1842. Lynn, Mass. 1847; Groton, Mass., 1849.

FOX, ARTHUR C.: Cherry Valley, N.Y. 19th century. Many Chrons., using both raw material and some English blanks. (Chamberlain)

—, ASA: Buffalo, N.Y. Ca.1810.

—, PHILETUS: Boston. Dir. 1842.

FOXCROFT (James A.) & CLARK (Gabriel): Baltimore, ca.1831–1839.

—, JAMES A.: Baltimore, 1839. Aw. 1822–1839. Apt. of Gabriel Clark; partner ca.1831–1839.

FRAGERCRANS, P.: Princeton, Ill. 1860's.

FRANCIS, FIELD & FRANCIS: Phila. n/d. Toy clocks.

— (Basil) & Vuille (Alexander): Baltimore. Adv. 1766. Pos. first recorded C. in Baltimore. (Abbott)

—, BASIL: Baltimore, Market St. Adv. 1768, "Watchmaker from London . . . makes, sells and repairs all sorts of watches." Pos. later in Albany, N.Y.

—, E.: Lee's Bridge, Va. n/d. C. (Burt)

FRANCISCUS, GEORGE, SR.: Baltimore. Ca. 1776–1791.

FRANCK, PHILIP: New Berlin, Pa. Tall clocks. Early 19th century.

FRANCONY, JACOB HAGEY: Listed in (FT), pos. Hagey.

FRANK (L.) & LICHTENAUER (M.): N.Y.C., 105 John St. Dir. 1854.

—, L.: N.Y.C., 17 Cortlandt St. Dir. 1872.

FRANKFIELD, A., & Co.: N.Y.C. Cuckoo clocks patented 1866. (BCL)

FRANKLIN & MARSHALL: Seneca Falls, N.Y. 1830's. Pos. Conn. movts. in Munger cases.

—, BENJAMIN: 1706–1790. Designed three-wheel clock. Model pos. by Edward Duffield, associate, or Gawen Brown of Boston; improved in Eng. by James Ferguson ca.1758. (Hoopes)

FRANKS, J. & S.: Phila. Dir. 1850 and later.

—, JACOB: Phila. Dir. 1845–1849.

FRANKSEN, B.: N.Y.C., 778 Ninth Ave. Dir. 1872.

FRARY, OBEDIAH: Southampton, Mass. C. Aw. 1745–1775. Made some good brass movts. for families and meeting houses. (Abbott)

FRASER, ALEXANDER: Menallin Twp., Pa. ca.1840.

—, JACOB: Phila. 1801–1877. Aw. ca.1822–1860.

—, WILLIAM: 1801–1877. Lincoln, near Ephrata, Pa. Aw. Phila. to 1821, also 1828; later New Holland, Pa. Apt. of Solomon Park in Phila. One of the older Cs. in continuous business in the U.S.

Aw. New Holland for Esterlie. Maker many fine Tall clocks. Grandsons successors. Pos. two William Frasers. (Lan. Co.)

FRAZER, ROBERT & ALEXANDER: Phila. before 1799; Paris, Ky., 1799. Robert to Lexington, Ky., 1799, Dir. 1818; Alexander after 1803. (LB)

—, H. N.: Vienna, N.Y. Adv. 1839.

—, SAMUEL: Baltimore, Ross and Anne Sts. Aw. 1822–1824 and later.

FRAZIER, WILLIAM: Phila. Dir. 1824. See "Fraser."

FREDONIA WATCH Co.: Fredonia, N.Y. Succeeded Independent Watch Co. 1884. Sold 1885 to Peoria Watch Co. Moved to Peoria, Ill. (Evans)

FREEMAN BROTHERS: Atlanta, Ga. Ca. 1850–1860.

—, D. M., & Co.: Atlanta, Ga. Succeeded J. P. Stevens Watch Co. Dir. 1885–1887.

—, HENRY B.: West Chester, Pa., Church St. Aw. 1857–1858 for T. H. F. Baldwin of Coatesville; 8-day clocks and bull's-eye watches. Watch Paper in Chester Co. Hist. Soc. (James)

—, WILLIAM: Baltimore. Ca.1810. Cabinet-maker and clockcases.

FREEPORT WATCH MFG. Co.: Freeport, Ill. Org. 1874, bought Rock Island Watch Co. assets; factory burned; discontinued 1875. "Produced no watches." (Evans) (Bowman)

FRENCH, CHARLES: Brattleboro and Rutland, Vt., before 1825. To Ohio, Adv. 1825, "Clockmaker from Vt." Aw. St. Albans, Del., Granville, O. With bro.-in-law Brace at Knowles Linnell's St. Albans, O. factory 1826. (Knittle)

—, JAMES ORMSBY: Baltimore. Adv. 1771.

—, LEMUEL: Boston. Ca.1790–1820. Tall clocks, inlay cases.

FRICK CLOCK Co., FRED: Waynesboro, Pa. Peculiar and complicated Shelf clock 17″ high, 46″ wide signed as above. Example in O. T. Lang Col. (James Gibbs)

FRIEND, ENGELL: N.Y.C. Middle 19th century. Brass founder.

—, GEORGE: N.Y.C. Ca.1820.

FRIES, JOHN & P.: Phila. Dir. 1837.

—, JOHN: Phila. Dir. 1830–1850 and later.

—, P.: Phila. Dir. 1839 and later.

FRINK, URBAN: Brattleboro, Vt. Ca.1880.

FRISBIE, L. & J., & Co.: Chittenango, N.Y. *Ca.*1840.

FRITZ, C.: Phila. Dir. 1848 and later. "Clock repairer." (Brix)

FROMANTEEL & CLARK: Providence, R.I. *Ca.*1710. Prob. English movt. in American case. (MFM)

FRONT, DANIEL: Reading. In (FT). Error for Jonathan Frost of Reading, Mass., in Pratt & Frost 1832–1835. (See Am. Col. Jan. 1948)

FROST, MERRIAM, & Co.: Bristol. Bought out Mitchell & Atkins 1836–1837.

— & MUMFORD: Providence, R.I. 1810. (Moore)

—, BENJAMIN: 1826–. Reading, Mass. Small 30-hour brass movt. spring driven Shelf clock *ca.*1850 owned by Mr. and Mrs. Charles Greenough, N.Y.C. Only reference in vital records, "Benjamin, son of Benjamin and Mary, b. June 28, 1826." Not in Eaton's history of Reading, Mass. (Grace J. Abbott)

—, JONATHAN: Reading, Mass. 1798–1881. Started spring of 1832 buying clocks and parts from Burr & Chittenden, Lexington, Mass. Partner Daniel Pratt, Jr., Reading 1832–1835. C. alone 1838–*ca.*1850. Looking glass Shelf clocks, wood movts. 30-hour, with and without alarm. (See ill. No. 207.) (Am. Col. Jan. 1948)

—, N. A.: Hanover, N.H. *Ca.*1885. W. J. at Dartmouth College.

—, OLIVER: Providence, R.I. *Ca.* 1800.

FRYE & SHAW: N.Y.C. Aw. *ca.*1830.

—, JACOB: Woodstock, Va. Tall C. (MFM)

—, JAMES: Haverhill, Mass., Main and Water Sts. Dir. 1853. Green Watch Paper, "40 Merrimack St., Watchmaker," in Bir. Col.

FRYER, PETER: Albany, N.Y., Dir. 1824–1825; Norwich, N.Y., 1828–1840. (Cutten)

FULLER & IVES: Bristol. On 1837 Conn. map as "Manufacturers." (Hill Clock House, Goshen, Conn.)

—, ARTEMAS: Lowell, Mass. *Ca.*1840–1850.

"—, ASA," used by United States Watch Co. *ca.*1870.

—, F. A.: Rutland, Vt. *Ca.*1830. Watch Paper BCL Col.

—, RUFUS: Francistown, N.H. n/d. White Watch Paper Bir. Col.

FULLER, THOMAS FRANKLIN: His death, Feb. 5, 1848, ended partnership of Birge (John) & Fuller. Son-in-law was Wallace Barnes.

FULTON WATCH Co.: Lancaster, Pa. Successor to Dudley Watch Co. 1923–1924. Inexpensive Swiss type bracelet watch, thin pallet escapement. f., building sold to J. F. Apple Mfg. Co., who made school jewelry. (Bowman)

—, JAMES: Shelby Co., Ky. Patent Dec. 30, 1835, for "Escapements for clocks."

FUNK, JACOB: Lebanon, Pa. *Ca.*1850.

FURNISS, SAMUEL: 1735–. New Castle, Md. Son of William. "At age 13 bound as apprentice to Benjamin Chandlee till age 21." (Chandlee)

—, WILLIAM: –1748. Newcastle Co., Del. Aw. *ca.*1740–1748. C. Father of Samuel. Tall clock marked on dial "S. Evans & Wm. Furniss, New Castle Co. Fecit." (Conrad)

FURNIVAL, JAMES: Marblehead, Mass. *Ca.* 1780.

FUSSELLI, PETER: Bowling Green, Ky. Adv. 1850, C. "from Italy"; to Italy 1877. In various Ky. firms. (LB)

FYLER, —: Torrington or Torringford, Conn. *Ca.*1830. Large 8-day wood movt. Shelf clock with this name.

—, ORSAMUS ROMAN: b. Newfield, Conn., Nov. 4, 1793. To Vermont; mfd. whetstones. Studied geology and chemistry; well versed in scientific subjects. Pos. to Conn. 1820's; later to Vt. Two patents: one from Chelsea, Vt., June 13, 1831, for "Wooden clocks"; another Bradford, Vt., Sept. 6, 1833, for "Escapements." Used by Riley Whiting on 8-day wood Shelf clocks. Label, "Fyler's Patent 8-day clocks / made and sold by / Riley Whiting." (Col. Mr. and Mrs. Francis D. Cooley, Windsor, Vt.) (Lane Kendall Fyler, Pittsfield, Mass.)

GAGE, HIRAM: Conn. or N.H. *Ca.*1842. n/p. Repaired old J. Masters Tall clock. (Mrs. B. K. Little)

GAILLARD, PETER: Reading, Pa. Tall clocks. Adv. 1794, "From France." Adv. 1798. (Steinmetz)

GAINES, JOHN: Portsmouth, N.H. 1800. (Moore)

GAINES, RICHARD: Patent with James Goodwin on "Balance Pendulum clocks," Baltimore, Jan. 22, 1806.

GAINEY, W. B.: Pendleton, S.C. Adv. 1859.

GALBRAITH, PATRICK: Phila., 286 Front St., 4 and 9 Dock St. Dir. 1794–1817. (Gillingham)

GALE, DANIEL JACKSON: 1830–1901. Bristol. b. Waitsfield, Vt. To Sheboygan Falls, Wis., June, 1855. Apt. to shoemaker; had shoeshop, in which completed Calendar clock Aug. 17, 1865, patented Nov. 16, 1869. Made by Welch, Spring Co. 1870 for royalty of $100. To Bristol April 12, 1871, aw. for Welch, Spring Co. for $2.25 for 10-hour day. Adv., "Inventor of the Best Calendar clock in existence. One of the most useful and important inventions of the age, elegant and beautiful article of great utility. Mfd. and for sale by the Welch, Spring Co., Forestville, Conn." (LB)

—, JAMES: 1791–. Salem, Mass., Neptune and Waters St. 1815–1819. Math. insts.

—, JOSEPH: Fayetteville, N.C. Pos. apt. of Peter Strong. In Lord & Gale 1792. Adv. 1798, "Low state of health, called for watches." (Cutten)

—, ROBERT: 1834–1896. Adv. Fish reels; prob. no clocks after Civil War. (LB)

GALIAY, JOHN P.: Boston. Dir. 1825.

GALLOME, C.: Baltimore, 19 Broad St. Dir. 1819.

GALPIN, MOSES: –1822. Bethlehem, Conn. "Not a maker but a peddler, though he put his name on clocks." Bought clocks from C. Jerome and others; went to La. to sell them, fall of 1821. Died there during winter. Jerome lost $740. (Jerome)

GALT, JAMES: Williamsburg, Va. Adv. 1766, "Plans to move to Shockhoe, near Richmond, Va."

—, PETER: 1777–1830. Baltimore. Aw. 1802–1830. Bro. Stirling. (Moore)

—, SAMUEL: Williamsburg, Pa. "1751."

—, STIRLING: Baltimore, 1802. Bro. Peter.

—, WILLIAM: Washington, D.C. Aw. ca. 1815–1840.

GANNET, AARON: Troy, N.Y. Dir. 1842–1844.

GARDINER (Barzillai) & McBRIDE (Andrew): Charlotte, N.C. Aw. ca.1810.

GARDINER, BALDWIN: N.Y.C., 149 Broadway. Aw. 1827–1835. Later in B. Gardner & Co. Aw. Phila. before 1827.

—, BARZILLAI: 1778–. Charlotte, N.C. Adv. 1807, "Moved from Guilford, to begin Watch and Clock making." G. S. Partner Andrew McBride. (Cutten)

—, JAMES P.: Columbia, Pa. Patent Dec. 5, 1843. "Sundial."

—, JOHN B.: Ansonia, Conn. "1857." (Moore)

GARLAN, JOHN R.: Greensboro, N.C. Adv. 1843; 1845, "Cleaned and repaired 742 watches." (Cutten)

GARNER, EDWIN T.: Utica, N.Y. Dir. 1842–1843.

GARRETT & HARTLEY: Phila. Dir. 1827.

—, PHILIP, & SON: Phila., 20 Strawberry Alley. Dir. 1828–1835. "Importers of watches, Mfger. J. S."

—, THOMAS C., & CO.: Phila. Dir. 1841 and later. Watch Paper BCL Col.

—, BENJAMIN: 1771–1856. Goshen, Pa. Aw. ca.1800–1825. C. to 1825. "Joiner" in tax records 1796. Cases for Tall clocks, native lumber; assembled English movts.; 17 Tall clocks known with "Benj. Garrett-Goshen" on dials: one brass dial, others painted iron. Farmer, operated grist mill, wool-carding machine; cabinetmaker; saw mill. (James)

—, PHILIP: Phila., 138 (144) High St. 1805–1816. Aw. 1801–1835. H. E. Gillingham, Phila. owns Tall clock dial so marked, belonged to great-grandfather, Joseph Gillingham, also silver spoons marked with this name. Dir., "Watchmaker." (Gillingham)

—, THOMAS C.: Phila. Dir. 1829–1840.

GARRISH, D. D.: Boston. Dir. 1854.

GARTNER, JACOB: Pa. Aw. 1790–1800.

GATES, ZACHEUS: Harvard and Charlestown, Mass. Aw. early 19th Cent. (See ill. No. 148.) Banjo and rocking ship Tall clocks. (Dr. W. S. Horton)

GAW, WILLIAM P.: Phila., 84 North Front St. Dir. 1816–1822.

GAYHART, S.: Camden, N.J. Aw. 1846–1849.

GAYLORD, C. E.: Chicago. Aw. ca.1850.

—, HOMER: Norfolk, Conn. Made clocks on father's farm in Norfolk till 1812; flood destroyed dam, moved to Homer, N.Y.

GEBHARD, R. L.: Aw. *ca.*1850. Maker of astro. C. (Dre.)

GEDDES, CHARLES: Boston, N.Y.C. 1776. Adv. 1773, "Clock and watch maker and finisher from London." Bracket clock at Edison Inst.

GEDDY, JAMES: Williamburg, Md. Adv. 1774, "Lost gold watch J. D. scratched inside case rim and watch paper in the bottom." (Prime)

GEER, ELIHU: Hartford, Conn. Printer. Made many labels for Conn. Shelf clocks. 26 State St., 1838–1847; 1 State St., 1847–1850; 10 State St., 1850–1856; 16 State St., 1856–1887. These addresses tend to give approximate date of manufacture of clocks. (Coleman) (Ingraham)

GEGYE, REME: Charleston, S.C., Elliot St. Adv. 1740, "Clock and watchmaker and mender."

GEHRING, JOHN G.: Baltimore, Ensor St. Aw. 1827–1831.

GEIGER, JACOB: Allentown, Pa. 1787–1790. To Md. Tall clock owned by Mrs. Joseph H. L. Ward, Upper Darby, Pa.

GEISSLER, C. A.: N.Y.C. 1899. Succeeded H. H. Heinrich, "Chronometers." Last Adv. 1903. (MFM)

GELSTON, GEORGE S.: N.Y.C., 189 Broadway. Aw. 1833–1837. Adv. 1833, "Orders left with Hugh Gelston of Baltimore particularly attended to." (FT)

—, HUGH: Baltimore. 1832. "Importer of watches." (FT)

GEMMEL, MATTHEW: N.Y.C. 1805. (Baillie)

GEMMILL, JOHN: Lancaster, Carlisle and York, Pa. *Ca.*1756–1760. Tall clocks. Walnut case, broken arch top, hood with rosettes, and bracket feet, brass movt. and dial with spandrels.

GENERAL ELECTRIC CO.: Bridgeport, Conn., Schenectady, N.Y. Electric clocks.

— TIME CORPORATION: N.Y.C. Successor to General Time Instruments Corp. 1949. (Darrot)

— TIME INSTRUMENTS CORP.: N.Y.C. 1930–1949. Merger of Seth Thomas Clock Co., Western Clock Co., and others.

GERBIE, CHARLES: Atlanta, Ga. Dir. 1871. (MFM)

GERDING & SIMEON: N.Y.C. 1832. "Importers of mantelpiece clocks." (Moore)

GERE, ISAAC: 1771–1812. Northampton, Mass. b. Preston, Conn., son of Nathan. W. S. Aw. 1793. (Cutten)

GEROULD, S. A.: Keene, N.H. *Ca.*1825. Watch Paper BCL Col.

GERRISH, OLIVER: Portland, Me. *Ca.*1826–1834. Hill Jewelry Co. owns Banjo clock with Curtiss type hands, "patent" on waist tablet; Box tablet Italian scene; good movt., knife-edge pendulum suspension, dead beat escapement.

GERWICH, H.: Hartford, Conn. n/d. Watch Paper BCL Col.

GERY, HERMAN: Phila. Dir. 1804 and later.

GETZ, PETER: Lancaster, Pa. Aw. 1791–*ca.*1820. David Rittenhouse called him an ingenious workman.

GIBBONS, THOMAS: Phila., Front St. Adv. 1751, "From London, makes and mends." (Prime)

—, THOMAS: Boston, 1739. Cabinetmaker only. Partner Leneir Kenn.

—, WILLIAM: Phila. n/d.

GIBBS, BENJAMIN: Newburyport, Mass. *Ca.*1820.

—, JAMES: Phila. Dir. 1847. Watch Paper James Gibbs Col.

GIFFORD, S. K.: Camden, S.C. Adv. 1836. W. J.

GIFFT, PETER: Kutztown, Pa. *Ca.*1810 and later. Fourth group. (May be GRIFFT.) (Steinmetz)

GILBERT CLOCK CO., WILLIAM L.: Winsted, Conn. 1871–1934.

— CLOCK CORP., THE WILLIAM L.: Winsted, Conn., Laconia, N.H. 1934–.

—, JORDAN & SMITH: N.Y.C. Dir. 1832. (Moore)

— MFG. CO.: Winsted, Conn. 1866–1871. Joint stock company, Gilbert, Woodruff, George B. Owen, Noah S. Pond. First company brick building, built 1825 by Riley Whiting, burned 1871, with loss of all company records.

— (Wm. L.), MARSH (George), & CO.: Farmington, Conn. 1830–1835. Square case, side painted columns, painted and stenciled top. Flint Sale 1926.

—, RICHARDS & CO.: Chester, Conn. 1830's. (Moore)

—, J. F.: Rochester, N.Y. 1830. Mfr. "Patent Improved Looking Glass Clocks." Pos. Conn. movts.

GILBERT, JESSE: Brooklyn, N.Y. Dir. 1843.
—, JESSE: Brooklyn, N.Y. *Ca.*1840.
—, T.: Atlanta, Ga. Dir. 1867. (MFM)
—, WM. L: Winsted, Conn. *Ca.*1850–1866. With Lucius Clarke and Ezra Baldwin, org. Clarke, Gilbert & Co. 1841; weight-driven brass movt. Shelf clocks. *Ca.*1850 bought out partners; took into business bro.-in-law Isaac B. Woodruff, using this label.
—, WILLIAM LEWIS: 1806–1890. Farmington, Bristol, Winsted, Conn. School teacher. To Bristol 1828 with bro.-in-law, George Marsh as "Marsh & Gilbert." Farmington, Conn. 1830–1835. Also Bristol 1828–1834. With John Birge as Birge, Gilbert & Co. in Bristol 1835–1837, successors to Birge, Case & Co. In Jerome, Gilbert, Grant & Co. 1839–1840; 30-hr. brass weight movt. clocks. To Winsted (Winchester) Conn., 1841 with Lucius Clarke in Clarke, Gilbert & Co., which *ca.*1850 became Wm. L. Gilbert Co. to 1866. Then Gilbert Mfg. Co. to 1871. Then William L. Gilbert Clock Co. to 1934. Then William L. Gilbert Clock Corp., continuing in business today. Gilbert made fortune as C.
GILES, WALES, & CO.: N.Y.C. n/d. Watch Paper BCL Col.
—, JOSEPH: Trenton, N.J. 1800–1820. Adv. 1804, "Moved to Market St." (MFM)
GILL, CALEB: Hingham, Mass. 1785. (Moore)
—, ISAAC: Charleston, S.C. Patent "Marine timekeeper" Jan. 15, 1810.
—, LEAVITT: Hingham, Mass. Late 18th century. (Moore)
GILLIAM, EDWARD: Pittsburgh, Pa. *Ca.*1830.
GILLMAN, —: Hallowell, Me. n/d.
GILMAN, B. C.: Exeter, N.H. *Ca.*1790–1830. Tall, Wall, and Shelf clocks. (Burt)
—, JOHN: Kensington, N.H. Blacksmith, pos. C. Shop at Eastman's corner, sold to Reuben Swain. (Ant. July 1948)
—, JOHN H.: Portsmouth, N.H. n/d. Watch Paper BCL Col.
—, THOMAS: Mass. or N.H. Name found under name plate of Haverhill Hist. Soc. Blaisdell clock, ill. No. 27. (Mrs. J. B. Mason)
GILMARTIN, JOHN: Augusta, Ga. *Ca.*1820.
GILMORE, WILLIAM: Pittsburgh, Pa. *Ca.*1830.

GILMUR, BRYAN: Phila. *Ca.*1800. Insts.; pos. clocks.
GIRARD, A.: Mobile, Ala. 1849. Invented altitude recorder and sun transit.
GIRAUD, VICTOR: N.Y.C. Dir. 1847. (Moore)
GLADMAN & WILLIAMS: N.Y.C. Aw. 1764.
GLEASON, F. A.: Rome, N.Y. Adv. 1848. (Cutten)
GLIGEMAN, —: Reading, Pa. 1784. May be Klingerman, A. (FT)
GLOBE CLOCK CO.: Milldale, Conn. Patent Jan. 8, 1883, on Globe clock. 8-day brass movt. by Laporte Hubbell & Son, Bristol; 9″ globe, height 18″, cast iron base; name on outer belt, patent date on brass ring; minutes indicated on chapter ring at North Pole, hours on inner equatorial belt; hour hand on bowed rod; showed time on any part of globe. Prob. not many made; one in F. B. Platt Col.
GLORE, —: N.H. *Ca.*1830. (Dre.)
GLOVER, EDWIN: Fayetteville, N.C. Adv. 1843, "Continued to repair watches and jewelry." (Cutten)
—, HENRY: Brooklyn and N.Y.C. Dir. 1846.
—, WILLIAM: Boston. Dir. 1818–1825.
GOBEL, HENRY: N.Y.C. Dir. 1853.
GOBRECHT, DAVID: Hanover, Pa. Aw. 1798–1817. Tall clock owned by Mrs. D. Gilbert Houck, New Oxford, Pa.
—, ELI: Pa. Early 19th century. Tall clocks.
—, JACOB: Pa. Early 19th century. Tall clocks.
"GODDARD & CIE., D. & P.," used by Luther Goddard on watches *ca.*1809–1817.
"—, & CO., I-L.," used *ca.*1809–1817 by Luther Goddard. (See ill. Nos. 289, 290.)
—, (GEORGE S.) & GRUBB (William, Jr.): Boston. Dir. 1816.
"—, L. & P.," used by Luther Goddard on watches *ca.*1809–1817.
"—, L. & SON," used by Luther Goddard on watches *ca.* 1809–1817.
—, GEORGE S.: Boston. Dir. 1816–1825.
—, JOHN: 1723–1785. Newport, R.I. Aw. 1748–1785. Celebrated cabinetmaker and joiner. With Townsend created Block Shell. John Townsend bro.-in-law. Marr. Hannah, daughter of Job Townsend 1746. (See ill. Nos. 20–22.)

GODDARD, JOHN: 1789–1843. Newport, R.I. Bridge and Second Sts. Grandson of first John. Cabinetmaker.

—, LUTHER: 1762–1842. Shrewsbury, Mass. Responsible for first quantity production of watches in America. Preacher and evangelist. Pos. training with Willards in Grafton. Set up small shop, Shrewsbury, 1809. Europe-trained helpers. Tariff restrictions favorable, imports blocked by "Jefferson Embargo"; imports flooded market again, 1815. Production ended by 1817. Ca.500 watches made. Names on movts., "L. Goddard & Son," "L. & P. Goddard," "D. P. Goddard & Cie." Pos. foreign-made or assembled with foreign parts. No. 155 ill. Nos. 289, 290. As described by owner Frank Bogenrief, Hinton, Iowa, the outside diameter of case is 2$\frac{3}{16}$", verge and fuzee type, and appears to be on the order of the English make of this period. The American Eagle and Shield are engraved on the balance cock. The hour hand is like the type prevalent on wood movt. Shelf clocks. No hall mark on the case. According to George V. White, Wollaston, Mass., there are few Goddard watches before 1812. To Worcester, Mass., ca. 1817; resumed preaching, continued repair W. and C. Died aged 80.

—, STEPHEN: –1804. Newport, R.I. Fourth son of first John. Aw. with and succeeded father. With bro. Thomas, fifth son.

—, NICHOLAS: 1773–1823. b. Shrewsbury, Mass. Northampton, Mass., 1794–1797, Rutland, Vt., 1797–1823. Partner in Lord & Goddard. Excellent clockmaker. Made Tall clocks, brass movts., some musical; clock dials; pos. made first American watch; no watches extant.

GODFREY, THOMAS: 1704–1749. Phila. Aw. ca.1730–1749. Invented improved Davis quadrant or stack Staff, popular with English seamen in 16th century. Great mathematician; also glazier. Pos. C. (Gillingham)

—, WILLIAM: –1763. Phila. Aw. 1750–1763.

GODSHALK, JACOB: No. Ward, Phila.; Kowamencin, Pa. C. Adv. 1771, pos. earlier. Tall clock owned by Harry G. Kauffman, Jr., Waynesboro, Pa.; Chippendale broken-arch hood, walnut case, 8-day brass movt.; two weights. Tall clock owned by W. H. Richter, Bethlehem, Pa. (Gillingham)

GODSOE, B. F.: N.Y.C. Dir. 1848.

GOELTZ, HENRY: N.Y.C. n/d. Watch Paper BCL Col.

GOEWEY, P. F.: Albany, N.Y. Aw. 1855–1880.

GOFF, CHARLES: n/p. n/d. Pos. Hoff.

"GOLDEN GATE," used by Otay Watch Co. 1889. (Chamberlain)

GOLDER, JOHN: N.Y.C. Aw. ca.1810.

GOLDSBURY, —: St. Albans and Granville, O. Adv. 1828. With French & Brace. (Knittle)

GOLDSMITH & Co.: Salem, Mass. Ca.1850. Pos. D. Wm. Chase, Caleb Newcomb, Nat'l Goldsmith, James Fairless.

GOLDSTONE, B.: Phila. Dir. 1839.

Goletiel, S.: Lancaster, Pa. Aw. ca.1850–1860. (J. L. Ruth)

GOODELL, DAVID: Pomfret, Conn. Late 18th century. Made Tall clock for Aaron Stevens owned by John Grosvenor, Pomfret, Conn.

GOODFELLOW & SON: Phila. Dir. 1799.

—, WILLIAM, & Co.: Phila., ca.1795–1815. (Baillie)

—, JOHN: Boston. Dir. 1800–1803.

—, WILLIAM: Phila., 64 Dock St. Dir. 1793–1818.

—, WILLIAM, Jr.: Phila. Dir. 1799.

GOODHART, JACOB: Lebanon, Pa. Early 19th century.

GOODHUE, D. T.: Providence, R.I. 1824. (Baillie)

—, RICHARD S.: Portland and Augusta, Me. 1830's. (MFM)

GOODING, ALANSON: New Bedford, Mass. Ca.1810–1840.

—, HENRY: Boston, and pos. Duxbury, Mass. Ca.1815. Boston Dir. 1820–1842.

—, JOHN: Plymouth, Mass. Pos. early 19th century. Watch Paper John Gooding, Jr., N.Y.C.

—, JOSEPH: Dighton and Fall River, Mass. Early 19th century. Name on dial of Tall clock owned by Gerald Donovan, N.Y.C.

—, JOSEPHUS: Bristol, R.I. Ca.1820.

—, JOSIAH: 1788–1867. Dighton, Mass., and Bristol, R.I. Boston. Dir. 1842. Made 25 Tall clocks.

GOODMAN, JOHN: Cleveland, O. *Ca.*1850.
—, THOMAS: –1738. Charleston, S.C. Adv. 1733, "From London." (Prime)
GOODRICH, CHAUNCEY: Bristol and Forestville, Conn. Aw. *ca.*1828–1857. Before 1830 in Ingraham & Goodrich, with J. C. Brown 1845–1847, in Smith & Goodrich 1847–1852, later alone. (See ill. No. 257.)
—, JARED: Bristol. In Forestville Mfg. Co., 1835–1839. In Hills, Goodrich & Co., Plainville, Conn. 1841–1845.
GOODSPEED, LOT: Middletown, Conn. *Ca.* 1820–1830. Pos. made cases and used Samuel Terry movts. (LB)
GOODWIN & DODD: Hartford, Conn., Main St. Adv. 1816, "Clock and watchmaker's tools." (J. H. Thompson)
— & FRISBIE: Unionville, Conn. *Ca.*1830–1850.
—, E. O.: Bristol, Queen and Goodwin Sts. (tx) 1852–1855. C., made cases; bought movts. from Matthews & Jewell and others. Adv. 1851. Small 8-day Shelf clocks, Empire cases. "Traveling Agent" for Forestville Clock Mfg. Co. (Am. Col. Sept. 1947)
—, HENRY: Boston. Dir. 1820–1821.
—, HORACE, JR.: Hartford, Conn. *Ca.* 1830–1840. Pos. D.
—, JAMES: Baltimore. Patent with Richard Gaines on "Balance Pendulum Clocks" January 22, 1806.
—, SAMUEL: Baltimore. Patent on "Balance Pendulum Clocks" July 7, 1809, different from James Goodwin patent.
—, SAMUEL: Phila. Dir. 1820–1822.
—, V. C. (V. O.): Unionville, Conn. 1830's. Made cases and assembled clocks; pos. case maker only. (LB)
—, WALLACE: Attleboro and North Attleboro, Mass. 1850's. Banjo clocks Howard type, wood bezels, no side arms, wood, also black and gold painted glass tablets; height *ca.*28"; good timekeepers.
—, WILLIAM: Hartford, Conn. n/d. (FT)
GORDON, ALBERTUS S.: –1920. Laconia, N.H. R. J. Nephew and successor (1883) of Richard Gove. (A. L. Childs)
—, GEORGE: Phila. Dir. 1847 and later.
—, GEORGE I: N.Y.C., 335 Hudson St. Dir. 1854 and later.
—, SMYLEY: Lowell, Mass., Merrimack St. Dir. 1832. "Made watchcases."

GORDON, THOMAS: N.Y.C. Adv. 1758, "Watchmaker from London, cleans and repairs." Adv. 1758, "Moved to the shop of Mr. Histier in Hanover Sq. adjacent to Wall St." Pos. Boston as "Goron." (Prime)
GORGAS: Family of Pa. C. Many fine Tall clocks. John is first generation, Jacob and Benjamin his sons; third generation Joseph and Solomon, fourth generation William. (Lan. Co. and others)
—, BENJAMIN: Ephrata, Pa. Aw. late 18th century. Son of John, bro. Jacob. Second generation.
—, JACOB: 1728–1789. Ephrata, Pa. Aw. 1763–1798. One of earliest and best known Tall Cs. Marr. 1763. *Ca.*150 brass movt. 8-day and 30-hour Tall clocks. Second generation.
—, JOHN: Germantown, Pa. Aw. *ca.*1720–1760. Marr. Sophia Rittenhouse. Father of Jacob and Benjamin. First generation. Pos. taught David Rittenhouse.
—, JOSEPH: 1770–. Ephrata, Pa. Aw. 1791–1816 and later. Son of Jacob. To Running Rumps near Elizabethtown, Pa. 1816. Third generation.
—, SOLOMON: 1764–1838. Ephrata, Pa. Aw. 1785–1800. Son of Jacob; with bro. Joseph in father's business. To Cumberland Co., Pa. *ca.*1800. Third generation.
—, WILLIAM: Greensburg, Pa. Aw. *ca.*1850. Tall clocks. Fourth generation.
GORHAM, BROWN & CO.: Providence, R.I. n/d. Watch Paper BCL Col.
—, CHARLES L.: Barre, Mass. n/d. Name on dial Tall clock.
GORON, THOMAS: Boston. Adv. 1759, "From London . . . sells all kinds Timepieces."
GOSLER, GEORGE ADAM: York Co., Pa. Early 19th century.
GOSTELOWE, JONATHAN: 1744–1806. Phila., Church Alley; later 66 Market St. Exquisite furniture and Tall clock cases. Marr. niece of Edward Duffield, C.; prob. made some of his cases.
GOTSCHALK, JACOB: Phila. *Ca.*1770. Tall clocks owned by H. G. Kauffman, Jr., Waynesboro, Pa., and Ludlow Strong, N.Y.C.
GOTSHALK, HENRY: New Britain, Pa. *Ca.* 1760. Tall clocks.

GOTTIER, FRANCIS: Charleston, S.C. *Ca.* 1750.

GOULD, ABIJAH: Nashua, N.H. Early 19th century. Rochester, N.Y. *ca.*1830. Patent from Henrietta, N.Y., on "Clocks" Oct. 1, 1830. Adv. 1834, "To be found at Starr's Cabinet Shop." Dir. 1841.

—, JAMES: Baltimore. Dir. 1842.

GOVE, Richard: –1883. Laconia, N.H. Aw. 1833 Meredith Bridge. J. W. Watch with name on dial owned by Andrew L. Childs, N.Y.C.

GOVETT, GEORGE: Phila. Dir. 1811–1819. Prob. Norristown, Pa., 1820–1841.

GOWAN, PETER D.: Charleston, S.C. *Ca.* 1820.

GRAFF, JACOB: Lancaster, Pa. *Ca.*1775. Tall clocks owned by Lewis E. Yirget, Sheridan, Pa.; M. P. Van Buren, N.Y.C.; Mrs. John Harrison, Merion, Pa. (Orr)

—, JOSEPH: Allentown, Pa. *Ca.*1800. Partner Jacob Blumer. (Roberts)

GRAFFENBERG, THOMAS: n/p. n/d. Wood movt. Tall clock extant.

GRAHAM & Co.: n/p. n/d. Shelf clock Essex Inst.

—, DANIEL: N.Y.C. 1805. (Baillie)

—, MITCHELL: Phila. Dir. 1837.

—, WILLIAM: Phila. Adv. 1733.

GRANT & MATTHEWS: Bristol. (tx) 1841. Pos. C.

—, ALFRED: New Haven, Conn. *Ca.* 1850.

—, ISRAEL: St. Louis, Mo. *Ca.*1820.

—, JAMES: Hartford, Conn. Aw. 1794. C. London-trained. Adv. 1795, "Clock and watchmaker from London, but now mender and repairer." To Wethersfield, 1796; R. W. C (Hoopes)

—, JAMES: Albany, N.Y. Adv. 1789.

—, WILLIAM: Boston. Aw. 1815–1830. Banjo clock ill. No. 145.

GRAV ELECTRIC CLOCK CO.: N.Y.C., 177 Broadway. Adv. 1899. (MFM)

GRAVES, ALFRED: Willow Grove, Pa. 1845. (Moore)

GRAY (DeMory) & ALDER (W. D.): N.Y.C. 1868 and later. Succeeded George C. A. Baker. Chrons. (BCL)

—, JAMES: N.Y.C. *Ca.*1840.

GREEN, J.: Albany, N.Y. Adv. 1797–1798.

—, JOHN: Boston. Dir. 1796.

—, JOHN: Phila. Dir. 1794, 1796.

—, JOHN: Carlisle, Pa. Early 19th century.

GREEN, SAMUEL: Boston. Dir. 1820.

—, SAMUEL, JR.: Boston. Dir. 1825.

—, WILLIAM: Milton, (?). n/d. Old one-hand Wag-on-Wall clock owned by W. L. Robinson, Kingston, N.Y. Eight William Greens listed by Baillie in England, none located in Milton.

GREENAWALT, WILLIAM: Halifax, N.C. Adv. 1826. W. C.

GREENLEAF, DAVID, JR.: 1765–1835. Hartford, Conn. Apt. of Thomas Harland. Aw. 1788. Some clocks before 1796. Adv. May, 1796, Found it difficult to carry on a number of lines and to confine work to watch repair. With Frederic Oaks as Greenleaf & Oaks, 1804, J. Dealings with Harland till Harland's death 1807. Pos. sold Harland Tall clocks in Hartford; adv. clocks for sale long after gave up making. Dentistry, 1811. (Hoopes)

GREENOUGH, NORMAN CUMMINGS: 1820–1866. Newburyport, Mass. b. Lebanon, N.H. Chronometer watches and nautical insts. Fine W. Frank B. Kenrick was Apt. (Chamberlain) (Britten) (AJ July, 1950)

GREENWICH CLOCK & INSTRUMENT CO.: N.Y.C. Org. 1888. Succeeded by Shrewsbury Clock Co. 1935. (Phillipse Greene)

GREER, JOHN: –1774. Carlisle, Pa. "Watch and clockmaker."

GREGG, JACOB: Alexandria, Va. Aw. *ca.*1810–1820. Uncle of William Gregg, successful W. Mfr. spinning machinery. *Ca.*1821 to Ga. with William Gregg, estab. one of first cotton factories in South. (LB)

GREINER, CHARLES: Charleston, S.C. *Ca.* 1780.

GREISHABER, E.: Louisville, Ky. *Ca.*1840. (LB)

GRIBBEN, —: Belfast, Me., 15 High St. n/d. Gray Watch Paper Bir. Col.

GRIDLEY, L. P. & C. E.: Logansport, Ind. *Ca.*1860.

—, F. R.: Attica, Ind. n/d. Watch Paper BCL Col.

—, MARTIN: Logansport, Ind. *Ca.*1840.

—, TIMOTHY: Sanbornton, N.H. *Ca.*1808. C. with Messrs. Peck and Holcomb; sold out to Col. Simeon Cate. Mrs. James Connor painted and lettered dials for them.

GRIFFEN & HOYT: N.Y.C. *Ca.*1820–1830.
—, HENRY: N.Y.C. and Brooklyn. Aw. 1793–1818.
—, PETER: N.Y.C. *Ca.*1810.
—, W.: Atlanta, Ga. Dir. 1871.
GRIFFITH, EDWARD: Litchfield, Conn. Late 18th century. Adv. 1790, "From London, makes plain watches and clocks." Later adv. for two apprentices. Shortly after to Savannah, Ga., adv. 1796 as watchmaker. (Hoopes) (Prime)
—, L.: Phila. Dir. 1842–1843.
—, OWEN: Names reversed; see Owen.
—, SAMUEL: Phila. Dir. 1847.
GRIFFITHS, JAMES: Glens Falls, N.Y. Adv. 1836.
—, JOHN: Greenville, S.C. Adv. 1855, "Long experience in Europe."
GRIFFT, PETER: Kutztown, Pa. *Ca.*1810 and later. Brass movt. 8-day Tall clock, cherry case, name on dial, owned by Mrs. F. P. Donatelli, Allentown, Pa. (Steinmetz)
GRIGER, JACOB: Pa. n/d. (Steinmetz)
GRIGGS, EBENEZER: Bristol. (tx) 1810 "clockmaker."
—, SOLOMON: Bristol. (tx) 1810. C.
GRILLEY, SILAS: Waterbury, Conn. In Abel, Porter & Co. 1808. (Hist.)
GRIM, GEORGE: Orwigsburg, Pa. *Ca.*1820. Tall clocks. (Orr)
GRISWOLD, A. B., & Co.: New Orleans, La. *Ca.*1850–1860.
—, CHAUNCEY D.: Troy, N.Y. Dir. 1838–1839.
—, DANIEL WHITE: 1767–1844. East Hartford, Conn. Aw. *ca.*1788–1800. Son of White and Elizabeth Cheney Griswold, nephew of Benjamin and Timothy Cheney. Apt. of Timothy *ca.*1782. Four Tall clocks extant, wood movt. engraved brass dials. Trader between N.Y.C. and Boston; also owned powder mill. (Hoopes)
—, H. D. C.: Framingham, Mass. n/d. (BCL)
—, JOAB: Buffalo, N.Y. Dir. 1835.
GROFF, AMOS: Rawlinsville, Pa. *Ca.*1850.
GROPENGIESSER, J. L.: Phila. Dir. 1841 and later. Tall clock owned by E. F. Luppe, Reading, Pa., one weight, 30-hour movt., square top hood, dial 12″ square, seconds hand above VI. (Moore)

GROSCH, SAMUEL: Marietta, Pa. Early 19th century. Lumber merchant, not recorded as C.
GROSH, PETER LEHN: Lan. Co., Pa. Adv. 1830. Portrait painter, Clock dials. Not C. (Lan. Co.)
GROTZ, ISAAC: Easton and Bethlehem, Pa. 1810–1835. (Abbott)
GROUT, WILLIAM: Phila. Dir. 1816.
GROVE, CHRISTIAN: Heidelberg Twp., Pa. *Ca.*1800. Tall clocks.
—, WILLIAM: Hanover, Pa. Aw. 1830–1857. Tall clocks, one owned by Mrs. N. F. Derry, Westfield, N.J., dated 1837.
GRUBB, WILLIAM, JR.: Boston. Dir. 1816–1818. Partner with Goddard. (Baillie)
GRUBY, EDWARD L.: Portland, Me. Dir. 1834.
GRUEN, D., & SONS: Cincinnati, O. 1890–1898; became D. Gruen Sons & Co. Also operates Gruen Watch Case Co.
— & SAVAGE: Columbus, O. Aw. 1879–1882. Succeeded by Columbus Watch Co. (MFM)
GRUEZ, JOHN: N.Y.C. Dir. 1821. Cabinet worker, succeeded S. Lannuier. Not C.
GRUMBINE, DANIEL: Hanover and East Berlin, Pa. 1824–1850.
GUILD, JEREMIAH: Cincinnati, O. *Ca.*1831.
—, JOHN: Phila. Dir. 1818–1824. Name spelled various ways.
GUIMERIN, T. J.: Atlanta, Ga. Dir. 1871. (MFM)
GUINARD, F. E.: Baltimore. *Ca.*1810.
GULICK, NATHAN: 1777–1826. Easton, Pa. Aw. *ca.*1800–*ca.*1818. C. S. Son of Samuel, pos. C. Marr. Elizabeth Erb. To Maysville, Ky., 1818. Tall clock, cherry case, owned by Mrs. Shirk, Harrisburg, Pa. (Mrs. W. W. Wiess, Maysville, Ky.)
—, SAMUEL: 1756–1825. Northampton, Pa. Father of Nathan. Tall clock known, "S. Gulick" on dial.
GUNKLE, JOHN: Ephrata, Pa. Aw. 1830–1840. Pos. Kunkle. German descent, good maker Tall clocks. (Lan. Co.) (Baillie)
GURNEY, L. F.: Bridgeport, Conn. *Ca.*1870.
GUYER, BENJAMIN: Phila. Dir. 1848.

HAAS, JOHN, & Co.: N.Y.C., *ca.*1825. Musical Clockmakers.

HAAS & GOETZ: N.Y.C. *Ca.*1820–1830.

—, GOTTLIEB: Red Hook, N.Y. *Ca.*1830. (Arthur Stout)

—, JAMES A.: Phila. Dir. 1846–1849.

—, N.: –1796. Phila. Dir. 1846 and later.

HACKER, MICHAEL: –1796. Tewksbury, N.J., Germantown, Pa. *Ca.* 1757. Moravian. Tall 8-day clocks marked "New Germantown," "Tewksbury." One owned by D. Cameron Smith, Chicago.

HADDER, WILLIAM: Phila. Dir. 1837.

HADLEY BROS. & ESTELL: Chicago, 41 Madison St. Patent on Estell's program regulator January 11, 1870. Example Mitchell Col.

HAETTICH, ANDREW: Cleveland, O. *Ca.*1850.

HAGEY: Pa. Family for three generations made many Tall clocks. Samuel; son Jacob; Jacob's sons, George, John, Jonas. Also spelled Hage, Hege, Heagey. (Steinmetz)

—, GEORGE: –1850. Trappe, Pa., Sterling, O. Most noted of the family. Third generation.

—, JACOB: Lower Salford Twp., Pa., until 1831. Aw. *ca.*1790–1820. Second generation, son of Samuel. More than 100 clocks. Sons George, John, Jonas apts. Tall clocks owned by J. W. Fried of Feasterville, Pa., marked "Somersalfort," and by Mrs. B. C. Sexton, Kensington, Md.; others known.

—, JOHN: Phila. and Germantown, Pa. Aw. *ca.*1820. Tall clocks, one owned by Mrs. James A. Scatterfield, Dover, Del. Third generation.

—, JONAS: Springtown and Hallertown, Pa. Middle 19th century. Twelve or more Tall clocks. Later R. (Orr) (Funk)

—, SAMUEL: Franconia and Germantown, Pa. 1820–1840's. First generation. Many Tall clocks.

HAGUE, B.: N.Y.C. Dir. 1854.

HAHL MFG. CO., THE: Baltimore. *Ca.*1875. Name on movts. of Wenzell air clocks. Ex. Smiths. Inst.

HAHN, C. G.: Phila., 162 N. 3rd St. Dir. 1789. (Prime)

—, HENRY: 1754–1843. Reading, Pa. 3rd group. "One of his clocks traveled as far as Massachusetts." Tall clocks numbered. (Steinmetz)

HAIGH, T. JEFFERSON: Baltimore, 26½ W. Pratt St. 1829–1831.

HAKES, A. H.: Norwich, Conn. *Ca.*1860.

HALE, DAVID R.: Lowell, Mass., Merrimack St. n/d. White Watch Paper Bir. Col.

—, JOSHUA: Lowell, Mass. *Ca.*1840.

—, NATHAN: 1772–1859. Windsor, Vt. Aw. *ca.*1800–1810. To Chelsea, Vt.

—, WILLIAM C.: Salem, Mass. *Ca.*1850.

HALL & BLISS: Albany, N.Y. Dir. 1816–1818.

—, SEYMOUR & Co.: Unionville, Conn. *Ca.* 1830.

— & WADE (Nathaniel): Newfield, Conn. *Ca.*1796. (Hoopes)

—, A. B.: Ohio City and Cleveland, O. 1820–1830. (Knittle)

—, AMASA W.: Atlanta, Ga. Dir. 1859–1860.

—, ASA: Boston. Dir. 1806. "Name on dial of Tall clocks."

—, ASAPH: 1800–1842. Goshen and Hart Hollow, Conn. Marr. Hannah C. Palmer. Son of John Hall. Captain in Rev. War. Built house in Goshen 1797; friend of Ethan Allen. State Legislature. Son Asaph prepared for Yale but mother refused to let him go; set him up in clock business. d. Clinton, Ga., selling clocks made in Goshen factory. Shelf clock Flint Sale 1926, square case, fine carved side column, claw feet, carved eagle at top, tablet in door.

—, CHRISTIAN: 1775–1848. Lititz, Pa. Aw. *ca.*1800–1830. Many good Tall clocks. One owned by B. H. Lebo, Lebanon, Pa., 8' high, walnut case, two 14 lb. iron weights, seconds hand, moon dial, strikes hours only.

—, D. G.: Lewiston, Me. *Ca.*1850.

—, DAVID: Phila. and Burlington, N.J. 1777–1778. S.

—, HENRY WILLIAM: Lititz, Pa. *Ca.*1830–1840.

—, JOHN: 1793–1867. West Chester, Pa., Gay Street. Aw. *ca.*1810–1815. Watch Paper in Chester Co. Hist. Soc. One Tall clock known. Uncle George Cochran willed him tools 1806. In charge of West Chester town clock many years. Not marr. (Gillingham) (James)

—, JOHN: Phila., 55 So. Front St. Dir. 1806–1840.

—, JOHN: Geneva, N. Y. *Ca.*1810. C. Tall clocks, brass 8-day movts.

HALL, JOHN H.: New Haven, Conn. Watch Paper. "Clocks made and watches carefully repaired." Label engraved by A. Doolittle *ca.*1780.

—, JONAS G.: Montpelier and Roxbury, Vt. *Ca.*1870. Made excellent watches but could not compete with machine-made watches; turned to mfr. of fine tools. Two watches in A. O. Dodge Col., Schenectady, N.Y.; full plate movt., No. 23, made at Montpelier; ¾ plate movt. made Roxbury; both 15 jewels, compensated balances. (Dodge) (Chamberlain)

—, PETER: Phila. Dir. 1818–1824.

HALLE, A.: Louisville, Ky. *Ca.* 1840 (LB)

HALLER, JACOB: Cannonsburg, Pa. n/d.

HALLIDAY, ELIAS H.: Phila. Dir. 1828–1833. Pos. also Camden, N.J.

—, HIRAM: Albany, N.Y. Dir. 1834–1844.

HALLIWELL, GEORGE: N.Y.C. 1805. (Baillie)

HAM, GEORGE: Portsmouth, N.H. *Ca.* 1810.

—, HENRY H.: Portsmouth, N.H. n/d. Watch Paper BCL Col.

—, JAMES: N.Y.C., Smith St. Aw. 1754. Math. insts. Prob. not C. or W. (LB)

—, SUPPLY: 1788–1862. Portsmouth, N.H. Own shop *ca.*1810. Dir. 1860–1861.

HAMILTON & ADAMS: Elmira, N.Y. Dir. 1837–1842.

— SANGAMO CORP.: Springfield, Ill. 1928–1930. Subsidiary jointly owned by Hamilton Watch Company and Sangamo Electric Co. Assembled and sold synchronous electric clocks and electrically wound clocks combining jeweled watch movements and synchronous motors. Merged 1930 with Seth Thomas Clock Co. and others in General Time Instruments Corp.

— WATCH COMPANY: Lancaster, Pa. 1892–. Named for Andrew Hamilton, to whom William Penn granted land now Lancaster, and who, with son James, laid out and founded Lancaster. End result of series of reorganizations of watch companies: Adams & Perry Watch Co. 1874–1876; Lancaster Watch Co., Ltd., *ca.*1877; Keystone Watch Co. 1884, f. 1890; assets merged with those of Aurora Watch Company of Aurora, Ill., 1892 to become Hamilton Watch Company. First watch and movt. ill. Nos. 302, 305. Made only

jeweled movts., cases after 1909. Bought Illinois Watch Co. 1927. Later bought name "Howard." Org. 1928 with Sangamo Electric Co. to form Hamilton Sangamo Corp. to produce and sell fine electric clocks; sold 1930 to General Time Instruments Corp. Temperature-resistant alloys for balance-wheels and hair-springs. World War II mass-produced Marine Chrons. Continue to make fine jeweled watches. Numbering system too complex for presentation here. (R. Waddell) (John Hall)

HAMILTON, DANIEL S.: Elmira, N.Y. Adv. 1848.

—, JAMES: Phila. Dir. 1848.

—, R. J.: Phila. Dir. 1837–1846.

—, S. P.: Savannah, Ga. *Ca.*1860.

—, SAMUEL: Phila. Dir. 1837.

HAMLEN, NATHANIEL: Augusta, Me. 1790–1820. Dwarf Tall clock 43½″ × 10½″. One in Edison Inst. (Abbott)

HAMLIN, WILLIAM: Providence, R.I. Adv. 1797.

HAMMAN, PETER: Phila. Dir. 1817.

HAMMOND CLOCK CO.: Chicago. 1936.

—, SAMUEL: N.Y.C. *Ca.*1840–1860. Chron. No. 1554 owned by B. S. Albertson, Jr., Lewes, Del.

HAMPDEN WATCH CO., THE: Springfield, Mass. 1877–1888. Bought by John C. Dueber, Newport, Ky., 1886. To Canton, O., 1888 as Dueber-Hampden Watch Co. One of largest makers of watches in America until 1925.

HAMPSON, ROBERT: N.Y.C. n/d.

HAMPTON (James B.) & PALMER (John C.): Salisbury, N.C. 1830–1832. Palmer alone after death of Hampton, mostly S.

—, JAMES BRANDON: 1801–1832. Salisbury, N.C., Main St. Aw. 1822. With bro.-in-law John C. Palmer org. Hampton & Palmer, 1830.

—, SAMUEL: Chelsea, Mass. *Ca.*1840.

HAMSON, CLARK: Waterbury, Conn. 1812. Involved in law suit with Heman Clark.

"HANCOCK, JOHN," used by N.Y. Watch Co. 1872–1875.

HANEYE, NATHANIEL: Bridgewater, Mass. n/d. Tall clock, 30-hour wood pull-up type movt. engraved brass dial mounted on plaque, Selchow Col.

HANKS, BENJAMIN: 1755–1824. Windham, Mansfield, and Litchfield, Conn. "Skilful, energetic mechanic." Son of Uriah and Irene Case Hanks. Pos. apt. of Thomas Harland. Adv. Windham 1777, "Clock and Watch Maker, Chiming and Repeating and Common 8-day clocks, watches . . . and Repair." Also stocking weaving; petitioned Conn. General Assembly for patent on new type loom. Adv. 1779 to Litchfield, built homestead, "made Clocks and Watches." Tower clock for Old Dutch Church at corner of Nassau and Liberty Sts., N.Y.C. Petitioned for patent on Tower clock wound by Windmill attachment. Adv. 1785, "Still makes and warrants Horizontal Watches, shewing 2nd's from center and Day, Skeleton and 8-day watches . . . repeating and Pneumatick Clocks in mahogany and cherry cases, also Church Clocks that will go without winding . . ." Bell casting 1786. Shortly after 1790 to Mansfield, "continued to make Clocks and Bells"; also in woolen business. Bell foundry Troy, N.Y., 1808 with son Truman, b. 1782. Patent 1816 for "Moulding and Casting Bells." d. Troy, N.Y. (Hoopes)

HANNA, HUGH: Wabash, Ind. Dir. 1834. Pos. sales only.

HANNUM, JOHN: Northampton, Mass. 1837–1849. (Cutten)

HANSELL, JAS.: Phila., Market St. below 7th. Dir. 1816–1850 and later. Tall clock at Smiths. Inst. Tall clock owned by Van Leer Heyburn, Chester, Pa. Watch Paper in Bir. Col., "at 226 Market St."

HANSEN MFG. CO.: Princeton, Ind. *Ca.* 1936. (LB)

HARDEN, JAMES: Phila., 18 Dock St. Dir. 1818–1824. "Clock dial maker."

HARDER, W. A.: N.Y.C. Dir. 1848.

HARDING, NEWELL: 1796–. Haverhill, Mass.; Boston until 1862.

HARDMAN, J.: Lebanon, O. Adv. 1832, "Clock and Watch maker lately from Va. has commenced the above business in the house formerly occupied by Mr. Griffith on Main St." (Phillips)

HARDY, WILLIAM: Charleston, S.C., Queen St. Adv. 1773, "From London." To England 1775.

HARLACHER, BENJAMIN: Washington Twp., Pa. Early 19th century.

HARLAND, THOMAS: 1735–1807. Norwich, Conn. Aw. 1773–1806. One of America's great Cs. b., learned trade, in England. To Boston 1773 on ship later in Boston Tea Party. Adv. 1773, "near the store of Christopher Leffingwell." Norwich town of 7,400 half size of Boston, prosperous. Nathan Hale a customer. First shop burned 1795; continued at new location. Adv. 1800, "Spring and plain 8-day clocks with enameled and silvered faces completely finished and regulated, in mahogany and cherry cases." Adv. 1802, "New Warranted Watches, etc." *History of Norwich*, p. 608, "Harland's factory produced 200 watches and 40 clocks a year." No watches now known. Fine C. Many apts.: Daniel Burnap, William Cleveland, Seril and Ezra Dodge, David Greenleaf, Nathaniel Shipman, Gurdon Tracy, Jedidiah and Jabez Baldwin, and others. (Eli Terry apt. of Daniel Burnap, not Thomas Harland, despite statement by Henry Terry.) Employed 10–12. Pos. made parts for several clocks at a time. Tall clocks Metropolitan Museum of Art. (See ill. Nos. 59–62.) Prob. only Tall clocks; last one made is in Charles Terry Treadway Col. Marr. Hannah Clark 1779. Father of Thomas, Jr. Much of fine Conn. Clockmaking stems from this master C. Died heartbroken 4 mos. after death of son Thomas, Jr. (Hoopes)

—, THOMAS, JR.: 1781–1806. Carefully taught by father; promise of brilliant career cut short by early death. (Hoopes)

HARMSON, —: Newport, R.I. 1720's.

HARPER, BENJAMIN: Phila. Dir. 1843.

—, JOHN M.: Phila. Dir. 1841 and later.

— (HARPUR), W. E.: Phila. Dir. 1839 and later. Ernest Cramer owns watch No. 9 with "W. E. Harper" on movt. and "Wm. Harper" on dial.

HARRINGTON, CHARLES: Brattleboro, Vt. *Ca.*1830. Watch Paper BCL Col.

—, HENRY: 1832–. Salem, Mass., 155 Federal St. Aw. 1855.

—, SAMUEL: Amherst, Mass. 1842–1845. Adv. watches and jewelry.

—, WILLIAM: Phila. Dir. 1849 and later.

HARRIS & CO.: Phila. 1830's. Imp. Wag-on-Wall clocks.
— & HARRINGTON: N.Y.C., 22 Cortlandt St., 23 Vesey St. 1880–1919. Successor Jacques Clock Co. 1897. Sole agent Ellicott & Co. English Cs. Also imp. French clocks.
— & STANWOOD: Boston. Dir. 1842.
—, JOHN: –1739. Charleston, S.C. Aw. 1729–1739.
HARRISON, —: Highland Co.,O. 1792.(Knittle)
—, JAMES: 1767–. Waterbury, Conn. Son of Lemuel and Lois Barnes Harrison; bro. of Wooster and Lemuel, Jr.; nephew and apt. of Timothy Barnes. Aw. 1791. Tall clocks, brass movts., enameled dials; first clock sold to Maj. Morris, second to Rev. Mark Leavenworth, third to Capt. Samuel Judd. Installed water wheel on Little Brook ca.1800, "first use in Waterbury of water power for driving machinery." Ingenious mechanic, not too good business man. Boston Aug. 2, 1814, patent on "Time Part, Wood, for Clocks" (date of Asa Hopkins patent). Later aw. in Waterbury shop of nephew. d. N.Y.C. (Anderson)(Hoopes)
—, JOHN: Phila. n/d.
—, JOHN MURRAY: Phila. n/d.
—, LEMUEL, JR.: Waterbury, Conn. Bro. James and Wooster. Handmade clocks before 1800; pos. wood movts. Ephraim Downs worked for him ca.1811.
—, S. (Susannah): N.Y.C. Ca.1855. Pos. another lady C. or W.
—, WOOSTER: 1772–. Trumbull and Newfield, Conn. Son of Lemuel, Sr., bro. James and Lemuel, Jr. C. Aw. ca.1795. Adv. 1800, "Removed to Newfield, Conn., over the store of Sherman & Wheeler, and employed a good workman for watch repair." (Hoopes)
HART & BREWER: Middletown, Conn. 1800–1803. (Hoopes)
— & TRUESDALE: Hartford, O., in Conn. Western Reserve. Pos. some connection with Conn. Clockmaking. Wood movt. Shelf clocks. (Hull)
— (Judah) & WILLCOX (Alvin): Norwich, Conn. 1805–1807.
—, ALPHA: Goshen, Conn. Ca.1820. Bro. of Henry.
—, ELIPHAZ: Norwich, Conn. Ca.1810. "On the Green by the Court House." (Hist.)

HART, G.: Bridgeport, Pa. Ca.1850.
—, HENRY: Goshen, Conn., Hart Hollow. Ca.1830. Bro. Alpha.
—, JUDAH: Norwich, Conn. 1805–1816. With Alvin Willcox bought business of Abel Brewster "at the Landing." (Hoopes) (Hist. p. 608)
—, M.: Pittsburgh, Pa. Ca.1820. In Morgan & Hart.
—, ORRIN: Bristol, Peaceable St. Aw. 1824–1833. Bought 1824 brick house of Edward Barnes and clock business of Charles G. Ives. Sold house and business to John Bacon 1833. (Hist.) (tx.)
HARTH, H. C.: N.Y.C. Ca.1850.
HARTLEY, JEREMIAH: Phila. Dir. 1837 and later.
—, JOHN: York, Pa. Early 19th century.
HARTMAN, EMIL: N.Y.C. Ca.1840.
—, EMIL: San Francisco, Cal. 1875–1876. Wenzell air clocks.
HARTZLER, JOSEPH: Bear Town, Pa. Ca. 1850.
HARVARD CLOCK CO.: Boston. Patent in 1880. Became Boston Clock Co., then Chelsea Clock Co. (James Conlon, Jr.)
HARWOOD BROS.: Boston. n/d. Watch Paper BCL Col.
—, GEORGE: Rochester, N.Y., 39 Buffalo St. Ca.1830.
HASCY, SAMUEL, & SON (Alexander): Albany, N.Y. Dir. 1829–1831.
—, ALEXANDER R.: Albany, N.Y. Dir. 1831 and later. Son of Samuel.
—, SAMUEL: Albany, N.Y. Ca.1825. Father of Alexander.
HASELTINE & WENTWORTH: Lowell, Mass., Central St. Dir. 1832.
HASIE, MARK: N.Y.C. Ca.1855.
HASSAM, STEPHEN: Charlestown, N.H. Ca. 1787. From Boston. Mass. Shelf and Tall clocks, some extant. Marr. 1787. (DKP)
HASTING, B. B.: Cleveland, O. Adv. 1837.
HASTINGS, T. D.: Boston. Dir. 1854.
HATCH, GEORGE D.: No. Attleboro, Mass. Striking Banjo and Wall regulator clocks. (See ill. No. 176.)
—, JOHN B.: Attleboro, Mass. Ca.1880.
—, JONATHAN: Westtown, Pa. 1810–1815. From Conn. with Russell Vibber and Thomas DeWolf. Fitted wooden movts. in cases by Henry Darlington. (James)

HATTON, THOMAS: Conn. n/d. "Every boy ought to be taught the art of hammering (planishing) with great care and to obtain which, he should practice well on clock dials."

HAUGHTON, S.: New Haven, Conn. Pos. case maker for Simeon Jocelin. Letter dated 1810 in Tall clock, "Mr. Hewitt, Sir, Rec'd the wood . . . your acquaintance. Shall be glad to let them have it at a fair price. Yours as ever, S. Haughton."

HAUGHWOUT, E. V., & Co.: N.Y.C. Adv. Ca.1850. Bronze clocks.

HAUSBURG, E. O.: N.Y.C., 41 Maiden Lane. 1897–1900. "Watchmen's clock."

HAUSHALL, JOHN: Phila. Dir. 1816–1817.

HAWES, J. H.: Ithaca, N.Y. Invented Calendar clock mechanism, patent 1853 (did not compensate for leap years). Sold patent to Huntington & Platt. Mfd. by Mix Bros., Ithaca. Other patents 1860–1862, sold to Seth Thomas. Many Calendar clocks mfd. in Ithaca.

HAWXHURST & de MILT: N.Y.C. Ca.1790.

—, NATHANIEL: N.Y.C. 1786–1793. (Stow)

HAYDEN & FREEMAN: N.Y.C., 47 Water St. Adv. 1788, "Near Fly Market, adjoining Mr. Andrew Van Tuyl's store, carrying on business of watch and clock making."

—, S., & SON: Boston. Dir. 1803.

—, DAVID: Waterbury, Conn. Ca.1808. In Abel Porter & Co. Not listed in Anderson as C.

—, SAMUEL: Boston. Pos. 1786. Dir. 1796–1809.

—, STEPHEN: Butler, O. Ca.1804. Cases from cherry slabs. "Friendly Indians, gathered outside cabin door to hear hour struck." Two panes of glass joined to cover dial. (Knittle)

HAYDOCK, C. G.: Phila. Dir. 1785–1798. (Prime)

—, Jos.: Manchester, N.H. n/d. "Patent lever watchmaker." Orange Watch Paper Bir. Col.

HAYES, PETER B.: 1788–1842. Adv. 1826–1842. W. D. S.

HAYNES, LAFAYETTE: Troy, N.Y. Dir. 1836–1837.

HAYS, MICHAEL S.: N.Y.C. 1769. (MFM)

"HAYWARD," used by Hampden Watch Co. ca.1881.

HAZELTON (or Haseltine), E. L.: Springfield, Vt. n/d. Watch Paper BCL Col.

HAZEN, N. S.: Cincinnati, Ohio. Ca.1840.

HEADMAN, WILLIAM: Phila. Dir. 1828, 1850.

HEAGY, JACOB: See Hagey.

HEALY, CHARLES W.: Syracuse, N.Y. Ca. 1850.

—, JOHN W.: Worcester, Mass. Ca.1850.

HEATH, REUBEN: –1818. Scottsville, N.Y. 1791–1818. Vt. earlier. In Nettleton & Heath Co.

—, STEVENS: Chillicothe, O. Adv. 1815. (Knittle)

—, WILLARD B.: Bangor, Me. Ca.1830–186

HEDDERLEY, CHARLES: Phila. Ca.1790. Brass founder; clock parts.

HEDGES, GEORGE: Buffalo, N.Y., 8 Cheapside, Dir. 1828–1848; Waterford, N.Y. Ca.1825.

HEFFARDS, S. M.: Middleboro, Mass. n/d.

HEFFLEY, ANANIAS: Berlin, Pa. Ca.1825–1860. Tall clock, name on dial and movt. (PG)

—, DANIEL: Berlin, Pa. Ca.1831–1849. (Steinmetz)

HEGE, JACOB: See Hagey.

—, SAMUEL: See Hagey.

HEILBURN, MICHAEL: Baltimore. Ca.1840.

HEILIG, FREDERICK: Phila. n/d.

—, HERMAN: Germantown, Pa. Ca.1850.

—, JACOB: 1770–1824. Phila. and Lancaster, Pa. Watches.

—, JOHN: Germantown, Pa. Dir. 1801–1850. Watch Paper Cramer Col.

HEINEMAN, GEORGE: Phila. Dir. 1847–1849.

—, L. C.: Phila. Dir. 1849 and later.

HEINITSCH, CHARLES: Lancaster, Pa. Late 18th century. Sold parts, tools and complete Clocks. Considered merchant. Some sales to John Eberman.

HEINRICH, H. H.: N.Y.C. n/d. (Chamberlain)

HEINTZELMAN, HIERONYMUS: Lampeter Sq., Pa. Ca.1750. Father of John, grandfather of Peter. b. Switzerland. With C. & D. Forrer. Tall clocks, Bachman cases; marked "H. H." or without full name. (Chamberlain)

—, JOHN CONRAD: 1776–1804. Manheim, Pa. Well-known maker. Father of Peter. Aw. 1787–1805. Tall clocks.

—, PETER: Manheim, Pa. Ca.1800. Son of John. Continued father's business briefly; eyesight failed. (Lan. Co.)

HEINY, CLEMENTS: N.Y.C. Dir. 1842.

HEISELY, FREDERICK: 1759–1839. Frederick, Md. In Rev. War. 1783–1793 Math. Insts. To Lancaster, Pa., 1793 with George Hoff. To Harrisburg 1801. To Pittsburgh 1820's. Dir. 1837, 6 St. Clair St. Marr. Catharine Hoff 1783. Tower clock Smiths. Inst. (Lan. Co.)

HEISS, JAMES P.: Phila. Dir. 1849 and later.

HELLER, J. H.: N.Y.C. n/d. Watch Paper BCL Col.

HELM, CHRISTIAN: Phila. Dir. 1802–1804.

HEMINGWAY, A.: Chicago, Ill. Dir. 1856. Pos. sales agent.

HEMLEY, NATHANIEL: Kensington, N.H. Ca.1760. Blacksmith. Doubtful C. Bought Purington shop from John Fifield. (Ant. July 1948)

HEMPHILL, THOMAS J.: Phila. Dir. 1836–1841.

HEMPSON, ROBERT: N.Y.C. Ca.1825.

HEMPSTED, DANIEL BOOTH: 1784–1852. New London, Conn. Early S., C., cabinetmaker. Succeeded by son until 1882. (Am. Col. June 1947)

HENDEL, BERNARD: Carlisle, Pa. Ca.1800.

—, JACOB: Carlisle, Pa. Ca.1810.

HENDERSON & LOSSING: Poughkeepsie, N.Y. Ca.1835.

—, ADAM: Poughkeepsie, N.Y. Ca.1831. Adv. 1846. W. (Arthur Stout)

—, WILLIAM: Appoquinimink, New Castle, Del. 1770.

HENDRICK, BARNES & Co.: Forestville, Conn. (tx) 1849–1852. Marine clocks. Same as Hendrick, Hubbell & Co.

— (Ebenezer M.) & CHURCHILL (John): Bristol, Frederick St. (tx) 1847–1848. Shop where Elisha Manross commenced Clockmaking. Succeeded by Hendrick, Hubbell & Co.

— (E. M.), HUBBELL (Laporte) & Co.: Bristol. 1848–1853. With Daniel Clark, W. B. Barnes, Rodney Barnes. Marine clocks as invented by Bainbridge Barnes, "the first successful Marine Clock ever made" (see Charles Kirke). Also self-winding clocks.

—, HUBBELL & BEACH (Levi): Bristol, 1854. Marine 30-hour clocks and 8-day timepieces. Some purchased by Jerome Mfg. Co. of New Haven.

HENDRICK, EBENEZER M.: Bristol. Credit report 1850, "Makes marine clocks. He is easy in circumstances, pays well, gives no bank notes, owns R. E. and personal property, all clear. Safe to trust, no fear of this man. Mr. Wm. Barnes of Bristol may be a partner with him. He is a good mechanic and industrious." (EI)

HENDRIE, WILLIAM A.: Chicago, Ill., 87 Franklin St. 1880–1882. Also "W. A."

HENDRIX, URIAH W.: N.Y.C. 1756 and later. "Next to the sign of the Golden Key in Hanover Sq."

HENEBERGER, PETER: 1784–1869. Harrisonburg, Va. Aw. 1850 or later. From Harrisburg. Flat silver, also Tall clocks, "Some of which are still in use here." Harrisburg, Pa., 1790–1830. (John W. Wayland)

HENRY, JAMES: Maysville, Ky. Patent on "clocks" Sept. 13, 1820.

HEPPLEMAN, JOHN: Manheim, Pa. Late 1790's to ca.1810.

HEPTON, FREDERICK: Phila. Dir. 1785.

HEQUEMBOURG, C.: New Haven, Conn. Ca.1818. "In business many years and adv. freely. Sold watches. At one time had 36 watches stolen from his shop window." (Moore)

HERANCOURT (G.) & DRESBACHE (C. T.): Columbus, O. Ca.1830.

HERCULES WATCH Co.: Chicago, Ill. n/d. "Swiss Movts." (MFM)

HERDSAL, JOSEPH: Florida, N.Y. n/d. Inlay Tall clock, French feet, double arch, moon.

HERMAN, JOHN: Lancaster, Pa. n/d. Tall clocks. (Bowman)

HERON, ERSKINE: Charleston, S.C. Aw. 1762. Adv. 1765, "From London."

—, ISAAC: Phila. 1763; Bound Brook, N.J. 1763; N.Y.C. 1765; to Ireland 1778. John Thompson took over shop. (Williams) (Am. Col. June, 1948)

—, JAMES: Newtown, Pa. Ca.1780. Tall clock, rocking ship, brass dial.

HERR, WILLIAM, JR.: Providence, R.I. Adv. 1849.

HERRICAN, WILLIAM: Phila. Dir. 1850.

HERSHEIDE CLOCK Co.: Cincinnati, O. 20th century. Still making Tall clocks.

— HALL CLOCK Co.: Cincinnati, O. 1936.

HERTZ, JACOB: Lancaster, Pa. Early 19th century. Tall clocks, 8-day brass movts. painted iron dials.

HERVEY, C. P.: N.Y.C. Early 19th century.

HERWICK, JACOB: Carlisle, Pa. 1779. Pos. "Hardwick."

HETZEL, JOHN: Newtown, N.J. Adv. 1795. Pos. took over S. and C. after Symmes left. (Williams)

HETZELL, —: Milford, Pa. Ca.1834. Tall clock owned by Mrs. Richard F. Nicholas, Colmar, Pa., 8-day brass movt., cherry case, hour strike, calendar, on bronze gong. (C. Ainsworth)

HEURTIN, WILLIAM, JR.: 1703–1765. N.Y.C., John St. Aw. 1729. Sons, Wm. III and Joshua. S. C. Joshua succeeded father.

HEWITT, A. E.: No. Bridgewater, Mass. Ca.1860.

HEYDORN (C.) & IMLAY (R.): Hartford, Conn. 1808–1811. Bought Doolittle business. Offered for sale. At death of E. Hinsdale 1810, this firm listed as debtor. (Hoopes)

—, C.: Hartford, Conn. 1808–1811 (Hoopes)

HIBBARD (HIBBERD), CALEB, JR.: 1781–. Williston, Pa. Aw. 1809. S. Grandfather of Isaac Thomas, nephew of Mordecai Thomas. To Ohio 1818. Marr. 1819 Mirgalla Stowe. (James)

"—, H. M.," used by Cornell Watch Co. 1871–1874.

HIBBEN, ANDREW: –1784. Charleston, S.C. Aw. 1764. Adv. 1765, "moved from Elliot St. to Broad St."

HICKCOX, SAMUEL R.: Humphreysville, Conn. Ca.1830. Ray W. Sherman has wood movt. clock, label printed by "Whitemore & Buckingham, New Haven."

HICKS, WILLET: N.Y.C. Ca.1790.

HIGBY, S. S.: New Hartford Center, Conn. Ca.1830. Wood movt. Shelf clock, label reads, "Improved clocks made and sold by . . ." Wood dial, 30-hr. weight-driven movt., mahogany veneer. Top of door stamped "31," ball feet. (Ingraham Col.)

HIGHT, CHRISTIAN: Phila. Dir. 1819–1822.

HILBURN, JOHN JACOB: 1836–1877. Bowling Green, Ky. Apt. to uncle Franch Shrock, St. Louis. With E. L. Mottley & Co. ca.1858; Peter Fuselli 1866, 1877.

HILDEBURN & BROS.: Phila. Dir. 1849 and later.

HILDEBURN (Samuel) & WATSON: Phila., 72 Market St. Dir. 1833. Watch Paper Cramer Col.

— (Samuel) & WOODWORTH: Phila. Dir. 1819.

—, SAMUEL: Phila., 72 High St. Dir. 1810–1837.

—, WOOLWORTH: Phila. Dir. 1816–1819.

HILDRETH, JONAS: Salisbury, Vt. 1805.

HILEINGER, JOSHUA: n/p. Pa. n/d.

HILL & ROSS: Zanesville, O. Ca.1830.

—, BENJAMIN MORRIS, JR.: Richmond Twp., Pa. 4th group. Tall clock owned by Mrs. Andrew R. Wight, Glenside, Pa., date on case "1771," brass 30-hr. movt. one weight.

—, CHARLES: Zanesville, O. 1815. "Not the one at Steubenville." (Knittle)

—, CHARLES: Steubenville, O. Adv. 1823–1825. (Knittle)

—, D.: Reading, Pa. 1820–1840. (Abbott)

—, E. J.: Albion, N.Y. Ca.1850.

—, HENRY: N.Y.C. Ca.1750. Tall clock, Metropolitan Museum of Art.

—, J. W.: Kansas. 1873. Century clocks, weight-driven, "to run 100 years." Weight fall designed to drop less than 1" per year.

—, JOACHIM: 1783–1869. Flemington, N.J. Aw. 1804–ca.1820. Son of Isaac and Mary Hill. Apt. of Thomas Williams after 1800. Tall clocks. Cases by Matthew Egerton, John Tappan, or John Scudder. Dials in four styles, showing orderly development from beginner to sophisticate, as do cases, with Scudder cases pos. best. Tall clock owned by Mrs. J. B. Frelinghausen, Far Hills, N.J., and John F. Schenk, Flemington. (J. F. Schenk)

—, JOHN B.: Beverly, Mass. Ca.1850.

—, PETER: Mt. Holly and Burlington, N.J. Aw. 1796 and later. Negro apt. of John Hollinshead. W.C. Took over Gamaliel Bailey shop 1821. (Williams)

—, SAMUEL: Hamburg, Pa. Ca.1800. Learned Clockmaking in England.

—, WILLIAM: N.Y.C. Ca.1810.

—, WILLIAM F.: Boston. Dir. 1810.

HILLARD, CHRISTOPHER: 1802–1871. Hagerstown, Md. Ca.1825. (LSS)

—, GEORGE W.: Fayetteville, N.C. Adv. 1823 and later.

HILLARD, JAMES: –1749. Charleston, S.C. Aw. *ca.*1730. Adv. 1738, "At the Sign of the Clock on King St."

—, WILLIAM: Fayetteville, N.C. Adv. 1801, accepted Wm. Dye as apt. Adv. 1805.

HILLDROP, THOMAS: Hartford, Conn. 1773. "At the Sign of the Dial."

HILLDRUP, THOMAS: Hartford, Conn. Aw. *ca.*1775–1790. "From London." W. J. S. R. Prob. no clocks. (Hoopes)

HILLER, JOSEPH: Boston, Salem, Mass. 1770.

HILLMAN, F.: N.Y.C. Dir. 1854.

HILLS (Wm.), BROWN (J. C.) & Co.: Bristol. (tx) 1840–1841. Succeeded Forestville Mfg. Co. J. C. Brown bought out Hill's interests 1841; continued as J. C. Brown & Co.

—, GEORGE, & SON: Plainville, Conn. *Ca.*1870. Metallic clock cases, sold some clocks. (*Mem. Hist. of Hartford, Conn.*)

— (Wm.), GOODRICH (Jared) & Co.: Plainville, Conn. 1841–1845. Partners J. C. Brown. "Brass 8-day clocks," one in R. Newcomb Col.

—, AMARIAH: N.Y.C. Dir. 1845.

—, CHARLES C.: Haverhill, Mass., Main and Water Sts. Dir. 1853.

—, DWIGHT B.: Bristol, Frederick St. (tx) 1895–1896. "Bronze and nickel-plated clocks."

—, D. B.: Plainfield, N.J. 1888–1889. (MFM)

—, WILLIAM: Farmington, Conn. In Forestville Mfg. Co. 1835–1839, J. C. Brown & Co. 1840–1841, Hills, Goodrich & Co., 1841–1845. Ex. in Walter C. Robinson Col.

"HILLSIDE," used by American Watch Co. from 1882.

HILLWORTH, FREDERICK: Phila. Dir. 1844–1849.

HILLYARTINER, PHILIP: Phila. Dir. 1844.

HILSINGER CLOCK: Size of dial and movt. resemble Tall clock, but plates of wood and gears and axles of metal. Hung on wall, hence a "wag." (H. H. Funk)

HIMELE, JAMES: N.Y.C. 1786 (MFM)

HIMELY, JOHN JAMES: Phila. *Ca.*1786; Charleston, S.C. Adv. 1796, "moved from 43 Broad St. to 117 Tradd St." (Prime)

HINKLE, JOHN P.: Phila. Dir. 1824.

HINMAN, ALONZO: New Haven, Conn. *Ca.*1840.

HINSDALE, EPAPHRAS: 1769–1810. Newark, N.J. Aw. 1795–1810. Made gold jewelry at outset of vogue. Prosperous. Later in E. Hinsdale & Co. Large wholesale business. Money owed at death recorded. (Williams)

HINSHON, J. P.: Terre Haute, Ind. *Ca.*1850.

HITCHCOCK, H.: Lodi, N.Y. Early 19th century.

—, R.: n/p. Patent 158084, Dec. 22, 1874, model Smiths. Inst.

—, S. R.: Humphreysville, N.Y. *Ca.*1810.

HOADLEY, SAMUEL, & Co.: Winchester, Conn. Mentioned in lawsuit *ca.*1809. Hoadley & Whiting, Winchester, Conn. on clock label. Origin of William Gilbert Clock Co. (Amos Avery)

—, AMMI: 1762–1834. Bethany and Plymouth, Conn. Grist mill. Father of Silas. Prob. no clocks.

—, LUTHER: –1813. Winsted, Conn. Aw. 1807 with Riley Whiting. Bro. Samuel "died in war service." (Vail)

—, SAMUEL: Winchester or Winsted, Conn. Aw. 1807–1813. C. With bro. Luther and Riley Whiting. Wood movt. clocks. In Army 1813, and retired from C.

—, SILAS: 1786–1870. Hoadleyville, Plymouth, Conn. Son of Ammi. b. Bethany, Conn. Taught carpentry by uncle Calvin. Marr. Sarah Painter, becoming bro.-in-law Ephraim Downs. Aw. *ca.*1808–1849. With Eli Terry in Hoadleyville or Greystone. C. Wood movt. 30-hour clocks, many with tall pine cases. (See ill. Nos. 67, 68.) Tradition of partnership Terry (Eli), Thomas (Seth) & Hoadley. With Seth Thomas bought interests of Eli Terry. Jerome says competition keen and price of wooden movt. reduced from $10 to $5; Roberts, Rich, Barnes, Ives, and others making same article in Bristol. Thomas sold out to Hoadley in 1813, purchasing shop of Heman Clark on site of present Seth Thomas Clock Co., Plymouth Hollow, now Thomaston. Shifted to Shelf clocks with wooden movts. of own devising, many unique. Label, "First Quality Timepieces, with Alarm, Pivots Bushed with Ivory." Franklin clock marked, "Time is Money, Franklin Clocks, with Improvement of Burling Pivots." Pendulum *ca.*19″. "Time is Money" on many labels; one, Pillar and Scroll case with "upside down" wood movt., in Peter Mitchell Col. Later some 8-day wood and 30-hour brass movt. Shelf clocks. Many Tall clocks extant. One at Essex Inst. Amassed fortune; retired 1849; rented factory to knife company. d. Plymouth age 84. (See ill. No. 208.)

HOBART, AARON: Abington, Mass. Adv. 1770, "Bells being cast of any size suitable for churches, equal to and cheaper than can be imported." Brass founder, clock parts. This enterprise led Paul Revere to add bell casting to his accomplishments. Sent one of his sons to Abington to learn. First Paul Revere bell cast 1792. (BCC)

HOBBS, JAMES: Baltimore. *Ca.*1800.
—, NATHAN: Boston. Dir. 1842.

HOCKERS, G.: Ephrata, Pa. *Ca.*1850. Tall clocks. (Lan. Co.)

HOCKLEY, THOMAS: Phila. *Ca.*1800.

HODGES (Erastus) & NORTH (Norris): Torrington Hollow, Conn. *Ca.*1830 or earlier. Cs. (J. H. Thompson)

—, EDWIN H.: Torrington Hollow, Conn. Son of Erastus. Also listed as having made clocks. (Floyd Thoms)

—, ERASTUS: Torrington Hollow, Conn. Father of Edwin H. Acquired cotton mill 1827 for debt. C. Later with Norris North. Torrington type Pillar and Scroll clocks; two in Flint Sale 1926. (See ill. No. 193.) Ex. at Edison Inst.

HODGSON, WILLIAM: Phila. Dir. 1785.

HOFER, CHARLES: Macon, Miss. *Ca.*1850.

HOFF (John) & HEISELEY (Frederick): Lancaster, Pa. 1793–1801. (Burt)

—, GEORGE: *Ca.*1740–1816. Lancaster, Pa. Aw. 1765–1816. b. Germany. Marr. 1761. To U.S.A. Aug. 1765. Tall clocks, also watches. Two clockmaking sons, John and George, Jr. 1793 took partner Frederick Heiseley. One Tall owned by Mrs. Harold E. Rassmussen, Westfield, N.J., marked "Geo. Hoff, Lancaster, Pa. 1780."

—, GEORGE, JR.: 1765–1818. Lancaster, Pa. Aw. *ca.* 1790–1816.

—, GEORGE FREDERICK: 1810–. Lancaster, Pa.

—, JOHN: –1819. Lancaster, Pa. E. King St. Aw. *ca.*1800. Son of George. With father, in Hoff & Heiseley. Tall clocks, some

with quarter hour strike; more than 100 known. Active and prominent.

HOFF, JOHN GEORGE: Lancaster, Pa. Prob. George Hoff. (Brix)

HOFFARD, SAMUEL: Berlin, Pa. 1825–1850. (Stow)

HOFFMAN, C. M.: Lebanon, N.H. *Ca.*1850.

HOFFNER, HENRY: Phila., 148 N. Front St. Dir. 1791.

HOGUET, AUGUSTUS: Phila. Dir. 1814–1833.

HOKE, GEORGE: Hanover, Pa. n/d.

HOLBROOK, H.: Medway, Mass. Made clock for Unitarian meeting house in Keene, N.H., *ca.*1830.

—, MAJOR GEORGE: 1767–1846. Wrentham, Brookfield, Medway, Mass. Bell founder. b. Wrentham. Leicester town clock 1803. First bell recast 1810, again 1834. To E. Medway 1815. Poor health and financial reverses. Returned to Wrentham. Holbrook Bell Foundry carried on by four generations to 1880. Patterns sold to West coast interests. (BCC)

HOLDEN, ELI: Phila. Dir. 1843 and later. Banjo clocks.

—, HENRY: New Haven, Conn. *Ca.*1840.

—, J.: Boston. *Ca.*1830. Watch Paper BCL Col.

—, JOSEPH: Dayton, O. J. Am. Col. Dec. 1947: "About 1836 expanded clockmaking shop into factory using water power. Made up to 2500 clocks a year." (Geo. D. Smith, Dayton, O.)

HOLDREDGE, A. A.: Glens Falls, N.Y. Adv. 1841.

HOLLENBACH, DAVID: Reading, Pa. Aw. for Daniel Oyster, 1822–1826. Adv. *ca.* 1826–1840.

HOLLER WATCH CO.: Brooklyn, N.Y. n/d.

—, HENRY: Center Co., Pa. Date on dial "1818." Tall clock owned by Mrs. James McAlister, McAlisterville, Pa.

HOLLINGER, A.: Phila. Dir. 1839.

HOLLINSHEAD, GEORGE: Woodstown, N.J. Aw. 1775–1779. (PG) Son of Morgan. A. Somers apt. and successor, 1800–1820. (Williams)

—, HUGH: –1786. Mt. Holly and Moorestown, N.J. Marr. 1775.

—, JACOB: Salem, N.J. Aw. 1768–1778. Adv. 1772.

—, JOB: Haddonfield, N.J. Succeeded by John Whitehead 1821.

HOLLINSHEAD, JOHN: 1745–. Mt. Holly and Burlington, N.J. Ca.1780.

—, JOSEPH: Burlington and Moorestown, N.J. Aw. 1740–1775. C. Apt. and later partner of Isaac Pearson. Marr. Sara Pearson, Isaac's daughter; Quakers. Brass dials marked "Pearson & Hollinshead." Inherited Pearson's tools and equipment. More than 12 Tall clocks known; one owned by Mrs. Ronald W. Sheppard, Montclair, N.J.

—, JOSEPH, JR.: 1750–. Burlington, N.J. Aw. after Rev. War. Tall clock owned by Mrs. Lester Brown, N.Y.C.

—, MORGAN: –1832. Moorestown and Chester, N.J. Aw. after Rev. War to 1822. Father of George. Adv. 1775, "Opened shop in Moorestown on the Great Road leading from Phila. to Mt. Holly. Makes repeating dead beat clocks. Superior to recoil, they will last much longer. Watchwork done, etc. Also wants an apt." Tall clocks owned by Mrs. Thos. B. Stockham, Morrisville, Pa.; No. 55 by Edmund Zelly, Haddonfield, N.J.; No. 96 by Mrs. R. O. Bentley, Phila.

HOLLIS, J. M.: West Chester, Pa. Adv. April-October, 1821. "Short duration." (James)

HOLLISTER, J. H.: Springfield, Mass. Orange Watch Paper Bir. Col.

HOLLOWAY, ROBERT: Baltimore. Ca.1820.

HOLMAN, D.: Baltimore. Ca.1810. Pos. Banjo clocks.

—, SALEM: Hartford, Conn. Ca.1820. Mrs. Jane Large has wood movt. Shelf clock marked "Made and Sold by . . ." Edward Ingraham has 30-hr. wood stencil column Shelf clock.

HOLMES, AARON: Boston. Dir. 1842.

—, A. B.: Newark, N.J. n/d.

—, J.: Phila. Dir. 1842.

—, WEAVER: Newport, R.I., Meeting St. "Cabinet and chair maker." Label in Tall clock of Henry A. Hoffman, Barrington. (See ill. No. 3505. (FT))

HOLMGREEN, CHARLES: Hamilton, N.Y. Ca.1850.

HOLTON, HARRY: Wells River, Vt. Ca.1850.

HOLWAY, PHILIP: Falmouth, Mass. Ca. 1800. Prob. in Boston, Hanover St. Dealer or R. Clock in Worcester with his name. Prob. learned trade Marblehead or Lowell. Pos. Philip Holway of Falmouth. (E. F. Holway, N.Y.C.)

HOMAN, SAMUEL: Marblehead, Mass. Gray Watch Paper Bir. Col.

"HOME WATCH CO.," used by American Watch Co., Waltham. No. 5190283 made ca.1868. "Not old enough to be among the American-made watches to be rare. Value possibly only in case, in collector's market." (Bul.)

— WATCH CO.: Boston, ca.1890. Watch owned by Russell Hughes, Atlantic City, N.J. No. 299847 with 1891 scratch mark.

HOMER, WILLIAM: Moreland, Pa. 1849.

HOOD, FRANCES: N.Y.C. 1810.

—, JOHN: Phila. n/d.

HOOK, MICHAEL: Lancaster, Pa. Ca.1708. "Little known." (Lan. Co.)

HOOKER & GOODENOUGH: Bristol. Ca.1840.

— & MORGAN: Pine Plains, N.Y. Ca.1815–1820.

HOOLEY, RICHARD: Flemington, N.J. From England; in U.S. 1796–1840. C.W. Most Tall clocks have Sheraton or Hepplewhite cases. Dials often marked with name and "Flemington." One known with his name and "New York." (J. F. Schenk)

HOOPS, ADAM: Somerset, Pa. Ca.1800.

HOOVER, JOHN: Emmetsburg, Md. Ca.1850.

HOPE, F. M.: Sag Harbor, N.Y. 1870. J. Tall clock in Sag Harbor Library; spent 30 years in its construction.

HOPKINS (Edward) & ALFRED (Augustus): Harwinton, Conn. 1820–1827. Excellent wood movt. clocks. "Made by them and sold by Thos. Moses." Original building still standing 1947. Hopkins lived in Northfield, walked to work; Alfred lived in Harwinton. Dials hand painted by Alfred's two sisters, Louisa Sperry and Cynthia Gunn. Pos. sold out to Seth Thomas. (Ben Hopkins)

— & LEWIS: Litchfield, Conn. Ca.1825. Wood movts. for 30-hr. Tall clocks. Tall clock in Mitchell Col.; one owned by Bruce E. Marks, Harrisburg, Pa., solid walnut case.

—, ASA: 1799–. Northfield and Fluteville, Conn. Inventor; C. Patent on cutting wheel engine 1813. Shop and clockmaking business in Fluteville, 4 miles S. of Torrington. Sold out to Orange Hopkins, who made flutes and clarinets, who in turn sold to New York firm. To New York State with Orange. Patent from Litchfield, "Wheels for Wooden clocks, August 22, 1814." Inventive genius. Many uncredited improvements. (Ben Hopkins)

HOPKINS, HENRY P.: Phila. Dir. 1831–1833. Dealer.

—, JASON R.: Washington, D.C. Perfected 1875 model of watch planned to make for 50¢. (Later attempted by H. W. R. Fowle and Auburndale Watch Co.; ended in failure.)

—, JOSEPH: Waterbury, Conn. Ca.1750. Prob. no clocks. S.

—, ORANGE: 1791–. Litchfield, Campville, and Terryville, Conn. Ca.1820–1830. Pos. with Terry 1804, to Terryville, but name of town not established until early 1830's. Shelf clock, 30-hr. Tall wood movt. pull-up type, Selchow Col. Bought out Asa Hopkins, Fluteville. Also Mus. insts. Prosperous; Pillar and Scroll, Tall clocks; most cases fine; one cherry known. Tall clock owned by Geo. Hartman, Phila., 30-hr. wood movt. Shop, near Castle Bridge, still stands. Original plant enlarged. (S. A. Beckwith)

—, ROBERT: Phila. Dir. 1833.

—, WILLIAM R.: Geneva, N.Y., Patent on "Barometer" Jan. 25, 1841.

HOPPER, B. C.: Phila. Dir. 1844–1848.

—, BENJAMIN: Phila. Dir. 1850 and later.

—, JOHN M.: Phila. 1819. (Baillie)

—, J. M. (or Joseph): Dir. 1835–1841.

—, JOSEPH M.: Phila. Dir. 1816–1822.

HORAH, JAMES: 1826–1864. Salisbury, N.C. Father S. Adv. 1849.

HORN, ELIPHALET: Lowell, Mass., Central St. Dir. 1832–1847. C. N.H. Mirror clock with alarm extant. (BCC)

—, E. B.: Boston, Washington St. 1847–1860.

HORTON & BURGI: N.Y.C. Ca.1776.

— & PECK (Timothy): Litchfield, Conn. 1808. Timothy Peck's business reorganized. Clocks or paper. (Hoopes)

—, ALFRED: New Haven, Conn. Ca.1840.

—, HENRY BISHOP: 1819–1885. Akron, O. 1845–1860. b. Winchester, Conn. Apt. to Geo. Whinston, cabinetmaker. Seven patents on "Calendar Clocks" 1864–1867. Formed Ithaca Calendar Clock Co. Aug.

1868. Forty different styles. Invented 1868 perpetual calendar mechanism adjusted for Leap Year.

HORWOOD, CHARLES: Bristol, England. Aw. 1750. English Tall clock in Museum City of N.Y.

HOSTETTER, JACOB, JR.: Hanover, Pa. To Ohio 1822; father joined him 1825. C. until ca.1831. (LSS)

—, JACOB, SR.: Hanover, Pa. Aw. 1786; Ohio 1825–1831. (LSS)

—, S.: Hanover, Pa. Ca.1820. Watch Paper.

HOTCHKISS & BENEDICT: Auburn, N.Y. Ca.1830. Shelf clocks.

— & Co., A. S.: N.Y.C. Ca.1869–1870. Assembled Tower clocks by Seth Thomas and sold by American Clock Co. Catalog dated May 1, 1877, extant. First dial clock made in Thomaston 1872.

— & FIELD: Burlington, Conn. Ca.1825. Pos. OG clocks. (John H. Thompson)

— & PIERPONT: Plymouth, Conn. Ca.1810. "They had been selling Wag-on-Walls in N.J." (Jerome)

—, ROBERT & HENRY: Plymouth, Conn. Ca.1840.

—, SPENCER & Co.: Salem Bridge, Conn. Ca.1830. Buttons and 8-day brass Shelf clocks.

—, A. S.: Brooklyn, N.Y. Tower clocks.

—, ALVA: Poughkeepsie, N.Y. 1825–1835. N.Y.C. 1835–1845.

—, ELISHA: Burlington, Conn. Ca.1820. On 1836–1837 Conn. map. Shelf clock, label printed by C. Canfield, in G. B. Davis Col.

—, HEZEKIAH: 1721–1761. New Haven, Conn. Elder son of Caleb and Ruth. Apt. early age; aw. 1748 at 19 own shop New Haven. Bro. John partner. Jack-of-all-trades; blacksmith and dentistry. (Hoopes)

—, JOHN: Rochester, N.Y. Dir. 1845 and later.

—, WILLIAM: "Md." 1775.

HOUGH, J. G.: Bridgeport, Conn. n/d. Dwarf Tall 8-day clock known.

—, JOHN: 1801–. Ind. Aw. 1820's. Son of John and Mary Mills Howe. With William and Mary Hough, grandparents, to Wayne Co., Ind., 1814. First shop New Liberty, near Fountain City, Ind., cabinet work. Clocks in New Liberty;

HOUGH, JOHN (*cont'd*)
Newport, Ind., by 1830. Two Tall clocks, wood movts. solid cherry cases, one flat top, other scroll top. Pos. cases only. (AAJ Sept. 1949) (W. C. Heiss)

HOUGUET, AUGUSTUS: Phila. 1819–1825. (Baillie)

HOUSE & ROBINSON: Bristol. (tx) 1851. Pos. C.

—, GEORGE: Hanover, Pa. n/d. C., S.

—, GEORGE V.: N.Y.C., 107 Fulton St., 175 Chatham St. Pos. dealer. Shelf Empire clock, 30-hr. brass movt., brass dial, owned by Willis Milham, O.G. in E. Rossi Col., label, "Improved clocks made and sold by . . ."

HOUSTON, JAS.: Johnstown, Pa. n/d.

—, WILLIAM: Phila. *Ca.*1800. Tall clock No. 4, brass dial, owned by Mrs. Anthony Morris, Bryn Mawr, Pa. (R. Franks)

HOVEY, S., & Co.: Manchester, N.H. n/d. Watch Paper BCL Col.

—, CYRUS: Lowell, Mass. *Ca.*1870.

—, J. R.: Norwich, N.Y. Aw. 1817.

HOWARD, A., & Co.: Boston. Name used by Albert Howard.

— CLOCK Co., E.: Roxbury, Mass. 1903–1934. Discontinued watches 1930.

— CLOCK PRODUCTS Co.: Waltham, Mass. 1934–.

— CLOCK & WATCH Co., THE: 1861–1863. Formerly E. Howard & Co. Watches marked "E. Howard & Co."

— & DAVIS: Boston. 1842–1859. Succeeded by E. Howard & Co.

—, DAVIS & DENNISON: Roxbury, Mass. *Ca.*1850.

—, E., & Co.: Roxbury, Mass. 1857–1861. Clocks so marked to present day. Movts. numbered. Banjo clock movts. generally heavier construction than Willards. Prob. made all Riggs Banjo clocks. Made Ws. (See ill. Nos. 294, 295.)

—, E., WATCH & CLOCK Co.: 1881–1903.

— WATCH & CLOCK Co., THE: Boston. 1863–1881. Business shifted from watches to clocks.

— WATCH Co.: Waltham, Mass. 1910–1927. W. Keystone Co. bought factory of U. S. Watch Co. at Waltham. (AJ Mar., Apr. 1950)

— , ALBERT: –1893. Boston. *Ca.*1878. Son of Watters Howard, bro. and apt. of

Edward. Gen. Mgr. of firm 1881–1893. C. and scale maker. Name on some clocks. "HOWARD, CHAS. E.," used by N. Y. Watch Co. 1871–1875.

—, E.: N.Y.C. "Of Boston." Showroom in N.Y.C. and Chicago. Watch Paper BCL Col.

—, EDWARD: 1813–1904. Boston, Waltham, Mass. Apt. at 16 to Aaron Willard, Jr. W. C. Partner 1842 David P. Davis, Howard & Davis, office Boston, 34 Water St. Roxbury factory. Mechanical genius, many inventions, mass-production machinery. With Aaron L. Dennison 1848 (beginning of Waltham Watch Co.); Howard, Davis & Dennison 1850; American Horologe Co. 1850; Warren Mfg. Co. 1853; Boston Watch Co. 1853; Waltham Improvement Co. 1853–1857; E. Howard & Co. 1857; Howard Clock & Watch Co. 1861; Howard Watch & Clock Co. 1863; E. Howard Watch & Clock Co. 1881; retired 1882. Fine jeweled watches, "E. Howard & Co." For story of his part in Waltham Watch Co. see *Timing a Century*, by Chas. W. Moore.

Famous for Banjo, Regulator, Tower and Wall clocks. Banjo clocks in five sizes, wooden bezels, moon type hands, rounded or square side boxes. (See ill. No. 177.) Many wall clocks for offices and factories. Excellent Tower clocks, many used for replacement in old church buildings; continue to be made today.

—, J.: Boston. "1870's." Prob. R. only. Card or label in clocks. (Buhler)

—, THOMAS: Phila., 26 So. 2nd St. Adv. 1775. (Prime)

—, WILLIAM: Boston. Dir. 1813–1821.

HOWCOTT, NATHANIEL: Edenton, N.C. Adv. 1828, "would work on clocks and watches." Marr. 1828.

HOWE, ELIAS: Boston. Inventor of sewing machine. Before 1843 apt. to Ari Davis, maker Chron. No watches or clocks known.

—, JUBAL: Boston. Dir. 1830.

HOWELL & HALL: Albany, N.Y. Adv. 1801.

—, NATHAN: 1741–1784. New Haven, Conn. Son of Stephen Howell, Jr. Brass clocks; one owned by New Haven Colony Hist. Society. (Hoopes)

HOWELL, SILAS WHITE: 1770-. New Brunswick, N.J.; Albany, N.Y. S. b. Morristown, son of Captain Silas and Hannah. Adv. 1794. Adv. 1797 Albany, N.Y., as Howell & Arnold; dissolved 1798.

HOYT, BADGER, & DILLON: N.Y.C., 266 Pearl St. n/d. Watch Paper Cramer Col.

—, GEORGE A., & Co.: Albany, N.Y. Dir. 1829–1833.

—, GEORGE A., & SON: Albany, N.Y. Dir. 1845–1846. Watch Paper Bir. Col.

—, S., & Co.: N.Y.C., 266 Pearl St. Ca. 1836. Ex. Museum City of N.Y.

—, FREEMAN: 1805–1869. Sumter, S.C. Adv. 1832, "12 years experience in NYC."

—, GEORGE A.: Albany, N.Y. Dir. 1822–1844. S.

—, GEORGE B.: Albany, N.Y. Dir. 1846 and later.

—, HENRY: N.Y.C. ca.1810; Albany, N.Y. Dir. 1828–1836.

—, JAMES H.: Troy, N.Y., 242 River St. Dir. 1838 and later. Watch Paper BCL Col.

—, SEYMOUR: Brooklyn, N.Y. Ca.1840.

HUBBARD BROS.: N.Y.C., John and Nassau Sts. Adv. 1862, "Importers of watches." (BCC)

—, GILBERT & Co.: Bristol. (tx) 1857. Pos. C.

—— & HITCHCOCK: Buckland, Mass. Early 19th century. "Before Sherwin." Power from Taylor Brook. (Ant. Sept. 1938)

—, C.: Boston. n/d. Tablet in Banjo clock owned by William Meanix, "C. Hubbard, 18 State Street, Boston." (BCC)

—, C. K.: Hartford, Conn. Ca.1860.

—, DANIEL: Medfield, Mass. Ca.1820.

HUBBELL (Laporte) & BEACH (Levi) (BEACH & HUBBELL): Bristol. (tx) 1859–1863. Marine clocks. Hubbell bought out Beach heirs, continued alone.

—— & BOARDMAN: New Haven, Conn. Adv. ca.1860–1870 "Calendar Clocks."

—, L., & SON: Bristol, Frederick St. (tx) 1874–1879. "Marine Shop." Marine movts., bank lock clocks, 8-day and 30-hour lever and pendulum clock movts.

—, LAPORTE: –1889. Bristol, Frederick St. Aw. 1849–1889. Clocks. Burned out 1873; built "Marine Shop." In Hendrick, Hubbell & Co., 1849–1852; Hendrick, Hubbell & Beach, 1853–1854; Hubbell &

Beach, 1859–1863; Laporte Hubbell & Son, 1874–1879. Patents October 10, 1865, Nov. 28, 1865. Patent model No. 51184 at Smiths. Inst. (Coleman)

HUBER, CHRISTIAN: –1789. Cocalico Twp., Pa. Clock tools bequeathed to bros. and sisters. (Lan. Co.)

HUCKEL, SAMUEL: Phila., 38 Cedar St. Dir. 1818–1829.

HUDSON, EDWARD: Mt. Holly, N.J. 1810–1814. (Stow)

—, J. C.: San Francisco, Calif. Ca.1860.

—, WILLIAM: Mt. Holly, N.J. Ca.1810–1816. Clock with copper silvered dial known to have been made by him. (Stow)

HUGHES & HALL: Middletown, Conn. n/d. "Watchmakers," Watch Paper Bir. Col.

—, EDMUND: Hampton and Middletown, Conn. C. S. Ashford, Conn., 1788. (Hoopes)

—, GEORGE W.: Phila. Dir. 1829–1833.

HUGUENAIL, CHARLES T.: Phila., 83 Callowhill. Dir. 1799–1828. See Huguenin.

HUGUENIN, CHARLES FREDERICK: Phila. Dir. 1797–1802. From Switzerland. Adv. 1798 at Halifax, Wilmington, Fayetteville, S.C. Pos. Huguenail.

HUGUS, JACOB: 1768–1835. Greensburg, Pa. Bought property 1784. Bro. Michael. W. J. Owned farm in Hempfield Twp., flour mill operated after 1816. Great-granddaughter said he made Tall clocks; one owned by A. H. Torrence, Indiana, Pa. (A. H. Torrence)

—, MICHAEL: Berlin, Pa. Early 1800's. Tall clocks. Bro. Jacob. (A. H. Torrence)

HULBURT, HORACE: New Haven, Conn. Ca.1850.

HUMBERDROZ, —: Phila. 1799. (Prime)

HUMBERT, CHARLES: N.Y.C. Ca.1810.

—, DROZ: Phila. 1795. (Baillie)

HUMMELY & THOMAS: Piqua, O. Adv. 1829, "Clockmakers." (Knittle)

HUMPHREY (Humphries), DAVID: Lexington, Ky. Adv. 1789–1793. S. and engraver. Pos. did Ky. State Seal. (LB) (MFM)

—, NORMAN: N.Y.C. 1840's. Pos. cases only.

HUMPHREYS, JOSHUA: Charlestown, Tredyffrim, East Whiteland, Pa. Ca.1744-. Six Tall clocks known. W. R. Hines, Phila., owns 7½' Tall clock, mahogany case, two 25 lb. weights, brass pulleys, large dial. (James)

HUNT, E.: N.Y.C. 1789.
—, HIRAM: 1806–1866. Robbinston and Bangor, Me. Tall and Shelf clocks. (Abbott) (E. A. Battison)
—, JOHN: Farmington and Plainville, Conn. Ca.1830–1840. Wood movt. Shelf clock owned by Mrs. Harry Robbins, Elmira, N.Y.; Carved 8-day brass movt. Shelf clock known.
HUNTINGTON, M. P., & Co.: Milton, N.C. Dealers. Adv. 1819. M. Palmer and bro. William. (Cutten)
— & PLATTO: Ithaca, N.Y. 1855–1868. Came from Plymouth, Conn. Became Ithaca Calendar Clock Company, 1868 to 1919, using Horton patents. Bought Hawes patent on Calendar clocks, later sold it to Seth Thomas.
—, GORDON: 1763–1804. Windham, Conn. Adv. 1784, "a few rods north of Major Ebenezer Backus's store in Windham." To Walpole, N.H. Oct. 1789; postmaster. Died insolvent. Estate administered by Asa Sibley, C., Woodstock, Conn. (Hoopes)
HURDUS, ALLEN: Cincinnati, O. From England 1806. Minister. Tall clock known in England exhibited U.S. Prob. no American clocks. (A. Lockett)
HURST, DAVID: Lancaster, Pa. Ca.1850.
HURTIN (William) & BURGI (Frederic): Bound Brook, N.J. Adv. 1776.
HURTIN, CHRISTIAN: Goshen, N.Y. Adv. 1792–1793. (Cutten)
—, JOSHUA: 1738–1780. Bro. William III, son and successor (1765) of William, Jr. "Shop robbed" 1775. Business depleted by Rev. War. (Williams)
—, WILLIAM, III: Bound Brook, N.J. Adv. 1776 N.Y.C. on "Golden Hill," John St. Son of Wm. Hurtin, Jr. (Williams)
HUSTON, JAMES: Trenton, N.J. 1761–1770. C. Phila., Walnut Ward, 1774. (Stow)
—, JOSEPH: Albany, N.Y. Ca.1850.
—, WILLIAM: Phila., Middle Ward. Adv. 1754–1771. C. Tall clock, name on dial; case by Nathaniel Dowdney, Phila. cabinetmaker. Name also on dial of Tall clock case made by Edwin James, label inside, in Phila. Museum of Art. (Gillingham) (Chandlee) (Am. Col. October 1937)
HUTCHINS, ABEL: 1763–1853. Apt. of Simon Willard 1783. Aw. 1786, Roxbury, Mass.

To Concord, N.H. 1788, with bro. Levi till 1821. Fine Tall clocks.
HUTCHINS, LEVI: Abington, Conn.; Concord, N.H. Apt. of Simon Willard. Training as W., Abington. To Concord, N.H., 1786; with bro. Abel 1788. Had apts. Some Tall clocks marked "Levi & Abel Hutchins." "Possibly they are the earliest." Banjo clock reported. Mass. Shelf clock in J. C. Wells Col. (DKP) (Hist.)
—, NICHOLAS: Baltimore. Ca.1810.
HUTCHINSON, SAMUEL: Phila. Dir. 1828–1839.
—, THOMAS: –1820. Phila. Dir. 1816–1820.
HUTINSON, WILLIAM: Phila. After 1800.
HUVER, I.: n/p. Pa. Name on clock bought near Pittsburgh, Pa. (Barny)
HYDE, JOHN E.: 1885. N.Y.C. (MFM)
—, J. O.: N.Y.C., 22 Maiden Lane. Dir. 1854.
HYLAND, WILLIAM C.: N.Y.C. Dir. 1848.
HYMAN, HENRY: Lexington, Ky. Adv. 1799. (LB)
—, SAMUEL: Baltimore, 8 Market Square, 1799; Phila., ca.1800.
HYVER, G. A.: New Orleans, La. Ca.1850–1860. (Dre)

IHRIE, EDWARD: Easton, Pa. Early 19th century.
ILLINOIS SPRINGFIELD WATCH Co.: Springfield, Ill. 1869–1879. Reorg. 1875, same name; reorg. 1879 as Springfield Illinois Watch Co.; later became Illinois Watch Co.; 1927 sold to Hamilton Watch Co. (*Timing a Century*)
— WATCH Co., THE: 1885–1927. Sold to Hamilton Watch Company 1927. Approx. numbers

1872	5,000	1895	2,560,000
1873	12,000	1900	3,200,000
1874	40,000	1905	3,500,000
1875	50,000	1910	3,800,000
1876	160,000	1915	4,140,000
1877	220,000	1920	4,500,000
1878	300,000	1925	4,800,000
1879	400,000	1930	5,100,000
1880	460,000	1935	5,360,000
1885	1,120,000	1940	5,650,000
1890	1,810,000		(MFM)

— WATCH CASE Co.: Elgin, Ill. Acquired remaining stock of Rockford Watch Co. 1915. (Evans)

Imay, K. K.: n/d. (Dre)

Imbery, J. & A.: N.Y.C., 231 Grand St. Dir. 1840.

—, John: N.Y.C. *Ca.*1820–1830.

Imhauser & Co.: N.Y.C., 212 Broadway. Patent April 4, 1873, "Watchman's Improved Time Detectors."

Imhoff, Jacob: N.Y.C. *Ca.*1840.

Imlay, —: New Haven and Hartford, Conn. *Ca.*1801–1807. Pos. in Heydorn & Imlay. (Hoopes)

Imperial Clock Co.: Hyland, Ill. *Ca.* 1936.

Inch, John: Annapolis, Md. Adv. 1745–1749.

Independent Watch Co.: Fredonia, N.Y. J. C. Adams helped organize. Bought Cornell Watch Co. and its successor Calif. Co. 1877. Sold other watches 1880 marked "Fredonia Watch Co." First watches completed called "Marion" movts.; new model 1882, succeeded 1884 by Fredonia Watch Co. Sold 1885 to Peoria Watch Co.

Ingersoll, Robert H., & Bro.: Waterbury, Conn., Trenton, N.J. (factories); N.Y.C. (office). Started 1892; developed huge business in inexpensive watches. Bought Trenton Watch Co. 1908. Contract with Waterbury Clock Co. f. 1922, result of overexpansion after World War I. (See ill. Nos. 308, 310.) (Brearley)

—, Daniel G.: Boston. 1803–1813. (Abbott)

—, Daniel III: Boston. Dir. 1800.

—, Robert Hawley: 1859–1928. N.Y.C. b. Delta, Mich., son of Orville and Mary Elizabeth Ingersoll. Came to N.Y., at 20, making and selling rubber stamps. Mail order business; added first "dollar" watch to his list 1892, made for him by Waterbury Clock Co. (who eventually made most of nearly 70 million sold). Lantern pinion helped production of nonjeweled watch. Business was later expanded to include jeweled watches. Younger brother, Charles Henry Ingersoll, became plant manager. f. 1922; sold to Waterbury Clock Co.

Ingraham, E. & A.: Bristol, Conn. 1852–1855; Ansonia, 1855–1856. Shelf clocks so marked.

— & Co., E.: Bristol. 1857–1880. Elias and Edward. Successors to E. & A. Ingraham. Leading Cs. Several factories.

Ingraham & Co., The E.: Bristol. 1880–1884. Joint stock company, Elias Ingraham Pres.

—, Co., The E.: Bristol. 1884 to present day. One of largest mfgers. of Cs. and Ws. in the world. Present mgt. fifth generation. Bought 1912 Bannatyne Watch Co. Large current production nonjeweled watches.

—, Elias, & Co.: Bristol. n/d. Label so marked. Edward Ingraham suggests dates 1857–1861.

— E. (Elias) & A. (Andrew), Co.: Bristol, North Main St. near present Ingraham plant. 1852–1856. Factory burned Dec. 1855. Operated about a year in Ansonia, Conn.

— & Bartholomew: Bristol. 1831–1832.

— (Elias) & Goodrich (Chauncey): Bristol. 1832–1833. Made Cases.

— & Steadman: N.Y.C. and Conn. *Ca.* 1850.

—, Elias: 1805–1885. Bristol, Ansonia, Conn. b. Marlboro, Conn. Cabinetmaker, joiner, C., case maker. Aw. 1827. Foremost clock case designer of period. Sharp Gothic Shelf clock, nicknamed "Steeple," most famous; excellent proportions kept by few imitators. Founded 1831 clock business now one of largest in world; carried on by fifth generation. d. Bristol Aug. 16, 1885, at 80. In Ingraham & Bartholomew 1831–1832; Ingraham & Goodrich 1832–1833; alone 1835–1840; Ray & Ingraham 1841–1844; Brewster & Ingraham 1844–1852; E. & A. Ingraham 1852–1855; Ansonia 1855–1856; E. Ingraham & Co. 1857–1880; The E. Ingraham & Co. 1880–1884; The E. Ingraham Co. 1884 to present. Many clocks extant. (Edward Ingraham)

—, Henry: Phila. Dir. 1829–1833.

—, Reuben: 1745–1811. Preston and Plainfield, Conn. Son of John, Jr. Apt. of John Avery. Tall clock in Garvin Col.; one Tall clock marked "Plainfield" known. (Hoopes)

Inskeep, Joseph: Phila. *Ca.*1800. Tall clocks.

International Time Recorders: N.Y.C. 1936.

"Inter-Ocean," used by Elgin National Watch Co. from *ca.*1877.

Irish, Charles: N.Y.C. 1822.

Ithaca Calendar Clock Co.: Ithaca, N.Y. 1865–1914 (1919). Calendar clocks with two dials, under H. B. Horton patents. Liquidated and sold out either 1914 or 1919. (See ill. No. 266.)

Itnyer, —: Hagerstown, Md. Before Rev. War. (LSS)

Ives, Amasa & Chauncey: Bristol. 1811–1812. Shop on Pomeroy's Brook near present Thompson Clock Company. Sometimes known as Amasa Ives, Jr., & Co. Joseph Ives prob. in company.

—, Amasa, Jr., & Co.: Bristol. Another name for Amasa & Chauncey Ives.

—, Blakeslee & Co.: Bridgeport, Conn. *Ca.*1870–1880. Novelty motion clocks.

— Brothers: Bristol. Six bros. famous in Bristol clock history. Ira; Amasa; Philo, father of Lawson C. and Philander; Joseph or "Uncle Joe"; Shaylor; Chauncey. Eleven patents on clocks. Ira received two: 1809, clock, time and strike, 1812, pinions; Shaylor two for clock spring, 1836 and 1828; Joseph seven, from clock case patent Mar. 21, 1822, to final patent on "Watch No. 25934, October 25, 1859."

— (Shaylor) & Brewster (Elisha C.): Bristol. (tx) 1840–1843. Less expensive spring-driven movts.

—, C. (Chauncey) & L. (Lawson) C.: Bristol. (tx) 1830–1838. Built "Eureka shop." Elias Ingraham made cases for them. Joseph Ives 8-day patent brass clocks and 30-hour wood movts. Lawson alone 1839 as Lawson C. Ives & Co. Shelf clock at Edison Inst.

—, Lawson C., & Co.: Bristol. (tx) 1839–1843. Son of Philo. Made clocks in Eureka shop.

—, Amasa: 1777–1817. With bro. Chauncey as Amasa & Chauncey Ives. 1811–1812.

—, Charles Graneson: Bristol, No. Peacedale St. 1816–1824. Son of Enos. Sold 1824 to Orrin Hart.

—, Chauncey: 1787–1857. Bristol. Aw. 1811–1838. Pillar and Scroll clocks, wood movts. In C. & L. C. Ives 1830–1838. f. Friend of Elias Ingraham. In Hartford after 1845. Pillar and Scroll clock in G. B. Davis Col.

Ives, Enos: N.Y.C., 105 Fulton St. Dir. 1848.

—, George: Lebanon, Pa. n/d. Tall clocks. (Conrad)

—, Ira: 1775–1848. Bristol, North Main St. near north end of present Ingraham shop. Aw. 1809. Two patents from Bristol, "Time and Strike Clock" June 24, 1809, and "Pinions for Clocks" Feb. 24, 1812. Sold to Josiah Davis, Jr., who sold 1835 to Elias Ingraham. With bro. Chauncey active in real estate 1830–1845. Sons Joseph Shaylor and Ira A. (LB)

—, James S.: Bristol. Patent May 23, 1836, "Spring for Clocks." Prob. Shaylor.

—, John: Bristol. Patent on Clock cases March 21, 1822. Prob. Joseph.

—, Joseph: 1782–1862. Bristol. Famous C. Aw. *ca.*1805. Tall hang-up wood movts. (See ill. No. 69.) Invented "roller pinions" (see ill. No. 70). In business for himself 1812. Pos. then made Tall wood movt. clocks, some 30-hour, some 8-day. In Amasa Ives, Jr., & Co., 1811–1812. Interested in process of producing rolled brass. *Conn. Gazeteer* 1819 gives space to "factory in Bristol then making brass clocks." With Thomas Barnes, Jr., and Lot Newell in Joseph Ives & Co. 1818–1819 making movts. with cast brass wheels and iron plates (see ill. No. 225); became Thomas Barnes & Co. *ca.*1820. In Merriman, Birge & Co. 1819–1822. With Levi Lewis 1819–1823. Invented and patented Mirror clock (see ill. Nos. 225, 227); some wood movts., roller pinions; long pendulum required longer case. Three examples experimental wood type in Pillar and Scroll case known (see ill. No. 231). To Brooklyn, N.Y., 1825; first produced famous Wagon-spring clocks there (see ill. Nos. 230, 232). In financial difficulties 1830; John Birge bailed him out, took him back to Bristol. Pos. clocks with own labels before 1833 (see ill. Nos. 243, 244), including ladder-type brass strap movt. The name Birge & Ives appears on label of Empire 2- and 3-decker clocks *ca.*1832–1833. In Birge, Case & Co. 1833–1834. Patents April 12, 1833, "Rolling Pinions" and "Striking Parts of Clocks" (striking part a long brass arm extended to the left). Constantly aw. on wagon spring clocks. His 8 day and 30-hour Wagon-spring clocks in Steeple on Steeple cases made by Birge & Fuller 1844–1848. See ill. Nos. 233–238.

Devised and made 1850–1856 best of the wagon-spring movts., ran one month on a winding; wall case or box Shelf case (see ill. Nos. 239–241). In attempt to compete with coil spring clocks, to Farmington or Plainville, Conn. Produced bow type wagon-spring 30-hour clock; few extant. One in LSS Col. Patent 1859 on round tin plate movt. (See ill. No. 247.) d. Bristol, April 18, 1862. Worthy of complete book, for his development of rolled brass in clock business. (LB)

IVES, JOSEPH SHAYLOR: –1887. Bristol. Son of Ira. Worked in father's shop. Patent 1828 on "Striking part." To West Farms, N.Y.C., 1848 as "organette maker." Patent 1836 on "Brass Spring" when foreman for E. C. Brewster. Patent 1838 on "Steel Spring." Pos. one of first to devise successful American clock spring.

—, PHILO: 1780–1822. Bristol. Father of Lawson C. (1805–1867) and Philander.

—, PORTEUS R.: 1805–1867. Bristol. Son of Joseph; father of Rollin and Joseph II.

—, ROLLIN: Bristol. (tx) 1861–1865. Son of Porteus, grandson of Joseph. Marr. daughter of Alfonso Barnes, sister of Wallace Barnes. (Hull)

—, SHAYLOR: 1785–ca.1840. Bristol. Pos. one of first to make low-priced spring-driven clock. With Elisha C. Brewster 1840–1843.

JACKS (James) & GIBSON (Thomas): Charleston, S.C. Ca.1780. Dissolved 1800.

—, JAMES: –1822. Jamaica, West Indies, ca.1777; Charleston, S.C., 5 Broad St., 1784–1797; Adv. Phila. 1797, Dir. 1799; Charleston 1822.

JACKSON, ALFRED: Norwalk, Conn. n/d. Watch Paper Bir. Col.

—, CHARLES: Schenectady, N.Y. Adv. 1816.

—, GEORGE, JR.: Ca.1778–1836. East Marlborough, Pa. Aw. 1788–1812. C., S., and carpenter. One Tall clock known, case by Edward Brooks 1808. No record after 1812. To Del. 1833. (James)

—, ISAAC: 1734–1807. London Grove and

New Garden, Pa. Aw. 1761–1807. Pos. apt. of Benjamin Chandlee. C., W., S., pewterer, brass caster. Elisha Kirk, apt. Tall clocks, 15 known, some with moons. (James)

JACKSON, JOHN: 1746–. Marlborough, Pa. Aw. ca.1770–1777. Tory leanings; to Nova Scotia. Two Tall clocks known.

—, JOHN: Boston. 1791. (Baillie)

—, JOSEPH A.: Mill Creek, Del. b. England. Aw. 1790. Phila. 1802–1810. Two Tall clocks known marked "J. H. Jackson, Mill Creek Hundred, Del.," owned by Robert C. Justis and James G. Longfellow, Clayton, Del.

—, RICHARD: East Springfield, O. Aw. 1801–1812. Tall clocks. "An early resident." (Knittle)

—, THOMAS: Ca.1727–1806. b. England. To Portsmouth, N.H., Kittery, Me., Boston, and Preston, Conn. C. Tall clock in Lewis Dyer Col.; two others known.

JACOB (Charles) & CLAUDE: Annapolis, Md. Adv. 1775.

—, CELESTIN: Phila. Importer of Watches. Dir. 1840.

—, CHARLES: Annapolis, Md. Adv. 1773–1775. Adv. Port Tobacco, Baltimore 1778.

JACOT, A.: Baltimore. Dir. 1842.

JACQUES CLOCK CO., CHARLES: N.Y.C., Cortland St. Ca.1880. Dealer. "Agent for V. Blanpain of Paris."

JAEGER WATCH CO.: N.Y.C. 20th century. Timers and automobile clocks.

JAMES, EDWARD: Phila. Late 18th century. Cabinetmaker. Name on Tall clock dials; label in case of Tall clock owned by William Huston in Pa. Museum. (Stretch)

—, HENRY B.: Patent No. 120, 385, Oct. 31, 1871, model at Smiths. Inst.

—, J. J.: Augusta, Ga. Ca.1820.

—, JOSHUA: Boston. Dir. 1810–1820.

—, WM.: Portsmouth, R.I. Early 18th century.

JAMESON, JACOB: –1830. Columbia, Pa. Pos. apt. of John Maus. Made Tall clocks, Front St. Sold these at $65, "no profit." To Dayton, O., 1823; pos. with Marsh, Williams & Hayden, who operated first clock factory in new territory. Springfield, O., census 1828 as "Clockmaker." Tall clock owned by John B. McGrew. (Lockett) (Lan. Co.)

JAMIN, JEAN BAPTISTE: Baltimore. *Ca.*1800.

JARRET, SEBASTIAN: Germantown, Pa. Taxed as C. 1772. Tall clock owned by I. LeRoy Bush, Oxford, Pa., brass dial, scroll work in corners, center top inscribed "Sebastian Jarret fecit"; two iron hands, one weight, 30-hour chain drive, strikes hour and half hour. (Gillingham)

JARVIS, JOHN JACKSON: Boston. Adv. 1787, "Cabinet, chair and Clockmaker from London." Several John Jarvis's in Eng. (Baillie)

JEANES, THOMAS: Phila. Pos. Joyce. Dir. 1835–1837.

JEANNERET, THEOPHILUS H.: Phila. Dir. 1818.

JEFFERIS, CURTIS G.: 1785–. Aw. 1817–1819. Glasgow, Ky., 1820–1834. Watch Paper Chester Co. Hist. Soc.

JEFFERSON, THOMAS: Monticello, Va. Letter 1813 tells of wish for certain materials to make clock pendulum to complete certain experiments he was making. Made sun dials.

JEFFREYS, SAMUEL FULLER: Phila. Aw. 1759–1776. Prosperous C., and W. till Rev. War. To England. Adv. 1771, "Just imported from London watches, moved to Front St." (Prime) (Ant. Jan. 1929)

JEFFRIES, REV. GEORGE: Franklintown, O. 1814. Tall clock cases. (Knittle)

JENCKS, JOHN E.: Providence, R.I. *Ca.*1800.

JENKINS, I. (Ira) & H. (Harman): Albany, N.Y. Dir. 1815–1816.

—, HARMAN: Albany, N.Y. Adv. 1817–1823.

—, IRA: Albany, N.Y. Dir. 1813.

—, OSMORE: 1837–. Lowell, Mass., Merrimack St. W. at Fenno's.

—, W.: Richmond, Ind. *Ca.*1820.

JENNE & ANDERSONS: Big Rapids, Mich. *Ca.*1860. (Dre)

JENNERER, CHARLES F.: St. Louis, Mo. *Ca.*1820.

JENNINGS BROS. MFG. CO.: Bridgeport, Conn. n/d. Shelf clock Essex Inst.; Mrs. N. H. Johnson, Burlington, Ind., owns desk clock, pewter case, inkstand, pen tray, pewter horse head at back, on back right leg "J. B. 10."

JENNIS, F. S.: Barnstead Parade, N.H. Dir. 1884. (A. L. Childs)

JENSEN, FRED, & SON: N.Y.C., West St. 20th century. Clock museum and store.

JEPSON, WM.: Boston. Dir. 1830.

JEROME & BARNES: Bristol. 1833–1837. Wood movts., weight-driven; one marked "and sold by Geo. D. Wadhams, Wolcottville, Conn." (Paul Swartz Col.)

—, C. (Chauncey) & N. (Noble): Bristol. Bros. (tx) 1834–1839. Successors to Jeromes & Darrow. Wood movts., some 8-day brass.

— & Co.: New Haven, Conn. ca.1850. Label printed by "Benham, 55 Orange St., New Haven, Conn." on looking glass Shelf clock, brass movt.

— & Co.: Phila., 88 Market St. "Clock dealers." Catalogue dated 1852.

— (Noble) & GRANT (Zelotes C.): Bristol. (tx) 1842–1843.

—, Darrow & Co.: Bristol. *Ca.*1825.

— (Noble), JEWELL (Lyman) & Co.: Bristol. (tx) 1847–1849.

— MFG. Co.: New Haven, Conn. 1845–1855. Name also used by New Haven Clock Co. after 1855. Some known with "1870." Pos. for export.

— MFG. Co.: Boston. Adv. 1852. Dir. 1854. Prob. predecessor of B. Bradley & Co., 147 Hanover St. ca.1862.

—, CHAUNCEY & NOBLE: Richmond, Va., and Hamburg, S.C. 1835–1837. Assembly plant in Richmond; tools and workmen, parts and cases from Bristol. Labels printed in Richmond by "Thomas White." Hamburg office sales only.

—, S. B., & Co.: New Haven, Conn. Adv. 1856–1878, "Extra quality clocks in tasteful styles, detached lever timepieces, travel clocks and small shelf clocks."

—, THOMPSON & Co.: Bristol. Wood movt. Shelf clocks known with broken-arch top, finials, 31″ by 16″, 3-panel mirror door.

—, ANDREW: New Haven, Conn. *Ca.*1850.

—, CHARLES: New Haven, Conn. *Ca.*1850.

—, CHAUNCEY: June 10, 1793–Apr. 20, 1868. Plymouth 1816–1822, Bristol 1822–1845, New Haven, Conn. 1845–1855. b. Canaan, Conn. C.; important, colorful figure in Conn. clockmaking business. Apt. as carpenter and joiner. With Eli Terry at Plymouth making clock cases 1816; claims to have made first Pillar and Scroll clock for Terry winter 1816. Later alone making or buying movts. or cases; one known. Bought house from George Mitchell 1821 for 214 "Terry Patent" wood movts. Made wood movt. clocks, 30-hour, 8-day, from 1824–1833 as Jeromes & Darrow. Claimed "invention of looking glass clock (but see Joseph Ives 1822 patent). In C. & N. Jerome 1834–1839; Jeromes, Gilbert, Grant & Co. 1839–1840 (Hiram Camp supt.). In 1843 two large Bristol factories, New Haven assembly plant; prob. largest C. in Conn. Bristol plants destroyed by fire 1845; severe financial loss. Org. Jerome Mfg. Co., at New Haven with Hiram Camp 1850, joint stock company. (Camp in his own business 1853, as New Haven Clock Co. making movts. for Jerome.) Absorbed Terry & Barnum of Bridgeport; f. 1855; taken over by New Haven Clock Co. (See his *History of the American Clock Business for the Past Forty Years*, 1860; also Phineas T. Barnum autobiography.) *Ca.*1866 supt. at Austin or Chicago, Ill., for U. S. Clock and Brass Co. Clock made by this company owned by Samuel W. Jennings, 30-hour weight OG; label printed by "Chicago Evening Journal Printery." d. New Haven 1868. At depth of 1837–1838 depression financed huge mfr. of 30-hour weight-driven strip-rolled brass clock movts. devised by bro. Noble in OG cases; copied by many others; made in tremendous quantities up to *ca.*1914. (See ill. Nos. 250–251.)

Successful, prosperous, energetic, leader in industry. Super salesman, not efficient business man. Many clocks known.

JEROME, CHAUNCEY: N.Y.C., 500 Fifth Ave. Adv. Jewelers Keystone Circular, Mar. 1931. Difficult to believe, but vouched for by Mark F. Massey.

—, CHAUNCEY: Morristown, N.J. *Ca.*1812. Made clock cases near here.

—, C. (Chauncey): Phila. Dir. 1846–1849. Sales outlet or store.

—, NOBLE: Bristol. *Ca.*1824–1849. Bro. Chauncey. In Jeromes & Darrow 1824–1833; C. & N. Jerome 1834–1839; Jeromes, Gilbert, Grant & Co. 1839–1840; Jerome & Grant 1842–1843; Jerome, Jewell & Co. 1847–1849. Invented and perfected one-day weight movt. of strip-rolled brass (see ill. No. 250). Patent at Bristol on "Striking Part of Clock" June 27, 1839.

JEROMES & Co.: Bristol. n/d. OG, round dial, this name on paper in Mitchell Col.

— (Chauncey, Noble) & DARROW (Elijah): Bristol, Main St. (tx) 1824–1833. Chauncey made cases, Nobel movts., Darrow tablets. Factories both sides of Main St., near Requabuck River. Looking glass clocks, wood movts., some 8-day.

— (Chauncey, Noble), GILBERT (Wm. L.), GRANT (Zelotes) & Co: Bristol. (tx) 1839–1840. Low-priced 30-hour brass weight movt.

JESSUP, JONATHAN: York or Yorktown, Pa. Apt. to Elisha Kirk; succeeded Kirk *ca.*1787; continued to *ca.*1850. Friend of Phineas Davis, taught him Watchmaking (Davis built early steam locomotives for B. & O.). Brass movt. Tall clocks. Watch owned by Mrs. Harry Miller, Croyden, Pa., name and No. 490 engraved on inner case, key wind. Tall clock in Michael Col.

—, JOSEPH U.: York, Pa. *Ca.*1820–1850. Son and apt. of Jonathan.

JEWELL, JEROME & Co.: Bristol. (tx) 1847–1849. Same as Jerome, Jewell & Co.

— (Lyman), MATTHEWS (Daniel) & Co.: Bristol. 1847–1853. Also Samuel Botsford. See Matthews, Jewell & Co. (Hist.)

— & WARNER: Bristol. (tx) 1846. Pos. Cs.

JEWETT, AMOS: 1753–1834. New Lebanon, N.Y. "Shaker Clockmaker." (Andrews)

—, AUGUSTINE: Newburyport, Mass. Dir. 1860.

JOB, JOHN: Phila. Dir. 1819.

JOCELIN, SIMEON: 1746–1823. New Haven, Conn. C. Prob. apt. to Isaac Doolittle. Adv. 1771. Owing to Revolutionary War turned to other interests; mfd. salt, watch crystals. C. again before 1790. March 8, 1800, patent for "Silent Moving Timepiece." Adv. Oct. 1800, "Clock Manufacturing." Tall 8-day clock, moon face $45; plain face $40; 8-day timepiece $20. Also 32-day patent silent moving timekeeper $30, "moves on different principles from other timepieces with fewer wheels and pinions with less friction and not a sixth part of the usual weight, as a 5-pound weight will run it for 32 days"; 4-lb., pendulum vibrating 3″ at bob. Tower and House spring clocks. Pos. imported clocks. Active until d. July 13,

JOCELIN, SIMEON (cont'd)
1809. Patented and mfd. "improved pruning shear." Mathematician. (Hoopes)

JOCELYN, ALBERT HIGLEY: 1827–1900. New Haven, Conn. Son of Nathaniel, grandson of Simeon. Mechanically inclined; wood engraver. (Foster W. Rice)

—, NATHANIEL: 1796–1891. New Haven, Conn. Son of Simeon; father of Albert H. Apt. to father at 11 as W.; skilful but turned to drawing, painting, engraving. (Am. Col. Dec. 1947) (Foster W. Rice)

—, SIMEON SMITH: 1825–1879. Son of Simeon, bro. Nathaniel. Engraver; clergyman. Org. bank note engraving company. (Rice)

JOHNSON BROS.: Sanbornton, N.H. Second quarter 19th century. Factory.

— & CROWLEY: Phila. Dir. 1830–1833.

— & LEWIS: Phila. Dir. 1837–1842.

—, R. S. & R. D.: Sanbornton, N.H. Dir. 1844. (Childs)

—, —: Ithaca, N.Y. n/d. Tower clocks.

—, ADDISON: Wolcottville, Conn. Ca.1825. Pillar and Scroll clocks and OGs. Ex. in Floyd Thoms Col.

—, ANDREW: Boston. Ca.1840.

—, CALEB: Boston. Dir. 1805.

—, CHARLES F.: Patent from Owego, N.Y., on "Turret or Town Clocks" July 28, 1846.

—, CHAUNCEY: Albany, N.Y. Dir. 1824–1841. "Musical, Ornamental and Common Clocks." (Cutten)

—, DANIEL B.: Utica, N.Y. Ca.1834–1843.

—, EDWARD: 1774.

—, ELI: Boston. Dir. 1821.

—, ELISHA: Greensboro, N.C. Adv. 1841.

—, F.: Belmont, N.H. J. Dir. 1884. (Childs)

—, ISRAEL H.: Easton, Md. 1793. (Pleasant & Sills)

—, J. J.: N.Y.C. Ca.1860. (Prime)

—, JABEZ: Charleston, S.C., 29 Broad St. 1795.

—, JOHN: Charleston, S.C. Adv. 1763, "Late from London."

—, M. B.: Watertown, N.Y. Adv. 1838.

—, MICHAEL: Yellow Creek, O. Adv. 1816. "Was a Clockmaker." (Knittle)

—, MILES: Wallingford, Conn. n/d. Tall clocks.

—, NELS: Manistee, Mich. Dane. Self-taught. Fifty Tower clocks; two in Detroit, three in Milwaukee, one in N.Y.C., one in Michigan, one in Los Angeles, one in Memphis, one in India. (BCC) (Am. Mag. June 1915)

JOHNSON, P.: Sheward, Del. Apt. of Charles Canby. (Conrad)

— (Johnston), ROBERT: Phila. Dir. 1832–1850.

—, SAMUEL: Hagerstown, Md. n/d. W., J., and dentist. (LSS)

—, WILLIAM S.: N.Y.C., Dir. 1841–1861. 16 Cortlandt St. 1841–1848; 20 Cortlandt St. 1848–1849; many other addresses. Not known if he made Cs.; may have only assembled, or possibly purchased them; many extant with name. Shelf clock at Essex Inst.

JOHNSTON, A. (Arthur) & W. (Walter or Wm.): Hagerstown, Md. Bros. Aw. ca.1785–1815. "On the Public Square." Succeeded after 1800 by A. Johnston. Tall clock in LSS Col.

— & FISCHER: Hagerstown, Md. Ca.1846. (LSS)

— & MELHORNE: Hagerstown and Boonsboro, Md. Ca.1785–1818.

—, J. H., & Co.: N.Y.C., 150 Bowery. Ca.1820. Ex. Museum City of N.Y.

—, ARTHUR: –1846. Hagerstown, Md. Aw. 1785 to ca.1820. Succeeded A. & W. Johnston. Tall and Tower clocks, pos. watches. Bro.-in-law George Fischer, Frederick, Md. In Johnston & Simpson, Johnston & Price, Johnston & Melhorne, A. & W. Johnston. Bank director 1831–1837. (LSS)

—, ROBERT: Cincinnati, O., 186 Vine St. Dir. 1851. Small factory.

JONAS, JOSEPH: Phila. Dir. 1817.

—, JOSEPH: Cincinnati, O., Main and 3rd Sts. Adv. 1817–1825, "From England." (Knittle)

JONCKHEERE, FRANCIS: Baltimore, Md., Bond St. 1807–1824.

JONES & ASPINWALL: Boston. Dir. 1809.

JONES, BALL & Co: Boston. Dir. 1840–1846.

—, BALL & POOR: Boston, Mass. See Shreve, Crump & Low.

— & Co., GEORGE A.: Bristol and N.Y.C., 6 Cortlandt St. (tx) 1870. Dir. 1872. With James Wood. "Clock Manufacturers." Bought W. H. Nettleton clock parts business. Also made a William A. Terry patent Calendar clock. Succeeded by James Wood & Co. (MFM)

JONES & FRISBEE: New Hartford, Conn. Ca.1830–ca.1840. OG in Geiger Col.

—, Lows, & BALL: Boston. Ca.1835. Dir. 1839. A. L. Dennison aw. for them ca. 1837–1839. See Shreve, Crump & Low.

— & OLNEY: Newark, N.Y. Ca.1835. Another Tioga Co. Dealer.

— & PARDMORE: Troy, N.Y. Charles E. DeLong aw. for them ca.1887. (Chamberlain)

—, SHREVE, BROWN & Co.: Boston. Dir. 1852.

— & WOOD: Syracuse, N.Y. Adv. 1846–1847. (Cutten)

—, ABNER: Weare, N.H. 1780 and after. Made 8-day Tall clocks with brass movts. for $50.

—, ALBERT: Greenfield, Mass. n/d. Red Watch Paper Bir. Col.

—, DANIEL: Steubenville, O. 1808. (Knittle)

—, EDWARD K.: Bristol. On 1837 Conn. map.

—, EZEKIEL: Boston, Mass. Dir. 1813–1825. Aw. 1790. Fine C. Mass. Shelf and Banjo clocks. With Daniel Monroe, Jr. 1807–1809. Later alone. (See ill. No. 133.)

—, GEORGE: 1782–1867. Wilmington, Del., 29 and 407 Market St. Aw. 1803–1850 with Samuel McClary, important Wilmington figure. Apt. of Thomas Crow. Dentist. Adv. 1833, "Repairs Clocks and Watches, also cleaning and filing and plugging teeth and teeth brushes." Succeeded ca.1850 by Benjamin S. Clark. (Conrad)

—, GRIFFITH D.: Baltimore. 1824–1827.

—, HARLOW: Canandaigua, N.Y. Adv. 1811–1812. (Cutten)

—, J. B.: Boston, 37 Market St. Authorized by Simon Willard in adv. Oct. 2, 1822, to sell his Lighthouse clocks. (See ill. Nos. 150 and 151.)

—, JACOB: Baltimore, 39 Germain St. 1817–1818.

—, JACOB: Pittsfield, N.H. Tall clocks. Ca.1800.

—, JOHN: Phila. Adv. 1772.

—, NOEL: Hudson or Troy, N.Y. Ca.1800. Tall 8-day brass clock in Amos Avery Col.

JONES, ROLAND: Utica, N.Y. Dir. 1837–1838.

—, SAMUEL G.: Phila. 1799. With Patton & Jones ca.1800.

—, SAMUEL G.: Baltimore, 93 Baltimore St. 1815–1829. W. C. Adv., "Late of Patton & Jones."

—, WILLIAM: N.Y.C., 275 Spring St. Dir. 1846. Astronomical Chron. displayed at American Inst. Fair 1846, won silver medal. None known.

—, WILLIAM H.: Charleston, S.C. Dir. 1837–ca.1841. (Prime)

JORDAN, R.: Richmond, Va. Ca.1820–ca. 1830.

JOSEPH, ISAAC: Boston. Dir. 1823.

—, J. G.: Cincinnati, O. Ca.1830. Pos. Jonas.

JOSLIN, GILMAN: Boston. Globe maker 1855–1876. Globe used on Timby clock (see ill. No. 269). These clocks shipped from Saratoga. Patent 1860 covered map and method of applying. Printed from drawing and engraving by William B. Annin. (BCC)

—, JAMES: New Haven, Conn. "Not C." (Hoopes)

JOYCE, ROBERT: –1811. N.Y.C. Aw. 1794.

—, THOMAS F.: Phila. Dir. 1820–1825. Tall clocks. One owned by Harry B. Hess, N.Y.C., 7½' high, moon, calendar; another by Harry C. Hallowell, Atlantic City, N.J.

JUDD, HENRY: Wolcottville (Torrington), Conn. n/d. Name on Shelf clock paper.

—, HENRY G.: N.Y.C., 382 Greenwich St. Dir. 1846–1847.

JUSTICE, JOSEPH (J. J.): Phila. Dir. 1844–1848.

JUVET, LOUIS PAUL: Glens Falls, N.Y. 1879–1886. Two patents on "Improvement in Time Globes" Jan. 1 and May 21, 1867. Partner with James Arkell and A. G. Richmond, Canajoharie, N.Y., 1879. Harry V. Bush, History of Canajoharie, Chap. 42: "For a few years prior to 1866 the Juvet Time Globe Co. had been mfg. these globe clocks in the village, James Arkell and A. G. Richmond being interested in the concern. The building stood just north of the engine room of the Arkell & Smiths. These time globes were made in several sizes and were operated by clock

JUVET, LOUIS PAUL (cont'd)
work so that the revolutions of the earth
were correctly timed on the globe. The
Co. had exhibited them at all the great
expositions in various parts of the world
and had been awarded many prizes for
the differing styles of globes. Shipments
were being made to all parts of the world,
the markets being libraries, schools and
colleges. On Oct. 18, 1886, the Globe
factory was destroyed by fire, the company
did not rebuild and the industry as far
as Canajoharie was concerned passed out
of existence. All the boys in the village
were on hand the next morning after the
fire, combing the ruins and the creek bed
for map segments, all hoping to find the
necessary number of pieces to make a
globe. Later Arkell and Smith rebuilt the
building as part of their plant."

KABEL, JOSEPH: N.Y.C. Ca.1850.

KADMUS, J.: Dubuque, Ia. n/d. Watch
Paper BCL Col.

KALLMAN, CHARLES: Newburg, N.Y.
Patent No. 88718 April 6, 1869, on combined clock and fly trap. (ALP)

KARN, A. L.: Phila. 202 South 3rd St. Dir.
1809–1810.

KARNER (KARRAR), C.: Phila. Dir. 1809–
1811.

KEARN, FELIX: New Haven, Conn. Ca.1840–
ca.1850.

KEARNEY, HUGH: Wolcottville, Conn. Aw.
ca.1825. Pillar and Scroll Shelf clocks.
One owned by Charles H. Lawten, Torrington, Conn.; another in Collins Clock
Museum.

KEDZIE, JOHN: Rochester, N.Y. Dir. 1838–
1846.

KEEL, JOHN: Phila. Dir. 1835–1837.

KEELER, JOSEPH: Norwalk, Conn. Ca.1870.

KEHEW, WILLIAM HENRY: 1829–. Salem,
Mass., Essex St. 1855–1864.

KEIM, JOHN: 1745–1819. Reading, Pa. 2nd
Group. Aw. 1777–1819. Son of Nicholas.
Proprietor "White store," later Stichters.
Prominent in county and city affairs. Tall
clock owned by Mrs. Stanley Bright,
Reading, Pa.

KELLEY, ALLEN: Sandwich, Mass. 1810–
1830. (Abbott)

—, BENJAMIN: Atlanta, Ga. Dir. 1874.

—, DAVID: Phila. Dir. 1806–1816.

KELLOGG, DANIEL: 1766–1855. Hebron,
Conn. Son of Rev. Ebenezer and Hannah.
Apt. of Daniel Burnap. C. G. Aw. ca.
1787. Marr. 1794. Held town offices.
To Colchester, Conn., 1811; Hartford
1833–1855. (Hoopes)

KELLY, EZRA: New Bedford and Hanover,
Mass. "Kelly Watch Oil." (Abbott)
(Burt)

—, HEZEKIAH: Norwich, Conn. 1793.
(Hoopes)

—, JOHN: New Bedford, Mass. 1836.

—, MICHAEL: N.Y.C., 60 Ridge St. Dir.
1854.

—, O. H.: N.Y.C. n/d. Watch Paper BCL
Col.

KELVEY, THOMAS: West Union, O. Pos.
itinerant Cabinetmaker from East. 8-day
clocks known with "New Holland" on
dial; one, cherry case, owned by Mrs.
Roswold H. Branson, Dobbs Ferry, N.Y.

KEMBLE, WILLIAM: N.Y.C. Pos. Kumbell
or Kimball.

KEMLO, FRANCIS: Chelsea, Mass. Ca.1840.

KENDALL, CALEB: So. Woodstock, Vt. Ca.
1811. "Hung out a sign telling the public
that he worked on silver, gold and brass.
Made jewelry and watches and did repair
work." (Wilder)

—, D.C.: Boston. Dir. 1842.

KENDRICK, FRANK B.: 1845–1936. Lebanon,
N.H. Learned watchmaking with Carlos
Buswell. Year at Newburyport, Mass.,
with N. C. Greenough. Bought Dust
Proof Watch Key Factory 1876, moved it
to Lebanon, employing as many as 125;
destroyed in "great Lebanon fire" of 1887.
Retired 1910. (Chamberlain)

KENNARD, JOHN: Newfields, N.H. Ca.1820.
Tall clocks and Banjo clocks.

KENNEDY ELECTRIC CLOCK CO.: N.Y.C.
Ca.1860. Adv. 1860.

—, ELISHA: 1766–. Middletown, Conn.
Aw. 1788; adv., "Intends to work at clock
and watchmaking and repair in Middle-
town in the shop formerly occupied by
Samuel Canfield and now by William
Johonnot." (Hoopes)

—, PATRICK: Phila., 87 So. 2nd St. Dir.
1795–1801.

—, S. A.: N.Y.C. Ca.1860. Invented an
electric clock. Friend of S. F. B. Morse.

KENNEY, ASA: West Milbury, Mass. *Ca.*
1800.

KENT, LUKE: Cincinnati, O. *Ca.*1820–*ca.*
1840.

—, THOMAS: Cincinnati, O. Aw. 1821–1844.
Son of Luke. (Knittle)

KEPLINGER, JOHN: Baltimore. Early 19th
century. Pos. son of Samuel, bro. of
William.

—, SAMUEL: 1770–1849. Baltimore. Late
18th century. Father of William and
John. Formerly at Gettysburg, Pa.

—, WILLIAM: Baltimore. Dir. 1829. Son
Frederick to Lancaster, Pa., as case maker.
(Stow)

KERN, HERMAN: Lancaster, Pa. *Ca.*1850.

KERNER & PAFF: N.Y.C., 254 Water St.
Adv. 1796. Mus. and Cuckoo clocks.
Pos. imp. (MFM)

—, LOUIS: Muskingum Co., O. *Ca.*1850–
*ca.*1870.

—, NICHOLAS: Marietta, Pa. *Ca.*1850.
(Lan. Co.)

KERNOCHAN, FRANK D.: Middletown, N.Y.
Watch Paper BCL Col. Peter Mitchell:
"Ran a jewelry store for many years.
Did minor clock and watch repair, but did
not make clocks."

KERR, WILLIAM, JR.: Providence, R.I. Pos.
clock factory 1850's.

KERRISON, ROBERT M.: Phila. Dir. 1842
and later.

KERSEY, ROBERT: Easton (?), Md. 1793.

KESSELMEIR, FREDERICK: Wooster, O.
Patent "Clock Pendulums" April 10,
1844.

KESSLER, JOHN, JR.: Phila. Dir. 1806–1808.

KETCHAM & HITCHOCK: N.Y.C. *Ca.*1810.

KEW, GEO.: Phila. Dir. 1840.

KEYES, RUFUS: Lowell, Mass. Dir. 1833–
1834.

KEYSER, JOSEPH: Phila. Dir. 1828–1833.

KEYSTONE WATCH CASE CO., THE: Phila.,
19th & Brown Sts. Org. 1899. *Ca.*1903
bought rights to make "E. Howard"
watches and bought U. S. Watch Co. factory, Waltham, Mass. Watches. Became
Keystone Watch Corp. 1927.

— WATCH CORP.: Phila. 1927 and later.
Name changed from Keystone Watch
Case Co.; combined following: Howard
Watch Co., N.Y.; Standard Watch Co.,
Jersey City; Crescent Watch Case Co.,
Newark; Philadelphia Watch Case Co.,
Riverside, N.J.; others.

KEYSTONE STANDARD WATCH CO., THE:
Lancaster, Pa. 1886–1890. F. See Lancaster Watch Co. (Bowman)

KEYWORTH, ROBERT: Washington, D.C.
*Ca.*1820. (MFM)

—, T.: York, Pa. *Ca.*1850.

"KIDDER, C. L., SAN FRANCISCO," used by
Cornell Watch Co. 1870's.

KILBOURN, HENRY: New Haven, Conn.
*Ca.*1840–*ca.*1850.

KILBOURNE, LEMUEL J.: n/p. Pa. Patents
Oct. 12 and 13, 1809, "Wheels for casting
clocks"; "Clocks, Striking Part."

KILBURN, HIRAM: Lowell, Mass. Dir. 1837.

KILLAM & CO.: Pawtucket, R.I. Name on
movt. of Banjo clock owned by T. H.
Laing, West Nyack, N.Y.

—, GEORGE ROLAND: 1873–1930. "Made
Banjo movts., cased and sold by Tilden-
Thurber, Providence, R.I. A native of
Nova Scotia, he began in 1908 to make
Banjo clock movts. Cases possibly made
by someone else." (TP)

—, GUY: Pawtucket, R.I. 1939–1940. Mfd.
Willard type movts. (Ant. 1939–1940)
(PG)

KIMBALL & GOULD: Haverhill, Mass. Dir.
1865. Succeeded by James C. Bates 1879.

"—, F. A.," used by Otay Watch Co. *ca.*
1889. (Chamberlain)

—, JAMES: Montpelier, Vt. *Ca.*1810.

—, JOHN, JR.: Boston. Pos. 1820.

—, N.: Boston. *Ca.*1820. Banjo clocks.

KIMBERLY, R.: Ansonia, Conn. n/d. 30-
hour OG brass "superior bushed movt."
in Richard Newcomb Col.

KING, HENRY: Hamburg, Pa. *Ca.*1800.
4th Group. Real name Henry Roi.
(Steinmetz)

—, HENRY N.: N.Y.C. *Ca.*1810.

"—, JOHN L.," used by N.Y. Watch Co.
1870's.

—, SAMUEL: 1748–1819. Newport, R.I.
Math. insts., portrait painter, pos. some
clocks. (Am. Col. June 1947)

—, THOMAS: Baltimore. *Ca.*1820.

—, W. B.: Boston. n/d. Name on Tall
clock dial; tag inside, "B. M. Boyce, 49
Cornhill, Boston." (BCC)

KINGSMAN, MATTHEW: Woburn, Mass. n/d.
Watch Paper BCL Col.

KINKAID, GEORGE: Cincinnati, O. *Ca.*1830. (Knittle)

KINKEAD, JOSEPH & ALEX'R: Christiana Bridge, Del. *Ca.*1790. Tall clock so marked in old Allen Homestead there.

—, ALEXANDER: Christiana Bridge, Del. *Ca.*1788. Pos. son of Joseph. (Abbott) (Conrad)

—, JAMES: Adv. Phila. 1765, "On Front St. from Strabane, in Ireland, but late of Salisbury Twp., Chester Co., Pa. Follows his business at Emanuel Rouse's, Front Street, near the drawbridge."

—, JOSEPH: Christiana Bridge, Del. Aw. after 1788. Father of Alexander. Owned lot in Newark, Del. *ca.*1781, sold 1796. Tall clock known with "Joseph and Alex'r. Kinkead" on dial. (Conrad)

KINNAN, JOHN: Phila. n/d. Tall clock owned by Mrs. M. P. Beans, Denver, Col.

KIPPEN, GEORGE: Bridgeport, Conn. 1822.

KIRCHOFF, J. H.: Phila. Dir. 1805.

KIRCKHAFF, E. H.: Phila., 141 No. 2nd St. Dir. 1803.

KIRK, AQUILLA: York, Pa. *Ca.* 1795. Later Baltimore.

—, (KIRKE), CHARLES: Bristol, Wolcott, New Haven, Conn. Tax list 1828–1831. Sold clock business 1833 to E. C. Brewster, but ran it for him till *ca.*1837. Invented fusee for Brewster's brass spring. C. With sons to Wolcott, Conn., 1837. Patent on clocks Aug. 26, 1843; also New Haven 1847 on marine type striking spring-driven movt. Brass marine movts. in New Haven. Two models at Smiths. Inst., patent No. 3233, Aug. 1843 and No. 5045, Apr. 3, 1847.

—, ELISHA: Yorktown, Pa. Aw. 1780–1790. Apt. of Isaac Jackson. Mrs. James L. Hannon, Alexandria, Ind. owns Tall clock, walnut case, one weight, "No. 12." (James)

—, JOHN: Bristol. (tx) 1831.

—, TIMOTHY: Hanover, Pa. *Ca.*1783. Joiner and C. (Am. Col. Apr. 1948)

KIRKE (Charles) & TODD: Wolcott, Conn. Early 1840's. Large brass movt., heavy cast iron back plate, spring barrels, retaining spring E. C. Brewster type in elaborate Musical clock, in Edw. Ingraham Col.

KIRKLAND, SAMUEL W.: Northampton, Mass. Aw. after dissolution of Howell & Kirkland *ca.*1835. (Cutten)

KIRKPATRICK, THOMAS: N.Y.C. *Ca.*1846. Metal Lighthouse clock about 10″ high known.

KIRKWOOD, ALEXANDER: Charleston, S.C. Adv. 1768, "next door to Post Office." (Prime)

—, JOHN: Charleston, S.C. Adv. 1761, "Just arrived from London. Shop on Church St." (Prime)

KITTS, JOHN: Louisville, Ky., 2 West Main St. Dir. 1838–1878.

KLECKNER, SOLOMON: Mifflinburg, Pa. *Ca.* 1830.

KLEIN, JOHN: Phila. Dir. 1838 and later.

KLEISER, JACOB: Phila. Dir. 1822–1824. (Brix)

KLINE & Co.: N.Y.C. Dir. 1862.

—, B.: Phila. 1841.

—, JOHN: Amity, Pa. 4th Group. Lancaster, Pa. *ca.*1800; Phila. 1812–1820; Reading, Pa., 1820–1830. (Abbott) (Steinmetz)

KLING (KLINGMAN), JACOB: 1758–1806. Reading, Pa. 3rd Group. Aw. 1790–1806. Tall clock owned by Women's Club of Reading, Pa.

KLINGLE, JOSEPH: Phila. Dir. 1823–1825.

KLINGMAN, DANIEL: York, Pa. *Ca.*1820.

"KNAPP, CHAS. G.," used by U. S. Watch Co. *ca.*1870.

—, JESSE: Boston. Dir. 1825–1842.

—, WILLIAM: Annapolis, Md. Adv. 1764, "Opened a shop—mends watches—instructions from the most imminent in London and Dublin." (Prime)

KNEEDLER, JACOB: Horsham, Pa. 1791.

KNEELAND & ADAMS: Hartford, Conn. 1792–179–. Tall clocks. Pos. case makers.

—, SAMUEL: Hartford, Conn. Aw. 1788–1793. (Hoopes)

KNICKERBOCKER WATCH Co.: N.Y.C. Adv. *Ca.*1891. Imp. Swiss watches.

KNIGHT, BENJAMIN: Statesville, R.I. Patent Sept. 10, 1840, "Alarm to Clocks and other Timepieces."

—, LEVI: Salem, Ind. *Ca.*1845. Wood movts. (Knittle)

KNOWER, DANIEL: Roxbury, Mass. *Ca.* 1800. Tall clocks.

KNOWLES, JOHN: Phila. Adv. 1784, "Watchmaker and store keeper. Moved to 2nd St." (Prime)

—, ROBERT: Bangor, Me. *Ca.*1830–1840.

KOCH, JACOB: York, Pa. n/d. Prob. not C., but name on dials of some Tall clocks. Cases for J. Albert.

—, RICHARD: York, Pa. Aw. 1805–1836. Tall clock owned at Stissing, N.Y., painted iron dial, moon calendar in slot, dial marked "York-town."

KOCKSPERGER, HENRY: Phila. Dir. 1837.

KOHL, NICHOLAS: Willow Grove, Pa. 1830.

KOLB, MARTIN: Pa. (Franks)

KOPLIN, T.: Norristown, Pa. *Ca.*1850.

—, WASHINGTON: Norristown, Pa. 1850.

KORFHAGE, CHARLES: Brooklyn, N.Y. "Estb. 1877."

KRAEMER, F.: N.Y.C. Dir. 1848.

KRAFT, JACOB: Shepherdstown, W.Va. *Ca.* 1800. See Craft.

KRAHE, WILLIAM: San Francisco, Cal. Partner with Wenzell on air clock. Dir. 1861.

KRAMER, M., & CO.: Boston, 48 Cornhill. Adv. 1830. Dir. 1841. Clock Dealer.

—, J. C.: Phoenixville, Pa. n/d. Gold cased watch so marked owned by G. L. Lunberg, Norristown, Pa.

KREUZER, FIDEL: n/p. Pa. n/d. Name on Tall clock dial, floral decoration.

KRINGE, JACOB: New Market, Va. *Ca.*1790.

KROEBER CLOCK CO., F.: N.Y.C., 360 Broadway. Used Seth Thomas No. 89 movt. first made for them 1880. Adv. 1894, "Eclipse Movement, patented Oct. 9, 1894. No more trouble with pendulum clocks. Can be carried about." Adv. 1895. E. L. Kroeber, son of president, d. 1899.

—, FREDERIC J., CLOCK CO.: N.Y.C., 360 Broadway. 1887. Label so marked in clock owned by Mrs. Meyer Divoritsky, N.Y.C.

—, F.: N.Y.C., 8 and 10 Cortlandt St. Dir. 1872–1878. Mfr. of clocks. Wood cased brass movts. Ex. Essex Inst.

KRONENBERGE, F.: N.Y.C., 1992 Third Ave. n/d. Labels printed by "Fred Binzen." (J. T. Collins)

KROUSE, JOHN J.: Northampton (Allentown), Pa. *Ca.*1830. (Eckhardt)

—, JOHN SAMUEL: Bethlehem, Pa. n/d. (Orr)

KROUT, JACOB: Plumstead, Pa. *Ca.*1830.

KRUEGER, ADOLPH: Camden, N.J. 1850–1862.

KRUGER, L.: Cleveland, O. *Ca.*1850.

KULP, JACOB: Franconia, Pa. n/d. Watch Paper Cramer Col.

—, WILLIAM: Lower Salford, near Sumneytown, Pa. *Ca.*1800. Tall clocks. (Orr)

KUMBELL, WILLIAM: N.Y.C. Adv. 1775. Also S.

KUNKLE, JOHN: Ephrata, Pa. 1830–1840. Pos. Gunkle.

KUNSMAN, HENRY: Raleigh, N.C. Adv. 1820–1823. Pos. in Savage & Kunsman, Salisbury, N.C.

KUNTZ, M. S.: South Whitehall Twp., Pa. n/d.

LABBART, JOHN: N.Y.C. 1805. (Baillie)

LABHART, W. L.: N.Y.C. *Ca.*1810.

LACEY, JOHN: Phila. Dir. 1819–1825.

LACKEY, HENRY: Phila., 13 Elfuth's Alley. Dir. 1808–1811.

LADD & BIGELOW: N.Y.C. n/d. Watch Paper BCL Col.

LADOMUS, CHARLES A.: Chester, Pa. *Ca.* 1825–1855.

—, JACOB: Phila. Dir. 1843 and later.

—, JOSEPH: Chester, Pa. *Ca.*1850.

—, LOUIS: Phila. Dir. 1845–1846.

LADUE, S. P.: Rockford, Ia. Patent on "Improvement in Calendar Clock" Sept. 24, 1859. (F. S. Collins, Eastham, Mass.)

LAFEUER & BEARY: N.Y.C., White and Elm Sts. "Town clock makers." Dir. 1854. (Trow)

"LAFLIN, MATTHEW," used by National Watch Co. of Chicago *ca.*1870.

LAFOY, THEODORE: Newark, N.J. 1848–1852.

LAKEMAN, EBENEZER KNOWLTON: Salem, Mass. Aw. 1819. In Stevens & Lakeman. Succeeded Jabez Baldwin.

LAMB, ANTHONY: N.Y.C. Adv. 1749 Math., surveying, mus. insts.; pos. clocks. (LB)

—, CYRUS: Oxford, Mass. *Ca.*1830. "Not regularly a clockmaker."

LAMBERT, L. C.: N.Y.C. Dir. 1872.

LAMBERTOZ, D.: Wilmington, N.C., Dock St. Adv. 1797.

LAMOYNE, AUGUSTUS: Phila. Dir. 1816.

LAMPE, JOHN: Annapolis, Md. Adv. 1779–1780; 1780 Baltimore, "Late from Annapolis."

LAMSON, CHARLES: 1817–. Salem, Mass. Junior partner with James Balch, 234 Essex St., Salem, 1842; still in firm 1864.

LAMVINE (LEMVINE), AUGUSTUS: Phila. Dir. 1811–1816.

LANCASTER, PENNSYLVANIA, WATCH CO.: Lancaster, Pa. Reorganization 1877 of Adams & Perry Watch Co.

— (PENNSYLVANIA) WATCH CO. LTD., THE: Name changed Oct. 1878. To May 1879 used names "New Era," "West End." (Bowman)

— WATCH CO., THE: Lancaster, Pa. 1879–1892. Control passed 1884 to Abram Bitzner; later became "Keystone Watch Co." (trademark). f. 1890; bought 1892 by Hamilton Watch Co. (Bowman)

LANDAH, JOHN: n/p. Pa. Ca.1792. Tall walnut case, broken-arch top, large rosettes, 8-day moon, sweep seconds hand. Name difficult to decipher.

LANDIS, C. E.: Newburgh, N.Y. n/d. Watch Paper BCL Col.

—, ISAAC: Coatesville, Pa. Ca.1845. Apt. of David Anderson. "Active Watchmaker of Coatesville." (James)

—, ISAAC C.: Coatesville, Pa. 1898–1914. (James)

LANDRY, ALEXANDER: Phila. Ca.1790. Adv. 1790, "Importation of clocks from Europe with and without cases." (Gillingham)

LANE & STURGEON: Lancaster, O. Adv. 1827, "Clocks of every description made." (Knittle)

—, AARON: 1753–1819. Elizabethtown, N.J. Aw. 1782–1800. C. S. Mgr. Town lottery 1786. Tall clocks owned by Robert Hoffman, Venice Park, N.J.; Mrs. Fred Wright, Pelham, N.Y., engraved brass dial. Another ex. in Bement House, Old Deerfield, Mass. Some Mus. clocks. One known marked "Boundbrook"; pos. there before 1780.

—, J.: Southington, Conn. n/d.

—, JAMES: Phila., 151 No. Second St. Dir. 1803–1818.

—, LYMAN J.: New Haven, Conn. Ca.1840–ca.1850.

—, MARK: Elizabethtown, N.J. 1835–1837.

Pillar and Scroll clock, 30-hour wood movt., Phillipse Greene Col. (PG)

LANE, N.: N.Y.C., 212 6th Ave. Dir. 1848.

LANGDON (William) & JONES (George A.): Bristol. (tx) 1845–1855.

— (Edward) & ROOT (Samuel E.): Bristol, Main and School Strs. Aw. 1851–1854. (tx) Root alone 1854–1896.

—, EDWARD: Bristol, Main and School Sts. (tx) 1851–1854. In Langdon & Root. Clock dials and trimmings.

LANGE & WYLEYS: Charleston, S.C., 5½ Church St. Aw. ca.1785. Robert Clark aw. for them.

LANGMACK, H.: Davenport, Ia. Ca.1850.

LANGWORTHY, WILLIAM ANDREWS: Saratoga Springs, N.Y. Adv. 1822.

LANNUIER, CHARLES HONORE: N.Y.C. "A French-American cabinetmaker with an extensive business. His work is sometimes confused with Duncan Phyfe." (FT)

LANNY, DAVID F.: Boston. Adv. 1789, 21 Marlboro St., "Late from Paris." Adv. for apt. 1790. To N.Y.C. ca.1793–1802. (Prime)

LANSING, JACOB H.: Rochester, N.Y. Dir. 1847–1848.

LAPIERRE, BENNET: Baltimore. 1802.

LaPLACE, CHARLES: Wilmington, N.C. Adv., "Watchmaker from Paris." Bought store from Alex Young. Adv. 1795. Left 1796. Later at Phila.

LaQUAIN, M.: Phila. Dir. 1794.

LARGE, "SQUIRE": Putnam, O. Ca.1810. Clockcase maker; also coffins. (Knittle)

LARGEN, ROBERT: Phila., 1310 South 3rd St. and 1320 Moyamensing Ave. Late 1840's. Sold clocks. Blue overpasted label in Birge & Fuller Empire 8-day, weight-driven, brass movt. Shelf clock.

LARKIN, JOSEPH: Boston, 5 Endicott St. 1841–1848. Charles R. Delaney, Santa Barbara, Cal., has Banjo clock, all mahogany case, with this name on dial.

LATCHOW, JOHN: Baltimore, Pearl and Saratoga Sts. 1829.

LATHAM & CLARK: Charleston, S.C., 125 Broad St. 1790.

LATHAM, —: n/d. "Del. Co." on dial of Tall clock, mahogany case, inlay.

—, JAMES: Albany, N.Y. Adv. 1795.

LATIMER, JAMES: Phila. Dir. 1813–1822.

LATOURNAU, JOHN B.: 1796–1853. Baltimore. Aw. 1820–1853.

LATSHAR, JOHN: York, Pa. Aw. 1780–1784.

LATTA, A.: Phila. Dir. 1837.

LAUGHLIN, A. S.: Barnett, Vt. *Ca.*1860.

LAUNDRY, ALEXANDER: Phila. n/d.

LAUNY, DAVID F.: N.Y.C. Patent on "Timepieces" Mar. 21, 1823. See D. F. Lanny.

LAW, WILLIAM: Phila. Dir. 1839–1841.

LAWING, SAMUEL: 1807–1865. Charlotte, N.C. Adv. 1841, opened shop. In Lawing & Brewer 1842–1843; later alone. (Cutten)

LAWRENCE, GEORGE: Lowell, Mass. Dir. 1832.

—, JOHN: –1798. Phila.

—, SILAS H.: N.Y.C. *Ca.*1840.

—, WILLIAM: Mt. Pleasant, N.Y. *Ca.*1850.

LAWSE, JONATHAN: Amwell, N.J. 1778–1809. (PG)

LAWSHE (LAASHE), JOHN: Amwell Twp., near Flemington, N.J. *Ca.*1750. Flat top hood Tall clock, English dial, so marked owned by John J. Schenk. Pos. made case and imp. movt. "Earliest clock in area."

LAWSON, WILLIAM H.: Waterbury, Conn. n/d.

LAWYER, LORING: Newark, N.Y. *Ca.*1835. Pos. Tioga Co. clock dealer.

LAY, ASA, JR.: Hartford, Conn. *Ca.*1784. C. W. (E. H. Whitlock, New Haven)

LEACH & BRADLEY: Utica, N.Y. J. and dealer. Dir. 1832–1834.

—, CALEB: Plymouth, Mass. 1776–1790. Ex. in J. Cheney Wells Col. (Abbott)

—, CHARLES B.: Utica, N.Y. Dir. 1843–1847.

LEACOCK, JOSEPH: Phila. n/d. Tall clocks. (Prime)

"LEADER," used by Elgin National Watch Co. 1877 and after.

LEAVENWORTH (Mark) & Co.: Waterbury, Conn. *Ca.*1830.

—, MARK, & SON: Waterbury, Conn. n/d. Pillar and Scroll clocks 28 × 16½. In Flint Sale 1926.

— & SON: Albany, N.Y. Col. Wm. Leavenworth & Son after moving from Waterbury.

—, WILLIAM, & SON: Waterbury, Conn. *Ca.*1807–1810. Name pos. on clocks.

—, MARK: 1774–1849. Learned Silversmith trade. *Ca.*1795 made axes and guns.

Successful C. Purchased property on Great Brook and made wood movt. clocks for a long time. Stored in warehouse as high as the top of the room. Wall clocks had no cases. Weights were about 8″ long and an inch and one-half in diameter, cylinders of tin, filled with sand. Sometimes as many as 40 men employed. Continued in clock business having various partners at various times till 1837 when brass took place of wood movt. Then made gilt buttons. (See ill. No. 191.) Pillar and Scroll clocks, both standard and miniature. (Anderson)

LEAVENWORTH, WILLIAM: Waterbury, Conn. Clocks on Mad River *ca.*1802; f. 1810; Albany, N.Y. 1817–1823.

LEAVIT, M. F.: Kalamazoo, Mich. 1870.

LEAVITT, DR. JOSIAH: Hingham, Mass. *Ca.*1772. C. Later Boston organ builder. (BCC)

LEBOSQUET, CALEB: Haverhill, Mass. Prob. tinsmith only. Michael Cowden, apt.

LEE & GODDARD: Rutland, Vt. *Ca.*1820.

—, STEPHEN: Charleston, S.C. *Ca.*1780.

—, WILLIAM: Charleston, S.C., Broad St. Adv. 1768.

LEEDS, GIDEON: Phila. Dir. 1841–1842.

—, HOWARD G.: Phila. Dir. 1840.

LEFFERTS & HALL: Phila., 61½ South 2nd St. Dir. 1818–1822.

—, CHARLES: Phila. Dir. 1818–1822.

—, CHARLES: Ovid, N.Y. Adv. 1827–1828.

LEGOUX, J. F.: Charleston, S.C. Late 18th century.

LEGROS, JOHN F.: Baltimore, St. Paul and Market Sts. Adv. 1793–1794. (Prime)

LEHURAY, NICHOLAS: Phila., 79 Front St. Dir. 1809–1831. From Germany. Tall clocks. Father of Nicholas, Jr.

—, NICHOLAS: –1834. Ogletown, Del. C. Son of Nicholas from Guernsey.

—, NICHOLAS, JR.: Phila., 79 Front St. Dir. 1809–1846.

LEIBERT, HENRY: Norristown, Pa. *Ca.* 1850. (Moore)

LEIGH, DAVID: Pottstown, Pa. Adv. 1849. (Moore)

—, W.: Newtown, Pa. n/d. Edwin Burt owns Mus. Tall clock, brass movt., brass dial, silvered ring, sweep seconds hand, days of month as in other Pa. clocks; has pine backboard and sub-dial plate

LEIGH, W. (*cont'd*)
marked "Wm. Whitaker, Halifax," plays seven tunes on ten bells.

LEINBACH, ELIAS & JOHN: Reamstown, Pa. 1788–1810. Mostly 30-hour type Tall clocks, wound like Cuckoo clocks; dials reported excellent.

LEINHARDT, CHRISTIAN: Carlyle, Pa. 1782.

LEMIST (Wm.) & TAPPAN (W. P.): Phila. Dir. 1816–1819.

—, WILLIAM KING: 1791–1820. Apt. Simon Willard ca.1806–1808. Banjo and Mass. Shelf clocks. Phila. ca.1816–1819. Banjo clocks used Simon Willard door lock, hooks to fasten dial, shape of hands. d. in shipwreck 1820. Bro. John lived opposite Willard, families intimate; John d. 1840 in *Lexington* fire on L.I. Sound. (JWW)

LEMOINE, A.: Phila. Dir. 1810–1817.

LEMON, J. J.: Louisville, Ky. Adv. 1845.

LENHARDT, GODFREY: 1779–1819. York, Pa.

LENTZ, GEORGE K.: Phila. Dir. 1825.

LEONARD WATCH CO.: Boston. Inc. 1911 "for selling and distributing watches." (Evans)

LEONI & CO.: N.Y.C. Ca.1840.

LEPPLEMAN, EDWARD: Buffalo, N.Y. Dir. 1836–1839.

LEROW, LEWIS: Boston. Dir. 1813–1825.

LEROY, ABRAHAM: Lancaster, Pa. Before 1750. Swiss. Father-in-law of Wilmer Atkinson. Daughter, Mrs. Atkinson, "as expert a mechanic as her father." To Switzerland ca.1750, back in 1757, d. 1765. (Lan. Co.)

LESCHEY, THOMAS: Middletown, Pa. Early 19th century.

LESCHOT, LOUIS A.: –1838. Va. Swiss. C. and mathematician. Induced to come to U.S. by Thomas Jefferson. Constructed clock in Jefferson's home in Monticello. d. Charlottesville, Va., buried in Jefferson family plot. (J. Sternfeld)

LESCOIT, LAMBERT (LAMBIER): Aw. Providence, R.I.; later Hartford, Conn., adv. 1769, "From Paris at the shop of James Tiley on King St." Adv. 1769, "Removed to the store of Lathrop & Smith." Adv. 1770, "Intending for London, please pay all accounts." Tall clock in Joe Kindig, Jr., Col., York, Pa., fine block front, shell case, Chippendale; case prob. by Goddard; brass dial engraved, "Lambert Lescoit, Providence." (Hoopes)

LESLIE & PARRY: Phila. Dir. 1803.

— & PRICE: Phila. Dir. 1793–1800. Tall clock, 8-day brass movt., and Tall clock painted metal dial owned by Mrs. Robert Heyl, Pelham, N.Y.; another by Mrs. McKay, Lykens, Pa., mahogany case, domed hood, bracket feet, decorated dial, brass capped corner reeding. Price d. 1799, Leslie d. 1803. Leslie & Price, Baltimore, adv. 1795 as branch of the Phila. firm at 119 Market St., Abraham Patton, representative.

—, ROBERT, & CO.: Baltimore, 19 Baltimore St. 1796

— (William J.) & WILLIAMS: New Brunswick, N.J. 1791–1806. Pos. Benjamin Williams, bro.-in-law Aaron Lane. Mus. Tall clock owned by Monmouth Co. Hist. Assn., case by Matthew Edgerton, Jr. (his label).

—, ROBERT: –1803. C. W. London 1793–1799; from Eng. with parents. In Leslie & Price. Three patents Jan. 30, 1793, "Pendulum for Clocks"; also others. Adv. 1788; Dir. 1791–1795. "Ingenious workman." (Prime)

—, WILLIAM J.: –1831. New Brunswick, N.J., ca.1791; prob. before that in Phila. Trenton, Warner St., 1799, in shop of Joseph Yates. Adv. Trenton papers till 1817. Operated Trenton tavern. Partner New Brunswick and Trenton with one Williams. Adv., "Native of N.J., not from London, Paris, or Boston."

LESQUEREUX, L., & SON: Columbus, O. 1804–1805.

LESTER, J. U.: Oswego, N.Y. Adv. 1843–1845. (Cutten)

—, ROBERT: Phila. 1791–1798.

LETELLIER, JOHN: –1793. Phila. Adv. 1770–1780. Dentist, Wilmington, Del., 1800.

LEUBA, HENRY: Lexington, Ky. Dir. 1818. (LB)

LEVELY, GEORGE: Phila. Adv. 1774. Later adv. Baltimore, "Opened a shop on Market St." (Prime)

LEVI, MICHAEL & ISAAC: Baltimore. Adv. 1785.

—, GARRETSON: Phila. Dir. 1840–1843.

—, ISAAC: Phila., Front St. Adv. 1790, "Watchmaker lately from London." In Michael & Isaac Levi. (Prime)

LEVI, MICHAEL: Phila., 151 Mulberry St. *Ca.*1750. Baltimore Dir. 1802–1816.

LEVIN & FERGUSON: Alexandria, La. *Ca.* 1850.

LEVY, M., & Co.: Phila. Dir. 1816–1817.

—, HENRY (H. A.): Phila. Dir. 1841 and later.

—, LEWIS B.: Phila. Dir. 1841–1845.

LEWIS, BENJAMIN B., & SON: Bristol. (tx) 1871–1872. Calendar clocks.

— & CATLIN: Litchfield, Conn. n/d. Tall clock, cherry case made by "Norton" who made fine coaches, wooden movt., in Floyd Thoms Col.

— & Co., C. S.: Bristol. (tx) 1875.

— & IVES: Colebrook, Conn. (See Bristol for same name.) "The late Rocelia De-Wolf of Colebrook said: 'Above the river was a clock shop operated by Lewis & Ives quite successfully. As a little girl, before 1849, I remember going to the clock factory and getting blocks and pieces of painted glass used in clocks to play with.'" (H. H. Vining)

— (Levi) & IVES (Joseph): Bristol. (tx) 1819–1823. Wall and Shelf wood movt. clocks.

LEWIS, —: Phila. Dir. 1796. (Prime)

—, BENJAMIN B.: Bristol. (tx) 1864–1870. Patented Calendar clock; made them in Manross shop. Sold patent to Welch Spring Co.

—, CHARLES: St. Albans, O. Adv. 1823–1825.

—, CURTIS: 1770–1847. Reading, Pa. 4th Group. Tall clocks. (Steinmetz)

—, ERASTUS: New Britain and Waterbury, Conn. *Ca.*1825.

—, FREDERIC H.: Rochester, N.H. Dir. 1849 and later.

—, G. H.: N.Y.C. n/d. Watch Paper Bir. Col.

—, GEORGE: Cannonsburg, Pa. *Ca.*1830. Case maker. Wood movts. Wag-on-Wall clocks with name on dial.

—, ISAAC: Newark, N.J. Adv. 1782. (Williams)

—, JACKSON: San Jose, Cal. *Ca.*1870.

"—, JOHN," used by U. S. Watch Co. *ca.*1870.

—, JOHN (JOHN M.): Phila. Dir. 1830 and later.

—, LEVI: Bristol. (tx) 1809–1823. Assessed as C. 1809. With Joseph Ives as Lewis & Ives, or Ives & Lewis.

LEWIS, R. W.: n/p. n/d. Tall clock owned by Wm. Wallace, Uniontown, Pa., wood movt.

—, SHELDON: Bristol. Farm near John Birge. In Birge, Mallory & Co.

—, TUNIS: N.Y.C. After 1800.

LIDELL, THOMAS: Frederick, Ind. *Ca.*1860.

LIEBERT, HENRY: Norristown, Pa. Adv. 1849.

LILIENTHAL, J.: New Orleans, La., 28 Camp St. *Ca.*1850–*ca.*1860. (Dre)

LIMEBURNER, JOHN: Phila. Census 1790. Dir. 1791.

LINCOLN & REED: Boston. Dir. 1842. "—," used by Auburndale Watch Co. 1879.

LIND, JOHN: Phila., 39 Keyes Alley. Adv. 1775. Census 1790. Dir. 1805.

LINDER, CHARLES: Geneva, N.Y. *Ca.* 1810.

LINDSAY, W. K., & Co.: *Ca.*1830.

—, MORTON: Rising Sun, Md.

—, THOMAS: Frankford, Pa. *Ca.*1810. "Contemporary of Seneca Luckens." Tall clock, painted iron dial, good walnut case *ca.*1810. (Franks)

—, W. K.: Pittsburgh, Pa. *Ca.*1825.

LINDSEY, THOMAS: Adv. 1799. (Prime)

—, W. R.: Davenport, Ia. *Ca.*1850. (Dre)

LINDSLEY, WILLIAM: Portsmouth, O. Adv. 1828, 1839–1841. (Knittle)

LINDSLY, TIMOTHY: –1825. Reading, Pa. Aw. 1815. Adv. 1821–1825.

LINEBAUGH, H. W.: Keokuk, Ia. *Ca.* 1860–*ca.*1870. W. R.

LINERD, JOHN: Phila. Dir. 1816.

LINGO, J. W.: Phila., 1206 Pine St. n/d. Watch Paper Cramer Col.

LINNEL, KNOWLES: St. Albans, O. *Ca.*1825. "Clock factory." (Knittle)

LISNEY, WM.: N.Y.C. *Ca.*1840.

LITCHFIELD MFG. Co.: Litchfield, Conn. Org. *ca.*1850 to make clocks with marine movts. prob. obtained from Bristol to *ca.*1856. J. G. Beckwith, pres. P. T. Barnum gained first experience with this firm, later joined with Theodore Terry in Bridgeport. Clocks cased in papier-mâché, mother-of-pearl inlay, movts. regulated by both pendulum and escape wheel, powered by both weight and spring drives. Many running today. Mrs. Thomas Jarman, Charlottesville, Va., has Shelf clock 14″ × 9″, wood case, mother-of-pearl inlay, label "Patent Eight

LITCHFIELD MFG. CO. (cont'd)
Day / Brass Clocks / Springs with equalized power, warranted not to fail; / Forestville Manufacturing Co., / J. C. Brown, Bristol, Conn.," small overpasted label at/ bottom marked "Litchfield Mfg. Company / CAVEAT." (AAJ Nov. 1950)

LITTLE & ELMER: Bridgetown, N.J. Ca. 1830. Watch Paper BCL Col.

—, ARCHIBALD: Reading, Pa. Ca.1810–1820. Camden, N.J., 1839; Phila. 1840. Also Chrons.

—, PETER: Baltimore. 1799–1807.

LITTLEJON, JAMES: Charleston, S.C., Elliot St. Adv. 1761.

LLOYD, THOMAS R.: West Chester, Pa. Watch Paper Chester Co. Hist. Soc.

—, WILLIAM: 1779–1845. Springfield, Mass. Adv. 1802, "Sideboards and clock cases."

LOCKE, JOHN: Cincinnati and Newark, O. Scientist and professor of chemistry, Ohio Medical College. Invented 1840 "electro-cronograph, a combination clock and telegraph, by which a current transmitted the beats which were printed at some distance on a paper roll." (TP)

LOCKWOOD & PALMQUIST: N.Y.C. n/d. S. Steinman, Phila., has 30-day clock, month and date.

— & SCRIBNER: N.Y.C. 1847. W., R. and Dealer.

—, FRED: N.Y.C., 44½ Canal St. Ca.1831. "Clock, Watchmaker, chronometers, repeating horizontal watches repaired." Watch Paper owned by R. Reiter, Washington, D.C.

—, JOSHUA: Charleston, S.C., Elliot St. and 1 Broad St. 1751–1781. Arthur Downs worked for him. In West Indies 1771, later returned and continued work. (Prime)

—, WILLIAM: Charlestown, Mass. n/d. Tall clocks.

LOEW, JOHN J.: Phila. Dir. 1846–1848.

LOGAN, ADAM: N.Y.C. 1805. (Baillie)

—, A. SIDNEY: 1849–1925. Goshenville, Pa. (James)

—, ROBERT: St. Louis, Mo. Ca.1820.

LOHE & KEYSER: Phila. Dir. 1831–1835. Imp. watches. (Prime)

LOMAS, JOHN: Chambersburg, Pa. n/d.

LOMBARD, NATHANIEL & DANIEL: Boston. Dir. 1825.

LOMBARD, DANIEL, JR.: Boston. Dir. 1830.

LOMES, WILLIAM: N.Y.C. Ca.1840.

LONG, GEORGE: Hanover, Pa. Aw. ca.1800–1811. Some mus. Tall clocks.

—, JOHN: Hanover, Pa. n/d. Tall clocks known.

—, SAMUEL (S. R.): Phila. 1842–1846.

LONGIN, R.: n/p. Patent No. 173410, Feb. 15, 1876, model at Smiths. Inst.

LOOMIS, HENRY: Frankfort, N.Y. Ca.1830. Name on Pillar and Scroll clock owned by Mrs. William Wiley, Massapequa, L.I.

—, WILLIAM B.: Middletown and Wethersfield, Conn. Ca.1825. Adv., "Premium clocks made by . . ." Edward Ingraham has 30-hour clock, decorated column, wood movt.

LORD & GALE (Joseph): Fayetteville, N.C. Adv. 1792.

— & GODDARD: Rutland, Vt. 1797–1823. Tall clocks. See Nicholas Goddard.

—, JAMES: Woodbury, N.J. 1821–1835. Tall clocks.

LORING, HENRY W.: Boston. Ca.1812–1840.

—, JOSEPH: Sterling, Mass. 1791–1812. Tall 8-day brass movt. clocks, cases by John Hill of Leominster. (A. W. Farwell)

LORTON, WILLIAM B.: N.Y.C., 3 and 15 Dutch St. 1810–1825. Dir. 1854. Mfr. and wholesale American clocks.

LOSS, AUGUSTUS: Pittsburgh, Pa. Ca.1840.

—, P.: Germantown, Pa. Ca.1850.

LOUCHEIM, P.: N.Y.C. n/d. (BCL)

LOVE, JOHN: Baltimore. 1802.

LOVELL & CO., G.: Phila. Ca.1880.

—, MFG. CO., LTD.: Erie, Pa. Adv. 1893, "The wonderful luminous dial clock that shines all night. Solid bronze front covered back with an alarm, price $5.50. Also manufacture clothes wringers." (TP)

— & SMITH: Phila. Dir. 1841–1843. Later Lovell & Co. until ca.1880.

—, A. E.: Phila. Dir. 1841–1843. 1844–1849. In Lovell & Smith.

LOVEREN & RITZ: Boston. Watch Paper BCL Col.

LOVETT, JAMES: 1728–1814. Mendon, Mass. Tall clocks.

LOVIS, CAPT. JOSEPH: Hingham, Mass. 1775–1804. (BCC)

LOW & CO., JOHN J.: Boston. 1832. "Importer of Watches."

Low, DANIEL: 1842–. Clerk with Smith & Chamberlain 1859; 207 Essex St. 1861. Founder Daniel Low & Co. Still in business.

Lowe, THOMAS: Phila. James McCallum apt. 1772. (Gillingham)

Lownes, DAVIS: –1810. Phila., Market and Chestnut Sts. 1785, 3rd St. till 1807. Dir. 1785.

—, HYATT: Hagerstown, Md. *Ca.*1792. (LSS)

Lowrey, DAVID: 1740–1819. Newington, Conn. Son of Thomas and Ann Lowrey. Pos. apt. of Ebenezer Balch. Marr. 1771. C. Blacksmith. Chosen to inspect and approve Wethersfield town clock 1791. Made guns during Rev. War. Several clocks extant, "creditable pieces of work." (Hoopes)

Lows, BALL & Co.: Boston. Dir. 1842.

Lucke, JOHN P.: Phila. Dir. 1849.

Lucy, D. E.: Houlton, Me. *Ca.*1860.

Luden, JACOB: Reading, Pa. n/d. Watch Paper Cramer Col.

Ludwig, JOHN: Phila., 88 No. 6th St. Census 1790. Dir. 1791.

Lufkin & Johnson: Boston. 1800–1810. (Abbott)

—, ASA: Bucksport, Me. n/d. Tall clocks, brass movts. (E. O. Sugden, Orlando, Me.)

Lukens, ISAIAH: 1779–1846. Horsham and Phila., Pa. Aw. *ca.*1800–1837. Dir. 1823–1831. George Eckhardt, Oct. 1949, Frontiers Magazine: "Strong, self-reliant, diligent and self cultured, and of indomitable perseverance. Father was Seneca, farmer who carried on clockmaking, who taught his son at Horsham, Pa. Isaiah when young made some improvements in surgical instrument. He visited Europe and obtained work as a watchmaker; gained recognition for his methods of tempering steel. Remained in England and France three years and returned to the U.S.A., established himself as town-clock and watch maker and machinist. Made his first tower clocks for the Hatboro Academy 1812, made State House clock replacement, *ca.*1828." A founder and vice-pres. Franklin Inst. Interested in papermaking, mechanical inventions, science. (William E. Camp) Made clock 1820 for Second U. S. Bank,

Phila. (building later became U. S. Custom House). Clock fully restored 1949 by Philadelphia Chapter of Natl. Assoc. of Watch and Clock Collectors under supervision of Robert Franks, national pres.; movt. ill. No. 71.

Lukens, J.: Phila. Dir. 1837. (Brix)

—, SENECA: March 14, 1751–Dec. 9, 1829. Horsham, near Phila., Pa. C. Farmer. Father of Isaiah. Made 41st clock by 1795; No. 37 owned by A. Lincoln Spencer, Hatboro, Pa. (Gillingham)

Lupp, —: Family of N.J. C., W. and S. Also spelled Leupp. (Williams)

—, CHARLES: 1788–1825. New Brunswick, N.J. Aw. 1810–1825. Bro. Laurence, Wm., son of John.

—, HARVEY: New Brunswick, N.J. 1809–1815.

—, HENRY: New Brunswick, N.J. 1760–1816. Aw. 1808–1816. Marr. 1788. Son of Peter; father of Samuel V. Made artificial teeth. (Williams)

—, JOHN: 1734–1805. New Brunswick, N.J. Aw. 1782–1805. S. C. Father of Charles, Laurence, Wm. Succeeded by son Wm. 1805. (Williams)

—, JOHN H.: New Brunswick, N.J. *Ca.*1830. "Son of Wm. who had been active with father a number of years and who received his tools by will." (Williams)

—, LAURENCE: 1783–. New Brunswick, N.J. Bro. Wm. and Charles. Employed as journeyman by Wm. Adv. own shop 1806. (Williams)

—, PETER: –1807. New Brunswick, N.J. Aw. 1760–1807. Father of Henry. Will 1802 calls himself C.; none extant.

—, SAMUEL VICKERS: 1789–1809. New Brunswick, N.J. Aw. 1809. Son of Henry. Apt. of Peter. Pos. took over grandfather Peter's business.

—, WILLIAM: 1766–1845. New Brunswick, N.J. Aw. 1790–1845. Son of John. Succeeded to father's business and tools. Took care of town clock 1805. Son John H. "active with him and received his tools." (Williams)

Luscomb, SAMUEL: d. before 1781. Salem, Mass. Town clock in East Meeting House 1773.

Lux Clock Mfg. Co., THE: Waterbury, Conn., 21 Hanson St., Inc. Jan. 1917 by

LUX CLOCK MFG. CO. (*cont'd*)
Paul Lux. Timers, alarms, novelty clocks.
(Pape)

—, PAUL: –1947. Waterbury, Conn. Aw.
1914 E. Farm St.; 1915 to large loft in
Printer's Court. Founded 1917 The Lux
Clock Mfg. Co.

LYMAN, G. E.: Providence, R.I. *Ca.* 1840.

—, ROLAND: Lowell, Mass., Central St.
Dir. 1832–1837.

—, THOMAS: 1770–. Windsor, Conn., Marietta, O. Son of Deacon Thomas and Ann
Lyman. Apt. of Daniel Burnap. One
Tall clock marked "Windsor" known,
dial like Burnap's. Marietta, O. *Ca.*1791
with bro. Jeremiah. (Knittle) (Hoopes)

LYNCH, ABRAHAM: Baltimore. *Ca.*1800.

—, JOHN: Baltimore. 1802–1832.

LYNDALL, WILLIAM: Phila. Dir. 1844.

LYON, GEORGE: –1844. Wilmington, N.C.
Adv. 1819–1844. (Cutten)

LYONS, JOHN, JR.: New Haven. *Ca.*1840.

MAAG, HENRY: Phila. n/d. Tall clocks so
marked. (Conrad)

MAAS (MANNS), FREDERICK: Pa. n/d.
Name on Tall clock, Pa. type. Prob.
Maus. (FT)

MACALLISTER, A. L.: n/p. Tall clock dated
1821.

McBRIDE (A.) & GARDNER (B.): Charlotte,
N.C. Adv. 1807. (Cutten)

McCABE, JOHN: Baltimore. Adv. 1774,
"From Dublin, watch and clockmaker in
Market St., Baltimore. Having con-
ducted business for many of the most
eminent artists in London, Dublin, and
Liverpool, he considers the testimony of
their approbation of his abilities to finish
watches, clocks and either spring or
weights, also turret or steeple clocks constructed to endure for a long continuance
of time. Spring clocks for mariners."
(Prime)

—, WILLIAM: Richmond, Va. *Ca.*1790–
*ca.*1820.

McCARTER, JOHN: N.Y.C., 116 Seventh
Ave. Dir. 1854.

McCLARY, SAMUEL: 1788–1859. Wilmington, Del. Apt. of Thomas Crow. Father
of Samuel II, Thomas. Partner with
Jacob Alrichs operating machine shop
1810–1814; machinery business after 1816.

Tall and Shelf clocks. Tall clock in Old
Town Hall at Wilmington. (Conrad)

McCLARY, SAMUEL II: Wilmington, Del.
Early 19th century. Son of Samuel, bro.
Thomas.

—, THOMAS: Wilmington, Del. Early 19th
century. Son of Samuel, bro. Samuel II.

McCLINTOCK, O. B.: Minneapolis, Minn.
Aw. 1945. Electric clocks. (John Hall)

M'CLOSKEY, F.: Phila. Dir. 1850.

McCLUER, HEMAN: Hamburg, N.Y. Patent on "Sun dials of cast iron" Sept. 17,
1834.

M'CLURE, DAVID: Boston. Dir. 1810.

—, JOHN: Boston. Dir. 1825.

McCOLLIN, THOMAS: Phila. Dir. 1824–1833.

McCONNELL, J. CLEMENS: Waynesburg, Pa.
*Ca.*1845. Apt. of David Anderson.
"Made one clock, then went into another
business." (James)

McCORMACK, HENRY: Phila. Dir. 1833.

—, ROBERT: Phila. n/d.

M'COY, GEORGE W.: Phila. Dir. 1837 and
later.

M'CROW, THOMAS: Annapolis, Md. Adv.
1767, "Watchmaker from Edinburgh."

M'CULLY, WILLIAM: Phila. Dir. 1841 and
later.

McDANIEL, WILLIAM H.: Phila. Dir. 1825.

McDONALD, CHARLES: Lexington, Ky. Dir.
1818. (LB)

McDOWELL, F.: Phila. *Ca.*1800. "Shop
two doors above draw bridge."

—, JAMES: Phila., 136 N. Front St. and
82 N. 4th St. Dir. 1794–1808.

—, JAMES, JR.: Phila. Dir. 1817. "Clockmaker." (Brix)

—, JOHN: Phila. Dir. 1817.

McELWAIN, DAVID & GEORGE: Rochester,
N.Y. *Ca.*1840–*ca.*1850.

McELWEE, JAMES: Phila. Dir. 1813–1814.
Also Ferris & McElwee.

McFADDEN, JOHN B., & CO.: Pittsburgh, Pa.
*Ca.*1840.

—, J. B.: Pittsburgh, Pa. *Ca.*1835.

MacFARLANE, JOHN: Boston. Dir. 1796–
1813. (Abbott)

—, WILLIAM: Phila. Dir. 1805.

McGRAW, DONALD: Annapolis, Md. Adv.
1767, "Watchmaker from Edinburgh."
(Prime)

McGREGOR, J.: San Francisco, Cal. *Ca.*
1850–*ca.*1860. Clocks and Chrons.

McGrew, Alexander: Cincinnati, O. C. W. S. J. Dir. 1829. (LB)

—, Wilson: Cincinnati, O. Dir. 1829–1864.

M'Harg (Alex.) & Selkirk: Albany, N.Y. Dir. 1815.

—, Alexander: Albany, N.Y. Dir. 1817–ca.1850 and later. Also M'Harg & Selkirk.

Machen, Thomas W.: New Bern, N.C. Adv. 1812, 1830.

McHugh, James: Lowell, Mass. Ca.1860.

McIlheny (J. E.) & West: Phila., 13 No. 3rd St. Dir. 1818–1822.

—, Joseph E.: Phila. Dir. 1825.

McIntyre Watch Co.: Kankakee, Ill. 1905. (Chamberlain)

McIvor, Murdo: Rochester, N.Y. Dir. 1844.

McKay, Spear & Brown: Boston, 195 Washington St. Succeeded Wm. P. McKay & Co. 1854. (Buhler)

—, William P., & Co.: Boston. Dir. 1842, 1846–1854. Label overpasted on a Joseph Ives, Farmington, Hour Glass clock owned by E. T. Chichester, Darien, Conn. (Ant. Mar. 1949)

Mackay, C.: Charleston, S.C. Adv. 1790, "Watchmaker from London." From 1 Broad St. to S.W. corner Union St. 1799.

MacKay, Crafts: Boston. Dir. 1789. (First Boston Dir.). Pos. also Phila., 1 Broad St. n/d. Prob. from London. English bracket clock owned by Lewis Dyer, Newburyport, Mass.

McKay, H.: Haverhill, Mass. 20th century.

M'Kee, John: Chester, S.C. Name variously spelled. Adv. 1816, "Continues to carry on in all its various branches." Tall clock owned by Cecil Reid, Frederick, Va. (Prime)

M'Keen, Henry: Phila., 161 Market St. Dir. 1823–1850. Watch Paper Cramer Col.

M'Kinley, Edward: Phila. Dir. 1830–1837.

McKinney, Robert: Wilmington, Del. Adv. 1845.

M'Manus, John: Phila. Dir. 1840.

M'Masters, Hugh A.: Phila. Dir. 1839 and later.

M'Mullen, Edward: Phila. Dir. 1846–1848. "Clockmaker." (Brix)

McMyers, John: Baltimore, Bond St., Fells Point. Adv. 1799.

M'Namara, —: Phila. Adv. 1765, "Watch finisher." (Brix)

McNeil, E.: Binghamton, N.Y. Adv. 1813. (Cutten)

McNeish, John: N.Y.C. Ca.1810.

Macomb Co., The: Macomb, Ill. Ca.1885. Calendar clock. (Dre)

McParlin, William: Annapolis, Md. Ca. 1800. Apt. and successor to Wm. Faris. (LB)

M'Pherson, Robert: Phila. Dir. 1837 and later.

—, Sweeney Eugene: Boston. Dir. 1830.

M'Stocker, Francis: Phila. Dir. 1831 and later.

Magann, Patrick: Charleston, S.C., 122 Broad St. "From Ireland." Adv. 1792. Later 64 Bay St. Adv. 1794 at 3 Champney St. (Prime)

Magnin, David: N.Y.C. Ca.1810.

Maher (Mahva), Matthew: Phila. Adv. 1761, "Watch finisher. From London on 2nd St. Has wrought for some of the most iminnant watch makers of both London and Dublin." (Prime)

Maholland, Robert: Phila. Dir. 1850.

"Maiden Lane": 18 size watch, 7 position adjusted, by Seth Thomas Co. ca.1893. "Took highest awards at 1893 Chicago World's Fair." See ill. No. 303. (Paul Darrot)

Maire, Charles: Louisville, Ky. Adv. ca.1840. (LB)

Maker, Matthew: Charleston, S.C. Before 1776.

Mallory & Merriman: Bristol. (tx) 1831. Pos. Cs.

—, George: N.Y.C., 333 Pearl St. Dir. 1846–1847. Dealer.

—, Ransom: 1792–1853. Bristol. Son of David. Apt. at cabinetmaking and carpentry seven years. To Bristol 1821; clock cases at Jerome shop. With John Birge, Sheldon Lewis, Thomas Fuller, Ambrose Peck in Birge & Mallory ca.1837. (AAJ June, July 1949) (Hist.)

Malloy, George: Lowell, Mass. Dir. 1859.

Malls, Philip: Washington, D.C. Ca.1800. Tall clock No. 220 known.

Manchester, Cyril B.: Pawtucket, R.I. Adv. 1867, "Tin toy clock banks."

—, G. D.: Plainfield, Conn. Ca.1850–ca. 1860.

MANHATTAN CLOCK CO.: N.Y.C. 1899. "Eureka clocks." (MFM)

— WATCH CO., THE: N.Y.C. 1883–*ca.*1892. (MFM)

MANNING BOWMAN CO.: Meriden, Conn. 20th century. Electric clocks. One owned by Mrs. Wm. Lovelace, Westbury, L.I.

—, RICHARD: Ipswich, Mass. *Ca.*1748–1760. Wag-on-Wall clock, plain wood case dated 1767, Essex Inst. (See ill. No. 2.) Pos. made guns during Rev. War. Britten lists as "Clockmaker."

—, THOMAS: Salem, Mass. Gunsmith. Admitted to Ipswich 1685. Prob. son of Nicholas (both names in Ipswich). Thomas Fuller had land on Rock Hill, Ipswich, 1685; built wheelwright shop. Prob. C. only. (Trades and Tradesmen)

MANROSS BROS.: Bristol, Frederick St. (tx) 1856–1861. Sons of Elisha. Fought in Civil War, except Elijah who carried on Manross clock business till 1869.

—, E. (Elijah) & C. (Charles) H.: Bristol. (tx) 1854–1856. Sons of Elisha. Succeeded by Manross Bros.

— (Elisha) & NORTON: Bristol. (tx) 1839–1840.

—, PRICHARD & CO.: Bristol. (tx) 1841–1842.

—, ELIJAH: 1827–1911. Bristol. Son of Elisha. (tx) 1862–1869.

—, ELIJAH, JR.: Bristol. (tx) 1862–1870.

—, ELISHA: 1792–1856. Bristol. Aw. 1813–1854. In War of 1812. Father of Elijah, Charles Hayden, Newton Spalding, Eli, John, Henry, Roberts. Bought from Joseph Ives et al. shop on brook west of Frederick St., S. of W. Washington St., later known as "Laporte Hubbell Shop." *Bristol Hist.* said after 1813 made wooden clock parts for Chauncey Boardman; up to 25 clocks finished in advance, salesmen out on horseback and eventually sold them. Pos. first C. to use jeweled movts. With son Newton S. devised machinery to cut jewels from garnets found near Buffalo, N.Y. Woodturning business; made clock parts for Ortons & Preston, Boardman & Wells. In Manross & Wilcox 1840, Manross, Prichard & Co. 1841–1844. Built factory 1845 near center of Forestville on Church St. Prob. bought out partners, continued alone. f. 1854,

sold out to E. N. Welch. Report 1850, "He makes say 15,000–20,000 clocks annually, has valuable real estate, all clear, is good." In G. B. Davis Col. Fuzee Shelf clock, label "Patent Spring 8-day brass clocks made and sold by Elisha Manross. Press of Elihu Gear" (no street or number); wood cones taper toward backline attached to big end, small end blocked by wood disc, springs sunk in solid block of wood, supporting seat board; roller pinion movt., strip brass frame. Another in Davis Col., label printed by Elihu Gear, 26 State St., Hartford, 1838; brass movt. OG by him 9 × 14, inlaid, several fine lines of light-colored wood, in H. Grant Rowell Col. (EI)

MANS, JOHN: Columbia, Pa., Front St. Before 1818. (Lan. Co.)

MANSFIELD, SAMUEL A.: Phila. Dir. 1848 and later.

MANUEL, JULES: Phila. Dir. 1849 and later.

MARACHE, SOLOMON: N.Y.C. 1759.

MARAND, JOSEPH: Baltimore, Harrison St. 1804.

MARANVILLE, ALUSHA: Winsted, Conn. Patent 1861 Wall Calendar clock. Ex. Ray Walker Col.

MARBLE, SIMEON: New Haven, Conn. 1801–1807. "Made and sold clocks, watches and Silverware." (Hoopes)

MARCHISI, JOSEPH: Utica, N.Y. Dir. 1845–1846.

MARIE, M.: Charleston, S.C., 34 Church St. Adv. 1796. (Prime)

MARIEN, JOHN: N.Y.C. Dir. 1848.

MARINE CLOCK MFG. CO.: New Haven, Conn. *Ca.*1847. "8-day and 30-hour marine T.P. and clocks, mfd. by . . ." Patented by Charles Kirk(e). Striking clock regulator slot in dial for adjustment of striking mechanism by running pin through hole between 10 and 11 and raising wire; dial and movt. inscribed "C. Kirk's Patent"; unusual escapement, two escape wheels; single spring furnishes power for running and striking. Similar double escape wheels were used by Munger, Auburn, N.Y. *ca.*1825 and Fasoldt, Albany, 1851–1865. (BCC) (Coleman)

MARION WATCH CO.: Marion (now Jersey City), N.J. (See U. S. Watch Co.) 1872–

1875. Machinery sold 1875 to E. F. Bowman, Lancaster, Pa. (Bowman sold this machinery to J. P. Stevens Watch Co., Atlanta, Ga., 1882; pos. part to Auburndale Watch Co.) (Evans) (*Timing a Century*) (Bowman)

MARKHAM & CASE: Columbia, S.C. *Ca*.1845.

MARKS, ISAAC: Phila. Dir. 1795–1799. "Dealer in watches."

MARLOW & CO.: York, Pa. 20th century. 14″ miniature Tall clock, reproduction of Jonathan Jessup's Tall clock. One owned by George Raymond, Mt. Kisco, N.Y.

MARQUAND & BROS.: N.Y.C. Aw. 1823. Pos. Dealer and imp.

—, FREDERIC: N.Y.C., 166 Broadway until 1825. (Miller)

—, ISAAC: 1766–1838. Edentown, N.C. Adv. 1791–1796, "From London." N.Y.C. Dir. 1804–1805, "Merchant" 183 Front St. (Cutten)

—, ISAAC: 1776–1838. Fairfield, Conn. Son of joiner from Guernsey 1761, d. 1772 left books and tools to son. Aptd. to uncle Jacob Jennings, S., *ca*.1787. Later alone. With B. Whiting as Whiting & Marquand, Cs. To N.Y.C. after 1801, mfg. J. and merchant. (Hoopes)

MARRIAN, JOHN H.: N.Y.C. Dir. 1847

MARRIS, JOHN: Middletown and Hartford, Conn. n/d. (Hoopes)

MARSH, B. B. & T. K.: Paris, Ky. Bros. according to Steele Marsh of Paris, Ky., grandson of B. B.; S. and makers of Tall clocks. (LB)

—, GEORGE, & CO.: Farmington, Conn. George Marsh in Curtis (Lewis) & Marsh in Farmington, 1830's. Factory may now be village library. (Wallace W. Gray, Hartford)

—, GILBERT & CO.: Bristol. *Ca*.1830 or later.

— & HOFFMAN: Albany, N.Y. *Ca*.1890. Charles E. DeLong worked for them. (Chamberlain)

—, WILLIAMS & CO.: Dayton, O. *Ca*.1830. Label, "Made and sold by . . . clocks with improvements of ivory bushings." Walnut wheels; one 8-day wood movt. (Am. Col. Dec. 1948)

—, WILLIAMS, HAYDEN & CO.: Dayton, O. After 1833; with Hayden as partner. Pos.

2,500 wood movt. clocks a year. (Am. Col. Dec. 1947)

MARSH, GEORGE C.: Aw. Winchester, Winsted, Bristol 1828–1831. Bought factory 1828 from Thomas Barnes. Also Wolcottville and Farmington, Conn. Reported at Dayton, O., *ca*.1830, in Marsh, Williams & Co. Good clocks. See ill. No. 216 for 8-day brass movt. hollow column, no place name on label. Shelf clocks Conn. type, most kinds, mostly brass movts., 30-hour and 8-day. Some wood clocks, wood movts.

—, T. K.: Paris, Ky. *Ca*.1804. Bro. B.B.

MARSHALL & ADAMS: Senaca Falls, N.Y. *Ca*.1825. Shelf clock in Flint Sale, 1926. "A large mahogany mantel clock with claw feet and 8-day. 40¼ × 23½″."

— & WHITE: Petersburg, Va. *Ca*.1825.

—, GEORGE: Bristol. n/d. Flint Sale 1926, "Square case painted stencil columns at the sides and top."

MARTIN (Thomas) & MULLIN (Robert): Baltimore. Adv. 1764.

—, ALEX: N.Y.C., 100 Hudson St. White Watch Paper Bir. Col.

—, GEORGE: Lancaster, Pa. Rope maker; pos. C. Catgut and ropes. Aw. 1780–1830. Succeeded by son George, Jr. (Catgut used on 8-day clocks.) (Lan. Co.)

—, GEORGE A.: Bethel, Me. *Ca*.1870.

—, JOHN: N.Y.C., 184 and 288 Spring St. 1831. Watch Paper Bir. Col.

—, JOHN J. (J. L.): Phila. Dir. 1844 and later.

—, PATRICK: Phila. Dir. 1820–1850.

—, PETER: N.Y.C. *Ca*.1810.

—, SAMUEL: N.Y.C. Early 19th century. Tall mahogany quarter column clock, arched painted dial.

—, THOMAS: Baltimore. Adv. 1764, "Opened his shop." (Prime)

—, VALENTINE: Boston. Dir. 1842.

MASCHER, JOHN F.: Phila. Dir. 1845 and later.

MASHAM, SAMUEL: Wiltshire, Md. 1774.

MASI & CO., F.: Washington, D.C. 1833.

—, SERAPHIM: Washington, D.C. *Ca*.1830. Dealer.

"MASON": Used by Illinois Springfield Watch Co. 1870–1875.

—, GEORGE: Waseca, Minn. *Ca*.1870. "Wag-on-Walls." (Dre)

MASON, H. G.: Boston. 1844–1849.
—, P.: Somerville, N.J. Early 19th century.
—, SAMUEL, JR.: Phila. Dir. 1820–1830. (Prime)
—, TIMOTHY B.: Boston. Dir. 1830.
—, WILLIAM H.: Mt. Holly, N.J. 1834–1861. Tall clocks. (PG)
MASSEY, CHARLES R.: Phila., 409 No. 2nd St. Dir. 1837–1839. Watch Paper Cramer Col.
—, JOHN: Charleston, S.C. Ca.1736. Pos. Joseph.
—, JOSEPH: –1736. Charleston, S.C. Aw. 1722–1736. (MFM)
MASSOT, HORACE: Charleston, S.C. Ca. 1780.
MASTERS, JOHN: 1770–1846. Bath, Me., Boston. Aw. 1820–1846. b. England; Newfoundland 1786, inherited business of uncle William, C. Burned out 1818; to Boston. Adv. Dir. 1820. To Bath, Me.; cared for town clock. Son William with him. Mrs. B. K. Little owns Tall clock.
—, WILLIAM: 1806–1854. Bath, Me. Son of John. C., W. with father. Adv. Bath papers, "Clockmaker, Dealer, and Repairer." (Mrs. B. K. Little)
MATHER, ELI: West Bradford Twp., Pa. Sold Eli Terry & Sons patent clocks 1828. (Francis D. Brinton)
MATHEWS, DAVID & EDWIN: Bristol. (tx) 1832. Pos. Cs.
— (David), JEWEL (Lyman) & Co. (Samuel Botsford): Bristol, Union St. (tx) 1851–1853. Brass clock movts.; some sold ca.1852 to E. O. Goodwin. (LB)
MATHEWSON & HARRIS: New Hartford Centre, Conn. Ca.1830. Modified Pillar Shelf clock in Robert Dickey Col., Haverhill, Mass.
MATHEY, LEWIS: Phila., 173 High St. Dir. 1797–1803.
MATHIEU, GASTON: N.Y.C. Dir. 1845.
MATLACK, WHITE & WILLIAM: Phila. Adv. 1780, "All kinds of clocks and watches made or repaired at the South side of Market St. near 4th. Likewise buy and sell old or new clocks and watches." (Prime)
—, WHITE: N.Y.C. Aw. 1769–1777. To Phila. 1777. Adv., "Lately from N.Y.C. on Market St. near 4th St." (Prime)
—, WILLIAM: Phila. 1787; Charleston, S.C.; to Phila. Dir. 1797 South 3rd St., Dir.

1828 11 Strawberry Alley. Aw. 1787–1828. (Prime) (Gillingham)
MATTHEWS & PENNOYER: Bristol. (tx) 1830–1831. Pos. Cs.
MATTHEWSON, J.: Providence, R.I. Dir. 1849
MAUREPAS, M. (E.): Bristol. Pos. Manross.
MAUS, FREDERICK: Phila., Brewer's Alley between 3rd and 4th Sts. Adv. 1782. Dir. 1785–1793. Tall clocks; one owned by A. Keller, Phila., motto on dial, "Time Shews the Way of Life's Decay." (Ritter)
—, JACOB: Phila.; Trenton, N.J. Aw. 1780–1790. Adv. 1780; 1781, shop robbed. (Prime)
—, PHILIP: Lebanon, Pa. Ca.1800. Tall clocks; one owned by Mrs. Ruth L. Bomberger, Harrisburg, Pa., another by C. W. McDavitt, Louisville, Ill.
—, SAMUEL: Pottstown, Pa. Ca.1790. Tall clocks. No. 20 owned by Harry M. Denzler, Washington, D.C.
—, WILLIAM: Quakertown or Hill Town, Pa. Ca.1810. (Baillie)
MAUSER M'F'G. Co.: N.Y.C. n/d. Name in Tall clock owned by Mrs. Jeffrey Granger, N.Y.C.
MAUTZ, JOHN: Phila. Dir. 1841.
MAWDSLEY, JOHN: Phila. Dir. 1846–1847.
MAXANT, E. M. L.: n/p. Patent No. 220401, Oct. 7, 1879, model Smiths. Inst.
MAXWELL, A.: Phila., 157 S. Front St. Dir. 1805–1811.
—, JAMES: Boston. Early 1700's. Hourglasses. (Buhler)
MAY & PAYSON: Baltimore, Market St., Adv. 1789, "Displayed springs made by J. Deverell of Boston." (Prime)
—, SAMUEL (May & Clark): Phila. Adv. 1765.
MAYER, ELIAS: Phila. Dir. 1831–1832. J. and dealer.
MAYNARD, GEORGE: N.Y.C. 1703–1730.
MEAD, ADRIANCE & Co.: Ithaca, N.Y. Adv. 1831–1832. C., W., S., and dealer.
—, BENJAMIN: Castine, Me. Early 19th century. Tall clock owned by Hill Jewelry Co. (Abbott)
MEAGEAR, THOMAS J.: Wilmington, Del. Apt. of Ziba Feris. In Phila. Dir. 1833–ca.1850. Mrs. Buhler reports name on dial of Tall clock by Patton & Jones ca.1790.

MEARS, CHARLES: Phila. Dir. 1828–1835.
—, WILLIAM: Reading, Pa. (tx) 1785, "Clockmaker." Adv. 1901 mentions Tall clock by him for sale, dated "1785." (Steinmetz)
MEATH & FRAZER: n/p. Ca.1831. Pos. Heath. On brass movt. watch owned by R. Kister, Washington, D.C.
MECHLIN, JACOB: Reading, Pa. Ca.1759. "A pioneer maker. With Urletig, one of the earliest." 1st Group. (Steinmetz)
MECKE, JOHN: Phila. Dir. 1837 and later.
MECOM, JOHN: –1770. N.Y.C., Rotten Row. Adv. 1763–1770. J., sold watches.
MEDINGER, THOMAS G.: N.Y.C. n/d. Chrons. No. 9194 in Andrew Shiland Col.
MEDLEY, A. F.: Louisville, Ky. Adv. ca.1840. (LB)
MEEKS, EDWARD, JR.: N.Y.C. Adv. 1796, "Makes and has for sale 8-day clocks."
MEER BROS.: Frankfort, Ky. Adv. ca.1835. (LB)
MEGARY, ALEXANDER: N.Y.C. Ca.1820–1830.
MEGONEGAL, W. H.: Phila. Dir. 1844.
MEIER, FELIX: N.Y.C. Ca.1880. "Astronomical clock." (BCL)
MEILY, EMANUEL: Lebanon, Pa. Ca.1810.
MELCHER, —: Plymouth Hollow, Conn. Ca. 1790. (FT)
MELHOM, MICHAEL: Boonsboro, Ind. Ca. 1830. (Dre)
MELLY ("Brothers Melly"): N.Y.C. Ca. 1829. Pos. Dealer.
MELVILLE, HENRY: Wilmington, N.C. Adv. 1798, "From London, took shop lately occupied by D. Lambertoz, on Dock St." Adv. 1798 for apt. (Cutten)
MENDENHALL, THOMAS: Phila. and Lancaster, Pa. Adv. 1775. King and Queens Sts., borough of Lancaster. Made and repaired clocks and math. insts. (Prime)
MENDS, BENJAMIN: Phila. Ca.1800.
—, JAMES: Phila. Dir. 1796–1797. (Prime) (Baillie spelled it "Mens.")
MENZIES, JAMES: Phila., 140 and 159 So. Front St. Ca.1800.
—, JOHN: Phila., 140 and 159 So. Front St. Dir. 1804–1851.
—, JOHN, JR.: Phila. Dir. 1835 and later.
—, THOMAS: Phila. 1806–1825. (Baillie)
MERCHANT, WILLIAM: Phila. n/d.

MEREDITH, JOSEPH P.: Baltimore. 1824–1828.
MERGENTHALER, OTTMAR: 1854–1899. From Germany 1872. Completed apprenticeship as expert W. Invented linotype, patented 1885. Employed to inspect and repair clocks in Govt. buildings in Washington, D.C. After 1876 in Baltimore; perfected linotype. (Mittman) (HIA Jan. 1948)
MERIDEN CLOCK CO.: Meriden, Conn. n/d. Emerson C. Terry worked for them.
MERIMEE, WILLIAM: n/p. Ky. 1796. (MFM)
MERRELL, A.: Vienna, O. Ca.1828. Clock label in J. S. Fuchs Col.
MERRIAM, SILAS: New Haven, Conn. Pos. Merriman.
MERRIE, JOHN P.: Utica, N.Y. Dir. 1833.
MERRIMAN (Dr. Titus), BIRGE (John) & Co. (Joseph Ives): Bristol. 1819–1822 or later. (See ill. No. 228.) In Frank Beaven Col. label, "This clock was invented by Joseph Ives and manufactured by . . ." Metal and wood movts. (See ill. Nos. 225–229.) Ives type, 30-hour, long pendulum, two weights, no guides, direct fall, long case Mirror Clock. Pos. mentioned in Conn. 1819 *Gazetteer*.
— & BRADLEY: New Haven, Conn., 58 State St. 1825. "Carried on general business, jewelry, silverware and gold beads, watches and clocks repaired." (Moore)
—, BRADLEY & Co.: New Haven, Conn. Ca.1810. Pos. sons of Silas.
— & Co.: New Haven, Conn. Org. by sons of Silas. Continued business after 1805. Mahogany case Tall clock owned by Mrs. Harriette Beecher, Torrington, Conn.
— (Titus) & DUNBAR (Butler): Bristol. 30-hour wood Tall clocks before 1812, when Dunbar sold Merriman blacksmith shop.
—, R., & Co.: Bristol. Early 1820's. "Clocks of Joseph Ives type." (LB)
—, BUTLER: Bristol. Baillie error for Butler Dunbar.
—, MARCUS: New Haven, Conn. Ca.1805 and later. Son and apt. of Silas. Bro. Samuel.
—, REUBEN: Cheshire and Litchfield, Conn. In Litchfield Adv. 1842, "One door East of Presbyterian Church." Floyd Thoms reports Tall clock, brass 8-day movt.,

MERRIMAN, REUBEN (cont'd)
mahogany case, moon, marked "Chesshire." (J. H. Thompson)

—, SAMUEL: New Haven, Conn. Ca.1805. Son and apt. of Silas. Bro. Marcus.

—, SILAS: 1739–1805. New Haven, Conn., State St. Son of John and Jemima. Pos. apt. of Macock Ward. Marr. 1760. Brass movt. Tall clocks. Trained two sons, Marcus and Samuel. Simeon Joscelyn an apt. (Hoopes)

—, TITUS: 1768–1848. Bristol. Early 1800's. C. Other industries. In Merriman & Dunbar ca.1812; Merriman, Birge & Co. 1819 and later. A leading doctor.

MERRY (MERY), F.: Phila. Dir. 1799.

MESTIER, B.: Phila. Dir. 1817.

METCALF, F.: Hopkinton, Mass. Ca.1825.

—, LUTHER: Medway, Mass. Ca.1800 or later. Case maker. Clocks extant with name on dial.

METTEN, LAURENS: St. Louis, Mo. Ca.1850.

MEVREY, F.: Phila. Ca.1799.

MEYER, ALBERT: Cincinnati, O. Ca.1850.

—, DAVID: Meyerstown, Pa. n/d. Tall clocks.

—, FELIX: N.Y.C. 1880. Spent 10 years making clock which gave local time, hour, minute, second, day of week, month, seasons, zodiac signs, earth revolutions, planet movement, moon phases; also time in Washington, San Francisco, Chicago, Cairo, Melbourne, Constantinople, Peking, London, Paris, Berlin, Vienna, Leningrad; child strikes quarter hour, youth half-hour, old man three-quarter hour, and death the hour while Washington rises from seat, presents Declaration of Independence. Servant opens door, other U. S. Presidents up to time clock was made come forward, salute, go out through other automatic door. Clock 18' high, 8' wide, 5' deep; contained over 2,000 wheels. (G. Gould)

—, J. H.: N.Y.C. 1803. Pos. imp. Canton, O., ca.1850.

MEYERS, JOHN: Fredericktown, Md. 1793–1825. (Abbott)

MICHAEL, LEWIS: York, Pa. n/d. Adv. insts.

MIDDLETON, AARON: Burlington, N.J. Adv. 1732 by Isaac Pearson, from whom he ran away. (Williams)

MIETY, EMANUEL: Lebanon, Pa. n/d. Tall clocks. (Conrad)

MILK, THOMAS: Md. "1775." (FT)

MILLARD, SQUIRE: Warwick, R.I. Ca. Rev. War. Tall clock, cherry case, OG feet, plain brass dial, silvered, unusual hands, James Conlon Col.

"MILLER," used by Illinois Springfield Watch Co. ca.1870.

MILLER: n/p., n/d., Tall clocks so marked; one owned by A. W. Roat, Huntington Valley, Pa., prob. Wag-on-Wall, case pos. by George Wellington ca.1776; date and name on case; case with hand-wrought nails, handmade dowel pins, face marked "Miller," painted bird and floral design; one weight, endless chain 30-hour brass movt.

— (Herman) CLOCK Co.: Zeeland, Mich. 1929–1930. Banjo, Shelf, and Electric clocks. (PG) (MFM)

—, W. H. C., & Co.: Chicago. 1860's. J. W.

— & WILLIAMS: Cincinnati, O. Ca.1830–ca.1840. "Made clocks and tools." Employed Warren Warner, C.

—, AARON: –1777. Elizabethtown, N.J. Adv. 1747 N.Y. papers: "Clockmaker who makes and sells all kinds of clocks after the best manner with expedition. He likewise makes compasses, chains for surveyors, also church bells of any size, having foundry for that purpose, and has cast several that have proved to be good, and will supply Persons on a timely notice with any of the above articles at very reasonable rates." Left tools to son-in-law Isaac Brokaw. (Prime)

—, ABRAHAM: Easton, Pa. 1810–1830. (Abbott)

—, COL. ALEXANDER: Uniontown or Ashland, O. n/d. (Knittle)

—, BENJAMIN: Germantown, Pa. n/d.

—, CORNELIUS: New Jersey. Late 18th century. Tall clock owned by Paul Bigelow.

—, EDWARD F.: Providence, R.I. 1824.

—, GEORGE: Germantown, Pa. Pos. Apt. of Christopher Witt. C. and W. ca.1771. Apt., David Fisk, Jr. Tall clock owned by Mrs. Byron Jones, Bendersville, Pa., brass dial, days, heavy black figures, marked "Geo. Miller, Germantown"; walnut case pegged together, wind chains and weights.

Tall clocks also owned by Mrs. E. Greenwalt, Phila., George Collo, Quakertown, Pa., and Ralph Turn; white iron dial Tall clock in Milford, Pa. (Gillingham)

MILLER, GEORGE: Phila. Dir. 1809.

—, GEORGE II: Phila. 1828–1833. Pos. same as above.

—, HENRY: Patent on "Astronomical clock" May 5, 1825 from East Hanover, Pa.

—, HENRY A.: Southington, Conn. Ca.1830. Tall clocks.

—, J. B.: Portland, Ore. 1860's.

—, JOHN (JOHAN, JNO.): Germantown, Pa. Tall clock owned by Mrs. Johannes Nabhof, New Brunswick, N.J., "1735" on dial and inside case, brass movt.

—, JOHN JAMES: Germantown and Phila., Pa. n/d.

—, KENNEDY: Elizabethtown, N.J. 1830–1833. Pos. Miler. "The case shows the heights of craftsmanship of which the N.J. cabinetmakers were capable in the days of the young Republic. The case and brass movt. have come down through the years absolutely untouched, even the glass door being original." (PG) (FT)

—, PARDON: Providence and Newport, R.I. Ca.1820–ca.1840.

—, PETER: 1772–1855. Lynn Twp., Pa.; Ephrata, Pa. ca.1800. Aw. 1793–1837. "Best known maker in Lehigh Co. Worked with brass and wood, probably made more Tall clocks than any other maker." Two Tall clocks owned by Dr. Walter F. Kistler, Wilkes-Barre, Pa., and Paul C. Hohl, San Francisco, Cal. (Roberts) (Stow)

—, PHILIP: N.Y.C. 1763–1769. Adv. 1763, "Robbed"; Adv. 1769, "Robbed again."

—, RICHARD: Pa. n/p. Tall clock owned by K. R. Bowen, Kennett Sq., Pa., "55" on dial is where "50" should be.

—, S. W.: Phila. Dir. 1843.

—, THOMAS: Phila. Dir. 1819–1841. (Millar in Baillie)

—, WILLIAM S.: Phila. Dir. 1844–1848.

MILLINGTON, ISAAC: Lancaster Co., Pa. Ca.1850.

MILLIS & CHASE: N.Y.C. Dir. 1853.

—, J. R., & Co.: N.Y.C., 109 Fulton St. "Crane's patent month clocks, manufactured by . . .," label printed by "John Henry, printer, Franklin Bldg., cor. Ann & Nassau Sts., N.Y.C." Adv. 1845 on Crane clocks. (FMS)

MILLIS, JOSEPH: Pos. Willis. 1700–1799. Pennsylvania Tall clock, brass dial, applied rings, applied cast spandrels, 8-day brass movt., owned by Mrs. Robert Heyl, Pelham Manor, N.Y.

—, WILLIAM: N.Y.C. Ca.1840.

MILLUM, MOSES: Baltimore, 25 Caroline St., Fells Pt. 1819.

MILNE, ROBERT: N.Y.C. 1798–1802. Phila. Dir. 1817.

MINCHIN & WILLIS: Boston. n/d. Name on clock dial. (Burt)

MINDEL, GUSTAVUS: Phila. Dir. 1850.

MINOR, E. C.: Jonesville, Mich. Ca.1870.

—, RICHARDSON: 1736–1797. Stratford, Conn. ca.1758. Son of Rev. Richardson and Elizabeth Munson Minor. G. C. Marr. 1764. (Hoopes)

MINOT, J.: Boston. Ca.1800–1810. Painted dials. Prob. not C.

MITCHELL (George) & ATKINS (Rollin, Irenus): Bristol. (tx) 1830–1836. Bought and moved old Baptist meeting house for shop. Later Atkins & Downs, then R. & I. Atkins, finally Frost, Merriman & Co. Atkins shop burned 1880. Flint Sale 1926 No. 262 mahogany Shelf clock, square case, black and gold trimmed double columns, gold carved top, mirror in extreme lower section.

—, BAILEY & Co.: N.Y.C. 1854–1860. Bronze and gilt clocks; one in S. C. Robinson Col., Stamford, N.Y.

— & HINMAN: Bristol. (tx) 1828–1830. Prob. Cs. Assessed as "traders."

— (Henry) & MOTT (Jordan): N.Y.C., 27 Pearl St. Ca.1790–1809. Watch so marked in Museum City of N.Y.

—, VANCE & Co.: N.Y.C. 1860 and later. Bronze metal clocks and lamps. Display room 1880, at 597 Broadway, factory 10th Ave. bet. 24th and 25th Sts.

— (Phineas) & WHITNEY (Moses): Boston. Dir. 1813–1821.

—, GEORGE: 1774–1852. Son of William. C. With uncle in Mitchell & Hinman 1802–1830; later Mitchells Clothing Store. Shrewd trader, large banker; successful business man; leading spirit in community. Helped young men come to Bristol. (See Jerome's book). Bought clocks; pos. made

MITCHELL, GEORGE (cont'd)
some. Large landowner; took clocks in payment for land.
—, HENRY: N.Y.C. 1786–1802. Name on dial of Tall rockingship clock. Pos. in Mitchell & Mott, 1793–1809.
—, JESSE C.: Buffalo, N.Y. Dir. 1835–1836.
—, PHINEAS: Boston. Dir. 1809–1830.
—, PROF.: Cincinnati, O. Ca.1850. Astronomical electric clock.
—, WILLIAM, JR.: Richmond, Va. 1843–1849.
MITCHELSON, DAVID: Boston. 1774. "Clocks and watches."
MIX BROS.: Ithaca, N.Y. 1854–1863. Hawes patent Calendar clocks for Huntington & Pratt.
—, ELISHA: New Haven. Ca.1840–ca.1850.
MOHLER, JACOB: 1744–1773. Baltimore. Adv. 1773, "Watchmaker, shop under the printing office on South St. near Market St."
MOIR, WILLIAM: N.Y.C. Dir. 1878. Dealer, imp. Name on Shelf clock dial, brass movt., "G. Japy Freres" owned by S. W. Trivit, Hawthorne, N.Y.
MOLL, JOHN: Wilmington, Del. Ca.1680. Edward B. Humphries said 1880 he saw Old Dutch clock by John Moll, old and well-known magistrate; clock was sent to Holland to have movt. put in; Moll armorial bearings. Pos. first C. in Del. Moles prominent in Newcastle and Del. during Duke of York's government 1676–1682. Son John, Jr. (Conrad)
MOLLINGER, HENRY (Henri): Phila., 100 Race St. Dir. 1794–1804.
MONGIN, DAVID: Charleston, S.C. Adv. 1840, "Watchmaker now being settled in Charleston, makes and mends on Broad St." Adv. 1743, "Moved to King St." Adv. 1747, "Still in business despite the rumors, on King St." (Prime)
MONNIER, DANIEL: Phila. Dir. 1825–1850.
MONROE, E. & C. H., & Co.: Bristol. Ca.1850.
—, CHARLES: Bangor, Me. Ca.1840.
—, JOHN: Barnstable, Mass. n/d.
MONTANDON (Hannah) & ROBERTS (Oliver): Lancaster, Pa. Adv. 1802–1803.
—, HANNAH (Mrs. H. L.): Continued after death of husband 1802–1810.
—, HENRY LEWIS: –1802. Lancaster, Pa. W. No known Tall clocks with name;

Will inventory shows he made them. Widow Hannah with Oliver Roberts as Montandon & Roberts 1802–1803. (Roberts to Eaton, O.) (Lan. Co.)
MONTCASTLE, WILLIAM R.: Warrenton, N.C. 1844. Adv. 1856. (Cutten)
MONTEITH & Co.: Phila. Dir. 1845.
— & SHIPPEN: Phila. Dir. 1817.
—, BENJAMIN: Phila. Dir. 1818.
—, CHARLES: Phila. Dir. 1847–1848.
MONTGOMERY, ANDREW: Baltimore, Calvert and Baltimore Sts. 1822–1823; 46 Baltimore St. 1824.
—, ROBERT: N.Y.C. 1786.
MOOAR (?), LOT: Nashua, N.H. Ca.1830. (Dre)
MOON, ROBERT: Phila. 1768. Case maker.
MOONLINGER, HENRY: Phila., 100 Race St. Dir. 1794–1804.
MOORE, FREDERICK: New Haven, Conn. Ca.1840.
—, GEORGE H.: Lynn, Mass. Ca.1860.
—, NELSON A.: Newark, N.J. Ca.1850.
—, ROBERT: Phila., Front St. near Vine. 1798–. (Prime)
MORGAN & HART: Pittsburgh, Pa. Dir. 1819.
—, ELIJAH, JR.: 1783–1857. Poughkeepsie, N.Y. Adv. 1807–1831. W. D. S. Father of William S. Morgan. (Stout)
—, GIDEON: Pittsburgh, Pa. Dir. 1826. In Morgan & Hart on Wood St., bet. 4th and Diamond. Dir. 1819. Tall clock, 8-day brass movt. date, center seconds, moon, scrolled top, cherry inlaid curly maple case, owned by Dr. R. E. Wise, Hanover, Pa.
—, LUTHER S.: Salem, Mass., 243 Essex St. 1842–1846. Prob. grandson of Lucas Morgan, West Springfield, W. and J.
—, THEODORE: 1778–1845. Salem, Mass. 1831–1842. Marr. 1806. C. W. In former Post Office.
—, THOMAS: Phila. before 1772; Baltimore 1772–1779; Phila., Arch St., 1779, 1782, 1793.
—, WILLIAM S.: 1807–1886. Poughkeepsie, N.Y. S. Son of Elijah. (Cutten)
MORIN, AUGUSTUS: Phila. Dir. 1835.
MORPHY, JOHANAS: See Murphy. (Orr)
MORRELL & MITCHELL: N.Y.C. 1816–1820.
—, JOHN: Baltimore, 27 Charles St. 1822–1823.

MORRILL, BENJAMIN: 1794–. Boscawen, N.H. Aw. 1816–1845. Two clock shops; made mostly 8-day N.H. Mirror clocks. Machinery later used to make counter scales and reed mus. insts. Mass. Shelf clock at Essex Inst.; N.H. Mirror clocks and Tower clock at Dover, N.H. Label of one, "8-day clocks and timepieces manufactured by, . . . South of the Academy. To make the timepiece go faster, turn the screw up at the bottom of the pendulum and the contrary way to make it go slower." No printer's name. (Ray Walker) (DKP)

—, H. C.: Baltimore. 1835–ca.1840. Brass repeating 8-day alarm clock, which also lights lamp.

MORRIS (William) & WILLARD (Simon): Grafton, Mass. Ca.1770. Tall clock, both names on pendulum ball. (Sack)

—, ABEL: Reading, Pa. Taxed 1774 as "Clockmaker." No Tall clocks known.

—, BENJAMIN: 1748–1833. Hilltown Twp. and New Britton, Pa. Aw. 1768–1830. Credited with making more than 300 Tall clocks. (Conrad)

—, ELIJAH: Canton, Mass. Ca.1820. Son-in-law of William Crane.

—, ENOS: Hilltown Twp., Pa. Ca.1780. J. S. Bailey said he was son and for a few years successor of Benjamin.

—, HENRY: Canton, Mass. Ca.1820. With Elijah Morris.

—, ROBERT: New Britain, Pa. n/d. Tall clock owned by Mrs. Anna K. Garges, Doylestown, Pa.

—, SHELDON: Litchfield, Conn.

—, WILLIAM: Bridgetown, N.J. n/d. Watch Paper Cramer Col.

—, WILLIAM: Grafton, Mass. Ca.1770. Pos. trained Simon Willard (Willard aptd. to older brother Benjamin).

—, WILLIAM: Utica, N.Y. Dir. 1832–1833.

—, WILLIAM: Phila. Dir. 1837.

—, WILLIAM, JR.: Phila. Dir. 1844.

—, WOLLASTON: Md. 1774. (FT)

MORRISSEY, C. R.: Phila. Dir. 1837.

MORSE & BLAKESLEE: Plymouth, Conn. 1841–1855. Low-priced brass movt. clocks. (Hoopes)

— CHAIN Co.: Bridgeport, Conn. 20th century. Formerly made Poole Electric Battery Clocks.

MORSE (Miles) & Co.: Plymouth Hollow, Conn. Aw. 1846–1855. With Thomas Davis. Small factory on Naugatuck River. Low-priced brass clocks. Shop burned 1855. OG clock in Arthur Little Col.

— & MOSLEY: Albany, N.Y. Dir. 1823. (Cutten)

—, ANDREW, JR.: Bloomfield, Me. Patent Sept. 18, 1835, "Clocks and Timepieces Propelled by Atmospheric Air."

— CELEBRATED PERPETUAL CALENDAR CLOCK: Chicago, Ill. Ca.1893. (BCL)

—, JOSEPH: Walpole, Mass. n/d. Mass. Shelf clock known. (BCC)

—, MILES (Myles): Plymouth, Conn. 1841–1845. C. Ca.1820, pos. with H. Clark. With Jeremiah Blakeslee. With Gen. Thomas Davis, N.Y.C., built clock factory on W. branch of Naugatuck and Plymouth 1846; burned 1855.

—, MOSES L.: Boston. Dir. 1813.

—, R. C.: Baltimore. Dir. 1842. "Chronometers and watches." (MFM)

MORT (MOTT), JORDAN: N.Y.C. Aw. 1802–1825. Adv. 1810. Later Mort & Mitchell.

— & MITCHELL: N.Y.C., 247 Pearl St. "Extensive stock of clocks, etc."

MORTON, E. DANIEL, & Co.: Bristol. (tx) 1855. Pos. Cs.

MOSELEY, ROBERT E.: Newburyport, Mass. Ca.1848. Pos. C. or W.

MOSES, THOMAS: Wolcottville, Conn. Ca. 1830. Label, "Improved clocks made by Hopkins & Alfred and sold by . . ." (J. H. Thompson)

MOSHER, S.: Hamilton, N.Y. Adv. 1830. Mosher & Davis, S., Adv. 1834. (Cutten)

MOSS, —: Rochdale, Mass. "1818." Imperfect Watch Paper extant.

MOTT & MORRELL: N.Y.C. 1802–1810.

— & MOURNE: N.Y.C. "Evidently importers or assemblers, but at any rate engraved as the maker of a pear cased silver watch with a London 1790 hallmark"; owned by Ames A. Castle, Chicago.

—, JAMES: N.Y.C. Ca.1830.

MOULTON (William) & CARR (James): Lowell, Mass., 44 Merrimack St. Dir. 1834–1835.

—, EDWARD (E. G.): Rochester, N.H.; Saco, Me. 1807–1825. Tall clocks. (DKP)

—, FRANCIS E.: Lowell, Mass. Dir. 1832–1835.

MOULTON, JOSEPH: 1694–ca.1756. Newbury, Mass. S., pos. R. Blacksmith; gold beads. Later to Newburyport, Mass. Became Towle Ss.

—, THOMAS: Rochester, N.H. Early 1800's. (DKP)

—, THOMAS M.: Dunbarton (pos. also Rochester), N.H. Ca.1800. Fine Tall cased clocks.

MOUNTAIN, SAMUEL P.: Phila. Dir. 1842.

MOUNTFORD, JOHN: Phila. Dir. 1818–1819. Imp. of watches.

MOUNTJOY, JOHN: N.Y.C., 265 William St. Ca.1810.

—, WILLIAM: N.Y.C. Ca.1805.

MOUNT VERNON WATCH CO.: Mt. Vernon, N.Y. Ca.1936. "American made watches." (MFM)

MOUTOUX, CARL: Brooklyn, N.Y. Ca.1850.

MOWROVE, FRANCIS: N.Y.C. 1816.

—, PETER: –1739. Charleston, S.C. Aw. ca.1735–1739.

MOYER, JACOB: Skippackville, Pa. n/d. Tall clocks. (Orr)

—, JOSEPH D.: Skippackville, Pa. Name on dial 30-hour Tall clock, chain one-weight drive. (Orr)

MOYSTON, JOHN HUGAN: 1772–1844. Schenectady, N.Y. Adv. 1798. (Cutten)

MOZART (Don J.) WATCH CO., THE: Ann Arbor, Mich. 1868–1870. Ca.30 watches. f. Sold 1871 to Rock Island Watch Co., Rock Island, Ill.

—, —: Boston. From Italy. 1823–1830. Father of Don J. (Chamberlain)

—, DON J.: 1820–1877. To Boston 1823 with father. Shanghaied 1829. At sea 1829–1836. Came back and found his family gone. Marr. 1854. "Was an excellent inventive genius. Went into business at Xenia, O., making mechanical devices for watches. He was excitable with a restless desire for horological invention." Bristol 1863 to make a year clock; failed. Providence, R.I. 1864 making three-wheeled train watch, chron. lever escapement. Org. Company at Springfield, Mass., in 1867 as N.Y. Watch Co., became 1877 The Hampden Watch Co., Canton, O. Org. Mozart Watch Co., Ann Arbor, Mich., 1868 (ill. Chamberlain); ca.30 made. Org. another company at Freeport, Ill., 1874; factory burned 1875. (Chamberlain)

MUELLER, FREDERIC: –1747. Savannah, Ga. 1736. Prob. Wood Wag-on-Wall clocks, rope drive. None known. (Hob. July, 1949.)

MULFORD, E.: Princeton, N.J. n/d. Watch Paper Cramer Col.

—, JOHN H.: Albany, N.Y. Invented watch escapement 1842. "A high standard of work set in Albany." (Chamberlain)

MULLER, NICHOLAS: N.Y.C., 8 Cortlandt St. Aw. 1850. Dir. 1872. Founder; cast iron cases. Iron front Shelf alarm clock owned by Helen Lord, Phila.

MULLER'S SONS, NICHOLAS: N.Y.C. Ca.1880. Fancy bronze and iron cased Shelf clocks.

MULLIKEN: Early Mass. family of Cs. (AJ Feb., June, 1950)

—, BENJAMIN: Bradford, Mass. Ca.1740's.

—, JOHN: Bradford, Mass. 1690–. b. Boston. "Lived on an island in the Merrimac River near his father's home." Father of Samuel and Nathaniel. Blacksmith; pos. C. No clocks known.

—, JONATHAN: Ca.1810–. Bradford, Mass. Son of Robert. Bro. John. Marr. Martha Marsh 1742. Samuel and Nathaniel prob. his apts. Tall clocks known with "Jonathan Mulliken, Falmouth," on dial. Ex. in F. G. Reed Col., Lexington, Mass.

—, JONATHAN: 1746–1782. Newburyport, Mass. 1772. Son of Samuel I. Father of Samuel and Nathaniel of Newburyport and Me. Bought land and buildings in Newburyport. C. W. Employed others. Later merchant and ship owner. (AJ June, 1950.)

—, JOSEPH: –1804. Newburyport, Mass. "Clockmaker."

—, JOSEPH: 1771–1795. Salem, Mass. Aw. 1793–1795. Prob. son of John. Prob. apt. to Jonathan. W. at Stearns & Waldo's.

—, JOSEPH: Concord, Mass. Aw. ca.1777. Son of Nathaniel. Bro. Nathaniel II. Prob. brass movt. Tall clocks.

—, NATHANIEL I: –1767. Lexington, Mass. Son of John. Bro. Samuel I. Father of Nathaniel II. Learned clockmaking in Bradford, Mass. Marr. Lucy Stone of Lexington. Flat top hood Tall clock, cherry case, brass dial inscribed "For Jacob Abbot. Nath'l Mulliken, Lexington," in Edwin Hale Abbot Col. Tall clock in J. Cheney Wells Col., maple case, flat top hood, brass dial, applied hour and seconds dial, brass spandrels, name plate, exhibited Harvard Tercentenary. Another in Albert L. Partridge Col., pine case. *Boston Evening Post*, Dec. 4, 1767: "Monday, Mr. Nathaniel Mulliken of Lexington, clockmaker, who to all appearances has been as well that day as at any time, as he was coming in the door of his house, instantly fell notwithstanding all possible Endeavors for Relief, expired in a few moments to the great Grief of his disconsolate widow and children. His remains were interred on Thursday." Sons Nathaniel II and Joseph continued business.

MULLIKEN, NATHANIEL II: Lexington, Mass. Aw. 1767–1777 and later. Son of Nathaniel I. Shop burned by British on retreat from Lexington 1775.

—, NATHANIEL: 1776–. Newburyport, Mass. Later Hallowell, Me. Son of Jonathan of Newburyport. Learned clockmaking from father.

—, ROBERT: 1665–. From Scotland to Boston 1683; to Bradford *ca.*1638–1688. First Essex County gravestone marker 1723–1737. Pos. taught his sons clockmaking. No clocks extant.

—, SAMUEL I: 1720–1756. b. Bradford. Son of John. C. Learned clockmaking, pos. from uncle Jonathan. To Newburyport 1750; d. there. Succeeded by son Jonathan. Tall clocks extant with name "Bradford" on dial. Tall clock owned by Miss Morrow, Amesbury, Mass.

—, SAMUEL II: 1761–1847. Son of Samuel I. Friend of Jonathan; marr. Jonathan's widow 1783. To Salem, Mass., 1790–1796; Lynn, Mass. 1803–1807, postmaster, tanning, store owner. Adv. for "Partner for English West Indian trade." Tall clock at Edison Inst.

—, SAMUEL: Haverhill, Mass. n/d. Several by this name. Tall clock so marked owned by Mrs. Kinney Chase.

—, SAMUEL: 1769–. Newburyport, later Hallowell, Me. Son of Jonathan. Bro. of Samuel. (Miss Sarah Mulliken)

MULTER, PETER A.: N.Y.C. Dir. 1854.

MUMFORD, —: Providence, R.I. *Ca.*1810. Watch Paper MFM Col.

MUNCHIN, M.: n/p. Patent No. 156674, Nov. 10, 1874, model at Smiths. Inst.

MUNGER: Family of N.Y. Ss., Cs. Joseph had sons Asa, Perley, Sylvester. Asa's son was Austin; Sylvester's son was James. (Cutten)

—, A., & SON: Auburn, N.Y. *Ca.*1839–1847.

— (Asa) & BENEDICT (J.H.): Auburn, N.Y. Adv. 1826–1833.

— (S.) & DODGE (Abraham, Jr.): Ithaca, N.Y. 1824–1825.

— (S.) & PRATT (Daniel): Ithaca, N.Y. 1826–1832. Clocks and silver. Dissolution announced Dec. 12, 1832; Pratt continued (not Daniel Pratt of Reading, Mass.).

—, ASA: 1778–1851. Auburn, N.Y. Aw. *ca.*1820–1840. "N.Y. State style Shelf clocks." (See ill. Nos. 223, 224.) Hollow columns shown in ill. No. 221 are of sheet iron. Frequently used flying eagle pendulum ball. Some brass movts., double escape wheels. In A. Munger & Son, Munger & Benedict, and used own name.

—, AUSTIN E.: 1811–1892. b. Herkimer, N.Y. C. S. *Ca.*1839 in A. Munger & Son. Syracuse with Pliny Dickinson 1847. Alone *ca.*1850. (Cutten)

—, SYLVESTER: 1790–1857. Clinton, Onondaga, Elmira, Ithaca, N.Y. b. Ludlow, Mass. Son of Joseph. Bro. Asa. Marr. 1816 Achsah Tower. "Was first watchmaker and silversmith in Clinton, N.Y." Onondaga 1822. Ithaca 1823. In Munger & Dodge 1824–1825; Munger & Pratt 1826–1832. Elmira 1833. (Cutten)

MUNK, D.: N.Y.C. n/d. Watch Paper BCL Col.

MUNRO & CO.: Charleston, S.C., 230 Broad St. and 7 Elliott St. Adv. 1795. (Prime)

—, JOHN: Charleston, S.C. Adv. 1785, "Watchmaker from Edinburgh, last from London, makes, repairs, cleans . . . at 6 Broad St." Dir. 1809 7 Elliott St. and East Bay St. (Prime)

MUNROE FAMILY: Cs. Principally at Concord, Boston, Mass. Three bros.; Daniel, Nathaniel, William.

—, DANIEL & NATHANIEL: Concord, Mass. 1800–1807. Cs. Some brass founding.

— (Daniel) & JONES (Ezekiel): Boston. 1807–1809.

— (Nathaniel) & WHITING (Samuel): Concord, Mass. 1808–1817. Banjo clock ill. in Moore.

MUNROE, DANIEL: 1775–1859. Concord, Boston, Mass. C. Aw. 1796–1858. Apt. to Simon Willard seven years. Recommendation 1796, ". . . one of the best workmen in America." Clocks chiefly for Boston market with fluctuating success. Bro. Nathaniel with him 1800. With Ezekiel Jones in Boston 1807; 1809 alone, 51 Newbury St. "Continued at the bench till he retired at age 83 in 1858." Mass. Shelf (ill. in Moore), Banjo clocks, and others. (BCC)

—, DEACON NEHEMIAH: Boston. Late 18th century. Cabinetmaker. Lived at Roxbury, Mass., some years before coming of Willards. Successful; acquired considerable estate. Pos. teacher of Samuel and William Fisk, cabinetmakers. (BCC)

—, NATHANIEL: 1777–1861. Concord, Mass. Aptd. to Abel Hutchins. With bro. Daniel 1800–1807. Cs. and brass founding. With Samuel Whiting 1808–1817 as Munroe & Whiting. Large business, using mostly 8-day brass movts. "Mostly Hand Made." Seven or eight apprentices; in two-story building, 30′ front, 15′ deep. Small brass foundry "on the other side of the Dam," wheels and other brass parts, also bells. Industrious, genial. Most of his business with South. To Baltimore 1817. (Coupled with activities of Lemuel Curtis, at this time a number of fine clocks were made in Concord, Mass.— not to be confused with Concord, N.H., also center of fine clockmaking.)

—, WILLIAM: Concord, Mass. Bro. Daniel and Samuel. "Short time with his brothers as a clockmaker, better known as a cabinetmaker. Also made pencils with which he did well." Shop 35′ × 28′. (BCC)

MUNSELL, WILLIAM: n/p. O. n/d. Shelf clocks. (Knittle)

MUNYAN BROS.: Pittsfield, Mass. Ca.1860.

—, A. H.: Northampton, Mass. Adv. 1848. "Opened a shop." (Cutten)

MURDOCK & CO., J.: Utica, N.Y. Ca. 1820.

— & MELLISH: Woodstock, Vt., Central St. Name in Shelf clock. Pos. sales only. Dealt in East India goods. (Wilder)

—, JOHN: Woodbury, N.J. 1777, 1785–1786. Prob. S. only. (Williams)

MURPHY, JAMES: Boston. Dir. 1803–1806.

—, JOHN (Johannes): Northampton and Allentown, Pa. Aw. after Rev. War. "From Ireland." "Said to be the earliest clockmaker in Lehigh Co." "Tall clock purchased from him in 1787 for 18 Pounds." (Roberts) (Funk) (Conrad) (Orr)

—, JOHN: Charlestown, Pa. Tax record of Pikeland Twp., Pa., lists a "John Murphy" owning "14 acres of land" and taxed for "Trade." Tall clock with this name on dial ca.1790, enameled dial, 30-hour brass movt., walnut case, Q columns, owned in Charlestown, Pa. (James)

—, ROBERT (R. E.): Phila. Dir. 1848.

—, THOMAS: Allentown, Pa. Late 1830's.

MURRAY & SON: Fredericksburg, Va. 1805 (MFM)

—, ROBERT: Trenton, N.J. n/d. "Made 8-day clocks." (Stow)

MUSGRAVE & KELLY: Buffalo, N.Y. Adv. 1812. (Cutten)

MYER, GEORGE: N.Y.C. Dir. 1846.

MYERS & CO., S. F.: N.Y.C. Succeeded Prentiss Calendar & Time Co. 1889. Catalogue in BCL Col.

—, FREDERICK: Md. Late 18th century. Tall clocks.

—, MOSES: Poughkeepsie, N.Y. 1840's. (Stout)

MYGATT, COMFORT STARR: 1763–1823. Danbury, Conn., Canfield, O. Son of Eli and Abigail Starr Mygatt. C. S. Aw. Danbury ca.1783. Adv. 1804 for one or two boys as apts. To Ohio 1807. d. Canfield. (Hoopes)

MYLE, SAMUEL: Lebanon, Pa. Ca.1810.

NARNEY, JOSEPH: Charleston, S.C. Adv. 1753, "Makes, mends, cleans . . . Regularly bred to the watchmaking business which followed for several years in Dublin with credit and reputation. Several watches made by him in Dublin for sale." Adv. 1761, "Watchmaker, being returned to Charleston, carries on his business as usual."

NASH, THOMAS: –1638. New Haven, Conn. Gunsmith according to Penrose Hoopes; pos. first American C. None known.

NASHUA WATCH CO.: Nashua, N.H. Org. 1859. 1,000 movts. f. 1862; sold to interests that became Waltham Watch Co. (MFM) (Evans) (Crossman)

NATIONAL CLOCK CO.: n/d. Brooklyn, N.Y. Calendar clock "made by Seth Thomas for . . ." in MFM Col.

— SELF WINDING CLOCK CO.: Bristol, Frederick St. 1903–1904. N.J. company in Hubbell's marine shop. Made a good self-winding clock, a number of which are still running.

— WATCH CO.: Elgin, Ill. Org. 1864. Became Elgin National Watch Co. 1874. Still making fine watches. Smaller watches 1870. First stem winds 1873. Movts. numbered. See Elgin and ill. Nos. 296–298.

"NATIVE SON," used by Otay Watch Co., Cal., 1889. (Chamberlain)

NEAL, J., & Co.: Phila. n/d. "Watchmaker from London." Baillie lists three.

—, DANIEL: Phila. Dir. 1823–1833.

—, ELISHA: New Hartford, Conn. Label, "Patent Clocks—Invented by Eli Terry. Movements made by Samuel Terry. Finished and cased by Elisha Neal." Pillar and Scroll clocks in Mitchell Col. and in Flint Sale 1926, 29″ × 16½″.

NEGUS, T. S. & J. D.: N.Y.C., 69 Pearl St. 1845 to present. Ws., Chrons. (A. Dyke)

NEILSON, —: Annapolis, Md. 1734. (Brix)

—, GEORGE: Boston. Dir. 1830.

NEISSER, AUGUSTIN: –1780. b. Moravia. To Georgia 1736; Phila. 1739. "Watchmaker," Germantown. Adv. 1772, "Moved, makes as before all kinds of new clocks." Adv. for apt. Adv. 1778, "$8 reward, a repeating 30-hr. clock with alarm by some of the British Troops on Sept. 25, 1777, with the maker's name 'Augustine Neisser' engraved on the face 11″ sq., taken without pendulum & wgt." Germantown 1739–1780; pos. to Bethlehem, Pa.

NELSON, ALEXANDER: West Chester, Pa. 1820–1821. (James)

—, JOHN A.: Boston. Ca.1825.

—, R. J.: Davenport, Iowa. Ca.1850. (Dre)

—, THOMAS: Phila. Ca.1800.

NEMERT, GOTTLIEB CHRISTIAN: Reading, Pa. 1841. "C., W., J., S. and fine gilder."

NERLE, JOHN L.: Tall clock, name on dial, "S. F. Deibert, Catawissa, Pa." Clock paper Brandt Col.

NETTLETON, HEATH & Co.: Scottsville, N.Y. Ca.1820. Sold "Riley Whiting's improved model clock."

—, WILFRED H.: Bristol, 1850–1870. Lock work for striking mechanisms; other special clock parts. Sold ca.1870 to Geo. A. Jones.

—, W. K.: Rochester, N.Y. Ca.1830.

NEWALL, THOMAS: Patent from Sheffield, Mass. July 7, 1809 on astro. clocks. (Abbott)

NEWARK WATCH CO.: N.Y.C. 1863. Org. Louis S. Fellows of Fellows & Schill, N.Y.C. Js. Arthur Wadsworth in charge of production. To old Newark hat factory for larger space 1864. Pos. name adopted then. Few watches till 1867, then 400; 1868, 1,000; 1869, 1,500; 150 workers, many of them women. Names used: "Fellows," $25; "Newark Watch Co.," $20; "Edward Biven," $15. Total ca.3,000. Cost stopped production 1869; machinery and watch parts sold 1871 to Cornell Watch Co. (Paul Cornell and J. C. Adams). Machinery to San Francisco, Cal., 1874, Cornell Watch Co. of Cal.; then to Berkeley, Cal., as "California Watch Co." 1876; then bought by Independent Watch Co. of Fredonia, N.Y., 1878 (became later in 1880 Fredonia Watch Co.). Machinery again sold 1886 and moved to Peoria, Ill., as The Peoria Watch Co. Production ceased 1889. Pos. some used by Otay Watch Co., Otay, Cal. Machines sold and sent to Osaka, Japan, 1890. (Sources—not all in agreement—Dr. W. Barclay Stephens, Crossman, and Chamberlain)

NEWBERRY, J. & R.: Phila. Dir. 1816.

—, JAMES: Annapolis, Md. Adv. 1748, "Watch and clockmaker . . . just removed from the shop of John Inch to that of Samuel Soumaien."

—, JAMES W.: Phila. Dir. 1819–ca.1850.

NEWCOMB, HENRY: Lowell, Mass. "At Brastow's, Central St." Dir. 1837.

—, THOMAS: 1784–. Boston. Ca.1808. W. S. Later shoe findings business Haverhill, Mass. with son John D. (Mrs. Mason)

NEWELL, A.: Boston. Ca.1785.

—, JAMES J.: Utica, N.Y. Dir. 1834.

—, LOTT: Bristol. 1818–1819. Partner J. Ives & Co. (Hull)

NEWELL, NORMAN: Rochester, N.Y. Dir. 1844.

—, SEXTUS: Bristol. (tx) 1809–1811.

—, THEODORE: Poultney, Vt. Patent Apr. 12, 1820, on "planetarium."

—, THOMAS: Sheffield, Mass. 1810–1820.

NEW ENGLAND CLOCK CO.: Bristol. Prob. sales; 1851 only. Small Shelf clocks, spring wound. Label printed by "Jewett's Steam Press, 26 State St., Hartford." (J. T. Collins)

— WATCH CO., THE: Waterbury, Conn. Waterbury Watch Co. till 1898; f. 1912; bought by Ingersoll 1914. (Evans)

"NEW ERA," used by Lancaster (Pa.) Watch Co. Ca.1878.

NEWHALL, FREDERICK AUGUSTUS: 1818–. Salem, Mass. 1853–1859. W. Lived in Lynn, Mass.

—, WILLIAM: Boston. Ca.1850.

NEWHART, —: Lebanon, Pa. Ca.1840.

NEW HARTFORD MFG. CO.: New Hartford, Conn. Shelf clock, 30-hr. brass movt., weight-driven, mahogany veneer, 25″ × 15″, in Selchow Col.; labels printed by Elihu Geer, Hartford. n/d.

"N.H. MIRROR CLOCK": Mostly wall clocks, some with base board; 29″ to 32″ high, ca.14″ wide, 4″ deep. Upper glass 8½″ × 10″, opening for dial ca.7″ diam. Lower mirror 10¼″ × 16½″; cases usually hinged on right. Sometimes scroll top; occasionally plain; some pine and hardwood. Four or more types brass movts. Chadwick used solid plates. Mirror combined with clock pos. to compete with Banjo clocks as cases cost less. (DKP) (BCC)

NEW HAVEN CLOCK CO.: New Haven, Conn. Org. 1853, Hiram Camp pres. Movts. for Jerome Mfg. Co. Successfully enlarged. First clocks OGs (ill. in 1914 catalogue), both one-day and 8-day brass weight movts. Also smaller spring wound Shelf clocks. Marine movts., balance wheel instead of pendulum control, ca.1875; nickel-plated round back wind alarm clocks available. Used similar smaller movt. in watches ca.1880; by 1915 movts. small enough for wrist watches. Electric clocks made from 1929. Production 1941 was 70% watches, automobile clocks using watch movts., and self-wind 6-volt battery clocks. Some earlier New Haven labels have picture of old factory. Produces 1950 ca. 3 million timepieces a year. Clocks date from 1856. (Jerome) (Camp)

NEW HAVEN WATCH CO.: New Haven. Org. 1883. To Chambersburg, N.J., 1886. Became Trenton Watch Co. 1887. Sold to Ingersoll 1908. Ira Leonard has No. 910,279, "resembles Manhattan Watch Co."

NEW JERSEY WATCH CO.: N.Y.C., 16 John St. 1888.

NEWLIN, EDWARD G.: Phila. 1848.

NEWMAN CLOCK CO.: Chicago, Ill. Org. 1878. Later prob. in New Haven Clock Co. Watchmen's clocks. Patents May 20, 1890, July 7, 1891. Catalogue in author's Col.

—, JOHN: Boston, King St. Adv. 1764.

NEWTH, WILLIAM: Schenectady, N.Y. Adv. 1837–1842.

NEWTON, ISAAC L.: Salem, Mass., Essex St. 1796.

—, J. L.: Trenton, N.J. Adv. 1804, "Watchmaker from London." To 1820.

—, WILLIAM: N.Y.C., 7 Christie St. 1840's. Prob. case maker.

NEW YORK CHRONOGRAPH WATCH CO.: N.Y.C. n/d. Watch Paper.

— CITY WATCH CO: N.Y.C., 43 Downing St. "Mfg. dollar watches but sold at Sheriff's sale 1897." (MFM)

— STANDARD WATCH CO., THE: Jersey City, N.J. Org. 1885. Sold 1902 to Keystone; continued under original name. (Evans)

— WATCH CO.: Providence, R.I. Org. 1866 by Don J. Mozart. Succeeded Mozart Watch Co. Moved to Springfield, Mass., 1867. Plant burned 1870. Cain & Perry entered Company ca.1874, took name 1875. Became Hampden Watch Co. Sold to John C. Dueber and successor companies; watches in Canton, O., till 1927. Movts. named "John L. King," "No. 5," "H. G. Norton," "Homer Foot," "Springfield," "Albert Clark," "J. A. Briggs," "Geo. Walker," "Frederick Billings," "John Hancock," "Chas. E. Hayward," "Geo. Sam Rice," "New York Watch Co." (MFM)

— WATCH MFG. CO.: Springfield, Mass. 1875–1876. Successor N.Y. Watch Co. After one year failed and became Hampden Watch Co. (Bowman)

NEYSSER (NEISSER), AUGUSTINE: Tall clocks owned by Mrs. A. B. Scheibner, Audubon, N.J., Miss Louise Bergen, Allentown, Pa., Mrs. W. G. Emmott, Media, Pa., Robert Kutz, Gladwyne, Pa.

—, WILLIAM: Germantown, Pa. Late 18th century. Pos. relative of above.

NICAISE, GABRIEL: Nauvoo, Ill. 1848–1893. Hand-wrought iron bird-cage type clocks resembling 17th century European. (Dre)

NICHOL, JOHN L.: Belvedere, N.J. Aw. 1790–1818. Tall clock owned by Dr. William S. Magee, Phila. (ill. Ant. Feb. 1940).

NICHOLAS, WM. C.: Winchendon, Mass. Ca.1840. Watch Paper owned by Chesley Bixby, Haverhill, Mass.

NICHOLS, C. R.: Fulton, N.Y. 1860's.

—, GEORGE: N.Y.C. 1728–1750. "An early maker." (Moore)

—, Walter: Newport, R.I. 1849–1850.

NICOLET, JULIAN: Baltimore. 1819–1831. To Pittsburgh, Pa.

NICOLLET, JOSEPH M.: Phila. Dir. 1797. Other spellings.

—, JOSEPH W.: Phila. Dir. 1798.

—, MARIA (Mary): Phila. Dir. 1793–1799. "First woman watchmaker in America." (Ritter)

NIEBERGALL, FREDERICK: Rondout, N.Y. ca.1850.

NIEILLY, EMANUEL: Lebanon, Pa. Name on dial Tall clock, cherry case, over 6', brass movt., two weights, in family of Rufus T. Strohm, Scranton, Pa., 1848.

NINDE, JAMES: Baltimore. 1799–1835.

NIXON, JOHN: N.Y.C. Adv. 1773, "Musical, Repeating, and Plain Clocks and Watchmaker opp. Hill's Tavern in the Broadway . . . has set up business."

"No. 5," used by N.Y. Watch Co. ca.1870.

NOBLE, PHILANDER: Pittsfield, Mass. Ca. 1830.

NOEL, THEODORE: Frankfort, Ky. Ca.1830. Also hand made reels.

NOLEN & CURTIS (Samuel): Boston, 8 Washington St., Phila., 8 So. 3rd St. Dir. 1809. Made and decorated dials, tablets, mirrors. Some dials so marked on back.

—, SPENCER: Boston ca.1806 with bro.-in-law Aaron Willard, Jr. as Nolen & Willard. Clock dial and Sign painters. Dir. Phila. (JWW)

NORMAN, JAMES S.: Lincolnton, N.C. Adv. 1840. Claimed long experience.

NORRIS, BENJAMIN: New Britain, Pa. n/d. Tall clocks.

—, PATRICK: Phila. Dir. 1844–1845.

—, WILLIAM: n/p. ca.1815. Tall clock reported.

NORTH, ETHEL: Wolcottville (now Torrington), Conn. Ca.1820. Bro. Norris. Male despite name; belonged to Masonic Lodge. Shelf clocks, wood movts. "Torrington" type. (See ill. Nos. 192, 193.)

—, NORRIS: Wolcottville, Conn. Bro. Ethel. Engaged in the clock business ca.1820 and Erastus Hodges may have been a partner. Clocks were first made at Harvey Palmer's old carding machine shop then part of Ormel Leach's grist mill and after that in a bldg. called "the Clock Factory." Pillar and Scroll and other clocks, "Torrington" type wood movts. (See ill. Nos. 192, 193.)

—, PHINEAS: Torrington, Conn. 1762–1810. Son of Asbel and Ruth Lyman North. In Rev. War. Marr. 1787. Freeman 1790. Farmer, blacksmith, S., brass movt. Tall clocks, one dated "1794." (Hoopes)

—, SIMEON: Conn. Contract with Govt. 1812 to make 20,000 pistols. Wrote, "the component parts of the pistols are to correspond so exactly that any limb or part of one may be fitted into any other pistol." Pos. clock experience.

NORTHEY, ELIJAH: Phila. Dir. 1844–ca.1850.

—, R. E.: New Haven, Conn. Ca.1820.

NORTHROP & SMITH: Goshen, Conn. 1820's. Wood movt. mirror Shelf clocks. One at Torrington Hist. Soc.

NORTON, THOMAS & SAMUEL: Phila. Ca. 1800. Tall clock owned by Mrs. Frank Zesinger, Phila., has rocking ship, Union Jack on stern; hemispheres have "New Holland" for what is now Australia.

—, ELIJAH: Utica, N.Y. Ca.1820.

—, JOHN: Yorktown, Pa. Late 18th century. Three Tall clocks known.

—, NATHANIEL: New Haven, Conn. Ca. 1840.

—, SAMUEL: Hingham, Mass. 1785.

—, THOMAS: Phila. Adv. 1789. Dir. 1800–1811. Tall clocks. On dial of one owned by Donald Fenster, Churchville, Pa., "Rising Sun, Md."

NORTON, T. B.: Pa. Pos. Thomas. "Tall clocks." Mrs. Joseph Carson has mahogany Shelf clock marked "T. N. Norton, Northern Liberties."

NOWLAND, THOMAS: Phila. Dir. 1806–1808.

NOWLENS MFG. CO.: Boston. n/d.

NOWLIN, L.: Chicago. 1840's.

NOXON, MARTIN: 1780–1814. Edenton, N.C. Aw. ca.1800. Adv. 1810, Clock and Watch maker. (Cutten)

NOYES, L. W.: Boston, 64 Cornhill. Dir. 1841.

—, LEONARD W.: Nashua, N.H. Ca.1825–ca.1840. Tall and Banjo clocks, "Warranted by L. W. Noyes." Striking Banjo clock in Robert Dickey Col.

NUSZ, FREDERICK: Frederick, Md. Adv. 1819. (LSS)

NUTTER, E. H.: Dover, N.H. Ca.1825. Striking Banjo clock in DKP Col.

—, JOHN D.: Mont Vernon, N.H. Ca.1825.

NUTZ, —: Cincinnati, O. Ca.1830.

NYE, WILLIAM F.: New Bedford, Mass. 1862–. Not C. "Nye's Fine Clock Oil."

OAKES, HENRY, & CO.: Hartford, Conn. Ca.1830.

OAKES, FREDERICK A.: Hartford, Conn. 1828. W. G.

—, HENRY: Hartford, Conn. Ca.1830. "Dealers in watches."

OBER, HENRY: Elizabethtown, Pa. Ca. 1820. (Lan. Co.)

O'BRIEN, JAMES: Phila. Dir. 1850.

—, JOHN: Phila. Dir. 1844–1849.

OCHS, G.: N.Y.C., 81 Nassau St. Dir. 1872.

O'CLAIR, NARCIS: Albany, N.Y. Dir. 1819. (Cutten)

O'CONNELL, MAURICE: Boston. Dir. 1842.

O'DANIEL, PERRY: Phila. Dir. 1837–ca.1850.

"OGDEN, M. D.," used by Elgin National Watch Co. from 1876.

—, THOMAS: West Chester, Pa. Adv. 1824–1830. 8-day Tall clocks, movts. by George Baldwin. (James)

OGLE, WILLIAM: Phila. Dir. 1828–1829.

O'HARA, CHARLES: Phila. Dir. 1899–1900.

OHIO WATCH CO.: O. n/d. (MFM)

OLEWINE, ABRAHAM: –1866. Pikeland, Pa. "Classed as watchmaker; also kept general store." Adv. 1834, "For sale one 8-day brass and two 30-hr. Tall clocks."

To Phila. ca.1837. Prob. C. Bro. Henry. (James)

OLEWINE, HENRY: –1867. Pikeland, Pa. Taxed 1812 as W., 1813 as C. Bro. Abraham. Adv. 1814, "Making and repairing clocks and watches." Marr. 1813. Phila. 11th St. Dir. 1845–1849. d. Phila. (James)

OLIVER, D.: Plainfield, N.J. 1800's.

—, GRIFFITH: Phila. Dir. 1785.

—, JOHN: N.Y.C., 96 John St.; home, Brooklyn, 34 Chapel St. Dir. 1854.

—, JOHN, JR.: Charleston, S.C. Adv. 1765, "Watchmaker from London in Broad St., watches and clocks." (Prime) (MFM)

—, JOHN S.: Reading, Pa. Ca.1830.

—, WELDEN: Bristol. Ca.1820–1830. "Made Shelf clocks with wooden movts. bell strike." One owned by Oliver B. Glass, L.I.

OLMSTEAD, GIDEON: Charlotte, N.C. Adv. 1832, "New establishment for business as clock and watchmaker." (Cutten)

—, NATHANIEL: New Haven, Conn., 117 Chapel St. Ca.1820. W. J. S. R. (Moore)

—, NORMAN: Brooklyn, N.Y. Ca.1829. Correspondence with Samuel Terry about large order for clocks. (LB)

OLMSTEAD, NATHANIEL, & SON: New Haven, Conn., Marble block, Chapel St. "Clock and Watchmaker." Yellow Watch Paper in Bir. Col.

O'NEIL, CHARLES: New Haven, Conn. Ca. 1820. "Clock and watch repairer. Informs his friends and the public he is at work at Messrs. Merriman and Bradley and solicits their patronage." (Moore)

OOSTERHOUDT, PETER E.: Kingston, N.Y. Ca.1800.

OOSTERHOUT, DIRK: Yonkers, N.Y. Ca.1840.

ORMSBY, HENRY: Phila. Dir. 1839–ca.1850 and later.

—, JAMES: Baltimore. 1771.

ORNE, R. S.: Boston. Ca.1840.

ORNSTEAD & BARNS: Brooklyn, N.Y. Name on case, Shelf type wagon spring. (FMS)

OROIDE WATCHES: Newark, N.J. Ca.1870. "N. H. White." BCL Col.

ORR, THOMAS: Phila. Dir. 1809–1817. To Louisville, Ky., ca.1825. (LB)

OTTICK, M.: Baltimore. Ca.1790.

ORTON, PRESTON & CO.: Farmington, Conn. Ca.1820–ca.1830.

OSBORN, ROBERT: Rochester, N.Y. Dir. 1847–1848. (Cutten)

—, W. R.: Watertown, N.Y. *Ca*.1850.

"OSBORNE": See Osborne & Wilson.

— (Thomas) & Co.: *Ca*.1800–1842. Prob. after Osborne & Wilson.

"— MFG. Co.": Birmingham, England. *Ca*.1805–. Dial makers, iron founders. Name on cast iron "false plate" of Tall clock dials fastening dial to front plate.

— & WILSON: Birmingham, England. 1772. English dial makers. Dissolved 1778; partners continued alone.

—, JOHN: –1827. Lynn, Mass. W. Watch Paper BCL Col.

OSGOOD, JOHN: Andover, Mass., 1790–1795; Haverhill, N.H. 1795–1840. Tall clock. Fine 8-day brass movt., butternut hood, pine waist and base, owned by Peter Shattuck, W. Andover, inherited by son (d. 1898), now owned by Dr. Charles A. Currier, Andover, Mass. Two Tall clocks, dials marked "Haverhill," F. Thoms Col.

—, JOHN, JR.: Boston. Dir. 1825–1842. Mahogany case Tall clock.

—, ORLANDO F.: Haverhill, Mass. Marr. 1843. S., pos. C.

OTAY WATCH CO.: Otay, Cal. Adv. 1888–1890. P. H. Wheeler's Co. used "Golden Gate"; "Native Son"; "Overland Mail"; "F. A. Kimball"; "California"; "R. D. Perry" on watches; 11 to 15 jewels, numbers known from 1,208 to 1,340, 30,110 to 30,637. (Chamberlain)

OTIS, F. S.: N.Y.C. *Ca*.1860. "Patent N.Y. No. 2" iron front Shelf clock owned by Harry E. Bleu, Weissport, Pa.

—, FREDERICK S.: Forestville, Conn., East Main St.; Bristol. (tx) 1853–1856. Pearl inlay fancy cased Shelf clocks. f. 1856; absorbed by E. N. Welch.

OTTO, A. F.: Chicago. 1855.

OUDIN, JOSEPH: Phila. Dir. 1814.

"OVERLAND MAIL," used by Otay Watch Co., Cal., 1889.

OVES, GEORGE: Lebanon, Pa. Only record, "Marr. 1805." (Stow)

OWEN, CHARLES F., & CO.: N.Y.C. *Ca*.1850.

— & CLARK: N.Y.C., 25 John St. Dir. Adv. 1857, "Manufacturers and dealers in American clocks of every description."

—, G. B., & CO.: N.Y.C. Dir. 1854.

OWEN (S.) & READ: Cincinnati, O. 1840's. (Knittle)

— & SILE: Chester, Pa. 1800's.

—, E.: Prob. English dial maker. Name occasionally found cast in iron subframe of Tall clock dials.

—, GEORGE: Winsted, Conn. "Operated as small manufacturer in 1870's and 80's. Business later merged with the Gilbert Co. of which he was an officer for many years." (Vail)

—, GEORGE B.: N.Y.C., 325 Hudson St. Dir. 1854–1864.

—, GRIFFITH: Phila., 73 Mulberry St. Census 1790. Dir. 1791–1793, 1801–1814. Tall clock marked "Owen." Ill. in Moore. Other Tall clocks owned by Mrs. Raymond S. Cox, Malvern, Pa., first cleaning date 1809; Horace C. Jenkins, Gwynedd, Pa., marked "Griffith Owen of Towamencin"; another at Halfestock House, Haverford, Pa. Many in Phila., one described "bomb shaped Tall clock."

—, JOHN: Phila. Dir. 1818–1819.

—, M. T.: Abbeville, S.C. *Ca*.1848–1860. When Bailey moved to Newbury, Owen continued as Bailey & Owen. (Prime)

OWENS, WILLIAMS: Utica, N.Y. Dir. 1839–1850 and later. (Cutten)

OYSTER, DANIEL: 1764–1845. Reading, Pa. Aw. 1779. 3rd group. "Probably left to posterity more Tall clocks than any other Reading, Pa. maker." One prob. made for Gen. Lafayette 1824–1825, Lafayette medallion on door. Prob. best known of Reading makers. Tall clocks owned by Mrs. V. Esplenshade, Reading, Pa.; Mrs. Kathryn Bentz, West Lawn, Pa., metal dial, calendar hand, sweep seconds, two weights, moon and ship on dial, cherry case. (Steinmetz)

—, JOHN: Herndon, Va. n/d. (MFM)

PACE, C.: San Francisco, Cal. *Ca*.1850.

PACKARD (Jonathan) & BROWN: Albany, N.Y. Dir. 1815.

— (Jonathan) & SCHOFIELD: Rochester, N.Y. Adv. 1818–1819.

—, ISAAC: Brockton, Mass. Early 19th century. With Rodney Brace.

—, JONATHAN: Albany, N.Y. Adv. 1815. In Packard & Brown. Later J. in Roches-

PACKARD, JONATHAN (cont'd)
ter, N.Y. Adv. 1818–1819 as Packard & Schofield.

PAILLOT, LEON: Baltimore. Dir. 1842.

PAINE (PAYN) & HEROY: Albany, N.Y. 1813.

PALLWEBER, JOSEF: Salzburg, Austria. U.S. Patents 312,754, Feb. 24, 1885, and 359,227 March 8, 1887. "Timepiece which indicated the time by means of numbers on rotary wheels read through slots instead of the customary hands and dial." "Three-dial or jumper clock." Model or attempt at production of Conn. mfr. in author's collection. Neither patent exactly describes model. Patents show rotors mounted on horizontal axles at right angles to clock face; model has rotors mounted on common horizontal axle parallel with clock face. Patent 359,227 based on watch, but mechanism applicable to "timepiece." Pallweber later turned to cash registers. March 3, 1891, received patent 447,473 for watch case spring.

PALMER (Beriah) & CLAPP: N.Y.C., 145 Reade St. Dir. 1831.

— & Co.: Boston. Early 19th cent. (Baillie)

— & OWEN: Cincinnati, O. n/d. Watch Paper BCL Col.

— (John C.) & RAMSAY: Raleigh, N.C. 1847–1855. Watch repair & J. Palmer bought out Ramsay 1855 and continued alone. (Cutten)

—, W., & Co.: Boston and Roxbury, Mass. 1857. (Stallcup)

— (D. D.) WATCH Co.: Waltham, Mass. Ca. 1864–1875. Ca.1,500 watches. (Crossman)

—, D. D.: 1838–. No. Bridgewater, N.Y. In 1858, West Winfield, N.Y.; later Newport, N.Y. To Waltham, Mass. 1864; made ca.1,500 watches, sold in South. Later with American Watch Co. to 1875. (Crossman)

—, JOHN: Phila., 263 No. Front St. Dir. 1795–1796.

—, JOHN C.: 1806–1893. Oxford, Haywood, Salisbury, Raleigh, N.C. Aw. 1830–1889. Apt. John Y. Savage, Raleigh. In Hampton & Palmer 1830–1832, Palmer & Ramsay, 1847–1855. Interested in daguerreotype. (Cutten)

—, SAMUEL: Dedham, Mass. Name on Tall clock, tapered axles, steel integral pinions. (Bryon Briggs, Forest Hills, N.Y.)

PALMER, WILLIAM: N.Y.C., 2 Nassau St. Ca.1802–1818. Pos. case maker.

PARDEE, WILLIAM: Albany, N.Y. Dir. 1834–1835. Patents Albany May 22, 1835, "Clocks & Timepieces"; Poughkeepsie, N.Y., Feb. 10, 1836, "Timepieces."

PARKE: Family made many Tall clocks.

—, SOLOMON, & Co.: Phila., 146 No. 2nd St. Dir. 1797–1801.

—, SOLOMON, & SON: Phila. Dir. 1806. (Steinmetz)

— & SON: Phila. Dir. 1806.

—, AUGUSTUS: Phila., 126 Race St. Dir. 1817–1822.

—, CHARLES B.: Phila. Dir. 1806–1810.

—, SAMUEL: Pos. Solomon.

—, SETH: Parktown, Pa. 1790.

—, SOLOMON: Newtown, Pa. "Settled in Newtown in Colonial days and continued as a clock maker for many years." Southampton Twp., Pa. 1782. Mention of robbery by eight men. Phila. Dir. 1791–1796, 1802–1822. In 1814–1822 "Large clock manufactory in Phila. and employed workmen of different nationalities as French, German, and Swiss." Tall clocks owned by Mrs. Frank Deedmeyer, Freehold, N.J., A. K. Frankes, Ventnor, N.J., 93" high, mahogany case, sun, moon, Calendar. (Lan. Co.) (Conrad) (J. S. Bailey) (Brix)

PARKER CLOCK CO., THE: Meriden, Conn. Took over Parker & Whipple Co. 1893, dissolved 1934. Small pendulum desk clocks, later round alarm clocks under Hotchkiss patents, excellent marine clocks, three in E. I. Col. (Charles Parker)

— & PIERCE: Boston. Dir. 1809.

—, THOMAS, & Co.: Phila. Dir. 1818–1819.

— & WHIPPLE Co., THE: Meriden, Conn. 1868–1893. Org. by John E. Parker, H. J. P. Whipple, John Parker, Horace C. Wilcox, Lemuel J. Curtis, Jennette B. Parker, John Douglas. Various products including clocks. Became Parker Clock Co. (Charles Parker)

—, DANIEL: Boston. Ca.1760.

—, GARDINER: 1772–1816. Westborough, Mass. C. Pos. apt. of Willards. Aw. 1793. Tall clocks often have on dial name of purchaser with "Made and Warranted by . . ." Clock 1801 for Westborough

Church tower, now in Historical Society. Later Tower clocks for Shrewsbury & Northboro. Built organ 1809. Financial difficulties 1816; found d. of bullet wound, pos. self-inflicted. Tall clock owned by Samuel P. Horne, Bradford, Mass. (Charles H. Reed) (BCC)

PARKER, GEORGE: Patent Apr. 7, 1832, Ithaca, N.Y., on "Striking Parts of Clocks." Later Utica, N.Y.

—, ISAAC: Deerfield, Mass. 1780.

—, ISAAC: Phila., 13 So. 3rd St. Dir. 1818–1825, 1835–1850.

—, JOHN: Md. 1774. "Watch movement maker." (FT)

—, JOSEPH: Princeton, N.J. Adv. 1785 as G., J. and S. (Williams)

—, T. H.: Phila. Dir. 1833.

—, THOMAS: 1761–1833. Phila., 13 So. 3rd St. 1786–1793. Dir. 1785–1817. Apt. of Rittenhouse and J. Wood. Aw. 1783. President Mechanic Bank 1816.

—, THOMAS, JR.: Phila. Dir. 1817–1822. Tall and Shelf clocks.

—, WILLIAM: Phila. Dir. 1823–1824.

—, WILLIAM, JR.: Phila. Dir. 1835.

PARKINS, JOSEPH: Phila. Dir. 1837.

PARKS, G. D.: Cincinnati, O. 1850's. Pos. agent for Conn. clocks. (Knittle)

—, HUGH: N.Y.C. Ca.1840.

—, JONAS: Bennington, Vt. Ca.1770. Tall clock with brass dial known.

PARLIN, A. S.: Norwich, Conn. Ca.1860.

PARMELE, ABEL: 1703–ca.1766. Branford, Conn. b. Guilford, Conn. Son of John and Betty Edwards Parmele. Nephew and apt. of Ebenezer Parmele. To Branford 1731. Tall clocks. Petitioned Conn. General Assembly 1736 to cast bells; not granted. Promissory note "Branford, Feb. 13, 1741–1742 for 30 £ 4 s. courant money or a good 8-day repeating clock to be delivered at or before the 10th day of June next for value rcd." (Hoopes)

—, EBENEZER: 1690–1777. Guilford, Conn. Son of Isaac, cabinetmaker, and Elizabeth Hyland Parmele. Pos. first C. of Conn. Colony. Cabinetmaker, boat builder; operated cargo sloop Long Island Sound; Town treasurer. Guilford meeting house Tower clock 1726 "first tower Clock in Conn."; freed by 1741 town meeting from holding town offices in return for taking care of clock. Movt. in Hist. Soc., described as "well built mechanism of hand wrought and cast metal except winding barrels and wood hands and it's maker was unquestionably a thoroughly trained and skillful Clock Maker." Milford Tower clock 1742. "A prominent and respected citizen, a man of means, and of varied attainments." d. Guilford. (Hoopes)

PARMIER, JOHN PETER: Phila. Dir. 1793.

PARROT, FREDERICK (F. W.): Phila. Dir. 1847.

PARROTT, JOSEPH: Phila. Dir. 1835–1843.

PARRY, JOHN: Trenton, N.J. 1788–1814. (PG)

—, JOHN F.: Phila., 38 So. 2nd St. Dir. 1824.

—, JOHN I.: Phila. Dir. 1795–1797.

—, JOHN J.: Phila., 38 So. 2nd St. Dir. 1793–1835.

PARSONS, HENRY R.: Phila. Dir. 1840–1841, 1849.

—, SILAS: Conn. n/d.

PARTRIDGE, HORACE: Bristol, North St. Did C. in "Eureka Shop." Bought out Eureka Mfg. Co. 1868. Sales agency, Boston, Hanover St.

PASS & STOW: Phila. Late 18th century. Brass founders, bell casters. Brass parts for Cs. Recast Liberty Bell, first cast Eng. 1751 by Thomas Lister, London, cracked 1752, recast by Pass & Stow, hung in tower of State House (now Independence Hall) 1753. Weights 2,080 lbs., 12' around lip, 7' 6" around crown, 3' high, lip to crown, 3" thick at lip and 1¼" at crown. To save it from capture by British, taken to Allentown, Pa., 1777, buried under floor of Zion Reformed Church; returned to Philadelphia 1778. Inscription (Lev. 25:10), "Proclaim Liberty throughout all the Land unto all the Inhabitants thereof." (Pa. Ins. Co.)

PATCHIN, T. A.: Syracuse, N.Y. Adv. 1846.

PATTEN (Richard) & FERRIS: N.Y.C. Ca. 1820.

—, RICHARD: N.Y.C. Ca.1820.

PATTON (Abraham) & JONES (Samuel G.): Phila. Dir. 1804–1814. Also listed in Baltimore. Name on plate on back of white enameled dial.

—, ABRAHAM: Phila., 79 High St., 1799–1819. Represented Leslie & Co., 1799–1803.

PATTON, ABRAHAM (*Cont'd*)
Later with Patton & Jones, 1804–1814.

—, DAVID: Phila. 1799.

PAVEY, JOHN: Phila., 32 So. 2nd St., Dir.
1803, and 245 High St., 1820.

PAYNE, LAWRENCE: N.Y.C. 1732–1755.

PEABODY, ASA: Wilmington, N.D. Adv.
1821. C., W., G. and S.

—, JOHN: Fayetteville, N.C. Pos. son of
John. Bought stock of Alvin Wilcox 1823.
Marr. 1825. (Cutten)

PEALE, CHARLES WILLSON: Annapolis, Md.,
Church St. 1764. Adv. 1764, "Makes,
cleans and repairs clocks and mends
watches as well as carrying on the saddler's
business." Best known as portrait painter.
First self portrait includes clock by him.
(Prime) (Gillingham)

—, JAMES: Phila. Dir. 1814–1817.

PEARCE, WILLIAM: Charleston, S.C. After
1780.

PEARMAN, WILLIAM: Richmond, Va. *Ca.*
1834. (MFM)

PEARSALL & EMBREE: N.Y.C. *Ca.*1786. S. W.
Frost, State College, Pa., owns 8′ Tall clock,
mahogany inlaid maple case, brass dial.

—, JOSEPH & JAMES: N.Y.C. *Ca.*1770–1773.

—, JOSEPH & THOMAS: N.Y.C., Beekman St.
and Burling Slip. Adv. 1770. Dissolved
1773.

—, JOSEPH: N.Y.C. Adv. 1773, "Carries on
the business in the watch and clock way as
usual, imported from London, 8-day clocks
in mahogany and Japan cases and
watches." Adv. 1775, "Moved. Imported very neat 8-day clocks in mahogany
cases—moon'd, and plain elegant Spring
do. Black ebony cases, gold watches, cap.
& jeweled hammered plain do. in Shagreen
cases; French do."

—, THOMAS: N.Y.C. Adv. 1773, "Left for
sale with him gold watch." Adv. 1774,
"Neat clocks in mahogany cases, moon'd,
plain and Japanned Spring do. and assortment of new watches."

PEARSE, ISAAC T.: Enfield, Conn. *Ca.*1830.
Flint Sale 1926, Mahogany Shelf clock
31½ × 17½.

PEARSON & GREY: Georgetown, S.C. Adv.
1768. (Prime)

— (Isaac) & HOLLINSHEAD (Joseph): Burlington, N.J. 1750–1760, (PG); 1740–1749.
(CMW).

PEARSON, ISAAC: N.J. *Ca.*1685–1749. C., G.
and W. First New Jersey S., Quaker.
Ingenious, versatile. Blacksmith, general
metal work. Prop. Mt. Holly Iron Works
1730–1749. Marr. 1710 Hannah Gardiner.
Active in politics; Gen. Assembly 1738.
Tall clocks. (PG) (Williams)

—, WILLIAM, JR.: N.Y.C., Adv. 1768–1775.
"At the Sign of the Dial in Hanover Sq."

PEASELEY, ROBERT: Boston. Adv. 1735.

PECK & CO., JULIUS: Litchfield, Conn. *Ca.*
1830.

—, HAYDON & CO.: St. Louis, Mo. *Ca.*1840.
"Improved clocks mfd. and sold wholesale
and retail." Samuel W. Jennings, Plainfield, Ill., prob. sales agent Conn. clocks.
Birge, Mallory & Co. 1838–1842 Shelf
clock, Joseph Ives roller pinion strip frame,
pillared and carved case in G. B. Davis
Col., San Antonio, Texas.

— & HOLCOMB: Sanbornton, N.H. *Ca.*1820.
In Thomas Gridley's clock factory.
(Childs)

— & JEROME: Liverpool, Eng., 43 Bold St.
Listed 1843. Some clocks have name on
label.

—, AMBROSE: Bristol. In Birge, Mallory &
Co., and Birge, Peck & Co. With William
Richards sold land and buildings and
water rights 1864 to S.C. Spring.

—, BENJAMIN: Providence, R.I. 1824.
(MFM)

—, EDSON: Derby, Conn. 1827.

—, ELIJAH: Boston. Dir. 1789.

—, EPAPHRODITUS: 1811–1857. Nephew of
clock peddler in South Carolina, 1811. To
England 1842 for Chauncey Jerome with
first shipment of Jerome clocks. Pos.
disagreed with Jerome, Jr. Signed contract 1848 with Brewster & Ingraham to
represent them overseas. Did large business. d. and buried in London. (Jerome)
(LB)

—, MOSES: Boston, King St. Adv. 1753,
"South side of Town House, tickets in the
Phila. lottery." Adv. 1763, "Imported
watches for sale." Adv. 1765, "Sell
watches made in London by Samuel
Toulmin and others, and 8-day clocks."
Adv. to 1789.

—, TIMOTHY: 1765–1818. Middletown,
Litchfield, Conn. Son of Timothy and
Sarah Plumb Peck. Related to Miles

Beach; pos. his apt. Aw. Middletown 1787; shop taken over by Antipas Woodward. To Litchfield *ca.*1790; shop in brick bldg. south of Court House; Tall clock brass movts.; S.; repaired clocks. Later interested in sawmill as partner in papermaking with Aaron Smith & Co. Reorg. 1808 as Horton & Peck. (Samuel A. Beckwith) (Hoopes)

PECKHAM & KNOWER: Albany, N.Y. Adv. 1814, "Have for sale 7 Willard patent timepieces and 8-day clocks of best workmanship."

PEELE, J. B.: Salem, Mass., 27 Essex St. Adv. 1818.

PEERLESS WATCH CO.: San Francisco, Cal. Org. 1892. "Did not make any watches."

PENFIELD, JOSIAH: Savannah, Ga. *Ca.*1820.

—, SYLVESTER: N.Y.C. Dir. 1847.

PENNIMAN, JOHN R.: 1783–. Boston. *Ca.* 1806–1828. Dial painter for Simon Willard, "a versatile artist." (JWW)

PENNSYLVANIA WATCH CO.: Phila. n/d. (MFM)

PENNWOOD CO., THE: Pittsburgh, Pa. *Ca.* 1940. Electric three-dial clocks under patent No. 1990645 and others. John J. Purcell, N.Y.C., owns one.

PEORIA WATCH CO.: Peoria, Ill. "Bought Independent Watch Co. of Fredonia, N.Y., but did not continue long, soon failed. In 1885 only." (MFM)

PEPPER, HENRY J., & SON: Phila. Dir. 1846–*ca.*1850.

—, H. J.: Phila. *Ca.*1850.

—, H. S.: Phila. Dir. 1837.

PERKINS, JOHN: Fitzwilliam, N.H. Tall clock, wood movt., No. 67, "Made Sept. 18, 1821," owned by Mrs. B. K. Little, Brookline, Mass.

—, ROBINSON: Jaffrey, N.H. *Ca.*1825.

—, THOMAS: Phila., Front St. below Walnut, 17 New St. Dir. 1783–1799. Pittsburgh, Pa., 1820's. Elected *ca.*1840 Commissioner of Alleghany Co. (Stow) (Gillingham)

PERPIGAN, PETER: Phila. Dir. 1809–1825.

PERRET, PHILIP H.: Cincinnati, O., 37 Main St. 1820's. "From Switzerland." (Knittle)

PERRIGO, JAMES: 1737–1808. Wrentham and pos. Dedham, Mass. Aw. 1760–1800.

—, JAMES, JR.: Wrentham, Mass. *Ca.*1800.

PERRINE, W. D.: Lyons, N.Y. Aw. 1850. (Cutten)

PERRY, THOMAS & MARVIN: N.Y.C. Adv. 1767, "Watches imported."

—, ALBERT: 1828–. Salem, Mass., 25 Carlton St. till 1864. Gunsmith; R. after 1861.

—, ELIAS: Phila. Dir. 1804.

—, MARVIN: N.Y.C., Hanover Sq. Son of Thomas. Adv. 1768–1776, "From London."

"—, R. D.," used by Otay Watch Co. 1889. (Chamberlain)

—, THOMAS: –1774. N.Y.C., Hanover Sq. and Dock St. Adv. 1749–1774. Father of Marvin. "From London." "Thomas Perry, apprentice, 1726." (Baillie)

PETERS, A. R.: Marietta, Pa. *Ca.*1850.

—, EDWARD: N.Y.C. Dir. 1846.

—, JAMES: Phila. Dir. 1821–1850. Tall clocks.

PETTEE, SIMON: Wrentham, Mass. n/d. (Burt)

PETTIBONE & PETERS: N.Y.C., 35 John St. Dir. 1848.

—, LYNDES: Brooklyn, N.Y. *Ca.*1840.

PETTY, HENRY: Phila. Dir. 1829–1833.

PETZ, JOHN: Nicholasburg, Pa. n/d. Tall clock reported by E. Cramer, Phila.

PFAFF, AUGUSTUS P.: Phila. Dir. 1830–1850 and later. "Clock in Empire style, a cabinet with pipe organ which played two minutes before the hour," mus. part by Dominibus Nuhle, owned by Mrs. J. M. Young, Chicago.

—, HENRY: Phila. Dir. 1829–1833.

PFALTZ, J. WILLIAM: Baltimore. *Ca.*1800–1812. Partner Philip Stadtler; later alone.

PFLUEFFER, HERMANN: Phila. Dir. 1849–.

PHARR, BENJAMIN Y.: Atlanta, Ga. Dir. 1874.

PHELPS & BARTHOLOMEW: Ansonia, Conn. *Ca.*1880.

— (E. S.) & WHITE (G. W.): Northampton, Mass. 1828–1830.

—, SILAS: *Ca.*1720–*ca.*1785. Lebanon, Conn. (Ant. March 1935) (Hoopes)

"PHILADELPHIA MERCHANTS' EXCHANGE": Famous print on many clock tablets, prob. decalcomania; drawn from nature by August Kollner; litho. by Deroy; erected Dock & Walnut Sts. 1832–1834; William Strickland architect; still standing. For 25 y. most frequently pictured

"Phila. Merchants' Exchange" (cont'd) building in Phila. Mentioned because may assist in dating clocks as being made after 1832. (George H. Eckhardt)

— Watch Case Co.: Riverside, N.J. 1927–. Owned by Keystone. (Evans)

— Watch Co.: Phila. Ca.1868. Typical models "pos. Swiss made" in Ira Leonard Col. C. A. Thompson, Newark, N.J., owns No. 88, "Patented 1868," given his father 1872.

Philip, John: N.Y.C. Ca.1717. "Brass and bell foundry. Made clock parts."

Phillippe & LeGras: Baltimore. 1796.

Phillips, James: Charleston, S.C. Ca.1790.

—, Joseph: N.Y.C. "1713–1735."

Phinney & Mead: East Randolph, Vt. Watch Paper H. Fleischer Col.

— Walker Co.: N.Y.C. 20th century.

"Phipps": n/p. n/d. Name on Banjo clock reported by Mrs. Ralph M. Robinson, Longmeadow, Mass.

Phyfe, Duncan: 1768–1847. N.Y.C., Fulton St. Celebrated cabinetmaker, Clock cases. (See ill. No. 230.)

Piaget, L. A., & Co.: Paterson, N.J. n/d. Watch Paper owned by Mrs. Harold Hastings, N.Y.C.

Picard, J. C.: Cincinnati, O. Ca.1830.

Pickering, George: Cincinnati, O. Dir. 1867. "Clock mfr." (Knittle)

—, John: Cincinnati, O. Ca.1830.

—, Joseph: Phila., 315 No. Front St. Dir. 1816–1846.

Pickett, Richard, Jr.: 1815–1840. Newburyport, Mass. Dir. 1836–1840.

Pickrell, J. L.: Greenville, S.C. Adv. 1851.

Pierce, William S.: Phila. Dir. 1841.

Pierpont & Co.: Unionville, Conn. 1840's. After the fire at the Seymour, Williams & Porter factory on Roaring Brook, 1836–37, clockmaking never seemed to have flourished again, although it was carried on by this firm in the Screw factory after abandoning the screw business.

Pierret, Henry S.: Portland. Dir. 1834.

—, Mathey: Phila., 143 No. Front St. Dir. 1795–1796. "French watchmaker."

Piggot, Samuel: N.Y.C. Ca.1830. "Clock and S. Mfr."

Pike, William: n/p. Pa. Late 18th century. Tall clocks.

Pine, David: Strasburg, Pa. "1772." (Brix)

Pink, Osborne & Conrad: Phila. Ca.1840.

Pinkard, Jonathan: Phila. Adv. 1773, "Ran away from Samuel Jeffreys on 2nd St., by trade a watchmaker." (Prime)

Piper, James: 1749–1802. Chestertown, Md. Aw. 1772–1791.

Pitel, K.C.: n/p. Patent No. 32144, Apr. 23, 1861. Model at Smiths. Inst.

Pitkin (Henry) & Bro. (James F.): Hartford, Conn. Ws. Apts. Amander Hills, N. P. Stratton (later of American Watch Co.), Samuel Alexander, E. Howard. Ca.1000 movts. 1837–1841. To N.Y.C., Nassau St. and Maiden Lane as Pitkin & Co.; out of business 1841. Second attempt at machine mfr. in America. (Crossman)

— & Co.: N.Y.C., Nassau St. and Maiden Lane. 1841. From Hartford, Conn.

"—, H. & J. F.," used by Pitkin Bros., Hartford, Conn., 1837–1841.

—, John O.: Hartford, Conn. n/d. Watch Paper James Gibbs Col.

—, Levi: 1774–1854. Hartford, Conn., Rochester, N.Y. Youngest son of Joshua and Hannah Stanley Pitkin, member of well-known family pioneer Conn. mfrs. Tall clocks before 1800. "Clever mechanic." To N.Y. State after 1800. Patent Rochester 1828 on beer pump. Prob. no Tall clocks in N.Y. (Hoopes)

Pitman, John: Phila. Dir. 1818.

—, Saunders: Providence, R.I. "1780."

—, William R.: New Bedford, Mass. 1836. Pos. Dealer.

Pitt, W.: N.Y.C. Dir. 1853.

Pittman & Dorrance: Providence, R.I. Ca.1800.

—, John: Wilmington, Del. 1813–1825. (Hist. Soc.)

—, John: Chester Co., Pa. "Itinerant clock repair man. Periodically traversed Chester Co. in early 1800's." (James)

Place, W. S.: Charleston, Md. n/d.

Platt, A. S., & Co.: Bristol, Main St., 1849 –1856. Platt, John Pomeroy, Filbert L. Wright. Adv. 1851, "Manufacturers of 8-day and 30-hour Spring pendulum clocks, also 8-day and 30-hour balance chronometer and lever escapement clocks. Mainsprings, steel cylindrical and flat helix hair springs, made to order of best material and warranted as wholesale. All orders respectfully solicited." "J. Pomeroy process manufacturing springs followed by this Co. 1851." Prospered, larger shop same site. f. 1857 because of failure of Jerome Clock Co., large customer. Succeeded by Wallace Barnes Co. (Hull) (EI) (LB)

PLATT & BLOOD: Bristol. 1840's.

—, G. W. & N.C.: N.Y.C. Aw. 1816–1820.

—, ALANSON S.: Bristol. Before 1849. Made 30-hour Spring movts. Report 1850, "Made some clock movts. and some clock trimmings. . . . Creditors two years ago were afraid of him. . . . He has improved and I believe he now pays well. . . . Real estate may be worth $2,000." (EI)

—, AUGUSTUS: Columbus, O. 1844. Math. insts. (Knittle)

—, BENJAMIN: 1757–. Danbury, Conn.; Litchfield, Conn. 1780. G., S. and C. Grandson of William Augustus. Marr. 1776. Brass movt. Tall clocks. New Milford, Conn., 1787. Compasses 1790. Lanesboro, Mass., 1800. To Columbus, O., 1817. With William Augustus.

—, CALVIN: Columbus, O. Math. insts. Ca.1840–ca.1870.

—, CHARLES D.: Bloomington, Ill. Watch, duplex gold escape wheel and balance, fine handmade specimen, owned by Orville R. Hagans, Denver, Col. (Ira Leonard)

—, EBENEZER SMITH: N.Y.C. Adv. 1774, "Clocks made and sold by cheaper than can be imported from Europe."

—, JOHN: Phila. Dir. 1843.

—, SAMUEL: Boston. Dir. 1825.

—, WILLIAM A., JR.: Columbus, O. Ca. 1840–ca.1870. (Knittle)

—, WILLIAM A., SR.: Columbus, O. Ca. 1830–ca.1850. Grandson of Benjamin.

—, WILLIAM AUGUSTUS: 1809–. Dir. 1843–1844. Grandson and apt. Benjamin. Mother d. at birth; reared by Benjamin. To Columbus 1817, learned Watchmaking. First W., C. and J. in Columbus. Sons continued business. (Hull)

PLELPA, CARL: N.Y.C. 20th century.

PLUMB, JAMES M.: Berlin, Conn. n/d. In Flint sale 1926 a mahogany Shelf clock 31 × 16¼.

PLUMMER, ELIJAH T.: Atlanta, Ga. Dir. 1871.

POINDEXTER, WILLIAM: Lexington, Ky. Dir. 1818–1848. W. S. (LB)

POLACK, FRANCIS C.: York, Pa. Ca.1850.

POLLHANS, ADAM: St. Louis, Mo. 1879–1890.

—, HENRY: St. Louis, Mo. Ca.1860.

—, PHILIP: St. Louis, Mo. Ca.1870. Tower Clocks.

POLSEY, JOHN & Co.: Boston. n/d. (Burt)

POMEROY (Noah) & HILL (Edw.): Report ca.1850, "Makes superior marine clocks, good mechanics, young and industrious, have great prospects, do a small business. . . . Fair men doing well." (EI Col.)

—, JOHN, & Co.: Bristol. Patent 1845 or 1848 on method of making springs. "Used even today." Allowed Anson L. Atwood to use method. (Hull)

—, NOAH, & Co.: (tx) 1849–1851. Formerly Pomeroy & Robbins. Bought Chauncey Ives shop 1849. Made only Clock movements, prob. marine type.

— (Noah) & PARKER (Geo. H.): Bristol, 1852–1857. Clock trimmings. Brass 8-day spring movt., standard steeple Shelf case, mahogany veneer, label, "Pomroy & Parker," owned by E. L. Lovely, Bradford, Mass.

— & ROBBINS: Bristol. (tx) 1847–1849.

POMEROY, —: Hartford, Conn. 1886–1900. Jigsaw cases, Seth Thomas movts.

—, CHAUNCEY: Bristol. Ca.1835.

—, ELTWEED: Bolton, Mass. Ca.1640. Gunsmith pos. C.

—, HUNT: Elmira, N.Y. Adv. 1832.

—, NOAH: 1847–1878. Bristol. C. In Pomeroy & Robbins, 1847; org. Noah Pomeroy & Co. 1849; in Pomeroy & Parker, 1852–1857; successful alone 1858–1878. Adv. Conn. Bus. Dir. 1851, "N. Pomeroy & Co., Bristol, Conn., manufacturers of 8-day and 30-hour marine TP at wholesale. All others promptly attended to." Sold 1878 to Hiram C. Thompson. (LB) (EI)

POND & BARNES: Boston, 71–73 Hanover St. Dir. and Adv. 1848, "Manufacturers. Large and small lots for export." Twin Steeple Brewster & Ingrahams clock, brass springs, overpasted label, in Ray Walker Col.

—, WILLIAM, & Co.: Boston. Dir. 1830.

POND, C. H.: New Haven, Conn. 1888. In Standard Electric Time Co. Electric master controlled clocks. (Catalogue)

—, L. A.: Boston and Chelsea, Mass. *Ca.* 1845.

—, PHILIP: Bristol. 1840.

—, WILLIAM: Boston. Dir. 1842.

PONSON, PETER: Phila. Dir. 1796.

POOL, DAVID L.: 1810–1861. Adv. 1832. Learned clockmaking Phila. C. W. J. S. Engraver.

—, JAMES M: Washington, N.C. Adv. 1846, "Articles for sale. Watch and clock repairs." (Cutten)

—, THOMAS: Cincinnati, O. *Ca.*1830. (Knittle)

POOLE CLOCK CO.: Westport, Conn. 20th century.

POPE, JOSEPH: Boston. Adv. 1790, "Respectfully informs his friends and the public, that he is lately returned from London and now carries on the clock and watchmaker's business in their different branches at No. 49 Marlborough St., a few doors north of 7 Star Lane. He has neat silver watches for sale." (Moore)

—, ROBERT: Boston. Adv. 1786, "On Orange St. South end Boston. Makes chime and plain clocks. Time pieces, etc. of various constructions. Warranted to be equal to any and superior to many imported from Europe. Table clocks, either chime or plain. Clock and watch springs, warranted as above. Spiral springs of almost any size, spring saws, spring tresses, etc." (Moore)

PORTER, ABEL, & CO.: Waterbury, Conn. Pos. first to roll brass in America *ca.*1802. Benedict & Upson's mill. Aaron Benedict 1805 sold his interest to Lemuel Harrison: Harrison sold his 1808 to Abel Porter, David Hayden, Daniel Clark, Silas Grilley, as Abel Porter & Co. Gilt buttons; later clocks. Became Scoville Mfg. Co. See Eli Terry. (Hist.) (LB)

— & ATKINS: Bristol. n/d. Label in Shelf clock owned by John McGinley, New Canaan, Conn.

— (Eleazar), HORACE & CO.: Boston. Dir. 1830.

—, DANIEL: Williamstown, Mass. *Ca.*1790. Tall clocks. "He purchased his house and lot on Main St., Feb. 14, 1799 — 10 rods west of a well with a pump in it, and a few rods west of the College." Three Tall clocks, 8-day brass movts., extant in Williamstown. (Milham)

PORTER, REV. EDWARD: 1765–1828. Waterbury, Conn. Graduated Yale 1786. Marr. Dolly Gleason 1789. Pos. Cabinetmaker and C. with Levi Porter. Contracted 1807 with Eli Terry to make 4000 clocks at $4 in three years, Porters to supply stock, Terry to make movts., dials, hands. Installed 1795 pastor First Church of Waterbury. To Farmington, Conn., 1812. d. New Haven. (Anderson) (Hoopes) (Hist.)

—, GEORGE: Boston. *Ca.*1835.

—, GEORGE E.: Utica, N.Y. Dir. 1834.

—, RUFUS: Billerica, Mass. Patent on "Clocks" June 22, 1832.

—, WILLIAM: Waterbury, Conn., Williamstown, Mass. *Ca.*1814. Pos. Daniel. Waterbury clock factory with Zenas Cook, Daniel Clark. Tall clock ill. in Milham. (Baillie)

POSEY, F. J.: Hagerstown, Md. Watch Paper Ritter Col.

POST, SAMUEL, JR.: 1760–1794. New London, Conn. Son of Samuel and Susanna Grant Post. Adv. 1783, "Carries on clock and watch business at shop near Mr. Milner's tavern. Makes new warranted watches and clocks of different kinds, such as repeating, moon, day and 2nd's, plain 8-day and common 30-hour clocks, desk and hanging timepieces in neat mahogany cases." To Phila. *ca.*1785; metal buttons. (Hoopes)

POTTER BROS.: Chicago, Ill. 1872–1875. Two bros. Wm. C. Potter alone after 1875.

—, J. O. & J. R.: Providence, R.I. Dir. 1849.

—, ALBERT H.: 1836–1908. N.Y.C. 1855–1861. Chicago, 1870. W. "In 1852 he was three years an apprentice of Wood & Foley, Albany, N.Y." N.Y.C. 19 John St., later 84 Nassau St. *Ca.*35 watch movts., gold cases, sold for $225 to $350. Same work in Cuba 1861–1866. To N.Y.C. 1866. Patent on watch escapement 1868. To Minneapolis, pos. Milwaukee; Chicago 1870. With bro. Wm. Cleveland org. Potter Bros. 1872; dissolved 1875; continued by Wm. C. Patent October 1875 on "Compensating balance." Invented steam propelled tricycle 1895; "ran well." One of America's greatest watchmakers. (Chamberlain) (Crossman)

POTTER, ELI: Williamstown, Mass. n/d.

—, EPHRAIM: Concord, N.H. 1775–1790. "Made wooden movt. clocks, serviceable wooden timekeepers at East Concord to 1790." (Hist. Soc.) (E. M. Hunt) (Abbott)

—, H. J.: Bristol. "1849." (FT)

—, JOHN: Farmington, Conn. *Ca.*1780.

POULTNEY, JOHN: Phila. 1780's. Son of Thomas and Elizabeth Poultney. Marr. Ann Savery 1781, dau. of William Savery, famous cabinetmaker. (Friends' Meeting Records at Hist. Soc. of Pa.) (Gillingham)

POUND, ISAAC: Charleston, S.C., Elliot St. Adv. 1746, "Clock and Watchmaker, lately arrived here." (Prime)

—, JOHN: n/p. South Carolina. "1746." C.W.

POWELL, JOHN: Baltimore. *Ca.*1745. Bound servant from Eng. Pos. paid for passage to America by clockmaking.

—, JOHN: Annapolis, Md. W. C. Indentured to William Post. Adv. 1745, "Ran away from Wm. Roberts, alias Charles Lucas, London born, by trade clock and watchmaker." (Prime)

POWERS, HIRAM: 1805–. b. Woodstock, Vt. Aw. 1822–1828. Moved to Cincinnati *ca.*1819. Apt. of Luman Watson 1822–1828. Later employed in wax museum. Marr. Elizabeth Gibson 1832, "who helped him." To Washington 1834, sculpturing. Later studio in Italy. (A. Lockett)

PRAEFELT, JOHN: Phila., 5th St. bet. Lombard and Pine Sts. Dir. 1897–1898. (Prime)

PRATT (Daniel, Jr.) & FROST (Jonathan): Reading, Mass. 1832–1835. Mostly looking glass Shelf clocks, wood movts., 30-hour, labels, "Improved Clocks manufactured and sold by Pratt & Frost, Reading, Mass.," printed by J. Howe, 39 Merchants Row, Boston. Pos. Conn. clocks or movts., though some made in Reading. Dissolved 1835.

— & WALKER: Boston, "Rear 843 Washington St." Cabinetmakers. (JWW)

PRATT, WILLIAM, & BRO.: Boston. "1847." Pos. Daniel Pratt, Jr., or associate.

—, AZARIAH: Marietta, O. Early 19th century. (Knittle)

—, DANIEL, JR.: 1797–1871. Reading, Mass. C., Dealer. In Pratt & Frost 1832–1835 with Jonathan Frost; dissolved; alone till *ca.*1858. Extensive business; also exported, India and elsewhere. Labels, "Extra Clocks, Mfd. and sold by Daniel Pratt, Jr., etc.," many dated. Brass movts. after 1838, prob. Conn. Boston store, 49 Union St., 1846–1871; continued as Daniel Pratt's Sons 1871–1880; became Benjamin Boyce, 49 Union St., later 119 Hanover St. 1880–1895; Daniel Pratt, Son, 339 Washington St. 1895; discontinued 1916 on death of Frank W. B. Pratt. (See ill. No. 207.) (Am. Col. Jan. 1948)

—, JOSEPH: Boston, "145 Court St., formerly 119." n/d. W. C. Yellow Watch Paper Bir. Col.

—, PHINEAS: 1747–1813. Saybrook, Conn. *Ca.*1768. Son of Azariah and Agnes Beebe Pratt. In Rev. War. Deacon Second Church of Saybrook. With David Bushnell, inventor of American Turtle, earliest submarine or torpedo boat; made one successful trip in it. With son Abel built machinery for ivory combs made by Abel at Deep River, Conn. (Hoopes)

—, WILLIAM: Boston. Dir. 1842.

—, WILLIAM T.: Washington, N.C. Adv. 1834. (Cutten)

PRENOT, HENRY: N.Y.C. 1805.

PRENTISS CALENDAR & TIME CO.: N.Y.C. Sold to S. F. Myers & Co. 1892.

— CLOCK CO.: N.Y.C. Later Prentiss Calendar & Time Co.

—, C. M. C.: n/p. Patent No. 164210 June 8, 1875, model at Smiths. Inst.

—, JOHN H.: Utica, N.Y. Dir. 1832.

PRESCOTT, JONATHAN: Kensington, N.H. *Ca.*1765. Blacksmith. Prob. C. (Ant. July, 1948)

PRESTON, J. W.: Castleton, Vt. *Ca.*1830. Watch Paper BCL Col.

—, PAUL: Buckingham, Pa. *Ca.*1860.

—, STEPHEN: N.Y.C. n/d. Watch Paper BCL Col.

PREVEAR (Edw.) & HARRINGTON (Samuel, Jr.): Amherst, Mass. Adv. 1841, "At old

PREVEAR & HARRINGTON (cont'd)
Stand of Dickenson & Newbury."
(Cutten)

PREY, H. W.: Newport, R. I. "Estb. 1830."
Timepiece with standard recoil escapement in Selchow Col.

PREYLE, J.: Charleston, S.C. *Ca.*1780.

PRICE, E. D.: Kingston, N.Y. 1850's.
(Mrs. L. Mallory)

—, ISAAC: 1768–1798. Phila., 18 Strawberry St. Dir. 1791–1798. Son of Philip and Hannah Bougall Price. Bro. Phil. With Robert Leslie as Leslie & Price, 1794–1798, 86 Market St. 1791, 79 Market St. 1793. d. of yellow fever while member Phila. Board of Health. Pos. West Chester, Pa. Marr. Mary Fentham, dau. William Wygatt Fentham, Sussex Co. at Kinsessing Twp., Pa. 1791. (Friends' Meeting House Records) (Prime) (Gillingham) (Brinton)

—, JOSEPH: Baltimore, 35 Baltimore St. 1799. Pos. Rice.

—, PHILIP: Chester Co., Pa. Bro. Isaac. Marr. Rachel Kirk 1791. Pos. confusion with Philip Price, Jr. F. D. Brinton states he was farmer and educator, not C.

—, PHILIP, JR.: Phila., 71 High St. Dir. 1813–1825. "In Philadelphia as a clock and watchmaker 1813 to 1824, by 1830 as a copper plate and type printer at 66 Lombard St. One tall clock is in Chester, Pa., with his name on the dial. Difficulty in connecting him with the present Price family of Chester Co." (Brinton)

—, PHILIP P.: Cincinnati, Lebanon, O. Adv. 1815, "From Phila." Adv. 1823, "Late from Cincinnati." (Knittle) (Phillips)

—, ROBERT: N.Y.C. *Ca.*1830.

—, WILLIAM H.: –1879. West Chester, Pa. Adv. 1822–1823 as C. and W. on High St. (taxed) as "clockmaker." "No evidence of making found." (James)

PRIEST, JOSEPH: "Port of Bristol," Md. 1775.

PRIM, WILLIAM W.: West Chester, Pa. *Ca.*1823. (James)

PRINCE, GEORGE W.: Dover, N.H. *Ca.*1825. "Maker of N.H. Mirror strikers and orthodox in every way." (Brad Harvey)

PRIOLLAUD, E.: New Orleans, La. *Ca.*1850–*ca.*1860.

PRIOR, DANIEL: New Haven, Conn. *Ca.* 1840.

PRITCHARD & HOLDEN: Dayton, O. Succeeded Pritchard & Spining. Pos. agent for Pritchard & Munson 1840's. (Lockett)

— (Eben) & MUNSON (Lemuel H.): Bristol. (tx) 1844. Conn. Shelf clocks; some sold in O., wooden movts.

— & SPINING: Dayton, O. 1830–1833. Prob. Buel Pritchard. Label printed by J. Wilson, Dayton, O. (J. J. Neihaus, Dayton, O.)

—, BUEL: Dayton, O. *Ca.*1830. Shelf clock 19¾" high, flat 30-hour OG, "unusual tablet with picture of lady, raven tresses, white skin and cheeks that match the rose she so coyly holds," owned by Hilda Torrop, Dayton, O. (Lockett)

PROBASCO, JACOB: Phila. Dir. 1822.

—, JOHN: Trenton, N.J., Lebanon, O. 1800–1823. C. W. S. Employed James Huston. To Lebanon, O. Adv. 1823, "Now on cor. of Broadway in Lebanon." (Stow) (PG)

PROCTOR, CARDEN: N.Y.C. Adv. 1734, 1747, "Watches made and mended." Adv. 1755, "Watch movements made and purchased at Hanover Sq." Adv. till 1768. Tall clock, claw and ball front feet, bracket feet behind, double arch chamfered corners below, Q col. above.

—, G. K.: Beverly, Mass. 1860. Invented burglar and fire alarm. Mfd. by Seth Thomas to *ca.*1880. (Darrot)

—, W. M.: N.Y.C. 1737–1760. (MFM)

PRONTAUT, ANTHONY: N.Y.C. *Ca.*1840.

PROUD, JOHN: Newport, R.I. n/d. Very early dealer.

PROVAUX, —: Charleston, S.C., Broad St. Adv. 1775, "Lately arrived in this town, undertakes to make and mend all sorts of watches, after the French and English manner." (Prime)

PUDNEY, G.: N.Y.C., 104½ Catherine St. Aw. 1824–1825. Ex. Museum City of N.Y. Watch Paper owned by Elsworth Gosling, Pennington, N.J., "Clock & Watch Maker."

"PUFFIN BETSY": Nickname of old type steam locomotive on labels of Birge & Fuller and others. On label of William Markam, Mobile, Ala., printed by Elihu

Geer, 10 State St., Hartford, Conn. See Geer.

PULSIFER, F. L.: Boston. Dir. 1854.

PURCELL, CHARLES: Richmond, Va. *Ca.* 1819.

PURINGTON, ELISHA: Kensington, N.H. Son of James. Prob. C. Sons Elisha, Jr., Jonathan B. (Ant. July 1948)

—, ELISHA, Jr.: 1736–. Son of Elisha. C., gunsmith, blacksmith. Sold shop 1758 to Nathaniel Hemley.

—, JAMES: 1663–1718. Kensington or Hampton, N.H. "Clockmaker." No clocks known. Father of Elisha. b. Europe. Drowned at sea 1718.

—, JAMES: 1759–. Kensington, N.H. Son of Jonathan B. Tall clocks. To Marietta, O. 1816. (Ant. July 1948)

—, JONATHAN B.: 1732–1816. Kensington, N.H., South Road. Son of Elisha. Father of James. "A capable craftsman, selectman, Quaker." Dial of Tall clock "Jonathan Purintun, Kensington," in L. Dyer Col.

PURSE, JOHN: Phila. Dir. 1803.

—, THOMAS: Baltimore, 1796–1812.

—, W.: Charleston, S.C. *Ca.*1810.

PUTNAM, JONATHAN: N.Y.C. Dir. 1848.

PYLE, BENJAMIN: –1812. Washington, N.C. "Left excellent set of clockmakers' and watchmakers' tools." (Cutten)

—, BENJAMIN II: Fayetteville, N.C. Adv. 1838–1841, "Going West." Adv. 1841, "Commenced clock and watch repairing and had long experience." (Cutten)

QUANDALE, LEWIS: Phila., 92 Market St. Dir. 1813–1845. C. W. S. Watch Paper Cramer Col.

QUEST, HENRY: Marietta, Pa. *Ca.*1810–1830. Bro. Samuel.

—, SAMUEL: Maytown, Pa. Bro. Henry. *Ca.*1813. Tall clocks. On dial Australia marked as "New Holland." (Ant. Nov. 1944) (Lan. Co.)

QUICK TRAIN ROCKFORD WATCH Co.: Waldoboro, Me. n/d.

QUIMBY, HENRY: Portland, Me. *Ca.*1830.

—, PHINEAS: Belfast, Me. 1830–1850. (Abbott)

—, WILLIAM: Belfast, Me. 1821–1850. Succeeded by Abel Eastman. (Abbott)

QUINN, THOMAS: N.Y.C. 1775; Phila., Chestnut St., 1776. Congratulated on regulating watches by Command of American provincial regiment. (Ant. Jan. 1929)

RACINE, DAVID: Baltimore. *Ca.*1800.

RADCLIFF, J. N.: Birchrunville, Pa. *Ca.* 1874. C. W. (James)

RAHMER, G.: N.Y.C. *Ca.*1840.

RAILROAD WATCH Co.: Albany, N.Y. Inc. 1896.

RAINE, NATHANIEL: Phila. Adv. 1773. Aptd. to Jacob Godschalk.

RAIT, ROBERT, & Co.: N.Y.C. n/d. On dial regulator Tall clock, with mercury pendulum, in Barny Col.

RAMSAY, WALTER J.: –1856. Raleigh, N.C. Apt. of John C. Stedman. Org. W. J. Ramsay & Co. 1831; then alone; then in Ramsay & Beckwith; to New Bern, N.C., 1840. To Raleigh alone; in Palmer & Ramsay 1847–1855.

RAMSDELL & WHITCOMB: n/p. Patent No. 108390, Oct. 18, 1870, model at Smiths. Inst.

RAMSDEN, WRIGHT: Brooklyn, N.Y. *Ca.*1830.

RAND, DANIEL: Boston. Dir. 1830.

RANDALL, O. E.: Woodstock, Vt. n/d. Watch Paper BCL Col.

"RANDEL, HENRY," used by U. S. Watch Co. *ca.*1869–1870.

RANKIN, ALEXANDER: Phila. Dir. 1829–1833.

—, JOHN A.: –1896. Del. Apt. of Charles Canby. d. at Elkton, Md. (Conrad)

RANLET, NOAH: 1777–. Gilmanton, N.H. *Ca.*1800. Son of Charles and Elizabeth Lougee Ranlet. Marr. 1800 Rachel Osgood of Gilmanton. Name on dwarf Tall clocks. Ex. in Mitchell Col.

— (Raulet), SAMUEL: Monmouth, Me. *Ca.* 1800. Tall clock owned by Hill Jewelry, North East Harbor, Me. Sheraton type mahogany case Tall clock, 8-day brass movt., seconds, cal., painted iron dial, fan spandrels, owned by Robert F. Kurtz, Gladwyne, Pa. (Abbott)

RANSINGER, M.: Elizabethtown, Pa. *Ca.* 1850. (Lan. Co.)

RAPP, WILLIAM D.: Phila., Race St. 1831. Dir. 1828–*ca.*1850. Pos. Norristown, Pa. (Moore)

RATHBURN, VALENTINE W.: Stonington, Conn. n/d. Tall clock in Dr. Wm. Horton Col.

(263)

RAUS, EMANUEL: Phila. n/d. Tall clocks.

RAWSON, JASON R.: Holden, Mass. Wood movt. Mirror clock, alarm on top like D. Pratt's; Watch Paper 1839. "Extra improved clocks Mfd. and sold by . . . wholesale and retail, warranted if well used." Barny Col.

—, SMITH, E. G.: Saratoga Springs, N.Y. Patent Jan. 22, 1867, "Improvement in Globe Clocks." Also Timby type Globe clocks. (See ill. No. 269.) (BCC)

RAY (Benjamin) & INGRAHAM (Elias, Andrew): Bristol, North St. (tx) 1841–1843.

—, DANIEL: Sudbury, Mass. Ca.1790. Sudbury, Eng. Early 18th century. (Baillie)

"RAYMOND, B. W.," used by National Watch Co. 1867–1875.

—, BENJAMIN W.: 1801–1883. Elgin, Ill. Founder, first pres., Elgin National Watch Co. Retired as pres. 1867; director till 1877.

RAYNES, JOSEPH: Lowell, Mass., Central St. Dir. 1834–1847. W. J. With Wentworth.

REA, ARCHELAUS, JR.: 1750–1792. Salem, Mass., Court St. 1791. Formerly blacksmith. Marr. 1777 at Danvers, Mass. Diary of Rev. Wm. Bentley, Dec. 16, 1792: "Died at Danvers by a secondary fever after inoculation, a Mr. Rea of this town leaving a wife and 7 children. He was bred a blacksmith but having an adventurous rather than ingenious turn of mind, he commenced jack, clock and watch maker. His principal business was cleansing such machines and being intoxicated with his success, he came proverbially a conceited man. In regard to the Small pox, he knew everything about it, rejected the prescriptions of his physicians and lived as he pleased and died in consequence of his folly." (Buhler)

—, GEORGE: –1838. Flemington, and Pittstown, N.J. Aw. 1795–ca.1810. Farmer, public official. Tall clock, Chippendale cherry case, name, "1796." (John F. Schenk)

READ (REED), ABNER, EZRA & ISAIAH: Ohio. Ca.1809. "Three bros. in Read & Watson. All from Mass." (Champagne County records, Ezra from Conn.) "Were making clocks between Springfield, O. & Xenia, and Ezra eventually moved to Urbana, ca.1809."

READ (Abner, Ezra, Isaiah) & WATSON (Thomas): Cincinnati, and pos. Dayton, O. Ca.1809. Clocks similar to Luman Watson's Tall wood movt. clock.

—, G. A.: New Jersey. Night clock, opaque dial, candle socket behind, watch type movt., attached to dial made in N.J., 1874 stamped on cover of movt.; N.Y. standard mainspring, 18 size, 7 jewels, No. 2189, Serial No. 165427, in G. B. Davis Col.

—, ISAAC: Phila. Dir. 1819–1822.

—, SILAS G.: New Brunswick, N.J. 1812–1814.

—, WM. H. J.: Phila. Dir. 1831–ca.1850 and later. C. W. and Dealer.

REASNORS, JOHN: Rochester, N. Y. Dir. 1841. (Cutten)

REED, ISAAC, & SON: Phila., 176 No. 2nd St. Dir. 1830–1850. Tall clocks, imp. Watch Paper Cramer Col.

—, BENJAMIN: Bristol. Ca.1775.

—, DANIEL I.: Phila., 217 S. Front St. Dir. 1798.

—, EZEKIEL: Brockton or Bridgewater, Mass. Before 1800. "Tall clock, pine case, 8-day brass movt., striker, painted arch dial." In James Conlon Col.

—, FREDERICK: Norwalk, Conn. Watch Paper Charles Terry Treadway Col.

—, FREDERICK: Phila. Dir. 1814–1823. (Prime)

"REED, G. A.," used by U. S. Watch Co. ca.1870.

—, GEORGE P.: 1827–1908. Boston. "Only maker of chronometers in quantity in U.S.A." Ex. Chicago Museum and Chamberlain Col. (Baillie)

—, G. WASHINGTON: Phila. Dir. 1839–1850 and later.

—, ISAAC: 1746–ca.1808. Stamford, Conn. Aw. 1808. Ca.1768–1776. C. Son of William and Rachel Kellogg Reed. Tory; to Shelburne, Nova Scotia. To Stamford 1790; joined M. E. Church; meetings held in home many years. Master Stamford Masons. Tall clock sold at Riefsnyder Sale 1929. (Hoopes)

—, ISAAC: Frankford, Pa. n/d. Tall clocks. Pos. Phila.

—, ISAAC: Phila. Dir. 1820–1829, 1837–1846. In Reed & Son. See Read.

—, JAMES R.: Pittsburgh, Pa. Ca.1840.

REED, JOHN W.: Phila. Dir. 1846–1847.
—, OSMON: Phila. Dir. 1831–1841.
—, SILAS: New Brunswick, N.J. n/d. Tall clocks.
—, SIMEON: Cummington, Mass. *Ca.*1770. Father of Zelotus.
—, STEPHEN: N.Y.C. 1802–*ca.*1830. (Baillie)
—, ZELOTUS: Goshen and Cummington, Mass. *Ca.*1796. Son of Simeon.
REEDER, ABNER: 1766–1841. Phila., 38 No. Front St. 1793–1796. In McFee & Reeder. To Trenton, N.J., 1798. Dealer in English watches. Marr. 1796 Hannah Wilson of Southampton, Pa. Org. State Bank of Trenton, N.J. 1804. (Williams)
REET, GEORGE P.: 1828–. Melrose, Mass. 1868–1887. Apt. of Jacob Carter, Concord, N.H. Invented patent barrel 1857. W. Chrons.
REEVE & CO.: N.Y.C., 187 Center St. Dir. 1854.
—, RICHARD & GEORGE: Phila. Dir. 1804.
—, BENJAMIN: Phila. and Greenwich, N.J. Aw. *ca.*1760–1801. Son of Joseph and Ellen Bagnall Reeve. Fine Tall clocks. Apt. of Peter Stretch; witnessed his will. Tall clock in Phila. Hist. Soc. (Stretch) (Chandlee)
—, GEORGE: Phila. Dir. 1804–1805.
—, GEORGE, SR.: Zanesville, O. 1809. Tall clocks. Father of Richard. (Knittle)
—, JOSEPH: Phila. Early 1700's. From Salem, N.J., to learn Clockmaking with Peter Stretch. (Stretch)
—, JOSEPH: Brooklyn, N.Y. *Ca.*1840–1850.
—, RICHARD: Phila. Dir. 1804.
—, RICHARD: Zanesville, O. *Ca.*1815. Son of George, Sr. (Knittle)
—, THOMAS: N.Y.C. *Ca.*1840–1850.
—, Y.: Phila. Dir. 1808.
REEVES, DAVID S.: Phila. Dir. 1830–1835.
—, STEPHEN: *Ca.*1738–. Bridgeton, N.J. "Most important N.J.S." J. Adv. 1776. (Williams)
REGALLY, M.: Boston, 4 School St. Dir. 1842. Adv. 1846.
REGENSBURG, MOSES A.: West Chester, Pa. 1835–1843. W. C. "Adv., Watch Papers, no record after 1843." (James)
REIBLEY, JOSEPH: Phila. Dir. 1845–1846.
REILLY & CO., J. C.: Louisville, Ky. Aw. *ca.*1816. C. W. S. J. (LB)

REILLY, JOHN: Phila., 11 So. 4th St. Dir. 1797.
REISER, AUGUSTIN: Phila. 1772. (Prime)
RELIANCE WATCH CO.: Chicago. n/d. "Swiss Watches." (MFM)
REMINGTON, O. H.: Akron, O. 1860's.
RENTZHEIMER, HENRY (HEINRICH): Salisbury Twp., Pa. 1785–1788. Tall clock, pine case, dial marked "Allentown," before 1812. (Roberts)
REVERE CLOCK CO., THE: Cincinnati, O. *Ca.*1930. Electric Shelf clocks, telechron movts. One in author's col.
—, PAUL, & SON: Boston. 1804. Cast 398 bells (stockbook). Marked "Paul Revere," "Paul Revere & Son," "Revere & Co." Elder son Paul with father till 1801. Bells then marked "Revere." Paul, Sr., d. 1818. Son Joseph continued till 1828; sold to Revere Copper Co.
—, PAUL: Boston. —1818. Aw. 1792–1818. Not C. Cast bells for Tower clocks.
REYMOND, M.: Charleston, S.C. Adv. 1785, "Clock and watchmaker from Paris. Makes and mends all sorts of watches in his trade." (Prime)
REYNOLDS (E. J.) & BENTON (J.): Rochester, N.Y. *Ca.*1850.
—, HENRY A.: Rochester, N.Y. Dir. 1847–1848.
—, JOHN: Hagerstown, Md. *Ca.*1790–1832. C., W. and brass founder. (LSS)
—, THOMAS: N.Y.C., 19 Union Sq. 1891.
RICE (Joseph) & BARRY (Standish): Baltimore. Adv. 1785, "Having entered into partnership, removed to shop N. W. Cor. Market & Calvert Sts., and thanks for the business there in their short continuance in business." Also engraving. (Prime)
— (Charles W.) & HARRINGTON (John E.): n/p. Patent No. 26008, Jan. 19, 1859, model Smiths. Inst.
—, CHARLES: Lewiston, Minn. After 1850.
"—, GEO. SANCE," used by N.Y. Watch Co. 1872–1875.
—, GIDEON: N.Y.C. *Ca.*1840.
—, H. P.: Saratoga Springs, N.Y. Adv. 1827–1830. Watch Paper BCL Col.
—, JOSEPH: Baltimore, Adv. 1784–1801. Adv. with Standish Barry, Calvert and Water Sts., "Clocks."
—, JOSEPH T.: Albany, N.Y. Dir. 1813–1850.

RICE, LUTHER G.: Lowell, Mass. 1835. W. Worked for Hazen Elliot.

—, PHINEAS: Boston or Charlestown, Mass. 1830.

—, WILLIAM (W. C.): Phila. Dir. 1835–1850 and later.

RICH & WILLARD (Benjamin Franklin): Boston. Ca.1842–1844. (BCC)

—, ALEXANDER: Charleston, S.C. Ca.1790.

—, GIDEON: N.Y.C., 140 Broad St. Ca.1840. "Mfger." on label. (PG)

—, JOHN: 1763–1812. Bristol. Son of William and Mary Rich. Pos. aptd. to Gideon Roberts. With Roberts, one of Bristol's first Cs. Wood movts., Tall clocks, gold watches. Many clock movts. (100 in process at death). Sold 1809 "Forge saw mill, near my dwelling house, reserving to myself the privilege of working up what coal I have on hand, likewise the privilege of making one ton of iron each year for five years." Estate inventory indicates general drygoods and jewelry; Cs. supplies. Not assessed as C. (LB) (Hoopes)

—, WILLIAM: Salem, Mass. Before 1857. W. "boarding at 56 Derby St."

RICHARD, C. A.: Columbus, O. 1835. C. W. (Knittle)

RICHARDS, B. (Bryan) & A. (Alanson): Bristol. (tx) 1828–1835.

— (Gilbert) & Co.: Chester., Conn. Ca. 1830 "Manufacturer of Patent Clocks."

— & MORRELL: N.Y.C. 1809–1832.

— (Seth) & SON: Bristol. (tx) 1815. Assessed as Cs.

—, W. & S. R.: Phila. Dir. 1818–1829.

—, ALANSON: Bristol. Ca.1825–ca.1840.

—, BRYAN: Bristol. (tx) 1823. 1828–1833. In B. & A. Richards. C. W. R.

—, FRANK L.: Boston. n/d. Watch Paper BCL Col.

—, S. R.: Phila. 1805.

—, SAMUEL: Paris, Me. Ca.1860.

—, SETH: Bristol. Ca.1815.

—, THOMAS: N.Y.C. 1805. Authorized by adv. October 2, 1822 of Simon Willard to sell his Lighthouse clock in N.Y.C.

—, WILLIAM, JR.: Phila. Dir. 1813.

—, WILLIAM RUSH: 1816–1885. Bristol. Father G. Aptd. carpenter at 16. To St. Louis, later St. Paul; aw. at trade. Marr. Sarah C. Champion 1840 in Win-

sted. Father of Wm. C. Partner in Birge, Peck & Co. 1849–1859. Later employed by Welch, Spring & Co. 1869–1884. With Ambrose Peck sold land, bldgs., water rights to S.C. Spring 1864.

RICHARDSON, J. & N.: Boston. Dir. 1803.

—, FRANCIS: 1681–1729. Phila. 1710–1729. "Bought movts. from Peter Stretch." (Stretch)

—, JOHN: Boston. Dir. 1805.

—, JOSEPH: –1784. Adv. 1733. 1736–1771.

—, MARTIN: Little Falls, N.Y. Adv. 1837–1839.

—, WILLIAM: Norfolk, Va. Ca.1796. Tall clocks. (MFM)

RICHMAN, ISAAC: Phila. Dir. 1850.

RICKSECKER, ISRAEL: Dover, O. 1834–1872. "From Bethlehem, Pa." Tall clocks, brass movts. (Knittle)

—, J.: St. Clairsville, O. Ad. 1839. "Clockmaker." (Knittle)

RICHMOND, A.: Providence, R.I. Ca.1810. (MFM)

—, FRANKLIN: Providence, R.I. 1824–1849.

—, G.: Providence, R.I. Ca.1810.

RIDDLE, JAMES: Fermanaugh Twp., Pa. Ca.1780.

RIDER, ARTHUR: Baltimore. 1822–1824.

RIDGWAY, JOHN, & SON: Boston. Dir. 1842.

—, C. T.: Nashua, N.H. n/d. "Watches, jewelry and spectacles." White Watch Paper Bir. Col.

RIEL, GEORGE: Phila. Dir. 1805.

RIESLE, EGIDIUS: N.Y.C. Ca.1840.

RIGGS & BROTHER: Phila., 310 Market St. 1949. J., Chrons., charts, nautical insts. Some clock works. (George Eckhardt) (AJ. Mar., Apr. 1950.)

— (Daniel) & BROTHER (Robert): Phila. 1866–1870. "Nautical instruments" added 1871.

— BROTHERS: Phila., 11 and 116 S. 4th St. 1872–1875; 211 Walnut St. 1878–1879.

— (Daniel) & Co.: Phila., 244 S. Front St. 1864–1865.

— (William H. C.) & SON (Daniel): Phila., 244 S. Front St. 1863.

—, WILLIAM H. C.: Phila. Dir. 1819 to 1861. Agent for E. Howard & Co. C., W. Sold many clocks to various railroads in and around Phila.; name sometimes on dial; prob. all by Howard. Addresses: 89 Chestnut St., cor. 3rd (1819–1821);

29 4th St. (1822); 112 High St. (1825); 34 Chestnut St. (1828–1829); 67 S. Front St. (1831–1833, 1837, 1839), W., Chrons.; 126 S. Front St. (1840–1842); 126 S. Front St., 13 Dock St. (1843–1858); 244 S. Front St., 13 Dock St. (1859–1861).

RIHL, ALBERT (A. M.): Phila. Dir. 1849.

RILEY, JOHN: Phila. Adv. 1773, "Imported watches for sale . . . also apprentice wanted." Dir. 1785–1818. "Repairer of equation clocks and watches of unusual construction." (Ritter) (Prime)

—, ROBERT: Phila. Dir. 1806–1808.

—, RILEY: N.Y.C. 1805. (Baillie)

RIOU & BOELL: N.Y.C. Ca.1840. Imp. French clocks.

—, E.: N.Y.C., 63 Liberty St. Dir. 1840.

RITCHIE, BENJAMIN: Maryland. 1774. "Of Scotland." (FT)

—, F. J.: n/p. Patent No. 143847, Oct. 21, 1873, model at Smiths. Inst.

—, GEORGE: Phila. Dir. 1785–1793, 1807–1811.

RITTENHOUSE & POTTS: Morristown and Phila., Pa. Ca.1770. Name on transit.

—, BENJAMIN: 1740–. Partner with older bro. David. ca.1760. Tall clocks, insts. Adv. 1786 for apt. "to learn the art and mistery of clocks." "Working as late as 1819." Clocks marked "Worcester Twp.," "Phila. Co." Tall clock marked "Worcester" owned by Walter B. Sheppard, Denver, Col.; one 7½' owned by W. A. Ramsey, Big Stone Gap, Va., mahogany case, brass movt., one lead weight, 30-hour, 10" brass dial with filigree border, base 10¾" sq., "Benjamin Rittenhouse, Worcester, Fecit" inscribed on crescent. (See ill. No. 34.) (Gillingham) (Pa. Mag. July 1932)

—, DAVID: 1732–1796. Norristown, Phila., Pa. Scientist, C., mathematician, astronomer. Great-grandfather, William Rittenhuysen, from Holland, estab. first American paper mill ca.1690. Early interest in science and mathematics. Pos. apt. of uncle John Gorgas. Little instruction. At Norristown made splendid Tall clocks; insts. (See ills. Nos. 29–33.) Made at least two Orreys. Commissioned by Govt. 1763 to survey Mason-Dixon Line; used own surveyors' insts.

Calculated transit of Venus 1769; later observed it successfully from own observatory. To Phila. 1770. Provincial Legislature 1775. Member Phila. Committee of Safety, president 1776. Member Pa. Constitutional Convention. Pa. State Treasurer 1777–1779. Professor of Astronomy at U. of Pa. 1779–1782. Member Am. Phil. Soc. president 1791, succeeding Benjamin Franklin. Fellow London Royal Soc. 1795. Great figure in American clock history. Life by William Barton, Phila. 1813.

RITTERBAND, HENRY: N.Y.C. Ca.1830.

"RIVERSIDE," used by Am. Watch Co. from ca.1877.

R. & J. CLOCK Co.: Pittsfield, Mass. "Like Gilbert, made 8-day brass with the lifting wire for the strike, flattened on the end, as I find in some of the not too old brass movts. Movt. only and no other identification. Name stamped on movt." (G. B. Davis)

ROATH, R. W.: Norwich, Conn. Ca.1830. Mfr. of ever-pointed pencil cases, and window springs, dealer in watches.

ROBBINS & APPLETON: N.Y.C. Ca.1871. Agents for Waltham watches.

—, GEORGE: Phila. Dir. 1833–1851.

—, JEREMIAH: Phila., 819 Chestnut St. n/d. On dial and plate of watch movt. in Cramer Col.

—, ROYAL E.: –1902. With Tracy and Baker, watch case mfgrs. of Phila., bought watch company at Waltham in 1857.

ROBERT, H.: n/p. Patent No. 154717, Sept. 1, 1874, model at Smiths. Inst.

ROBERTS, ELIAS, & Co.: Bristol. (tx) 1808–1809. "Clockmakers." Sons of Gideon.

— & LEE: Boston. Adv. 1772. (Buhler)

—, CANDACE: Bristol. Dau. of Gideon. Famous for her handpainted dials for Cs.

—, ELIAS: 1727–1778. Bristol. Father of Gideon and Elias. C.; pos. taught them. Pos. aw. by 1760. Killed by Indians near Wilkesbarre, Pa. One of first forty settlers of Bristol.

—, ENOCH: Phila. Dir. 1816.

—, F.: Phila., 47 So. 4th St. Dir. 1828–1829.

—, G. E.: New Milford, Conn. n/d. Watch Paper BCL Col.

ROBERTS, GIDEON: 1749–1813. Bristol. Son of Elias. Father of Wyllys. In Rev. War; imprisoned by British. Became Quaker. Wood movt. hang-up clocks, in Tall cases, in quantity in shop near house on Fall Mt. pos. *ca.*1790. Peddled them as far south as Pa. (See ill. Nos. 63–65.) Numbered all clocks. Some have painted paper dials on wood. Pos. mass production pioneer. (Hull) (Hoopes) (LB)

—, GIDEON J. C.: Bristol. (tx) 1811–1812. Pos. Gideon or son.

—, JACOB: Easton, Pa. 1810–1830. (Abbott)

—, JOHN: Phila. Dir. 1797–1799.

—, JOSEPH: 1808–. Newburyport, Mass. 1849–1852.

—, N. H.: Phila. Dir. 1848–.

—, OLIVER: Lancaster, Pa. *Ca.*1800. Partner in Montanden & Roberts 1802–1808. Later Eaton, O. Tall clocks. Came from Lancaster as journeyman maker with Henry L. Montanden, later continuing with his widow Hannah. 30-hour, wooden movt. Tall clock with cal. pull movt. illus. in (TP). Tall clock owned by Guy W. Kidwell, Springfield, O. (Lockett)

—, SILAS: Trenton, N.J. 1790–1820.

—, THOMAS: Easton, Pa. 1815–1835.

—, TITUS MERRIMAN (T. M.): 1793–1856. Son of Gideon. Marr. Lucia Parmelee 1817. Sold clocks in South. Clocks for E. C. Brewster *ca.*1835. Aw. 1837 in shop in carriage factory. Mahogany Shelf clock 31½ × 17 LG clock, label "Made by T. M. Roberts for E. C. Brewster" in Newcomb Col. Flint Sale 1926, "sq. cased, double side columns, carved sqs. at center, mirror in bottom, and another in upper molding."

—, WILLIAM: Phila. Dir. 1821.

—, WILLIAM: Annapolis, Md. Adv. 1745.

—, WYLLYS: 1795–1841. Bristol. Son of Gideon. Bro. Titus. C. In Thomas Barnes, Jr., & Co. 1819–1823. "He received a thorough training in Clock-making." (Hull)

ROBERTSON CLOCK & INSTRUMENT CO.: Detroit, Mich. 1929–1930. Special clocks on order. (MFM)

ROBESON, ISAAC: Phila. Dir. 1843–1846.

ROBIE, J. C.: Binghamton, N.Y. Adv. 1835. (Cutten)

ROBIE, JOHN: Plattsburg, N.Y. *Ca.*1817.

ROBINSON, BURNHAM & CO.: Danvers, Mass. Adv. 1831.

—, ANTHONY: –1802. Trenton, N.J. Aw. 1788. To Phila. 1796. In Dickman & Robinson (dissolved 1798). Alone till 1802. (Williams)

—, ISAAC: Phila. Dir. 1829–1835.

—, JACOB F.: Wilmington, Del., 3rd and Market Sts. *Ca.*1840. Apt. Charles Canby. (Conrad)

—, JEREMIAH A.: Lowell, Mass. 1835–1837.

—, JOHN: Haverhill, Mass. With first settlers 1640. Blacksmith. To Exeter, N.H., before 1653; clerk of market. Pos. C. (Trades & Tradesman)

—, OBED: Attleboro, Mass. *Ca.*1790.

—, SAMUEL: Pittsburgh, Pa. *Ca.*1830.

—, WILLIAM: Chillicothe, O. Adv. 1809, "From Scotland in 1809, one door left of Red Iron Inn." (Knittle)

—, WILLIAM F.: Phila. Dir. 1835.

—, WILLIAM K.: Brownville, N.Y. Adv. 1828. (Cutten)

ROBJOHN, THOMAS: N.Y.C. *Ca.*1840.

ROCK ISLAND WATCH CO., THE: Rock Island, Ill. Bought Mozart Watch Co. 1871; f. 1874. "Produced no, or few, watches and went out of existence." Sold to Freeport Watch Mfg. Co. (Evans) (Bowman)

ROCKFORD WATCH CO., THE: Rockford, Ill. 1873–1901. f. 1896, operated by receivers till 1901. Became Rockford Watch Co., Ltd.

— WATCH CO. LTD., THE: Rockford, Ill. 1901–1915. Succeeded Rockford Watch Co. Remaining stock finished by Illinois Watch Case Co.

ROCKWELL, HENRY: N.Y.C. *Ca.*1840.

— (ROCHWELL), SAMUEL: 1722–1773. Providence, R.I., Middletown, Conn. (*ca.*1762). Son of Joseph and Suzanna. Aptd. pos. Providence, R.I.; aw. 1746-*ca.* 1763. Tall clocks extant, with name and "Providence." Also trader selling coffee, sugar, molasses in N.Y.C. Died insolvent. (Hoopes)

RODE, WILLIAM: Phila. Dir. 1795.

RODGERS, WILLIAM: Phila. Dir. 1824.

RODMAN, JOHN: Burlington, N.J. 1760–1768.

—, ISAAC: Burlington, N.J. n/d.

RODMAN, THOMAS: Burlington, N.J. n/d. Son-in-law Isaac Pierson. Tall clock.

ROGERS, ABNER: 1777-. Berwick, Me. Son of Paul. N.H. Mirror clocks. Pos. to Portland, Me., 1799. (L. Dyer)

—, CALEB: 1765-1839. Newton, Mass. n/d. Shop had dial sign. Watch Paper.

—, ISAAC: Marshfield, Mass. 1800-1828. (Abbott)

—, JAMES: N.Y.C., 45 Liberty St. Dir. 1872. Steamship clocks. Watch Paper in Museum City of N.Y., "410½ Broadway"; also BCL Col.

—, JAMES M.: Troy, N.Y. Dir. 1836-1840.

—, JOHN: Billerica, Mass. to 1770. Newton, Mass. till ca.1800. Pos. Boston 1765.

—, NATHANIEL: Windham, Me. Ca.1800.

—, PAUL: Berwick, Me. Late 1700's. Father of Abner. Tall clock in Lewis Dyer Col. Pos. Mirror clocks.

—, PETER: N.Y.C. Ca.1830.

—, SAMUEL: 1766-1839. Plymouth, Mass. 1790-1804. (Abbott)

—, THOMAS: N.Y.C. Ca.1820.

—, WILLIAM: Hartford, Conn., Exchange Bldg. 1837. Chrons.; repeating patent lever, horizontal, plain watches. Watch Paper Bir. Col.

—, WILLIAM: Boston. 1860.

—, WILLIAM H.: Brooklyn, N.Y., 131 Myrtle St. Ca.1850. Formerly of Rice & Roberts. "C., W., engraver, plater, gilder and galvanizer."

ROHR, JOHN A.: Phila. Dir. 1807-1813.

ROI, HENRY: Hamburg, Pa. Early 19th century. Sometimes signed Henry King. 4th group. (Steinmetz)

ROLAND, HENRY: Albany, N.Y., 106 State St. "Estb. 1832." Shelf clock extant, stenciled columns, carved eagle top. (PG)

"ROLLO, EDWIN," used by U.S. Watch Co. ca.1868.

RONSON, PETER: Phila. Ca.1796. (MFM)

ROOME, JAMES H.: N.Y.C. Dir. 1854.

ROORBACK, M.: N.Y.C. Ca.1770.

"ROOT, GEO. F.," used by Cornell Watch Co. ca.1871-1874.

—, JOEL C.: Bristol. Ca.1852. Son of Samuel and Philotheta Ives Root; bro. Samuel E. "Clock trimmings." Built shop 1867 on Root's Island. Later hardware. Succeeded by son Charles J. Beginning of present Veeder, Root Co.

ROOT, LAFAYETTE: New Haven, Conn. Ca. 1850.

—, SAMUEL EMERSON: 1820-1896. Bristol. C. Lived with uncle Chauncey Ives. Aw. 1851. With Edward Langdon; later alone. Marine type clock movts. Patent on "Paper Clock Dial with Brass Sash." Built factory 1853 Main and School Sts. (Hist.)

—, SYLVESTER S.: Bristol, Downs St. (tx) 1842-1844. Wood clocks in Downs Shop ca. two years. N.Y.C., 125 Maiden Lane. Dir. 1848; prob. sales outlet.

ROSE, DANIEL: 1749-1827. Reading, Pa. 2nd Group. Best work late 18th century. Listed 1779 as Clockmaker. Lt. in Rev. War. Later Pa. Legislature, with John Kiem. (See ill. No. 39.) (Steinmetz) (Abbott)

—, DANIEL, JR.: Reading, Pa. Ca.1820-1837.

ROSS, ALEXANDER COFFMAN: 1812-1883. Zanesville, O. Son of Elijah, gunsmith. From Brownsville, Pa., 1804. Aw. 1833. S., J., "Clock and watchmaker," Aptd. to local Watchmaker. To N.Y.C. 1829 to complete training. In Hill & Ross ca.1830-ca.1870. Invented daguerreotype camera 1839. Student of science; prizes in photography. First telegraph operator Zanesville, O. Org. Gas Co. Other activities, including water-color painting. Composed "Tippecanoe and Tyler Too." (Knittle)

—, ROBERT: N.Y.C. Dir. 1854.

ROSSELOT, P. A.: N.Y.C. Dir. 1849. Dealer in clock parts.

ROSSET, T. E., & MULFORD: Elizabethtown, Pa. 1860-1873. "Near the stone bridge." Cabinetmakers, Veneered and inlaid clock cases. (PG)

ROTH, HARRY: N.Y.C., 23rd St. Middle 20th century. Chrons.

—, N. (Nelson): Utica, N.Y. Dir. 1837.

ROTHROCK, JOSEPH: York, Pa. Aw. 1783-1790. Tall clocks owned by Mrs. Dora Houck, New Oxford, Pa., and in Dr. Wm. Horton Col.

ROULSTONE, JOHN: Boston. Adv. 1768. Dir. 1789-1803.

ROUSE, EMANUEL: Phila. Adv. 1747-1768.

—, WILLIAM MADISON: 1812-1888. Charleston, S.C., 139 King St. and 211 Meeking St. Ca.1875. Aw. 1831-ca.1875. (Prime)

"Royal," used by American Watch Co. *ca.* 1889.

— Gold American Watch Co.: N.Y.C. n/d. Watch No. 11470, size 18, 11 jewels, in MFM Col.

Royce, Charles E.: Jersey City, N.J. n/d. Watch Paper BCL Col.

—, Harvey: Morrisville, N.Y. Adv. 1834. (Cutten)

Roydor, Francis: Boston. Dir. 1813.

"Rubie, Francis," used by National Watch Co. *ca.*1870–1878.

Rudisill, George: Manheim, Pa. *Ca.*1820.

Rudolph, Samuel: Phila., 157 No. Front St. Dir. 1803.

—, William F.: Del. n/d. Apt. Ziba Ferris. (Conrad)

Rue, Henry: Phila. Dir. 1835.

Ruff, William E.: Washington and Halifax, N.C. W. S. Adv. 1822, 1829.

Rugheimer, Moses: N.Y.C. Dir. 1854.

Rumsey, Charles: –1841. Salem, N.J. W. S. J. Adv. 1820–1841. (Williams)

Russel, Jonathan: Geneva, N.Y. Adv. 1807.

Russell & Clark: Woodstock, Vt. *Ca.*1830. Pos. Russell, Clark & Randall.

— & Jones Clock Co.: Pittsfield, Mass. 1884–1888. Succeeded Terry Clock Co.

—, A. L.: Lynn, Mass. n/d. Printed sticker in Banjo clock owned in Pittsburgh, Pa., reported by John McGinley, II.

—, Charles H.: Lynn, Mass. *Ca.*1848.

—, D. N.: Greenfield, Mass. n/d. "Patent level watchmaker." Orange Watch Paper Bir. Col.

—, George: Phila. Dir. 1832.

—, Major John: Deerfield, Mass. 1765. Son of John.

—, Samuel: Middletown, Mass. 1846. "Clock Worker."

—, Thomas: Charleston, S.C., Dir. 1855; Columbia, S.C., Dir. 1856.

—, William: Augusta, Ga. *Ca.*1830.

Rutter, Moses: Baltimore. 1804.

"Ryerson, J. T.," used by National Watch Co. 1867.

Saber, George: Reading, Pa. Early 19th century. (Conrad)

Sadd, Harvey: 1776–1840. Son of Dr. Thomas and Delight Warner. Moved to New Hartford, 1798. Adv., "Carrying on Clockmaking, different kinds as may suit the purchaser, at the North End of New Hartford." Marr. 1801. In 1802 moved to Hartford, worked in shop of Miles Beach as plater. Name appeared in Beach's adv. of 1803. Also engaged in the foundry business, casting stoves, kettles, etc., and possibly brass for clock parts. In 1829 moved to Austinburgh, O. Died there October 11, 1840. (Hoopes)

Sadd, Thomas: 1750–. East Windsor, Conn. "A Doctor, not a clockmaker, the father of Harvey of New Hartford." (Hoopes)

Sadtler, Philip B.: Baltimore. 1804.

Safford (Chas. B.) & Kail (Emil): Kingston, N.Y. *Ca.*1850. Possibly only agents for Conn. clocks, although their names appear on them. (TP)

Sage, A., & Co.: n/d. Savannah, Ga. Tall clocks.

Sailor, Washington: Phila. Dir. 1825–1833. Tall clock with painted iron dial. Robt. Franks Col.

Salede: See Solliday.

Salliday: See Solliday.

Salmon, Alfred: Cincinnati, O. *Ca.*1820.

—, William H.: Morrisville, N.Y. Adv. 1830. Also at Cazenovia, N.Y. Adv. 1830–1836. (Cutten)

Salybacker, I.: Columbia, S.C. *Ca.*1850.

Sample, William: Boston. *Ca.*1850.

Sampson, Alexander: Hagerstown, Md. 1799–1805. (LSS)

—, William: Phila., 316 No. Front St. Dir. 1802–1803. (Prime)

Samuel, Hyman: Charleston, S.C., 142 Broad St. Aw. Dir. 1806–1809. (Prime)

Samuels & Dunn: N.Y.C. *Ca.*1844. Supposedly sold clocks that were not Chauncey Jeromes with Jeromes' labels.

Sandell, Edward: Baltimore. 1817.

Sandoz, Charles H.: Phila. Dir. 1800–1802. (Prime)

—, Frederick: Charleston, S.C. *Ca.*1800.

—, Louis: Phila. Dir. 1845.

Sands, Stephen: N.Y.C., near Pecks Slip. Adv. 1772, "Clock and Watchmaker opened his shop." Adv. 1786.

Sanford, Abel: 1798–1843. Hamilton, N.Y. Adv. 1834–1843. D. (Cutten)

—, Eaton: Plymouth, Conn. After 1810. Tall clock owned by E. B. Belcher, Portland, Me. Tall wood movt. as in ill. No. 67, name across dial "E. Sanford — Plymouth."

SANFORD, ISAAC: Conn. Hoopes said, "Engraver, minaturist, and inventor, but not a clock maker, although at one time a partner of Miles Beach."

—, JUDSON: Hamilton, N.Y. Adv. 1843–1844.

—, RANSOM: Plymouth, Conn. 1840. "Made brass pinions and barrels for Seth Thomas movts."

—, SAMUEL: Plymouth, Conn. 1845–1877.

SANFORDS, T. & E.: Goshen, Conn. A modified Scroll Shelf clock with Torrington type wood movt. owned by F. L. Thoms, Litchfield.

SANGAMO ELECTRIC CO.: Springfield, Ill. Org. 1926. In 1928 combined with Hamilton Watch Co. to make electric clocks. In 1930 sold to General Time Instruments Corporation of N.Y.C. "Sangamo Electric clocks made 1926–1928. Carl W. Drepperd was Vice President. Name changed to Hamilton-Sangamo Corp., and clocks electrically wound with Hamilton 7-jewel escape movts. and also synchronous motor clocks marked 'Hamilton-Sangamo Corp.'" (Dre)

SAN JOSE WATCH CO.: San Jose and Alviso, Cal. Inc. 1891, absorbed Otay machinery. Probably made no watches, but may have assembled some from Otay parts. Machinery was shipped to Japan. 1891 only. (Chamberlain)

SANSON, JOHN: N.Y.C. Case maker. d. 1847.

SARGEANT, EBENEZER: Newburyport, Mass. n/d. "No. 2" Tall clock in Lewis Dyer Col., "a 30-hour very early brass dial with cherry case." Another "made for Ensign Sanborn." (L. DYCK)

—, JACOB: 1761–1843. Mansfield, Hartford, Conn., and Springfield, Mass. Son of Samuel and Hannah Baldwin Sargeant. Marr. in 1785, and shortly after started in business as C. in Mansfield, Conn. First adv. 1784 shop south of the meeting house in Mansfield, also G. J. Seems to have moved to Springfield, Mass., ca.1787, where he continued as C. and J. and employed his younger brother, Thomas, as apprentice. In 1795 moved to Hartford and adv. 1795, "Established business at the Sign of the Golden Watch, a few rods south of the State House." Continued and became leading J. and S. in Hartford. Apparently devoted himself to Silversmithing. Adv. 1796 stated he had received a number of warranted 8-day brass clocks for sale, and some imported from London. Watches, 8-day clocks, imported. Adv. 1800, "For sale, Chime and common 8-day clocks"; Adv. 1803, "A store a few rods north of the State House." In 1813 was selling Willard's "Elegant patent timepieces." Dials of many of the imported clocks which he sold were marked with his name. A few examples of his own work are known. d. Hartford 1843. (Hoopes)

SARGENT, JOHN: Wilmington, N.C. Adv. 1821. Employed James Beckett as apprentice in 1822.

—, JOSEPH: Springfield, Mass. 1820 and after.

SARTWELL & CHAPPELL: Chautauqua Co., N.Y., also Busti, N.Y. n/d. Made Wagon-Wall and Tall clocks. One owned by C. B. Sampson of Jamestown.

SAUER, FREDERICK: West Chester, Pa. Dir. 1857–1858. (James)

SAUSSE, RICHARD: Phila. before 1778, then moved N.Y.C. "Also hardware." (MFM)

SAUTER, RICHARD: Hanover, Pa. Ca.1770.

SAVAGE (John Y.) & KUNSMAN (Henry): Salisbury, N.C. W. J. Adv. 1823 that they had a first-class workman on clocks. Were independent Watchmakers in Raleigh, N.C. (Cutten)

—, JOHN Y.: Raleigh, N.C. Adv. 1808. In Savage & Stedman, 1819–1820. In 1829 as dentist in Richmond. His Silver mark unidentified by Ensko. (Cutten)

—, W. M.: Columbus, O. Adv. 1838–1841, "Maker and expert repairer of clocks." (Knittle)

—, WILLIAM: Glasgow, Ky. "First Clockmaker in Barren Co." Kept a tavern and a cotton gin, was a blacksmith, S. and W. Aw. 1805–1820, then with Joseph and James Eubank. Approx. dates 1805–1820 William Savage, 1820–1834 Eubank & Jeffries, 1834 James Jeffries, 1834–1841 Joseph and James Eubank, 1841–1856 Joseph Eubank. (LB)

SAVOYE, N.: Boston.

SAW, WILLIAM: New Haven, Conn. *Ca.* 1840.

SAWIN & DYER: Boston. Firm of John Sawin and John Wild Dyer, 1822–1828, when Dyer met with financial reverses and the firm dissolved. Sawin continued alone. Lyre clock in Metropolitan Museum. Banjo clock in Edison Inst. Made Lyres, tablet and mirror, and Banjos. (Moore) (JWW) (BCC) (See ill. Nos. 159–161.)

—, JOHN: 1801–1863. b. Roxbury; apprentice of Aaron Willard, Jr. Sawin & Dyer at 33 Market St., now Cornhill, Boston, 1822–1828. Cs. from Me. and N.H. came to them for tools and parts. Many N.H. dealers' names on Sawin lyres. Made most beautiful of lyres. Gave up his shop in 1856 and worked at home until he died Mar. 28, 1863. Shelf clock in Edison Inst. Adv. 1829 at 33 Cornhill, "His manufacturery is now in full operation making all kinds of clocks and timepieces, such as church, gallery, bank, insurance office, counting room, alarm and parlor timepieces—8-day striking clocks, watchmakers regulators, factory watch clocks with alarms attached to them at any and every given period." Frequently employed by Simon Willard, Jr., to make clocks; made excellent ones. Principally on Court St. Adv. 1850 at 66 Court St., "and keeps a set of tools at his house in Chelsea." (See ill. Nos. 126, 147, 162.) (JWW)

—, SILAS W.: N.Y.C. *Ca.*1820.

SAWYER, C. & H. S.: Colebrook, Conn. "Henry Sawyer built a cotton mill about a 100 yards north of the mill. His brother, Charles, operated a grist mill connected with the mill by an overhead bridge. They also had a blacksmith shop on the river bank. No record of clockmaking, although a clock exists with this label." (H. H. Vining)

—, LEVERTT: 1804–1839. Salem, Mass., at 222 Essex St. W. and J. *Ca.*1830–1839.

SAXTON & LUKENS: Phila. *Ca.*1830–1840. (Moore)

—, JOSEPH: Phila. Dir. 1823–1824.

SAYRE & FORCE: N.Y.C. *Ca.*1810. Succeeded C. Brickerhoff as brass founders.

—, I. & R.: N.Y.C. 1805.

SAYRE, (John) & RICHARDS (Thomas): N.Y.C. 1802–1811. (Miller)

— & RICHARDS: N.Y.C. at 240 Pearl St. 1802–1810.

—, CHARLES: Easton, Pa. "Name on the dial of a Tall clock." (Moore)

—, ELIAS: Elizabethtown, N.J. Tall clock with Osborn dial reported. (Stow)

—, JOHN: 1771–1852. N.Y.C., at 281 Pearl St., 1796. Partner of Thomas Richard, 1802–1811.

SCHAFFER, T. C.: Portsmouth, N.H. *Ca.* 1840. Invented a fan driven by a clock movt.

SCHARF, J.: *Ca.*1778–1859. Selinsgrove, Pa. A Pillar and Scroll cased 8-day brass Shelf clock, *ca.*1830. Came from Switzerland *ca.*1810, first near Ephrata, later at Selinsgrove, Pa.

SCHEID, DANIEL: 1782–1876. Sumneytown, Pa. Had two brothers and two sisters. At 16 apprenticed to John Hagey. Worked for him for several years as journeyman, then came back to Sumneytown and started for himself. Marr. Sarah Zepp. Aw. 1809–1860. Made many Tall clocks. All his wheels he made by hand. (Morris E. Houseman, Ocean City, N.J.) (See ill. No. 51.)

SCHEIDT, —: Late 18th century; Sumneytown, Pa. (May be Scheid.)

SCHELL, SAMUEL F.: Phila. Dir. 1829–1835.

SCHEM & FALCONNET: Charleston, S.C. *Ca.* 1800.

—, J. F.: Charleston, S.C. *Ca.*1785–1790.

SCHERR, LEWIS: Phila. Dir. 1843 and later.

SCHEY, F.: Lewes, Del. n/d. Watch Paper Cramer Col.

SCHINKLE, JOHN: Phila. Dir. 1810.

SCHMALZE, F.: York Co., Pa. *Ca.*1850.

SCHMID, JOHN G.: Phila. Dir. 1850.

SCHMIDT & TAYLOR: N.Y.C. n/d. Square cased mahogany Shelf clock. Flint Sale 1926.

—, JOHN: Lakecourt, Cal. "Of London," a Dane. Patented clock "Father Time" made at Lakecourt, Cal.; now in Essex Inst.

SCHNEIDER, PETER: Pa. *Ca.*1840. Tall clock owned by Joseph V. Donahue, Jr., Flowertown, Pa.; mahogany, handmade throughout, brass movt., hour strike.

SCHOEMAKER, PETER: N.Y.C. *Ca.*1810.

SCHOLLABERGER, JOHN: Either Pa. or Md. *Ca.*1800. (LSS)

SCHOLLET, JOHN BAPTIST: Boston. Dir. 1796.

SCHOMO, (Schumo) (Scumo), THOMAS: Phila. *Ca.*1820.

SCHREINER, P., & SON: Columbia, Pa. *Ca.* 1850.

—, CHARLES W.: Phila. Dir. 1813–1833.

—, HENRY M.: Lancaster, Pa. *Ca.*1855. Grandson of Martin, son of Martin 2nd; "Skillful watchmaker, living in retirement at age 84 in 1939."

—, MARTIN AND PHILIP: Lancaster, Pa. Sons of first Martin. Because the Conn. clock killed the sale of the Tall clock, after they had been at work six to eight years they turned to making fire engines Aw. 1830–1838. (Abbott)

—, MARTIN I: 1767–1866. For over 40 years made many fine Tall clocks and numbered them. Highest known No. 356. Also with sons made "best of their time fire engines which became their main business." W. T. Brandon, LeMoyne, Pa., has No. 242; B. Schreiner, Marshfield Hills, Mass., his grandson, owns a musical Tall clock, one of only five made. (Lan. Co.)

—, MARTIN II: 1833–. Lancaster, Pa. Son of the first Martin. Also made fire engines. His son was Martin 3rd. (Lan. Co.)

—, PHILIP: Lancaster, Pa. Worked with his brother Martin II. Aw. 1830–1838.

—, THOMAS, JR.: n/d. Phila., 13 South 3rd St.

SCHULLER, J.: Phila. Dir. 1845–1846.

SCHULTZ, GOTTLIEB: Phila. Dir. 1821–1824. Dir. 1831–1844.

—, JACOB: Lancaster, Pa. *Ca.*1850.

SCHUMO (Scummo), THOMAS: Phila. Dir. 1823–1825.

SCHUYLER, P. C.: N.Y.C., at 48 John St. Adv. 1802, "Commenced business again." (Moore)

SCHWALBACH, M.: n/d. Patent No. 232,073, Sept. 7, 1880, model Smiths. Inst.

SCHWARTZ, GEORGE: York, Pa. 1775 to 1776, when he enlisted in Army. No record of return to York. (Michael)

—, PETER: York, Pa. May have been Schutz. Brother of George. 1758–1790. Tall clock with brass dial with pewter circle, No. 124 known with "Schutz" on dial. (Brix)

SCHWETZER (Schuetzer), GEORGE: Fredericktown, Md. Late 17th century. Tall, 30-hour, chain drive, Huygens type movt.

SCHWING, JOHN G.: 1783–1868. Louisville, Ky. Adv. 1803–1832. (MFM)

SCMOLTZ, WILLIAM: San Francisco, Cal. *Ca.*1850.

SCOTT (David) & ANDERSON: Greensboro, N.C. Adv. 1829 as prepared to do clock and watch work. In existence only a few months. (Cutten)

—, W. D., & CO.: Louisville, Ky. 1848–1849.

—, ANNE: Harrisburg, Pa. *Ca.*1850. C.

—, DAVID: 1797–1875. Greensboro, N.C. Adv. 1826. In Scott & Anderson, 1829. Died there 1875. "A successful business man." (Cutten)

—, JOHN: Charleston, S.C. Dir. 1803–1809. d. 1809. At 111 Broad St. (Prime)

—, JOHN: Peters Twp., or Chambersburg, Pa. Late 18th century.

—, ROBERT: Richmond, Va. *Ca.*1779. (MFM) (Baillie)

—, SAMUEL: Concord, N.C. Adv. 1825 on Main St. (Cutten)

—, THOMAS: Downington, Pa. 1834–1850. Watch in Chester Co. Hist. Soc. No clocks known. (James)

—, WILLIAM D.: Louisville, Ky. Dir. 1841. In 1843–1844 Scott & Kitts (John); alone 1845–1847; W. D. Scott & Co. 1848–1849. (LB)

SCOVILLE MFG. CO.: N.Y.C., 4 Beekman St. and 36 Park Row. Dir. 1872. "Clocks."

SCRAFTON, WILSON: Wilmington, Del. Dir. 1868, "did make clocks here." (G. Brinckle)

SCRIBNER, LEVI: N.Y.C., 74 Fulton St. n/d. Watch Paper Bir. Col.

SCROCK, JOHN M.: With John G. Fischer from Millersburg, O., a patent "Improvement in Clocks," Oct. 3, 1846.

SCUDDER, CAPT. JOHN: 1767–1848. Westfield, N.J. Made clock cases for Aaron Brokaw and other N.J. Clockmakers. One Tall clock had label, "Made & Sold by John Scudder, Cabinet Maker, Westfield, N.J." Dial marked "Wilson" on back. (Wm. R. Ross)

SEAMAN, THOMAS: Edenton, N.C. Adv. 1790 that he had imported a complete set

SEAMAN, THOMAS (cont'd)
of tools and was commencing Clock and
Watch making. Adv. to 1802. Then
possibly N.Y.C. (Cutten)

SEARS, JOHN: Chillicothe, O. Ca.1810.

SEARSALL, THOMAS: N.Y.C. Ca.1780.

SEARSON, JOHN: N.Y.C. 1757.

"SEASIDE," used by American Watch Co.
from 1886.

SEDDINGER, MARGARET: Phila. Dir. 1846.

SEDGWICK & BISHOP: Waterbury, Conn.
"1820." (Moore)

— & BOTSFORD: Watertown, Conn. Wooden
movt. clocks. Ca.1820.

SEELY & FREEMAN: Ogdensburg, N.Y. Ca.
1830. Watch Paper BCL Col.

SEGAR, DORNICK: Cleveland, O. Ca.1830.
(Knittle)

SEGER, JAMES S.: Received two patents from
N.Y.C. on "Clocks," Nov. 27, 1832, and
May 22, 1833.

SEIP (Sipe) DAVID: "near Doylestown, Pa."
n/d. A. W. Herstine, Bethlehem, Pa.,
owns Tall clock, 30-hour, endless chain
drive, single weight. (Steinmetz) Also
Northampton, Pa. (Orr)

SELF WINDING CLOCK CO.: N.Y.C. and
Brooklyn, N.Y. Ca.1888 to present.
Synchronized electric and battery clocks,
with hourly correction. Some movements
were made in Bristol by Hiram Thompson.
Self-winding Clock definition: "Runs on a
self-contained power source, usually 2
No. 6 dry cell batteries, supplying power
for motor which winds main spring once
an hour." Movements are either pendulum or lever escapement.

SELF WINDING CLOCK CO.: Bristol, Conn.
n/d. (Hist.)

SELF WINDING WATCH CO.: N.Y.C. Adv.
1887. (MFM)

SELKIRK, SAMUEL: Kalamazoo, Mich. Ca.
1850. (Dre)

SENG & HESS: N.Y.C. Dir. 1854.

SENNERT, F. L.: Lititz, Pa. Ca.1850. Tall
clocks.

SERVOSS, CHARLES: Phila. Dir. 1849.

—, JOSEPH S.: Phila. Dir. 1850.

SESSIONS CLOCK CO.: Bristol-Forestville,
Conn. Founded 1903. One of the largest
clock companies in business today. Plant
on East Main St., Forestville. This is
the continuation of the combination of

former clock companies amalgamated by
E. N. Welch in 1855, which included the
J. C. Brown interests, Manross, and the
Birge Companies. After the death of
Elisha N. Welch in 1887, the business
languished for a number of years. William E. Sessions was in the foundry
business in Bristol. In 1903 he purchased
the company, reorganized it, and made
it one of the largest modern producers
of Connecticut clocks.

SESSIONS, CALVIN: Burlington, Conn. Before 1845 operated a small clock manufactory. His three sons, Albert, John H., and
Samuel W., came to Bristol ca.1845 and
established manufacturing concerns. (LB)

—, WILLIAM E.: Feb. 21, 1857–Aug. 20,
1920. Bristol, Conn. Son of John H.
Entered father's trunk hardware business
in Bristol 1876. He and father purchased
a foundry in Bristol, and reorganized it
in 1879 as The Sessions Foundry, producing gray iron castings. (See Sessions
Clock Co.)

SEVERBERG, C.: Prob. Syberberg. (Baillie)

SEWARD: "Name on 8-day brass movt.
Lyre Wall clock." (FT) Or could be
Sawin.

SEYMOUR, BALL, & CO.: Unionville, Conn.
Ca.1830. Wood movt. Shelf clocks.
Transition type Pillar clock owned by H.
W. Hopkins, San Diego, Cal., with label
reading, "Patent Clock with Brass Bushings, Invented by Eli Terry. Mfg & Sold
by Seymour, Ball & Co."

— (H. A.) & CHURCHILL (John): Bristol,
Conn. (tx) 1846–1852. Factory cor.
Farmington Ave. and Brook St.

—, WILLIAMS, & PORTER: Unionville, Conn.
1833–1837. Began making clocks ca.1833,
till fire of 1837 burned down plant.
"Clockmaking never again flourished in
Unionville, although carried on in the
screw factory after abandonment of screw
business by Pierrepont & Co." May also
have made clocks in Farmington. Shelf
clock 33 × 18 in Flint Sale 1926. (Hist.)

—, HENRY ALBERT: 1818–. b. New Hartford, Conn. Marr. Electra Churchill 1844.
Moved to Bristol 1846 and started clockmaking in the Boardman & Wells Shop in
partnership with John Churchill, his
brother-in-law, and Ebenezer Hendrick.

Because of conflict with Nobel Jerome's patents, gave up business, and manufactured ivory and boxwood rules. Later sold to Stanley Rule & Level Co. of New Britain. Was first President, Bristol Savings Bank. (Scudder)

SEYMOURE, ROBERT: Waterbury, Conn. "1814." (Moore)

—, SYLVESTER: Pittsburgh, Pa. Ca.1840.

SHADE, DANIEL: Sumneytown, Pa. n/d. Tall clocks. Possibly Scheidt. (Orr)

—, JOHN V.: Phila. Dir. 1845–1847.

SHADFORTH, WHITACKER: Richmond, Va. Ca.1796. (MFM)

SHAEFFER, BENJ.: Elizabethtown, Pa. Ca. 1850.

SHAFFER, PHILIP: Lancaster, Pa. 1788–1802. (Bowman)

SHALLENBERGER, JNO.: n/p. Name on dial of Tall clock, brass movt., sweep 2nd hand, with "John Willbank, Phila.—1839–1841—" cast in bell; found in Richmond, Va., and owned by B. C. Waldenmaier, Washington, D.C.

SHARF, JOHN: Mifflinburg, Pa. 1820–1826. Tall clocks.

SHAW, G. & A.: Providence, R.I. 1810.

—, B. E.: Newport, Vt. Ca.1860.

—, CALEB: 1717–1791. Kensington, N.H. Lived near the shop of the Puringtons and was their apprentice. Tall clock known with "1749" date on dial. (Ant. July 1948)

—, DAVID: 1792–1882. Plainfield, Mass.

—, GEORGE: N.Y.C., at 18 Maiden Lane. Ca.1840

—, JOHN: Phila. Dir. 1819.

—, JOSEPH K.: Phila. Ca.1770.

—, P.: Olney, Ill. Adv. ca.1860 that he made clocks and watches. (Dre)

--, SETH W.: Providence, R.I. 1856.

SHEAM, FRANCIS: N.Y.C. Ca.1810.

SHEARER, MARVIN: Akron, O. Made the "Electric Wonder Clock," containing 5,000 pieces of wood and several miles of electric wiring. Exhibited Chicago World's Fair, 1933. (PG)

SHEARMAN, M.: Andover, Mass. n/d. Name on dial reported by E. L. Burt.

—, MARTIN: Hingham, Mass. 1821. (FT)

—, ROBERT: Wilmington, Del. 1768–1770. Tall clocks. "In 1768 owned 3 lots of land. Wife was Ellenor Derrickson." Phila. Dir. 1799–1804.

"SHEID": Sumneytown, Pa. Tall clocks. See Scheid.

SHEPARD & PORTER: Waterbury, Conn. Ca. 1800–1807. Noah Shepard, C.; Edward Porter, ex-minister; Levi Porter, cabinetmaker.

—, NOAH: Waterbury, Conn. "A regular clockmaker from Southford, with Edward and Levi Porter. They hired others to make their movts., fitted them up and finished them in Judge Hopkins' shop. Some movts. made by Eli Terry." (Anderson)

—, TIMOTHY B.: Utica, N.Y. Dir. 1834.

SHEPHERD, MATTHEW: N.Y.C., Charleston, S.C. Adv. 1760, "Clock and Watchmaker from London." Adv. 1774, "at Church and Tradd Sts. Cleans and repairs watches; proposes fair terms. 'No cure, no pay.'" (Prime)

—, NATHANIEL: New Bedford, Mass. Ca. 1810 a partner with Ezra Kelly in watches and clocks and clock oil.

SHEPPERD & BOYD: Albany, N.Y. 1810–1829.

SHERMAN, C. R., & Co.: New Bedford, Mass. Ca.1860.

—, ROBERT: Phila. at 339 No. 2nd St. Dir. 1799.

—, WILLIAM: Phila. Early 19th century. (MFM)

SHERMER, JOHN: Phila. at 132 No. Front St. and 384 No. 2nd St. Dir. 1803–1813.

SHERRY & BYRAM: Sag Harbor, N.Y. Adv. 1851, "Clocks for Churches, public buildings, railroad stations, etc. The subscribers having made important improvements in the apparatus for counteracting the influence of the changes of temperature upon the pendulum and in the retaining power, together with a most precise method of adjusting the pendulum to correct time . . . All clocks ordered and not proving satisfactory may be rejected."

SHERWIN, WILLIAM: Buckland, Mass., at "Clock Hollow." Ca.1830. Wood movt. Shelf clocks. (See ill. No. 204.) One owned by Harold Crosier, Shelburne Falls. B. J. Kemp of Shelburne Falls owns his clock engine. (Ant. Sept. 1938)

SHERWOOD, R.: San Francisco, Cal. Ca. 1850. See Barrett & Sherwood.

SHETHAR, SAMUEL: Litchfield, Conn. Adv. 1795. Partnership 1796–1798 with Isaac Thompson in the Red Shop as G. & S. Also repaired clocks and watches and gave cash for old brass. 50 rods west of Court House. Wanted, a journeyman who understands brass work, also wanted an apprentice. (Hist.)

SHIDE, CHARLES: Sumneytown, Pa. May have been Scheid. (W. H. Bergey)

SHIDET, V.: Shreveport, La. *Ca.*1850. (Dre)

SHIELDS, THOMAS: Phila. Adv. 1769–1776. Dir. 1785–1794. (Prime)

SHIMER, JOHN: Phila. Dir. 1811.

SHINKLE, JOHN P.: Phila. Dir. 1824–1825.

SHIPHERD, ARTHUR: N.Y.C. 1764. (Brix)

SHIPMAN, N., & SON: Norwich, Conn. Nathaniel had a son Thomas. Tall clock so marked. n/d.

—, NATHANIEL: 1764–1853. Norwich, Conn. Son of Nathaniel and Elizabeth Leffingwell Shipman. b. Norwich. Apprenticed to Thomas Harland. *Ca.*1785 set up a shop in Norwich as Clockmaker and Silversmith. His Tall clocks resembled Harland's. "It is probable that a close friendship and some measure of cooperation existed between them." Shipman settled Harland's estate. Probably made Tall clocks to *ca.*1800, when he gave up the trade, became a farmer, and investor in the West Indian trade. Occupied a position of trust in the community. Died Norwich July 14, 1853. (Hoopes)

—, THOMAS: 1796–. Norwich, Conn. Only son of Nathaniel; afterward became a clergyman. (Hoopes)

SHIPP & COLLINS: Cincinnati, O. *Ca.* 1830.

—, S. A. M.: Cincinnati, O., at 27 Main St. From Va. C. W. S. 1820. (Knittle)

SHIPPEN, WILLIAM A.: Phila. Dir. 1818–1824.

SHOEMAKER, ABRAHAM: Phila. Dir. 1846.

—, BENJAMIN: Phila. *Ca.*1800.

—, DAVID: Mt. Holly, N.J. 1802–1810. Tall clocks. (PG) (Stow)

SHORT, JOHN: –1819. Halifax, N.C. Adv. 1792, "from London, where he was apprentice . . ." (Cutten)

SHOURDS (Shrouds), SAMUEL: 1718–. Bordentown, N.J. Pro. clockmaking 1740 to 1758.

SHREINER: See Schreiner.

SHREVE, BROWN & CO.: Boston. 1856.

—, CRUMP, & LOW CO.: Boston. Predecessor Companies: Jones Lows & Ball, Dir. 1839; Lows, Ball & Co., 1840; Jones, Ball & Poor, 1846; Jones, Ball & Co., 1852; Jones, Shreve, Brown & Co., 1854; Shreve, Brown & Co., 1856; Shreve, Stanwood & Co., 1860; Shreve, Crump, & Low Co., 1869. (Buhler)

—, STANWOOD, & CO.: Boston. Dir. 1860.

—, G. C. & CO.: San Francisco, Calif. *Ca.* 1860.

SHREWSBURY CLOCK & INSTRUMENT CO.: N.Y.C. 1935–1947. Formerly the Greenwich Clock & Instrument Co. (1888–1935). Phillipse Greene (1889–1949) purchased it and changed name to above.

SHROETER, CHARLES: Baltimore. 1807–1817. (Baillie)

SHULER, DAVID C.: 1847–. Trappe, Pa. "*Ca.*1867 made about 15 clocks selling at $12 to $15, 3′ high, 8-day. He purchased the movts. and materials and in a measure assembled them. In 1901 moved to Norristown, Pa." (Orr)

—, JOHN: Phila. Dir. 1849.

SHUMAN, JOHN: Easton, Pa. *Ca.*1790. (Roberts)

SHURLEY, JOHN: Albany, N.Y. Dir. 1839–1840.

SHUTZ, GUSTAVUS: Phila. Dir. 1825–1833.

—, PETER: York, Pa. "A Swiss clockmaker." Name spelled various ways. Aw. 1758–1790. (Dre)

SIBLEY & MARBLE: New Haven, Conn. Adv. 1801, "swords and cutlasses, clocks & Watches, Math. & Surgeon's Inst. carefully repaired." Until 1807. (Hoopes)

—, ASA: 1764–1829. Woodstock, Conn. Son of Col. Timothy and Anne Wait Sibley. b. Sutton, Mass. Apprentice of Peregrine Whire in Woodstock, Conn., where he settled and carried on Clockmaking and Silversmithing. Marr. 1787 Irene Carpenter, daughter of Joseph Carpenter of Norwich, C. In 1790's moved with family to Walpole, N.H. After 1808 moved to Rochester, N.Y., where he died Feb. 25, 1829. Tall clock owned by Col. C. S. Haight, Pelham, N.Y. (Hoopes)

—, CLARK: New Haven, Conn. 1810–1817. (Hoopes)

SIBLEY, GIBBS: 1765–. b. Sutton, Mass., where he learned Clockmaking. Marr. Hannah Rice, 1788. Later moved to Canandaigua, N.Y., and carried on his trade. (Moore)

—, JAMES: Rochester, N.Y. Dir. 1847–1848.

—, RICHARD S.: Boston. Dir. 1842.

—, STEPHEN: Great Barrington, Mass. Made Tall clocks from ca.1790. One in Public Library, Lenox, Mass., made in 1816. (Benjamin Hill) (Irene M. Poirier)

SIDLE & BARTBERGER: Pittsburgh, Pa. Ca. 1840.

—, MATTHIAS & NICHOLAS: Pittsburgh, Pa. Dir. 1850. Also as individuals.

SIGOURNEY, CHARLES, JR.: Hartford, Conn. Ca.1800 imported brass clock parts, hardware, and tools.

SILL, M. & F.: N.Y.C. Ca.1840.

SILVER & WAY: Bristol, Conn. (tx) 1864–1866.

SILVERTHAW & SON: New Haven, Conn. "Established 1846." Watch Paper BCL. Col.

SIMMONS, ABEL: Buffalo, N.Y. Dir. 1836.

SIMNET, JOHN: Albany, N.Y. Adv. 1783.

—, JOHN: Boston. Adv. 1769. Adv. N.Y.C. 1770–1775, though he adv. 1771, "Dwelt in City (N.Y.C.) 4 years. Watches . . ." Adv. 1775, "Removed next to the white house lower corner of Coffe House Bridge."

SIMONS, ELIJAH: Mass. Ca.1800.

SIMONTON, GILBERT: N.Y.C. 1820. (FT)

SIMPLEX CO.: Gardner, Mass. Late 19th century. Made time recorders, using Seth Thomas movts.

SIMPLEX TIME RECORDER CO.: Gardner, Mass. 20th century. Made time clocks with long lever and punch dial.

SIMPSON, ALEXANDER: Hagerstown, Md. 1799–1805. Alone 1801; later in A. Johnson & Simpson, which dissolved 1804. (LSS)

—, JONATHIN: Ky. Made clocks ca.1820. (MFM)

—, WILLIAM: Phila. Dir. 1801.

SINCLAIR, WILLIAM: Phila. Dir. 1837.

SINDLER, ANDREW: New Church, Va. n/d.

SINGER, GEORGE: Baltimore. Dir. 1842.

SINGLETON, ROBERT: Greensboro, N.C. Adv. 1839. (Cutten)

SINNETT, JOHN: See Simnet.

SINNOTT, PATRICK: Phila. until 1760. Baltimore adv. 1761.

SINWELL, RICHARD: Pittsburgh, Pa. Shop on 5th St. between Liberty and Market. Dir. 1837.

SITWELL, RICHARD: Probably Sinwell.

SKELLHORN, RICHARD: N.Y.C. Adv. 1775, "in Beaver St. Brass Founder, Likewise Clock, Watch & Gun Work."

SKIDMORE, THOMAS: Lancaster, Pa. 1767.

SKINNER & SAWYER: Boston. n/d. Name on dial of clock reported by E. L. Burt.

—, ALVAH: Boston. Dir. 1830–1842. Two Watch Papers, Bir. Col.

—, G. M.: Montpelier, Vt. n/d. Watch Paper BCL Col.

SLICER, WILLIAM: Annapolis, Md. Adv. 1769 that he made clock cases. Tall clocks with this name known. (MFM)

SLIGH, SAMUEL: West Cahn, Pa. Taxed as W. and C. 1796–1797; as "plasterer" 1799–1800. (James)

SMART, GEORGE: Lexington, Ky. Aw. 1794–1810. Adv. 1794, "A Clock & Watch Maker from Britain; offered for sale neat assortment of 13 inch plain, double moon & seconds from the center 8 day and 30 hour Clocks." (LB)

—, JOHN: Phila. Dir. 1839, 1850, and later.

—, THOMAS: N.Y.C. Adv. 1773, "At the Sign of File & Hammer in Division St. near St. Paul's Church. Makes and Sells all sorts of clocks."

SMILEY, DAVID: Peterborough, N.H. n/d. Watch Paper Bir. Col.

SMITH, BLAKESLEY & CO.: Bristol. Ca.1840. Firm composed of Levi Smith, Augustus Blakesley, and Edwin Ray. Smith continued alone after 1842, making clocks till 1846, in what was later known as the Noah Pomeroy Shop on Federal St. Also N.Y.C. office ca.1840. (Hull)

— (Levi) & BLAKESLEY (A.): Bristol. Ca. 1830. Possibly same firm as above. Mrs. Ester Ross, Ardmore, Pa., has wood movt. OG.

— & BRO.: Phila. Dir. 1843–1844.

— & BROTHERS: N.Y.C., at 7½ Bowery. Dir. 1841.

— BROS. CLOCK ESTABLISHMENT: N.Y.C., 74 Bowery and Bowery and Division Sts. Label has picture of building still located there. Shelf clock owned by C. R. Nale, Reedsville, Pa., 28″ high, 17¼″ wide, 5¼″ deep. Roman numeral dial, gold

SMITH BROS. (cont'd)
embellishments on tablet, 30-hour wood movt., cherry case.
— & Co.: Canton, O. 1831. Clock and math. inst. makers. (Knittle)
— Co., THE: Phila., 18th and Market Sts. Started before 1850, still in business. Mostly watches. (Eckhardt)
—, E. A. (Edward) & D. T. (Daniel T.): Salem, Mass. Ca.1850.
— & FENN: Baltimore. Dir. 1842.
— & GOODRICH: Bristol. (tx) 1847–1852. Did an extensive business. At one time had four factories, one on Brook St., two on Stafford Ave. and one on East Main St. Both Samuel C. Smith and Chauncey Goodrich had been with J. C. Brown ca.1844 until forming this Company. In 1850 it was said of them, ". . . make about 15 thousand clocks annually, owning a factory, dwelling houses and some land. . . . They are doing a fair business, good industrious men, love work, and have lost by bad debts in Phila." Adv. 1851, "Smith & Goodrich, Manufacturers of all kinds of Brass and 8 Day Clocks, of the latest and best styles. All orders attended to promptly and sent to any part of the Union or the World."
Shelf clock in George B. Davis Col. has name on dial in script and "Bristol, Conn." This has reversed fuzee with line attached at largest diameter, toward front part of clock. Label reads, "Thirty Hour Spring Brass Clocks, Springs with Equalized Power, warranted not to fail, Manufactured and Sold by . . . Power Press of Elihu Geer, No. 10 State St., Hartford, Conn." 1850–1856. Ingraham type twin-steeple Shelf clock at Smiths. Inst. (EI) (LB) (See ill. No. 257.)
— & GOODRICH: Phila. Dir. 1850. See above.
— & HOLMAN: Hartford, Conn. n/d. Shelf clock owned by Mrs. Charles Phelps, N.Y.C., 30-hour wood movt., transition pillar type, with label reading, "Improved Clocks made and sold by Smith & Holman, Hartford, Conn. Warranted if well used." One in Flint Sale 1926.
—, R., & Co.: Watertown, Conn. Ca.1830; definite data lacking. Shelf clock, 30-hour wood movt., finely carved half col-

umns, carved feet, and eagle top; resembles Eli Terry, Jr., only it is plainer. One in John A. Lamond Col. (ALP)
SMITH & SEARS: Rochester, N.Y. Ca.1830.
— & SILL: Waterbury, Conn. 1831. Possibly Henry T. Smith. (Moore)
—, S. B., & Co.: N.Y.C., 3 Cortlandt St. Dir. 1854, where he was listed as "Agent of the American Clock Co." Dir. 1867 at 34 Pine St., home in N.J.
— & TAYLOR: N.Y.C. Ca.1840.
SMITH, —: Sudbury, Mass. Pos. early clockmaker ca.1640.
—, A.: Boston. Dir. 1854.
—, A. B.: N.Y.C., 7½ Bowery. Dir. 1835. Clockmaker at Bowery and Division Sts. Dir. 1840.
—, A. D.: Cincinnati, O., 12 E. 5th St., as "Smith's Old Established Clock House." Ca.1860.
—, AARON: Ipswich, Mass. "1775–1785" and "making bayonets for the Rev. Army." No further data. (Abbott)
—, B.: Phila. Dir. 1835.
—, B.: N.Y.C. Early 19th century. Name on Banjo clock, lower tablet with figure of Liberty placing wreath on head of eagle supporting American coat of arms. (Ill. in Miller)
—, C. C.: Fayetteville, N.C. Adv. 1841, "from London," 1843 sold to Edwin Glover. (Cutten)
—, CHARLES: Reading, Pa. 4th group. Early 19th century. (Steinmetz)
—, CHARLES A.: Brattleboro, Vt. Made many all wood clocks ca.1890 to ca.1940.
—, CHARLES N.: Phila. Dir. 1835–1850 and later. "Equilibrium Clock."
—, DANIEL TREADWAY: 1824–. Salem, Mass. at 262 Essex St. 1846–1864.
—, EBENEZER: Brookfield, Conn. Late 18th century. Also S. House in Brookfield still standing. Made Tall clocks with brass movts. at Brookfield and Newtown, with brass or silvered brass dials marked "EBEN'R." Much of his silver still extant. Tall 8-day brass movt. clocks owned by Floyd Thoms, Litchfield, Conn., and Jerome Jackson, Newtown, Conn. Others known. (John H. Thompson) (Jackson)
—, EDMUND: New Haven, Conn. Ca.1837.
—, EDWARD AUGUSTUS, JR.: Salem, Mass., at shop of Jesse Smith, Jr., 1850–1864.

Smith, Capt. Elisha: Sanbornton, N.H. Early 19th century.

—, Elisha, Jr.: Sanbornton, N.H. Early 19th century. Pos. apprentice of A. Hutchins. Sanbornton spelled with a "d" on some dials.

—, Ernest: Phila. Dir. 1830–1833.

—, F. C.: Phila. Dir. 1844.

—, George: Carlisle, Pa. n/d.

—, H. C.: N.Y.C., at 105 John St. Ca.1840.

—, Henry A.: Rochester, N.Y. Ca.1830.

—, Henry C.: Waterbury, Conn. Ca.1814. Later Plymouth Hollow, Conn. Ca.1840. Example Essex Inst. Shelf clocks owned by Lamar Rankin, Ocean City, Md., and H. L. Hutchinson, Ambler, Pa., with label reading, "Mfgered & Sold by . . . Keeps very accurate time."

—, Hezekiah: Phila. Dir. 1845.

—, I.: Skippackville, Pa. n/d. "Name on Tall clock dial."

—, Isaac: Phila. Dir. 1840–1843.

—, James S.: Phila., 82 No. 3rd St. Dir. 1837–1850 and later. Adv., "Wholesale Clock Establishment . . . year, month, 8-day, 30-hour, and alarm."

—, Jesse: Concord, N.H. Ca.1800. Apt. of Levi Hutchins. (Williams)

—, Jesse, Jr.: 1756–1844. Salem, Mass. Watchmaker and partner of Benjamin Balch, 1807 to 1832, when he adv. "late of Balch & Smith, removed to 10 Essex St. opp. Mr. Thompson's warehouse." 1837 at 262 Essex St.

—, Jesse Rogers: 1835–. Son of Jesse Jr. 1857–1861 at 262 Essex St.

—, John: Charleston, S.C. Adv. 1754, "moved to Elliot St., continues business of making and mending all sorts of Clocks and Watches." (Prime)

—, John: Lancaster, Pa. Ca.1800. Tall clocks. (Lan. Co.)

—, John: N.Y.C., at 90 Nassau St. Watchmaker. Dir. 1841; at 105 Fulton St., Dir. 1848.

—, John: Phila. Dir. 1835.

—, Joseph: Reading, Pa. 4th group ca.1800. (Steinmetz)

—, Joseph: Brooklyn, N.Y. Ca.1830.

—, Joseph L.: N.Y.C. (or Brooklyn), 75 Fulton St. Dir. 1841. Doubt as to whether he actually made clocks; possibly bought them in Conn. In George B.

Davis Col. a pillar Shelf clock with label of Wm. S. Sperry, 75 Barclay St., N.Y.C., has name "J. L. Smith" stamped on front plate of movt.

Smith, Josiah: 1778–1860. Reading, Pa. 4th group. Early 19th century. (Steinmetz) (Conrad)

—, Levi: Bristol. In Smith & Blakesley, ca.1840–1842; also ran livery stable. Wood movt. Shelf clocks known. Prob. made clocks in 1820's. (Hist.)

—, Luther: Keene, N.H. Ca.1785–1840. Tall clock (ill. Moore) "about the same period as T. Chandler." Made Tower clock for Keene, 1794.

—, Lyman: Stratford, Conn. "A Clock and Watchmaker, Silversmith and Jeweler; took over Nathaniel Wade's business in 1802." (Hoopes)

—, Nathaniel: Columbus, O. Made Tall clocks and movts. Ca.1814. (Knittle)

—, Philip L: Marcellus, N.Y. Shelf clock in Flint Sale 1926, "mahogany, square and round columns having carved caps, a mirror, 36 × 20½." Ca.1830.

—, Ransom: N.Y.C., at 7½ Bowery. Dir. 1848. Described in Howard Palmer's article on 8-day wood movt. Shelf clocks as one who used overlapping drive. Label on 8-day wood movt. Shelf clock owned by Mrs. H. T. Jaffery, Palmyra, N.Y., reads, "Superior 8-day clocks made and sold wholesale and retail by R. Smith, 243 Bowery, New York." May have had connection with Smith Bros. Clock Establishment. (AAJ Oct. 1949)

—, Robert: Phila. Dir. 1818–1822.

—, S.: Lyons, N.Y. Ca.1830. Watch Paper BCL Col.

—, Sam.: Brooklyn, N.Y. n/d. "Watch Mfger" on Watch Paper owned by Elsworth Gosling, Pennington, N.J.

—, S'm'l: N.Y.C. Tall clocks. Late 18th century.

—, Samuel: Phila. Dir. 1845.

—, Samuel G.: Coatesville, Pa. 1865. (James)

—, Stephen: n/d. (FT)

—, Walter C.: 1831– Louisville, Ky., Main St. Aptd. to father at Greensburg, Ky., late 1850's. (LB)

—, William: Possibly at N.Y.C., then Phila. Dir. 1818–1825. (Prime)

SMITH, WILLIAM: N.Y.C. Dir. 1810, Cabinet-maker at 48 Orchard St.

—, WILLIAM: N.Y.C. Dir. 1831, Watch-maker at 130 Bowery.

—, ZEBULON: Bangor, Me. *Ca.*1830. Watch Paper BCL Col.

SMITH'S CLOCK MANUFACTORY: N.Y.C., at Bowery and Division Sts., or 17½ Division St. Dir. 1841. Their adv. ill. in Drepperd. (AAJ Oct. 1949)

SMITTEN, R. T.: Phila. Dir. 1844–1847.

SNATT, JOHN: Ashford, Mass. *Ca.*1700. (TP)

SNELLING, HENRY: Phila. Adv. 1776, "Watchmaker from London who carries on the business at the above address [Front St.] is not, nor has been any way connected with the said Wood [John]." After this John Wood adv. that Snelling was not connected with him. (Gillingham) (Prime)

SNOW, R. R., & SON: Ripon, Wis. n/d. Watch Paper Bir. Col.

SNYDER, GEORGE: Phila. Dir. 1801.

—, PETER, JR.: Exeter Twp., Pa. 2nd Group. 1779 and later. (Steinmetz)

SOLLIDAY: Spelled in various ways, as: Salede, Solede, Sallady, Salliday, Soladay, Salida, Soliday, and Solliday. This list assumes the last form, though the others appear on dials of Tall clocks, which more than three generations of this family made in large numbers for at least three quarters of a century. Much is known about the splendid achievements in many fields by men with this name, but little about their clockmaking activities. Five brothers and possibly five or six others by this name came to America. Some of them made various types of clocks. All made Tall clocks.

— & SONS: Factory at Dublin, Pa. His-torical Society has receipt from them for clock purchased 1830. Salesroom in Doylestown.

—, BENJAMIN: Son of Frederick. Rock Hill near Sellersville, Pa., late 1700's. Brother of Jacob. Tall clock, with one weight drive, owned by Mrs. Ray Garrett, West Lawn, Pa. At least two C. sons, George and Samuel.

—, CALVIN: –1915. New Hope, Pa.; moved to Lambertville, N.J., about 1900 and opened Jewelry store and repaired Tall clocks. Son, Christopher.

SOLLIDAY, CHARLES: –1860. W. and C. at Doylestown, Pa. Son of Jacob. Watch Paper at NAWCC., Phila. Exhibit 1949.

—, CHRISTOPHER: –1941. Son of Calvin; continued store and repaired clocks after father's death till *ca.*1935.

—, DANIEL H.: –1873. Aw. Sumneytown, Pa., after 1800. Phila. Dir. 1829–1850. Watchpaper Cramer Col., "D. H., 186 Callowhill St." (See ill. No. 40.)

—, ELI: New Hope, Pa. Son of Samuel. Prob. made clocks. Tall clock reported by Lewis Dyer, "New Hope, Pa." Re-tired 1887.

—, FREDERICK: 1717–1774, or 1792. Father of Jacob and Benjamin; to America 1740; marr. 1742 Anna Maria Weisel. May have made clocks.

—, GEORGE: Rock Hill, Pa.; Son of Benj.; most of his later work in Montgomery Co. Tall clock owned by Mrs. Kenneth Keen, Greenwich, N.J., marked "Montgomery-ville." Two Watch Papers Cramer Col. spelled "SOLLIDAY – C & W Makers – Green, near 5th, Phila."

—, GEORGE, JR.: Mentioned by Orr; no further data.

—, HENRY: –1814. Towamensin, Pa. Two sons, Jacob and Samuel. Tall clock owned by Mrs. Frank Histand, Doyles-town, Pa.

—, JACOB: 1748–1815. Reading, Pa. Aw. Bedminster and Northampton, Pa. Brother of Benj. Son Peter working after Revolution to *ca.*1807. F. S. Stein-metz: "Records carefully preserved. 8-day movt. sold @ $40, 30-hr. @ $21 to $25. Cases made by local cabinetmakers to fit movts. and sold *ca.* $25 with slight variations for quality of woods and em-bellishments. Walnut and wild cherry pfd., also curly maple and mahogany. Less expensive cases of soft painted white wood." (Funk)

—, JOHN: Richland Twp., Pa. "1782"; no other data. (FT)

—, JOHN N.: 1794–1881. Reading, Pa. Adv. 1816; moved to Bucks Co. *ca.*1821; Tinicum and Point Pleasant, Pa. Made many Tall clocks; considered one of the better makers. Made musical Tall clock

1830 playing 3 tunes. Watch Paper Cramer Col.

SOLLIDAY, PETER: Son of Jacob. Continued with father 1795 to 1807, Bedminster, Pa.

—, SAMUEL: 1805–1880. Son of Benj., brother of George. Aw. *ca.*1828–1834 at Doylestown. Made at least 5 Tall clocks "of superior quality." (J. S. Bailey) When Shelf clocks ruined business *ca.*1834 moved to New Hope, Pa., where for 50 years was in coal and lumber business as well as Jeweler and clock repairer. Had son Eli.

—, WILLIAM: Pa. n/d. Tall clock owned in Lancaster, Pa.

SOLOMAN, HENRY: Boston. Dir. 1820–1825. "Patent Lever Watches made."

SOMERS & CROWLEY: Phila. Dir. 1828–1833.

—, ALBERTUS: Apprentice of George Hollinshead; succeeded him as only Clockmaker in Woodbury, N.J., *ca.*1820. Moved 1821 to Woodstown to succeed John Whitehead. Brix listed as W. Gloucester Co. 1821. (Williams)

SOUTH, JAMES: Charlestown, Mass. *Ca.* 1810.

"SOUTH BEND," used by South Bend Watch Co. 1902–1930.

SOUTH BEND WATCH Co.: South Bend, Ind. In 1902 inc. as American National Watch Co. but name changed to above almost immediately. In 1903 purchased Columbus Watch Co., Columbus, O.; voluntary liquidation 1933. Used names "South Bend," "Studebaker," "Studebaker of Canada."

SOUTHERN CALENDAR CLOCK Co.: Inc. March 2, 1875, St. Louis, Mo., by three Culver brothers at 802 Washington Ave. Mechanisms made by Seth Thomas Co. in Conn. — sturdy 8-day brass clock movt. with perpetual calendar, "practical household Clock." Two standard models, and some others. Prices from $11 to $85; $42 average. No exact record of number sold. Sales force of 100; sold direct to customer. If cash not available, 6 months' notes with 10% interest. In business till Sept. 1889, when the Culvers began making stoves. W. L. Culver revived operations for short time in 1890's. Example owned by Frank Klassi, N.Y.C. See ill. No. 265. (Coleman)

SOUTHWORTH, ELIJAH: N.Y.C. 1793–1830.

SOUZA, SAMUEL: Phila. Dir. 1819.

SOWER, CHRISTOPHER: Germantown and Phila. *Ca.*1724–1740. Talented C., also math. insts., doctor, farmer, author, printer, papermaker. Name also Souers, Sauer, Souers on clock dials. (Stretch)

—, DANIEL: Phoenixville, Pa. On Watch Paper, Chester Co. Hist. Soc., listed as Watchmaker in Schuylkill Twp., Chester Co. 1845–1849. (James)

SPACKMAN, GEORGE: Phila. Dir. 1824–1825.

SPANGLER, JACOB: Hagerstown, Md., and York, Pa. 1790–1810. Eldest son of Rudolph. Cut his clock hands to include an "S." (LSS)

—, RUDOLPH: Hagerstown, Md., and York, Pa. *Ca.*1764–1805. Father of Jacob. Tall clocks. (LSS)

—, RUDI: York, Pa. Late 18th century.

SPARCK, PETER: Phila., 86 No. 4th St. 1797.

SPAULDING & Co.: Providence, R.I. *Ca.* 1800. "Tall clocks."

—, ABRAHAM: Brooklyn, N.Y. *Ca.*1840.

—, EDWARD: 1732–1785. Providence, R.I. *Ca.*1770–1785. Tall clocks. (Ant. Aug. 1942)

—, EDWARD, JR.: Providence, R.I. *Ca.* 1800.

SPEAR & Co.: Charleston, S.C. *Ca.*1850.

—, JAMES E.: Charleston, S.C. Adv. as "Watch Dealer" 1846–1871.

SPELLIER: Doylestown, Pa., State and Main Sts. "Perfected electric tower clock." (George S. Hotchkiss)

—, AUGUST: Phila. *Ca.*1870.

SPENCE, GAVIN: N.Y.C. *Ca.*1810.

—, JOHN: Boston. Dir. 1823–1830.

SPENCER, HOTCHKISS, & Co.: Salem Bridge (now Naugatuck), Conn. *Ca.*1830.

—, WOOSTER, & Co.: Salem Bridge, Conn. "1828–1837." "8-day brass Shelf clocks." (Moore)

—, JULIUS: Utica, N.Y. *Ca.*1820.

—, NOBLE: Adv. 1796, "Lately from London at his shop in Wallingford (Conn.)." Later in 1796 moved to Stratford, Conn. where he adv. 1797, "shop a few rods south of the Church ... making and repairing Clocks and Watches. He wants to purchase Old Gold, Silver, Brass & Copper." (Hoopes)

SPERRY & BRYANT: Williamsburg, L.I. *Ca*.1850. (See ill. No. 255.) Steeple Shelf clock in Selchow Col.

— & BUNKER: N.Y.C., 272 5th Ave. Dir. 1848.

—, HENRY, & Co.: N.Y.C., 338 Broadway. Dir. 1854. Green label printed in black, "Clock and Looking Glass Manufacturers no. 18 Maiden Lane, New York." OG case, Barny Col. n/d.

— & GAYLORD: N.Y.C. Dir. 1854.

— & SHAW: N.Y.C., 10 Cortlandt St. Dir. 1848. Said to have sold clocks with labels of Chauncey Jerome. Adv. 1846 that they made 100,000 clocks a year and had large export business in England.

—, ANSON: Waterbury, Conn. Patent Aug. 22, 1814, on "Wire Pointing for Clock." "Clockmaker, not the cooper." (Anderson)

—, C. S.: N.Y.C. Dir. 1848. Pos. Mfr.

—, ELIJAH: N.Y.C., 526 Broadway. Dir. 1848.

—, F. S.: N.Y.C. Dir. 1854.

—, HENRY: N.Y.C. Dir. 1848.

—, J. T.: N.Y.C. *Ca*.1830.

—, SILAS: New Haven, Conn. *Ca*.1840.

—, TIMOTHY S.: N.Y.C., 339 Hudson St., Dir. 1848, and 25 John St., Dir. 1854. Shelf clock at Smiths. Inst.

—, WILLIAM: Baltimore. Dir. 1842.

—, WILLIAM: Phila. Dir. 1843–1849.

—, WM. S.: N.Y.C., 40 Gold St., 75 Fulton St., 70 Barclay St. Pos. Case maker. Dir. 1840 and later. Shelf clock G. B. Davis Col.

SPICE, WILLIAM: Hanover, Pa. Early 19th century.

SPILLER, JOHN: N.Y.C. *Ca*.1820.

SPOTSWOOD & Co.: Baltimore. Adv. 1785, "A. Clarke does the Watchmaking." (Prime)

SPRATT, I. M.: Epping, N.H. n/d. Yellow Watch Paper Bir. Col.

—, SAMUEL L.: Elkton, Md., prior to 1831, then sold property and tools to Thomas Howard, Jr. Business not continued.

SPRING, SOLOMON C., & Co. (or S. C. Spring & Co.): Bristol. (tx) 1864–1868. Successor of Birge, Peck, & Co.; factory located S.W. cor. Riverside and East Sts., later known as "The Codling Plant." Made Shelf clocks, including fine roller leaf

pinion movt. In 1869, S. C. Spring and Elisha Welch formed partnership as Welch, Spring & Co. Business transferred to Manross Shop on Church Ave. Shelf clock at Essex Inst. (LB)

SPRING, SOLOMON CROSBY: 1826–1906. Bristol. Worked for S. B. Terry in Terryville. Date he came to Bristol not known exactly; with Irenus Atkins at Divinity and Park Sts. In 1858 went into business for himself. Shelf clock label, "S. C. Spring, Successor to Birge, Peck, & Co., Bristol, Conn." His three brothers, Charles, Edwin, and George, worked with him. In 1868 he and Elisha N. Welch formed "Welch, Spring, & Co.," which operated successfully until 1883, when Spring sold out to Welch, though he remained with the firm. Made Shelf clocks, high grade regulators, and Calendar clocks, using Gale patents. Spring retired 1895, d. Bristol May 16, 1906. His name on clocks has caused some confusion with clocks run by springs.

"SPRINGFIELD," used by N.Y. Watch Co. *Ca*.1870.

SPRINGFIELD ILLINOIS WATCH Co., THE: Springfield, Ill. Successor 1879 to Illinois Springfield Watch Co. Made watches with names "Mason," "Miller," "Hoyt," "Currier," "Bunn." In 1885 became Illinois Watch Co.; made large numbers of jeweled movt. watches. Business sold to Hamilton Watch Co. 1927.

SPRINGFIELD WATCH Co.: Springfield, Mass. This name may have been used *ca*.1877. See N.Y. Watch Co.

SPROGELL, JOHN: –1794. Phila. Aw. 1764–1794. Adv. 1764–1799 "Watch & Clock Maker on Front St. near cor. Market or High St. Said Sprogell has worked for John Wood, the Watchmaker, to the complete satisfaction of his customers." Adv. 1779, "moved to 2nd St. and continues. . . ." Dir. 1791. Tall clocks; one with brass dial at Williamsburg, Va., one owned by Mrs. L. H. Fish, Ridgewood, N.J., and one by A. H. Darnell, Jr., Rochester, N.Y. (Gillingham) (Prime)

—, JOHN, JR.: Phila. Late 18th century.

SPRUCK, PETER: Phila., 2 No. Front St. Dir. 1794–1806. Name given also as Spruch, or Spurck.

SPYCHER, PETER, JR.: Tulpehocken, Pa. 4th group. Aw. 1784–1800 and later. (Steinmetz)

SPYERS, MOSES: Phila. Dir. 1830.

SQUIRE & BROS.: N.Y.C. *Ca.*1860.

—, HORATIO N., & SON (Geo. H.): N.Y.C., 1 Maiden Lane. "Established 1838." According to Milford B. Squire, Ashfield, Mass., watch movts. may have been imported, but his name appeared on dials and he "handled quality merchandise only."

— & LANE: N.Y.C., 97 Fulton St. Adv. 1857.

STADLINGER, JNO. R.: Buffalo, N.Y. Adv. 1891 as mfr. and jobber of clocks and watches. (MFM)

STADTER, P. B., & Co.: Baltimore, 1871. (MFM)

STANDARD ELECTRIC TIME CO.: New Haven, Conn. *Ca.*1888 made electrically wound clocks controlled by master clock, system invented by C. H. Pond. (New Haven Clock Co. catalogues)

— WATCH CO.: Syracuse, N.Y. Org. 1888; W., but 1895 turned to Silverware. (MFM)

— WATCH CO.: Minneapolis, Minn. Inc. 1893. (MFM)

STANLEY, J.: Chillicothe and Zanesville, O. 1807. (Knittle)

—, PHINEAS: Lowell, Mass. Dir. 1837.

—, SALMON: Cazenovia, N.Y. Adv. 1831. (Cutten)

STANTON FAMILY: S.s, possibly some clock or watch work. At least two families. Phineas Stanton had three sons: Daniel (1755–1781), Enoch (1745–1781), and Zebulon (1753–1828). Born and worked in Stonington, Conn. William (1772–1850) and his two sons, William P. (1794–1878) and Henry (1803–1872), worked mostly in Rochester, N.Y. (Cutten)

— & BROTHER: Rochester, N.Y. 1845–1866. (Cutten)

—, W. P. & H.: Rochester, N.Y. 1826–1845. William P. and Henry, brothers. Became in 1845 Stanton & Brother.

—, GEORGE S.: Providence, R.I. 1824.

—, JOB: N.Y.C. *Ca.* 1810.

—, W.: Providence, R.I. *Ca.*1810.

STANWOOD, HENRY B., & Co.: Boston. *Ca.* 1850. H. B. and J. D. Stanwood and G. D. Low.

STAPLES & DOBBS: N.Y.C. *Ca.* 1780.

—, JOHN L., JR.: N.Y.C. 1793.

STARK, W. T.: Xenia, O. *Ca.*1830.

STARR, FREDERICK: Rochester, N.Y. "Clock & Cabinet Factory" 1834.

—, THEODORE B.: N.Y.C. Name on dial of late Tall clock at Dartmouth Club, N.Y.C.; probably European make.

STARRETT, JAMES: East Nantmeal, Pa. n/d. Tax record as "Clockmaker" 1796–1804. (James) At Brandywine Manor as "Watch Maker." (Brix)

STATZELL, P. M.: Phila. Dir. 1845 and later.

STAUFFER (Samuel) & EBY (Christian): Manheim, Pa. Tall clocks *ca.*1800. (Bowman)

—, SAMUEL C.: 1757–1825. Manheim, Pa. Also in partnership with Christian Eby. Aw. 1785–1825. "Seems to have been proficient and paid minute detail to finish and appearance. Made several Q hour striking tall clocks which are rare." (Magee) Some Musical? No. 25 with brass dial known. (Bowman)

STEBBINS & Co.: N.Y.C. 1832. "Store, W., J., S. & Fancy Goods."

— & HOWE: N.Y.C. *Ca.*1830.

—, LEWIS: Waterbury, Conn. 1811. "A singing master, Chauncey Jerome, worked for him making dials for old fashioned clocks." (BCC)

—, THOMAS: N.Y.C., 134 Chatham St. Dir. 1830.

STECKELL, VALENTINE: Frederick, Md. Adv. 1793.

STECKMAN, H.: Middletown, Pa. *Ca.*1850. Tall clocks.

STEDMAN, JOHN C.: –1833. Raleigh, N.C. Aw. 1819–1833. In Savage & Stedman 1819–1820. Auctioneer 1821. Adv. 1822 commenced W. and S. Killed in railroad accident Nov. 11, 1833, returning from N.Y.C. (Cutten)

STEEL, JOS.: Carlisle, Pa. n/d. Tall clocks. (James)

—, R. F.: Adams, N.Y. *Ca.*1850.

—, SAMUEL: New Haven, Conn. *Ca.*1840.

—, WILLIAM: Albion, Mich. *Ca.*1860. (Dre)

STEELE & CROCKER: Hartford, Conn., 195 Main St. n/d. Watch Paper Cramer Col.

—, THOMAS: Hartford, Conn., 195 Main St. n/d. Watch Paper Cramer Col.

STEIKLEADER, JOHN: Hagerstown, Md. 1791–1793. Adv., "makes and mends all kinds . . ." (LSS)

STEIN, JACOB, & SON (George): Allentown, Pa. Tall clocks; possibly to 1840.

—, ABRAHAM: Phila., 86 No. 3rd St. Dir. 1795–1825.

—, ALBERT H.: Norristown, Pa. 1837.

—, DANIEL: Norristown, Pa. Ca.1830. (Moore)

—, GEORGE: Allentown or Northampton, Pa. Ca.1820. Son of Jacob. Tall clocks marked "Jacob Stein & Son." (Orr)

—, JACOB: 1771–1842. Allentown, Pa. Made many Tall clocks. In 1814 assessed $40 for his occupation. Father of George. (Roberts) (Orr)

STEINMAN, GEORGE: Lancaster, Pa. n/d. Possibly case maker only.

STEINSEIFFER, JOHN: 1743–. Hagerstown, Md. Ca.1777; possibly later at Williamsport, Pa. (AAJ Dec. 1948) (LSS)

STELLWAGEN, CHARLES K.: Phila. Dir. 1840–1848.

"STEM WIND, LADIES," used by Cornell Watch Co. ca.1874.

STEPHENS, T. C. & D.: Utica, N.Y. Dir. 1840–1841.

—, WILLIAM: Albany, N.Y. Dir. 1840–1842.

STEPHENSON (L. S.), HOWARD (E.), & DAVIS (D. P.): Boston or Roxbury, Mass. Ca.1849. Led to mass production of watches. See Howard & Davis, and Waltham Watch Co. (AJ Mar., Apr. 1950)

STERLING, RICHARD: So. Woodstock, Vt. "Began in 1811 to make clocks and chairs." (Hist.) (Wilder)

STERN, WILLIAM: Phila. Dir. 1820–1822.

STEVENS & HEATH: Chillicothe, O. Ca.1815. (Knittle)

—, HODGES, & CO.: N.Y.C., 1 Cortlandt St. Dir. 1872.

—, J. P., WATCH CO.: Atlanta, Ga. Dir. 1877–1887. f. U. S. Watch Co., Marion, N.J., sold to Ezra Bowman, Lancaster, Pa. In 1882 Bowman sold watchmaking machinery to J. P. Stevens, who made about 10 watches a day ca.1884. (See ill. No. 300.) Machinery resold to D. N. Freeman after production ceased. Stevens continued in sales department of business

to ca.1920. (Bowman) (Evans) (Coleman)

STEVENS & LAKEMAN: Salem, Mass. Succeeded Jabez Baldwin, 1819; dissolved 1830, with John Stevens continuing.

—, AARON: Pomfret, Conn. Late 1700's. 2 Tall clocks known with this name on dial; workmanship described as excellent. One owned by J. P. Grosvenor, Providence, R.I., cherry case, brass engraved dial.

—, B. F.: Peabody, Mass. n/d. Watch Paper BCL Col.

—, CHARLES G.: N.Y.C. Ca.1840.

—, E.: West Springfield, Mass. Ca.1800. Tall clocks reported with wood movts.

—, GEORGE M.: Boston. Name on Tower clocks in 1880's. One at Roslindale, another at Groveland, Mass. (AJ Feb. 1950)

—, J. P.: Utica, N.Y. Dir. 1837–1838.

—, JOHN: Bangor, Me. Ca.1840.

—, JOHN: New Haven, Conn. Ca.1840.

—, JOHN: Salem, Mass. Stevens & Lakeman 1819–1830; then alone at 1 Holyoke Place.

—, M.: Chillicothe, O. 1815. (Knittle)

—, S.: Lowell, Mass. Dir. 1853.

STEVER (J.) & BRYANT: Burlington, Whigville, Conn. Ca.1845. Built large shop, but later failed. Labels marked "Bristol." Mentioned as at Bristol ca.1830, but this may be error. (Hist.)

— (J.) & HILL (Wm. S.): Bristol; shop in S. E. Root factory, School St.; (tx) 1852–1856.

— (J.) & PRINDLE: Burlington, Conn. n/d. (pos. 1850's). Labels on Shelf clocks marked "Bristol."

— (J.) & WAY (John A.): Bristol. (tx) 1864–1866.

STEWARD, AARON: Phila. Dir. 1843.

STEWART & CO.: Phila. Dir. 1824.

—, ARTHUR: N.Y.C. Ca.1820.

—, DANIEL: 1734–1802. Salem, Dorchester, Fitchburg, Mass. d. Fitchburg June 2, 1802. Estate inventory included clock tools, parts, four partly completed clocks, and one complete clock.

—, GEORGE: Phila. Dir. 1837.

—, JAMES: Baltimore, Baltimore St. Adv. 1792. (Prime)

—, WILLIAM P.: Funkstown, Md. Adv. ca. 1820.

STICHLER, JOHN: Marietta, Pa. *Ca.*1850.

STICKNEY, MOSES: Boston. 1823. (Moore)

STILES (Samuel) & BALDWIN (Jedidiah): Northampton, Mass. 1791–1792. (Cutten)

—, SAMUEL: Northampton, Mass. 1785. *Ca.*1795 pos. to Windsor, Conn.

STILLAS, JOHN: –1793. Phila. Adv. 1783, "opened a shop in Front St. . . . elegant assortment of Clocks, Watches, & Jewelry." To Baltimore 1790.

STILLMAN, BARTON: Burlington, Conn. Aw. 1790–1795; Westerly, R.I., *ca.*1810 or 1820, pos. later. Bro. Paul. A. P. Sherwood, Bayside, L.I., owns Tall clock, solid mahogany Sheraton case with inlay, broken arch hood, name and "A.D. 1814" cut in back of strike cam.

—, IRA: Newport, R.I. *Ca.*1830.

—, PAUL: 1782–1810. Aw. *ca.*1803–1810. Son of Joseph and Eunice Stillman. Family all inventors, excellent craftsmen. Cousin William Stillman to Westerly 1793; pos. his apt. Succeeded by bro. Barton. (Bul.)

—, DEACON WILLIAM: 1767–. Pos. Burlington, Conn., *ca.*1786–1791. Westerly, R.I., aw. 1793. "Hired a young man [pos. Paul] who served his time at goldsmithing and silversmithing." "Made a comfortable living till Embargo of 1809." Tall clocks reported, brass and wood movts. Patent 1801 for "Veneering Plough" which "cut grooves in wood." (Bul.) (TP)

STILLSON, DAVID: Rochester, N.Y. *Ca.*1830.

STOCKTON, SAMUEL W.: Phila. Dir. 1823–1831. Pos. N.Y.C., *ca.*1840.

STODDARD & KENNEDY: N.Y.C. 1794.

STODDARD, —: Litchfield, Conn. "Another clockmaker, who in the 1820's specialized in Shelf clocks." (S. A. Beckwith)

STOKEBERRY, GEORGE: Phila. Dir. 1837.

STOKEL, JOHN: N.Y.C. 1820–1843.

STOLL & FUNK: Lebanon, Pa. *Ca.*1850.

—, GEORGE: Lebanon, Pa. *Ca.*1850.

STOLLENWERCK & BROS.: N.Y.C. *Ca.*1820.

—, P. M.: Phila. Dir. 1813–1814. N.Y.C. 1815–.

STONE, EZRA: Boston, Dir. 1810.

—, J. W.: East Randolph, Vt. n/d. Watch Paper Cramer Col.

—, WILLIAM G.: Somers, N.Y. Adv. 1809.

STONER (STEINEN), RUDI: 1729–1769. Aw. 1753–1769, Lan. Co. (Lan. Co.)

STORRS (Nathan) & COOK (Benj. F.): Northampton, Mass., 1827–1833. Branch store Amherst, 1829. (Cutten)

—, C. D.: Portland, Me., "cor. Clark and Summer Sts." on paper inside clock owned by Helen G. Buzzell, Maplewood, N.J. n/d.

—, N.: Utica, N.Y. Early 19th century. Tall clocks. One with maple inlaid case, 12″ enameled dial at Metropolitan Museum. (See ill. No. 46.)

—, NATHAN: Northampton, Mass.: Adv. 1791. Partner 1792–1794 Baldwin (Jedidiah) & Storrs. Partner 1827–1833 Storrs & Cook. (Cutten)

—, THOMAS: Boston. Dir. 1803.

STORY, GUSTAVUS: Lebanon, Pa. n/d.

STOUT, SAMUEL: 1756–1795. Princeton, N.J. Aw. *ca.*1779–1795. Prob. only S. (Williams)

STOVER & KORTWRIGHT: N.Y.C. n/d. Name on Tall clock dial.

STOW, D. F.: N.Y.C. *Ca.*1830.

—, P. M.: Phila. *Ca.*1810.

—, SOLOMON: N.Y.C., Southington, Conn., 1823. Cabinetmaker. C. Aw. 1828. Built dam 1834 for water power. With Seth Peck & Co. 1837 making tinning machines. Pillar and Scroll clocks, one owned by Mrs. W. Wiley, Massapequa, L.I.

STOWE, L. G.: So. Gardner, Mass. n/d. Watch Paper BCL Col.

STOWEE, FREDERICK: Phila. Dir. 1802–1803.

STOWELL & SON: Charlestown, Mass. *Ca.*1845. Name on Tower clock movt.

—, A.: Charlestown or Boston, Mass. *Ca.*1850.

—, ABEL: Worcester, Mass., Boston, *ca.*1800 to *ca.*1820. Father of Abel, Jr. Tower and house clocks. One Tower clock for Worcester Old South Meeting House *ca.*1800.

—, ABEL, JR.: Boston. *Ca.*1820–1856. Son of Abel. Tower clocks; one 1852 for Codman Sq. Church, Dorchester, Mass., bell by Revere & Son.

—, JOHN: Charlestown, Mass. 1825–1836. (Abbott)

—, JOHN: Boston and Medford, Mass. 1815–1825. Abbott lists two Cs.

—, JOHN J.: Boston and Charlestown, Mass. *Ca.*1831. (Moore)

STOY, GUSTAVUS: Lancaster, Pa. Adv. 1806, "Carries on his business of Clock & Watch making." Later Lebanon, Pa. (Lan. Co.)

STRAEDE, CHARLES: Lititz, Pa. *Ca.*1850. Tall clocks. (Dre)

STRATTON, CHARLES: Worcester and Holden, Mass. Looking glass clocks *ca.*1830–*ca.* 1840. Shelf clock, wood movt., in G. B. Davis Col., label, "Extra Clocks / manufactured & Sold / Wholesale & Retail by / Charles Stratton / Worcester, Mass. / 1841 / The Public may rest assured that CLOCKS made at this factory are superior to any made in this Country. / Lewis Metcalf, Printer, 15 Central Exchange, Worcester, Mass." / Large type date "1841" similar to those of D. Pratt. Two Shelf clocks in Flint Sale 1926, one "Worcester," other "Holden, Mass."

"—, FAYETTE," used by U. S. Watch Co. *ca.*1868.

STREETER, GILBERT L.: Salem, Mass. W. Lived 1846 at 38 Summer St. Publishing business 1850.

STRETCH: Famous name early Phila. Clockmaking. Data largely based on research of Miss Caroline Stretch, Albert L. Partridge, Harrold Gillingham, and others.

—, ISAAC: Phila. Aw. 1732. Adv. 1752. Prob. C., W., Stretch's Corner. Grandson of Peter.

—, PETER: 1670–1746. Phila. b. Leek, Eng. Aptd. to uncle Samuel Stretch in Leek, Eng. Knew work of great English Cs. To Phila. 1702. Sons Daniel, Thomas, William. Quaker. Tower and Tall clocks, brass movts., 30-hour, one weight, 8-day. Some cases (one flat top hood by William Savery). Made or took care of Phila. Town Clock 1717. Shop cor. Front and Chestnut Sts., famous "Peter Stretch's Corner." Clientele included most of prominent families. *Ca.*25 Tall clocks known. Those made 1702–1705 one hand; minute and seconds hands added by 1710. Flat top cases; domed top hoods used by 1720. "In Phila. he rapidly acquired substance and became a factor in social and political life of the City." Tall clocks owned by E. W. Zelley, Haddonfield, N.J., Elizabeth R. Lippincott, Riverton, N.J., and E. K. Tryon, Phila. (ALP)

STRETCH, SAMUEL: –1732. Phila. Aw. 1711–1732. Son or nephew of Peter Stretch. From Leek, Eng. 1711. Admitted as Freeman to Phila. 1717. Noted maker of lantern clocks Eng. *ca.*1660.

—, THOMAS: –1765. Phila. b. Eng. Son of Peter. C. W. Watches with his name reported; Tall and Tower clocks; seven Tall clocks known. Sold Front St. corner after 1746, opened shop 2nd and Chestnut Sts. A founder Penna. Hospital. Pos. succeeded by Edward Duffield. Robbery Hopewell Twp. 1782, "Among the articles taken was a very good plain silver watch, engraved No. 25, Thos. Stretch, Phila." Tall clocks owned by Mrs. F. C. Henkels, Phila., Mrs. B. Kane, Phila.; one in Governor's Palace, Williamsburg, Va.

—, WILLIAM: Phila. b. Eng. Aw. *ca.*1720–1755. Son of Peter. "Also a clock maker." Two Tall clocks known.

STRIEB, C. H.: Wooster, O. 1822–1847. (Knittle)

STRIEBY, GEORGE: Pa. n/d. (Orr)

—, MICHAEL: Greensburg, Pa. Pos. Lampeter, Pa. *Ca.*1790–1830. Tall clocks. Tall clock owned by Mrs. G. D. Stoll, Mechanicsburg, Pa. (LB)

STROMBERG ELECTRIC CO.: Chicago. Active business today.

STRONG, PETER: 1764–1797. Fayetteville, N.C. Aw. 1788–1797. "Clock and Watch Maker." Apts. Joseph Gale –1788, Alexander Campbell –1793. (Cutten)

"STUART," used by Illinois Springfield Watch Co. 1870.

—, JAMES: Phila. Dir. 1837–1850.

—, THOMAS: Phila. Dir. 1839.

"STUDEBAKER," used by South Bend Watch Co. 1903–1930.

"— OF CANADA," used by South Bend Watch Co. 1902.

STUDLEY, DAVID: Hanover, Mass. Apt. John Bailey *ca.*1806. Adv. 1834 No. Bridgewater and Brockton, Mass., "Came from Hanover, made watches & jewelry and Repaired Clocks." Later with bro. Luther; sold out to him. Mass. Shelf clock ill. No. 132. (DKP) (BCC)

—, LUTHER: No. Bridgewater or Brockton, Mass. 1840's. With bro. David; later bought business.

STUMP, JOSEPH: Reading, Pa. Early 19th century. 4th Group. (Steinmetz)

STUNTZ, C. W., & KEATH, T. C.: Pittsylvania, Va. n/d. Watch Paper BCL Col.

STURGEON, SAMUEL: Shippensburg, Pa. *Ca.* 1810. (Dre)

STURGIS, JOSEPH: Phila. Dir. 1813–1817.

STUTSON, JAMES: Rochester, N.Y. Dir. 1838.

SUFFOLK WATCH Co.: N.Y.C., 37–39 Maiden Lane. Adv. 1901. "Factory in Boston."

SUGGS, G. W., & Co.: Yorkville, S.C. n/d. Wood 30-hour movt., half-column Shelf looking glass clock, name on label, owned by W. F. Hall, Jr., Statesville, N.C.

SULEY, JOHN: Baltimore. 1810–1812.

SULLIVAN, C. D., & Co.: St. Louis, Mo. *Ca.* 1850.

—, J. T.: St. Louis, Mo. *Ca.*1850.

SUMMERHAYS, JOHN: N.Y.C. *Ca.*1810.

SUMNER, WILLIAM: Boston. "July 28th, 1684. Agreed with Wm. Sumner, blacksmith, to pay him 41ds. in mony to keepe the clocke at ye North end of the Towne for one yeare to begin the 1st of Augt. next and to pay him for worke done about sd clocke the yeare past, 14 s mony." (Boston Town Records)

SUTTON, ENOCH: Boston. Dir. 1825–1842.

—, ROBERT: New Haven, Conn., 30 State St. Adv. 1825, "Continues to carry on his business at the old stand of the late Simeon Joscelyn—died 1823—where clocks, Patent Lever, Horizontal, Repeating & Plain Watches are repaired." Watch Paper Cramer Col.

SWAIM, JAMES: Phila. Patent June 29, 1833, on "Astronomical Machine."

SWAIN, REUBEN: Kensington, N.H. Bought blacksmith shop of John Gilman 1778. Pos. C. (Ant. July 1948)

SWAN, B. & M. M.: Augusta, Me. n/d. Watch Paper Cramer Col.

—, BENJAMIN: 1798–1867. Haverhill, Mass., Augusta, Me. Apt. of Frederick Wingate. Pos. Haverhill *ca.*1810. Tall clocks, 8-day brass movts. Two in Floyd Thoms Col. marked "Augusta." Tall clock owned by Mrs. G. C. Putnam, Westfield, N.J. (Crossman) (Mrs. J. B. Mason)

—, JUSTUS: Richmond, Va. *Ca.*1819. (MFM)

SWAN, MOSES M.: Augusta, Me. *Ca.*1840. Son of Benjamin; with him.

—, TIMOTHY: Suffield, Conn. 1787–1795. (Hoopes)

SWARTZ, A'B'M.: Lower Salford, Pa. n/d. Tall clocks. (Conrad)

—, PETER: York, Pa. *Ca.*1790.

SWAYNE, E. J.: N.Y.C., 34 Dey St. *Ca.*1830. "Agent" on label in 8-day wood movt. Shelf clock, alarm, and "fancy pendulum," owned by Mrs. J. C. Jarvis, Butler, N.J.

SWEET, JAMES S.: Boston. Dir. 1842.

SWENEY, THOMAS: Phila. *Ca.*1850. Banjo and Regulator clocks. (Dre)

SWIFT, JOHN D.: Cazenovia, N.Y. Adv. 1816–1821. (Cutten)

SYBERBERG, CHRISTOPHER: Charleston, S.C., "on Broad St. fronting Union." Adv. 1757, 1768. N.Y.C. 1756, "Watchmaker, lately imported neat silver & pinchbeck watches, sell reasonable for ready money." Adv. Dec. 27, 1756, "Robbed." (Prime)

SYDERMAN, PHILIP: Phila. Dir. 1785–1794.

SYMMES, CLEADON: Newton, N.J. Aw.1789. Bro. Daniel. Later Ohio. S. (Williams)

—, DANIEL: 1772–1827. Walpack Twp. or Newton, N.J. Son, apt., of Timothy. Aw. 1792. Sold out 1793. To Ohio to join uncle, Judge John Cleves. Lawyer, Cincinnati, O., 1802. (Williams)

—, TIMOTHY: 1744–1797. Walpack Twp. and Newton, N.J. b. Aquebogue, L.I. Son of Rev. Timothy and Mary Cleves Symmes. Apt. of Elis Pelletreau, Southampton, L.I. Marr. Abigail Tuthill 1765. Farmer, judge, S. To Newton 1780; later to Ohio. Pos. some Clockmaking with son, Cleadon. (Williams)

TABER, ELNATHAN: 1786–1854. Roxbury, Mass. b. Dartmouth, Mass. Son of Thomas and Elizabeth Swift Taber. Bro. Stephen. Quaker. C. Aw. 1784. Apt. of Simon Willard ("his best"); life-long friends. Marr. Catherine Partridge 1797. Shop, described as "a very pretty one, dwelling with garden and cherry trees in front," on Taber St. (renamed for him). Tall, Mass. Shelf, Banjo clocks; tablets prob. painted by Charles Bullard. "Tireless worker." Given privilege of marking "S. Willard's Patent" on Banjo clocks. Bought Willard's business, tools, good

TABER, ELNATHAN (cont'd)
will. Clocks for S. Willard, Jr., 1838–
1854. Some Banjo clocks sold for $16.
Succeeded by son Thomas. Tall clock in
Edwin Hale Abbot, Jr. Col. (JWW)
(BCC) (See ill. Nos. 125, 130.)

—, H.: Boston. Ca.1850.

—, J.: Saco, Me. Ca.1820. N.H. Mirror
long Wall clock.

—, STEPHEN N.: 1777–1862. Aw. New Bedford, Mass., Providence, R.I. Ca.1798–
ca.1825. Tall clocks. Bro. Elnathan.
(See ill. No. 85.)

—, THOMAS: 1797–1878. Son and successor
of Elnathan. No clocks known. Marr.
Harriett Wyman. (Sister marr. Isaac
Wyman, name on dials of Roxbury Banjo
clocks.) (JWW) (BCC)

TABOR, L. A.: Holyoke, Mass. Ca.1860.

TAF, JOHN JAMES: Phila. Dir. 1794.

TALBOT, SYLVESTER: Dedham, Mass. Ca.
1815–1817.

TALLMADGE, ELLIOTT: Wolcottville, Conn.
Tall clock reported by Paul Hollinshead,
Youngstown, O.

TAPPAN, J. F.: Manchester, pos. N.H. or
Mass. N.H. Mirror clock known. No
Tappans in Manchester, N.H., some in
Mass. (BCC)

—, WILLIAM B.: Phila. Dir. 1818–1819.

TAPPEN, JOHN: Flemington, N.J. 1839–
1843. (PG)

TARBELL, EDMUND: Boston. Dir. 1842.

TARBOX, H. & D.: N.Y.C. Ca.1830.

TARRELL, SEBASTIAN: n/p. n/d. Tall clock
in W. Michael Col., engraved dial.

TAWS, CHARLES: Phila. Dir. 1802. Insts.
Pos. C.

TAYLOR (John) & BALDWIN (Isaac): Newark,
N.J. Ca.1825. (Williams)

—, GEORGE, & Co.: Providence, R.I. Ca.
1875. "Makers of banjo, wall, and other
clocks." "Banjos resembling Howard,
name on movt. and serial No. on all parts."
(H. M. Baker) (E. A. Battison)

— (John) & HINSDALE (Horace Seymour):
Newark, N.J. Ca.1810.

—, P. L., & Co.: Brooklyn, N.Y., 9 Fulton
St. Ca.1830. Ex. Museum City of N.Y.

—, ANDREW: N.Y.C. Dir. 1854.

—, CHARLES: Sedalia, Mo. Ca.1870. (Dre)

"—, H. H.," used by National Watch Co.
ca.1867.

TAYLOR, HENRY: –1760. Phila. Tall clock,
brass dial, moon, days, walnut case, in
Penrose Hoopes Col.

—, JOHN: Aw. ca.1773–ca.1816. C. Aw.
before Rev. War. Enlisted from Mt.
Holly, N.J. Later York, Pa. Among
Capt. Spangler's Volunteers, who marched
from York to Baltimore Aug. 1814 to op-
pose British at No. Point. Repaired
Jessop clock in Michael Col. (Michael)

—, JOSEPH: York, Pa. Ca.1785.

—, LUTHER: Phila. Dir. 1823–1835.

—, NOAH C.: Salisbury, N.C. Adv. opened
shop 1844. (Cutten)

—, RICHARD: Boston. Boston Town Records
No. 11, 1657: "Richard Taylor is allowed
30 shillings for repairing the clock for his
direction to ring by, and is to have five
pounds per annum for the future provided
hee bee att charges to keepe a clock and
to repayre itt."

—, RICHARD: York, Pa. Ca.1785.

—, SAMUEL: Phila., Water and High Sts.
Dir. 1798–1799.

—, SAMUEL: 1780–1864. Worcester, Mass.
C. Dir. "S. E. Taylor." Partner Jona-
than Barker to 1807; alone to 1856. Not
Samuel E. Taylor of Bristol.

—, SAMUEL E.: Bristol. Partner Birge,
Peck & Co. (tx) 1849–1858. Shop in
Forestville, where he made clock verges,
other clock parts.

—, W. S.: Troy, N.Y. Dir. 1847–1849.

—, WILLIAM: Buffalo, N.Y. Dir. 1835.

TAZEWELL, S. S.: Bridgeton, N.J. Ca.1864–
1868. Tall clocks.

TEMPLETON, ROBERT: Newport, R.I. Ca.
1785.

TENNENT, THOMAS: San Francisco, Cal.
Ca.1850. (TP)

TENNEY, WILLIAM: Nine Corners, now
Washington, N.Y. Tall clocks ca.1790.
(Moore) (Arthur Stout)

TERHUNE & BOTSFORD: N.Y.C., 50 Cortlandt St. "Corner of Greenwich, Warranted Good. D. Murphy, Book & Job
Printer, 153 Water St., & 384 Pearl St.
N.Y." Label in OG clock, brass weight,
movt. stamped "Chauncey Jerome, New
Haven, Conn." Case pos. made by this
firm in N.Y.C. John T. Collins Col.

— & EDWARDS: N.Y.C., 48 Cortlandt St.
in 1860's; 18 Cortlandt Dir. 1872. Shelf

clock, 30-hour wood movt., Conn. type, known.

TERHUNE, H.: N.Y.C., Warren St., W. of Broadway. Dir. 1853.

TERNBACH, M.: St. Louis, Mo. *Ca.*1830.

TERRY, —: Famous name in Conn. clock history and U.S. industrial development. *1792–ca.*1870. Authoritative articles based on personal research by Albert Partridge, Penrose Hoopes, Lockwood Barr, Charles Terry Treadway, and others.

— (Ralph, Theo.) & ANDREWS (F. C.): Bristol, "Old Bit" Shop, Frederick St. (tx) 1842–1850. Made Shelf and gallery type clocks, later bit braces. Sales agency N.Y.C., 3 Cortlandt St. Report 1850, "R. & T. Terry of Bristol and F. C. Andrews of N.Y.C. They make say 30 or 40 thousand clocks annually. They own as partners and as individuals good and valuable real estate and it is all clear. They are called as safe a firm as any in town, pay well, you can trust them all they ask for. . . ." Excellent 8-day brass lyre-shaped movts. (EI)

— (Theo.) & BARNES (Horace): Boston, 123 Washington St. Dir. 1854, "Clocks and Mirrors."

— (Theo.) & BARNUM (P. T.): Bridgeport, Conn. *Ca.*1850–1855. Brass movt. clocks. Merged with Jerome Mfg. Co., later f. Terry into oil business in Pa. (AAJ Sept., Nov. 1949.)

— CLOCK CO.: Winsted, Conn. Org. after 1852 by sons of Silas Burnham Terry. With father produced unusual clocks. Silas B. head of firm till 1876; sons to Pittsfield, Mass. Mahogany wall clock Flint Sale 1926 marked "Plymouth."

— CLOCK CO.: Pittsfield, Mass. Org. by George Bliss 1880 with sons of S. B. Terry. Reorg. 1884 as Russell & Jones Clock Co.

— CLOCK CO.: Waterbury, Conn. Pos. such a firm existed. (FT)

— (R. E.) & DOWNS (George): Bristol. (tx) 1853–1856. Succeeded Terry, Downs & Burwell. Factory burned.

— (R. E.), DOWNS (Franklin, George) & BURWELL: Bristol, Downs St. (tx) 1851–1852. In E. Downs shop. Brass 8-day clocks invented by Ralph E. Terry and Hiram Camp. Succeeded by Terry & Downs.

TERRY, ELI, JR., & CO.: n/d. Name on clock label as successors to H. Welton & Co. (G. B. Davis Col.)

—, ELI, JR., & HENRY: Plymouth, Conn. *Ca.*1822. Label reported.

—, ELI & SAMUEL: Plymouth, Conn. 1824–1827. Bros. Fine Pillar and Scroll clocks label, "Patent Clocks / invented by Eli Terry / Made and Sold at Plymouth, / Conn. / by Eli & Samuel Terry / warranted etc."

—, E., & SON: Plymouth, Conn. 1825–1836. After 1836 Henry Terry continued business alone; Eli, Jr., and S. B. Terry on their own. "Henry Terry" label also known.

—, E., & SONS: Plymouth, Conn. 1818–1824. Eli, Sr., Jr., Henry. Pillar and Scroll clocks in volume; label, "Patent Clock / Invented by Eli Terry / made and sold at Plymouth, Conn. / by / Eli Terry & Sons / warranted if well used / The Public may be assured etc." Printed by "Goodwin & Co. Hartford, Conn."

—, R. (Ralph) & J. B. (John Burnham): Bristol. 1835–1836. Took over Samuel's business. Shelf clocks, 8-day, 30-hr. wood and brass movts.; label, "Eight Day / Brass / Clocks / mfg. by / R. & J. B. Terry / Bristol, Conn." Succeeded by Terry & Andrews.

—, S. B., & CO.: Terryville, Conn. Late 1840's. One of Silas Burnham Terry's firms.

—, THOMAS & HOADLEY: Greystone or Plymouth, Conn. "1809." Name first in Moore. Prob. Eli Terry, Seth Thomas, Silas Hoadley. Wood movt. Tall and Hang-up clocks. Dials so marked seen; none known. After Terry left, Thomas and Hoadley formed partnership; Tall clocks dials marked "Thomas and Hoadley" are extant. (See ill. No. 66.)

—, ELI: April 13, 1772, E. Windsor, Conn.; Feb. 24, 1852, Terryville. Son of Samuel and Hildah Burnham Terry. First American to actually produce clocks in volume. Invented and perfected wood movt. Shelf clock. Master of difficult horological principles. Nine patents 1797–1845. Fine Tower clocks. Good business man. Made and merchandised large numbers of clocks. Initiated important principles. Apt. to master Conn. C., Daniel Burnap, East Windsor, Conn.; pos. also

(289)

some instruction from Timothy Cheney, East Hartford. (Hoopes) Aw. 1792, East Windsor; Tall clocks. To Northbury (now Thomaston and Plymouth) 1793, clocks, engraving, repairing clocks and watches; Brass and wood movts. known. Marr. Eunice Warner 1795. Made own tools for quantity mfr. of clocks. First patent 1797 "equation clock," showed apparent as well as mean time. By 1800 (pos. one or two workmen) making several wood movt. clocks at a time; used waterpower-driven saws. Contract ca.1806 with Levi and Edward Porter of Waterbury to make the then unheard-of number of 4,000 wood "hang-up" clock movts. (see ill. No. 67), dials, and hands. Sold shop on Plymouth hill; to Hoadleyville, Ireland or Greystone near Waterbury line, for more waterpower.

Invented machine to cut gear wheel teeth. Label, "Clocks / Made by / ELI TERRY / for / Levy G. and E. Porter / and warrented if cased and well used. / Let the Clock be set in perpendicular position. This is necessary, in order to have its having an equal beat; and if it fails to beat equally, it may be put in beat by raising one or the other side of the Clock. And having found the right position, there let it be fastened. If the Clock goes too fast, lengthen the pendulum; but if too slow, shorten it by means of the screw at the bottom. / If the hands want moving, do it by means of the longest, or by turning the face wheel on the time side of the Clock; turning, at any time, forward, but never backwards, when the Clock is within 15 minutes of striking; nor farther than to carry the longest hand up to figure XII. So, in Clocks which shew the day of the month, the hand, if it varies from the truth, may be put forward with the finger. And if the Clock fails to strike the proper hour, press downward, with your finger, the small wire on the striking side of the Clock, and it will strike as often as you repeat the pressure. / Keep the Clock as much as possible from dust, and apply no oil, at any time, to it, unless it be a very small quantity of sweet oil, or the oil of Almonds, with a feather,

to the brass or crown wheel./ Waterbury, Conn." These movts. were housed in Tall cases, or used as "Hang ups" or Wag-on-Walls; many of these were cased later. All 4,000 clocks for Porters finished by 1809-1810. Joined in this work by Seth Thomas and Silas Hoadley to whom he sold Greystone plant 1810; returned to Plymouth Hollow. Simon Willard had patented "Improved Timepiece" 1802. Terry ca.1808 determined to produce Shelf clock less expensive than Tall clock. Worked out gear ratios, to run clock 30 hrs. with 20" weight fall and overcame problems of friction. First model of Shelf timepiece, housed in hood like that of Tall clock, in Charles Terry Treadway Col. Successful by ca.1814. Patent June 12, 1816, signed by Pres. James Madison. The strap wood movement in this clock (ill. No. 179), with rack and snail strike control, has escape wheel and pendulum in front of front plate (never done before). (Ill. No. 181.)

According to patent, "... The Construction and plan and how it differs from other clocks is as follows: ... The swing wheel, pallet, crutch, and pendulum are placed between the dial plate and the hands in equal distance from the glass, and all move and vibrate on the same plane. The pallet, on what the wooden Clockmakers call the verge, is not fixed on an arbour, as in other clocks, but has a small hole through it and turns on a small steel pin, which is fastened to the dial plate under side the swing wheel ..." To insure extra inches for weight fall, Terry compounded cords and placed fixed pulley each side of movt. at top inside of case. Patent said, "... The weights run one on each side of the clock, the whole length of the case. The cords or lines on which the weights hang go *to the top* of the case over a pulley, thence down to the barrel of the cylinder of the clock. The pendulum is hung under the centre socket and the swing wheel pivot turns in a bridge which is pinned or screwed to the dial plate and can be taken off, and the swing wheel taken out and cleansed without taking any more of the work apart ..." Before this the weights fell directly down from movt., as in Tall and Banjo clocks.

Patent said about the case, ". . . The Clock is fixed in a case about 20 inches long, 14 inches wide, and 3 inches in depth on the thickness; the door or sash of which is the full length and width of the case, there is no face except the glass, the dial figures and hands are on or near the inside of the glass; the dial plate is a frame or open work, so that the whole movement, weights, pendulum, bell, and all are in full view . . ."

Patent covered both wood and brass movts., ". . . the main time wheel turns the centre arbour by a small centre wheel with 24 teeth in the *brass clock*. Both main wheels in the brass clocks have 72 teeth . . . The swing wheel both to brass and wooden clocks have 60 teeth . . . The two main pinions to brass clocks have 12 leaves each . . . The two main wheels to the wooden clocks have 54 teeth . . ."

Terry continued to improve Shelf clock. Second movt. (ill. No. 180) had large round count wheel in center, replacing rack and snail, to control striking. The Pillar and Scroll clock was first made in model (ill. No. 182) called "Outside Escapement"; escape wheel and pendulum were in front of dial. Jerome asserted he made first one for Eli Terry winter of 1816. Perfectionist that he was, Terry continued to perfect minor troubles. Next prob. "Inside/Outside" *ca*.1818 (ill. No. 186), though picture is of a Seth Thomas. Then prob. "Off Center" (ill. No. 184); lastly *ca*.1818–1819 "Standard" (ill. No. 185); in this clock movt. and inside arrangement (ill. No. 187) he used for the first time vertical weight channeling strips devised also to support dial. This clock completely successful; many still running.

Prob. originated Pillar and Scroll case (see *New York Sun* August 22, 1947). Charles Terry Treadway believes case evolved in Terry's factory, *ca*.1816, pos. with many minds at work on design. Certainly more such clocks with Eli Terry name than any other. Learned case design from a master, Daniel Burnap; had, besides ability, inventiveness, love of good proportion.

Took Sons Eli, Jr., and Henry into business which lasted *ca*.1818–1824. With bro. as Eli & Samuel Terry 1824–1827. Retired with fortune *ca*.1834. Continued, making occasional brass movt. clocks of extreme excellence; Tower clocks. Turned business into hobby. Penrose Hoopes says of him, "His shop was one where pride of workmanship and high personal skill were combined to produce fine clocks." d. in Terryville aged 80. Tall Shelf, Tower, Regulator clocks, brass and wood movts., 1792–1852.

Granted nine patents:

1797, Nov. 12: "Clocks" from Conn., Equation clock; signed by Pres. John Adams; ill. in Moore.

1816, June 12: "Thirty-Hour Wooden Clocks"; included brass; from Litchfield; Box clock (ill. No. 181), successful Shelf clock, wood movt., became Pillar & Scroll clock.

1822, May 26: "Wooden Wheeled Clocks"; Plymouth.

1825, May 18: "Thirty-Hour Wood Wheeled Clocks"; Plymouth.

1825, Sept. 9: "Thirty-Hour Wood Wheeled Clocks"; Plymouth.

1826, March 4: Two patents, same day, Wood Wheeled clocks; Plymouth.

1826, July 5: "Wooden Wheeled Clocks"; Plymouth.

1845, Aug. 9: "Device to reduce friction of Balance Wheel Clocks"; Plymouth (ill. NAWCC Bul. No. 33).

One patent ill. in Atwater's *History of Plymouth*.

TERRY, ELI, JR.: 1799–1841. Plymouth, Conn. Apt. to Eli, Sr.; with him *ca*.1818 in Eli Terry & Sons. Milo Blakeslee employed by him from 1825, later partner. Wood movt. clocks 1825, 8-day 6-axle wood movts. 1834–1837; label, "Patent Clocks / invented by Eli Terry / made and sold / at Plymouth, Conn. / by Eli Terry, Junior / warranted etc." Sold to Hiram Welton & Co. 1837. Marr. Samantha McKee 1821. "Terrysville" P.O. opened 1831, named after him; "s" dropped later.

—, ELI, III: 1840–. Bristol. Son of Eli, Jr. Tempered coiled springs in old S. B. Terry shop, Pequabuck River and Poland Brook.

TERRY, ELI, III (cont'd)

Soon sold to Seth Thomas Clock Co. *ca*.1862; to Minn.

—, HENRY: 1801–1877. Plymouth, Conn. Son and apt. of Eli. After E. Terry & Sons, continued as E. Terry & Son or with own name. Label, "Patent Eight Day Clocks / made and sold at Plymouth, Conn. / by Henry Terry / at the old Manufactory / of E. Terry & Sons /." Wrote article *Waterbury American* June 10, 1853, later pamphlet, *American Clockmaking, Its Early History and Present Extent of the Business* (J. Giles & Son, Waterbury, 1870), rev. edn. (In full in Drepperd.) Woolen business 1836. Three clocks in Flint Sale 1926.

—, DR. JOHN BURNHAM: 1806–1870. Son and apt. of Samuel. Invented machine to make pins. In R. & J. B. Terry 1835–1836. Left clock business to study medicine in Hartford.

—, LUCIEN B.: Albany, N.Y. Dir. 1830–1835. Conn. family relationship unknown.

—, RALPH ENSIGN: 1804–1892. Son and apt. of Samuel; succeeded 1834 as R. & J. B. Terry. In Terry & Andrews 1842–1850, Terry, Downs & Burwell 1851–1852.

—, SAMUEL: Jan. 24, 1774–May 4, 1853. Plymouth, Bristol, Conn. Clocks and saddles at East Hartford 1797–1818. Some Tower Clocks. Marr. Esther Gillette. Father of Samuel Steele, Ralph Ensign, John Burnham, Theo. 1818 to Plymouth; wood movts. and clock parts for E. Terry & Sons and others. With bro. Eli as Eli & Samuel Terry, Plymouth, 1824–1827. Sons R. E. and J. B. with him. To Bristol 1829, clocks in "an old grist mill." Successful. Wood movt. Pillar and Scroll clocks and others 1827–1829, label, "Patent Clocks / Invented by Eli Terry / Made and sold / at Plymouth, Connecticut / by / Samuel Terry." Shelf clock labels, "Patent / Clocks / made and Sold by / Samuel Terry / Bristol, Conn. / etc."; ". . . also manufactured by Samuel Terry / for / George Mitchell." Looking Glass Shelf clocks and others, 1829–1834. Succeeded 1835 by sons as R. & J. B. Terry. (LB)

—, SAMUEL STEELE: 1801–1867. Son of Samuel. Father of Wm. A. Pos. clocks or clock parts; none extant.

TERRY, SILAS BURNHAM: 1807–1876. Plymouth, Terryville, Waterbury, Winsted, Conn. Aw. *ca*.1824–1876. Inventive C., many unique movts., pioneer in clock springs. Not had full recognition. b. 1807, Plymouth, Conn. Son and apt. of Eli. Marr. Maria W. Upson, 1832. Father of S. B. Jr., Solon M., Cornelius, Simeon G. Preferred brass movts. to popular wood type. Many new type movts., particularly early models of Marine clock (name for Conn. clocks with balance wheel instead of pendulum control). (See ill. Nos. 248, 249.) Patent Nov. 3, 1830, from Plymouth for "Combined Spiral Spring for Clocks." Sold spring tempering process to Butler Dunbar after 1840.

To Bristol by 1831. Coiled spring movts. *ca*.1845. Aw. for Wm. L. Gilbert, Winsted after 1852. Not financially successful. Capable craftsman, unusual clocks and machinery; designed Seth Thomas 1 and 2 regulators. Others benefited from his inventions. Sons with him in Terry Clock Co.

Labels, "S. B. Terry & Co."; "The Terryville Clock Co."; "The Terryville Mfg. Co." "Patent / Craveat A. D. 1851 / S. B. TERRY & Co. / Manufacturers of / Clocks / Terryville, Conn. / Warranted etc" //; "Eight Day and Thirty Hour / Marine Clocks / and Timepieces / Warranted / Superior to anything offered to the Public / Manufactured by / Terryville Manufacturing Company / Terryville, Conn. U.S.A. / Patented by / S. B. Terry, Oct. 5, 1852"; some dials, "Terryville Mfg. Co., Terryville, Conn." No Plymouth labels known. Small Shelf clock in G. B. Davis Col., "Craveat filed in 1851. S. B. Terry, Manufacturers of Clocks, Terryville, Conn., Warranted etc. Geer's Press, Hartford"; movt., plates, two brass strips ¾" wide, long enough to take the wheelwork, one wheel above the other.

—, THEODORE: 1808–1881. Bristol, Ansonia, E. Bridgeport, Conn. Fifth son of Samuel. Aw. *ca*.1842–1855. In Terry & Andrews 1842–1850. A founder of Bristol Brass Co. 1850. To Ansonia 1850; clocks with name on label; plant burned. Contract with P. T. Barnum to make clocks at E. Bridgeport as Terry & Barnum. Sales outlets N.Y.C. and Boston, Dir. 1854. Merged with Jerome Mfg. Co.; f. 1855; had sold interest for $12,000. Oil business Pa. d. New Haven. (AAJ Sept., Nov. 1949)

TERRY, THOMAS: Boston. 1810–1823. (Abbott)

—, WILLIAM: Dutchess Co., N.Y., prob. Washington in Nine Partners Grant. Ca.1790. (Moore)

—, WILLIAM A.: 1828–1917. Bristol. Son of Samuel Steele Terry. Invented Calendar clock made by Atkins Clock Co. Patent Jan. 25, 1870, on "Calendar Clock" self-adjusting for leap years; sold mfg. rights to Ansonia Clock Co.; few made, specimens rare. Interested in photography.

TERRYVILLE CLOCK CO., THE: Terryville, Conn. Used by S. B. Terry ca.1850.

— MFG. CO.: Terryville, Conn. Silas Burnham Terry with the firm 1851–1852.

TEUFEL, H.: Chicago. Ca.1860.

THATCHER, GEORGE: Lowell, Mass. Dir. 1859.

THAYER, ELIPHALET, & SONS (Sears, Ezra, Willisson): Williamsburg, Mass. 1831–1837.

—, ELI: Boston. Dir. 1810.

—, ELIPHALET: Williamsburg, Mass. 1831–1837. C. With sons Sears, Ezra, Willisson as Eliphalet Thayer & Sons.

THIBAULT & BROTHER: Phila. "Mfr. & importer watches." Dir. 1810–1835.

THOMAS, SETH, CLOCK Co.: Plymouth, Conn. Joint stock co. org. March 31, 1853, to continue business of Seth Thomas, founder. Succeeded by son Seth, Jr. 1816–1888; he by son Seth E., 1841–1910; and he by his son Seth E., Jr. 1876–1932.
Calendar clocks (see ill. No. 264) made from ca.1860. First Southern Calendar clock by Seth Thomas 1875. With change of name from Plymouth Hollow to Thomaston 1866, clocks can be dated. Lever escapement clocks from ca.1866. Round alarm clocks ca.1875. (See ill. No. 276.)
Violin clocks (see ill. No. 272), 8-day brass movt., strike and time, ca.1890; prob. ten or fewer; five or six now known.
Watches 1883; first shipped 1884. Movts. never cased. Sizes 0, 6, 12, 16, 18, mostly with jewels 7, 11, 15, some 21, 23, 25. "Maiden Lane" fine stem wind, No. 18 size, seven position adjusted, won highest awards Chicago World's Fair 1893. (See ill. No. 303.) Watchmaking discontinued 1914.
Became 1930 part of General Time Instruments Co. Name changed 1949 to The General Time Corporation.
Tower clocks. Took over A. S. Hotchkiss business 1872. Colgate Clock in N.J., "The Biggest clock in the World," minute circle 50' diam., hands one ton each. Also clock on Paramount Building, Times Sq.; Consolidated Gas Co. clock on 14th St.; clock in Grand Central Station. Many others. Tower clocks shipped all over world.
Specialty Division estab. 1915; all kinds recording devices — range timers, taximeters, parking meters, etc.
Marine clocks during World Wars for U.S. Navy; also special and secret insts.
Round drum alarm clock (ill. No. 276), brass, drum shaped, copper drawstrings, drumstick hands, made 1879; in Paul Darrot Col.
Many examples; six in Essex Inst. (Paul G. Darrot)

THOMAS MFG. CO.: Plymouth Hollow, Conn. Ca.1850. Brass castings for jewelry.

—, SETH, & SONS: Plymouth, Conn., and N.Y.C. Org. 1866 to make lever type clock; successful. Absorbed into the Seth Thomas Clock Co. 1879. Glass-sided French type Shelf clock in 1868 catalogue. N.Y.C. 1868, 3 Cortlandt St., 115 Lake St. American Clock Co. "Sole Agents." (Co. Records)

— SONS, SETH, & CO.: N.Y.C. Used by Seth Thomas & Sons.

— (SETH) & HOADLEY (Silas): Plymouth, Conn. 1809–1813. Plant Hoadleyville or Greystone, near Waterbury line. Tall clocks, 30 hour wood movts. (see ill. No. 66) ill. Milham. Tall clock, 8-day wood movt. owned by Mrs. Matthew G. Ely, Pelham, N.Y., Tall clock Essex Inst. Thomas sold interest 1813; Hoadley continued successfully to 1849.

—, ENOS: Willistown, Pa. Ca.1800. Son of Isaac. Bro. Mordecai. Prob. R. (James)

THOMAS, ISAAC: 1721–1802. Willistown, Pa. Aw. 1768–1802. Chester Co.'s most prolific C. Father of Mordecai, Enos, Isaac, Jr. Clock cases walnut, cherry, brass dials, before 1768. Twenty-nine tall clocks known, one owned by Mrs. P. Burnley, Media, Pa. (James) (Orr) (Conrad)

—, ISAAC, JR.: Worcester, Mass. Ca.1800. Printer Simon Willard clock labels. Son of Isaac; succeeded him 1801. (JWW)

—, ISAIAH: Phila. and Lancaster, Pa. Ca.1870. (Lan. Co.)

—, JOSEPH: Phila. Dir. 1805–1808. Also Norristown and Penn. Square, Pa. Pos. two men same name. Tall clock owned by Mrs. E. F. Gable, Landsdowne, Pa., mahogany case, moon, months, days, hour strike; dial "Penn. Square."

—, MORDECAI: 1767–. Willistown, Pa. Son and apt. of Isaac. Ca.1790–1820. C., Cabinetmaker. Bro. Enos. (James)

—, SETH: Aug. 18, 1785–Jan. 29, 1859. Greystone, Plymouth, Conn. Famous C. b. Wolcott, Conn. Son of James and Martha Thomas. Little schooling. Learned trade of carpenter, joiner. Aw. on Long Wharf, New Haven, Conn. Later learned cabinet making. Ca.1808 aw. with Eli Terry on order for 4,000 clocks. Later with Silas Hoadley, wood 30-hr. movts., some Tall clock cases; Moore states firm was called Terry, Thomas & Hoadley. Terry sold interest 1809. Thomas & Hoadley (Greystone) continued successful. Thomas sold interest 1813 to Hoadley. To Plymouth Hollow 1813; bought Heman Clark shop; Tall cased wood movt. clocks. This was beginning of Seth Thomas Clock Co. still in business as part of General Time Corp.

Reported to have paid Eli Terry $1,000 for right to make wood movt. Shelf clocks (patented by Terry 1816). Label, "Patent Clocks / Eli Terry, Inventor and Patentee / Made & Sold by / Seth Thomas / Plymouth, Conn." (See ill. No. 181.)

Also Pillar and Scroll clocks. Label (Author's Col.): "Patent Clocks / invented by / Eli Terry / Made & Sold / at / Plymouth, Connecticut / by / Seth Thomas // Goodwin & Co., Hartford,

Printers." Used wood movts. successfully till 1838. Then adopted 30-hour brass movt. All clocks weight-driven till ca.1850 when springs were used.

Employing more than 900, 1853. Org. Seth Thomas Clock Co. 1853. d. Plymouth. Plymouth Hollow named "Thomaston" 1866 in his honor.

THOMAS, WILLIAM: Trenton, N.J. Adv. 1780 as G. and S. (Williams)

THOMEQUEX, PETER: Northampton, Mass. Adv. 1802, "Gold and silver watches, wholesale and retail at A. Pomeroy's Store." (Cutten)

THOMPSON & FLOYD: Glens Falls, N.Y. Ca.1830.

—, H. C., CLOCK CO., THE: Bristol. Org. 1903 to carry on business of H. C. Thompson. Partial destruction by fire 1906. New modern plant 1907.

— & RANGER: Brattleboro, Vt. Ca.1810.

—, AVERY J.: 1852–1917. Cherry Valley, N.Y. W. Son of Lyman. Father of J. Avery, Jr. With Lyman till 1910. (Chamberlain)

—, AVERY J., JR.: 1883–. Cherry Valley, N.Y. Son and successor of Avery J. Sr. (Chamberlain)

—, HENRY: Phila. Dir. 1847.

—, HIRAM C.: 1830–. Bristol. Learned Clockmaking while a student; aw. for Noah Pomeroy 1862; bought him out 1878. Mfd. clock movts. for Self Winding Clock Co. et al. (Hist.)

—, ISAAC: Litchfield, Conn. S. Adv. 1796.

—, JAMES: Baltimore. Ca.1800. Pittsburgh, Pa., ca.1820. Improvements on steam engines; later made engines. (Gillingham) (Stow)

—, JOHN: N.Y.C. Adv. 1780, "Took over Isaac Heron's Shop when Heron left this Country." (Am. Col. June, 1948)

—, JOHN P.: Phila. Dir. 1819–1824.

—, LYMAN W.: 1825–1910. Cherry Valley, N.Y. W. Self-taught. Father of Avery. Aw. 1853. Watch in Ira Leonard Col. (Chamberlain)

—, S. N.: Roxbury, Mass. Dir. 1853.

—, SILAS G.: New Haven, Conn. Ca.1850.

—, WILLIAM: N.Y.C. Adv. 1775, "Watch & Clock Maker, lately from London on Fair St. opp. North Church."

—, WILLIAM: Carlisle, Pa. 1780.

THOMPSON, WILLIAM: Baltimore. –1800. Adv. 1762, "Moved and now lives 5 miles on Road to Nottingham. Repairs Clocks & Watches." (Prime)

THOMSON, SIMON: Phila. n/d. "A Phila. Watch Manufacturer at 4th St. below Market."

—, WILLIAM: 1800–1850. Wilmington, N.C. Adv. 1834 as C. and W. (Cutten)

THORNTON, ANDREW: Phila. Dir. 1811.

—, JOSEPH: Phila. Dir. 1819.

THORP, H. W.: Beaver Dam, Wis. *Ca.*1870.

THORPE, E., & Co.: Upper Alton, Ill. *Ca.* 1860.

THOWNSEND, CHARLES: Phila., 106 Chestnut St., Dir. 1799; 136 Front St., Dir. 1804-1828.

—, CHARLES, JR.: Phila. 1829–1850. Took over father's business. (Gillingham)

THREADCRAFT, B.: Charleston, S.C. Before 1800.

THUM, CHARLES: Phila. Early 19th century. Tall clock reported by Ernest Cramer.

TICE & ROBERTS: Brooklyn, N.Y. *Ca.*1840.

TICHENOR, DAVID (Isaac): Newark, N.J. *Ca.*1820. (Moses Bigelow)

TIEBOUT, ALEXANDER: N.Y.C. 1798.

TIERNEY, JOHN: Phila. Dir. 1820–1824.

TIFFANY NEVER WIND CLOCK CORP.: Buffalo, N.Y. Patent March 8, 1904, on glass-domed, torsion pendulum, electric battery magnetic clock. One in Robert Dickey Col.

—, CHARLES LEWIS: 1812–1902. N.Y.C. Jeweler. b. Killingly, Conn. To N.Y.C. 1837. With John B. Young, opened store. Enlarged 1841; added partner J. L. Ellis. Imp. from Europe. Larger store 1847; diamonds, jewelry, watches, clocks, silverware, etc. Inc. as Tiffany & Co. 1868. Made clocks N.Y.C. before 1888 for special orders.

—, GEO. S.: N.Y.C., 30 Rose St. Adv. 1904 electric battery clock. One in Mark F. Massey Col.

TIFFT, HORACE: No. Attleboro, Mass. *Ca.* 1800 or 1840.

TILDEN, THURBER: Providence, R.I. "Established 1856." Prob. sold George Kellam Banjo clocks.

TIMBY GLOBE TIMEPIECE: First made 1863 by T. R. Timby, also by L. E. Whiting. About 600 made; all numbered. "Best

made in America and unsurpassed in Europe, the balance wheel is set in jewels, making it a timekeeper equal to the best lever watch and regulated in the same way. Wind once a week regularly." Movts. made in Saratoga; Gilman Joslin, Boston map maker, added globe. First type had flat top case; solid scroll later adopted as standard. Pos. also made by E. F. Rawson at Saratoga Springs, N.Y. (H. G. Rowell, Am. Col. May, 1938)

TIMBY, THEODORE RUGGLES: 1822–1909. Saratoga Springs and Baldwinsville, N.Y. Invented Timby Solar Clock (see ill. No. 269). Four patents on this clock: July 7, 1863, "Improvement in Solar Timepieces"; Nov. 3, 1863, "Improvement in Globe Timepieces," and "Globe Clocks," May 2, 1865. Invented revolving gun turret, turbine water wheel, and others.

TIMME, M.: Brooklyn, N.Y. *Ca.*1840. Invented mus. chime clock. (TP)

TIMSON, WILLIAM W.: Newburyport, Mass. 1854–1860.

TINGES, CHARLES: Baltimore. 1796–1815.

TISDALE, E. D.: Taunton, Mass. *Ca.*1870.

—, COL. NATHAN: New Bern, N.C. Adv. 1795, "John Tinley bought his shop." Later in military service. (Cutten)

—, WILLIAM, II: Washington and New Bern, N.C. 1816–1850 and later. Father pos. C., also S. (Cutten)

TISSOT, ALEXANDER: N.Y.C. 1805.

TITCOMB, ALBERT: Bangor, Me. *Ca.*1850.

—, ENOCH J.: Boston. Dir. 1834 only. Pos. later in N.H. Banjo clock in James Conlon Col., brass bezel and side arms, "like Cole of Rochester, N.H."

TITUS, JAMES: Phila. Dir. 1833.

TOBIAS, M. I., & Co.: N.Y.C. n/d. Ex. Museum City of N.Y.

—, S. I., & Co.: N.Y.C. 1829. Pos. above firm. (FT)

TODD, M. L.: Beaver, Pa. *Ca.*1830.

—, RICHARD: Strasbourg, Pa. *Ca.*1769. (Steinmetz)

—, RICHARD J.: N.Y.C. *Ca.*1830.

—, TRACY: Lexington, Ky. Adv. 1840's. (LB)

TOLFORD, JOSHUA: Kennebunk, Me. "Here about a year—1815—then moved back to Portland, Me."

TOLLES, NATHAN: Plymouth, Conn. "Made parts of clocks, sold out 1836." (Moore)

TOLMAN, JEREMIAH: Boston. Dir. 1810.

TONCHURE, FRANCIS: Baltimore. Early 19th century. (Baillie)

TORK CLOCK CO., INC.: Mt. Vernon, N.Y. 1918–current. Timers and industrial clocks. (E. Cantelo White)

TORREY, BENJAMIN B.: Hanover, Mass. Early 19th century. Dished dial mirror Shelf clock in DKP Col.

TOWER, REUBEN: Plymouth, Hingham, and Hanover, Mass. Ca.1810–1830. Dwarf Tall clock Edison Inst. (See ill. No. 97.)

TOWN, IRA S.: Montpelier, Vt. Ca.1860. Watch Paper Cramer Col.

TOWNSEND, CHARLES: Phila. Dir. 1799–1800.

—, CHARLES, JR.: Phila. Dir. 1824–1850.

—, CHRISTOPHER: Newport, R.I. Adv. 1773–ca.1810. Case maker.

—, DAVID: Boston. Dir. 1789–1806. Phila. 1789.

—, ELISHA: Phila. Dir. 1828–1829.

—, H.: Conway, Mass. Ca.1870.

—, ISAAC: Boston. Dir. 1789–1806. "Of 27 Cornhill, made gold and silver watches, Clocks, elegant watch chains, seals, keys, trinkets, and glasses." (Moore)

—, JOHN: Newport, R.I. Ca.1770. Bro.-in-law John Goddard. Cabinet-maker, case maker. Tall clock, case by him, "William Tomlinson" on 12" brass dial. (Baillie lists as 1699–1747.) (See ill. No. 18.)

—, JOHN: Phila., 2 No. 5th St. Dir. 1813–1833.

—, JOHN, JR.: Phila. Dir. 1849.

—, JOSEPH: Baltimore, "near Center Market." Adv. 1792. (Prime)

TRACY (E.) & BAKER: Phila. and Waltham, Mass. Watchcase makers. Bought Boston Watch Co. with Royal E. Robbins 1857.

—, C. & E.: Phila. Dir. 1847. Watchcase makers.

—, CHARLES: Phila. Dir. 1842–1850. Watchcase maker.

—, E.: Phila. Of Tracy & Baker.

—, ERASTUS: (1768–1796). Norwich and New London, Conn. Son of Isaac and Elizabeth Rogers Tracy. Bro. of Gurdon. Prob. apt. of Thomas Harland. Adv.

1790, "Opened a shop opp. Capt. Jabez Perkins' store at Norwich Landing where he carries on Clock and Watch Making. . . ." Ca.1793 to New London. (Hoopes) (Am. Col. June, 1947)

TRACY, GURDON: 1767–1792. New London, Conn. C., S. Apt. of Thomas Harland. Adv. 1787, "Opened a shop." On recommendation of Harland given charge 1790 of town clock at 40 shillings a year. Left complete set tools, completed Tall clock, another partly finished. Shop and equipment taken over by Trott & Cleveland 1792. (Hoopes) (Am. Col. June, 1947)

TRAHN, PETER, & CO.: Phila. Dir. 1843–1849. Watch Paper in Cramer Col., "P. C. Trahn, Hanover St."

TRAMPLEPLEASURE, JAMES: Jersey City, N.J. 1850–1854. (PG)

TRAVIS, JOHN: N.Y.C. Dir. 1859–1860.

TREADWAY, AMOS: Middletown, Conn. ". . . Borrowed 2 watches from Amos Treadway 1787." (FT)

TREADWELL, OREN B.: Phila. Dir. 1847–1849.

TREAT (Sherman) & BISHOP (Daniel F.): Bristol, 1830's. "Made for George Mitchell" on label wood movt. Shelf clock owned by Harry L. Miller, White Plains, N.Y. Small Shelf clock in Mitchell Col.

—, GEORGE: Newark, N.J. 1850–1858. (PG)

—, ORRIN: New Haven, Conn. Ca.1840–ca.1850.

—, SHERMAN: Bristol. (tx) 1828–1835. C. Cases for Treat & Bishop.

TREISS, G. P.: Brooklyn, N.Y. n/d. Watch Paper BCL Col.

TREMONT WATCH CO.: Org. 1864. Aaron L. Dennison factory manager at Boston. To Melrose, Mass., 1866. Closed 1868, lack of capital; machinery sold to Anglo-American Watch Co., Eng. (later The English Watch Co.). Tremont adv., "made only dust proof watch movt. in U.S.A." (Crossman)

TRENAMAN, —: Charlottetown, P. E. Island, Queen Sq. n/d. White Watch Paper Bir. Col.

TRENTON WATCH CO.: Chambersburg, N.J. Formerly New Haven Watch Co. operating 1883–1886, New Haven, Conn. f.

1907; Ingersoll interests bought plant 1908. (Crossman)

TRIBE, GILBERT: Newark, N.J. 1850–1852. (PG)

TRONE, PETER: Phila. Dir. 1844.

TROTH, JAMES: Pittsburgh, Pa. *Ca.*1820.

—, THOMAS: Pittsburgh, Pa. *Ca.*1820.

TROTT (John Proctor) & CLEVELAND (Wm.): New London, Conn. Bought 1792 stock and tools of Gurdon Tracy. (Am. Col. June, 1947)

—, PETER & ANDREW C.: Boston. Dir. 1805.

—, ANDREW C.: 1779–1812. Boston. Dir. 1805–1810.

—, JOHN PROCTOR: 1769–1852. New London, Conn. Bro. Jonathan, Jr. In Trott & Cleveland 1792.

—, JONATHAN, JR.: 1771–1813. New London, Conn. b. Boston. C. S. Shop 1800 "2 doors No. of J. & A. Woodward's on Beach St." Adv. 1800, "Made and repaired clocks and wished to employ a journeyman clockmaker." (Hoopes)

—, PETER: Boston. Dir. 1800–1805.

TROTTER, JEREMIAH: N.Y.C. *Ca.*1820–*ca.*1830.

TROW, EPHRAIM: Haverhill, Mass., Water St. Dir. 1832. C. W. Schoolmate of John G. Whittier. (Mrs. J. B. Mason)

TRUAX, DEWITT: Utica, N.Y. Dir. 1842–1843.

TRUMAN, JEFFERY: Waynesville, O. Adv. 1822, "Watchmaking. He has made arrangements for conducting the Repairing of Timepieces as here-to-fore." (Phillips)

TRUMBALL & HASKELL: Lowell, Mass. *Ca.* 1860.

TUCKER, J. W.: San Francisco, Cal. *Ca.* 1850–*ca.*1860.

TUERLING, JAMES: N.Y.C. Invented and patented Jan. 6, 1857, "American Screw Clock." (See ill. No. 280.) Gravity screw winds up by lifting Eagle, which raises weight, kettle-drum shaped; on dial, "Made to order of J. C. Kennedy, The American Screw Clock"; cast on base, "James Tuerling, N.Y. Pat. Jan 6, 1857, No. 12." (W. Hallet) (Barny)

TULLER, WILLIAM: N.Y.C. Dir. 1831.

TURELL, ANDREW C.: Boston. 1800–1810.

TURNER, ALLISON: Ashtabula, O. *Ca.*1830. Finely carved column Shelf clock, well-painted dial with gilt ornaments in cor-

ners, hour strike, wood 30-hr. movt., *ca.* 30" high, in Jean Louis Roehrich Col.

TURNBULL, JOHN: Baltimore. Adv. 1798. (Prime)

TURNER, FRANKLIN: Cheraw, S.C. Aw. *ca.* 1814. Adv. 1823, for "apprentice to learn Clock & Watch making."

—, JOHN: N.Y.C. Dir. 1848.

TURRELL, SAMUEL: Boston. Dir. 1789, 1796, 1813, 1820.

TURRET & MARINE CLOCK Co.: Boston, 5 and 13 Water St. Collins Stevens, Moses D. Crane. Adv. 1860. Tower clocks. George F. Walker, agent in N.Y.C.

TUSTEN, HIRAM S.: 1826–1912. Abbeville, S.C. Apt. of "Mr. Dusenbury" of Middletown, N.Y. Aw. *ca.*1842. Adv. 1885. To Monroe, La., with son as J.

TUSTIN, SEPTIMUS: Baltimore. 1814.

TUTHILL, DANIEL M.: Saxtons River, Vt. *Ca.*1842. Shelf clock cases; bought Conn. brass movts.

TUTTLE, ELIADA: Owego, N.Y. 1833. Shelf clocks. (L. Smith) (R. Franks)

TWISS, B., & H.: Meriden, Conn. Cs. Aw. 1828. On 1837 Conn. map. Bros. Benjamin, Ira, Hiram. Three clock patents. (G. Hill) (Moore)

—, J., & H.: Montreal, Canada. n/d. "Typical Conn. 30-hr. Shelf clock." (E. A. Battison)

—, HIRAM: Meriden, Conn. In B. & H. Twiss. Two patents May 13, 1834, on "Clocks and Timepieces" and "Balance Pendulum."

TWITCHELL, MARCUS: Utica, N.Y. Dir. 1829.

TWOMBLY & CLEAVES: Biddeford, Me. *Ca.* 1870. (Dre)

TYLER, E. A.: New Orleans, La. *Ca.*1840–*ca.*1850.

TYSON, LEECH: Phila. Dir. 1823–1831.

ULRICH, VALENTINE: Reading, Pa. See Urletig.

UMBRECT, JOHN B.: Chicago, 143 Claybourn St. 1878–1879. Case maker. (MFM)

UNDERHILL, DANIEL: N.Y.C. *Ca.*1810.

—, W. J.: N.Y.C., 141 West St. n/d. Green Watch Paper Bir. Col., "Watches, Clocks & Musical Boxes etc. repaired."

UNDERWOOD, DAVID: Goshen, Pa. 1796–1801. "Watchmaker." (James)

UNION CLOCK CO.: Bristol. (tx) 1843–1845. See Union Mfg. Co.

— MFG. CO.: Bristol, Union St. (tx) 1843–1845. Cs. "Cooperative." Made clocks, sold them N.Y.C. at reduced prices. Other makers reported combined against them. Shortly out of business.

— WATCH CO.: N.Y.C. n/d. Movt., 11-jewel, key wind and set, owned by A. O. Dodge, Schenectady, N.Y.

UNIONVILLE CO.: Bristol. n/d. Name in 30-hr. weight-driven OG brass movt. (LB)

UNITED STATES CLOCK CO.: N.Y.C., 18 Cortlandt St. Dir. 1872.

— STATES CLOCK & BRASS CO.: Chicago. 1860's. Brass clock, 30-hr. weight, vivid blue label, owned by J. J. Niehaus, Dayton, O. Pos. another name for U.S. Clock Mfg. Co. of Austin, Ill.; factory burned 1868. (Mrs. E. G. Snodgrass)

— STATES CLOCK CASE CO.: Cincinnati, O., John St. Ca.1870–ca.1880. Black moulded composition Shelf clock cases. "Did not exceed cost of iron cases by more than 10%." Seth Thomas movts. Clemens Hellebush, Pres. Another adv., "Manufacturers of the only clock case moulded and pressed jet black in a single piece, brilliantly polished and inlaid with Variegated Marble or Bronze, the material being very hard and durable and susceptible of a high polish." (MFM)

— STATES CLOCK MANUFACTURING CO.: New Haven, Conn. To Austin, Ill. in 1866; brought workmen from East. Pos. company of which Chauncey Jerome was supt. in 1866 (not mentioned in autobiography). (Samuel Jennings)

— STATES TIME CORP.: N.Y.C. and Waterbury, Conn. Succeeded Waterbury Clock Co. 1944. Now mfg. clocks and watches.

— STATES TIME & WEATHER SERVICE CO.: N.Y.C. Adv. Keystone 1897–1898. (MFM)

— STATES WATCH CO.: Marion, now Jersey City, N.J. Giles, Wales, & Co. org. 1863; f. 1872; briefly Marion Watch Co.; f. Machinery sold to E. F. Bowman, Lancaster, Pa.; later sold to J. P. Stevens, Atlanta, Ga. Watch names: "Fayette Stratton," "Edwin Rollo," "Frederick Atherton," "George Channing," "S. M. Beard," "United States," "John Lewis," "A. H. Wallace," "G. A. Reed," "Henry Randel," "J. W. Deacon," "Asa Fuller," "G. Knapp," "Alexander." (Crossman) (Baillie) (Bowman) (Coleman)

UNITED STATES WATCH CO.: N.Y.C. n/d. Prob. sales agency. (Crossman)

— STATES WATCH CO., THE: Waltham, Mass. Org. 1884 as part of Waltham Watch & Tool Co. by Charles Vander Woerd, supt. Waltham Watch Co. f.; plant purchased by Keystone Watch Case Co., which made "Howard" watch till 1927. (Crossman) (Evans) (Tim. Cent.)

UNIVERSAM CLOCK CO.: Boston. n/d. Clock in Essex Inst.

UPJOHN, JAMES: London, Eng. C. To America 1802. Pos. to Augusta, Me. (Gillingham)

UPSON BROTHERS: Bristol, Conn. n/d. Shelf clocks; brass mfr. Shelf clock 18 × 10 × 6, tablet American Eagle, "E. Pluribus" scroll, gold-leaf decoration on tablet, owned by E. P. Merritt, Boston.

—, MERRIMAN, & CO.: Bristol. (tx) 1831–1838. Partners were Rensselaer Upson, Henry E. and George Merriman, Philip Barnes. Mirror Shelf clock, 30-hour brass movt., in Richard Newcomb Col. (Moore) (H. Palmer)

—, LUCAS: N.Y.C. Dir. 1846.

URLETIG, VALENTINE: –1783. Reading, Pa. Aw. ca.1755–1783. 1st Group. First Reading C. With Jacob Mechlin, pioneer maker. Tall clocks, brass dials, calendar, moon, some with strike repeaters, brass movts. Tower clock for Court House, Penn Square, 1762; bell from London. Other spellings—Ulrich, Ulrick, Uhreledig —on clock dials. (Gillingham)

VAIL, EDWARD: Laporte, Ind. Ca.1840–ca. 1870.

—, ELIJAH M.: Albany, N.Y. Dir. 1840–1841.

VALENTINE, —: Wormelsdorf, Pa. n/d. Tall clocks. Pos. Valentine Urtelig, Reading, Pa., or John Vanderslice.

—, WILLIAM B.: Boston. Dir. 1821.

VAN ALLYN, —: Ca.1630. C. of Dutch Trading Post in Conn.

VAN BUREN, WILLIAM: Newark, N.J. N.Y.C. S. To N.J. 1792. Adv., "Opp. Col. Sam Hayes store at the sign of the Gold Watch." N.Y.C., 22 Maiden Lane, 1794–. (Williams)

Van Cott, A. B.: Racine, Wis. *Ca*.1850.

Vanderslice, John: Wormelsdorf, Pa. Early 19th century. 4th Group. Tall clocks. (Steinmetz)

Van Der Veer, Jos.: Somerville, N.J. Early 19th century.

Van Eps, George K.: N.Y.C. Pos. imp. Dutch clocks 1830's and 1840's.

Vanlone, James: Phila. Adv. 1775. (Prime)

Van Steenbergh, P.: Kingston, N.Y. *Ca*. 1780.

Vantine, John L.: Phila. Dir. 1829–1847.

Van Valkenburgh, Charles: N.Y.C., 422 Fourth Ave. Dir. 1854.

Vanvleit, B. C.: Poughkeepsie, N.Y. Adv. 1830–1847. C., W., S., Dealer. (Cutten)

Van Voorhis, Daniel: 1751–1824. Phila. Adv. 1780. Princeton, N.J. N.Y.C. with William Coley. S. Retired 1819. (Williams)

Van Wagener, John: Oxford, N.Y. 1843.

Van Winkle, John: N.Y.C. n/d.

Van Wyck, Steven: N.Y.C. *Ca*.1805–. "Watchmaker." Also spelled Wijck, Wyk. Movt. in Olin S. Nye Col.

Vaughan, David: Phila. Aw. 1695–1702. From London, 1695. Mentioned by William Penn. James Logan's account book 1702, "D. Vaughan, note for Work done to Clock and Watch." (Gillingham)

Veal (John) & Glaze (Wm.): Columbia, S.C. Adv. 1838. Dissolved 1841.

Veazie, Joseph: Providence, R.I. 1805.

Verdin, Jacob: Cincinnati, O. *Ca*.1850. Tower clocks.

—, Michael: Cincinnati, O. *Ca*.1850. Tower clocks.

Vermont Clock Co.: Fairhaven, Vt. *Ca*. 1891–1910 as Fairhaven Clock Co. Then Vermont Clock Co. 1910–1921. Pendulum and lever escapement Shelf clocks like those of Chelsea Clock Co.; French clocks in brass-bound glass cases. Movts. unusual with lever escapement; no pendulum to fill lower part of case. One reported sold in Cal. for special low price because "the pendulum was lost." See Fairhaven Clock Co. (MFM)

Vibber, Russell: Westtown, Pa. From Conn. Fitted wooden movts. with Hatch & DeWolf into cases made 1810–1815 by Henry Darlington. (James)

Vining, L. S.: Cincinnati, O. *Ca*.1830–*ca*. 1840. "From Conn."

Vinton, David: Providence, R.I. 1792.

Vogel, Frederick: Middleburg and Schoharie, N.Y. "Imported from England parts and movts. in 1820's–1830's"; some with "George Brouck." f. 1840's. (TP)

Vogt, Ignatius Christian: N.Y.C. "1764."

—, John: N.Y.C., Hanover Sq. Adv. 1758, "Watchmaker, also cleans and repairs."

Voight, Henry: –1814. Reading, Pa. Taxed as C. 1780. Settled Phila., 2nd St., bet. Race and Vine Sts. Dutch. Pos. with John Fitch. Friend of Rittenhouse. Father of Thomas. Appointed by Pres. Washington "Chief Coiner" at Phila. Mint for "his mechanical knowledge & skill, being a clockmaker by trade." (Prime) (Steinmetz)

—, Sebastian: Phila., 149 No. 2nd St. Dir. 1793–1800. (Brix)

—, Thomas H. (T. H.): Reading, Pa. 3rd Group. Later Phila., 44 No. 7th St. Dir. 1811–1835. Son of Henry. Tall clock in Pa. Hist. Soc., Phila.

Vorhees & Van Wickle: New Brunswick, N.J. Watch Paper extant. C. M. Williams mentions an Abraham Vorhees *ca*.1840.

Voute, Lewis C.: Phila. Dir. 1835. S. Adv. 1826, "Shop at 5 Franklin Row, nearly opp. Buck's Hotel, Bridgeton, N.J." (Williams)

Vuille, Alexander: Baltimore. Adv. 1766. In Francis & Vuille.

Waage & Norton: Phila. Dir. 1798.

Wade, Charles: Boston. Dir. 1830.

—, Nathaniel: Newfield, Stratford, Conn. Aw. 1793–1802. Aptd. Norwich, Conn. Moved Newfield, 1793. In Hall & Wade, 1793. Adv. 1796, "Clocks & Watches made and repaired, G.S." Dissolved *ca*.1798. Stratford, 1798–1802. Sold to Lyman Smith. (Hoopes)

Wadhams, George D.: Wolcottville, Conn. From Cornwall, Eng., 1825. Engaged in various manufacturing endeavours until 1837, which included making clocks or having them made for him. Name on labels Conn. Shelf clocks, some papier-mâché cases, pos. of later era. Shelf clock in Flint Sale 1926, "square case, moulded

WADHAMS, GEORGE D. (cont'd)
columns at sides, painted and stencilled pediment, turned legs, painted tablet." Weight-driven, wood movt. Shelf clock owned by Paul Swartz, N.Y.C., label, "made by Jerome & Barnes and sold by G. B. Wadhams." (J. H. Thompson)

"WADSWORTH, THE ARTHUR," used by Newark Watch Co. *ca.*1868.

WADSWORTH, J. C. (James) & A. (Amos): Litchfield, Conn. "Had a clock shop near site of Bigelow Bros. Saw Mill in 1830's." (Hist.)

—, JEREMIAH: Georgetown, S.C. 1820's.

WADSWORTHS, LOUNSBURY & TURNERS: Litchfield, Conn. *Ca.*1830. Pillar and Scroll clocks, wood movts. Examples owned by Floyd Thoms, O. Hockenson, and H. P. Tolander. "Terry Patent Clocks." (F. L. Thoms)

— & TURNERS: Litchfield, Conn. Shop near South Bridge. *Ca.*1820–1830. Pillar and Scroll clocks. Labels, "Terry's Patent." "Cases sawed at Bigelow's Mills." (S. A. Beckwith)

WADY, JAMES: Newport, R.I. *Ca.*1750–1755. (Abbott)

WAGSTAFF, THOMAS: London, Eng. 1756–1793. "A celebrated Quaker Clockmaker who supplied clocks frequently to American Quakers who had them cased in Philadelphia or Newport, R.I. A lacquer cased Tall clock by him is known." (FT) (Baillie)

WAIT, DEWEY & Co.: Ravenna, O. *Ca.*1855. (Knittle)

—, L. D.: Skaneateles, N.Y. Adv. 1838–1847.

"WAITE, GEO. W.," used by Cornell Watch Co. *ca.*1871.

WAITLEY, —: Worthington, O. *Ca.*1893–1894. "Bought the Columbus Clock (see ill. No. 281) business from 3 Italians to sell them at the 1893 Chicago World's Fair." For complete story of Columbus clock see Willis Milham's pamphlet *The Columbus Clock*.

WALES, SAMUEL H.: Providence, R.I., 6 Market Sq. Dir. 1849–1856. Watch Paper Phillip Jenkins Col.

WALHAUPTER, JOHN: N.Y.C. 1805.

WALKER & BAILEY: Pa. n/d. William Wallace, Uniontown, Pa., owns Tall clock,

8-day brass movt., moon. "On bob is a Knight in Armour, riding a Horse with 'A Don Cossack' in letters above the horse." (W. Wallace)

WALKER & CARPENTER: Boston. Dir. 1807.

— & HUGHES: Birmingham, Eng. Dial makers. Name on Tall clock false plate in L. Barr Col.

—, A.: Brockport, N.Y. Adv. 1831–1832.

"—, GEORGE," used by N.Y. Watch Co. *ca.* 1871.

—, ISAAC: Long Plain, Mass. *Ca.*1800.

—, JULIUS: Buffalo, N.Y. Dir. 1840–1848.

—, THOMAS: Fredricksburg, Va. 1760–1775. Tall clock with movt. by him in Mus. Fine Arts, Boston. (Buhler)

WALL & ALMY: New Bedford, Mass. 1820–1823. (Abbott)

—, WILLIAM A.: New Bedford and Hanover, Mass. Early 19th century. In Wall & Almy. "Renowned as an American Artist."

"WALLACE, A. H.," used by U. S. Watch Co. *ca.*1870.

—, JOHN: Pittsburgh, Pa. *Ca.*1830. Tall clock owned by L. L. Parvin, Bridgeton, N.J., 8-day brass movt., mahogany case, well-made weights and pendulum, brass-covered bob, conch shell spandrels, moon, calendar. (L. L. Parvin)

—, ROBERT: Phila. *Ca.*1860. Dwarf Tall timepiece, metal dial, *ca.*24" tall. (PG)

WALLEY, JOHN: Boston. n/d. Tall clock, brass dial, name, "fecit Boston." (PG)

WALLIN, ROBERT: Phila. Dir. 1845.

WALLINGFORD WATCH Co.: Wallingford, Conn. n/d. Movt. No. 137998 in Ira Leonard Col., "resembles Manhattan Watch Co."

WALSH, —: Forestville, Conn. "*Ca.*1825." (FT)

WALTER, JACOB S.: 1782–1865. Baltimore. 1815–*ca.*1860.

—, M. F.: Hartford, Conn. *Ca.*1850.

WALTERS, CHARLES D.: Harrisburg, Pa. *Ca.*1850–*ca.*1860.

—, HENRY: Charleston, S.C., Broad St. Adv. 1757, "From London."

WALTHAM CLOCK Co.: Waltham, Mass. Sold 1913 to Waltham Watch Co. (Evans)

WALTHAM WATCH Co.: Waltham, Mass. 1850–1950. The first successful American Manufacture of watches by machinery came about through the efforts of Aaron L. Dennison, W. and Edward Howard, of Howard & Davis, C. who organized in 1848 or 1849, and built a factory in Roxbury. Dennison made a trip to Europe for supplies and information. Machinery was designed and built, and able assistants were secured. The start was made in 1850, using firm name of "The American Horologe Co." The first model watch made was about size 20, designed to run 8 days using two main springs. This was not put into production. A 36-hour English lever type was developed. By 1853, some 900 watches had been made at Roxbury.

The problem of securing enough capital was always present. In ca.1857 Samuel Curtis joined the enterprise and the name was changed to "The Warren Mfg. Co.," locally known as "The Boston Watch Co." In 1854 the business was moved to Waltham where a new factory had been built on land of "The Waltham Improvement Co.," which had come into existence as a financing subsidiary.

In 1857, an assignment was made to Tracy, Baker, & Co. and Royal E. Robbins. Production of watches continued with Aaron Dennison as Superintendent till 1862. The name used from 1859 to 1885 was "The American Watch Company." The 1857 assignment cut production briefly but making of watches was resumed with A. L. Dennison as Supt. Many of the experienced personnel left in 1858. Some went with Edward Howard to Roxbury to produce the E. Howard & Company Watch, others to Nashua, N.H., to found the Nashua Watch Company. The Civil War brought better business to the Company. Expansion followed. Stem wind on watch was introduced after 1870.

Name was changed 1885 to American Waltham Watch Co., with Ezra Charles Fitch as pres. until his retirement in 1921. New machinery was continually introduced; many prizes won for timekeeping and workmanship. In 1906 became Waltham Watch Co.; 1923–1925 Waltham Watch & Clock Co.; 1925 Waltham Watch Co. Production suspended 1950.

According to George V. White, Wollaston, Mass., "The first production of watches in Waltham was late in the year 1854; and according to early writers these watches were engraved "Dennison, Howard & Davis, Waltham." Watches of this period are found bearing the names "C. T. Parker," "P. S. Bartlett." No. 1002 is lowest numbered watch Mr. White has seen.

Serial numbers on watches:

1855	2,100	1890	3,996,000
1856	3,400	1895	5,355,000
1857	5,200	1900	8,827,000
1858	6,734	1905	12,520,000
1859	9,000	1910	15,775,000
1860	15,100	1915	20,157,000
1865	178,200	1920	23,000,000
1870	427,600	1925	25,233,000
1875	961,235	1930	27,323,000
1880	1,373,000	1935	28,800,000
1885	2,587,000	1940	30,640,000

Names on watches:
Dennison, Howard & Davis
Appleton, Tracy & Co.
C. T. Parker
P. S. Bartlett
American Watch Co.
Sporting
Watson
Crescent Street
Crescent Garden
Wm. Ellery
Riverside
Adams St.
Lady Washington
Seaside
Hillside
Bond St.
Royal
(others)

See Charles Crossman, *Jeweler's Circular*, 1885–; Henry G. Abbott, *The Watch Factories of America, Past and Present*; H. C. Brearley, *Time Telling Through the Ages*; Willis I. Milham, *Time and Timekeepers*; and Charles W. Moore, *Timing a Century*. (Geo. V. White) (Mark F. Massey)

WALTON, HIRAM: Cincinnati, O. *Ca.*1820.
—, S. B.: Livermore Falls, Me. *Ca.*1850. Invented clock that would "run for a year." (S. B. Patterson)

WAPLES, NATHANIEL: Phila., 58 High St., Dir. 1816–1819.

WARD & GOVETT: Phila. Dir. 1813–1814.
—, J., & Co.: Phila. Dir. 1843.
—, J. (John) & W. (William): Phila. Dir. 1839–1842.
—, J. & W. L., & Co.: Phila. Dir. 1839.
—, ANTHONY: Phila. Admitted freeman of Phila. 1717. Tall clocks. Moved to N.Y.C. 1724. Tall clocks owned by Mrs. A. E. Brown, Phila., and J. D. Woodward, Sewell, N.J. (Prime)
—, EDWARD H.: Phila. Dir. 1839–1842.
—, ISAAC: Phila. Dir. 1811–1818.
—, JAMES: Hartford, Conn. Ca.1800. Pos. dealer and importer.
—, JOHN: Phila. Dir. 1803, 1839.
—, JOHN: Phila. Dir. 1808, 1813–1848. Some confusion on these. (Prime)
—, JOSEPH: N.Y.C. 1735–1760. (Baillie)
—, JOSEPH: Henniker, N.H. n/d. "Tall clocks with wood movts. like those made at Ashby, Mass., yet with different details." (E. A. Battison)
—, LAUREN: Salem Bridge, Conn. Ca.1830.
—, LEWIS: Salem Bridge, Conn. Ca.1830.
—, MACOCK: 1702–1783. Wallingford, Conn. Son of William and Lettice Beach Ward. May have been apprentice of Ebenezer Parmalee. In 1724 est. shop in Wallingford, Conn. Tower clock for Wallingford Meeting House 1738. Inventive; clocks, reeds for hand looms, clock cases, and other cabinet works. Shop attached to house. None now known. In Dr. Wm. Horton Col. bell of Tall clock marked "Macock Ward." Left complete set Clockmakers' tools. (Hoopes)
—, NATHAN: Fryeburg, Me. Ca.1800.
—, RICHARD: Salem Bridge, Conn., Nov. 5, 1829, received patent on "self-moving clock, for winding up," from Waterbury, Conn.
—, THOMAS: Baltimore. Adv. 1755, 1777.
—, W. W.: Winnsboro, S.C. Adv. 1841.
—, WILLIAM: Litchfield, Conn. Ca.1830. "Silversmith and Clockmaker." (Hist.)
—, WILLIAM L.: Phila. Dir. 1831 and later.
WARE, BEACON: Salem and Greenwich, N.J. 1789–1820. (PG)
—, GEORGE: Camden, N.J. 1820–1822.
WARFIELD, J. H.: Baltimore. Ca.1827.
WARING, GEORGE: N.Y.C. Dir. 1848.
WARK, WILLIAM: Phila. Dir. 1848 and later.

WARNER (Geo. J.) & SCHUYLER: 1798.
—, WINTHROP, & Co.: Bristol. (tx) 1853–1854.
—, ALBERT: Bristol. (tx) 1857–1888. Clock verges and other parts at shop E. side Main St., near Pequabuck R. Doubtful if name on any clocks.
—, CUTHBERT: 1780–1838. Baltimore, 1799–1807. Phila. Dir. 1837.
—, ELIJAH: –1829. Lexington, Ky. Dir. 1818–1829. "Wooden Clock Maker." Will inventory showed he sold clocks in nearly every county in Ky. (C. Frank Dunn)
—, (Geo.) and REED: N.Y.C. 1802.
—, GEORGE J. (or T.): N.Y.C. 1795–1806. Also in Warner & Reed 1802. (Baillie)
—, JOHN: N.Y.C. 1790–1802.
—, THOMAS: Cincinnati, O. Ca.1820.
—, WARREN: Cincinnati, O. Ca.1830. (Lockett)
WARREN MFG. Co.: Roxbury or Boston. See Waltham Watch Co.
"— MFG. Co., THE": Used on watches ca.1853 by Warren Mfr. Co.
— TELECHRON Co.: Ashland, Mass. First president Henry Warren, pioneer inventor of electric synchronous motor, ca.1914. Still in business. (Robert Buckley)
WARRINGTON, J. & S. R.: Phila. Dir. 1822–1825.
—, JOHN, & Co.: Phila. Dir. 1828–1831.
—, S. R., & Co.: Phila. Dir. 1841 and later.
—, JOHN: Phila. Dir. 1811–1822, 1833.
—, S. (Samuel) R.: Phila. Dir. 1828 and later.
WASBROUGH & SON: Bristol. n/d. Tall clock. Pos. Eng. (Dre)
"WASHINGTON, LADY," used by American Watch Co. ca.1880.
— STREET WATCH Co.: Chicago. n/d. Size 18 key wind in heavy nickel case. (NAWCC Bull. No. 26)
— WATCH Co.: Washington, D.C. 1872–1874. f. (Evans)
WATERBURY CLOCK Co.: Waterbury, Conn. 1857–1944. Org. March 27, 1857, as branch of Benedict & Burnham. Grew rapidly. Arad W. Welton first president. New factory 1873, No. Elm St. All types popular Shelf clocks; some Tall clocks. Began 1892 to make watches for Ingersoll. Purchased business of Robert H. Ingersoll

& Bro. 1922, when it failed. Became U.S. Time Corp. 1944. Shelf clock and "Travel" clock in Essex Inst.

— CLOCK Co.: N.Y.C.; sales office, 4 Cortlandt St. Sales agent for Waterbury Clock Co., E. Ingraham & Co., Wm. L. Gilbert Clock Co., Welch, Spring & Co., Jerome & Co., Terry Clock Co. 1875 catalogue with price list in Barny Col. lists four types blinking eye clocks — Topsey, Sambo, Continental and Organ Grinder, priced at $5.75. (See ill. Nos. 282, 283.)

— CLOCK Co.: Winsted, Conn. Joint stock company. f. Silas B. Terry reported to have worked for them. Ca.1850.

— WATCH Co.: Waterbury, Conn. 1878–1880. Watches marked Benedict & Burnham. Inc. 1880. Made first 1,000 Waterbury watches, sold for $3.50 to $4.00 retail. (See ill. No. 306.) Name changed 1898 to New England Watch Co.; f. 1912. Sold 1914 to Robert H. Ingersoll & Bro.; f. 1922. Purchased by Waterbury Clock Co. D. A. Buck of Worcester, Mass., patented original model of Waterbury Watch. Main spring about 9′ long; entire movt. had 58 parts. This type discontinued 1891.

—, M. AMBER: N.Y. Possibly had factory ca.1830. (Dre)

WATERS, GEORGE: Exeter, N.H. n/d. Yellow Watch Paper Bir. Col.

—, THOMAS: Frederick, Md. Late 18th century. Tall clocks.

WATSON, LUMAN, & SON: Cincinnati, O. After 1830. (Knittle)

— & REED: St. Albans, O. Wag-on-Wall clocks. 1828. (Knittle)

—: Paris Hill, Me. Ca.1840. (Ruth S. Brooks)

—, G.: Baillie lists at "Nassau-New Providence, R.I. Early 19th century."

—, G.: Cincinnati, O. Possibly dealer and agent of Ephraim Downs, Bristol, Conn., in 1820's.

—, J.: Chelsea and Boston, Mass. Ca.1840.

—, JAMES: Phila. Dir. 1820 and later. Of Hildeburn & Watson.

—, JAMES: –1806. New London, Conn. London-trained C. and W.; to New London, 1769, where he worked as journeyman. Adv. Dec. 1769. Made and repaired all kinds of clocks and watches.

In 1801 Jonathan Brooks, Merchant, adv. for clockmaker to go to West Indies; Watson died there. (Hoopes)

WATSON, JOHN: Boston. Dir. 1842.

—, LUMAN: 1790–1841. Son of Thomas; C. Dir. 1825, 1828, 1834. Adv. in 1819, "Ivory and Wood clock factory." Clock factory 1826 employed 18 workmen, "mfging $20,000 clocks, of which $15,000 exported." Factory possibly in Brighton (now Cincinnati) and may have used water power from canal on which it was located. Adv. 1836, "clock factory which is quite an extensive concern, making annually 2,500 clocks, and operated by waterpower." Later activities not known. Tall clocks which greatly resemble those of Downs, and other Conn. makers. "L. Watson" or "Luman Watson" on dials. Wooden 30-hr. movts. Shelf clocks later. Adv. 1829. Label, "Improved Mantel Clocks mfg & Sold Wholesale & Retail by L. Watson, 7th between Main & Syracuse Sts. Warranted Superior to any bought from the Eastern States." (Lockett) (Coleman)

—, THOMAS: Cincinnati, O. Father of Luman. In Read & Watson 1809. "Came from Mass." (Lockett)

WATT, JOHN IRVINE: Pa. n/d. Tall clocks. (Conrad)

WATTLES, W. W., & SONS: Pittsburgh, Pa. Ca.1850.

—, W. W.: Pittsburgh, Pa. Ca.1850. Name on dial French-type Shelf clock with glass sides, Barny Col.

WATTS, CHARLES: Rochester, N.Y. Dir. 1844 and later.

—, STUART: Boston. Tall clocks. Ca.1740.

WAUGH, JOHN: Schenectady, N.Y. Adv. 1803.

WAY, JOHN: 1766–. Waggontown, Pa. Taxed as C. 1796. (James)

WAYCOTT, RICHARD: "Newton." Tall clock reported by Ernest Cramer. Two English Cs. of this name listed in Baillie; neither listed from Newton.

WAYLAND, H. J.: Henry in England early 19th century. (Baillie)

WEATHERLY, DAVID: Phila., 29 Pewter Platter Alley, also 515 No. 10th St. and 93 No. 3rd St. C. and W. Dir. 1805–1850 and later. Tall clocks owned by

WEATHERLY, DAVID (cont'd)
Mrs. J. W. Sheets, Jr., Phila., Mrs. Helen M. McMeekin, Drexel Hall, Pa., Mrs. E. N. Wright, Phila.

WEAVER, HOLMES: Newport, R.I. 18th century. Picture on label in FT reads, "Cabinet & Chair Maker, Meeting St., Newport, R.I."

—, N. (Nicholas): 1791–1853. Rochester, N.Y. Aw. 1815–1823 and 1834–1846.

WEBB, ISAAC: Boston, on High St. Adv. 1708, "turning old clocks into pendulums . . ." "From England." (BCC)

WEBBER, WILLIAM: Norwalk, O. Ca.1830. "Tall and Mantel clocks." (Knittle)

WEBSTER, H.: Burlington, Bristol, Farmington, Conn. n/d. OG clocks with label, "Improved Brass Clocks made and sold by H. Webster." One in Ray Walker Col.

WEED, ALEX.: Stamford, Conn. n/d. Ira Leonard has watch movt. labeled No. 3596 "like Hampden." Has "WEED" on dial.

WEEKS, JASON: Bangor, Me. Aw. 1840–1860. (Dre)

WEIDA, SOLOMON: Rochester, N.Y. Dir. 1847–1848.

WEIDEMEYER, JOHN M.: Fredericksburg, Va. 1790–1820.

WEIGEL, HENRY: York, Pa. Ca.1820.

WEISS, JEDEDIAH: Phila. Adv. 1777. (Brix)

—, JEDEDIAH: b. Bethlehem, Pa., Feb. 21, 1796, d. there Sept. 3, 1873. Apprentice of L. Krause, earlier C. in Bethlehem. Weiss took over clock business of Krause ca.1817. Continued 45 years. Tall clocks owned by Mrs. Jennie V. Brown, Wilkes Barre, Pa., brass dial, cherry case, endless chain, one-weight drive; and Mrs. Charles Boehmer, Easton, Pa., 8′ tall, walnut case. (Funk)

—, JOSEPH (or J.): –1863. Allentown, Pa. Ca.1840. Tall clock owned by Mrs. R. E. Smith, Sidney, N.Y., cherry case, painted iron dial, strikes hour and half hour, one-weight drive. Dial marked "J. Weiss-Allentown," n/d. See Allentown. C. A. Roberts called him almost last of Lehigh Co. makers.

—, JOSHUA: Allentown, Pa. n/d. Tall clocks.

WEISSER, MARTIN: Pa. Ca.1830. Tall clocks. (Orr)

WELCH (E. N.) MFG. CO.: Bristol. 1864–1903. E. N. Welch consolidated his clock companies under this name in 1864. One of largest Bristol companies. Successful large scale production till his death in 1887. Company into receivership 1897. Reorganized 1903 as The Sessions Clock Co. Continues in business today as large producer of clocks.

—, SPRING, & CO.: Bristol. 1868–1884. Partnership of Elisha N. Welch and Solomon C. Spring. Made high grade Regulator and Calendar clocks under Gale and B. B. Lewis patents. Lewis Calendar clock patented by him in 1862, 1863, 1868. Automatically adjusted for leap years. Lockwood & Brainard Co. of Hartford printed labels for these clocks. Located in Manross clock factory in Forestville. Merged 1884 with E. N. Welch Mfg. Co. (LB)

—, ELISHA N.: b. Chatham, Conn., Feb. 7, 1809, d. Forestville, Aug. 2, 1887. Prominent citizen of Bristol. One of largest producers of Conn. clocks last half 19th century. First connection with clock business was operation of foundry to cast clock weights. When financial panic stopped all Clockmaking in 1850's, purchased entire J. C. Brown clock "empire" in 1855. F. S. Otis Company also acquired, as well as E. & C. H. Manross in 1856, with factories on Church St. Birge, Peck & Co. factory had been purchased by Solomon Spring. In 1868 Welch partner with Spring, as Welch, Spring & Co. The business he had built up continued successfully till his death Aug. 2, 1887. Also president Bristol Mfg. Co. and Bristol Brass & Clock Co.

—, GEORGE: York, Pa. n/d.

—, GEORGE W.: N.Y.C., 244 Greenwich St. 1851–1872. Ex. Museum of City of N.Y.

—, WILLIAM: N.Y.C. 1805. (Baillie)

WELDON, OLIVER: Bristol. (tx) 1841 only.

WELLER, CARTER A.: Stockbridge, N.Y. n/d. Might be Carter & Weller, possible assemblers of parts of clocks made in Conn. (MFM)

— (or Willar), FRANCIS: Phila. Ca.1778. Adv. 1777, "From London, removed to 2nd St., repairs all sorts of Clocks and Watches, horizontal wheels and cylinders made, repeating motions repaired." Adv. 1778, "To those gentlemen to whom he has sold and warranted watches . . . necessity to return to New York City. Apply to Mr. Willar, watchmaker, on 3rd St." (Prime)

WELLES, GELSTON & Co.: Boston. *Ca.*1825. S. and importer.

—, L. T., & Co.: Hartford, Conn., 206 Main St. Watch Paper Bir. Col. "At the old stand of J. Church, Watches."

WELLS, A. & G.: Boston. Dir. 1806.

— (L. T.) & FOSTER (J.): Cincinnati, O. Tower and Shelf clocks and math. insts. (Knittle)

— (Joseph), HENDRICK (Ebenezer N.) & Co.: Bristol. (tx) 1845.

— & WILCOX: Lynn, Mass. *Ca.*1860.

—, ALFRED: Boston. Dir. 1803–1805.

—, C. H.: Colebrook, Conn. *Ca.*1840. Shelf clock in Flint Sale 1926, "mahogany, in plain case 25¾" × 15"." Probably an OG. One of several Colebrook makers about whom there is little information.

—, CALVIN: Watervleit and New Lebanon, N.Y. "Tall clock dated 1817." (Andrews)

—, D.: Ogdensburg, N.Y. Adv. 1813.

—, JOSEPH A.: Bristol. (tx) 1832–1847. Made clocks under his own name. Also partner in Boardman & Wells, 1832–1843, and Wells, Hendrick, & Co. 1845. Received patent Jan. 1, 1847, No. 4,914, with "Chauncey Boardman" on reversed fuzee, used in earliest Conn. Acorn clocks. (Ant. Mar. 1949)

WELSH, ALEXANDER: Baltimore. 1800–1801.

—, BELA: Northampton, Mass. Adv. 1808, Repaired watches and jewelry at shop of Isaac Townshend. (Cutten)

—, DAVID: Lincolnton, N.C. There by 1849. Adv. as C. and W. Adv. 1851. (Cutten)

WELTON, HIRAM (Herman), & Co.: Terryville, Conn. 1841–1845. f. Bros. Shelf clocks, wood movts., then brass. Trouble *ca.*1841 with Chauncey Jerome over use of brass movt. Asked Eli Terry to design brass movt. differing from one Jerome used invented 1837 by bro. Noble. Jason Clemence aw. on brass movt. model. Weight-driven 30-hour OG Shelf clock, wood dial, label, "EXTRA BRASS CLOCKS, manufactured by H. Welton & Co., successors to Eli Terry, Jr., & Co., Terry-ville, Connecticut. Brownson & Co., Printers, 56 Gold St., N.Y.C." (G. B. Davis Col.)

WELTON, H. & H.: Plymouth, Conn. Another name for H. Welton & Co.

—, HIRAM & HERMAN: Plymouth, Conn. Another name for H. Welton & Co.

—, HIRAM: Terryville or Plymouth, Conn. Took over Eli Terry, Jr., clock business 1841. f. 1845. Factory later used to make locks.

—, M.: N.Y.C., 54 John St. 1840–1844. Label, "Improved Clocks . . ." Standard brass movt. OG. Later lawyer. (MFM)

WENDELL, —: Albany, N.Y. Dir. 1839–1842.

WENTWELL, H.: Charleston, S.C. –1795. (MFM)

WENTWORTH, JOSHUA L.: Lowell, Mass., Central St. Dir. 1834–1837. With Joseph Raynes.

—, R.: Buxton n/p. n/d. Name on clock dial. (Burt)

WENTZ, HILARY: Phila. Dir. 1822–1824.

WENZEL Co.: Washington, D.C. Office for promotion of Air clocks; others Baltimore and N.Y.C. 1880's.

—, HERMAN J.: 1830–1884. San Francisco, Cal. Aw. 1851–1906. b. Germany; aptd. to Adolph Lange. To America 1851. Patents July 8, 1873, Oct. 23, 1877, on "Wenzel Air Clocks." With son Rudolph 1876–1906. Biog. by Dr. William Barclay Stephens, Cal. Hist. Soc. Q., Vol. 27, No. 22. (W. Barclay Stephens)

WEST, EDWARD: 1757–1827. Stafford Co., Va., before 1788, Lexington, Ky. Adv. 1788, "Clock & Watch making will be done in the neatest and shortest manner." (LB)

"— END": Used by Lancaster, Pa., Watch Co. *ca.*1878.

—, H.: Southbridge, Mass. Adv. 1830, "Make and repair clocks & watches also works at Silversmith business at his shop about 1½ miles from Southbridge on the Woodstock Road."

—, JAMES L.: Phila. Dir. 1829–1833.

—, JOHN: Bloomingdale, Ill. Watch Paper BCL Col.

—, JOSIAH: Phila., 1 Carter's Lane. Dir. 1798, 1807–1808. Three by this name in Phila. Dir.

WEST, JOSIAH: Phila. –1780. Adv. 1776.
—, JOSIAH: Phila. Dir. 1832. (Prime)
—, THOMAS G.: Phila. Dir. 1819–1822.
WESTCOTT, J.: Brooklyn, N.Y. Dir. 1849.
WESTERN CLOCK CO.: La Salle, Ill. 1895–1930. Cs., Ws. Watches 1895. "Big Ben," "Little Ben," "Westclox" and others. Became division of General Time Instruments Corp. 1934.
— CLOCK MFG. CO.: Peru and La Salle, Ill. Org. 1888. Name changed 1895 to Western Clock Co.
— WATCH CO.: Chicago. Org. 1880; f. 1880. Machinery sold to Illinois Watch Co.
WESTFIELD WATCH CO.: N.Y.C. n/d. (MFM)
WESTGATE, BALDWIN & CO.: Fall River, Mass. Ca.1870.
WESTINGHOUSE, GEORGE: 1846–1914. Inventor, mfr. More than 400 patents. Some work on clocks and watches.
WESTON, JAMES & SON: Boston. Dir. 1859.
—, JAMES: Boston, 8 Eliot St. Dir. 1841–1854, "Clock Maker & Repairer."
WESTPHALL, FERDINAND: Phila. Dir. 1814–1824. "Watch case maker."
WETHERELL & MEAD: Montpelier, Vt. n/d. Watch Paper Cramer Col.
—, NATHAN: Phila. Ca.1830–1840.
WHARFE, JOSEPH: Frederickstown, Md. Adv. 1819.
WHEATON, CALEB, & SON: Providence, R.I., 81 and 165 Main St. Ca.1810–1827.
—, GODFREY, & SON: Providence, R.I. Ca.1824. (Moore)
—, CALEB: 1757–1827. Providence, R.I., 83 Main St. Quaker. Aw. 1785–1827. One of best known Cs. of his time. Tall clocks. (Abbott) (Moore)
—, CALVIN: Providence, R.I. Opposite Gov. Fenner's 1790. To shop in Ambrose Page's house "at the Sign of the Clock directly opposite the Friends' Meeting House," 1791. (Moore)
—, GODFREY: Providence, R.I. Ca.1790. (Moore)
WHEELER, BROOKS & CO.: Livonia, N.Y. Adv. 1835.
— & SON: Salem, N.J. n/d. Watch Paper Cramer Col.
—, CHARLES: New Brunswick, N.J. n/d.
—, D. C.: New London, Conn. Ca.1860.

WHEELER, DAVID: Boston, Newbury St. Blacksmith. Adv. 1765, "to make and fix iron rods with points upon houses or any other eminences for prevention from the effects of lightning." (Hist.)
—, HENRY: Boston. Dir. 1820.
—, PHILIP HENRY: 1849–1917. Pos. with U.S. Watch Co., Marion (Jersey City), N.J., 1871. With Rockford Watch Co. 1874. Patent No. 229215, June 22, 1880, on "Micrometer Regulator"; No. 238464 March 1, 1881, on "Stem Wind Watch." With Illinois Watch Co. 1881. Supt. Columbus Watch Co. 1884. Patent No. 352283 June 3, 1886, on "Watch Regulator." To Otay, Cal., 1889. Later to Japan. (Chamberlain)
—, SAMUEL, JR.: Rochester, N.Y. Dir. 1844.
WHEELOCK, GEORGE: Wilmington, Del. Ca.1790. Cabinetmaker. Name on Tall clock dials.
WHENGO, ZEKES: n/d. (TP)
WHERRITT, SAMUEL A.: Richmond, Ky. Adv. 1824, "Clock & Watch business in all its various branches." Principally S. (LB)
WHETCROFT, WILLIAM: Annapolis, Md. G., J. Adv. 1767, "He likewise takes care of clocks in this town and will keep them in good order, and send a man once a week to examine them and wind them for 15 shillings a week." Baltimore, Adv. 1773. Adv. 1778, "To be sold by the subscriber at Elkridge Landing, a great variety of material for the clock and watch business." (Prime)
WHINSTON, GEORGE: Winchester, Conn. Cabinetmaker. Apt. Henry B. Horton ca.1838 who later made Ithaca Calendar clocks.
WHIPPLE, ARNOLD: Providence, R.I. Ca. 1810.
WHITCOMB, A.: Stow, Mass. n/d. Shelf clock owned by Harold K. Mulford, Greenport, L.I.
WHITE, WILLIAM H. & CO.: Phila. Dir. 1835–1837. "Watch Dealers."
—, CHARLES: N.Y.C., 66 Fulton St. Dir. 1872.
—, D. C.: Newark, N.J. 1827–1832.
—, F.: Brooklyn, N.Y. Ca.1820. Ex. Museum City of N.Y.

WHITE, FRANCIS: Phila. Dir. 1849.

—, G. W.: Northampton, Mass. 1830–. W. alone after Phelps & White dissolved.

—, JOHN: Boston. Late 18th century. Tall clocks.

—, JOHN: N.Y.C. Early 19th century. Tall clock in Metropolitan Museum. (Baillie)

—, JOSEPH: Phila., 162 No. 3rd St. Dir. 1808–1818.

—, JOSEPH, JR.: Phila. Dir. 1811–1817.

—, L. W.: No. Adams, Mass. *Ca.*1850.

—, MATLOCK: N.Y.C. *Ca.*1770.

—, N. H.: Newark, N.J. *Ca.*1870. "Oriode Watches."

—, P. G.: West Chester, Pa. Dir. 1857–1858. "Watchmaker." (James)

—, PEREGRINE: 1747–1834. Woodstock, Conn. Son of Joseph and Martha Sawyer White. Descendant first Pilgrim child. Pos. aptd. in Mass. Shop W. of Muddy Brook Village well-equipped with metal-working tools. Tall clocks for many years, excellent brass movts.; some engraved dials; later enameled iron dials. (Hoopes) (See ill. No. 58.)

—, SEBASTIAN: Phila. Dir. 1795–1796.

—, THOMAS: Phila. Dir. 1810.

—, WM. W.: N.Y.C., 68 Bowery. n/d. White Watch Paper Bir. Col.

WHITEAR, JOHN: –1762. Fairfield, Conn. Aw. 1736. Adv. 1738. C., bell founder. Cast bell *ca.*1744 for Christ Church, Stratford, Conn. 1750 Tower clock installed; pos. maker. Early and successful. Succeeded by son John, Jr. (Hoopes)

—, JOHN, JR.: 1738–1773. C., Bell founder. Son and apt. of John. Tall 8-day brass movt. clock 1762 for Peter Perry. Cast bells for Cheshire, Colchester, and Farmington, Conn. (Hoopes)

WHITEHEAD, JOHN: Haddonfield, N.J. To America 1821. Took over business of Job Hollinshead, C. Tower clock, 2 dials, Cumberland Nail & Iron Co., Bridgeton, N.J., oldest public clock in Bridgeton. (Williams)

—, JOHN: Phila. Dir. 1831, 1848–1849. Norristown, Pa., Haddonfield, N.J. Tall clocks.

—, WILLIAM W.: Phila. Dir. 1850. Watch Paper Cramer Col., "459 N. 10th St."

WHITING (B.) & MARQUAND (Isaac): Fairfield, Conn. *Ca.*1790. (Hoopes)

—, ADNA: Bristol and Farmington, Conn. (tx) 1847–1857. Assignee Joseph Ives patents. In Atkins, Whiting & Co. (Hoopes)

—, B.: Fairfield, Conn. "Named but unknown." (Hoopes)

—, LEWIS E.: Saratoga Springs, N.Y. 1860's. *Ca.*600 Timby Solar Globe Clocks. (See ill. No. 269.)

—, RILEY: –1835. Winchester and Winsted, Conn. Aw. 1807. With Hoadleys. Wood movt., hang-up, Tall clocks. Alone 1813–. Built several shops. Later Shelf clocks, wood movts. d. 1835, causing flourishing Winsted clock business to stop for a time. Became Clarke, Gilbert & Co. 1841–; now William L. Gilbert Clock Corp.

—, SAMUEL: Concord, Mass. 1808–1817. With Nathaniel Munroe. Large business in Banjo clocks. Ex. in James Conlon Col., "gold fronts and base, brass side arms and bezel." (BCC)

WHITMAN, BENJAMIN: 1774–1857. Reading, Pa., Callowhill St. 4th Group. Adv. 1796, Adv. 1799. Dial painter. May have confined himself to that work after 1800. Tall clocks. One owned by Mrs. J. M. Poole, Haverford, Pa., movt. No. 4, No. 199 on back of dial; moon, calendar, seconds track "31" instead of "60."

—, EZRA: Bridgewater, Mass. 1790–1840. (Abbott)

WHITNEY, ASA: N.Y.C. Aw. 1798–1812. Tall clock mentioned *Ant.* Sept., 1948. "A man of mystery." (Stow)

—, EBEN: Norwalk, Conn. *Ca.*1845. White Watch Paper Bir Col., "Late of N.Y.C., on Down Town Road ¾ mile below bridge."

—, EBENEZER: N.Y.C. *Ca.*1825 or later. (MFM)

—, GEORGE: Boston. Dir. 1803.

—, M. F.: Schenectady, N.Y. Adv. 1823–1824.

—, MOSES: Boston. Dir. 1830.

—, THOMAS: Phila. *Ca.*1800. Math. insts. Pos. C.

—, WILLIAM H.: Rochester, N.Y. Dir. 1845–1846.

WHITTACKER & Co.: Providence, R.I. 1824.

WHITTACKER, THOMAS, & G. DANA: Providence, R.I. n/d. Bought out N. Dodge.

—, GEORGE: Providence, R.I. 1805. (FT)

—, GEN. JOSIAH: Providence, R.I. *Ca.* 1800–1805. Partner Nehemiah Dodge.

—, THOMAS: Providence, R.I. *Ca.*1820.

—, WILLIAM: N.Y.C. 1731–1755.

WHITTEMORE, J.: Boston. Dir. 1856.

WHITTON, E. J.: Boston. n/d. 100-day movt. clock in Essex Inst.

WHYLER, JOHN: Norwalk, Milan, and Fitchville, O. "Clockmaker, also coppersmith." "Early, no recorded data." (Knittle)

WICHITA WATCH CO., THE: Wichita, Kansas. Org. 1887; aw. briefly. "A few watches were finished by the workmen." (MFM)

WICKENS, OBED: N.Y.C. Dir. 1849.

WIDDIFIELD & GAW: Phila. Dir. 1820–1822.

—, WILLIAM: Phila. Dir. 1817.

—, WILLIAM, JR.: Phila. Dir. 1820–1822. Fayetteville, N.C., 1821; charge of Charles Clark's store; bought store 1823. (Cutten)

WIEDEMEYER, J. M.: Baltimore. 1800–1801.

WIELAND, FREDERICK: Phila. Dir. 1848.

—, JOHANN GEORGE: Salem, Mass. *Ca.* 1780. (Baillie)

WIGGIN, HENRY: Newfields, N.H. Early 19th century. Clock cases for John Kennard.

WIGGINS & CO.: Phila. Dir. 1831.

—, T., & CO.: (Wriggins, Thomas, & Co.): Phila. Dir. 1831–1846.

WIGHTMAN & SPERRY: N.Y.C. Shelf clock, brass, weight-driven movt., rack and snail strike, in Olin S. Nye Col.

—, ALLEN S.: N.Y.C., 243 Bowery. Dir. 1840.

WILBUR, CHARLES: N.Y.C. Dir. 1846.

—, JOB B.: Newport, R.I. 1815–1849.

WILCOX, CYPRIAN: New Haven, Conn. *Ca.* 1820.

—, WESLEY W.: Chicago. 1881. Stem-wind watch parts. (MFM)

WILDBAHN, THOMAS: 1763–1805. Reading, Pa. Dir. 1799. C. Tall clocks, some with sweep seconds hands. 3rd Group.

WILDER, JOSHUA & EZRA: Hingham, Mass. Adv. Nov. 17, 1845, "8-day brass, $16; 1-day brass, $6; 1-day wood, $3; 8-day brass TP, $10; Alarm Clocks, TP's, and Alarm Watches at various prices."

—, L. H., & CO.: Phila. Dir. 1845. "Clock Dealers."

WILDER, EZRA: Hingham, Mass. C. Aw. *ca.* 1825–1850. Son of Joshua. Marr. Rebecca, dau. of Reuben Tower 1841.

—, JOSHUA: 1786–1860. b. Hingham, Mass. C. Aw.*ca.*1808. Last adv. 1845. Father of Ezra. Quaker. Marr. Judith Shearman 1812. Pos. aptd. to Joshua Bailey. Tall and Dwarf Tall clocks. (See ill. Nos. 94, 95.) Tall clock at Museum Fine Arts, Boston. Dwarf Tall clock at Edison Inst. (BCC)

WILKINS, ASA: Wiscasset, Me. or R.I. *Ca.* 1810. (Dre)

WILKINSON, W. S. & J. B.: Chicago. *Ca.* 1880.

—, CHARLES: Canton, N.Y. 1820's. Tall, Banjo, Shelf clocks. (Dre)

WILLARD: Famous name in Mass. Clockmaking history. Two families. Benjamin, Sr., and Sarah Brooks Willard had 12 children, four of whom (Benj., Simon, Ephraim, Aaron) were Cs. Benj. Sr. was descendant of Col. Simon Willard, who founded Concord, Mass.; prominent leader against Indians in King Philip's War. Benjamin, 3rd child (no children of his in clock business). Simon (1753–1848), 8th child had three sons—Simon, Jr., John Mears, Benjamin Franklin, all connected with Clockmaking; son of Benjamin Franklin, Zabadiel Adams, Willard, was also C. Ephraim, 9th child, C.; no descendants in the business. Aaron (1757–1844), the 10th child, had two sons, Aaron, Jr., and Henry, Cs. These men chiefly at Grafton, Roxbury, Boston.

Second family, also descendants of Col. Simon Willard, consisted of two sons of Jacob (1734–1808), farmer at Ashburnham, Mass., and Rhoda Randall of Stow: Philander Jacob and Alexander Tarbell, both Cs.

Colony of allied artisans surrounded Simon and Aaron in Roxbury. Cabinet and case makers included: Deacon Nehemiah Munroe, Thomas Dudley, John Clapp, William and Samuel Fisk, Charles Crane and William Crehore, John Doggett, Samuel Doggett, Henry Willard.

Complete well-documented and illustrated story of Willard Clockmaking in John Ware Willard, *A History of Simon Willard, Clockmaker and Inventor*, 1911 (now out of print). Information developed in proceedings of Boston Clock Club 1934–1940, and research by Albert L. Partridge, et al. (See ill. Nos. 74–80, 106–123, 134–143.)

WILLARD (A., Jr.) & NOLEN (Spencer): Boston. 1806–1809. Dial and sign painters on Boston Neck. Pos. Phila. Edwin L. Burt has seen dials of Roxbury group including Simon Willard marked "Wilson" and "Osborne," on false plate or on moon or calendar ring, but not on dial proper. James Conlon reported dials with "Willard & Nolen" on false plate.

—, SIMON, & SON: Boston. Pos. Simon and either Simon, Jr., or Benjamin Franklin. Two Banjo clocks in James Conlon Col., "Banjo with half round mahogany fronts, tablets, brass side arms and bezel"; "Banjo, tablets of glass painted to simulate mahogany, brass bezel, no side arms."

—, AARON: Oct. 13, 1757, Grafton, Mass.–May 20, 1844, Boston, 843 Washington St. b. Grafton. Son of Benjamin and Sarah Brooks Willard. C. With bro. Simon most important of Willards. Prob. taught by bros. Benjamin and Simon. Aw. Grafton before Rev. War. In War. Clocks marked "Aaron Willard, Grafton" known. Followed Simon to Roxbury 1780 and settled near him making clocks. Ca.1792–1798 moved to 843 Washington St., Boston; estb. factory. Good business man; considerable fortune. Sons and apts. Aaron, Jr., Henry. Succeeded 1823 by son Aaron, Jr. Overshadowed by bro. Simon but made splendid clocks. Tall, Wall, Mass. Shelf, Gallery, Banjo clocks. Banjo clocks sometimes more ornate than Simon's. Arabic numbers on some dials; some marked "Aaron Willard, Boston." (See ill. Nos. 134–136.) Developed Wall and Mass. Shelf or Half clocks (first made in Grafton). Seven clocks in Metropolitan Museum, others in Boston Museum of Fine Arts, et al. Three in James Conlon Col., "Mass. Shelf, mahogany case, OG feet, fret, kidney dial, TP, delicate hands"; "Mass. Shelf, Presentation case painted white with stencil black trim, frames over dial and over bottom panel, gold-leafed like the Presentation Banjo, dished dial, painted tablet, paw feet"; "Mass. Shelf, early type mahogany case on case, kidney dial."

WILLARD, AARON, JR.: 1783–1864. Boston. Bro. Henry. Son, apt., successor of Aaron 1823. After father's retirement continued to make large number of clocks at Boston factory. Tall, TP, Banjo, Regulator, Gallery, Tower, Lyre clocks. Employed number of workmen. One timepiece numbered 3482. Comfortable fortune; retired 1850 to "Oak Hill, Newton." Pos. originated Lyre clock. "He made them in great quantity and variety after 1823; some with solid mahogany cases, some carved, and others with tablets." (JWW) Some Banjo clocks had wooden bezels. "Made a less expensive grade of clocks than Simon Willard. Inclined to use more gilding, and commonly added a base piece." (JWW) (See ill. No. 153.) Banjo clock in Essex Inst., another in Museum City of N.Y. Tower clock at West Church, Grafton. Letter to Samuel Terry, March 11, 1830: "Sir,—I would make a brief reply. Accordingly state that I have been in business say 25 years, been in the habit occasionally of putting looking glasses into the fronts of my clocks and timepieces of all descriptions and I believe it has been practiced by many others, some of whom are of longer standing in the business than myself. There is an 8-day clock owned by a lady in Roxbury which has a looking glass in the front, this clock I would judge to have been made one hundred years at least." Pos. answer to Jerome's claims about Looking Glass clock.

—, ALEXANDER TARBELL: 1774–1850. Ashburnham, Mass., 1796–1800, Ashby, Mass., 1800–1830. Son of Jacob and Rhoda Randall Willard. Was aptd. to Abraham Edwards or self-taught. Tall clocks, wood, brass movts.; mus. timepieces, Tower clocks.

—, B.: N.Y.C., 80 Broadway. n/d. Dir. 1818.

—, BENJAMIN: 1743–1803. Grafton, Lexington, Roxbury, Mass. b. Grafton. Son of Benjamin and Sarah Brooks Willard. Pos. taught Clockmaking by Cheneys in E. Hartford, Conn., where he was "Last maker" in house of Benjamin Cheney.

WILLARD, BENJAMIN (cont'd)
In Grafton, Tall clocks ca.1765–ca.1771. (See ill. No. 76.) Adv. 1783, "After 8 years absence from this country, he has again begun his business at his farm in Grafton . . ." Later in Lexington. Tall clock extant, "Benjamin Willard, Grafton" on dial, "Simon Willard and Mr. John Morris" on cast lead pendulum bob. Tall clock, "Benjamin Willard, Lexington" in James Conlon Col. Dwarf Tall clock ill. No. 90. Pos. taught bros. Simon, Ephraim, Aaron. d. Baltimore.

—, BENJAMIN FRANKLIN: 1803–1847. Boston. Son, apt., of Simon. "Inherited much ability, an exceptionally skilled workman, did not make many clocks. His astronomical clock, 1844, excellent. Also made a Revolving Light for the U. S. Government." (JWW) Pos. in Rich & Willard ca.1846.

—, EPHRAIM: 1755–. Grafton, Medford, Roxbury, Boston (Sheaf's Lane, now West St.), Mass. b. Grafton. Son of Benjamin and Sarah Brooks Willard. C., W. Bro. Benjamin, Simon, Aaron. Prob. aptd. to bro. Benjamin. Aw. Grafton until 1777, pos. Medford, Roxbury 1798. Living in Boston 1801–1805, on Sheaf's Lane, now West St. "Clockmaker, otherwise trader." Tall clocks only (see ill. Nos. 74 and 75). Moved to N.Y.C. No definite record of him there. N.Y.C. Dir. lists an Ephraim Willard 1811–1816 as "Shipmaster," 55 Elizabeth St.; another listing 1825–1826 as "Watchmaker," 56½ Bowery, appearing with variations till 1832–1833; then 180 Forsyth St.

—, HENRY: 1802–1887. Boston. Ca.1823–1847. Son of Aaron. Bro. Aaron, Jr. Famous Cabinetmaker. Clock cases for Aaron and Aaron, Jr., William Cummens, E. Taber, Simon, Jr. To Canton, Mass., to run farm; some clock cases for "Simon Willard and Son." d. Boston. (JWW)

—, JACOB P.: Ashby, Mass. Error for Philander Jacob. (JWW)

—, JOHN: Boston. Dir. 1803, 1842. (First date too early for John Mears Willard.) (Abbott)

—, JOHN MEARS: 1800–. Boston. Son of Simon Willard. Artist; with wife, Mary

Bird Willard, painted clock tablets. "Died young." (JWW)

WILLARD, PHILANDER JACOB: 1772–1840. Ashburnham, Ashby, Mass. Son of Jacob and Rhoda Randall Willard. Bro. Alexander T. Pos. apt. of Abraham Edwards; prob. self-taught. Aw. 1796. To Ashby and with Alex. T. in Ashby 1825–1840. Ca.1825. "Gravity clock." "A fine workman, persistent and patient." (JWW)

—, SIMON: 1753–1848. Grafton, Roxbury, Mass. C., inventor. Most famous of Willard brothers. b. Grafton, son of Benjamin and Sarah Brooks Willard. Father of Simon, Jr., B. F., J. M. Limited schooling; showed early mechanical skill. Aptd. to "a Mr. Morris, an Englishman then engaged in making clocks in Grafton." (JWW) (Morris's name with Willard's on Tall clock pendulum ball.) Prob. taught by bro., Benjamin. Prominent apts., Abel and Levi Hutchins, Elnathan Taber, Wm. Lemist, Daniel Munroe, Jr.

Aw. Grafton ca.1766–1780; Tall clocks; Wall Timepieces, and Mass. Shelf or Half clocks. Ca. 15 Wall clocks known; movt. usually round (to save brass), pendulum attached directly to anchor. First Banjo clocks prob. conceived in Grafton; later models led to final development in Roxbury.

To Roxbury, 1780. Clock jack (see ill. No. 113) was a revolving spit for roasting meats, powered by clockwork; sold by Paul Revere et al.; mentioned in bro. Benjamin's adv.

Banjo clock completed late 1790's, patented 1802. (See ill. Nos. 137 and 138.) Always called it "Improved Patent Timepiece"; it had no strike train. Immediate success and acceptance; finely proportioned, best materials, finest workmanship. Movt. brass, 8-day, compounded pulleys (see ill. No. 137). Wheels and axles reduced to a working minimum; plates farther apart; pendulum in front of movt. From 1802 confined efforts to Patent Timepiece, abandoning other models. Labels printed by I. Thomas, Jr., Worcester. According to John Ware Willard, Simon made ca.1200 Tall and Shelf clocks, 4,000 patent Timepieces, some Gallery, Tower (25 listed) clocks, and *ca*.25 Lighthouse clocks (1822). (See ill. Nos. 150, 151.) Little profit from inventions. Highly skilled. Great pride in clocks. Sold tools and good will to favorite apt., Elnathan Taber. (Taber allowed to use Willard name on own clocks.) Retired 1839. d. Boston aged 95.

Clocks in principal museums. Fine group in Museum Fine Arts, Boston. See John Ware Willard, *A History of Simon Willard, Clockmaker and Inventor*, 1911. (JWW)

WILLARD, SIMON, JR.: 1795–1881. Roxbury, Mass.; N.Y.C.; Boston, 9 Congress St. Son of Simon. Bro. John Mears and Benjamin Franklin. Father of Zabadiel. At West Point 1813–1815, resigned 1816. Aptd. to father from whom he inherited great mechanical ability. Crockery business in Roxbury 1817–1824; with father 1824–1826; N.Y.C. 1826–1828, where he learned to make Chrons.; Boston 1828–1881. Financially successful. Charge of Boston Tower clocks, also clocks at Harvard University (5 Willard clocks). Two Watch Papers Bir. Col., "Simon Willard, Jr., 9 Congress St., Boston. / Chronometers for ascertaining longitude / Chimney and Musical Clocks Repaired /" Also used "Simon Willard & Son." (See ill. No. 143.) (JWW)

—, SYLVESTRE: Bristol, Conn. (tx) 1835. In Case, Willard & Co.

—, THOMAS: n/p. n/d. Tall clock, wood movt., in Barny Col.

—, ZABADIEL: 1826–. Son of Simon, Jr., and Eliza Adams Willard. Aptd. to father 1841, partner 1850. Lecturer and chemist. Ret. 1870; last Willard C.

WILLBANK, JOHN: Phila. Dir. 1839–1841. Bell caster. Tall clock with bell so stamped owned by B. C. Waldenmaker, Washington, D.C. Cast bell 1836 for West Chester town clock. (James)

WILLCOX, ALVAN: 1783–1870. Norwich, Conn. With Judah Hart bought in 1805 Abel Brewster business. Fayetteville, N.C., 1819; to New Haven, Conn., 1823. (Hoopes)

WILLIAMS & HATCH: No. Attleboro, Mass. 1850's.

— & LESLIE (Wm. J) (Leslie & Williams): New Brunswick, N.J., 1780–1791. Tren-ton, N.J., 1791–1806; took over Yates & Kent 1798.

WILLIAMS, ORTON & PRESTON: Farmington, Conn. Shelf clock 29 × 19¼ so marked. n/d.

—, ORTON & PRESTON & CO.: Farmington, Conn. *Ca*.1830. "Improved Clocks with brass bushings, wooden movts." Shelf clock in Edison Inst.; others owned by J. W. Cooner, Upper Darby, Pa.; Mrs. J. A. Campbell, Lebanon, Pa.; Ben Milberg, N.Y.C.

— & VICTOR: Lynchburg, Va. *Ca*.1810.

—, BENJAMIN: Elizabeth, N.J. Aw. 1788–1794. Pos. in Williams & Leslie, New Brunswick, N.J. Later Trenton. (Williams)

—, DAVID: Newport and Providence, R.I. Early 19th Cent. Tall clock ill. No. 86; Mass. Shelf clock ill. No. 124.

—, DAVID: East Cahn, Pa. taxed as C. 1795. "Of short duration, none now extant." (James)

"—, E. S.," used by Cornell Watch Co. 1871–.

—, GEORGE ROBERT: Charleston, S.C., 21 Meeting St. and 41 King St. Adv. 1786.

—, HINDS P.: Boston, 379 Washington St. Dir. 1860. Watch Paper Bir. Col.

—, ICHABOD: Elizabeth, N.J. 1836–1842.

—, JOHN: Phila. Dir. 1818.

—, JOHN G.: Chicago. 1882. "Watch Mfr." (MFM)

—, N.: Portsmouth, N.H. (?) n/d.

—, NICHOLAS: Libertytown, Md. Adv. 1792.

—, STEPHEN: Providence, R.I. With Nehemiah Dodge 1799. Then alone. (Moore)

—, THOMAS: Flemington, N.J., Village St. To America 1792. Tall clocks 1792–1796 Queen Anne cases, 1796–1800 Chippendale cases, 1800–1808 Sheraton cases. Left Flemington 1808–. Joachim Hill his apt.; pos. took over business. (J. J. Schenk)

—, WILLIAM: Boston. Before Rev. War.

WILLIAMSON, HENRY: Baltimore. Adv. 1808.

WILLIS, JOHN: Burlington, N.J. 1745–1753. Tall clocks.

WILLMOTT, BENJAMIN: Easton, Md. "1797–1816." (FTO)

WILLOCK, JOHN: Pittsburgh, Pa. 1830's. Pos. Dealer.

WILLS, JOSEPH: 1700–1759. Phila. Aw. 1725–1759. Tall clocks. Ex. owned by Mrs. H. C. Hagar, Salem, Mass.; Mrs. E. N. Stent, Wayne, Pa.; Mrs. R. C. Heyl, Pelham, N.Y.; Mrs. R. M. Doyle, Phila.; Mrs. C. E. Bear, York, Pa.; Omar D. Fisher, Pittsburgh. All have brass movts., 8-day and 30-hr. endless drive, with single weight, some sweep seconds, moon, brass dials, some 10½″ sq.

WILMIRT, JOHN J.: N.Y.C. 1793–1798.

WILMOT & RICHMOND: Savannah, Ga. 1850's.

—, SAMUEL: Aw., adv. New Haven, Conn., –1808. Adv. 1825 Georgetown and Charleston, S.C. (Cutten)

WILMURT, STEPHEN M.: N.Y.C. 1802–1805.

"WILSON": Name on back of imported dials of Tall clocks; James Wilson, 1788–.

— & DUNN: N.Y.C. Dir. 1844.

— & OSBORNE: English dial makers. Sometimes Osborne & Wilson.

—, T. & J.: Phila. or Nottingham, Pa. "1796" and name on painted iron dial of Tall clock owned by Pauline W. Wheeler, Oxford, Pa. Pos. only case-maker.

—, ANDREW D.: Providence, R.I. Aw. ca. 1890–ca.1920. Gravity escapement Regulator clock 1899. (HIA Journal July 1947)

—, HOSEA: Baltimore. 1817.

—, JAMES: Ca.1745–. Trenton, N.J. Aptd. to S., N.Y.C. (John Fitch). Before 1768 to Trenton, King St. f. 1769. Employed John Fitch who bought tools and succeeded him 1773. (Williams)

—, ROBERT: Received patent on "Alarm Bell for Timepieces" July 3, 1832, from Williamsport, Pa.

—, ROBERT: Phila. Dir. 1835.

WILTBERGER, CHARLES H.: Washington, D.C. Ca.1825.

WIMER, ANDREW: Phila. Dir. 1818–1819.

—, GEORGE: Phila. Ca.1820. (Baillie)

WING, MOSES: 1760–1809. Windsor, Conn. Son of Samuel and Hannah Wing. G. Adv. 1803, "Maker of all kinds of brass clocks and timepieces." 1781–1809. In Rev. War. Built house and shop in Windsor. Brass movt. clocks, also S. (Hoopes)

WINGATE, FREDERICK: 1782–1864. b. Haverhill, Mass. Bro. Paine. C. To Augusta, Me. Marr. Hannah Page 1806. Tall clocks. N.H. Mirror clock in D. K. Packard Col. Benjamin Swan, apt., prob. followed to Augusta. Tall clock owned by Hill Jewelry Co., N. E. Harbor, Me. (Mrs. J. B. Mason)

WINGATE, GEORGE: Baltimore. 1816.

—, PAINE: 1767–1833. b. Haverhill, Mass. Bro. Frederick. Boston Dir. 1789. Adv. Newburyport, Mass. 1803. To Augusta, Me. prob. to join bro. ca.1811. Adv. Haverhill 1817, 1833. Tall clocks; one in Ray Walker Col.

WINSHIP, DAVID: Litchfield, Conn. Ca. 1830's. Clockcase maker; pos. Dealer.

WINSLOW, EZRA: Westborough, Mass. 1860. Brass movt. clocks.

—, JONATHAN: 1765–1847. b. Harwich, Mass. Aptd. to Cheneys. Pos. Warren, New Salem, Worcester, Palmer, Springfield, Mass. C. J. Cherry plates and wheels; pinions calmia or maple; 30-hour clock, 34″ pendulum; dial painted on back of glass panel; brass hands without glass protection. Sheraton grained poplar Dwarf Tall clock No. 87 known; ca.1820. (Ant. Vol. 33, Mar., p.133, *A Grandmother Clock with Wooden Works*, by Robert S. Dodge.)

WINSTANLEY, HENRY: Brooklyn, N.Y. Ca. 1840.

WINSTON, A. L. & W.: Bristol. Ca.1840. "Makers of brass clocks." (FT)

WINTERBOTTOM, THOMAS: Phila. 1750. "Indentured to Joseph Wills, a clock-maker, who ran away." (Prime)

WINTERHALDER, CHARLES: Santa Cruz, Cal. Ca.1860. (Dre)

WINTERMUTE, O.: Newton, N.J. Dealer R.R. watch inspector ca.1870–ca.1890. Dial sign owned by H. O. Wintermute, Mt. Vernon, O.

WINTERRODE, JACOB: Dauphin Co., Pa. n/d. Tall clocks.

WINTERS, CHRISTIAN: Easton, Pa. Ca.1800. Tall clocks. C. E. Dalrymple owns Tall clock, solid walnut case, OG feet, Chippendale hood.

WISE, WILLIAM, & SONS: Brooklyn, N.Y. To ca.1930.

—, WILLIAM: Brooklyn, N.Y. Ca.1835–.

WISMER, HENRY: –1828. Plumsted Twp., Pa. Ca.1798–1828. Tall clocks. According to J. S. Bailey "Made more than any other maker and employed several workmen."

WISTER, CHARLES J.: Germantown, Pa. *Ca.*1820–*ca.*1860.

WITHINGTON, PETER: Mifflinburg, Pa. *Ca.* 1820.

WITMER, ABEL: 1767–1821. Ephrata, Pa. Aw. 1790–1821. Member of Cloisters. Mostly 30-hr. movt. Tall clocks. (Lan. Co.)

WITT, DR. CHRISTOPHER: Germantown, Pa. Aw. *ca.*1710–1765. Doctor, scientist, C., teacher. Fine Tall clocks, Tower clocks, math. insts. Christopher Sower an apt.

WITTENMYER, MICHAEL: 1772–1850. Doylestown, Pa. Aw. 1808–1846. Tall clock movts. Forge in cellar of house, smelted brass; made brass wheels, hands, plates, etc. (Edward Greene)

WITWER, ISAAC: New Holland, Pa. *Ca.* 1850–1855. Tall clocks.

WOLF, HENRY: Marietta, Pa. *Ca.*1850. Tall clocks.

—, JACOB: Waynesburg, Pa. n/d. Tall clock, moon, sweep seconds hand, curly and bird's-eye maple case, 8-day movt. owned by Harold C. Shealer.

—, THOMAS D.: Westtown, Pa. *Ca.*1815. (James)

WOLTZ, GEORGE ELIE: Hagerstown, Md. 1820's. (LSS)

—, JOHN: Shepherdstown, West Va. Early 19th century.

—, MAJOR JOHN GEORGE ADAMS: 1744–1813. Aw. 1770–1813. Tall clocks, "George Woltz, Hager's Town." Ex. owned by L. S. Spangler. (LSS)

—, SAMUEL: Hagerstown, Md. *Ca.*1800. (LSS)

—, WILLIAM: Oakland, Md. (?) *Ca.*1825–1850.

WOOD & FOLEY: Albany, N.Y. Albert Potter apt. 1852. (Chamberlain)

— & HUDSON: Mt. Holly, N.J. Aw. *ca.* 1773–*ca.*1790.

—, JOHN, & SON: Phila. 1754–1761. Tall clocks so marked. (Conrad)

—, B. B.: Boston, 87 Washington St. Dir. 1841. Banjo clock in author's col.

—, B. F.: Winchester, N.H. n/d. "He made beautiful clocks and movts. for many years" (S. C. Robinson). Bought bell from Paul Revere, had small bells cast from it. Movt. in Dwarf Tall case by Rev. Frank A. M. Coad, Hillsboro, N.H.

WOOD, DAVID: Newburyport, Mass. 1766–*ca.*1850. Famous C. Son of John and Emmie Wood. Pos. aptd. to Mulliken or Balch. Marr. Elizabeth Bird 1795. Adv. June 13, 1792, "Set up a shop in Market Square, near Rev. Andrews' Meeting House," where he made and sold Clocks. Tall, Banjo, Mass. Shelf clocks. Successful. Adv. 1824, "New and second hand clocks for sale at the shop to which he has recently moved on the westerly side of Market St. opposite the Market House." No record place, date of death. Ill. in Moore, Milham. Tall clock owned by Herbert Kimball, Bradford, Mass. Mass. Shelf clock at Essex Inst. Fine ex. in Metropolitan Museum and J. Cheney Wells Col. (See ill. Nos. 127–129, 146.) (AJ July, 1950)

—, JAMES: N.Y.C. 1874. Succeeded Geo. A. Jones & Co.

—, JOHN: –1761. Phila. Adv. 1734, 1738. Pos. imp. dials.

—, JOHN: 1736–1793. Phila., Front and Chestnut Sts. Adv. 1760–1793. C. W. Adv. 1771, "Philadelphia made watches by some capital workmen from London." Adv. 1772, "Imported watches and Clocks and watch tools and materials for sale." Adv. 1775, "Watch Springs made in Phila. by Matthais Eyre, spring maker and by John Wood, Watchmaker, much cheaper than imported from England, 30 shillings a dozen, 3 shillings a spring." Adv. 1777, "Commenced business again on March 1st on Front St. Mr. Henry Snelling who now carries on business is not nor has been in any way connected with the said Wood." Clocks and watches for Phila., also county trade; watch and clock parts. His father, practical C. and W., purchased Peter Stretch's "Corner" for him; left ample income to carry on work. Succeeded by Ephraim Clark. Tall clock in Metropolitan Museum. (See ill. Nos. 35, 36.) (Prime) (ALP) (Miss C. Stretch)

—, JOHN: N.Y.C. "1775." Prob. Phila.

—, JOHN: Mt. Holly, N.J. 1790–1810. Pos. in Wood & Hudson.

—, JOSIAH: New Bedford, Mass. Early 19th century. (Abbott)

WOOD, M.: Rockport, Ind. *Ca.*1840.

—, N. G.: Boston, 9 Hanover St. Dir. 1856.

WOODCOCK & CO.: Baltimore. Dir. 1871.

—, WILLIAM: Baltimore. 1819–1829.

WOODFORD, ISAAC: New Haven, Conn. *Ca.*1845.

WOODIN, RILEY L.: Decatur, N.Y. 1830's. Mirror clock, 30-hr. wood movt. in R. Newcomb Col. Used Jeromes & Darrow 8-day wood movts. (Palmer)

WOODING, E.: Torrington, Conn. *Ca.*1830.

WOODRUFF & WHITE: Cincinnati, O. *Ca.*1840.

—, ENOS: Cincinnati, O. *Ca.*1820–*ca.*1830.

—, JESSE: 1744–1797. Aw. 1766. Apt. of Stephen Reeves. S. (Williams)

—, JOHN, II: New Haven, Conn. *Ca.*1850.

WOODWARD, ANTIPAS: 1763–1812. Middletown, Bristol, Conn. Aw. 1791. G. C. S. Shop burned 1792. Adv. 1792, "Benevolence of kind friends, resumes in shop lately occupied by Major Otis." To "No. of the Coffee House" 1792. Adv., "Goldsmith who also did Clockmaking." To Bristol; specialized in wire pendulum rods for wood clocks of Roberts, et al. (Hoopes)

—, JAMES: Phila. *Ca.*1795. Cabinetmaker, cases only. (MFM)

WOODWORTH, E. C.: Boston, n/d. Watch Paper BCL Col.

WOOLF, B.: Charleston, S.C. *Ca.*1800.

WOOLSON, THOMAS, JR.: Amherst, N.H. Early 19th century.

WOOLSTON, R.: Glastonbury, Pa. n/d. Tall clocks. (Orr)

WOOLWORTH, CHESTER: New Haven, Conn. *Ca.*1840.

—, R. C.: Phila. Dir. 1816–1817.

WORDEN, C. M.: Bridgeport, Conn. *Ca.*1850.

WORTON, ROBERT: Phila. Dir. 1849.

WRIGGINS & WARDEN: Phila. n/d. Watch Paper BCL Col.

WRIGHT, CHARLES CUSHING: N.Y.C. *Ca.* 1800–1812; Utica, N.Y., 1812–*ca.*1830.

—, FILBERT: Bristol. 1849–1856. Son of Harvey. Partner A. S. Platt & Co. Later made springs in competition with Dunbar & Barnes. (Hull)

—, HARVEY: Bristol, Main St. No. of Pequabuck R. (tx) 1831. Father of Filbert, Julius. Wood movt. clocks. Early pioneer spring maker. Built factory for springs *ca.*1830–1832–. (George Hull)

WRIGHT, JOHN: –1768. N.Y.C. Adv. 1753, "to leave city." One of earliest makers in N.Y.C. Tall clock, oak case, known. (Stow)

—, JULIUS: Bristol. Son of Harvey. Bro. Filbert. Took over A. S. Platt & Co. after 1857. Sold to Wallace Barnes. Experimented with wire for hoop skirts. (Hull)

—, SAMUEL: Lancaster, N.H. 1808–*ca.*1830. "Did well here for some years."

—, T. H.: Lancaster, N.H. Early 19th century.

—, WILLIAM: Baltimore. 1802–1803. (Baillie)

WRUCK, F. A.: Salem, Mass., 262 Essex St. Dir. 1864. Watch Paper BCL Col.

WVUILLE, THEOPHILE: Phila., 72½ Walnut St. n/d. (MFM)

WYAND, JOHN: Phila. Dir. 1847.

WYLEYS, —: Charleston, S.C. *Ca.*1785. (MFM)

WYMAN, ROGERS & COX: Nashua, N.H. *Ca.*1830–1837. Operated factory owned by L. W. Noyes.

—, BENJ.: Boston. n/d. Banjo clock in Barny Col.

—, CHARLES: St. Albans, Vt. n/d. Watch Paper BCL Col.

—, ISAAC: Boston. Marr. Katherine dau. of Elnathan Taber. n/d. (BCC)

WYNN, CHRISTOPHER: Baltimore. Dir. 1842.

WYNNE, ROBERT: Salisbury, N.C. Adv. 1827–1828. In Huntington & Wynne. Alone –1830; not too successful. Sold watchmakers' tools 1830. (Cutten)

YALE CLOCK CO.: New Haven, Conn. 1881–1883. (R. Franks)

YARNALL, ALLEN: 1803–1832. Sugartown and West Chester, Pa. Adv. 1825–1832. Aptd. to M. Thomas or Caleb Hibbard. Promoted legal lottery. To West Chester 1828. One Tall clock known. (James)

YATES (Joseph) & KENT: Trenton, N.J. 1796–1798. Dissolved. Succeeded by Williams & Leslie.

—, EDWARD J.: Freehold, N.J. 1805–1809. (PG)

—, JOHN B.: N.Y.C., 21 Maiden Lane. Adv. 1893, "Purchased Waltham Repeating Watches." (MFM)

—, JOSEPH: Trenton, N.J. Aw. 1789. Partner Yates & Kent. Adv. 1796. To Freehold, N.J. 1803.

YEADON, RICHARD: Charleston, S.C., Broad St. Adv. 1771. Bought stock of Richard Clark 1772.

YEAGER, WILLIAM: Phila. Dir. 1837.

YEAKLE, SOLOMON: Northampton, now Allentown, Pa. Early 19th century. Tall clocks. (Orr)

YEAR CLOCK CO., THE: N.Y.C. Pos. 1841; dates confused. Label, "Crane's Patent 12 Month Clocks Mfd. by The Year Clock Co., 35 Cortlandt St., N.Y.C." Crane Year Clock in Selchow Col. (See ill. No. 263.) Adv. 1903, "One year with one winding—no Batteries, no weights, no pendulum." (MFM)

YEISER, FREDERICK: Lexington, Ky. S. Patent No. 22193 Feb. 8, 1859, on "new and useful instrument for determining the True Meridian and for the taking of the Altitude of the Sun either in the forenoon or afternoon." (LB)

YEOMANS (James) & COLLINS (John): N.Y.C. Adv. 1767, "From London." Yeomans alone 1771–1773.

—, ELIJAH: –1794. Hadley, Mass. Leading C. Ca.1771. Tall clock, "Petersham No. 51" on dial, owned by Mr. & Mrs. Thomas Blake, N.Y.C. Middletown, Conn., Samuel Canfield's shop 1792. To Hartford, Conn.; aw. with David Greenleaf. d. Hartford. (Hoopes)

—, JAMES: –1773. W. From Birmingham, Eng., 1767; aptd. there to "the ingenious Mr. Neale." In Yeomans & Collins 1769. Death notice 1773, "Native of England, Father of Mathematician and Fellow of the Royal Society, himself a watchmaker. His song and story ever set the table in a roar and the cheerfulness . . . entitles his memory to this faithful record of his very pleasant and truly courteous disposition."

YERKES, WILLIAM: Pa. "1774." Tall clock owned by Mrs. J. D. Wolfe, Springfield, Pa.

YODDER, —: Phila. and Bethlehem, Pa. n/d. "Began to manufacture Tall clocks by and of machinery, conducting a business there which carried on to a certain extent." "Factory was in Phila." (Funk)

YONGUE, ROBERT A.: Columbia, S.C. 1852–ca.1857. Sold gold- and silver-cased watches; prob. not maker. (Cutten)

YORKEE, JACOB: Manheim, Pa. Early 19th century.

YOU, THOMAS: Charleston, S.C. Ca.1760–1780.

YOUNG, WM. J., & SON: Phila. Ca.1857. Sun dials. (James)

—, B.: Watervleit, N.Y. 1800–.

—, CHARLES: Chambersburg, Pa. Before Rev. War.

—, DAVID: Hopkinton, N.H. Pos. Case maker only. Tall clock so marked owned by Lewis L. Smith, Jr., N.Y.C. Hopkinton Town Records, "1776—signed declaration of Fidelity to the American cause. 1800 Taxed for stock in trade as 'cabinetmaker' . . . said to have been a maker of the first clock case constructed here." "Two young men, apprentices of David Young, were disbelievers in witchcraft." (L. L. Smith, Jr.)

—, FRANCIS: N.Y.C. Adv. 1780, "Set up a shop next to where Isaac Heron had worked." Pos. Phila. (Am. Col. June 1948)

—, FRANCIS: Phila. Adv. 1777, "Watch and Clockmaker in 2nd St., late from London. Makes, mends and Repairs . . ." (Prime)

—, JACOB: Phila. Ca.1769. Tall clock dial. "Manheim." Tall clocks.

—, JOHN S.: Norwalk, O. "Early, no date given." (Knittle)

—, JOSEPH: Newburgh, N.Y. n/d. Fine inlaid case Tall clock with French fret, double arch, moon, known.

—, S. E.: Laconia, N.H. 1884. Partner Edgar Covell in jewelry business. Later in S. E. Young & Co. & Cram (Elisha S.), 114 Main St. (Childs)

—, SAMUEL: Charles Town, W. V. Ca.1800.

—, STEPHEN: N.Y.C. 1810–1816.

YOUNGS, BENJAMIN: 1736–1818. Son and apt. of Seth and Hannah Lawrence Youngs. C., S. Aw. Windsor, Conn., 1761. To Schenectady, N.Y., ca.1766. Later to Watervleit, N.Y. Father of Isaac. Joined Shakers. Tall clocks extant. Account book extant. (Hoopes) (D. M. Andrews) Given as "Ebenezer" in (FT).

—, BENJAMIN: N.Y.C. Ca.1800.

—, EBENEZER: 1756–. b. Hebron, Conn. C. Son of Ebenezer and Eunice Youngs. Pos. apt. of David Ellsworth, Windsor, Conn., 1776. Adv. Hebron 1778, 1780. C. (Hoopes)

YOUNGS, ISAAC: 1793–1865. New Lebanon, N.Y. Grandson of Seth; son of Benjamin. "Shaker" clocks. (D. M. Andrews) (BCC)

—, JOSEPH: Windsor, Conn. n/d. Son of Seth.

—, SETH: 1711–1761. C. Prob. apt. of Ebenezer Parmele. Marr. 1735; to Hartford, Conn. Pos. first C. near Hartford; pos. trained Benjamin Cheney. Elaborate hourglass for pulpit of new meeting house 1739. To Windsor, Conn., 1742; Torrington 1760. Bequeathed tools to sons Joseph, Benjamin, Seth, Jr. (Hoopes)

—, SETH, JR.: Windsor, Conn. Son of Seth.

ZAHM & Co.: Lancaster, Pa. *Ca.*1850.

—, H. L. & E. J.: Lancaster, Pa. 1850's.

— & JACKSON: Lancaster, Pa. 1850's.

—, G. M.: Lancaster, Pa. 1843. (FT)

ZEISSLER, G. A.: Phila. Dir. 1848.

ZELLAKS, DROSSON: St. Augustine, Fla. n/d. "Of Greek descent." (Dre)

ZIMMERMAN, ANTHONY: –1788. Reading, Pa. Taxed as C. 1768. Tall clocks; none extant.

—, C. H.: New Orleans, La. *Ca.*1850–*ca.* 1860. (TP)

ZUBER, JOHN J.: Upper Hanover, Pa. n/d. Tall clocks. (Steinmetz)

BIBLIOGRAPHY

ABBOTT, HENRY G., *Antique Watches, and How to Establish Their Age*. Chicago: G. K. Hazlitt & Co., 1897.

———, *The Watch Factories of America, Past and Present*. Chicago: G. K. Hazlitt & Co., 1888.

ANDERSON, JOSEPH, *The Town and City of Waterbury, Connecticut*. New Haven, Conn.: Price & Lee Co., 1896.

ATWATER, FRANCIS, *History of the Town of Plymouth*. Meriden, Conn.: Journal Publishing Co., 1895.

BAILLIE, G. H., *Watchmakers and Clockmakers of the World*. London: Methuen, 1929. (2nd ed., London: N.A.G. Press, 1947).

BARBER, JOHN WARNER, *Connecticut Historical Collections*. New Haven, Conn.: B. L. Hamlen, 1836.

BELKNAP, HENRY W., *Artists and Craftsmen of Essex County, Massachusetts*. Salem, Mass.: Essex Institute, 1927.

BOOTH, MARY L., *New and Complete Clock and Watch Maker's Manual* (compiled from the French with an appendix containing a History of Clock and Watch Making in America.) New York: J. Wiley, 1860.

BOWMAN, JOHN J., *Lancaster's Part in the World's Watchmaking Industry* (pamphlet). Lancaster, Pa.: Lancaster County Historical Society, 1945.

BREARLEY, HARRY C., *Bristol, Connecticut: A History*. Hartford, Conn.: City Printing Co., 1907.

———, *Time Telling Through the Ages*. New York: Doubleday, for Robert H. Ingersoll & Bro., 1919.

BRITTEN, FREDERICK J., *Old Clocks and Watches and Their Makers*. 3rd ed., London: Batsford, 1911.

BRIX, MAURICE, *List of Philadelphia Silversmiths and Allied Artificers from 1682 to 1850*. Philadelphia: Privately printed, 1920.

BRONSON, HENRY, *History of Waterbury, Connecticut*. Waterbury: Bronson Brothers, 1858.

BURKE, EDMUND, *List of Patents for Inventions and Designs Issued by the United States from 1790 to 1847*. Washington, D.C.: J. & G. S. Gideon, 1847.

BURTON, E. MILBY, *South Carolina Silversmiths, 1690–1860*. Charleston: Charleston Museum, 1942.

CHAMBERLAIN, PAUL M., *It's About Time*. New York: Richard R. Smith, 1941.

CHANDLEE, EDWARD E., *Six Quaker Clockmakers*. Philadelphia: Historical Society of Pennsylvania, 1943.

CHASE, GEORGE W., *The History of Haverhill, Massachusetts, 1640–1860*. Haverhill: Stone & Huse, 1861.

CONRAD, HENRY C., *Old Delaware Clockmakers*. Wilmington: Historical Society of Delaware, 1897.

CONRAD, JOHN, "Pennsylvania Clock Makers," *Bulletin of the Historical Society of Montgomery County, Pa.*, Vol. III, No. 3 (Oct., 1942).

CROSSMAN, CHARLES T., "A Complete History of Watch and Clock Making in America," a serial published in the *Jewelers' Circular* between 1889 and 1891.

CURRIER, JOHN J., *History of Newburyport, Massachusetts*. Newburyport: Author, 1906.

CUTTEN, GEORGE B., *The Silversmiths of North Carolina*. Raleigh: State Department of Archives and History, 1948.

———, *Silversmiths of Northampton, Massachusetts, and Vicinity Down to 1850* (pamphlet). Northampton, 1942.

———, *Silversmiths, Watch Makers, and Jewelers of the State of New York*. Hamilton, N.Y.: Privately printed, 1939.

DOW, GEORGE F., *Arts and Crafts in New England, 1704–1775*. Topsfield, Mass.: Wayside Press, 1927.

DREPPERD, CARL W., *American Clocks and Clockmakers*. Garden City, N.Y.: Doubleday, 1947.

ECKHARDT, GEORGE H., *Early Pennsylvania Clocks*. Philadelphia: North Museum Commission, 1938.

FREISTADTER, J., "Development of the Watch Industry in the United States," *Northwestern Jeweler*, Aug., 1939.

FRIED, HENRY B., *The Watch Repairer's Manual*. New York: Van Nostrand, 1948.

FUNK, H. H., "Grandfather's Clocks," *Pennsylvania German Magazine* (Philadelphia), 1907.

GOTTESMAN, MRS. RITA S., *Arts and Crafts in New York, 1726–1776*. New York: New-York Historical Society, 1938.

HAYDEN, ARTHUR, *Chats on Old Clocks*. London: T. F. Unwin, 1917.

HERING, D. W., *The Lure of the Clock*. New York: New York University Press, 1932.

HOOPES, PENROSE R., *Connecticut Clockmakers of the Eighteenth Century*. Hartford, Conn.: E. V. Mitchell, 1930.

———, "Some Minor Connecticut Clockmakers," *Antiques*, Sept., 1935.

JAMES, ARTHUR E., *Chester County Clocks and Their Makers:* West Chester, Pa.: Author, 1947.

JEROME, CHAUNCEY, *History of the American Clock Business for the Past Sixty Years, and the Life of Chauncey Jerome*. New Haven, Conn.: F. C. Dayton, Jr., 1860.

KNITTLE, RHEA MANSFIELD, *Early Ohio Silversmiths and Pewterers, 1787–1847*. Cleveland: Author, 1943.

LOCKWOOD, LUKE V., *Colonial Furniture in America*. 3rd ed., New York: Scribner, 1926.

MAGEE, D. F., "Grandfathers' Clocks: Their Making and Their Makers in Lancaster County," *Papers Read Before the Lancaster Historical Society*, 1917, pp. 63–77.

MILHAM, WILLIS I., *Time and Timekeepers*. New York: Macmillan, 1923.

MILLER, EDGAR G., *American Antique Furniture: A Book for Amateurs*. Baltimore: M. S. Watkins, 1937.

MILLER, V. ISABELLE, *Silver by New York Makers: Late 17th Century to 1900*. New York: Museum of the City of New York, 1937.

MOORE, CHARLES W., *Timing a Century: History of the Waltham Watch Company*. Cambridge, Mass.: Harvard University Press, 1945.

MOORE, MRS. N. HUDSON, *The Collector's Manual*. New York: Stokes, 1906.

———, *The Old Clock Book*. New York: Stokes, 1911. (2nd ed., New York: Tudor Publishing Co., 1936.)

NUTTING, WALLACE, *The Clock Book*. Framingham, Mass.: Old America Co., 1924. (2nd ed., New York: Garden City Publishing Co., 1935.)

———, *Furniture Treasury*. Framingham, Mass.: Old America Co., 1928–1933. (2nd ed., New York: Macmillan, 1949.) 3 vols.

ORR, SYLVESTER H., "Clockmaking in Pennsylvania of the 18th and 19th Centuries,"

Bulletin of the Historical Society of Montgomery County, Pa., Vol. I, No. 2 (Apr., 1937).

PEASE, JOHN C., AND JOHN M. NILES, *A Gazetteer of the States of Connecticut and Rhode Island*. Hartford, Conn., 1819.

PLEASANTS, J. HALL, AND HOWARD SILL, *Maryland Silversmiths, 1715–1830*. Baltimore: Lord Baltimore Press, 1930.

PRIME, ALFRED COXE, *Arts and Crafts in Philadelphia, Maryland, and South Carolina, 1721–1785*. Topsfield, Mass.: Wayside Press, for Walpole Society, 1929.

———, *Colonial Craftsmen of Pennsylvania*. Philadelphia: Pennsylvania Museum, 1925. (Pamphlet.)

RAWLINGS, ARTHUR L., *The Science of Clocks and Watches*. 2nd ed., London: Pitman, 1948.

ROBERTS, CHARLES R., "Grandfathers' Clocks," *Proceedings and Papers of the Lehigh County Historical Society*, 1922, pp. 29–33.

SCUDDER, MARVIN, *Manual of Extinct or Obsolete Companies*. New York, 1926–1934.

———, *Souvenir History of the Town of Bristol, Connecticut*. Meriden, Conn., 1897.

STEINMETZ, MARY OWEN, "Early Clockmakers of Berks County," *Historical Review of Berks County*, Vol. 2, No. 1 (Oct., 1935), pp. 12–13.

STRETCH, CAROLYN WOOD, "Early Colonial Clockmakers in Philadelphia," *Pennsylvania Magazine*, Vol. LVI, pp. 225–235 (July, 1932).

SWEINHART, FRED C., "Early Pennsylvania Clocks and Their Makers," *Bulletin of the Historical Society of Montgomery County, Pa.*, Vol. III, No. 1 (Oct., 1941).

TERRY, HENRY, *American Clockmaking: Its Early History and Present Extent of the Business*. Waterbury, Conn., 1870. Pamphlet.

———, Review of Dr. Alcott's History of Clockmaking, *Waterbury American*, June 10, 1853.

WILLARD, JOHN WARE, *A History of Simon Willard, Inventor and Clockmaker*. Boston: G. W. Humphrey, 1911.

WILLIAMS, CARL M., *Silversmiths of New Jersey, 1700–1825*. Philadelphia: George S. MacManus Co., 1949.